SAGE was founded in 1965 by Sara Miller McCune to support the dissemination of usable knowledge by publishing innovative and high-quality research and teaching content. Today, we publish over 900 journals, including those of more than 400 learned societies, more than 800 new books per year, and a growing range of library products including archives, data, case studies, reports, and video. SAGE remains majority-owned by our founder, and after Sara's lifetime will become owned by a charitable trust that secures our continued independence.

Los Angeles | London | New Delhi | Singapore | Washington DC | Melbourne

An Introduction to the Business of Tourism

Bulk Sales

SAGE India offers special discounts
for bulk institutional purchases.

*For queries/orders/inspection copy requests
write to* **textbooksales@sagepub.in**

Publishing

Would you like to publish a textbook with SAGE?

Please send your proposal to **publishtextbook@sagepub.in**

Get to know more about SAGE

Be invited to SAGE events, get on our mailing list.

Write today to **marketing@sagepub.in**

An Introduction to the Business of Tourism

Venu Vasudevan

Principal Secretary, Department of Tourism, Government of Kerala, Thiruvananthapuram

Vijayakumar B.

Former Principal, Kerala Institute of Tourism and Travel Studies (KITTS), Thiruvananthapuram

Saroop Roy B.R.

Assistant Professor, Kerala Institute of Tourism and Travel Studies (KITTS), Thiruvananthapuram

Los Angeles | London | New Delhi
Singapore | Washington DC | Melbourne

First published in 2017 by

SAGE Publications India Pvt Ltd
B1/I-1 Mohan Cooperative Industrial Area
Mathura Road, New Delhi 110 044, India
www.sagepub.in

SAGE Publications Inc
2455 Teller Road
Thousand Oaks, California 91320, USA

SAGE Publications Ltd
1 Oliver's Yard, 55 City Road
London EC1Y 1SP, United Kingdom

SAGE Publications Asia-Pacific Pte Ltd
3 Church Street
#10-04 Samsung Hub
Singapore 049483

Published by Vivek Mehra for SAGE Publications India Pvt Ltd, typeset in Stone Serif 9.5/11.5 by Zaza Eunice, Hosur, Tamil Nadu, India and printed at Saurabh Printers Pvt Ltd, Greater Noida.

Library of Congress Cataloging-in-Publication Data

Names: Vasudevan, Venu, author.
Title: An introduction to the business of tourism / Venu Vasudevan,
  Vijayakumar B., Saroop Roy B.R.
Description: New Delhi : SAGE Publications India, 2017. | Includes
  bibliographical references and index.
Identifiers: LCCN 2016052230 | ISBN 9789386062253 (pbk. : alk. paper)
Subjects: LCSH: Tourism--Management. | Tourism--Management--India.
Classification: LCC G155.A1 .V375 2017 | DDC 338.4/791--dc23 LC record available at https://lccn.loc.gov/2016052230

ISBN: 978-93-86062-25-3 (PB)

SAGE Team: Amit Kumar, Indrani Dutta, Vandana Gupta and Ritu Chopra

Brief Contents

Contents

Detailed Contents

List of Tables

List of Figures

List of Charts

List of Abbreviations

10YFP	10-Year Framework of Programmes
AAI	Airport Authority of India
ADEME	French Environment and Energy Management Agency
AERO	Americas, Europe and Oceania
AGM	Annual General Meeting
AIACC	Assessments of Impacts and Adaptations to Climate Change
AIDS	Acquired Immune Deficiency Syndrome
AITO	Association of Independent Tour Operators
AMT	Asian Millennial Traveller
ARR	Average Room Rate
ASI	Archaeological Survey of India
ASTA	American Society of Travel Agents
ATF	Air Turbine Fuel
ATM	Air Traffic Management
ATMs	Automatic Teller Machines
B&B	Bread and Breakfast
B2B	Business to Business
B2C	Business to Customer
CAGR	Compounded Annual Growth Rate
CEO	Chief Executive Officer
CFO	Chief Financial Officer
CIP	Commercially Important Persons
CKL	Cox and Kings Limited
CNS	Communication, Navigation and Surveillance
COO	Chief Operating Officer
CP	Cleaner Production
CPGI	Country Potential Generation Index
CPSE	Central Public Sector Enterprises
CRS	Computerized Reservation System
CRZ	Coastal Regulation Zone
CSE	Customer Service Executive
CSMC	Central Sanctioning and Monitoring Committee
CSMVS	Chhatrapati Shivaji Maharaj Vastu Sangrahalaya
CSR	Corporate Social Responsibility
DGCA	Directorate General of Civil Aviation
DGLL	Directorate General of Lighthouses and Lightships
DIAL	Delhi International Airport Limited
DINKS	Double Income, No Kids
DMC	Destination Management Companies

DMO	Destination Management Organization
EBITA	Earnings Before Interest, Taxes and Amortization
ECOSOC	Economic and Social Council
e-CRM	Electronic Customer Relations Management
EDC	Eco-Development Committee
EIA	Environmental Impact Assessment
EMI	Equated Monthly Instalment
EMP	Environment Management Plan
EREC	European Renewable Energy Council
ESTC	Ecotourism and Sustainable Tourism Conference
ETA	Electronic Travel Authorization
ETP	Endogenous Tourism Project
e-TV	e-Tourist Visa
F&B	Food and Beverages
FCI	Food Craft Institute
FDI	Foreign Direct Investment
FHRAI	Federation of Hotel and Restaurant Association of India
FIT	Free Independent Traveller
FTO	Foreign Tour Operator
GA	General Assembly
GCET	Global Code of Ethics for Tourism
GDP	Gross Domestic Product
GDS	Global Distribution System
GHG	Greenhouse Gas
GHT	Great Himalaya Trail
GIT	Group Inclusive Tour
GoAP	Government of Andhra Pradesh
GoI	Government of India
GSA	General Sales Agent
GSTC C-D	Global Sustainable Tourism Council Criteria for Destinations
GSTC	Global Sustainable Tourism Council
HCMI	Hotel Carbon Measurement Initiative
HES	Hotel Energy Solutions
HITEX	Hyderabad International Trade Expo
HIV	Human Immunodeficiency Virus
HRH	Historic Resort Hotels
HSR	High Speed Rail
HSRT	Hunar Se Rozgar Tak
HVAC	Heating Ventilation and Air Conditioning
IAS	Indian Administrative Service
IATA	International Air Transport Association
IATO	Indian Association of Tour Operators
ICAO	International Civil Aviation Organization
ICCROM	International Centre for the Study of the Preservation and Restoration of Cultural Property
ICOMOS	International Council on Monuments and Sites
ICPB	India Convention Promotion Bureau
ICT	Information and Communications Technologies
IH&RA	International Hotel and Restaurants Association
IHCL	Indian Hotels Company Ltd
IHG	Intercontinental Hotel Group
IHM	Institutes of Hotel Management

IHMCT	Institutes of Hotel Management, Catering Technology and Applied Nutrition
IITTM	Indian Institute of Tourism and Travel Management
IMK	Institute of Management in Kerala
INTACH	Indian National Trust for Art and Heritage
IOF	Indian Oil Foundation
IPCC	Intergovernmental Panel on Climate Change
IRCTC	Indian Railway Catering and Tourism Corporation Limited
ISPA	International Spa Association
ITB	International Tourism Bourse
ITDC	India Tourism Development Corporation
ITES	Information Technology enabled services
ITF-STD	International Task Force on Sustainable Tourism Development
ITY	International Tourist Year
IUCN	International Union for Conservation of Nature
IUOTO	International Union of Official Travel Organization
IUOTPO	International Union of Official Tourism Publicity/Propaganda Organization
IYE	International Year of Ecotourism
JECC	Jaipur Exhibition and Convention Centre
JICA	Japan International Cooperation Agency
JV	Joint Venture
KITTS	Kerala Institute of Tourism and Travel Studies
KMVS	Kutch Mahila Vikas Sangathan
KoD	Kingdom of Dreams
KTM	Kerala Travel Mart
LAC	Limits of Acceptable Change
LCC	Low Cost Carrier
MAA	Meghalaya Adventurers Association
MAB	Man and Biosphere
MDG	Millennium Development Goals
MESCO	Maharashtra Ex-Servicemen Corporation
MICE	Meetings, Incentives, Conventions, Events and Exhibitions
MoCA	Ministry of Civil Aviation
MoT	Ministry of Tourism
MoU	Memorandum of Understanding
MP	Madhya Pradesh
MTA	Master of Tourism Administration
MTDC	Maharashtra Tourism Development Corporation
NAPA	National Adaptation Programmes of Action
NCHMCT	National Council for Hotel Management and Catering Technology
NDBR	Nanda Devi Biosphere Reserve
NGO	Non-Governmental Organizations
NHDP	National Highways Development Project
NP	National Park
NS&EW	North South and East West
NTO	National Tourism Organization
OTA	Online Travel Agent
OUV	Outstanding Universal Value
PAs	Protected Areas
PATA	Pacific Asia Travel Association
PIOs	Persons of Indian origin
PM	Project Manager
PMC	Project Management Consultant

PPP	Public–Private Partnership
PR	Public Relations
PRASAD	Pilgrimage Rejuvenation and Spiritual Augmentation Drive
PRIs	Panchayat Raj Institutions
PSU	Public Sector Undertaking
RTO	Regional Tourism Organization
RV	Recreational Vehicle
SCA	Scheduled Commuter Airlines
SDG	Sustainable Development Goal
SIDS	Small Island Developing States
SIT	Special Interest Tourism
SME	Small and Medium Enterprise
SNA	System of National Accounts
STDC	State Tourism Development Corporation
ST-EP	Sustainable Tourism Eliminating Poverty
STS	Systems of Tourism Statistics
SWOT	Strength Weakness Opportunity Threat
T&T	Travel and Tourism
TAAI	Travel Agents Association of India
TCI	Travel Corporation of India
TDCs	Tourism Development Corporations
TEPS	Thenmala Ecotourism Promotion Society
TFCI	Tourism Finance Corporation of India
TGV	Train à Grande Vitesse
TIES	The International Ecotourism Society
TSA	Tourism Satellite Account
TTDC	Tamil Nadu Tourism Development Corporation
TVC	Television Commercial
UD	Universal Design
UFTAA	United Federation of Travel Agents' Association
UNCED	United Nations Conference on Environment and Development
UNDP	United Nations Development Programme
UNEP	United Nations Environment Programme
UNESCO	United Nations Educational, Scientific and Cultural Organization
UNFCC	United Nations Framework Convention on Climate Change
UNWTO	United Nations World Tourism Organization
USAID	United States Agency for International Development
USP	Unique Selling Proposition
UT	Union Territory
VAT	Value Added Tax
VERP	Visitor Experience Resource Protection
VFR	Visiting Friends and Relatives
VMS	Visitor Management Plan
VMY	Visit Malaysia Year
VOC	Volatile Organic Compounds
VoF	Valley of Flowers
VRS	Voluntary Retirement Scheme
WCED	World Commission on Environment and Development
WES	World Ecotourism Summit
WHL	World Heritage List
WHS	World Heritage Site

WLS	Wildlife Sanctuary
WMO	World Meteorological Organization
WTD	World Tourism Day
WTM	World Travel Market
WTO	World Tourism Organization
WTTC	World Travel and Tourism Council
WWF	World Wide Fund for Nature

Preface

Every discipline has academic and application dimensions. While the academic side focuses on the theoretical and philosophical underpinnings of the subject, the application side refers to the skill sets needed for putting theory into practice. Educational institutions, engaged in preparing skilled human resources to serve the diversified requirements of the commercial world, attempt to synergize theory and practice with a view to mould competent employees and entrepreneurs. Tourism is a labour-intensive industry, contributing one in eleven jobs created across the world. Realizing the role of tourism in international trade as an invisible export item and in strengthening the local economy by generating income and employment, it is treated as a priority sector in the development paradigm in most of the countries.

Tourism is increasingly acknowledged as an important academic discipline in colleges and universities across the world in keeping with its immense potential to generate employment, particularly for the youth. The tourism industry is skill oriented, knowledge based and multi-disciplinary, and students are expected to learn the subject to gain an understanding of the practice of tourism. Unlike other disciplines, students undergoing undergraduate or graduate courses in tourism do not possess the basic knowledge of the subject, as it is not taught at the secondary or higher secondary levels. Moreover, on successful completion of the course, tourism students are expected to either be placed in the industry or start their own ventures in the industry or to start their own ventures. In both the scenarios, a clear understanding of the tourism business, beginning with the basic principles and concepts, moving on to their application and policy implications and culminating with a good grounding of the discipline as it is practised, is essential.

This needs to be contrasted with the situation prevailing in the tourism industry in India. Our discussions with industry leaders indicate that there is a huge gap between supply and demand, and also the tourism industry sees one of the highest attrition rates than in any other sector. An insightful comment made by several top executives is that they prefer general graduates to tourism degree holders, as the latter have unreasonable expectations about their jobs, stemming from their ignorance of how the business works.

To take a proactive role in this sunrise sector, students should possess knowledge along with clear understanding of the nuances, complexities and interlinkage of this multifaceted industry to become successful entrepreneurs and professionals. This warrants appropriate interventions in curriculum, pedagogy and teaching and learning aids. This book *An Introduction to the Business of Tourism* is intended to fill the existing gap in tourism academia, which is dominated by publications giving prominence to history and principles of tourism setting aside business realities and operational aspects.

We do not undermine the importance of history, philosophy and theories of tourism discipline which provide rich inputs for preparing this book. Our humble attempt is to translate this knowledge into practical propositions so that the reader will have easy access to business

operations with added confidence. The education process should enable the students to rein-
vent the secrets of success which are embedded in the domain they work. This book is designed
keeping this end in mind.

Positioning the learning objectives in the beginning, each chapter gives a quick scan of the
theories and principles of the subject dealt and leading the reader to business realities, expos-
ing them to the latest trends and giving insights into innovations which will enable them to
become successful players in tourism business. The reader's inquisitiveness to go deeper is fulfilled by placing relevant information in separate boxes and through the medium of case studies. While giving conceptual clarity in terminologies used in tourism business, the book quite
often delves into the Indian experience, drawing comparisons with international practices
and enabling the reader to perceive the tourism business from an international platform.
Apart from this, we have tried to kindle the spirit of enquiry and professionalism of the reader
through debates by providing discussion questions in each case study and placing activities at
the end of each chapter. The activities given are indicative and both teacher and student can
continue the deliberations and enrich knowledge by designing new activities that can be
drawn from tourism business environment.

This book is structured into four major sections detailing into 19 chapters. We start with
Section A by introducing tourism. This section leads through the basics of the subject, focusing on the evolution, key definitions in tourism and highlights the growth of the sector to a
global phenomenon. This is followed by introducing concepts and terminologies to get an
unambiguous idea of the terms used in the tourism sector. Concepts such as demand and
supply as relevant to the tourism sector are introduced. The section ends by discussing major
national and international organizations that play a key role in tourism business. Section B
spreads over six chapters and focuses on the components of tourism sector. The section which
starts by familiarizing destinations, discusses on its lifecycle, management and marketing.
This is followed by a scrutiny of the different aspects of attractions including their management. The overview, range and new trends in accommodation and transportation sector are
also discussed in this section. The complexities of travel and tour operation business are discussed in detail, while the final chapter deals with the fundamental principles of marketing
and their application in the tourism sector. Section C, covering five chapters, examines the
extent and scope of tourism in India. In the backdrop of the history and evolution of tourism,
students are exposed to several issues connected with tourism development in the country.
This is followed by detailing the rich cultural heritage as tourism products, giving emphasis to
natural and cultural heritage. This section takes students through some of the major biodiversity areas highlighting their linkages with tourism and probable impacts. This section also
examines the organized business sectors in Indian tourism, particularly the accommodation
and tour segments. Section C concludes by examining the role of government agencies in
shaping Indian tourism. The final part Section D focuses attention on issues that are currently
important to tourism worldwide. Beginning with an examination on different types of
impacts that tourism development has had on destinations and local community, this section
proceeds to various aspects of sustainability. Concurrently, this section examines the impacts
of climate change on tourism and concludes by raising issues that the industry will have to
face in the future.

In this endeavour, we intend to initiate a dialogue between teachers and students to
strengthen tourism business skills based on theoretical knowledge and practical experiences.
Being a vocational subject, the teaching-learning process should be closely linked to ground
realities, covering the latest trends, developments and probable impacts. We hope that the
book will give fresh insights on how to approach tourism studies from a business perspective
and widen the scope of this fledgling discipline.

Acknowledgements

This book is the outcome of our discussions and deliberations over many years. Our collective experience in the public administration, tourism management and academics provided a foundation for our thought processes, which examined the subject of tourism in the context of the Indian education system. It is our considered view that tourism education, in its present style, is in urgent need for reform and revision. The evolution of tourism as a practising discipline brings to focus the need to change the pedagogical approach from a narrow and academic theoretic approach to one that equips young graduates to deal with business operations and practice. The tourism industry has a thriving demand for young professionals with a sound knowledge of the subject and an understanding of the business processes that underpins the sector. We believe that this book is a small beginning towards the 'reinvention' of tourism education in India.

Our realization of the changing requirements of the sector has come about from the valuable insights gained through discussions with experienced professionals in the tourism industry. We are immensely thankful to the captains of the Indian tourism industry who have offered their views and suggestions during the time we were putting together a strategy for this book. Dr Venu remembers with gratitude the conversations he had with Mr Inder Sharma, the late Caption Krishnan Nair, the late Ram Kohli, Mr Amitabh Kant, Mr Arjun Sharma and Mr Jose Dominic, which greatly increased his understanding of the sector. While doing research for the book, Mr Dipak Deva and Mr Vineet Mahendru provided specific inputs on the tourism sector, as did Professor Nimit Chowdhary of Indian Institute of Tourism and Travel Management (IITTM). The small entrepreneurs of Kerala have influenced the thinking of the authors in no small measure, providing important counterpoints to the conventional approach on accommodation business and underlining the importance of local knowledge in tourism education. Our experience of interacting with community representatives, panchayat functionaries and non-governmental organizations (NGOs) was invaluable in providing new perspectives that find prominence in the book. The members of Ecotourism Society of India, businesses practising Responsible Tourism and activists have immensely contributed to increase our understanding of Responsible Tourism, which has contributed to many sections of this book. We are immensely thankful to all these stakeholders and well-wishers who contributed their views and experiences that expanded our horizons and vastly improved the contents of the book.

We take this opportunity to extend our heartfelt gratitude to tourism business operators, elected representatives, administrators, academia, NGOs and local community in India and particularly in Kerala for motivating us to take this course of action. We are also thankful to Mr Jishnu P. Thampy for designing the pictures and authors who permitted us to quote relevant portions and share pictures for bringing out this book in its present form. We would like to provide credit for all the material used in the book, and would be grateful if any inadvertent oversight can be pointed out.

We believe that the courses in tourism should produce quality human resources with the knowledge and skillsets that are required for the tourism sector. We had a series of deliberations with business operators, policy-makers, administrators, academicians and local community for initiating a change in the approach in tourism education in the country. This book is a humble attempt to initiate a change in tourism education system which we expect to be deliberated across the country.

We would also like to thank Dr Jitendra Mohan Mishra, Associate Professor, Department of Tourism Management, Indira Gandhi National Tribal University; Amarkantak and Dr Rekha Maitra, Assistant Professor, Hospitality and Faculty of Management Studies, Manav Rachna International University, for reviewing our book and providing invaluable comments which have added to the value of the book.

On a personal level, Dr Venu would like to thank his wife Sarada Muraleedharan for her thoughtful advice and support during the difficult times of writing this book. Dr Vijayakumar B. remembers with gratitude the unstinted cooperation and support of his wife R. Shylaja. Mr Saroop Roy B.R. would like to thank his wife Bindu S. Kumar for her tolerance and sacrifice.

About the Authors

Venu Vasudevan currently serves the Government of Kerala as the Principal Secretary, Tourism, and looks after three more departments. With over 15 years of experience in senior management positions, Dr Vasudevan is the longest serving officer in tourism in India. Dr Vasudevan joined the Indian Administrative Service (IAS) in 1990, and has served the Government of India and state Government of Kerala in various capacities. Born in 1964, Vasudevan earned a degree in medicine but later chose to take up a career in the civil services.

He has served the sectors of Tourism and Culture in a variety of assignments. It was during his tenure as Director, Kerala Tourism, and later as Secretary, Department of Tourism, that Kerala transformed its market positioning and built up a strong private–public partnership, culminating in Kerala being recognized by the National Geographic Traveller as one of the 50 'must-see' destinations of the world. Kerala Travel Mart, the biggest international travel mart in India, is his brainchild. He served the Ministry of Tourism, Government of India, and played a pivotal role in formulating the 'Incredible India' campaign.

Two projects designed by him have won international awards instituted by Pacific Asia Travel Association (PATA). Utsavam, a project to revive the traditional art forms of Kerala and provide income streams to artistes, won the PATA Gold Award 2008 (http://www.pata.org/update-from-past-winners). 'A Day with the Masters', a guided tour of Kerala Kalamandalam, a school for performing arts, won 'honourable mention' in 2005 (http://www.kalamandalam.org/adaywithmasters.asp).

He served as Secretary, Cultural Affairs, Government of Kerala (2007–2011), during which period the International Theatre Festival of Kerala (http://www.theatrefestivalkerala.com/) was established. He was instrumental in setting up and curating a new museum, Keralam (http://www.museumkeralam.org/). He played a key role in the improvement and upgradation of the museums and archives of Kerala.

Moving to the Union Government, he served as Joint Secretary, Ministry of Culture, with responsibility over apex cultural institutions, libraries, archives and Museums. As the Director General of the National Museum (from January 2013 to May 2015), he headed a team that worked on the revival of National Museum, initiating a range of projects that improved arrivals, enhanced visibility and involved stakeholders and the academic community. He was invited to be a participant in the Global Museum Leaders Colloquium of the Metropolitan Museum of Art, New York. He served as the Vice Chancellor, National Museum Institute of History of Art, Conservation and Museology.

In the tourism sector, Dr Vasudevan has deep interest in community-based tourism. He organized the 2nd International Conference on Responsible Tourism, and was instrumental in establishing a robust model for Responsible Tourism in Kerala. He writes extensively on communities, responsible tourism and the changing role of public sector in the tourism sector.

Apart from his official responsibilities, he is a keen theatre actor and an avid fan of Arsenal football club.

Vijayakumar B. served as the Principal of Kerala Institute of Tourism and Travel Studies for ten years from 2007 to 2017. He joined the Collegiate Education Department, Government of Kerala as Lecturer of Economics in 1981, and also served as Senior Lecturer and Reader of Economics in various government colleges. He also served as visiting faculty in tourism in University of Kerala for seven years.

Dr Vijayakumar is a post graduate in economics, tourism management and rural development and took degrees of MPhil and PhD in tourism from the University of Kerala. He is an accredited management teacher and life member of All India Management Association, editor of *Indian Journal of Tourism and Hospitality Management*, expert member of various committees of State Planning Board, vocational higher secondary education, Business Advisory Committee Hospitality Sector of Additional Skill Acquisition Programme Kerala, Post Graduate Board of Studies in Tourism at Central University, Puducherry and Anna University, Chennai. He also served as Chairman, Board of Studies (UG), member of Post Graduate Studies in Economics and Management and faculty of Social Sciences, University of Kerala.

He has coordinated 12 research projects, published 4 books in economics, 11 books in tourism and contributed research articles to various national and international journals. He has presented research papers in more than 75 national and international conferences. He is a recipient of National Award for Best Research Report in 2003, instituted by International Institute of Adult and Lifelong Education New Delhi and Vocational Excellence Award by Rotary Club, Thiruvananthapuram in 2014. His areas of expertise include sustainable tourism and community-based tourism activities. He is actively involved in propagating responsible tourism among tourism stakeholders at micro and macro levels through public meetings, workshops, print and electronic media.

Saroop Roy B.R. is currently Assistant Professor, Kerala Institute of Tourism and Travel Studies, and the project coordinator of the Responsible Tourism Initiative in Kerala, and he has played a significant role in the formulation and implementation of the project in the state. He finished his degree of Masters of Tourism Administration (MTA) from the University of Kerala after finishing his B.Tech in Electronics and Communication engineering. Starting his career in tourism field as a trainee at Thenmala Ecotourism Promotion Society (TEPS) in 2000, he was the Kerala co-ordinator of EQUATIONS, a Bengaluru-based research campaign and advocacy organization on tourism policies and issues, for eight years. In 2010, he moved to the tourism academic field as faculty MBA (Tourism) at the Institute of Management in Kerala (IMK) under the University of Kerala. In 2011, he joined KITTS as Assistant Professor in Travel and Tourism (T&T). His expertise includes areas in tourism policy formulation, ecotourism, responsible tourism, rural tourism and community-linked tourism projects.

During his tenure at EQUATIONS, he participated in the SBSTTA 13 meeting of the Convention on Biological Diversity held at Rome in February 2008. He also led the Indian delegation of ecotourism practitioners to attend the South African and Indian Practitioners' Workshop to exchange lessons and best practices on using nature tourism as a force for Poverty Alleviation at Johannesburg in May 2008. He was also the resource person at various sessions on Institution Building for Sustainable Tourism and Livelihoods, organized by UNDP at IRMA, Anand as part of the Endogenous Tourism Project in 2006 and 2008. He participated and presented papers at various international forums including the 'Canopy Tourism: Concept and Practice in the Indian Context,' at the 5th International Canopy Conference in October 2009, Bengaluru, and made the key note presentation on environmental responsibility at the International Conference on Responsible Tourism—Looking Back: Moving Ahead—held at Kumarakom in June 2013.

On the policy front, he was the drafting committee member of the Kerala Tourism Policy 2012, Revamping of Homestay Classification Scheme for Kerala 2015 and preparation of charter for Green Carpet initiative for Kerala Tourism 2016.

Vijayakumar and Saroop Roy jointly authored the books *Tourism and Livelihood: Selected Experiences from Kerala* (2011), *A Case Study on Kumarakom* (2013) and submitted research paper 'Community Based Tourism Business in Kumarakom: A Case Study of Innovative Products and Experiences' which was accepted for presentation at the 2nd UNWTO Knowledge Network Global Forum held at Mexico in 2014.

Section A: Tourism—An Overview

This introductory section is intended to provide an outline of tourism—the sector, the industry and the discipline—to students. Through the chapters, students are acquainted with the fundamentals of the tourism system, getting a glimpse of the size of the sector and its overall significance in the global economy. The section is organized into four chapters, covering aspects of tourism and its practice that are necessary to gain a clear understanding of the tourism business in subsequent sections.

Chapter 1 leads students through the basics of the subject, emphasizing the growth of the sector to a global phenomenon. The evolution of tourism as an economic activity is an interesting story in itself, but it is essentially a continuation of the travels undertaken by prominent travellers such as Faxian and Vasco da Gama, who came to India for very different reasons. It is in this context that students are taken through the definitions of tourism, and the fine differences between categories of travellers. Students advance to explore the concepts of typologies of tourists and the perspectives from which a visitor can be categorized. The chapter concludes by familiarizing students with a recurrent theme in the book—the pros and cons of this dynamic sector.

Chapter 2 enables students to get acquainted with some key concepts in tourism as well as a few important areas, which will repeatedly appear as the chapters unfold. Tourism is considered a part of the services sector, and it is appropriate to provide students an introduction to the basic concepts of goods and services. Sustainable tourism engages the attention of scholars and practitioners, but the frequent use and abuse of the term has rendered its specific meaning somewhat blurred. We thought that it is important for students to get an unambiguous idea of the term, the origins of the sustainability movement and the links between sustainable development and sustainable tourism. The term ecotourism has also been misused and hijacked so much so that it has lost its original meaning and has become jargonized. By tracing the different components that make up ecotourism, the chapter provides clarity and specificity to these terms. Moving on, other forms of tourism that are frequently used in practice are also elaborated with a view to provide distinctive identities to these. The chapter ends by introducing responsible tourism about which much will be heard in the coming chapters.

Chapter 3 deals with tourism demand, a critical element in the tourism system. The concept of tourism demand is introduced in simple terms, elaborating the elements in and factors influencing demand. The decision-making process of a consumer is explored, and the elements that affect consumer behaviour are fleshed out. Basic economic principles such as the demand curve and elasticity of demand are outlined. The basics of demand forecasting and its uses are elaborated. The measurement of demand and other components of the tourism system are explained, enabling students to gain an understanding on the applied aspects of statistics. Through a box, the basics of Tourism Satellite Accounting are presented.

Chapter 4 familiarizes the students with the major organizations that play an important role in tourism. Some international organizations have been prominent in assisting developing economies to make use of the opportunities presented by tourism development. The United Nations World Tourism Organization (UNWTO), the evolution of which is presented as a box, has emerged as a strong voice of tourism in the world, leading noteworthy causes like sustainability, standardization and assistance to least developed countries. UNESCO has a formidable reputation worldwide as the international voice for culture and heritage. The world heritage list is the most prestigious recognition of the universal value of a site. UNESCO also functions as a watchdog safeguarding cultural heritage, which is a priceless asset on which tourism depends. In this endeavour, UNESCO is supported by advisory bodies like International Centre for the Study of the Preservation and Restoration of Cultural Property (ICCROM) and International Council on Monuments and Sites (ICOMOS), which are also touched upon in the chapter. The bodies regulating and promoting international civil aviation, such a vital component for tourism, are also introduced. The chapter concludes by drawing attention to industry associations such as American Society of Travel Agents (ASTA) which have become attractive target for destination marketers because of their reach and membership.

At the Pushkar fair
Image courtesy: Department of Tourism, Government of Rajasthan.

CHAPTER 1

An Introduction to Tourism

By the end of this chapter students will be able to:

- Trace the evolution and growth of tourism.
- Distinguish between closely related terminologies in tourism.
- Classify different types of tourists.
- Get an overview of pros and cons of tourism.

Introduction

Humans have been travelling since time immemorial. Since the prehistoric period, when nomads roamed the land in search of food and prey, man has been on the move. Even after the establishment of settlements and the beginning of cultivation, people continued to travel—for conquest, exploration and adventure. For the quest to know the unknown, the prospect of wealth-stimulated exploration and adventure travel, mighty rulers crossed their geographical boundaries for conquest. Religious beliefs brought another reason to travel, with pilgrimages and spiritual pursuits providing the impetus. Pilgrims, holy men and philosophers travelled great distances in the face of adversity and danger in search of succour, fulfilment and knowledge.

Faxian
Faxian was a Chinese Buddhist monk who travelled to Nepal, Sri Lanka and India to acquire Buddhist scriptures between 399 and 414 AD. He was born at Shanxi during the fourth century. His original name was Sehi, who later adopted the spiritual name Faxian (splendour of dharma). He visited India during the period of Chandragupta Vikramaditya II. The details of his journey are described in his travelogue *Foguoji* (a Record of Buddhist Kingdoms). His writings give important information about early Buddhism. After his return to China, he translated many Sanskrit Buddhist texts he had brought back into Chinese. Among them, two of the most important were the *Mahaparinirvana Sutra*, a text glorifying the eternal, personal and pure nature of nirvana and the *Vinaya* (rules of discipline for the monks) of

(Continued ...)

the Mahasanghika School. Faxian visited the most important seats of Buddhist learning: Udyana, Gandhara, Peshawar and Taxila. His pilgrimage was completed by visits to the most holy spots: Kapilavastu, where the Buddha was born; Bodh Gaya, where the Buddha acquired the supreme enlightenment; Banaras (Varanasi), where the Buddha preached his first sermon and Kushinagara, where the Buddha entered into the perfect nirvana. Then he stayed for a long time at Pataliputra, conversing with Buddhist monks and studying Sanskrit texts with Buddhist scholars. When he had deepened his knowledge of Buddhism and was in possession of sacred texts that were not yet translated into Chinese, he decided to go back to China. Instead of once more taking the overland route, Faxian took the sea route, first sailing to Ceylon (now Sri Lanka), at that time one of the most flourishing centres of Buddhist studies. After returning to his homeland, Faxian resumed his scholarly tasks and translated the Buddhist texts he had taken so much trouble to bring back into Chinese.

Source: Arvon (2016).

In modern times, there are multifarious reasons that stimulate travel. Primary among them are business, leisure and socialization. Business and trade have driven people to establish links with fellow traders and buyers across great landmasses and oceans, and thus great trade routes were established. With economic development came leisure travel and the concept of travelling for pleasure. Our social obligations make us travel for family celebrations, social functions and community events.

Tourism, in the modern sense of the term, is a relatively recent development. However, as we will see in this chapter, the rapid emergence of T&T as one of the most important economic activities of the world is a key development of the twentieth century. Tourism is regarded as a significant economic driver, contributing in multiple ways to the global economy.

In this chapter, we shall familiarize ourselves with this multifaceted, dynamic and ever changing discipline. It is essential to obtain a clear understanding of the concepts that form the basis of the subject and definitions of key terms. We will start our examination of the different aspects of tourism, beginning with an appreciation of the factors that extend an influence on the business of tourism. We will also get a glimpse of some of the differing viewpoints that exist on fundamental matters in the subject.

The Complexity of Tourism

Tourism is a complex subject, as it can be approached from different viewpoints. For example, tourism may be seen as an economic activity that contributes substantially to the economy of certain regions and countries. It can mean a business, a study of enterprises set up to cater to the demand of the tourists in a destination. To the business community, tourism may mean an industry, comprising of small and large businesses and companies, which have common objectives and issues. To a planner, tourism is a tool for economic development and societal change. To make sense of this confusing picture, a student of tourism has to obtain a systematic understanding of the theoretical basis of the management of tourism.

Tourism consists of many sectors such as accommodation, transportation, tour operations, attractions and support infrastructure. Each of these sectors is characterized by a complex interplay of factors. To give an example, the transportation sector is influenced by a variety of related components such as oil prices, regulatory environments, the construction of high-speed railway systems and climate change. It is this interplay of diverse aspects that makes tourism a challenging and interesting discipline.

Students of tourism approached the subject very differently in the 1980s and 1990s, and many of the theories and viewpoints about the industry, popular a few decades ago, have been discarded or substantially modified, owing to the evolution of the tourism business in response to the developments that have occurred in the world during this period. Tourism is informed by several perspectives—environmental, cultural, economic, social and political. These perspectives are often conflicting and antagonistic, but a study of their influences provides students a deep understanding of how tourism changes and evolves through the years.

Tourism is a truly global discipline that has international and national linkages. A network of dynamic and complex processes creates these linkages that make tourism possible across continents and cultures. Students of tourism need to develop a perspective that understands the transnational elements of the discipline, even while developing an appreciation of the smaller and most local factors in destinations that may play a critical role in the development of tourism.

From an academic point of view, tourism is yet to completely establish itself as a full-fledged, recognized subject, although there have been several developments in recent years in that direction. The lack of universal agreement about definitions stands in the way of the development of common approaches. As tourism does not have its own set of well-established theories or time-tested laws, it tends to depend on the principles and formulations made in other subjects such as sociology, psychology economics and management. This is pointed out as an aspect that weakens the case of tourism to be treated as an academic subject on par with established subjects. Each related discipline approaches tourism from a perspective that has been developed within that subject. The paucity of interdisciplinary research that focuses attention on issues peculiar to tourism practice is pointed out as another limitation.

Tourism as a Global Phenomenon

Realising the importance of tourism, destinations are opening up for business, fuelling investments that in turn bring in tourists to new regions. Tourism drives socioeconomic progress, creating jobs and improving incomes. Global tourist arrivals have seen tremendous growth during the last six decades. Despite periodic setbacks and shocks, tourism has registered continuous growth. From 25.3 million (2.53 crores) in 1950, global tourist arrivals has increased to 1,133 million (113 crores) in 2014.

International tourism receipts earned by destinations worldwide grew from US$2 billion to US$1,245 billion (₹81,000 crores) in 2014. International tourism receipts refer to the total expenditure of international inbound visitors, including payments made for air transportation and for purchasing goods and services in the destinations (Table 1.1).

Economic Significance of Tourism

Tourism is regarded as one of the largest industries, capable of creating wide ranging impacts on various facets of human life. The significance of tourism is often highlighted in terms of its capacity to generate income, foreign exchange, employment and support to development initiatives. According to the UNWTO, travel and tourism (T&T) contributes about 10% of the world's gross domestic product (GDP), 6% of world exports and 30% of service exports, as well as creates 1 in 11 jobs worldwide. The rapid growth of tourism is clear from the sustained increase in the number of tourist arrivals, tourism receipts and employment generated.

Growth of tourism as a global economic phenomenon is one of the most important milestones of the twentieth century. WTTC, one of the international authorities on the economic and social contribution of T&T, calculated that the T&T sector generated US$ 7.6 trillion, or 5.04 lakh crores, annually. This staggering figure constitutes about 10% of the world's GDP, which is the total value of all goods and services produced in the world.

How is this figure arrived at, and what exactly does it tell us? WTTC collects statistics from 181 countries, particularly data on spending on T&T by diverse sets of people such as businesses, households, tourists, same-day visitors and governments, with a view to fully capture the economic contribution of the sector and assess the economic impact of T&T on the economy.

Table 1.1   Global tourist arrivals and receipts

Year	Tourist Arrival (million)	Tourism Receipts (million US$)
1950	25.3	-
1960	69.3	-
1970	165.8	-
1980	275.9	-
1990	436.1	271
2000	683.3	495
2010	949	966
2011	997	1,081
2012	1,038	1,116
2013	1,087	1,197
2014	1,133	1,245

Source: World Travel & Tourism Council (WTTC, various years).

This contribution will be examined in detail in subsequent chapters. For the present, it may be sufficient to note that the contribution of T&T arises from the direct, indirect and induced impacts. Figure 1.1 portrays the broad areas that lead up to the total contribution of T&T to GDP and employment (Table 1.2).

The 'direct' component is the total of the spending by residents and non-residents on T&T for business and leisure purposes as well as government spending on T&T services directly linked to visitors such as expenditure on museums or national parks. The 'indirect' contribution includes all investments related to T&T such as construction of hotels or purchase of aircraft, government spending that support and help T&T activities such as infrastructure services, promotion and marketing. The 'induced' contribution measures the impact of jobs supported by the spending of persons employed by the T&T sector.

Evolution of Tourism

Some form of leisure travel has been recorded during the Egyptian (3100–1090 BCE) and Babylonian (1894–619 BCE) periods. The religious festivals of the Egyptians attracted many devotees, who also visited the famous works of arts and buildings of the city. A number of people in the ancient period visited Egypt to see the pyramids. During the Babylonian empire, a museum of historic antiquities was opened for the public.

During the Classical period of the Greeks (776–197 BCE), citizens travelled to places of the healing gods, taking part in their religious festivals. Parthenon, a former temple on the Athenian Acropolis, was a popular tourist attraction. In order to provide accommodation facilities for travellers, inns were established in towns and sea ports. The celebrated historian Herodotus was a seasoned traveller and his writings describe his travels, making him one of the world's first travel writers. Guidebooks covering destinations such as Athens, Troy and Sparta were published during the period.

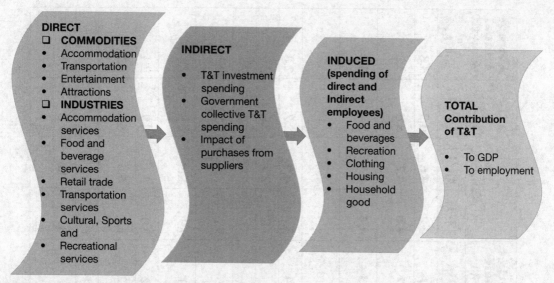

Figure 1.1 Contribution of travel and tourism sector
Source: Economic Impact, WTTC (2015).

During the Roman era (27 BCE–476 CE), excellent roads connecting cities coupled with way-side inns promoted travel. Regular patrolling by the Romans kept pirates at bay, and safe travel on sea routes to destinations like Sicily, Greece, Rhodes, Troy and Egypt became common. Some rich families constructed second homes near Rome and stayed there during spring time. Romans also introduced *itineraria*—road map in the form of a listing of cities, villages and other stops, with the intervening distances.

In the Middle Ages, people mainly travelled for business or as part of their official duty. Some adventurers from Europe tried to discover sea routes to India for trade purpose, resulting in the 'discovery' of America and some parts of Africa.

Vasco da Gama

Vasco da Gama (1460–1524) was a Portuguese explorer and navigator, and the first person to sail directly from Europe to India. Da Gama was born in 1460 into a noble family. Little is known of his early life. In 1497, he was appointed to command an expedition equipped by the Portuguese government, whose intention was to find a maritime route to the East.

Setting off in July 1497, da Gama's expedition took advantage of the prevailing winds by sailing south down the coast of Africa, then veering far out into the Atlantic and swinging back in an arc to arrive off the southern African coast. This established a route still followed by sailing vessels. The expedition then rounded the Cape of Good and, after sailing up the coast of east Africa, took on an Arab navigator who helped them reach the Indian coast at Calicut (now Kozhikode) in May 1498. This voyage launched the all-water route from Europe to Asia.

Source: BBC (2014).

The Silk Route, a 'highway' of trade and commerce, facilitated business travel, cultural exchange and strengthened the foundations for T&T in Central Asia. Missionaries also forayed into the new territories during the period, spreading the gospel. Leisure travel in India became popular with the Mughals building palaces and gardens in places with agreeable climate.

Table 1.2 International tourist arrivals

| | International Tourist Arrivals (million) | | | | | | | Market Share (%) | Change (%) | | | Average Annual Growth (%) |
	1990	1995	2000	2005	2010	2013	2014*	2014*	12/11	13/12	14*/13	'05-14'
World	**435**	**527**	**674**	**809**	**949**	**1087**	**1133**	**100**	**4.2**	**4.6**	**4.3**	**3.8**
Advanced Economies**	**296**	**336**	**420**	**466**	**513**	**586**	**619**	**54.7**	**4.0**	**4.7**	**5.8**	**3.2**
Emerging Economies**	**139**	**191**	**253**	**343**	**435**	**501**	**513**	**45.3**	**4.4**	**4.5**	**2.4**	**4.6**
By UNWTO Regions												
Europe	**261.5**	**304.7**	**386.4**	**453.0**	**488.9**	**566.4**	**581.8**	**51.4**	**3.9**	**4.9**	**2.7**	**2.8**
Northern Europe	28.7	36.4	44.8	59.9	62.8	67.4	71.3	6.3	1.5	2.9	5.9	2.0
Western Europe	108.6	112.2	139.7	141.7	154.4	170.8	174.5	15.4	3.6	2.8	2.2	2.3
Central/Eastern Europe	33.9	58.1	69.3	95.1	98.4	127.3	121.1	10.7	9.1	7.7	-4.9	2.7
Southern/Meditt. Europe	90.3	98.0	132.6	156.4	173.3	201.0	214.9	19.0	1.9	5.6	6.9	3.6
- of which EU-28	230.1	268.0	330.5	367.9	384.3	433.8	455.1	40.2	3.0	4	4.9	2.4
Asia and the Pacific	**55.8**	**82.1**	**110.3**	**154.0**	**205.4**	**249.8**	**263.3**	**23.2**	**6.9**	**6.8**	**5.4**	**6.1**
North-East Asia	26.4	41.3	58.3	85.9	111.5	127.0	136.3	12.0	6.0	3.4	7.3	5.3
South-East Asia	21.2	28.5	36.3	49.0	70.5	94.3	96.7	8.5	8.7	11.3	2.6	7.9
Oceania	5.2	8.1	9.6	10.9	11.4	12.5	13.2	1.2	4.2	4.6	5.7	2.1

	International Tourist Arrivals (million)							Market Share (%)	Change (%)			Average Annual Growth (%) '05-14'
	1990	1995	2000	2005	2010	2013	2014*	2014*	12/11	13/12	14*/13	
South Asia	3.1	4.2	6.1	8.1	12.0	16.0	17.1	1.5	5.9	11.4	6.8	8.6
Americas	**92.8**	**109.1**	**128.2**	**133.3**	**150.1**	**167.5**	**181**	**16.0**	**4.5**	**3.1**	**8.0**	**3.5**
North America	71.8	80.7	91.5	89.9	99.5	110.2	120.4	10.6	4.1	3.6	9.2	3.3
Carribean	11.4	14.0	17.1	18.8	19.5	21.1	22.4	2.0	3.1	2.8	6.2	2.0
Central America	1.9	2.6	4.3	6.3	7.9	9.1	9.6	0.8	7.3	2.6	5.6	4.8
South America	7.7	11.7	15.3	18.3	23.1	27.1	28.6	2.5	6.3	1.5	5.4	5.1
Africa	**14.7**	**18.7**	**26.2**	**34.8**	**49.5**	**54.4**	**55.7**	**4.9**	**4.8**	**4.7**	**2.4**	**5.4**
North Africa	8.4	7.3	10.2	13.9	18.8	19.6	19.8	1.7	8.7	6.0	0.9	4.0
Subsaharan Africa	6.3	11.5	16.0	20.9	30.8	34.7	35.9	3.2	2.8	4.1	3.3	6.2
Middle East	**9.6**	**12.7**	**22.4**	**33.7**	**54.7**	**48.4**	**51.0**	**4.5**	**-5.3**	**-3.1**	**5.4**	**4.7**

Source: World Tourism Organisation, May 2015.
Notes: *Provisional data.
**Classification based on the International Monetary Fund.

Silk Route

Eurasia was criss-crossed with communication routes and paths of trade, which gradually linked up to form what are known today as the Silk Roads; routes across both land and sea, along which silk and many other goods were exchanged between people from across the world. While the silk trade was one of the earliest catalysts for the trade routes across Central Asia, it was only one of a wide range of products that was traded between east and west, and which included textiles, spices, grain, vegetables and fruit, animal hides, tools, wood work, metal work, religious objects, art work, precious stones and much more. These routes developed over time and according to shifting geopolitical contexts throughout history. For example, merchants from the Roman Empire tried to avoid crossing the territory of the Parthians, Rome's enemies, and therefore took routes to the north, across the Caucasus region and over the Caspian Sea.

Travellers along the Silk Roads were attracted not only by trade but also by the intellectual and cultural exchange that was taking place in cities along the Silk Roads. Science, arts and literature, as well as crafts and technologies were thus shared and disseminated into societies along the lengths of these routes, and in this way, languages, religions and cultures developed and influenced each other. Perhaps the most lasting legacy of the Silk Roads has been their role in bringing cultures and peoples in contact with each other, and facilitating exchange between them. Knowledge about science, arts and literature, as well as crafts and technologies was shared across the Silk Roads, and in this way, languages, religions and cultures developed and influenced each other. One of the most famous technical advances to have been propagated worldwide by the Silk Roads was the technique of making paper, as well as the development of printing press technology. Similarly, irrigation systems across Central Asia share features that were spread by travellers who not only carried their own cultural knowledge, but also absorbed that of the societies in which they found themselves.

Religion and a quest for knowledge were further inspirations to travel along these routes. Buddhist monks from China made pilgrimages to India to bring back sacred texts, and their travel diaries are an extraordinary source of information. The diary of Xuan Zang (whose 25-year journal lasted from 629 to 654 AD) not only has an enormous historical value, but also inspired a comic novel in the sixteenth century, the *Pilgrimage to the West*, which has become one of the great Chinese classics. During the Middle Ages, European monks undertook diplomatic and religious missions to the East. Perhaps the most famous traveller was the Venetian explorer, Marco Polo, whose travels lasted for more than 20 years between 1271 and 1292, and whose account of his experiences became extremely popular in Europe after his death.

The routes were also fundamental in the dissemination of religions throughout Eurasia. Buddhism is one example of a religion that travelled the Silk Roads, with Buddhist art and shrines being found as far apart as Bamiyan in Afghanistan, Mount Wutai in China and Borobudur in Indonesia. Christianity, Islam, Hinduism, Zoroastrianism and Manicheism spread in the same way, as travellers absorbed the cultures they encountered and then carried them back to their homelands with them. Thus, for example, Hinduism and subsequently Islam were introduced into Indonesia and Malaysia by Silk Road merchants travelling the maritime trade routes from India and Arabia.

The process of travelling the Silk Roads developed along with the roads themselves. In the Middle Ages, caravans consisting of horses or camels were the standard means of transporting goods across land. Caravanserais, large guest houses or inns designed to welcome travelling merchants, played a vital role in facilitating the passage of people and goods along these routes. Found along the Silk Roads from Turkey to China, they provided not only a regular opportunity for merchants to eat well, rest and prepare themselves in safety for their onward journey, and also to exchange goods, trade with local markets and buy local products, and to meet other merchant travellers, and in doing so, to exchange cultures, languages and ideas.

Source: UNESCO (n.d.).

From the late sixteenth century, young nobles visited Paris, Venice, Florence and Rome, as the culmination of their classical education. The idea of the 'Grand Tour' was born and the upper classes travelled to appreciate the art and culture of France and Italy, seeking new cultural experiences and a sense of adventure.

The Industrial Revolution brought about profound changes in economic activities and lifestyles of people. The factory system and urbanization changed the outlook towards work and leisure. Till then, the concept of leisure was practically unknown to the masses and it was considered as the prerogative of the elite and the rich. The elite class travelled for hunting and pleasure, and to spas and hot water springs for rejuvenation and relaxation. The development of temporary accommodation near these attractions can be considered as the first step in development of resorts in the accommodation sector.

The Industrial Revolution gave rise to the continuous movement of people from rural to urban areas, in search of wage employment. Workers in factories were provided weekly offs and leaves with holidays and specific working hours. The factory workers/blue collar jobs were provided facilities that elevated them to a higher standard of living compared to farmers and casual workers. Factory workers and urban dwellers started spending part of their disposable income travelling short distances, eventually taking holidays with their families during their leisure time. The advent of railways promoted long-distance travel, passenger trains enabled the rapid transit to popular destinations on the seaside, and entrepreneurs like Thomas Cook developed tour packages. The introduction of steam boat service promoted regular passenger traffic between Europe and America in the nineteenth century. The opening of Suez Canal in 1869 transformed travel between Europe and Asian countries, dramatically reducing travel times.

During the Victorian Period in the latter part of the nineteenth century, establishments patronized by American tourists visiting Great Britain added dishes preferred by Americans to the menu, initiating another important innovation in hospitality. Increasing awareness of arts and culture, the opening of great colonial museums, the advent of photography and the publication of the first travel guidebooks are other noteworthy developments contributing to the growth of tourism during the period (Vijayakumar, 2008).

The period after the World War I witnessed the development of motor cars ensuring connectivity to remote and rural areas within the country. The introduction of private cars encouraged domestic travel in Europe. After the World War II, the use of air transport for civilian purposes played a crucial role in promoting mass international travel, popularizing seaside resorts of the Mediterranean, North Africa and the Caribbean islands. The introduction of jet engines, high-capacity aircraft and bullet trains have resulted in reducing travel times considerably. Seaside resorts became an annual family holiday destination, leading to the growth of the hotel industry and the establishment of hotel chains.

Defining Tourism

If a person working in a city returns to his house in his village, can he be counted as a 'tourist'? If someone in Delhi owns a house in Uttarakhand and stays there during the summer months, does that make him a tourist?

Finding a universally acceptable definition for tourism has been quite challenging. Numerous terms such as 'traveller', 'visitor', 'tourist' and 'guest' are used to denote the people who participate in this activity, and experts have debated whether certain aspects of the activity to be included in the definition or not. Even today, there are several grey areas which continue to be debated.

Here are a few categories of persons whose 'status' as 'tourists' have been discussed and debated:

- The elderly, who migrate seasonally during winter to warmer places.
- The day visitor who crosses international boundaries, like the Englishman who drives across the channel tunnel to France, and returns to his home in the evening.

- People staying in second homes they own in a tourist destination.
- Cruise passengers who visit the sites close to a port for a brief while on a shore visit.

While there will be continued debate on such matters, we will scan a few definitions that have been proposed, that may throw light on differing viewpoints:

> Tourism is about people being away from their own homes, on short term, temporary visits, for particular purposes. Davidson (1989)

> Tourism is the sum of phenomena and relationships arising from the travel and stay of non-residents insofar as it does not lead to permanent residence and is not connected to any earning activity. Hunziker and Krapf (1942)

> Tourism is the temporary movement of people to destinations outside their normal places of work and residence, the activities undertaken during their stay in those destinations and the facilities created to cater to their needs. Mathieson and Wall (1982)

> The sum of the phenomena and relationships arising from the interaction of tourists, business suppliers, host governments and host communities in the process of attracting and hosting these tourists and other visitors. McIntosh and Goeldner (1986)

Invariably, the above definitions indicate that tourism is related to a 'temporary' movement of people and focus on 'non-pecuniary' activities at destinations. Considering tourism as a socioeconomic phenomenon, and the need for a commonly accepted definition for operational purpose both from the industry and visitor perspective, UNWTO defined tourism as follows:

> Tourism comprises the activities of persons travelling to and staying in places outside their usual environment for not more than one consecutive year for leisure, business and other purposes not related to the exercise of an activity remunerated from within the place visited.

Related Concepts

We may come across a number of terminologies that are closely related to T&T. A clear understanding on the various terminologies would enable us to closely examine the processes involved and gain clarity on the economic activity termed as tourism.

Who is a 'traveller'?

Someone who moves between different geographical locations, for any purpose and for any duration.

Who is a 'visitor'?

A traveller making a trip outside his/her usual environment, for less than a year, for any purpose other than for employment, is termed a visitor.

An 'internal' or 'domestic' visitor is any person residing in a country, who travels to a place within the country, outside his/her usual environment for a period not exceeding twelve months and whose main purpose of visit is other than exercise of an activity remunerated from within the place visited.

Based on the Recommendations on Statistics of International Migration (United Nations, 1998), International visitors are persons who do not reside in the country of arrival and who are admitted for short stays for purposes of leisure, recreation and holidays; visits to friends or relatives; business or professional activities not remunerated from within the receiving country; health treatment or religious pilgrimages.

> A visitor is termed a 'tourist' if his/her trip includes an overnight stay. If it does not include an overnight's stay, the visitor is considered an 'excursionist' or 'same-day visitor'.

Travellers who commute regularly between their residence and place of work or study or who frequently visit places—homes of friends or relatives, houses of worship, healthcare facility—that might be at a distance from their residence regularly, cannot be termed visitors. This is because these places fall in the definition of his/her 'usual environment'. Travellers crossing a border on a regular basis for work including short-term work are excluded from visitors.

UNWTO defines tourists as 'people who are travelling to and staying in places outside their usual environment for not more than one consecutive year for leisure, business and other purposes not related to the exercise of an activity remunerated from within the place visited'.

Groups to Be Included as Tourists

- People travelling for pleasure for health or family reasons (including nationals who live permanently abroad).
- People travelling to attend meetings or for assignments (sports, management). Employees of large organizations on assignment abroad for less than one year are also included.
- People travelling for business (employees of commercial or industrial firms who are travelling to install machinery or equipment abroad).
- Students and young people at boarding schools or colleges and those who travel or work temporarily during their holidays.
- Visitors from cruise ships even if their stay is less than 24 hours. They can be registered in a separate group, which does not take into account their place of residence.
- Transit passengers who cross the country for more than 24 hours.
- Foreign airline and ship crew on stopover in a country.
- Musicians and artists on tour.

Travellers Not Considered as Tourists

- Diplomats.
- Representatives of consulates (travelling for duty purposes).
- Members of the armed forces.
- Refugees (as defined by the UN Commissioner for refugees, 1967).
- Transit passengers (who do not leave the transit area of the airport or the port including transfer between airports or ports).
- Nomads, as defined by the UN in the recommendations on statistics of international migration, 1980.
- Permanent and temporary immigrants.
- Border workers.

Types of Tourism

Tourism (and tourists) may be classified into different ways. The source/destination perspective divides them as coming to or going from a place. Geographically, tourists can be seen as national or international and can be classified on the basis of the purpose of their visit.

Destination Perspective

Inbound and Outbound Tourism: 'Inbound' tourism relates to tourism of non-resident visitors within the country. A French national visiting India for a week on a sightseeing trip is an example of an inbound tourist for India. 'Outbound' tourism refers to tourism of people visiting destinations in other countries. From an Indian perspective, an Indian citizen visiting France for a holiday is considered an outbound tourist.

Figure 1.2   Domestic tourist
Source: Authors.

Geographical Perspective

Domestic, Internal, National and International Tourism: Domestic tourism is tourism that takes place within the country. A domestic tourist is a resident visitor within the country of reference as part of a domestic tourism trip. In Figure 1.2, an Indian citizen residing in Kerala travelling to Goa for a holiday can be considered as an example of a domestic tourist.

Internal tourism is a combination of domestic and inbound tourism, that is, the tourism of resident and non-resident visitors within the country of reference as part of domestic or international tourism trip. National tourism comprises domestic tourism and outbound tourism that is the tourism of resident visitors within and outside the country of reference. International tourism comprises inbound and outbound tourism that is the total of tourism across countries.

Visitor Perspective

Leisure: Leisure time refers to the free and discretionary time available to an individual, after meeting basic and essential needs, during which the individual may or may not undertake activities without external compulsion for pleasure or otherwise. Let us elaborate this further. An individual has to spend time at work or for work-related matters such as commuting. He has to keep aside time for sleeping, eating, household chores, raising children and for religious pursuits. The time available to the individual after these needs have been met is to be spent by him on his discretion—to relax at home, watch a movie, play cricket or go for a holiday.

Travel for leisure itself can be for many reasons, such as relaxation, to satisfy one's curiosity, to indulge in hobbies or pastimes, to take part in an adventure or to satisfy one's desires. In India, family functions are the most common reasons for leisure travel, which in technical terms is called 'Visiting Friends and Relatives' (VFR) travel.

Business: People the world over travel for their business purposes, making business travel one of most important sectors within tourism. A whole genre has emerged recently, concentrating on the congregations of business travellers. The meetings, incentives, conferences, conventions, events and exhibitions business, collectively called MICE, is a major source of revenue for destinations. There is an increasing tendency among business people to combine business with pleasure to take some leisure time while working, to visit attractions, and for sightseeing, shopping and entertainment.

Education: Students generally travel to educational institutions or universities within the country or abroad for study, internship and research purposes. Educational tours are regularly organized for students with an objective to provide exposure and widen their viewpoints. Some organizations offer students a chance to offer volunteer service in selected destinations. Study tours have become part of the curriculum and a range of tours are organized, ranging from single day trips to long transcontinental tours.

Health: The first forms of travel for leisure were visits of the elite to hot springs and spas. The trend continues, and there are many people who travel across the globe for rejuvenation and revitalization. Traditional healing systems like Ayurveda offer programmes exclusively for tourists. People also travel for availing medical treatment, termed 'Medical Value Travel', taking advantage of sophisticated technology, cost-effective treatment and immediate attention.

Pilgrimage: Inspired by religious beliefs and in search for peace and salvation, pilgrims have been undertaking long journeys. Improved access and faster connectivity have dramatically increased the travel of this category of visitors. Pilgrims bound for Mecca for Haj and Umra, believers flocking to Rome and the Holy land and the multitudes visiting sacred *tirtha*s (places of pilgrimage, where devotees usually take a holy dip in sacred water bodies) are all examples of the great pull of religious places.

Tourist Typologies

In Chapter 3, we will dwell on the complex question of why people travel, and the motivations of a traveller. In this section, we will look at the approaches taken to create tourist 'typologies', examining the 'roles' played by the tourists. Scholars have tried to map out the motivations of different types of travellers, their attitudes and perceptions and finally, the goals they aim to attain through travel. The social needs of an individual and his craving for familiarity provide a frame of reference and analysis.

Erik Cohen (1972), adopting a sociological basis for analyses, put forward the theory that 'tourism combines the curiosity to seek out new experiences with the need for the security of familiar environment at his residence'. He proposed a continuum of combinations ranging from extreme familiarity to extreme novelty. Based on the degree of familiarities, Cohen developed a typology, dividing tourists into four roles (see Table 1.3).

Table 1.3 Cohen's classification

Role	Category	Characteristics
Organized mass tourists	Institutionalized tourism	• are dealt with in a routine way by the tourist establishments, such as travel agencies, travel companies, hotel chains and other tourism-related institutions which cater to the tourist trade.
Individual mass tourists		
Explorer	Non-institutionalized tourism	• are loosely attached to the tourist establishment;
Drifter		• act as a 'spearhead for mass tourism' as well as
		• a 'demonstration effect' to the lower socio-economic groups of the host community.

Source: Generated using the typology of Cohen's tourist typology, 1974.

The Organized Mass Tourist

These are tourists who prefer to enjoy facilities at the destination to which they are accustomed in their resident environments. They expect the same ambience, comfort and sense of security wherever they travel, and are not very interested in indulging in adventurous activities or experiencing anything that is locally significant or unique. They prefer to create and live in an 'environmental bubble' throughout their trip. 'Environmental bubble' means the tourist is surrounded by his similar living environment while he is abroad. Mass tourists are demanding in the sense that they insist on familiar facilities at destinations, expecting the tour operator to provide these as part of a package purchased by them.

Individual Mass Tourist

The 'individual' mass tourist is a traveller with similar tastes and requirements as the organized mass tourist, with the exception that the tour is not entirely fixed and some flexibility is built into the package. The tourist has a certain amount of control over his time and itinerary, and is not bound to a group. However, all the major arrangements are still made through an intermediary. They are still confined to their 'environmental bubble'.

Explorer

The explorer is a tourist who prefers to arrange his trips independently and tries to go somewhere new and do something unusual and different. While he is willing to explore new environments, he would look for the reassurance of comfortable sleeping places and reliable means of transportation. He tries to mix with the people of the destination, sample local cuisine and try to speak the local language. He dares to leave the familiar 'environmental bubble' more readily than the mass tourist, but may seek its comfort occasionally.

Drifter

The drifter is fundamentally different from the mass tourist. Interested in experiencing and enjoying the environment in its authentic form, he immerses himself in the lifestyle and culture of the destination. He rejects the comforts of organized accommodation, preferring to use locally available accommodation, consuming food and beverages and other facilities at the destination exactly like the residents. His attempt is to move as far away as possible from familiarity.

Pros and Cons of Tourism

The tourism sector, which is witnessing rapid growth, has strong advocates and vociferous critics. Considering its advantages in the socioeconomic and environmental fronts, tourism is being promoted by national-, state- and local-level governments. As an engine of growth, means of support to local community, a tool for strengthening understanding on world peace and environment friendly nature, tourism makes significant contributions to the modern world.

Engine of Growth

Tourism is a multifaceted industry with extensive links with many sectors and disciplines. Every visitor is a consumer, purchasing and consuming a range of products and services, from the point of origin to the destination. There is tremendous economic significance to these activities, as these spur production, provide employment and accelerate the process of development, particularly in less-developed areas. Relatively backward regions, blessed with rich natural and cultural heritage, are brought to the mainstream of development by developing tourism. Infrastructure development, particularly road, transport, communication, water supply and energy, supports overall economic development and benefits residents while laying the foundation to attract tourists to the destination.

Benefits to Local Community

Tourism has the potential to bring benefits to the local community in destinations. The primary link between tourism and the community is livelihood support—tourism influx spurs the demand for agricultural and dairy products, and generates regular wage employment in tourism enterprises such as hotels and restaurants. The labour intensive nature of tourism enables local community to acquire direct and indirect employment, putting money in the hands of the community members and stimulating the local economy. Since most of the tourism business revolves around small and medium enterprises, members of the local community often become entrepreneurs in the tourism sector. Investments to develop infrastructure that is undertaken to develop tourism benefits the local community, resulting in the enhancement of amenities and higher living standards. Besides economic advantages, the local community is benefitted socially as tourism encourages cultural exchange, protection and promotion of various art forms, heritage and other local cultural activities.

Contribution to World Peace

Tourism significantly contributes to world peace by promoting better understanding with people living in different regions. The underlying principle of tourism is the sound relationship between the guest and local community, an interaction that deepens insights about cultures, lifestyles and beliefs.

Society and Environment

Tourism depends on natural and cultural assets of a destination, and their degradation has a direct, negative impact on the sector. The negative impacts on society and environment generally associated with the manufacturing industry are relatively low in tourism. Tourism is often called 'smokeless' industry because of its relatively soft imprint. By encouraging eco-friendly practices in transportation and accommodation, tourism industry strives to reduce environmental impacts. In tune with increasing customer awareness of the need to adopt sustainable forms of consumption, tourism activities are continuously evolving with a view to provide more environment friendly solutions.

However, tourism is not free from disadvantages. Unless scientifically planned and practised, tourism can generate more harm than good even in areas that make positive contributions. The disadvantages are all the more prominent on socio cultural and environmental fronts.

Economic Leakages

The economic benefits of tourism by and large are determined by the chances of promoting linkages with other economic activities, particularly among the local community. In the absence of facilities for promoting these linkages, incomes generated through tourism may leave the destination—a phenomenon termed 'leakage'—leaving little economic benefit to local community. In such cases, tourism fails to contribute to the process of economic development of the destinations as expected.

Distorting Local Economies

Tourism may promote distortion of local economic activities by displacing labour from traditional activities like fishing, agriculture and small and cottage industries. By encouraging changes in land use patterns, tourism may interfere with local economic activities and drive many in the local community to be dependent on tourism. This over dependence on a seasonal activity like tourism can have deleterious consequences in the socioeconomic milieu of the destination. Many destinations such as Benidorm in Spain, featured in our case study, were created by mass tourism and are reminders of the consequences of unregulated development transforming destinations.

Case Study: Mass Tourism in Spain—The Story of Benidorm

On the Mediterranean coast of Spain, Benidorm is one of the biggest sun and sand tourist destinations of the world. A town of 80,000 registered inhabitants, Benidorm had close to 11 million visitors in 2012. It has the highest density of skyscrapers per inhabitant in the world, and is second only to Manhattan, New York, in the number of high-rise buildings per sq. m of available land. Mild climate and sunny weather is its chief attraction, as is its long Mediterranean coastline.

Benidorm became so popular in England during the 1960s and 1970s that it was known as the most visited 'English' beach destination. Apart from the long beaches and warm oceans, Benidorm had an abundance of cheap rooms, amusement parks for the family, golf courses and a vigorous nightlife with a plethora of nightclubs, casinos and bars. Benidorm attracted a wide variety of holiday makers, from families to youth, and also many long staying pensioners. Benidorm is often called the birthplace of package tourism (Tremlett, 2006).

The explosive growth of Benidorm as a monster tourist destination started in the late 1950s when the town council decided to plan for building hotels along the coastline to boost the local economy which was till then dependent on fishing. This coincided with a massive increase in leisure travel, particularly from North Europe to the French, Spanish and Italian towns on the Mediterranean coast. In the 1960s, alongside a huge boom in construction of hotels and apartments, infrastructure such as the Alicante airport and attractions such as the bull fighting square were built. Package tours run by tour companies offered cheap holidays at affordable rates, which attracted more middle-class families to travel overseas. The advent of tour operator companies, with their distribution networks offering travel and accommodation as reasonably priced packages, tempted many Britons to travel abroad for their holidays. The liberalization of the civil aviation regime, resulting in the beginning of charter operations providing cheap air passage, was another factor aiding the mass tourism boom.

Mass tourism brought an explosion of growth in tourist arrivals and with it numerous problems. Attracted by the cheap holiday offers, many British men came to Benidorm to 'binge drink' and enjoy themselves, resulting in disorderly conduct and law and order problems. The misbehaviour of these so-called 'lager louts' turned away families to less crowded and more peaceful destinations. Solid waste disposal, urban sprawl and traffic congestion were other problems that the town faced.

(Continued ...)

There has been a steady decline in the foreign tourist arrivals, partly as a result of over-crowding, decreasing popularity of package holidays and opening up of long haul leisure destinations. The tourism product offered by the destination is undergoing transformation, with upgradation of rooms to 4 and 5 star standards and conversion of many hotel properties into apartments and offices. There is less dependence on tour operators and a majority of hotel bookings are done directly online by the customers.

Discussion Questions

1. 'With some planning in the initial stages, Benidorm could have managed the tourism boom better'. Discuss.
2. How can a destination turn away 'undesirable' tourists? Is it at all practical? Debate the pros and cons of this approach.

Cultural 'Invasion'

Many undesirable effects have taken place in destinations because of the 'invasion' of tourism. These are particularly seen in the social and cultural spheres and leave lasting damage in the socio cultural fabric of the place. Commodification of arts and crafts, adoption of Western life-styles and habits, human trafficking, prostitution and child abuse and drugs and alcohol abuse have all been documented as direct effects of tourism. Abrupt changes in social equations and destabilized family relations have brought unforeseen challenges to some destinations.

Environmental Damage

Irresponsible tourism activities and businesses may damage the environment in many ways. Pollution of water bodies, dumping of solid and liquid waste, littering, construction in fragile areas, sound pollution and damage to visual integrity are some of the dangers of unregulated tourism development. Tourism often lays claim to common property resources, reducing access to the local population and damaging sensitive natural areas. Reckless exploitation of natural resources, such as groundwater, significantly contributes to the negative impacts of tourism. We will also examine the contribution of tourism to climate change, a global challenge.

Considering the diverse advantages and disadvantages of tourism, the global trend is towards solutions that can maximise positives and minimise negatives. Efforts are taking place at a global level to promote sustainable development of tourism. United Nations programmes like Sustainable Tourism Elimination Poverty (ST-EP), Millennium Development Goals and 10-Year Framework on Sustainable Consumption and Production are some of the international initiatives taken in this direction.

Conclusion

We have seen the immense contribution made by tourism to the global economy. Tourism is a vast and complex field, with many disciplines contributing to it and influencing it. Because of its global nature, there are some differences in precisely defining commonly used terms. However, a simple approach provides us with a clear idea of the concepts and definitions, and gives an indication of the nature and form of the subject. We will explore this further, a field where millions are actively involved in tourism business and billions participate as customers. Elsewhere, we will learn about the major stakeholders—the tourists, local community, travel agents, tour operators, accommodation sector, entertainment sector and state and local governments. The sum total of the actions and interactions of the stakeholders give shape to tourism industry. The roles, responsibilities and practices of various stakeholders along with theoretical underpinnings form the integral part of tourism industry, which will be discussed in the ensuing chapters.

Review Questions

1. Trace the evolution and growth of tourism as a global phenomenon.
2. Tourism is considered as a 'complex socioeconomic phenomenon'. Discuss.
3. Give an account of the Cohen's classification of tourists.
4. Define tourism and distinguish different types of tourism from the visitor perspective.

Activities

1. Survey five families in your neighbourhood to understand the travel patterns of the members. Identify the purpose, duration and period of travel of the members. Attempt a classification of the travels into leisure and business.
2. Visit a tourism destination close by and identify the advantages and disadvantages of tourism business to the local community.
3. Make a list of countries through which the Silk Route passes. Identify the major trade activities in these centres during the middle ages and try to compare these with the present economic activities prevalent there.
4. Make a poster exhibition featuring major explorers and invasions in the ancient and medieval periods.

References

Books

Cohen, Erik. 1972. 'Toward a Sociology of International Tourism'. *Social Research*, 39 (1), pp. 164–182.
Davidson, R. 1989. *Tourism*. London: Pitman.
Goeldner, C. R., and R.W. McIntosh. 1986. *Tourism: Principles, Practices, Philosophies*, 5th ed. Canada: John Wiley & Sons Inc.
Hunziker, W., and K. Krapf. 1942. Grundriss der Allgemeinen Fremdenverkehrslehre [Outline of General Tourism Doctrine]. Polygraphischer Verlag [Zürich: Polygraphischer Verlag].
Mathieson, Alister, and Geoffrey Wall. 1982. 'Tourism-Economic, Physical and Social Impacts'. *Annals of Tourism Research*, 6: 390–407.
Tremlett, G. 2006. *Ghosts of Spain: Travels Through a Country's Hidden Past.* London: Faber and Faber Limited.
United Nations. 1998. *Recommendations on Statistics of International Migration, Revision 1.* United States of America: United Nations.
Vijayakumar, B. 2008. *Tourism Growth and Development* (Malayalam), Thiruvananthapuram: State Language Institute Kerala.

Web Resources

Arvon, H. 2016. 'Faxian: Chinese Buddhist Monk'. Encyclopaedia Britannica. Available at: http://www.britannica.com/biography/Faxian (accessed on 20 December 2016).

BBC. 2014. 'Roman Empire Timeline. (n.d.). Available at: http://www.softschools.com/timelines/roman_empire/timeline_9/ (accessed on 20 December 2016). History: Vasco Da Gama'. http://www.bbc.co.uk/history/historic_figures/da_gama_vasco.shtml

Chandra, S. 2009. 'History of Travel and Tourism'. *Ezine Articles*. Available at: http://EzineArticles.com/2244859 (accessed on 20 December 2016).

Time Periods. 2003-12. 'Ancient Greece'. University Press Inc. Available at: http://www.ancient-greece.com/s/History/ (accessed on 20 December 2016).

UNESCO. n.d. 'Silk Road: Dialogue, Diversity and Development'. UNESCO Available at: http://en.unesco.org/silkroad/about-silk-road (accessed on 20 December 2016).

Suggested Readings

Books

Raina, A.K., and S.K. Agarwal. 2004. *The Essence of Tourism Development: Dynamics, Philosophy and Strategies*, 1st ed. New Delhi: Sarup & Sons.

'Roman Empire Timeline'. Available at: http://www.softschools.com/timelines/roman_empire/timeline_9/ (accessed on 20 December 2016).

Towner, J. 1988. 'Approaches to Tourism History'. *Annals of Tourism Research*, 15: 47-62.

A view of Ellora caves
Image courtesy: Shutterstock

CHAPTER 2

Concepts and Terms

Learning Objectives

By the end of this chapter, students will be able to:

- Recognize specific characteristics of tourism products.
- List the stakeholders in tourism sector.
- Understand the basic concepts of sustainable tourism.
- Distinguish between different types of special interest tourism.

Introduction

In the first chapter, we have familiarized ourselves with the basic definition of tourism and the distinction between different categories of tourists. In this chapter, we continue our exploration of the subject and get into grips with some concepts and terms that will engage attention throughout our enquiries into tourism. Frequent use—and abuse—of some of these terms has resulted in a lack of clarity about their meanings, and it is important at this early stage of our study to pin down important concepts in their specific contexts. Economic terms such as 'product' and 'service' will be explained, as these need to be understood accurately and specifically. We examine the components of tourism industry and the stakeholders in a tourism destination. Apart from clarifying the concept of sustainability, this chapter will introduce several types of tourism that are in the vogue.

Tourism Product and Industry

The acceptance of tourism as a business across the world is chiefly attributed to its ability to bring economic benefits. Tourism industry offers wide variety of goods and services that form tourism products. We will begin our examination by having a clear understanding of the economic terms that are used in the business of tourism.

25

Goods and Services

In simple terms, a product is anything that is manufactured and available for sale. A product is the result of a manufacturing or production process and satisfies a want. In the market, a product may mean a 'good' (which is a visible, tangible object that can be transferred from a seller to a buyer) or a 'service' (which is intangible, invisible and person dependent). A car is a 'good', which can be seen and felt by the buyer and is owned by him after the sale is concluded. A haircut is a service, bought by someone who wants to trim his hair, something that depends on the experience and skill of the service provider.

Tourism products are a combination of goods and services demanded by a tourist during travel to and stay at a destination. These include natural, cultural and manmade attractions and facilities such as hotels, transport and ancillary services. In this process, tourists derive an experience which varies from individual to individual. From a broader perspective, the sum total of experiences derived by the tourists during the entire trip can be considered as the product.

Tourism products satisfy the needs of tourists, and are bought by them from tourism businesses. Tourist products may be 'specific', individual units such as a room in a hotel or an airline seat sold by enterprises, or 'total' products which are 'bundles' of tangible and intangible elements based on an activity at a destination (Middleton, 1988).

An interesting concept of the tourism product is provided by Lewis and Chambers (1989). Tourism products are composed of 'goods, environment and services'. The 'formal' product is something that the tourist believes he is buying. This consists of a 'core' product that the tourist is actually buying, and the 'augmented' products are the features added on by the supplier. For example, in a restaurant, the formal product is the dinner that the guest has with his friend, the core product is the food and wine ordered and purchased by the guest and the augmented product is the service and the ambience of the restaurant.

Tourism products may be seen as consisting of core and supplementary (or secondary) services. The attraction is the core product in a destination. For travelling to the destination, and while at the destination, tourists demand other services like transport, accommodation, food and beverages and support services, all of which constitute supplementary services.

Characteristics of Tourism Products

Compared to manufacturing industry, the services sector has several features that make service products quite different from the goods which are manufactured and sold. Tourism products are good examples of service products and have the following distinct characteristics:

1. **Intangibility:** The experiences of flying with a particular airline or the feeling after witnessing a beautiful dance performance at a destination are examples of the intangible nature of the tourism product. The service cannot be heard, seen, felt or tasted before purchase, making it difficult to evaluate. The experiences embedded in attractions, facilities and support services and the enjoyment tourists derive are intangible.

2. **Inseparability:** A visitor has to travel to the destination to take a holiday, to be entertained at an amusement park or to marvel at a cultural attraction. Tourism products have to be consumed at the point of production or supply that is the destination.

3. **Perishability:** Most of the tourism products are 'perishable' in the sense that they cannot be stored for future sale. Unsold airline seats or rooms and even the climate on a particular day cannot be stored and made available for another day.

4. **Variability:** Tourism products vary in quality and defy standardization. The service of a front-office executive in a hotel may be different from the person in a previous shift. A chef may prepare a dish adding a personal touch, which makes it different from the same dish

on another day prepared by another chef. Tourism products with local specificities vary in quality and cannot be standardized.

5. **Instantaneous consumption:** Most tourism products demand instantaneous consumption as production and consumption takes place simultaneously. Food from a restaurant, performing arts, scenic beauty and so on are examples to this.
6. **Tourism products are localized:** Tourism products are generally moulded by local ambience and personal touch. The quality and standard of the product may change with a change in place and personnel.
7. **Tourism products cannot be sampled:** One cannot test a sample of a tourism product before making the purchase. A holiday has to be experienced by physically making the trip, after the product has been purchased.
8. **Many tourism products are supply inelastic:** The supply of most of the tourism products is fixed. It cannot be changed according to a change in demand. For example, a hotel cannot increase its room inventory when there is a rise in demand for accommodation.
9. **Many tourism products are seasonal:** Leisure destinations, to the most part, are dependent on the climatic conditions, and experience a periodic increase and decrease in arrivals.

Components of Tourism Industry

Tourism is a socioeconomic phenomenon resulting from the movement of people to destinations, interacting with local community members and involving in various activities, generating economic benefits to service providers. Tourists require a variety of services, particularly related to food and beverages, accommodation and transport, along with many ancillary services. All these services are drawn from various productive sectors of the economy. In other words, the inputs needed by the tourism industry are contributed by the primary, secondary and tertiary sectors of the economy. Various service providers constitute tourism industry. The major components of tourism industry are illustrated in Figure 2.1.

It may be noted that all the mentioned components are directly related to tourism business. Another segment, consisting of professionals such as construction workers, engineers, architects and technicians, work behind the scenes to facilitate infrastructure needed for the setting up and operation of tourism industry. However, the scope of this chapter is limited to service providers and their operations that have a direct bearing on tourist.

Stakeholders in Tourism

In tourism destinations, there are several individuals or groups which have an interest in the developments that take place on account of tourism. They may influence or be affected by these developments and have to be seen as significant participants in this dynamic system. The term 'stakeholders' refer to these players—the local community members, the business owners and employees, the visitors, the local government—who all have a stake in the development of tourism in a destination, and are influenced by tourism in a positive or negative way. The stakeholders in a destination may have competing or conflicting interests and interactions and linkages between themselves.

The local community is the central stakeholder group in a destination, which has the largest stake in the development of tourism as an economic activity. Members of the community stand to gain through the economic opportunities brought to the region due to tourism, but they have to bear the brunt of the negative effects of tourism as well. The local government represents the community, and has the mandate to regulate tourism, provide infrastructure

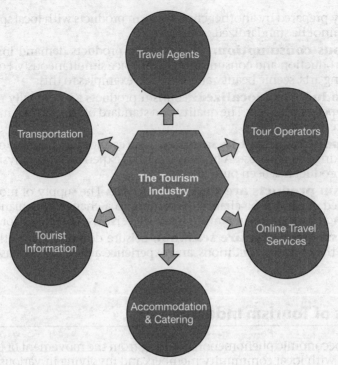

Figure 2.1 Components of tourism industry
Source: Authors.

and facilities, act as a watchdog and work to balance the type and extent of tourism to ensure positive developments benefiting the community. Tourism industry is another important stakeholder group, providing tourism services, building superstructure, creating jobs and bringing in visitors. Their interest is to recoup their investment and make profits through more business which translates to more tourists to the destination. Balancing the interests of the residents and visitors and ensuring that tourism does not lead to unsustainable consumption patterns or ecological damage are the concerns of governments and civil society organizations (Figure 2.2).

Tourism and Sustainability

The exploitation of natural resources in the name of human progress as part of rapid industrialization has brought about long-lasting impacts on the society and environment. Rising concerns about the reckless use of resources led to the environmental movements of the 1960s, which focused attention on the degradation caused by indiscriminate industrialization. There was growing realization that the world needed a system that aimed at an equilibrium between satisfying the requirements of the people and the judicious use of nature's bounty to man.

The UN Conference on Human Environment, held in Stockholm in 1972, agreed upon a declaration containing 26 principles related to environment and development. The most significant development was the release of 'Our Common Future' in 1987, the report of the United Nations World Commission on Environment and Development. On assessing the way in which resources are exploited and used indiscriminately for development purpose, the report

Figure 2.2 Stakeholders in a tourism destination
Source: Authors.

highlighted the need for adopting sustainable development. The Brundtland Report, as it was commonly known, defined sustainable development as

> Development that meets the needs of the present without compromising the ability of future generations to meet their own needs.

The triple bottom line framework, first used by John Elkington (1994), introduced social and environmental aspects along with the economic element. Businesses were encouraged to analyse their performance on the basis of economic, environmental and social parameters. These aspects were seen as pillars to sustainable development, helping us understand the concept in a more wholesome manner. Sustainability principles encompass all activities that are broadly put under three categories.

- **Environment:** The activity minimizes damage to or destruction of the environment, which includes air, land, water, flora and fauna. Ideally, the activity may benefit the environment, for example, by contributing to conservation efforts or recharging aquifers.
- **Social:** The activity does not damage the socio cultural milieu in which it is being conducted. Ideally, it may revive and revitalize skills, structures and knowledge of the community.
- **Economic:** Even while running a profitable business, the activity contributes to the community, bringing and sharing prosperity.

Sustainable Tourism

Sustainable tourism is the application of these principles in the context of tourism operations. Sustainable tourism can be defined as

> Tourism that seeks to minimize ecological and sociocultural impacts while providing economic benefits to local communities and host countries. (Mohonk Agreement, 2000)

The WTO (1993), taking the definition of sustainable development from the Brundtland Report as its basis, defined sustainable tourism at the 'Euro-Mediterranean Conference on Tourism and Sustainable Development' as that

> Which meets the needs of present tourists and host regions while protecting and enhancing opportunity for the future. It is envisaged as leading to management of all resources in such a way

that economic, social and aesthetic needs can be fulfilled while maintaining cultural integrity, essential ecological processes, biological diversity and life support system.

Simply put, sustainable tourism development refers to tourism which is ecologically sustainable, economically viable as well as ethically and socially equitable. The development of sustainable tourism meets the following requirements:

- Tourist resources—natural, historical, cultural and others—are preserved in a way that allows them to be used in the future, whilst benefiting today's society.
- The planning and management of tourist development are conducted in a way that avoids triggering serious ecological or socio cultural problems in the region concerned.
- The overall quality of the environment in the tourist region is preserved and, if necessary, improved.
- The level of tourist satisfaction should be maintained to ensure that destinations continue to be attractive and retain their commercial potential.
- Tourism should largely benefit all members of society.

It is important to note that the principles of sustainable tourism can be adopted by any tourism business. A large city hotel can be a model in their environmental management practices and socially responsible purchasing policy. A so-called 'eco resort', which does not recycle or dispose of its waste responsibly, is an example of unsustainable tourism development.

The main aims of making tourism sustainable are economic viability and competitiveness of destinations and enterprises, contribution of tourism to the economic prosperity of the destination, fair distribution of benefits throughout the host community, respect for the heritage and authentic culture of the host community, support of the conservation of natural areas and wildlife, minimal use of scarce resources and minimization of pollution of air, water and land by tourism enterprises and visitors (UNEP-WTO, 2005).

Imbibing the principles of sustainable development, different approaches were developed to design and promote tourism across the world. This includes a plethora of alternatives to mass tourism. Out of this, ecotourism has gained global acceptance and became a buzz word in the tourism industry.

Ecotourism

Ecotourism can be viewed as an overarching philosophy; a business sub-set; or a planning model for local economic development. The term ecotourism was coined by Hector Ceballos Lascurian, a Mexican architect who in 1983 while giving an interview during his tenure as the founding president of PRONATURA, a Mexican NGO dedicated to conservation efforts. The meaning of the term has itself evolved over the years. Initially, the term denoted travel to protected areas for recreation, with minimum possible interference and impact. Subsequently, the element of 'responsibility' became more relevant, as did the contribution to the economic status of the local people.

The International Ecotourism Society

The International Ecotourism Society (TIES) was established in 1990 as a program of the International Tourism Collective, a non-profit organization devoted to promote ecotourism. The main focus of the organization is the development of ecotourism. It sets up guidelines and standards, provide technical assistance, training and develop resources so as to position ecotourism as a global model for sustainable tourism development. TIES has currently a network of partner members in 120 countries which includes academicians, consultants,

(Continued ...)

conservation professionals and organizations, governments, architects, tour operators, lodge owners and managers, general development experts, and eco-tourists. By engaging and empowering these partners, TIES offers networking and professional development opportunities as well as take a lead role in making tourism a viable tool for conservation, protection of bio cultural diversity, and sustainable community development. TIES also organizes conferences, exhibits, industry outreach and educational programs to help organizations, communities and individuals to practice and promote ecotourism. The annual Ecotourism and Sustainable Tourism Conference (ESTC) organized by TIES is a leading international meeting place which provides practical solutions to sustainable tourism development.

There are several definitions of ecotourism, with no agreement on the specific nature of the term. TIES in 1991 produced one of the earliest definitions: 'Ecotourism is responsible travel to natural areas that conserves the environment and sustains the wellbeing of local people'. The International Union for Conservation of Nature stated that

> Ecotourism is environmentally responsible travel and visitation to relatively undisturbed natural areas, in order to enjoy and appreciate nature (and any accompanying cultural features - both past and present) that promotes conservation, has low negative visitor impact, and provides for beneficially active socio-economic involvement of local populations (IUCN, 1996).

While ecotourism is considered as a conceptual approach, the tourism industry has reoriented the term to a niche market that is governed by market forces and regulations. The term has been marketed as a form of nature-based tourism by the tourism industry and been studied as a sustainable development tool by NGOs, development experts and academics. The term ecotourism, therefore, refers on one hand to a concept based on a set of principles, and on the other hand to a specific market segment. Ecotourism is a form of sustainable tourism. Figure 2.3 offers a reflection of where ecotourism can be placed within the process of developing more sustainable forms of tourism.

From the bewildering array of definitions, discussions and approaches, it is relevant to glean out the important principles that may distinguish an enterprise that practices ecotourism. These are enumerated below.

1. Contributes to conservation of biodiversity, flora and fauna.
2. Includes an interpretation/learning experience.

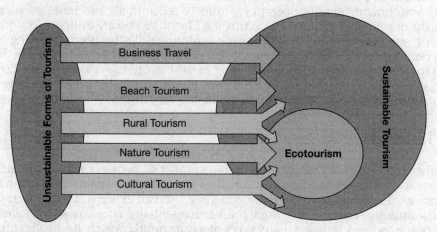

Figure 2.3   Ecotourism as a sustainable tourism concept
Source: Authors.

3. Involves responsible action on the part of tourists.
4. Is delivered primarily to small groups by small-scale businesses.
5. Requires the lowest possible consumption of non-renewable resources.
6. Stresses participation, ownership and business opportunities for the local community members.

The International Year of Ecotourism

In 1998, the United Nations Economic and Social Council (ECOSOC) proposed to designate the year 2002 as the International Year of Ecotourism (IYE). The UN General Assembly, while accepting the proposal, stated that the activities related to the Year should be taken within the broader framework of sustainable development of tourism, with four main motivations:

The objectives for the IYE were the following:

1. Generate greater awareness among public authorities, the private sector, the civil society and consumers regarding ecotourism's capacity to contribute to the conservation of the natural and cultural heritage in natural and rural areas, and the improvement of standards of living in those areas.
2. Disseminate methods and techniques for the planning, management, regulation and monitoring of ecotourism to guarantee its long-term sustainability.
3. Promote exchanges of successful experiences in the field of ecotourism.
4. Increase opportunities for the efficient marketing and promotion of ecotourism destinations and products on international markets.

The IYE witnessed many global events including World Ecotourism Summit (WES) at Quebec and more than 50 countries, developing strategies and policies in relation to ecotourism at national level. Although on one side, the concept of ecotourism got wide acceptance as it positions natural and cultural diversity as tourism's assets and stresses the need for local community participation and benefits, it was widely criticized as 'green washing'.

Unfortunately, the word was soon adopted by many in the tourism industry and soon lost any specific meaning associated to it. Ecotourism has come to mean a plethora of activities—adventure holidays, hunting and fishing tours, rural or farm stays, staying in hotels which practiced environment friendly operations, tours to see animals and birds, even cruises to watch whales or penguins. Visits to Antarctica and Machu Picchu are touted as 'eco-tours', and governments are investing millions to create ecotourism destinations. Prefixing 'eco' has become a fashion among industry operators, and there is growing tendency to use the terminology in tourism operations without adhering to the basic tenets of ecotourism. Eco-lodges, eco-shops, eco-tels and eco-tours are cited as examples to this. 'Ecotourism' has now become part of marketing jargon, sounding good but meaning very little.

'Rural' Tourism

Rural tourism can be defined as any form of tourism that showcases the rural life, art, culture and heritage at rural locations. The broad aim of rural tourism is to enable interaction between tourists and local community for a more enriching tourism experience which may benefit the local community economically. Rural tourism is essentially a holiday which takes place in the countryside and may indicate many types of leisure holidays such as soft adventure, farm visits, home stays, fishing, boating, literary festivals, local festivals and events and activities like bird watching and village visits. (Incredible India, n.d.) The emergence of rural tourism provides a means for the urban population to get away from the cities, and a source of income for some rural populations.

In a country like India, where 74% of the population resides in its 700,000 villages, the context is set for promoting tourism activities in many of these villages. The Endogenous Tourism project (ETP), a joined initiative of Ministry of Tourism (MoT) and United Nations Development Programme (UNDP) is an attempt to harness rural tourism to benefit the poor and vulnerable sections of the community. The project commenced in 2003 and involved the selection of 36 rural sites to be used as rural destination development pilot projects. The project was further extended to a total of 125 rural destinations in the country. The guiding principle of the project was the poverty eradication objective under the Millennium Development Goals (MDG). The project had two parts—hardware (infrastructure development) and software (capacity building). The hardware component of the project was under the purview of the Government of India (GoI) through its Destination Development Scheme, while the software component of the project was funded by the UNDP. The primary objective of the project was to create sustainable livelihoods for the local community.

The infrastructure development in ETP focused on visitor needs and concentrated on providing basic facilities like toilets, potable water, food and beverage facilities, signage, parking space and so on. Theatres and museums to showcase local arts and traditions were given priority. Accommodation units were designed and built in traditional style of the village to encourage overnight stay of tourists. As part of capacity building of the local community, workshops and education programmes were conducted among stakeholders for general understanding of tourism. In order to increase the participation level of women, training programmes were conducted for fetching direct and indirect jobs in tourism. Microfinance was also arranged for starting their own enterprises in tourism. In order to market the products, campaigns and promotional activities were conducted nationally and internationally. A website (www.explorerruralindia.org) was launched to showcase the ETP destinations. Our case study highlights the rural tourism initiative at Hodka, Gujarat.

Case Study: Experiencing the Banni through Hodka

One of the Endogenous Tourism Projects was established in the Banni area of Kachchh in Gujarat, a unique grassland habitat in the desert. The primary residents of this area are the Maldharis (cattle breeders) or Baniyaras who all practice Islam. Banni has 34 villages inhabited by approximately 5,500 families. Some of Gujarat's finest embroidery and leather work comes from the Banni area. In contrast to the stark landscape or perhaps to compensate for it, the embroidery is in bright vibrant colors and extremely intricate in nature. Hodka, in the Banni was established about 300 years ago by what is called the 'Halepotra' clan. In 2004, Hodka was shortlisted by the then District Collector, to be considered under the UNDP's ETP. Kutch Mahila Vikas Sangathan (KMVS) was considered as the nodal agency for the same/project, with support from Sahjeevan, an NGO that had been working in this region since 1991. A site, an old dried-up pond that belonged to the Jhuth Gram Panchayat (representing all the 13 villages of the area) was selected for this initiative. It was suggested that initially tented accommodation on a very small scale should be tried. The resort was named Shaam-e-Sarhad or quite literally, 'Evening at the Border'. The responsibility of the overall construction was given to Hunnarshala, a collaborative working with traditional architecture. The idea was to establish a place for people to stay, and serve them the local cuisine to recreate an authentic experience of an evening in a local village. However, as Shaam-e-Sarhad was opened for tourists and became more popular, the general feedback was to make available more permanent structures for accommodation. This was considered appropriate, as

(Continued ...)

the region is known for its unique dwellings called bungas. Bungas, because of their construction, were some of the few structures that had withstood the 2001 earthquake. There was sense of pride within the community for having this traditional knowledge and using it to combat natural disasters. Bungas were also ideal structures to combat the extreme temperatures in the desert without the use of air-conditioning. Shaam-e-Sarhad has been successfully running now for nine years and since 2012, it is owned and managed entirely by the community. It stands out as one of the most successful initiatives amongst the 36 projects that were supported through the UNDP/MoT. The gradual success of the project has reiterated in people the pride in their local culture and traditions.

It must, however, be emphasized that Shaam-e-Sarhad is a small enterprise, promoting niche tourism as opposed to mass tourism that focuses on the heritage of the Banni area. It will appeal to the tourist who wants to have a first-hand experience of rural life. Its success can be partially attributed to the fact that it is small in scale and operation and can thus operate at the level of each individual tourist.

Source: Bhatt (n.d.).

Discussion Questions

1. What are the features of the Hodka project that make it successful?
2. Discuss the possible constraints that may hamper the growth of Hodka as a destination, despite the establishment of 'Shaam-e-Sarhad'.

Special Interest Tourism

An interesting counterpoint to mass tourism is the emergence of Special Interest Tourism (SIT). SIT is otherwise termed as 'niche' tourism, because it seeks to provide interesting and meaningful experiences to tourists who are interested in specific fields of study, activity or cultural aspects. The definition of SIT is 'the provision of customized tourism activities that cater to the specific interests of groups and individuals' (SIT, n.d.). Most commonly, small groups of persons who share the same profession, hobby or area of interest come together to travel to such destinations that will enable them to further their interests, provide them meaningful and stimulating experiences and fulfil their personal needs and motivations. Usually SIT provides rewarding, enriching, adventuresome and learning experiences and the tourists expect high standards of service. The advent of social media platforms has enabled people with special interests to seek out and meet people with similar interests, resulting in substantial growth of this area of tourism. Improved marketing and communications, increasing access and the emergence of specialist operators have resulted in the tourism industry developing specific products and services to cater to this segment.

Some of the most popular SIT products include the following:

1. Hobbies such as flowers, gardening, horticulture.
2. Exploration such as Galapagos, Arctic Circle, Antarctica, Amazon.
3. Excitement such as trekking, mountain climbing, paragliding.
4. Activities such as sailing, skiing, cycling, hiking.
5. Educational such as cookery, architecture, museums.
6. Relaxation such as singles tours, cruising, boating.

Meghalaya plays host to a small band of dedicated caving enthusiasts, which is highlighted in our case study.

Case Study: Caving in Meghalaya

In the Khasi, Garo and Jaintia hills of Meghalaya, there are a series of cave systems that have attracted global attention. Speleologists—scientists who study caves, their structures, properties and life forms—have been exploring and mapping these caves for the last two decades. Caving—or Spelunking, as it is known in the United States of America and Canada—is a hobby that involves exploration of cave systems for recreation. Caving enthusiasts and adventure lovers have been exploring the *krems* (cave in Khasi language), with the help of some enthusiastic local partners of Meghalaya.

The Shnong Rim area has the most number of caves. Inside the caves, the explorer marvels at the formations created over millennia by rivers and streams, hollowing out the limestone, creating passages. Stalagmites, stalactites, cave curtains, cave pearls and candles are a few of the exotic formations to be found in the caves.

In the Khasi hills, Mawsmai cave is frequently visited by day trippers, as it is fully lit and easy to navigate. Krem Mawmluh is a popular cave, as are Krem Dam near Mawsynram and Krem Lymput near Nongjri. Krem Liat Prah, in the Jaintia hills is the longest natural cave in India, stretching over 30 km. It has an enormous trunk passage, titled the 'aircraft hangar'. Other prominent caves are Synrang-Pamiang, rich in coloured formations and the 'Titanic Hall' chamber with thousands of large cave pearls, Krem Lubon with its entrance hidden by a waterfall and Krem Shrieh. In the Garo hills, Siju cave is famous for the 'bat cave', with a huge bat colony and beautiful stalagmite and stalactite formations.

The formal documentation and exploration of the cave systems began in 1992, when the Meghalaya Adventurers Association (MAA), led by Mr B. D. Kharpran Daly, sought the help of international caving enthusiasts to help explore these caves. The collaborative project, involving speleologists, cavers and adventurers from many countries, is called 'Abode of the Clouds', continuously mounting annual expeditions that explore new caves, and further map known cave systems. Till 2015, 1,350 caves have been documented, mapping 387 km of cave systems.

These caves have begun attracting adventure and niche tourists, and tour companies such as Meghalaya adventure tours and Kipepeo offer cave expedition tours. These companies offer the services of experienced cavers and provide caving equipment, teaching the visitor the basics of caving and general safety rules to be followed. Visitors get to negotiate wet passages in wet suits, and swim for some distances to enter 'active' caves with rivers running through.

With a view to promote cave tourism and raise awareness, the Meghalaya tourism department in collaboration with MAA conducts workshop and training programme on cave tourism.

The pioneers in caving in Meghalaya are concerned about coal and limestone mining that cause damage to the caves and have been demanding action to protect the caves. They believe that involving local communities in caving tourism is a way to increase awareness and force government to protect the caves.

Discussion Questions

1. 'Although special interest tourism brings in only small numbers, it plays a prominent role in raising the profile of the destination'. Discuss.
2. What can stimulate the creation of SIT products? List the possible factors that can play a role.

Agritourism or Agrotourism

Agritourism or Agrotourism is where agriculture and tourism intersect. Here the tourists get the opportunity to visit farms, ranches, wineries and agricultural industries. It offers a huge variety of entertainment, education, relaxation, outdoor adventures, cuisine and shopping options for tourists while generating supplementary income for the owners. Visiting a farm would give the option for tourists to get a chance to climb the trees and pick up fruits, pluck vegetables, milk a cow or rope a calf and understand the different methods of farming practices. Most children, especially those growing up in cities, have little knowledge on how food is grown or where milk comes from, and agritourism offers the best chance for parents to take them to the field and show them these 'wonders' of nature. In the cases of certain crops like tea and coffee, tourists get the option to make factory visits and see the production process. Agritourism offers supplementary income to farmers facing dwindling incomes and rising production costs and the prospect of direct sales to customers from their farm stores, avoiding middlemen and marketing costs.

Wine Tourism

Wine tourism (other terms used are Eno-tourism, Oeno-tourism and Vinitourism) refers to tourism whose purpose is or includes the tasting, consumption or purchase of wine, often at or near the source (Wines of Balkans, 2011). It includes visits to wineries, vineyards and restaurants known to offer unique vintages, tasting wines as well as organized wine tours which involve taking part in the harvest, wine festivals or other special events. The winery tasting rooms now offer a complete tourism experience which include interaction with the wine maker and experiencing first-hand the product. This has developed direct relationship with customers and broken the traditional system of retail channels. The tasting room staffs are the brand ambassadors of the winery and they are given training on the product, the region and how to deal with the tourists in a professional way. The tasting rooms are no longer simply a place to taste and buy wine, but tourists are also provided with facilities like accommodation, restaurant and offered conducted tours to understand the rich diversity the wine region has to offer. Nowadays, many wineries build their tasting rooms in a location close to the main tourist route. Most of the wine regions in the world have found tourism promotion economically beneficial, and the growers association as well as the hospitality industry have pumped in money for tourism development. The 'Old World' producers of wine such as Spain, Portugal, Hungary, France, Italy as well as the 'New World wine' regions like Australia, Argentina, Chile, United States and South Africa have started promoting tourism as a means to advertise their products.

Lighthouse Tourism

Lighthouses have been beacons of navigation for the sailors for centuries, but now they are becoming major tourist attractions across the world. Many lighthouses attract tourists because of their situation as historic landmarks as well as for the scenic view of the coast. Many regions have carried out initiatives to promote lighthouses as tourism destinations, enhancing facilities for tourists. Since the lighthouses have been once maritime landmarks, tourism is being developed by building allied maritime infrastructures like maritime museums and lighthouse museums. Interpretation centres, communicating the history of the lighthouse, are also developed as parts of the tourism projects.

In India, lighthouses are under the control of Directorate General of Lighthouses and Lightships (DGLL). Currently, there are 189 lighthouses in India in the vast coastline, including

Table 2.1   Lighthouses identified for promotion of tourism

Sl. No.	Identified Lighthouse Sites	State
1	Dolphin Nose	Andhra Pradesh
2	Aguada	Goa
3	Dwarka	Gujarat
4	Veraval	Gujarat
5	Kadalur Point	Kerala
6	Minicoy	Lakshadweep
7	Chandrabhaga	Odisha
8	Gopalpur	Odisha
9	False Point	Odisha
10	Chennai	Tamil Nadu
11	Mahabalipuram	Tamil Nadu
12	Rameshwaram	Tamil Nadu
13	Kanyakumari and Muttom	Tamil Nadu

Source: Ministry of Shipping, light house tourism (n.d.).

the Andaman Nicobar islands in Bay of Bengal as well as the Lakshadweep islands in Arabian Sea. DGLL has decided to develop some of the 189 lighthouses in India as tourism destinations.
The major lighthouses identified by DGLL for promoting tourism are listed in Table 2.1.

Cemetery Tourism

Cemeteries have become a product of SIT in recent days with many countries promoting memorials, cemeteries and graveyards to attract tourists to trace roots or pay homage to their heroes (Graveyard Tourism and Cemetery Tourism, n.d.). This can also be considered as tourism that falls under the category of 'dark' tourism associated with tourists visiting places related to death and disaster (Cemetery Tourism, 2010). Many families can trace their ancestors who were buried in a land far from their home. Cemeteries have also become an attraction based on its cultural and heritage value. Cemeteries contain attractive and sometimes unusual tombs, grave stones and architecture which are linked to the culture and heritage of the country. The ancient graveyards also used arts and symbols on older tombs and graves which have a cryptic or hidden meaning. These symbols are different and vary from countries to countries, and tourists may get the opportunity to interpret and understand these symbols to identify facts and stories about the buried person. Interpretative programmes that include gravestone art and designs, historical past of the communities, social stories and conflict and funerary practices may be developed to attract tourists. As cemeteries may have emotional ties with the local population, special care should be taken that the programme does not conflict with the views of the local community.
Recently, the Uttarakhand Tourism Development Board has announced Cemetery tourism named 'Know Your Roots', and has started data collection about graves of renowned

people from across the world, people who made their home in the hills and died there. It is estimated that thousands of British citizens lived in the state before independence, and there are graves of many prominent personalities like John Lang, who was the lawyer of Rani Laxmi Bai, eccentric entrepreneur 'Pahari' Wilson and his Garhwali wife. The Department has now started making efforts to contact the descendants of these people, history lovers and foreign tourists who visit these graves (Sharma, 2015).

Avitourism

Avitourism or bird watching tourism is a specialized sector of nature-based tourism which focuses exclusively on watching birds and their activities. This type of travel encourages tourists to travel to areas that are hotspots to see the birding activities like forests, parks and water bodies, highlighting the endemic and endangered species of the locality. Some destinations have started promoting birding-related events and festivals as part of this. Bird watching has become an increasingly popular hobby and an income-generating activity for local community members. Local people, close to the sites of conservation, are selected and trained to identify different species of birds, their calls and understand their food habits and breeding patterns so that these could be interpreted to tourists. They would also play active roles in awareness building and local-level conservation. Avitourism is now being used as a tool for conservation in many countries. A portion of the income generated out of the activities is used for conservation purpose by the park authorities in protected areas. It is interesting to note that a large industry has developed worldwide in promoting birding tours. Hundreds of birdwatchers join the tour, some to increase their worldwide count on different bird species while some makes this as an opportunity to see the country side of destinations visited as bird watching tours take an off beaten track from normal tours. The tour companies which organize avitours need to be responsible in the sense that their tours should not be putting pressure on avian flocks. There are instances where the same flock of birds are visited by tourists a number of times the same day itself. Some enthusiastic birdwatchers try to photograph nesting as well as the nestlings which results in birds abandoning the nests and sometimes departing from the area (The Conservation Value of Avi-tourism, n.d.). Although these are some of the negatives that one would come across while promoting avitours, this activity is normally operated by responsible tour operators who would place the welfare of the birds before business.

Photography Tourism

Photography tourism may be defined as a combined passion for travel and photography. These types of tours provide opportunity for developing the photographic skills while travelling on holiday. Persons who have photography as a hobby are attracted to the experience of exploring a place with a camera with the help of professional photographers and guides who combine knowledge about the destination or the objects and sites to be photographed. The tour packages are usually designed with small group sizes allowing participants for mentor-participant interactions. Participants are provided with extensive off the field learning as well as hands on photography on the tour. They would get the opportunity to get appropriate guiding on the right locations, timings as well as tips on lighting options. Amateur photographers would be able to build upon their photography skills by interacting with professional photographers by which new avenues in photography could be explored. At the end of each day, image reviews of the participants are conducted to make corrective action in future. Tour companies usually provide good quality photographic equipment on rent for participants who may need these. A number of specialized photography tours are currently operational in India and abroad which includes wildlife photography, bird photography, cave photography, cultural photography, festivals and village photography.

Trekking

Enjoying the countryside on foot is one of the most pristine ways of recreation. This takes many forms and is described using different terms. 'Trekking' or hiking refers to multiday trips through rural, often hilly or mountainous territory. In some countries, this is referred to as simply walking, while other popular terms are tramping, backpacking and hillwalking. Trekking ranges from simple daylong walks to challenging trips through rugged and remote territory. Trekkers need to be physically fit and have an interest in adventure. Trekking generally involves camping outdoors, with trekkers themselves having to carry their tents and equipment for camping as well as preparation of food. For treks in well-laid out trails used continuously by trekking groups, accommodation may be arranged in guest houses or homestay and food would be served during their stay. Trekking is usually graded depending upon the altitude, level of difficulty, incline and surface conditions as soft and hard treks. Trekking requires some minimum equipment to be brought by the trekkers like sturdy hiking boots, backpack, compass, torch, first aid kit, sunscreen, knife, insect repellent and water bottle. Trekking companies usually provide specialized equipment for climbing and camping. Trekkers get to travel through spectacular landscapes often inaccessible to vehicular traffic, sparsely populated or unpopulated natural areas far from urban disturbances, making the effort worthwhile.

Biking

Bicycle touring means self-contained cycling trips for pleasure, adventure and autonomy rather than sport, commuting or exercise. The bicycle tour can range from single to multiday trips. Tours which go beyond a single day may require cycles that could carry heavy loads. Touring bikes are usually designed to carry appropriate loads and comfort for riding long distances. The types of tours are classified depending on the duration, terrain, speed and number of stopovers. The rider usually covers 100–150 km a day. In lightweight touring, the rider carries minimum of equipment and overnight stay will be arranged in youth hostels, lodges and hotels. In the case of fully loaded touring, the travellers carry everything they need including food, cooking equipment and tents for camping. In the case of expedition touring, the cyclists travel through remote areas carrying everything they may need, including spares and tools for repairing the cycle if needed. In the case of supported touring, the cyclists will be supported by a motor vehicle which carries the required equipment. These kinds of tours are usually taken by tourists who are on a holiday package, with tour companies selling places on guided tours which include booked lodging, food, luggage transfers, rental bikes and route planning (Bicycle Touring, n.d.).

Architecture Tourism

Architecture and tourism are very closely related elements and buildings of architectural value have become tourist attractions. Grand temples, churches and mosques, palaces, towers, theatres, stadiums, monumental public buildings and residences attract large crowds not only for their built purpose but for enjoying the architectural beauty. Architecture reflects the lifestyle and culture of the community in the period in which it was built. Many cities in Europe like Paris, Rome, Athens and Amsterdam are living examples of how the spirit of an epoch is depicted through the building architecture. Architecture tourism involves tour packages designed connecting architectural monuments. This includes proper interpretation on the history of buildings, its architectural style and material used for construction. Specialized packages have been introduced in India such as the British Raj tours which take tourists to examples of British architecture at various cities in the country like Delhi, Jaipur, Kolkata and Darjeeling. Major parts of New Delhi, designed by Edwin Lutyens and the magnificent colonial buildings of Kolkata, the capital of British Raj are included in the package.

Military Tourism

Military tourism can be defined as visits made to a destination that has military background and history. It could be a historical product like a visit to current or historically important military sites, museums that portray weapons, arms, paintings of war or new technological developments, or using military equipment for leisure purposes. In the case of military activities, tourists have the option to engage in activities like shooting with military arms, riding a tank and flying decommissioned combat aircraft (Hrusovsky and Noeres, 2011). The use of military equipment linked tourism can be seen as a part of adventure tourism. In certain cases, it could be a combination of historical product and a military product as in re-enactment of historical tank battles. Recently in India, the Maharashtra Ex-Servicemen Corporation (MESCO) has come up with the concept of military tourism. As part of the programme, they would be taking tourists to the borders to make them see and understand the tough terrain and conditions where soldiers have to undertake their duty. It would be the retired soldiers who would escort the tourists and explain to them the conditions prevailing in those areas and the difficulties they face during their national duties (Ganjapure, 2015).

Spa Tourism

Spas can be defined as destinations people visit for renewal of body, mind and spirit. The International Spa Association (ISPA), the professional organization and voice of the spa industry, representing health and wellness facilities and providers in more than 70 countries since 1991, has defined Spa as 'places devoted to overall well-being through a variety of professional services that rejuvenates mind, body and spirit' (SetuHealthCare, n.d.). From ancient times, people used to travel to hot or cold springs for rejuvenation purposes as referred earlier in Chapter 1. The emergence of resorts near the spas resulted in combining the benefits of spa with holidays. The main strength of spas is providing relaxation, de-stressing and preventative health. Increasing awareness on the importance of nutrition, exercise, beauty and relaxation has motivated people to include those elements in their holiday packages and spas, thus, have become unavoidable elements in the itinerary of the tourists. The demand for spas has resulted in industry coming up with facilities that meet their requirements. ISPA has categorized primary types of spas (ISPA, n.d.) as follows:

- *Club Spa*, whose primary purpose is fitness and which offers a variety of professionally administered spa services on a day-use basis.
- *Day Spa*, which offers a variety of professional administered spa services to clients on a day-use basis.
- *Destination Spa*, a facility with the primary purpose of guiding individual spa-goers to develop healthy habits. These spas provide a comprehensive program that includes spa services, physical fitness activities, wellness education, healthful cuisine and special interest programming.
- *Medical Spa*, a facility that has a full-time licensed health care professional on-site, which is further defined as a health professional with a degree in medicine.
- *Mineral Springs Spa*, which offers an on-site source of natural mineral, thermal or seawater used in hydrotherapy treatments.
- *Resort/Hotel Spa*, which is located within a resort or hotel providing professionally administered spa services, fitness and wellness components.

Film Tourism

Film tourism can be defined as a branch of cultural tourism (Zimmermann, 2003) and refers to the growing interest and demand for locations which became popular due to their appearance in films and television series. Scotland's National Tourism Organization has defined film tourism as a business where visitors are attracted to the area through the storylines in a film or through the portrayal of a certain place on a film or on television. It is also said that the number of visitors, coming to a place from the effect of a film, can be called film tourism (Roesch, 2009). Film tourism is often referred to as film-induced tourism, whereby tourist visits are motivated to view an on-screen film location. Film tourism can take a number of different forms and activities (Connell, 2012) as given below:

1. Visits to locations portrayed within a specific film/television production.
2. Visits to studio sets.
3. Visits to specific film/TV theme parks and attractions.
4. Visits to themed attractions with a film.
5. Visits to locations where filming is taking place.
6. Visits to a location marketed as a filmic location, where the film may not have been experienced by the tourist but attractive marketing imagery induces interest.
7. Participation in organized tours of film locations: e.g. commercially operated tours with tour guide of film locations.
8. Visits to film festivals like Cannes and Edinburgh International Film Festival.
9. Visits to destinations for film premieres, either to view or to watch the arrival of film celebrities.

MoT, GoI has taken some steps to promote Film Tourism in the country. A memorandum of understanding (MoU) was signed with Ministry of Information and Broadcasting to promote cinema of India as a sub-brand of 'Incredible India' at various international film festivals and markets abroad, to develop synergy between tourism and the film industry and to provide a platform for enabling partnerships between the Indian and global film industry (Press Information Bureau, 2014).

Responsible Tourism

A review of the different forms of tourism discussed above shows that none of them is giving due importance to socioeconomic and environmental aspects leading to sustainable development. In practice, it is observed that any type of tourism can be sustainable, provided it is able to ensure commitment to society, culture and environment when it is operational. This demands responsible practices by stakeholders at the operational level. It is in this context, the concept of Responsible Tourism emerged.

The broad objective of Responsible Tourism is to 'make destinations better places for people to live in and better places for people to visit'. It is an approach to manage tourism in destinations, with an aim to maximize economic, social and environmental benefits while minimizing costs to destinations. In the words of Krippendorf (1987), considered a pioneer in Responsible Tourism, 'rebellious tourists and rebellious locals' will lead to a 'development away from a manipulated tourist to an informed and experienced one, a critical consumer'.

Responsible tourism takes the agenda started by ecotourism forward. It goes beyond nature-based tourism and places more importance to the local community issues. It also crucially focuses on empirical evidence that is the tangible and measurable signs of how benefits reach the local people.

Responsible Tourism movement demands that all stakeholders in the tourism ecosystem act in a responsible manner. Travellers insist that they take holidays with companies that have clear policies of responsible action and act responsibly while on holiday. They respect local culture, act in deference to local beliefs and traditions and patronize local enterprises. Hoteliers adopt responsible practices in their premises, ranging from installing environment friendly measures, recycling and treating waste, hiring locals and sourcing from local farmers. Destination managers encourage responsibility in destination management, creating a regulatory framework that rewards responsible behaviour, planning the use of resources equitably and fighting exploitation and abuse. The local community is not only an active participant, but is involved in policy making and implementation, encouraging local enterprise, empowering members to take up skilled employment in the tourism sector and presenting an authentic version of their cultural assets before the visitor.

Though Responsible Tourism is in its infancy, the initiative has succeeded in generating several international declarations. The first International Declaration on Responsible Tourism took place at Cape Town, South Africa known as Cape Town Declaration in 2002, which was conducted as a side event preceding the World Summit on Sustainable Development (WSSD).

Conclusion

Several concepts and terms have been explained in the chapter, and students will encounter most of these in subsequent chapters. While obtaining an overview of the components of the tourism system and the stakeholders involved, it is necessary, at this early stage, to be clear of the issues confronting destinations and communities because of indiscriminate tourism development. In each chapter, in some form or another, concerns relating to sustainability will keep recurring, reminding us that all our actions in terms of developing tourism have to be taken with an understanding that the industry has to be handled sensitively and pragmatically, and the interests of the community has to be uppermost in our minds.

Review Questions

1. Do you consider tourism as a good or service? Elucidate the characteristics of tourism products.
2. Discuss the interrelationship among various components of tourism industry.
3. Who are the major stake holders in tourism? Examine their specific roles in tourism industry.
4. Discuss how different types of tourism are related to the socioeconomic environment where they operate.

Activities

1. Give five examples of tourism services that illustrate their intangible nature.
2. Through examples, explain how all nature-based tourism need not necessarily be ecotourism.

3. Identify the tourism-related terminologies and concepts used in the book and write down the definition/explanation in two sentences. Also develop a section depicting closely related terms/concepts.

References

Books

Elkington, J. 1997. *Cannibals with Forks: The Triple Bottom Line of 21st Century Business.* Oxford: Capstone.

Krippendorf, J. 1987. *The Holiday Makers: Understanding the Impact of Leisure and Travel.* Oxford: Butterworth-Heinemann.

Lewis, C.C., and R.E. Chamber. 1989. *Marketing Leadership in Hospitality.* New York: Van Nostrand Reinhold.

Middleton, V.T.C. 1988. *Marketing in Travel and Tourism.* Oxford: Heinemann.

Roesch, S. 2009. *Aspects of Tourism: The Experiences of Film Location.* Bristol: Channel View Publication.

UNEP-WTO. 1995. *Making Tourism More Sustainable: A Guide for Policy Makers.* UNEP-WTO.

Web Resources

Bhatt, S. n.d. 'Experiencing the Banni through Hodka'. Available at: http://www.vikalpsangam.org/static/media/uploads/Livelihoods/seema_experiencing_the_banni.pdf (accessed on 20 December 2016).

Bicycle Touring. n.d. Available at: https://en.wikipedia.org/wiki/Bicycle_touring (accessed on 20 December 2016).

Cemetery Tourism. 2010. 'Mother Linda's'. Available at: http://www.cemeterytourism.com/ (accessed on 20 December 2016).

Connell, J. 2012. 'Progress in Tourism Management: Film Tourism—Evolution, Progress and Prospects'. *Tourism Management.* Available at: http://media.bizwebmedia.net/sites/146527/upload/documents/21-film-tourism_evolution_progress.pdf (accessed on 20 December 2016).

Ganjapure, V. 2015. 'Exploring Armed Forces, the Military Tourism Way'. *Times of India*, Nagpur. Available at: http://timesofindia.indiatimes.com/city/nagpur/Exploring-armed-forces-the-military-tourism-way/articleshow/49249783.cms (accessed on 20 December 2016).

Graveyard Tourism and Cemetery Tourism. n.d. In *HDC International: The Heritage Interpretation Experts.* Available at: http://www.heritagedestination.com/cemetery-tourism.aspx (accessed on 20 December 2016).

Hrusovsky, M., and K. Noeres. 2011. 'Military Tourism'. In *The Long Tail of Tourism: Holiday Niches and their Impact on Mainstream Tourism*, edited by A. Papathanassis. Available at: http://link.springer.com/chapter/10.1007%2F978-3-8349-6231-7_10#page-1 (accessed on 18 June 2016).

Incredible India. n.d. Rural Tourism. Available at: http://incredibleindia.org/lang/images/docs/trade-pdf/product/rural-tourism/rural-guideline.pdf (accessed on 20 December 2016).

ISPA. n.d. 'Spa–Goers'. Available at: http://experienceispa.com/resources/spa-goers (accessed on 12 July 2016).

Ministry of Shipping. n.d. 'Directorate General of Lighthouses and Lightships'. Tourism at Light Houses. Available at: http://www.dgll.nic.in/content/320_0_TOURISMATLIGHTHOUSES.aspx (accessed on 20 December 2016).

Mohonk Agreement. 2000. Available at: http://www.rainforest-alliance.org/tourism/documents/mohonk.pdf (accessed on 20 December 2016).

Press Information Bureau. 2014. 'Potential for Film Tourism in the Country'. Ministry of Tourism, Government of India. Available at: http://pib.nic.in/newsite/PrintRelease.aspx?relid=103694 (accessed on 20 December 2016).

SetuHealthCare. n.d. 'What is Spa Tourism?' Available at: http://www.setuhealthcare.com/wellness-center/wellness-tourism/spa-tourism.html (accessed on 20 December 2016).

Sharma, S. 2015. 'Coming Soon: Cemetery Tourism for Descendants of Raj Luminaries'. *Times of India*, Dehradun. Available at: http://timesofindia.indiatimes.com/city/dehradun/Coming-soon-Cemetery-tourism-for-descendants-of-Raj-luminaries/articleshow/49963871.cms (accessed on 20 December 2016).

Special Interest Tourism. n.d. In ACS Distance Education. Available at: http://www.acsedu.co.uk/Info/...Tourism/Tourism/Special-Interest-Tourism.aspx (accessed on 17 July 2016).

The Conservation Value of Avitourism. n.d. 'Birding Ecotours'. Available at: http://birdingecotours.com/how-birding-tourism-benefits-birds-and-some-harmful-pitfalls/ (accessed on 20 December 2016).

The International Ecotourism Society. n.d. Available at: http://www.ecotourism.org/ (accessed on 20 December 2016).

Wines of Balkans. 2011. Available at: http://www.winesofbalkans.com/index.php?wine-tourism

Zimmermann, S. 2003. '"Reisen in den Film"—Filmtourismus in Nordafrika'. Available at: http://www.staff.uni-mainz.de/egner/Zimmermann.pdf (accessed on 14 July 2016).

Suggested Readings

Books

Goodwin, H. 2011. *Taking Responsibility for Tourism*. Goodfellow Publishers.

Pineda, F.D., and C.A. Brebbia, eds. 2012. *Sustainable Tourism V*. United Kingdom: Wit Press.

Weaver, D. 2006. *Sustainable Tourism*. Oxford: Elsevier.

The popular sport of Golf
Image courtesy: Ministry of Tourism, Government of India.

CHAPTER 3

Demand and Supply in Tourism

By the end of this chapter, students will be able to:

- Identify the factors influencing consumer behaviour in tourism.
- Recognize the relevance of Maslow's hierarchy model in tourism.
- Gain insights on the application of demand theory in tourism.
- Learn the basics of demand forecasting techniques.
- List the methods of collection of statistics in tourism.
- Understand the significance of measurement of tourism.

Introduction

Why do people go on holidays? What motivates us to take time off from work and travel to new places? What influences our choice to decide where to go? In this chapter, we shall try to find answers to these questions. We will explore the concept of tourism demand and try to link it with theories of motivation prevalent in other fields. The chapter will also examine the factors that affect consumer behaviour.

People choose to travel for many reasons. For most, a holiday is a welcome break from the humdrum of everyday existence, a hard-earned reward of leisure time—to relax, have fun and enjoy life's pleasures. While travelling, one encounters and interacts with people of different backgrounds and cultures, faces new situations and surmounts new challenges. These experiences provide an avenue for self-discovery and introspection. Travelling helps in acquiring new knowledge, adding new perspectives and learning about cultures. If one happens to be between jobs, schools or relationships, travelling is a perfect way to delineate these life stages and gain insights to prepare for the next phase in life. The underlying reasons for which people travel have been examined and studied in academic circles to gain an understanding of the patterns of behaviour among potential travellers. A study of this psychological phenomenon is critical for tourism, and continues to generate interest and controversy.

Travellers are diverse, and their age, financial situation, lifestyle and personal interests may influence their motivation to take a holiday. Economists tend to regard tourism in the same way as a form of consumption in economic terms, and the traveller as a consumer of goods and services. While there is strength in the argument that the general theories and laws of consumption will also apply in the case of tourism, certain characteristics of the tourism industry make tourism different from the general consumption model.

There has been extensive research on the reasons based on which people take their holiday decisions, with attention paid to psychological basis of such decisions and the factors that motivate travellers to purchase specific tourism products. Marketing professionals in tourism organizations use findings based on such research to create and modify tourism products.

Why Study Tourism Demand?

When people decide to travel, there is an increased demand for products and services that are needed for the activity of travel, and which are consumed as part of travel. The preconditions of demand include desire, purchasing power and willingness to pay. Products are produced and supplied in anticipation of demand. The volume of business and receipts are by and large influenced by the demand for the products. Understanding demand, therefore, is of vital importance in tourism business.

An understanding of the factors determining demand is essential for businesses to design products and for policy-makers to develop and implement programmes for sustainable development of tourism. The seasonal nature of tourism industry also calls for a clear picture of tourism demand, as the destination need to be equipped to provide hospitality services to tourists. Tourism products can be demanded individually as well as collectively.

Understanding Consumer Behaviour

Tourists are essentially consumers purchasing products that they need to fulfil their wants and desires. But approaching tourism demand as a function of consumer behaviour may be oversimplifying a complex type of consumption. Travel behaviour can be regarded as continuous process that includes varied yet interrelated stages and concepts that cannot be analysed separately (Mill and Morrison, 2002). There are three stages in the visitation process—pre-visit, on-site and post-visit.

Cohen et al. (2014) has summed up the main aspects influencing consumer behaviour as follows:

- **Attitudes:** An attitude is best described as a viewpoint or an outlook towards something. People develop attitudes by perceiving and assessing information or experiences, which then become 'settled' and affect their perceptions and decisions. Perceptions are interpretations of inputs (stimuli) in a meaningful way. For instance, perceptions on safety and security of a destination may be fashioned by visual stimuli such as television.

- **Expectations:** The standard that the consumer expects while evaluating a product or service is the 'expectation'. These expectations fashion a person's prediction of the outcomes. We will see in subsequent chapters that service providers aim to exceed consumer expectations, as that will create a positive memory of the holiday experience.

- **Motivations:** We shall be looking at established theories of motivation in subsequent chapters. Pearce and Lee (2005) explain that tourist motivations can be four-fold—novelty seeking, relaxation, relationship building and self-development. Of all the approaches, the 'push-pull' conceptualization appears most convincing. 'Push' factors are those which are intrinsic to the visitor, such as emotional needs and curiosity, and the attributes of a destination act as 'pull' factors.

- **Personality:** Consumers purchase products that are similar to their perception of themselves. This personal identity of the individual is a complex construct, comprising of one's beliefs, self-image, social aspects and aspirations. Research has shown that consumers prefer brands and destinations that enhance their perceptions about themselves and their identities.

- **Values:** The preference of a specific way of conduct or existence compared to others may be termed as a value. Our values, regarding actions which we believe are 'good' or 'preferable', guide consumers to purchasing certain products and services. Values can be personal or cultural.

- **Decision-making process:** The process of decision-making has been studied for many decades. The classical approach is to assume that decision-making is rational, and follows a clear sequence. In other words, a series of logical steps leads the consumer from an attitude to an intention to purchase and finally to the act of consumption. But these models have their critics, particularly in tourism, who contend that the multiple stages and elements in the tourism environment add to the complexity of decision-making in the context of tourism.

- **Trust and loyalty:** When a consumer places trust on a brand, it means that s/he has confidence in it, and believes that it is reliable. Trust is built over time, based on many experiences where expectations have been met or exceeded. The more a consumer trusts a brand, the more the chances of repurchase. This is known as brand loyalty, and is exhibited by patronizing products and services repeatedly. Staying in hotels of the same brand in different cities and in the midst of alternatives is a display of trust and loyalty, and indicates that the consumer has been satisfied with the service, and assumes that s/he will receive the same level of service and satisfaction. Trust in a brand is the cornerstone of long standing customer relationships.

Motivation

Motivation may be defined as some inner drive or impulse that causes a person to do something or act in a certain way. This act brings a level of satisfaction to the individual. Several factors—psychological, economic and social—motivate a person to travel. Theories of motivation propounded by Abraham Harold Maslow and Stanley C. Plog are widely discussed in the context of tourism.

Maslow's Hierarchy of Human Needs

Abraham Maslow (1943) developed the concept of hierarchy of human needs starting from basic physiological needs to self-actualization. Maslow's hierarchy theory passes through five distinct stages—physiological needs, safety and security, love and belonging, self-esteem and finally to self-actualization.

Physiological needs are related to primary requisites of life and it includes factors like breathing, food, shelter, clothing and sleep. People are motivated to work and earn to achieve these physiological needs. Once the socioeconomic conditions of an individual's life changes for the better, a person would be motivated by the needs of the next level in the hierarchy.

Given the different levels of tourism activities and business, one may find that tourists are guided by the motivation principles outlined in the Maslow model. Modern tourism is influenced by the tastes, preferences and socioeconomic environments of potential travellers. The complexities of modern life have led to a situation where rest has become an indispensable component of every day's life irrespective of the economic status. The inner drive of a person with a small disposable income will be to spend his evenings in a pleasant environment close by, without incurring much expense, as a means of relaxation. Once his disposable income goes up and he is financially sound, he may be motivated to go for a holiday in a new

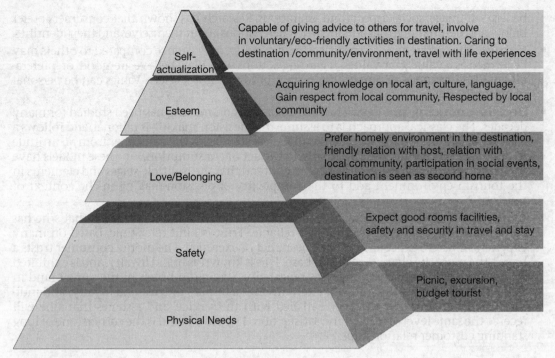

Figure 3.1 Maslow's hierarchy model and tourism
Source: Authors.

environment, which may be a tourist destination. Thus, the graduation process in motivation hierarchy begins, as the traveller, motivated by his needs of a higher level, consumes tourism products and services at a higher level in the hierarchy. Let us see how the five stages conceived by Maslow in his hierarchical model works in tourism (Figure 3.1).

The operation of this hierarchy model may be seen in different types of tourists who travel for varied reasons. Strategies related to product development, destination development and marketing were determined keeping in mind the postulates of this model.

The Maslow model has many critics, who argue that needs are not necessarily hierarchical and may occur simultaneously. However, it does provide a robust analytical platform, focusing attention on the need for personal growth and its application across disciplines. Subsequently, many researchers have used the Maslow hierarchy model as a base, and further analysed the motivations underlying the desire to travel.

Tourism Demand

Tourism demand can be defined as 'the total number of persons who travel, or wish to travel, to use tourist facilities and services away from their places of work and residence' (Mathieson and Wall, 1982). 'Demand may also mean the amount of products and services that people are willing and able to buy at a specified price ... during a specified period of time' (Cooper et al., 1993).

What are the factors that influence tourism demand? How does demand change and what are the implications?

The demand for products is influenced by social, economic and psychological factors. However, the size of disposable income and motivation to travel exercise considerable influence in the size of demand for tourism products. Consumers analyse the benefits derived and the costs to be incurred while making a purchase. For this reason, generally speaking, there is more demand for a product at a lower price and less at a higher price. This phenomenon is captured in the law of demand which expresses the inverse relationship between price and quantity demanded. The demand for a product varies at different price points. The relationship between the various quantities of a product demanded by an individual at different prices is represented by an individual demand schedule.

The Demand Curve

A demand curve depicts the relationship between the price of a certain product and the quantity of it that the consumer is willing and able to purchase at a given price. The price is denoted on the vertical axis and the quantity demanded is on the horizontal axis of the graph. As can be seen, the curve slopes from left to right, indicating that the quantity demanded goes up at lower prices, other factors remaining the same (Figure 3.2).

Elements of Tourism Demand

The demand for tourism products varies with factors like desire to travel, disposable income of the person travelling and knowledge about the tourism products. Some people desire to travel but cannot do so, as they do not have enough money or time or conducive health. There is another set of people who are not interested to travel as they are unaware of the benefits of travel. They may not have any knowledge about tourism products. Another category is highly price sensitive. The second and third set of people can be motivated to buy tourism products if the supply systems create and market their products attractively. Cooper et al.

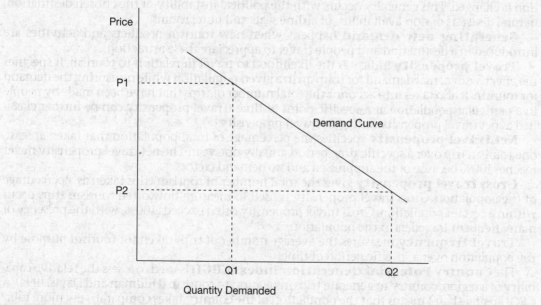

Figure 3.2 Demand curve
Source: Authors.

(1993) classified the demand for tourism products as 'Elements of Tourism Demand'. The elements of tourism demand and related concepts are discussed below.

Effective or actual demand refers to the number of tourists recorded in a given destination at a particular point of time. The increase in effective demand results in demand for creation of more infrastructure facilities at the destination.

Latent or suppressed demand is the number of people who would travel if they could but are prevented from doing so, either by their own circumstances (lack of purchasing power) or by external circumstances (lack of leaves from work). Suppressed demand can be divided into two—potential demand and deferred demand; both refer to those who do not travel for some reason.

Potential demand refers to those who have the will to participate in tourism activities but do not travel due to their own circumstances, basically lack of supporting socioeconomic environment. In other words, they do not have money or other resources to undertake tourism plans. Potential demand is more likely to become actual demand in the future when circumstances allow. They might be waiting for an increase in salary, holiday entitlement including paid leaves or a decrease in price of tourism products, in order to convert the suppressed but potential demand to effective demand.

Deferred demand refers to the number of people who do not travel because of the external circumstances, particularly from the supplier side. These include shortage of accommodation facilities, expensive accommodation, inadequate transport facilities, lack of supporting knowledge, safety and political instability of the destination, high crime rates and adverse weather conditions. The impassiveness of this type is mainly due to the inefficiency of the supply side to provide the required facilities or to market its products.

No demand refers to those individuals who are not interested to travel, or those who are unable to do so. The reasons for this may be lack of time, money or health issues.

Substitution of demand occurs when the demand for one type of tourism activity is replaced by another activity.

Redirection of demand occurs when the geographical location of the holiday destination is changed. This generally occurs with the political instability of the chosen destination, natural disasters or non-availability of airline seats and hotel rooms.

Generating new demand happens when new tourism products and activities are introduced in a destination and people travel to appreciate these attractions.

Travel propensity indicates the likelihood to travel in relation to tourism. It specifies the effective or actual demand for tourism in a given population while measuring the demand for tourism. It also takes into account the total number of trips that have been made by people in a particular population at a specific point of time. Travel propensity can be further classified as net travel propensity and gross travel propensity.

Net travel propensity specifies the percentage of total population that takes, at least, one tourism trip over a specific time period, usually one year. The net travel propensity never reaches 100% because of the suppressed and no demand factors.

Gross travel propensity gives the total number of tourism trips taken as a percentage of the population. Gross travel propensity is used to measure how often tourism trips occur within a certain population. Gross travel propensity often exceeds 100%, with the presence of many frequent travellers in the population.

Travel frequency measures the average number of trips taken for tourism purpose by the population over a specific period of time.

The **Country Potential Generation Index (CPGI)** is used to assess the relative capability of a region/country to generate trips in relation to tourism (Hudman and Davis, 1994). A CPGI greater than 1 means that the population of the country takes comparatively more tourism trips than its population share.

Measurement of Travel Propensity

$$\text{Net travel propensity} = \frac{\text{Number of population taking at least one trip}}{\text{Total population}} \times 100$$

$$\text{Gross travel propensity} = \frac{\text{Number of trips}}{\text{Total population}} \times 100$$

$$\text{Travel frequency} = \frac{\text{Gross Travel Propensity}}{\text{Net Travel Propensity}}$$

$$\text{CPGI} = \frac{Ne / Nw}{Pe / Pw}$$

Ne = Number of trips generated by country; Nw = Number of trips generated in the world; Pe = Population of the country; Pw = Population of the world

Factors Influencing Tourism Demand

In the backdrop of the discussion on various elements of tourism demand, let us examine the various factors influencing tourism demand:

- **Individual:** Individual propensities and characteristics play important roles in determining demand. These could be fundamental features such as age, gender, physical capacity, family circumstances and educational levels, or socio-psychological factors such as individual motivations, perceptions, attitudes and past experiences. Job-related factors such as amount of leave and leisure time, paid vacations and disposable incomes are major economic determinants affecting individual demand.
- **Economic:** People travel more when they are in a better economic situation. Economic factors include cost of living, relative prices of products, competitive prices, transportation costs and currency exchange rate differences.
- **Political:** Tourists prefer to travel to a destination where the political conditions are favourable. Examples of such factors include policies and regulations on visa procedures, health checks, ease of currency conversions, transport regulations and law and order.
- **Technological:** Advancement in technology plays a key role in stimulating tourism demand. High levels of infrastructure development in sectors such as transportation and aviation, urbanization, information technology and communication create favourable conditions directly influencing demand.
- **Destination:** Geographical factors in a destination such as attractions, accessibility, seasonality and climate are important in determining demand. Opening up of new destinations creates new demand. Other factors include destination image, facilities at the destination and the availability of and access to tourism products.

Changes in Demand

When there is a change in any of the factors that influences and determines demand, there is a change in demand, which can be an increase or a decrease. Increase in demand takes place when consumers demand more quantities of a product at the same price or they are willing to pay a higher price for the same quantity. A representation of this change is shown by a shift of the demand curve, outwardly or to the right. In the Figure 3.3, it can be seen that if M is the

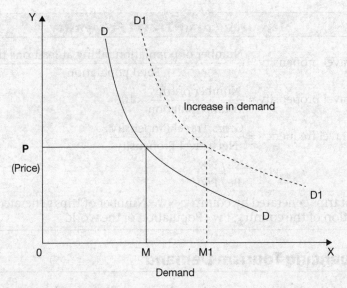

Figure 3.3   Increase in demand
Source: Authors.

quantity of goods bought by the consumer at price point *P*, the quantity increases to *M*1 even if the price remains unchanged.

Decrease in demand takes place when consumers demand less at the same price or are willing to pay a lower price for the original quantity. In such cases, original demand curve shifts inwards or to the left (Figure 3.4).

An understanding of changes in demand is important in tourism business as it help managers to design strategies to improve sales. For instance, if a destination attracts more tourists by adopting a strategy of price cut, it cannot be considered as an increase in demand for the destination. On the other hand, if the destination succeeds in attracting more tourists without changing the rates in hotels/restaurants, it could be termed as an increase in demand. Increase in demand could be realized by adopting strategies like quality enhancement, strengthening brand loyalty or adopting other successful marketing strategies. Increase in demand takes place when tourists are willing to pay a higher price for the services offered or when more people demand a product at the existing price. It follows that managers need to develop strategies to increase the demand for the destination rather than creating an extension in demand.

Let us consider an example of a beach destination. If the destination develops activities or attractions that supplement the core product (e.g., 'Beyond the Beach' package), some tourists may prefer to extend their stay, spending part of the time on the beach and the remaining part travelling to the attractions or involving themselves in the newly introduced activities. This changed behaviour can increase the demand for accommodation, longer stays and more incomes. This is the reason why destination managers are concerned with the development of value addition programmes to the core tourism product, focusing on local specific specialities.

Elasticity of Demand

The demand for a product may change when there is a change in the factors influencing demand. Broadly, a change in price, income, taste or preferences can bring about a change in demand. However, the influence of a change in price, income and the existence of substitutes

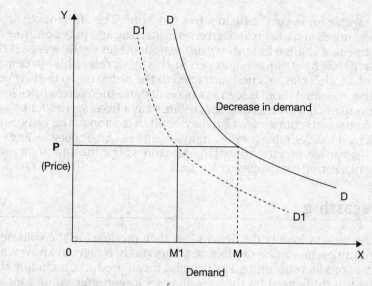

Figure 3.4 Decrease in demand
Source: Authors.

play a dominant role in creating a change in demand. Elasticity of demand shows the responsiveness to demand when there is a change in income, price or availability of substitutes. Price elasticity of demand shows a change in demand due to a change in price. It is measured using the following formula:

Price elasticity of demand=Percentage change in quantity demanded/Percentage change in price.

Elasticity of demand can be unity, greater than one, less than one, zero or infinite.

If the room tariff of a hotel is slashed by 20% and the demand changes by 20%, then price elasticity of demand is one, indicating that there is a proportionate change in demand due to a change in price. This situation is called unit elasticity of demand. Elasticity of demand could be more than one, provided there is a more than proportionate change in demand when price changes. Suppose room tariff changes by 20% and is followed by a 50% change in the demand for rooms, then the elasticity of demand will be 2.5. When the value is more than 1, demand is said to be more elastic as there is a more than proportionate change in demand due to a change in price. Suppose a 20% cut in room tariff creates only a 10% change in demand, then elasticity will be 0.5, indicating that there is a less than proportionate change in demand when price changes. Here, elasticity is said to be less than unity.

One may come across two extreme situations. First, perfectly inelastic demand, indicating that irrespective of a change in price, the quantity demanded remains the same. Here the value will be equal to 0, indicating that a change in price creates little or no impact on demand. Second, perfectly elastic demand, the opposite situation denotes considerable change in demand when there is a change in price. Normally, luxury goods have elastic demand and necessary goods experience inelastic demand. The concept of elasticity can be applied in the tourism sector also. An understanding of the nature of tourism products and customer preferences will help businesses to examine elasticity and determine the price accordingly. For instance, the demand for accommodation by pilgrim tourists and business travellers are more or less inelastic. Their primary purpose, that is, pilgrimage or business, needs to be fulfilled and cannot be postponed. Therefore, they may absorb wide price fluctuations. Hence, the demand for rooms in pilgrim destinations remains more or less the same even if accommodation rates are increased substantially.

Consider an example for luxury suite in a five star hotel. The affluent clientele who normally stay in luxury hotels are, to a great degree, price inelastic and may continue to patronize the hotel irrespective of a change in tariff within reasonable levels. However, if the property were to slash the tariff rate by 50% for a short period, this may create a hike in demand, spurred by the purchases of another class of guests attracted to the hotel due to the low pricing. Thus, we may observe that the same room is seen as a necessity and therefore, a price inelastic product by a certain group of consumers while it is regarded as a luxury product by another type of customers. (Of course, this course of action may result in erosion in the value proposition of the property, making it less desirable for the original clientele.) An understanding of the nature of customers and the various factors influencing demand is of prime importance in setting the price and creating marketing campaigns.

Demand Forecasting

Businessmen always observe keenly the demand for their products, as the volume of sales and sales turnover determines the success of a business. Everybody is eager to know what would be the demand for their products in future. The demand for all products, including those in tourism, is uncertain as it is influenced by the prevailing socioeconomic conditions and the psychology of consumers. To address the inherent uncertainty and to lead the business to success, businessmen rely on demand forecasting. In other words, demand forecasting is an attempt to predict the future so as to enable the organization to plan and execute programmes. Demand forecasting is of prime importance in tourism because the business itself is seasonal and the products demanded are perishable. In the tourism sector, forecasting demand is mainly done on tourist arrivals and its patterns, foreign exchange earnings, bed nights in hotels, outbound travel and expenditure pattern of tourists. Depending on the requirements, the organization can make short-term or long-term forecasting. Methods of forecasting adopted range from simple guesswork to econometric methods where statistical and mathematical theories are applied to economics for the purpose of testing hypotheses and forecasting future trends, involving qualitative and quantitative techniques (Investopedia n.d.). Usually, when there is a lack of data or irrelevant data available, qualitative forecasting methods are used. These methods are not purely guesswork, but well-structured approaches to obtain forecasts without using historical data. The important qualitative forecasting techniques include Executive Opinion Method, Sales Force Estimates, Delphi Method, Morphological Analysis, Relevance Tree and Scenario Planning.

Quantitative forecasting methods are applied when numerical information about the past is available or when it is reasonable to assume that some past trends will continue into the future. Quantitative forecasting methods use either cross-sectional data, collected at a single point of time or time series data, collected at regular intervals over time. In cross-sectional forecasting, prediction is made for values of something that has not been observed based on the information on cases that have been observed earlier. For instance, we have the room tariff of some hotels in a destination for the current year. We are interested in predicting the room tariff of hotels that are not in our dataset using various hotel characteristics like the star rating, position of hotel or facilities offered. Time series data is used to forecast something that changes over time. An example of time series forecasting is the prediction on tourist arrivals for a future period of a destination. This methodology uses only information on tourist arrivals in earlier periods to predict the future arrival pattern. It does not look at the factors that affect the arrival trend like marketing initiatives or competitor activity. The major quantitative techniques of forecasting are simple trend projection, arithmetic moving averages, decomposition analysis, exponential smoothing, auto regressive model, Box-Jenkins method, Clawson technique, multivariable regression demand analysis, growth scenario model, almost ideal demand system, system dynamics and input–output analysis. Of the above, smoothing techniques like arithmetic moving averages, decomposition analysis, exponential smoothing and auto-regressive models are used for time series analysis.

Tourism Supply

We have discussed the different aspects relating to tourism demand. Let us take a look at the supply side, its components and the environment in which supply occurs. It may be recollected that demand is generated in the source market, in the normal place of residence of the consumer. Supply takes place at the destination, which is geographically separate from the market. Demand and supply are linked by 'bridging elements', which set up the business system between the two. Examples of bridging elements are travel intermediaries such as tour operators, transportation providers and marketing agencies.

At the destination, 'supply' consists of mainly three types of elements—attractions, infrastructure and facilities.

In the manufacturing industry, products are stored in stock-awaiting sale. The portion of the stock that is brought to the market for sale is known as the supply. The quantity supplied is largely determined by the market price. Higher the market price, more will be supplied and vice versa. In other words, the law of supply exhibits a direct relation between the market price and the quantity supplied. As already discussed, tourism demand constitutes of whatever goods or services demanded by the tourists during their travel and stay at a destination. Transport, accommodation, food and beverages, entertainment, shopping, attraction and various ancillary services constitute the products that are supplied by different businesses to the tourists. Let us analyse the supply side further by examining the various components of this supply system.

Elements of the Supply System

Attractions: Natural attractions of a destination are important elements in the holiday experience. The local climate, physical features such as beaches, mountains, landscape, waterfalls and water bodies and the flora and fauna are primary natural resources. Much of this is 'common property resources', to be non-exclusionary and to be enjoyed by all.

Human-made attraction: Human-made attractions could be built structures, such as historic buildings, monuments, places of worship, archaeological sites or stadia, or they could be cultural attractions, based on what they have inside, such as museums, galleries and theatres. Some human-made attractions are built with tourists in mind, such as theme parks, marinas and festivals.

Built attractions, like palaces, forts, pilgrim centres and other constructions depicting the creativity, aesthetics, architecture and valour, contribute significantly in the promotion of heritage destinations. Similarly, parks, museums, art galleries, golf and marina also form part of human-made attractions which provide enjoyment and experience to the tourist. Heritage monuments and museums possess long history and culture. The protection, management and authentic interpretation of the same play a vital role in ensuring their uninterrupted supply to the tourist.

Infrastructure: The role of infrastructure is important, because it forms a vital pillar on which tourism services and facilities used by tourists are built. While general infrastructures, like different types of transport, road networks, pathways, parking areas, drinking water supply, streetlights, toilets, sewage system, banking and telecommunication, are used by the public and tourists, the supply of tourism-specific facilities like hotels, resorts, restaurants, theme parks, information centres are primarily oriented towards meeting the requirements of tourists. These buildings and facilities are often termed 'superstructure'. The importance of various modes of transport like air, water, rail and road need special mention. Thanks to global economic advancement, by and large, modern tourists are money rich and time poor. Fast and easy air access is therefore critical to the success of the destination. Quality roads along with wayside amenities like parking, information and public toilets strengthen the supply side of general infrastructure. Efficiently operated systems of public transport, such as coaches, cabs and tram services are important in the supply side.

Closely connected to this is the provision of various amenities and services. Tourists are interested in spending their time for entertainment, sports, shopping and other leisurely activities. Supply of these amenities of good quality will strengthen the value of core attraction of the destination. While considering the facilities for entertainment, tourists by and large, prefer local art forms and festivals that are capable of providing an experience that is entertaining as well as enriching. In an era of e-business, companies can ensure the supply of their products in any part of the world. Unlike travel to shopping destinations, tourists do shopping in all destinations, mainly to purchase products having a local flavour. Souvenirs of different types that can be gifted to friends/relatives and can be kept at home to make the journey memorable are largely demanded by tourists. Supply of innovative products of local specificity will strengthen the brand value of the destination.

Ensuring supply of local art forms with its full authenticity is another component of the supply side. Identifying and making them available with adequate interpretation need special mention.

In the backdrop of fast spreading urbanization, village visits have gained significance in tourism. Tourists prefer to spend their time with village people for close acquaintance to understand the lifestyle, culture, indigenous technology and practices. The continuous increase in demand for packages providing glimpses of village life is an indicator of this preference. With creativity and innovation, destinations can develop good number of village-based packages in tourism destinations across the world.

Accommodation

The provision of an adequate quantity of accommodation facilities is a key component of the supply side. It is the primary facility used by all tourists in a destination. Apart from sufficient quantity, the quality of accommodation supplies is an important consideration. Hotels, resorts, lodges, youth hostels, guest houses and homestays are common examples of accommodation. The ambience, connectivity, facility and hospitality along with service delivery decide the quality of product supplies. Accordingly, accommodation facilities are classified to enable the tourists to have a basic understanding of the facilities provided while ensuring standards based on identified criteria. Hotels are classified as premium, luxury, mid-price, economy and budget, based on specific criteria. Classification of homestays and restaurants are also done in some destinations to ensure quality standards. Accommodations adopting sustainable practices are well received by the tourists. Property management systems, use of appropriate technology, green technology and social commitment are some of the factors that strengthen the supply of accommodation units.

Food and beverage outlets such as restaurants, cafes and bars provide another important facility in a destination for the tourist. These are also important routes through which the tourist expenditure enriches the local economy, as a large majority of these establishments will be owned and operated by local residents. Other facilities like health services, pharmacies, theatres, sports and leisure centres are also important ingredients in a destination.

Market

The trend of tourism market is largely determined by demand and supply which are the invisible forces in the market. There is intense competition between suppliers and sellers to capture a slice of the tourist market. The characteristics of competition may vary based on the regulatory environment, the availability of land and resources, entry and exit constraints and price controls. Suppliers would ideally want a situation where the demand continues even in the face of sustained increase in prices, and competition is minimal. Though one may come across different models of competition, oligopoly is a common form in the tourism market. Oligopoly is defined as competition among a few. Tourism suppliers adopt different strategies such as backward and forward integration and mergers and acquisitions to create an oligopoly market situation.

Measurement of Tourism

The state of the tourism industry is reflected in the arrival of tourists, income generated, employment generated and foreign exchange earnings. The conclusions are derived by measuring the performance of tourism industry using appropriate parameters. What is the use of measurement of tourism? Is there any universally accepted methodology for measuring tourism? Who benefits from measuring tourism? Let us examine in brief the measurement of tourism, particularly in the context of tourism business.

The importance of the tourism sector to the economy has to be demonstrated in objective terms, which calls for reliable and authentic data. There are several ways to keep track of the demand and supply systems and to measure the impact of tourism activities that provide essential information for detailed economic analysis.

The simplest model of tourism data collection would be to equate demand to the number of arrivals and room nights, and supply to the number of rooms or beds in a destination. However, we need to realise that tourism is a multifaceted and complex economic activity, and its impact needs to be understood by creating and implementing measurement systems that capture this complexity.

The tourism business is constituted by various productive sectors. The role of different stakeholders is also equally important. Putting together the diverse interests and motives of stakeholders, we may conclude that measurement of tourism is warranted for making business decisions, pricing decisions, getting an insight into the economic contribution of the sector and as an early warning system.

Decision-making Process

Business decisions pertaining to investment in tourism infrastructure like hotels, resorts, restaurants, entertainment facilities, product development and marketing are taken after assessing the current status of the sector along with its future prospects. Analysis and assessment of these require authentic data related to the current demand. Demand forecasting enables the industry to plan investments for the future. An understanding of customer requirements by collecting feedback helps the industry to identify tastes and preferences of the customers, their changing needs and requirements and methods to improve customer satisfaction by providing improved services and facilities. Knowledge on emerging trends in tourism helps product development and marketing. Information on new market segments is helpful for designing and implementing suitable marketing strategies. Data related to customer feedback is used by businesses for developing customer retention practices.

Governments

Governments at national, state and local levels are interested in the measurement of tourism as the data provides vital information for designing policies and programmes for tourism development. Tourism, as a labour intensive industry, provides opportunities for direct, indirect and induced employment for citizens, which is an important imperative for governments, particularly in developing countries. Tourism also has ample scope for self-employment and entrepreneurship, creating prosperity in the local economy. Data on tourist expenditure provides clear and undeniable evidence of the profound impact and role of tourism, through information on linkages and multiplier effects of the sector. The multiplier effect, which shows the magnitude of recirculation of tourism income at the destination, ultimately throws light on the economic benefits generated through tourism in that area. The contribution of tourism to the economy is not limited to generation of income and employment. It cuts across other fields like exports and imports, with the sector bringing in foreign exchange and contributing to improving the balance of payments position of developing countries like India.

Tourism Satellite Account

The Tourism Satellite Account (TSA) is a standard statistical framework and the main tool for the economic measurement of tourism. The 'Tourism Satellite Account: Recommended Methodological Framework 2008' (also known as the TSA: RMF 2008) provides the updated common conceptual framework for constructing a TSA. It adopts the basic system of concepts, classifications, definitions, tables and aggregates of the System of National Accounts 2008 (SNA 2008), the international standard for a systematic summary of national economic activity, from a functional perspective. TSA, thus, allows for the harmonization and reconciliation of tourism statistics from an economic (National Accounts) perspective. This enables the generation of tourism economic data (such as tourism direct GDP) that is comparable with other economic statistics. Exactly how the TSA does this relates to the SNA logic of contrasting data from the demand side (the acquisition of goods and services by visitors while on a tourism trip) with data from the supply side of the economy. UNWTO has decided to release part of the material produced since 1979, the year when the term 'Tourism Satellite Account' was first coined in France. This compilation is divided into two parts. Both parts begin with an introduction of the now historical documents:

- Designing the TSA Methodological Framework (1995–2000).
- TSA: Past, present and future developments.

A Committee on Statistics and the TSA has been constituted which is a subsidiary advisory body of the UNWTO Executive Council. It acts in matters such as:

- Proposing initiatives related to the design and implementation of tourism statistics International standards.
- Promoting international comparability of tourism statistics by proposing initiatives relative to the collection, homogeneity, processing and dissemination of data.
- Helping member countries in their initiatives to improve their respective national systems of tourism statistics (STS) and in the development of the TSA.
- Liaising with other international bodies with delegated responsibilities for leadership and coordination of related international statistics and their standards within sphere of the UN system.

Promotion

Promotion is another area which is directly benefited from statistics on tourism business. Tourism promotion agencies under national or state governments undertake promotional campaigns within and outside the country, and the effectiveness of these campaigns can be assessed by measuring the impact of the campaigns in identified markets. This will enable the agency to redesign the campaign strategy, if needed.

An understanding on the current status and forecasting the future will help the government for formulating policy conducive for development of tourism. Policies related to taxation, investment, subsidy, discriminatory rates, environmental regulations, construction, micro-small and medium enterprises and human resource development are framed in the backdrop of the current status and future prospects of tourism business in a country.

NGOs and Local Community

Civil society organizations often act as watchdogs of tourism businesses. Much of the resources used in tourism fall under common property resources like grasslands, forests, beaches and backwaters. A careful examination of the business operations at the destination level will enable civil society organizations to give early warning to authorities for taking adequate corrective and precautionary measures. NGOs and local communities do this by assessing data on tourism business operations in prominent destinations.

What to Measure?

The above discussions have shown the need for measuring tourism activities and its relevance in planning and strategy making. To obtain a clear understanding of the magnitude of tourism business, we have to measure all prominent aspects related to tourism business operations. It is also important to understand the methodologies used in data collection. The main data collected can be broadly classified under two heads—demand side and supply side.

Demand Side Data

Demand side data mainly relate to tourist arrivals, duration of stay, expenditure, personal information of tourists, tourist preferences and visitor satisfaction.

Tourist arrivals: Here the data relating to arrivals of domestic and foreign tourists are collected. Tourist arrival data throws light on the situation prevailing in source markets. The number of arrivals to a destination is normally published on an annual basis.

Tourist expenditure: The contribution of tourism to the economy is calculated mainly by using statistics of expenditure. In other words, it reflects the value of tourism to the economy. Tourists spending on local transport, food and beverages, accommodation, entertainment, and shopping are included in this figure. Tourist expenditure data does not include the airfare to airline companies for air passage to the destination. The average per day expenditure is calculated by dividing the total tourist expenditure by total tourist days.

Personal information: This may include details such as age, profession, activities preferred in destinations, travel intermediaries used, number of nights of stay, purpose of trip, destinations to be visited and group size.

Consumer preferences: The data collected can give insights into potential demand, and serve marketing and promotional strategies. Socioeconomic trends in markets, perception of the image of a destination, relative strengths compared to competitors, use of internet-based channels such as portals and websites and efficiency of advertising campaigns may be measured using this data.

Visitor satisfaction: Accommodation units normally collect feedback from tourists. Destination management organizations engage researchers to conduct research on visitor satisfaction, with data being collected directly from the tourist. This data is used for improving quality service delivery and identifying problem areas.

Burkart and Medlik (1981) have summed up the various statistics collected on demand side of tourism under three categories viz. statistics of volume, statistics of expenditure, and statistics of characteristics. The number of arrivals made by tourists in a destination, normally one year, forms one component of statistics of volume. The average length of stay, which is measured in terms of the number of days tourists spend in the destination, is another component of statistics of volume. The arrivals along with duration of stay will help us to calculate average tourist days in a destination during a given period. It is calculated by multiplying the arrivals and average length of stay during a given period. Statistics of expenditure shows all data related to tourist spending in the destination. Data related to personal information, consumer preferences and visitor satisfaction constitute statistics of characteristics.

Supply Side Data

Data related to aspects like facilities, employment, transport, entertainment, raw materials to hotels and restaurants form the supply side data.

Accommodation: Accommodation statistics gives data on different types of accommodation, number of units in accommodation establishments, commercial and non-commercial accommodation, facilities within accommodation units, total employment of skilled, semi-skilled and unskilled labour, and data related to classified and non-classified units.

Employment: Employee turnover, training needs, skill gaps and satisfaction are some of the important aspects covered here. This data will help organizations for improving their human resource management systems.

Support services and products: The tourism industry uses several support services and products for its day to day operations. These may be sourced either from the local community or outside. Supply side data on support services and products will enable managers to assess economic linkages and leakages and design programmes for strengthening the local economy.

Methods of Collection of Statistics

Statistical data can be broadly classified into primary and secondary data. Primary data is collected for the first time and is original in character, while the secondary data are those which have been already collected by somebody else and has gone through a statistical process. The method of collection of primary and secondary data also varies as primary data has to be collected in original and secondary data involves compilation.

The primary data is usually collected by observation method, interviews, surveys using questionnaires and schedules.

In observation method, the data is collected by the investigator's own direct observations. The investigator personally goes and observes events, things, behaviour, activities and so on. While making observations, objectivity and purpose have to be maintained throughout by the investigator. The methods of observation employed also vary according to the situation and the type of data. Sometimes the investigator disguises himself as a participant of the group and observes the activities of other members of a group, a technique called participant observation. In non-participant observation, the researcher observes the group without participating in its activities. In order to maintain accuracy of observation, the investigator may sometimes use mechanical devices like cameras and audio recorders for data collection.

Interviews are done personally as well as telephonically. In personal interviews, the interviewer asks questions generally in a face-to-face context. These interviews are mostly done in a structured way with a set of predetermined questions asked in a prescribed form and order. In the case of unstructured interviews, the interviewer has the freedom to ask supplementary questions at times or sometimes omit questions that were pre-planned during the interview. The interviewer may change the sequence of the questions also depending on the situation. Telephonic interviews are conducted when the interviewer finds it difficult to meet the interviewee either because of distance or time constraints.

The Questionnaire method of data collection is used when a large number of people are to be surveyed. A structured questionnaire is prepared and sent to the respondents. Respondents are expected to read and understand the questionnaire and write down the reply in the space provided in the questionnaire by themselves. Questionnaire surveys have become popular online, because of ease of operation.

In the case of schedules, there will be a pro forma containing a set of questions which would be filled up by enumerators who are specifically appointed for this purpose. The enumerators go to the respondents, ask the questions in order and fill the answers to each question. Enumerators will be able to explain the aims and objectives of the investigation and remove the difficulties in case any for respondents to answer the queries. Enumerators have to be carefully selected and orientation should be given before sending them out to the respondents.

Secondary statistical data may be either published or unpublished. The published data can be available in various publications of foreign, central, state and local governments as well as international and national organizations and their subsidiary bodies, journals and publications of trade/industry, banks, stock exchanges, reports prepared by universities and research scholars in different fields, public records and historical documents. Unpublished data may be available in diaries, letters and unpublished biographies as well as with many individuals and private organizations.

Statistics pertaining to tourism are collected from primary as well as secondary sources. Three important methods are used for collecting statistics related to tourist arrivals. They include enumeration at the point of arrival/departure, accommodation records and surveys at the destination. Collection of statistics at the point of entry/departure is possible where the entry is controlled by an agency. The statistics of volume mainly focuses on arrivals and departure points. This is possible in the case of foreign tourists, as they have to enter through an immigration process where data capture is accurate. But for domestic tourists, most destinations do not have specific entry or departure points. Hence, it is difficult to follow this method. Accommodation record is another source. The effectiveness of this method depends on a proper maintenance of records by accommodation units. In many destinations, the law mandates that a record of resident guests have to be maintained by each accommodation establishment, and such records have to be compiled and made available to the concerned authority. Non-classified properties and households do not keep accommodation records, and hence pose a limitation to data collection. Accommodation data are valuable secondary sources of information on tourist arrivals. Field surveys are conducted for collecting primary data on tourist arrivals at destinations. Household surveys of persons conducted in places of residence provide primary data on frequency of travel, expenditure incurred and preferences. The domestic tourism data collected as part of the National Sample Survey in India is an example of the significant information obtained through an exhaustive household survey.

Tourist expenditure statistics are also collected through primary and secondary sources. Surveys among tourist are the most widely accepted method for collecting data on tourist expenditure. After deciding a sample size, tourists are directly contacted and surveyed using a questionnaire. Besides this primary source, secondary sources are also used for collecting statistics on expenditure. Accommodation units provide an average estimate of the expenditure incurred by the tourist, and other data such as expenditure per capita on food and beverages and expenditure on additional services provided by the unit. Taking data on average expenditure, the number of tourists and duration of stay, the total expenditure is estimated.

Data related to tourist characteristics are mainly collected by conducting field survey among tourists. Tourists are approached with pretested questionnaire and data is collected. The feedback of tourists collected by accommodation units and other establishments such as restaurants provides another source of data for collecting tourist characteristics. Besides this, departure surveys, household surveys, telephonic interviews and online surveys are also widely used for collecting statistics.

Limitations

Unlike other manufacturing or service sectors in the economy, it is not an easy task to collect accurate statistics on tourism, due to the peculiar nature of the discipline. Tourists make use of general utility services like public transport, water and electricity along with members of the community. It is difficult to delineate the tourist from other types of travellers in several situations. Similarly, there is no proper reporting system for the tourists who move from one destination to another within the same country, and the inclusion of such a person in multiple data points can distort the data. The available data with other organization/institutions quite often is incomplete. For administrative purposes like immigration, countries follow their own specific methods for data collection which may not be tourism specific. The statistics directly from tourists themselves may be rendered inaccurate based on the circumstances. While some may not be interested in sharing information with the enumerators, others may share only part of the information or sometimes provide false information. The approach and willingness of the tourist to share data on their activities is a major limitation while conducting surveys. Similarly, visitors may avail accommodation facility with friends, relatives or unclassified properties which are not accounted. The survey method for data collection is faced with other limitations which include small size of the samples, lack of clear-cut and universally accepted methodology in use and the presence of subjectivity elements.

Conclusion

Although there are several theories in the vogue relating to the motivations that encourage people to travel and take holidays, it is important to understand that human motivation and our decision-making patterns are complex and defy simplistic analysis. Economic principles of demand and supply are applicable to tourism, and segments of tourism display differing degrees of elasticity of demand. Tourism business is about providing goods and services to satisfy demand generated, and supply side components have destination-specific characteristics. In order to make sense of this complicated process, several methods of data collection and measurement are used by researchers and organizations. What is clear from all this is that a tourist may be seen as a consumer, a member of a group with common features or as an entity subject to manipulation by market forces, and yet many of the motivations behind his/her decision to travel and holiday are yet not clearly understood.

Review Questions

1. Discuss the factors that influence consumer behaviour in tourism.
2. Discuss how Maslow's hierarchy of Human Needs is relevant to the tourism sector. Do you agree with its application in tourism?
3. What is propensity to travel? How can we calculate different types of travel propensities?
4. Define elasticity of demand. Discuss its application in tourism business.
5. Explain the different methods of demand forecasting.

6. Discuss the major elements in tourism supply system.
7. Examine how tourism statistics are collected.

Activities

1. Make a list of 25 students of your institute, following simple random sampling technique, and collect data on their motivation to travel and types of tourism activities they are interested in. Based on this data, classify them into different groups using Maslow's hierarchy model.
2. Invite two tour operators to your institute and arrange informal discussions on current trends in tourism. What are the main determinants of demand, in their view? Which markets seem to have the greatest potential? Seek information from them regarding surveys they conduct with their clients.
3. Identify the major stakeholders in a destination and explore the ways in which they are connected to each other. Try to determine the relationships that have been built between stakeholders.
4. Conduct an interview with five hotel managers in your locality and examine how they use the concept of elasticity of demand in designing their business strategy.
5. Conduct a survey of 20 tourists visiting a tourist site. Prepare a questionnaire to bring out information on the profile of the tourists, their expectations on the destination and their expenditure pattern during their stay.

References

Books

Burkart, A.J., and S. Medlik. 1981. *Tourism: Past, Present and Future*, 2nd ed. London: Heinemarm.
Cohen, S.A., G. Prayag, and M. Moital. 2014. 'Consumer Behaviour in Tourism: Concepts, Influences and Opportunities'. *Current Issues in Tourism*, 17 (10): 872–909.
Cooper, C., S. Wanhill, J. Fletcher, and A. Fyall. 1993. *Tourism Principles and Practice*. London: Pitman.
Hudman, L.E., and J.E. Davis. 1994. 'Changes and Patterns of Origin Regions of International Tourism'. *Geojournal*, 34 (4): 481–90.
Mathieson, A., and G. Wall. 1982. *Tourism: Economic, Physical and Social Impacts*. Harlow, UK: Longman.
Mill, R.C., and A.M. Morrison. 2002. *The Tourism System*. United States: Kendal/Hunt Publishing Co.
Pearce, P.L., and U. Lee. 2005. 'Developing the Travel Career Approach to Tourism Motivation'. *Journal of Travel Research*, 43 (3): 226–37.

Web Resources

Investopedia. n.d. 'Econometrics'. *Investopedia*. Available at: http://www.investopedia.com/terms/e/econometrics.asp (accessed on 20 December 2016).
Maslow, A.H. 1943. 'A Theory of Human Motivation'. *Psychological Review*, 50: 370–96. Available at: http://www.newworldencyclopedia.org/entry/Abraham_Maslow (accessed on 20 December 2016).

Suggested Readings

Books

Archer, B.H. 1987. 'Demand Forecasting and Estimation'. In *Travel, Tourism and Hospitality Research: A Handbook for Managers and Researchers* 2nd edn, edited by Ritchie, J.R.B., and C.R. Goeldner. New York: John Wiley & Sons, Inc.

Kothari, C.R. 1990. *Research Methodology: Methods and Techniques*, 2nd edn. New Delhi: Wishwa Prakashan.

Dal lake, Srinagar, Jammu & Kashmir
Image courtesy: Ministry of Tourism, Government of India.

CHAPTER 4

Organizations in Tourism and Culture

By the end of this chapter, students will be able to:

- Identify the role of international organizations in tourism and culture.
- List the major functional areas of UNWTO.
- Understand the significance of UNESCO in protecting heritage.
- Gain an overview of organizations of tourism stakeholders.

Introduction

When we read that global tourism arrivals are poised to grow at 4%, we are enjoying the fruits of the labours of many people and organizations across the world which are sharing information on tourism arrivals. Statistics on tourism that inform us on the performance and trends of tourism activities are generated by tourism organizations which continuously monitor data and present reports that are useful to tourism professionals and planners. We hear about states promoting their destinations by holding events and advertising their attractions. These activities are driven by organizations which have been mandated to market destinations and improve arrivals to the states. In the continuing tussle between airlines and travel agencies, travel associations vigorously advocate the cause of their members in public forum, explaining their positions and canvassing public opinion. These are trade organizations which bring together businesses and plead their common cause. In this chapter, we will examine the major tourism organizations in the world, which play a vital role in multiple ways, providing frameworks and regulations, taking on business operations and advocating views, all of which are important for the travel and tourism sector.

Our examination is divided into two—international organizations and organizations which are national or regional in geographic distribution. International organizations are involved with matters which concern countries and multinational regions, focusing on the cooperation between nations for the advancement of travel and tourism. UNWTO, the International Civil Aviation Organization (ICAO) and the United Nations Educational, Scientific and Cultural Organization (UNESCO) are three great organizations that we will study in some depth, as they are concerned with three areas that are of supreme importance to tourism. Other international organizations are concerned with specific players in the international tourism scenario, such as WTTC, a forum of business leaders and the International Air Transport Association (IATA) serving the airline industry. Tourism organizations in the public sector are concerned with destination marketing, planning and operating public utilities, while private organizations mostly represent interests of stakeholders.

Role of International Organizations

With the rapid growth of the tourism sector as an international, multidisciplinary field, the role of international organizations has also developed and expanded. The potential of tourism as a powerful tool for economic development has also lent strength to the relevance of international organizations which work to ensure that the gains of tourism are enjoyed by more regions and communities. Tourism is a key driver for socioeconomic progress, but needs to be harnessed and supported, which requires the presence of specialized organizations. An increasing trend in transnational movements of people, goods and services used in the tourism sector has brought new and complex challenges.

Another important rationale for the formation of international organizations is the plethora of sectoral issues that have to be settled between countries, in order to ensure a smooth and safe international operation. International civil aviation is an excellent example involving numerous protocols, agreements and universal systems that have been negotiated and put in place. International organizations are also involved in expanding business opportunities across countries and regions, by creating forums, holding events and exchange programmes.

United Nations World Tourism Organization

UNWTO is the UN agency responsible for promotion of responsible, sustainable and universally accessible tourism. The precursor to UNWTO was Word Tourism Organization (WTO or OTM in French). Formed in 1970, WTO adopted its statutes on 27 September 1970, which is commemorated as World Tourism Day (WTD) all over the world. WTO was a grouping of countries, organizations and even individuals, involved in tourism. After intensive efforts, the WTO joined the United Nations system in 2003, changing its name to UNWTO, and being recognized as the specialized agency of the United Nations for Tourism.

Evolution of UNWTO
The evolution of UNWTO into the international organization today makes interesting reading. An organization named International Congress of Official Tourist Traffic Association was formed in 1925. Later, another organization, the International Union of Official Tourism Publicity/propaganda Organizations (IUOTPO) was formed in 1934. The IUOTPO transformed itself into the International Union of Official Travel Organization (IUOTO), which drew its members from national tourist organizations and industry entities. In 1947, the first Constitutive Assembly of the IUOTO was held at The Hague. The temporary headquarter was established in London. The IUOTO was granted the status of a consultative body of the United Nations in 1948. The headquarters was shifted to Geneva. The first major international conference on tourism was held in Rome in 1963, following an initiative taken by IUOTO. Among the important recommendations of the conference were the definition of the terms visitor and 'tourist', the simplification of international travel formalities and a general resolution on tourism development, including technical

(Continued ...)

cooperation, freedom of movement and absence of discrimination. The IUOTO persuaded the United Nations to declare 1967 as the International Tourist Year (ITY), with the slogan 'Tourism, passport to peace'. Urged by the United Nations, the IUOTO met in Mexico City and adopted the statutes of the World Tourism Organization (WTO) on 27 September. This day is celebrated as the WTD from 1980 onwards. The first WTO General Assembly was convened in Madrid in 1975 and decided to establish its headquarters in Madrid, Spain. In 1999, thanks to years of work done by the WTO, the World Conference on the Measurement of the Economic Impact of Tourism held in Nice approved the TSA, which has become a powerful tool in demonstrating the impact of tourism in economies. WTO has played a stellar role in leading the tourism industry in setting high professional standards. In 1995, the Cairo General Assembly of WTO adopted a resolution on the prevention of organized sex tourism. The 1999 Santiago General Assembly adopted the Global code of Ethics for Tourism. Year 2002 was declared the International Year of Ecotourism. The programme 'Sustainable Tourism-Eliminating Poverty' was presented at the World Summit on Sustainable Development at Johannesburg in 2002. In 2003, WTO transformed into UNWTO, as a specialized agency of the United Nations.
Source: UNWTO (n.d.).

The UNWTO has 157 member countries (or member states, as the official terminology goes), 6 associate members and over 480 affiliate members, consisting of organizations, educational institutions, tourism associations and local tourism authorities. The UNWTO functions through its organs. The General Assembly is the supreme decision-making body, where all members have right of representation and voting powers. There is an Executive Council, which has elected members. These bodies are served by the Secretariat, led by the Secretary General. The headquarters of UNWTO is in Madrid, Spain. The General Assembly (GA) is constituted by all full members and associate members. Affiliate members and other institutional organizations participate in the GA as observers. The GA normally meets every two years and the Secretary General is elected for a period of four years. The primary objective of the meeting of GA is to discuss topics of vital importance and decide on the budget for its operation.

The main executive body of the UNWTO is the Executive Council. The GA elects members to the Executive Council in a ratio of one for every five full members. Executive Council meets at least twice a year and carries out its operation based on the decisions taken and the budget approved by the GA. Being a host country of UNWTO headquarters, Spain has a permanent seat in the executive council.

For operational convenience, UNWTO has divided the world into six regions, namely Africa, the Americas, East Asia, the Pacific, the Middle East and South Asia. Each region is looked after by a Regional Commission which meets at least once a year. The Regional Commissions are composed of full and associate members from the region concerned, with the affiliate members of the region participating as observers in the meetings.

For effective implementation of various programmes of UNWTO, separate specialized committees of members are also formed, which give advice on programme content and management. The Secretariat headed by the Secretary General is responsible for implementing approved programmes and also looks after the day to day activities of the organization. The regional support office of UNWTO for Asia is located in Japan. English, French, Spanish, Russian and Arabic are recognized as the official languages of UNWTO. Mr Taleb Rifai of Jordan is the current Secretary General of UNWTO (Figure 4.1).

Functions of UNWTO

UNWTO discharges its responsibilities with the declared objectives of strengthening global tourism and ensuring sustainable development for the benefit of the stakeholders spread

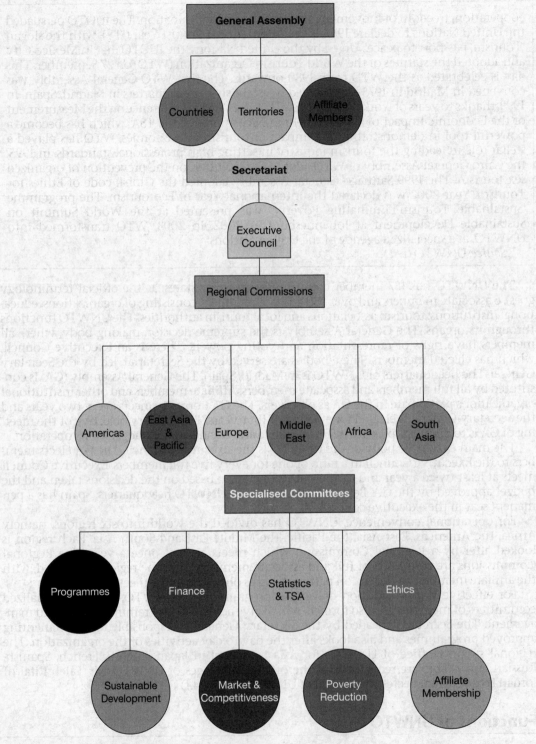

Figure 4.1   Structure of UNWTO
Source: Authors.

across the member countries. The programmes and policies are developed keeping in mind the optimal use of natural resources, respect to local culture and socioeconomic benefit to stakeholders. Guidelines and code of conduct are promulgated to promote sustainable tourism practices. The Global Sustainable Tourism Criteria and Global Code of Ethics are some examples towards this objective.

Knowledge and capacity building are other areas of activity for UNWTO. Appropriate methodologies are developed for collecting and analysing statistics and the preparation of periodic reports on various aspects of tourism. This is of immense use not only for tourism businesses but also helps in making policy decisions for appropriate tourism development. TSA initiative is an important step led by UNWTO to document and accurately account for the contribution of tourism in the world economy. UNWTO also provides networks for knowledge creation and exchange.

Human Resource development is another area of activity for UNWTO, by setting standards for education and promoting training with the objective of strengthening the pool of quality human resources. The TedQual Certification System for educational institutes and graduate aptitude test are efforts taken to make standardization in tourism education.

UNWTO offers support for projects that attempt to increase economic activities under the tourism sector that in turn will lead to job creation, profitability and economic development of destinations. UNWTO is an advocate of tourism as a tool for inclusive development and works to make tourism a priority in national and international policies.

UNWTO has been working to involve tourism as an instrument in achieving the UN MDGs, to address the global challenges of poverty, hunger, gender inequality and environmental degradation. To this end, UNWTO is committed to create global partnerships that will promote sustainable tourism development, particularly in developing countries. The UNWTO has identified priorities for action, which include

- Mainstreaming tourism in the global agenda.
- Improving tourism competitiveness.
- Promoting sustainable tourism development.
- Advancing tourism's contribution to poverty reduction and development.

UNWTO and World Tourism Day

WTD is celebrated every year on 27 September with the purpose of fostering awareness among the international community of the importance of tourism and its social, cultural, political and economic values. In the third session of the UNWTO GA held at Torremolinos, Spain, in 1979, it was decided to celebrate 27 September every year as WTD, the day chosen to commemorate the anniversary of the adoption of the UNWTO statutes on 27 September 1970. The theme for the WTD is selected by the UNWTO GA, on the recommendation of the UNWTO Executive Council, and a country is designated as the host country. The UNWTO invites all tourism stakeholders to take part in celebrations in their respective country or holiday destination to mark the day, and the Secretary General chairs the official celebrations and issues a message each year to mark the occasion (Table 4.1).

International Civil Aviation Organization

On an average, there are more than 100,000 flights being operated across the world every day, carrying more than 8,000,000 passengers. About 140,000 tonnes of cargo is transported by air every day. Civil aviation is the most reliable of mass transportation forms and has transformed the world. Safe and reliable air transport is dependent on the adoption of rules, regulations and

Table 4.1   World tourism day themes

Year	Host Country	Theme
1980		Tourism's contribution to the preservation of cultural heritage and to peace and mutual understanding
1981	–	Tourism and quality of life
1982	–	Pride in travel: Good guests and good hosts
1983	–	Travel and holidays are a right but also a responsibility for all
1984	–	Tourism for international understanding, peace and cooperation
1985	–	Youth tourism: Cultural and historical heritage for peace and friendship
1986	–	Tourism: A vital force for world peace
1987	–	Tourism for development
1988	–	Tourism: Education for all
1989	–	The free movement of tourists creates one world
1990	–	Tourism: An unrecognized industry, a service to be released
1991	–	Communication, information and education: Power lines of tourism development
1992	–	Tourism: A factor of growing social and economic solidarity and of encounter between people
1993	–	Tourism development and environmental protection: Towards a lasting harmony
1994	–	Quality staff, quality tourism
1995	–	WTO: Serving world tourism for twenty years
1996	–	Tourism: A factor of tolerance and peace
1997	–	Tourism: A leading activity of the twenty-first century for job creation and environmental protection
1998	Mexico	Public-private sector partnership: The key to tourism development and promotion
1999	Chile	Tourism: Preserving world heritage for the new millennium
2000	Germany	Technology and nature: Two challenges for tourism at the dawn of the twenty-first century
2001	Iran	Tourism: A tool for peace and dialogue among civilizations
2002	Costa Rica	Ecotourism, the key to sustainable development
2003	Algeria	Tourism: A driving force for poverty alleviation, job creation and social harmony

Year	Host Country	Theme
2004	Malaysia	Sport and tourism: Two living forces for mutual understanding, culture and the development of societies
2005	Qatar	Travel and transport: From the imaginary of Jules Verne to the reality of the twenty-first century
2006	Portugal	Tourism enriches
2007	Sri Lanka	Tourism opens doors for women
2008	Peru	Tourism: Responding to the challenge of climate change
2009	Ghana	Tourism: Celebrating diversity
2010	China	Tourism and biodiversity
2011	Egypt	Linking cultures
2012	Spain	Tourism and sustainable energy: Powering sustainable development
2013	Maldives	Tourism and water: Protecting our common future
2014	Mexico	Tourism and community development
2015	Burkina Faso	One billion tourists, one billion opportunities
2016	Thailand	Tourism for all: Promoting universal accessibility
2017	Qatar	Sustainable tourism: A tool for development

Source: UNWTO. *World Tourism Day.* Available at: http://wtd.unwto.org/content/past-wtd-celebrations-0 (accessed on 25 December 2016).

standards that cut across national boundaries. ICAO is the forum which creates these standards and agreements.

History of Global Civil Aviation

Civil Aviation celebrated its centenary in 2014. In 1914, the first 'commercial' flight took off with one passenger, who was charged $5 for a short trip across the bay in Florida, between Tampa and St Petersburg. This led to a twice daily flight across the bay, which became the first regularly scheduled commercial flight. The next noticeable landmark in the history of civil aviation is the flight of Charles Lindbergh. In 1927, Lindbergh flew the 'Spirit of St Louis', a single engine aircraft, across the Atlantic ocean, and completed the first solo, non-stop transatlantic flight in 34 hours. His epic journey brought aviation to the spotlight and resulted in a great increase in the number of Americans who opted to take an airline. Another landmark was the first commercial jet flight, between London and Johannesburg, in 1952. By the 1960s, aviation had become firmly established as the mode of choice for long distance passengers. But the quantum leap in numbers came with the introduction of the Boeing 747, the 'Jumbo Jet'. The 747 transformed aviation, and tourism, in unprecedented ways. It was the first wide-bodied aircraft capable of carrying over 500 passengers, and could fly vast distances without refuelling. Variants of the 747 are still being produced, more than 45 years after the first aircraft took to the skies.

Commercial Aviation
Over the last century, commercial aviation has transformed the world in ways unimaginable in 1914. The first flight provided a shortcut across Tampa Bay. Today the aviation industry reunites loved ones, connects cultures, expands minds, opens markets and fosters development. Aviation provides people around the globe with the freedom to make connections that can change their lives and the world. —Tony Tuler, DG and CEO, IATA

Development of International Systems

In 1944, an international civil aviation conference was held in Chicago, which was attended by 55 countries. The conference discussed the necessity to have uniformity in regulations and channels of communications to enable smooth operations. The convention on International Civil Aviation was signed by 52 states, resulting in the setting up of a permanent ICAO as well as agreements on international services transit and international air transport. The conference laid the foundation for a set of rules and regulations regarding air navigation which brought safety in flying, a great step forward and paved the way for the application of a common air-navigation system throughout the world. ICAO is a specialized body of the United Nations, and currently has over 190 members. Its headquarters is at Montreal, Canada, and there are seven regional offices catering to specific geographic regions. The office for Asia and the Pacific is located in Bangkok.

ICAO is engaged in creating standards and policies, undertaking studies and compliance audits and in assisting the aviation industry in myriad ways. Presently, there are over 10,000 standards and recommended practices which are vital for the safe and orderly development of international civil aviation. ICAO is concerned with the following strategic objectives:

- Enhancing global civil aviation safety.
- Increasing capacity and improving efficiency.
- Enhancing global civil aviation security.
- Developing a sound and viable aviation system.
- Minimizing adverse environmental effects of aviation.

United Nations Educational, Scientific and Cultural Organization

The UNESCO was formed in 1945, on the belief that world peace had to be established on the basis of 'humanity's moral and intellectual solidarity'. Headquartered in Paris, UNESCO strives to build networks among nations by

- mobilizing for education, to ensure universal access to quality education;
- building intercultural understanding through protection of heritage and support for cultural diversity; and
- pursuing scientific cooperation between nations and societies.

The relevance of UNESCO has never been better, as we live in a world in constant strife between cultures and faiths. UNESCO is the forum that promotes and celebrates intercultural dialogue that will lead to lasting peace and sustainable development. UNESCO works to promote human dignity, to help shape a new world for justice and equality and for deeper cooperation between countries and cultures.

The structure of UNESCO consists of the General Conference, consisting of representatives of UNESCO member states, which determines the policies and main lines of work. The executive board ensures the overall management of UNESCO. The work of the organization is supervised by the director general, who is assisted by the secretariat.

World Heritage

Although there are several themes which are active in UNESCO, yet the most important one is the mission to protect our heritage. Heritage constitutes a source of identity and cohesion for communities disrupted by changes and economic instability. UNESCO spearheads world-wide advocacy for culture and development while engaging with the international community to set clear policies and legal frameworks and working to support governments and local stakeholders to safeguard heritage, strengthen creative industries and encourage cultural pluralism.

UNESCO works through the numerous cultural conventions, which endeavour to protect and safeguard heritage in many manifestations. The major conventions are:

- The convention on the Means of Prohibiting and Preventing the Illicit Traffic of Cultural Property (1970).
- The convention on the Protection of the World Cultural and Natural Heritage (1972).
- The Universal Declaration on Cultural Diversity (2001).
- The convention for the Safeguarding of the Intangible Cultural Heritage (2003).
- The convention on the Protection and Promotion of the Diversity of Cultural Expressions (2005).

World Heritage Lists

The convention on the Protection of the World Cultural and Natural Heritage is more popularly known as the World Heritage convention. The convention linked together the concepts of nature conservation and the preservation of cultural properties. It defines the kind of sites that can be considered for inscription on the World Heritage List and sets out the duties and responsibilities of states parties in protecting and preserving such sites. It also explains how international financial assistance under the aegis of World Heritage Fund will be used and managed. In addition, UNESCO maintains a List of World Heritage in Danger, in order to focus attention on the threatened sites.

Inscription of a heritage property on the world heritage list signifies that the world heritage committee has deemed that the property has cultural or natural values that can be considered on outstanding universal value. It places the responsibility on each state party to protect, manage and preserve the cultural heritage that has been inscribed.

Cultural heritage is defined by the World Heritage Committee as 'monuments, groups of buildings and sites', including urban centres, archaeological sites, industrial heritage, cultural landscapes and heritage routes.

Natural heritage consists of natural sites of outstanding universal value from the point of view of science, conservation or natural beauty, natural features and geological and physiographical formations. While natural and cultural heritage were included in the 1972 convention, the general understanding of the term cultural heritage has changed along the years. Heritage today means the rituals, festivals, oral traditions, arts, traditional knowledge and skills and practices. These are understood today as 'intangible cultural heritage'—heritage that need not necessarily be tangible but are vital in understanding the traditions and knowledge of communities. Intangible heritage is traditional as well as contemporary, which means that the culture is 'living' and evolving. Intangible cultural heritage encourages a sense of identity and responsibility for individuals and communities. Intangible culture has to be recognized as such by communities or individuals that maintain and transmit it.

Diversity of Cultural Expressions

The convention on the protection and promotion of the diversity of cultural expressions is an international agreement that ensures artists, cultural professionals and practitioners can create and disseminate a range of cultural goods and services. The convention encourages the introduction of cultural policies and measures that nurture creativity.

UNESCO and Tourism

The tourism sector is increasingly seen as an important vehicle in preserving and managing natural and cultural heritage. While these assets are important ingredients in the tourism experience, the resources generated by the tourist arrivals constitute a significant revenue stream that funds conservation activities, helps in management of the site and also contributes to other projects that ensure the sustainability of the heritage site. Recognizing the vital role played by tourism, UNESCO has launched the World Heritage and Sustainable Tourism initiative, which represents a new approach based on stakeholder participation, integrating tourism and heritage management at the destination level.

Advisory Bodies

International Centre for the Study of the Preservation and Restoration of Cultural Property (ICCROM): ICCROM is an intergovernmental organization dedicated to the conservation of cultural heritage. Headquartered in Rome, ICCROM has 134 members. It collects information, conducts training and research and promotes awareness on the importance of preservation of cultural heritage. ICCROM has a community of around 18,000 professionals and experts, which offer technical knowledge and respond to the needs of member states. ICCROM is named as one of the advisory bodies to advise the World heritage Committee.

International Council on Monuments and Sites (ICOMOS): ICOMOS is a non-governmental organization dedicated to the conservation of the world's monuments and sites. ICOMOS collaborates with UNESCO as one of the advisory bodies. ICOMOS is a network of experts consisting of architects, historians, archaeologists, art historians, engineers and town planners. It works towards improving preservation of heritage, setting standards and techniques and exchanging information. It prepares reports for the World Heritage Panel, conducts training programmes, identifies sites which are threatened and suggests solutions to conservation problems. ICOMOS also has national committees which coordinate projects within individual countries.

International Union for Conservation of Nature (IUCN): IUCN is the world's oldest and largest environmental organization, with more than 1,200 members and 11,000 volunteer experts in 160 countries. Founded in 1948, it is a global conservation network, headquartered in Gland, near Geneva, Switzerland. It tries to find practical solutions to conservation and development challenges, with thrust on conserving biodiversity and setting standards. IUCN aims at sustainable management of diversity and natural resources. IUCN actively participates in UN negotiations on climate change and advocates natural solutions to global challenges.

Industry or Sectoral Organizations

World Travel and Tourism Council (WTTC): It is an organization comprising business leaders in the travel and tourism industry. It boasts of a membership of around 100 of the world's leading travel and tourism companies and works to raise awareness of travel and tourism as one of the world's largest industries (World Travel and Tourism Council, n.d.). Membership in WTTC is by invitation, and is restricted to the chairs, presidents and CEO's of the foremost companies. WTTC partners with many prominent companies in the sector, who provide products and services. It conducts research to show the value of travel and tourism in the world economy. To this end, WTTC invites select research organizations and academic institutions as knowledge partners.

Established in 1990 and headquartered in London, WTTC has emerged as the most influential voice of the private sector, producing research data and forecasts to influence governments and decision-makers on the impacts of travel and tourism in the economies. WTTC summits are important gatherings of the most prominent people in the tourism business, also bringing together political leaders, media and government officials to discuss on the important issues that affect the sector. To recognize best practices in sustainable tourism, WTTC organizes the annual 'Tourism for Tomorrow' awards, which are among the highest accolades for practitioners and businesses. Awards are given for the categories of community, destination, environment, people, innovation and sustainable business (WTTC, n.d.).

Pacific Asia Travel Association (PATA): PATA was established in 1951. It is an association focusing on travel and tourism in the Asia Pacific region. It is headquartered in Bangkok, Thailand, with offices in Sydney and China. PATA membership is open for organizations, including tourism bodies, international airlines, airports, educational institutions, travel and tourism companies and also travel professionals. It also has 43 local chapters. It is involved in generating data on the visitor economy, expenditure figures, accommodation, aviation and forecasts. It conducts the annual PATA Travel Mart, the PATA Adventure Travel and Responsible Tourism Conference, enabling networking and contracting opportunities. PATA gives away a variety of awards—PATA Gold Awards—recognizing excellence in operations (PATA, n.d.).

International Air Transport Association (IATA): It is the global trade association for the airline industry. Around 250 member airlines of IATA comprise 83% of air traffic. Established in 1945 and headquartered in Montreal, IATA has grown into the prime vehicle for inter-airline cooperation in promoting safe, reliable, secure and economical air services. IATA presently has around 260 members from 117 nations. Along the years, IATA was involved in setting standards in air navigation and flight operations. IATA provided vital inputs to ICAO in creating international frameworks, notable among which are the multilateral interline traffic agreements, passenger and cargo services conference resolutions, passenger and cargo agency agreements and sales agency rules. Later, IATA turned its attention to tariff coordination and also changed into a global association of the airline industry, particularly in the areas of safety audits, advocacy and issues relating to the viability of the aviation industry (IATA, n.d.).

United Federation of Travel Agents' Associations (UFTAA): UFTAA, as the name indicates, is an organization, the members of which are travel agents associations across the world. It was created in 1966 following the merger of two organizations and has its headquarters in the principality of Monaco. It is a confederation representing about 80 national associations. It aims to represent the interests of travel agents and tour operators, and participates in consultations and dialogues with other international organizations in the travel and tourism space. It works to offer services to its member associations, training programmes and conflict resolution (UFTAA, n.d.).

American Society of Travel Agents (ASTA): It is an association of travel professionals, said to be the largest of its kind in the world. Founded in 1931 as the American Steamship and Tourist Agents Association, ASTA has been fighting for the interests of travel agents over the years. It has been negotiating with IATA and airlines regarding issues like reduction of commissions and agency commission capping. In tune with the changing times, it has set a new mission for itself: to facilitate the business of selling travel through effective representation, shared knowledge and enhancement of professionalism. Providing its members with training modules to improve their knowledge and expertise and opportunities to network, ASTA aims to assist its members in growing their business and market share (ASTA, n.d.a.).

ASTA has grown into an influential forum, connecting thousands of active travel professionals. The significance of the organization can be gauged from the fact that destination marketing companies have to bid against each other in order to get an opportunity to host the ASTA annual conference. Our case study has the details.

Case Study: Bidding for ASTA Destination Expo

The annual events of some industry organizations have become strong tourism marketing opportunities. ASTA conducts an annual International Destination Expo, now renamed as ASTA Destination Expo, aimed at providing out of country knowledge and specialized training for their members, presented in a business format. The ASTA expo has been attracting hundreds of agents and tour operators and has become an important event for destination training.

The Expo has attracted the attention of destinations, as the event brings together American agents curious to learn about a destination, inclined to learn about the products and ready to strike deals. ASTA brings together all kinds of agents—small and big—and is committed to the professional development of its members through specialized education, industry information and networking opportunities. The Expo has grown into an event oriented towards providing the agent firsthand experience, intensive destination education and a trade show that exposes the agent to suppliers. ASTA works with destination marketing organizations to give a sustained communication campaign through all their media vehicles, apart from assisting with worldwide coverage of the destination expo (Sheats, n.d.).

Realizing the potential of the event to create visibility for exhibitions, ASTA has put in place a system by which destinations need to bid for hosting the ASTA Destination Expo. Destinations will provide commitments on the rooms that can be provided at discounted rates, infrastructural facilities available, including the exhibition venue to host the trade show, the details of the free lunches and dinners to be hosted, pre- and post-expo tours at highly discounted rates, the promotional programmes that will be conducted at the closing of the previous expo, the complimentary facilities to be extended to the event management team and so on. On receiving the bids, the ASTA business development team enters into discussions with bidders and finally makes the selection of the host destination for the expo (ASTA, n.d.b).

Discussion Questions

1. What are the reasons for the popularity of ASTA expo among destination marketers?
2. What role does the agent play in the tour operation process?

Sustainable Tourism for Eliminating Poverty Foundation

Tourism is the main source of foreign exchange for many poor regions of the world, particularly for the least developed countries. An important part of the work of UNWTO is the ST-EP (Sustainable Tourism Eliminating Poverty) initiative that provides for technical assistance and funding for tourism projects. Established in 2004 in Seoul, South Korea, the ST-EP Foundation aimed to harness the power of tourism to generate new opportunities for development, concentrating on least developed countries, particularly in sub-Saharan Africa.

The effort is to contribute to the reduction of poverty through funding and implementing projects aimed at achieving the MDGs or the UN sustainable development goals (SDG) by 2030. ST-EP projects have been funded initially by a grant of the Korean Government, but augmented by international donors and through partnerships with organizations like SNV, the Netherlands Development Organization.

Case Study: The Great Himalaya Trail

The Great Himalaya Trail (GHT) is an initiative in Nepal initially funded by ST-EP that aims at diversifying tourist arrivals in Nepal to new and unexplored areas to benefit rural communities. The GHT programme opened up remote regions in the North-western part of Nepal to international tourism by creating awareness of the great trail that traversed the entire length of Nepal, extending from Tibet to Pakistan. The GHT programme aims to support tourism to drive sustainable development and poverty alleviation through the creation of an iconic tourism product, which will give a boost to the tourism industry and generate investment and create employment opportunities for impoverished communities. GHT is involved in creating marketing opportunities for different destinations along the GHT, providing a new and peaceful image to Nepal, which had been affected by insurgency, increased media interest, attracting more tour operators to offer tour packages. Inbuilt into the project is the finance to local stakeholders to develop business enterprises along the GHT. Opportunities are both direct (accommodation, eateries, guiding, cooking, porterage) and indirect (agriculture, transport, handicrafts). Reviews have shown encouraging results, with increase in number of visitors, tour operators offering packages and incomes to local communities.

Source: Annual Review of GHT Development Programme, June 2013.

Conclusion

We have familiarized ourselves with several of the prominent organizations that perform important functions in the sectors of travel, tourism and culture. From the first chapter in this section, we have depended on the outcomes of the deliberations and initiatives of major organizations such as the UNWTO that clarified our understanding of many of the concepts in tourism. We have noted that there are significant global movements that have been led by international alliances and organizations which have pushed the agenda of travel and tourism forward. As the sector comes to terms with new challenges, such as the climate change, roles played by sectoral organizations and international associations will be increasingly important.

The ever increasing role of culture and heritage in promoting tourism necessitate guidelines, rules, regulations and institutional mechanisms to identify, preserve and protect both tangible and intangible heritages across the globe. Along with international organizations, institutional arrangements are being undertaken at national and state level also.

Review Questions

1. Trace the evolution and explain the functions of UNWTO.
2. Examine the role and functions of major tourism industry organizations.

3. Identify any one of the World Tourism Day themes of twentieth century and discuss its relevance today.

Activities

1. Prepare a list of monuments, rituals, festivals, oral traditions, arts and traditional knowledge available in your locality. Discuss the scope of promoting heritage/cultural tourism using these heritage assets.
2. Based on the UNWTO theme on World Tourism Day, organize a seminar in your college and disseminate the outcomes to stakeholders in tourism in any one destination of your choice.

References

Web Resources

ASTA. n.d.a. 'ASTA: A Living History'. Available at: http://www.asta.org/files/MainSite/images/pr/aLivingHistory.pdf (accessed on 20 December 2016).
——. n.d.b. 'ASTA's Destination Expo: Official Bid Document'. ASTA. Available at: http://asta.org/files/MainSite/images/ide/astaADEHostBid.pdf (accessed on 20 December 2016).
IATA. n.d. Available at: http://www.iata.org/Pages/default.aspx (accessed on 20 December 2016).
PATA. n.d. 'PATA Gold Awards'. Available at: https://www.pata.org/pata-gold-awards/ (accessed on 23 July 2016).
Sheats, S. n.d. 'Inspire'. ASTA Destination Expo, ASTA, ISSUU. Available at: http://issuu.com/amsoc-trvlagents/docs/astaadehostprospectus (accessed on 20 December 2016).
UFTAA. n.d. 'Our Mission'. Available at: http://www.uftaa.org/index.php/aboutus/mission (accessed on 20 December 2016).
UNWTO. n.d. 'History'. Available at: http://www2.unwto.org/content/history-0 (accessed on 20 December 2016).
World Travel and Tourism Council. n.d. Available at: http://www.wttc.org/ (accessed on 21 December 2016).
WTTC. n.d. 'Tourism for Tomorrow Awards'. WTTC. Available at: http://www.wttc.org/tourism-for-tomorrow-awards/ (accessed on 23 July 2016).

Suggested Readings

Web Resources

Foundation of the International Civil Aviation Organization. n.d. ICAO. Available at: http://www.icao.int/about-icao/pages/foundation-of-icao.aspx
IATA. n.d. 'No Country Left Behind'. Available at: http://www.icao.int/about-icao/NCLB/Pages/default.aspx

Johanson, M. 2014. 'How the Airline Industry has Evolved in 100 Years of Commercial Air Travel'. *International Business Times.* Available at: http://www.ibtimes.com/how-airline-industry-has-evolved-100-years-commercial-air-travel-1524238

Reed, T. 2013. 'First Trans-Atlantic Commercial Flight Landed 75 Years Ago'. Logistics & Transportation. *Forbes.* Available at: http://www.forbes.com/sites/tedreed/2013/08/10/first-trans-atlantic-commercial-flight-landed-75-years-ago-sunday/#40d808811642

Thomaselli, R. 2014. '10 Great Moments from Commercial Aviation's First 100 Years'. *Travel Pulse.* Available at: http://www.travelpulse.com/news/airlines/10-great-moments-from-commercial-aviations-first-100-years.html

UNESCO. n.d.a. 'Protecting Our Heritage and Fostering Creativity'. UNESCO. Available at: http://en.unesco.org/themes/protecting-our-heritage-and-fostering-creativity

——. n.d.b. 'Convention Concerning the Protection of the World Cultural and Natural Heritage'. UNESCO. Available at: http://whc.unesco.org/en/conventiontext/

——. n.d.c. 'What is Intangible Heritage?' UNESCO. Available at: http://www.unesco.org/culture/ich/index.php?pg=00002

——. n.d.d. 'Sustainable Tourism'. UNESCO. Available at: http://whc.unesco.org/en/tourism/

Tawang Monastery, Arunachal Pradesh
Image courtesy: Tourism India.

Section B: The Tourism Business

Our focus in this section is on the components of the tourism sector. The aim of each of the six chapters in the section is to explain the inherent core of each part of the tourism system, tracing the linkages and interconnections between components. The interconnectedness of these sub-sectors is one of the two themes that run through all chapters, the other being the elaboration of the business element.

Chapter 5 initiates the discussion by taking the student to the destination. Beginning with a discussion on the precise nature of a destination and the different perspectives from which a destination could be described, the student is familiarized with the comprehensive 6As framework for analysing destinations. The types of destinations based on various parameters are described, which provides a view of the variety and complexity of destinations. The theoretical construct of the destination lifecycle is examined, from the stages of which several real-life cases can be discussed. Managing destinations is a complex and collaborative task, and this important aspect is explored next. Destination marketing is at the heart of marketing products and services in tourism, and the topic is elaborated to understand the components and stakeholder engagements. We close the chapter by touching upon the impact tourism can have on destinations, which we will explore in greater detail in a chapter in Section D.

Continuing with our examination of the destination, Chapter 6 brings our attention to attractions, a segment that is diverse and interesting. The Taj Mahal is a compelling case, allowing the student to scrutinize the different aspects of an attraction and its relationship with stakeholders. Attractions are chiefly divided into natural and human made; however, we also attend to the theoretical constructs which are popular, and from what the visitor derives from an attraction—education, entertainment or spiritual. The management of attractions engages the students' attention, and the main organizations managing much of our cultural heritage are introduced. Significant aspects of attractions such as visitor management and carrying capacity are also brought to the students' notice. The importance of entertainment zones and theme parks is brought out through insightful case studies of Chokhi Dhani and Kingdom of Dreams.

The accommodation sector takes centre stage in Chapter 7. Accommodation remains at the centre of the tourism offering, and the chapter gives an overview of the sector and introduces the students to the range of options within it. The features of accommodation peculiar to the services sector are introduced, as are the concepts of serviced and commercial accommodation. Issues connected with accommodation such as classification of properties, management models and contribution to the economy are outlined. For the uninitiated students, a quick round up of the structures within a hotel and an introduction to its functional areas are useful. The trends within the sector from across the world are captured in a section, so that the student gets a perspective on the size and impact of the hotel industry.

Chapter 8 is concerned with travel and tour (T&T) operations, a dynamic and important part of the business of tourism. Much of the credit for the development of tourism to the huge economic activity goes to the packaging of the tourism product, and its marketing. The system of creating tour products, their distribution and the execution of the itinerary are all activities that need a high degree of knowledge, skill and acumen. The chapter introduces the components within a tour operation to the students in simple and familiar terms, and then presents the big picture, the world of transnational operators who own and operate airlines, hotels and cruise ships. The categories of tour operators, from the mass market company to the highly specialised niche operator are also brought into focus. Special attention is paid to describe the destination management company, which is ubiquitous in destinations like India. The chapter proceeds to outline sub-sectors such as MICE operators and then looks at the transformation of the traditional travel agent into travel management companies. The functioning of computerized reservations systems morphing into global distribution systems is also elaborated.

Chapter 9 'Transportation' reviews the transportation sector, examining the four 'surfaces'—air, rail, road and water. The evolution of air travel is traced, moving to the significance of the jet engines in transforming tourism. Recent trends in aviation such as the emergence of the low-cost carriers are examined closely. For students, an overview of the facilities and functions in airports and a brief introduction to international agreements such as the 'freedoms' are essential for a clear understanding of the sector. The possibilities and potential of rail and road travel and the burgeoning cruise industry are prominently covered in the chapter.

The last chapter, Chapter 10, in this section brings into focus the ever-important field of marketing. Beginning with the basics, students are guided through the fundamental principles of marketing such as the difference between sales and marketing, and the ingredients of the marketing mix. The features of the service industry are clearly brought out through the 7Ps framework. New thinking in marketing services is introduced for discussion and further reading. The importance of market research and its contours are briefly touched upon, as is the influence of environment on marketing. Moving to tourism, the important aspects of destination marketing are introduced, highlighting the activities under promotion and public relations. The significance of partnerships and alliances between stakeholders is revealed through a case study on Kerala, considered a model in destination marketing.

Dancers of Manipuri dance
Image courtesy: Ministry of Tourism, Government of India.

Destinations

By the end of this chapter, students will be able to:

- Define a destination and describe its main features.
- Classify the components of a destination.
- Identify characteristics and business dynamics of a destination.
- List the phases of a destination according to the life cycle theory.
- Recognize the role of destination management organizations and their operations in business.

Introduction

Destinations are central to any tourism experience. We take holidays to destinations, drawn by the attractions there, or lured by their image. In the tourism world, all the businesses attend to getting the tourist to a destination or to catering to the needs of the visitor at the destination. In order to understand the business of tourism, it is important for us to gain a clear understanding of destinations—the different types of destinations, their characteristics, the ways in which destinations are made and the issues involved in managing destinations. It is relevant to explore the relationship between the components of the tourism industry and the destination, and the ways in which one influences the other. Managing destinations is a challenge everywhere—with multiple stakeholders and often conflicting interests, the agencies that are in charge of destinations have to play a balancing role. These interesting dynamics are also explored in this chapter.

Definition

Destinations have been defined from different viewpoints. A simple definition of a destination, to start with, is 'a place or region which is well demarcated in terms of administrative setup, and is positioned and marketed as a specific entity'. In many countries, destinations can also be recognized by the planning and administrative framework which is in place. Definitions can get blurred, particularly when destinations are seen from the visitor's point of view. To the visitor, a destination is a distinct geographical location which he/she visits and where there is a feature or a set of features that the visitor experiences. The visitor, in many instances, is not concerned with the planning or administrative structure at the destination. This apparent contradiction between the local or 'supply', perspective, and a visitor or 'demand' perspective, can be explained by an example we are all familiar with, the Golden Triangle.

Is the Golden Triangle One Destination or Three?

The term Golden Triangle, in the context of Indian tourism, is specific. To the visitor, Golden Triangle denotes a particular set of tourism products that is experienced by the tourist in three places—Delhi, Agra and Jaipur (Figure 5.1). Indeed, all the tour operators, inbound and domestic, use this term as a ready reference to a tourism experience that is quintessentially Indian. The tour enables visitors to wonder at the monumental built heritage of the country, get a glimpse of the wonderful cultural traditions and peculiar lifestyles of Rajasthan, and of course to be dazzled by the Taj Mahal, one of the most beautiful sights of the world. It may be noted that the three points of the triangle are three cities governed by the different administrative entities, falling in three states. Delhi itself has a complex administrative mechanism: some of the monuments are under the administrative control of New Delhi Municipal Council, some come under the charge of the Government of the National Capital Territory of Delhi. Agra is a municipal corporation in the state of Uttar Pradesh, while Jaipur is the capital of the state of Rajasthan. Thus, we can see that while each of these cities is a destination in their own right, they combine to form a single destination that is recognizable across the world. From a local perspective, each destination has individual characteristics, attractions and administrative structures; but for a visitor, the Golden Triangle is a single destination, with different facets to be experienced.

Components of a Destination

Destinations can be regarded as the focus of facilities and services designed to meet the needs of the tourists (Cooper et al., 1998). The following model, devised by Dr Dimitrios Buhalis (2000) is useful for the analysis of products and services in a destination.

Six As frameworks for the analysis of tourism destinations are as follows:

- Attractions (natural, man-made, artificial, purpose built, heritage, special events)
- Accessibility (entire transportation system comprising of routes, terminals and vehicles)

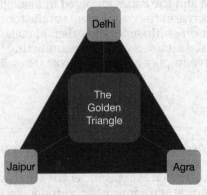

Figure 5.1   The golden triangle
Source: Authors.

- Amenities (accommodation and catering facilities, retailing, other tourist services)
  - Available packages (pre-arranged packages by intermediaries and principals)
  - Activities (all activities available at the destination and what consumers will do during their visit)
  - Ancillary services (services used by tourists such as banks, telecommunications, post, newsagents, hospitals).

Attractions

Features that form the core reason for the travellers to visit a destination are the most important components for any destination. It follows that the maintenance of these attractions and the provision of facilities for visitors to enjoy these attractions are important responsibilities of the managers of the destination. Natural attractions such as beaches have to be kept clean and pristine for the visitor to enjoy the attraction continuously, which calls for careful management and continuous monitoring. The conservation of built heritage is another concern for destinations which rely heavily on these assets to attract visitors. The management of visitors and the facilities for tourist attractions are important considerations in the minds of the visitor regarding the quality of the destination.

Contemporary tourists increasingly seek authentic and novel experiences in addition to the core attraction. There is a growing tendency among tourists to interact with local community to understand their culture, traditions and livelihood practices. In line with the changing tastes and preferences, tour operators are designing new products imbibing local specificities. With vision and creativity, innumerable tourism products which can provide authentic experiences to tourists can be developed while protecting the culture and environment of the destination. Innovations in product development enable destinations to provide a variety of products with diverse attractions and adding value to the core products. Product development focusing on indigenous knowledge, traditional art forms, livelihood practices and local cuisine are not only informative, but add to the unique selling proposition (USP) of the destination.

Accessibility

It goes without saying that the most beautiful attractions by themselves will not create destinations, unless these become accessible to the visitor. Improving access may dramatically alter the visitation pattern to destinations. For example, the opening of a new airport will throw open a whole new region before the tourism industry, attracting investments and creating destinations. A discussion on accessibility focuses on the different modes of transport and visa and other entry regulations that are used by or regulate visitors arriving at a destination.

Within destinations, managers are concerned with maintaining good access to attractions and creating new routes that will open up more attractions in the vicinity. Access to special groups, such as people with disabilities, is now assuming more importance. Easy access for visitor segments that need special attention, such as the elderly and the young visitors, is another area that is assuming importance, bringing in adaptations at tourist sites and on transport systems.

On a broader perspective on accessibility at destinations, signage, information materials such as brochures and pamphlets and interpretation facilities assume significance. Sign boards and 'Do's and Don'ts' in multiple languages are important devices contributing to easier accessibility. Access to communication systems—voice and data—is enabling visitors to remain connected to their loved ones while on holiday is another aspect.

Issues of accessibility are not confined to tourists, but are about access for the local community as well. The local community has to be provided access to attractions, common facilities and common property resources, protecting their customary rights.

Amenities

The provision of accommodation facilities at a destination is an important component and the popularity of destination is directly linked to the investment it attracts to create accommodation for the tourists. Apart from hotels, many destinations offer a variety of accommodation, such as apartments, bed-and-breakfast, hostels and paying-guest accommodation. Food and drink form an important part of a destination experience, and outlets such as pubs, bars, cafes and restaurants are important avenues for local entrepreneurship. This may include wide varieties of restaurants and other food outlets focusing on local cuisine, fruits and other beverages that can add to diverse and unique experiences ensuring authenticity. Other amenities that come up in destinations for tourists are shopping areas, bike and cycle hire, casinos and massage centres.

(Available) Packages

Packages (available) refer to packaged products offered to tourists by travel intermediaries that enable them to visit and explore the destination. It is important for the destination to have a variety of packages that the visitor can choose to purchase, such as city tours, cultural tours and excursions, village life experiences, which sustain the interest in the destination, encourage extensions of stay and bring revenue to the local community.

Activities

Tourism enterprises in the destination strive to create activities for the visitor. This may range from full-day tours to neighbouring places, nature walks, cultural visits and entertainment. Every destination would like to provide a variety of activities to suit the interests of all types of visitors. Again, the more a visitor takes part in activities, the more money is spent in the destination.

Ancillary Services

Services such as banks, post office and hospitals are important because these are significant signposts for the visitors. For example, an elderly visitor is reassured by the fact that the destination has well-equipped specialty hospitals to deal with any emergency. Banks and telecommunications are also important pointers to the level of development of a destination. Other ancillary services in the destination include car hire, catering companies, foreign exchange services, insurance, laundry services, tourism marketing services as well as entertainment options like bars, nightclubs and casinos.

Types of Destinations

Destinations are diverse by nature, and can be divided into different categories.

- **Geographical features:** Based on the distinct geographical features or locations, destinations can be islands, coastal, hill/mountain, desert or forest. Geographical location of a destination determines its attractiveness. The island destinations of India, Lakshadweep and the Andaman and Nicobar islands, offer an experience that is unique, and for that very reason attract a large number of visitors. 'Hill stations', located in higher altitudes, are popular destinations during the summer season in tropical countries. The desert destination of Jaisalmer and the cold desert of Ladakh have become big draws for visitors the world over because of their peculiar geographical features.

- **Urban:** Cities have been attracting tourists since time immemorial. Business travel, pilgrimages and events attracted visitors to urban destinations. Urban experiences such as a variety of cuisine, cultural attractions such as museums and monuments, fashion and shopping, theatre, concerts, bars and other entertainment options are important factors in an urban holiday.

- **Rural:** While great cities have been major destinations for many centuries, better access and availability of more information have resulted in many destinations located in the rural areas becoming popular. The Amalfi coast of Italy, the great outback of Australia and the backwaters of Kerala are examples of rural destinations that have become prominent. Of course, the wildlife sanctuaries and the national parks have become destinations in their own right.

- **Periodicity of tourist arrivals:** Generally speaking, cities can be regarded as year-round destinations receiving visitors across the year, although the numbers may fluctuate, based on climate and local weather conditions. The inflow of business visitors is one of the reasons why the cities see continuous business across the months of the year. On the other hand, most destinations have wide seasonal variations, with tourism drying up at certain periods of the year. A good example is Leh, where visitor numbers fall steeply during the harsh winter. Thus the destinations can be year round or seasonal.

- **Nature of attractions:** Cultural destinations and nature-based destinations. Destinations can also be grouped based on their offerings. Cultural destinations are those featuring cultural products such as monuments, museums or performing arts and festivals. Nature-based destinations depend on the natural resources and scenic beauty of the area, like wildlife sanctuaries, hill stations and coastal destinations.

Destinations may be classified as central, base or transit. Central destinations are those where the attractions are bunched around a central area, such as the city centre. Central London and Manhattan are examples of central destinations, where the visitor gets to experience the products offered within a limited area. Base destinations, on the other hand, are used by tourists as hubs from where a variety of products can be experienced through excursions. An example of a base destination in central India is Aurangabad, which offers accommodation and other services to tourists who have arrived to visit the Ajanta and Ellora caves. Transit destinations offer brief stays as part of a larger holiday elsewhere, adding a facet to the holiday experience. Singapore was a favourite transit destination to travellers flying to Australia from Europe, although it has evolved into a full-fledged destination in its own right in recent years.

Core and Periphery Attractions

Core attractions are those by which the destination is known to the outside world and form the base or nuclei of tourism in the destination. Periphery attractions are secondary nuclei to it and are optional to tourists. They add value to the core attractions by providing supplementary experience. The Taj Mahal and the backwaters of Kerala are examples of core attractions.

Seaside 'resorts' were established to cater to the steep rise in demand for accommodation. Budget travel and the emergence of no-frills airlines were important reasons for the establishment of many beach destinations, particularly in Europe. Benidorm and Ibiza are examples of such destinations. Mountain destinations provide interesting activities such as cycling, walking, expeditions and trekking.

Hill Stations are popular essentially for the cool weather, offering respite from the blazing summer temperatures of the plains. Similarly, destinations at higher altitude are popular during particular seasons. Skiing destinations attract visitors in winters, despite the extreme temperatures, as the setting is optimal for skiing and snow-based activities. Destinations offering trekking, mountain climbing and adventure are often open only during specific periods of the year, when the weather is favourable and the trails and passes are open. Then there are destinations that experience a spike in arrivals during the time of a particular event, such as an annual festival, a local celebration or a carnival. The cattle fairs of Pushkar and Nagaur are good examples.

Seasonality

Most seasonal destinations have fluctuations in visitor arrivals and volume of business. Beach and coastal destinations experience a heavy stream of arrivals when the weather is bright and sunny and the water comfortably warm. This accounts for the huge surge of tourist arrivals to beaches in the tropical regions, such as Maldives, becoming popular with visitors. Once the winter sets in and the weather turns cooler, the beaches favoured by travellers to Europe and America such as those on the French Riviera and Spanish coast are no longer attractive to tourists. The harsh winter of Europe also drives travellers to warmer countries during the winter months, and the destinations in the tropical and subtropical regions of the world become active with tourists. The beach destinations of Maldives, Thailand, Sri Lanka and India have a 'season' that lasts from November to March, mainly attracting visitors from Europe spending their time in a destination away from the cold winter weather at home.

Seasonal destinations are often faced with problems of low business during the lean period. Since investments are made in such destinations on the basis of the highest occupancy, hotels are faced with the challenge of filling their rooms during the off season. Hotels and destinations adopt different strategies to improve business during the lean season. The commonly adopted strategy is the offer of heavily discounted packages to the visitor, offering a combination of rooms, meals and excursions at attractive prices. Holding meetings, conferences and events has become a common practice to address business issues during off season.

Stakeholders in destinations often combine their resources in order to project the destination before specific segments of travellers and travel intermediaries. For example, city destinations, particularly in Europe, market their conferencing facilities to companies that organize conferences and meetings, aiming to attract major conferences, meetings and exhibitions during the low season. The efforts of destination managers are complemented by hotel associations which agree to offer discounts, and travel companies will also reduce their prices for their services, all of which make the destination more attractive to event organizers.

Another strategy frequently adopted by destinations is the organizing special events and celebrations, bringing in visitors who have specific interests. Festivals such as the Oktoberfest celebrating the beer making traditions of Germany and literary festivals are good examples of the strategy.

While some destinations will try to woo tourists fervently, there are several destination which are forced to bring down operational costs through measures like partial closure of facilities and laying off of employees as a direct consequence of the drying up of tourist arrivals. This seasonal unemployment and decrease in incomes are cited as one of the problems of overdependence on tourism.

The Destination Life Cycle

Butler (1980) attempted to provide a model of life cycle of destinations which depict the different stages of growth, development and finally the decline of the destination. According to

Butler, invariably all destinations experience these different stages and the model throw insight into the probable impacts of tourism business in the destination. The model also throws light into the need for feasible management system to arrest the declining stage ensuring sustainable development of the destination (see Figure 5.2).

- **The introduction stage:** The destination is 'discovered' by a few explorer visitors, who have travelled of the beaten path in search for 'different' experiences. These explorers are also called 'drifters'. The destination has very limited facilities and infrastructure—rooms are rented by the local community and most of the accommodation inventories are in guest houses, paying guest accommodations and basic hotels. Visitors are seen as valued guests by the locals, who appreciate the relatively high amounts paid by them for services provided. A small section of the community has turned to providing services for the visitors. The environment remains pristine, there is low density of tourists as compared to the locals and the relationship between them and the visitors is excellent. The number of visitors remains low in these years, and many are repeat visitors.

- **The growth stage:** The increasing number of visitors to the destination has attracted investors, and there is a spurt in new projects to provide quality accommodation facilities and improved tourism-related services like transportation and restaurants. The 'desirable' image of the destination is bringing in visitors, who are charged a premium by service providers as the demand is more than the supply. More people are employed in the sector, bringing in incomes and benefits to the community. Increased taxes and profits have encouraged the government to invest in marketing campaigns in source markets. There is migration of skilled labour to the destination, attracted by the jobs being created. The local community enjoys the benefits of improved infrastructure and access, but is concerned about the high migrant population, rising prices and does not share a warm relationship with the visitors, commercialization creeps in.

- **The maturity stage:** Driven by word of mouth and advertising, the number of visitors has increased to a high level, rising at a fast rate. Large numbers of accommodation units have been added, and occupancy levels are high, bringing profits, foreign exchange, jobs and taxes. Tourism has become an important economic activity in the destination,

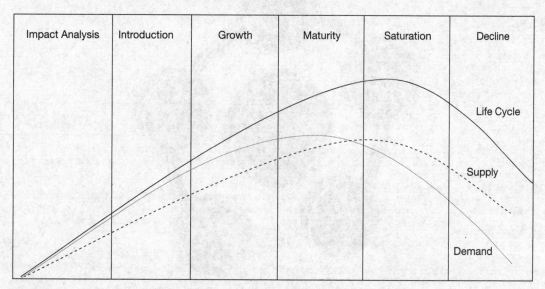

Figure 5.2 Destination lifecycle and tourism impact
Source: Authors.

employing both locals and a high number of migrants. The increased pace of development has resulted in impacts to environment, water pollution, traffic problems and crime.

- **The saturation stage:** There is a slowdown in the growth of the number of visitors, or even a decrease in the number. More inventories continue to be added, bringing down prices, although occupancy levels remain high. There is no addition to the attractions and activities in the destinations, and visitors merely follow the beaten path. There is a decrease in new investments, and reduced prices have affected tax revenues and incomes. Travel intermediaries control the price and the product, pushing down margins and the type of tourists visiting the destination changes. There is widespread degradation of the environment, visual pollution and cultural disruptions, leading to an antagonistic attitude on the part of the local population towards tourists.

- **The decline stage:** The number of visitors remains high, although declining. An abundance of supply, with little demand has resulted in very low prices, attracting visitors who do not spend on goods and services outside the hotels. The incomes of locals have dwindled, establishments have closed and jobs lost. Pollution and other environmental impacts remain at high levels.

Most destinations which have experienced rapid growth, sudden expansion and a steep increase in arrivals, have not been able to restrict and regulate the growth of tourism, and have been left with an overdeveloped and overexploited region, with declining arrivals and huge costs of repairing the damage on the environment caused by uncontrolled tourism development.

Managing Destinations

There cannot be a single model for managing destinations (Figure 5.3). The administrative models of the countries and regions in which destinations are situated determine, to a large

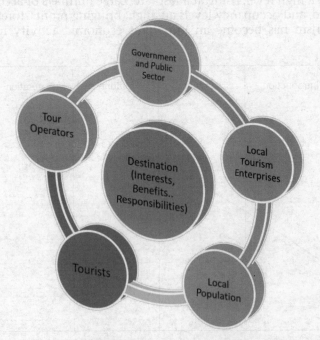

Figure 5.3 Stakeholders in destinations
Source: Authors.

extent, the way destinations are managed. Several factors influence the management of destinations. An important factor is the role played by tourism in the local economy, and its impact on the citizens of the destination. Destinations which are dependent on tourism to a substantial degree will lay greater emphasis on planning for tourism development and on marketing programmes. This is in contrast to those destinations where the local economy is driven by other forces and tourism plays a comparatively subsidiary role.

Destination Management Organizations (DMOs)

DMOs are 'part of the local, regional or national government and have political and legislative power as well as the financial means to manage resources rationally and to ensure that all stakeholders can benefit in the long term' (Buhalis, 2000). DMOs have regulatory and developmental functions, which are carried out because of the authority bestowed on them by legislation or administrative decree. In a complex environment, DMO takes the responsibility of ensuring that the different players carry out their roles efficiently under its direction and supervision. DMO coordinates with those agencies not under its direct control that have a bearing on the tourism experience. DMO regulates all major activities in the tourism ecosystem, including the supply of room inventory, the quality of services and the provision of a safe and secure environment. Lastly, DMO must also enjoy the trust of all partners and stakeholders to take the lead in developing strategies to promote the destination and bring in more visitors.

DMOs involve themselves in formulating tourism policies and strategies, building infrastructure, monitoring impacts and finding solutions for negative developments, regulating growth and licensing, developing human resources and skill training and developing products.

The stakeholders in the local community may have conflicting views about tourism development in the destination (Figure 5.4). Those who have direct benefits from tourism, such as hotel owners, employees, shopkeepers and transport providers may be in favour of increasing the tourist arrivals. But those who do not derive direct benefit from tourists would not support the increase in tourist traffic, as that can potentially create a strain on the resources

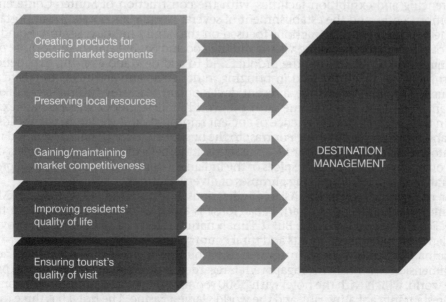

Figure 5.4   Role of destination management organizations
Source: Adapted from Manente (2008), UNWTO.

and infrastructure of the community. One of the most important challenges for any local government is to ensure that citizens continue to enjoy common property resources, such as access to scenic areas, beaches, public roads and the sea, without being displaced by tourists.

For destination managers, the aim is to develop tourism, from the perspective of the local population, is to increase incomes, provide employment and bring more business to local enterprises. From a visitor's point of view, destination planning should aim to improve the tourism experiences, enhancing the satisfaction levels of the visitor. From a long-term planning perspective, the aim is to ensure that tourism does not leave negative impacts on the social and environmental fronts. The Singapore Tourism Board is an example of a DMO with a strategic development plan, which is constantly working towards improving the product offering, working in tandem with private enterprises in creating new products and experiences by forging partnerships, driving innovation and promoting excellence in the tourism sector. The case study on Singapore illustrates the efforts of the Singapore Tourism Board.

Case Study: Destination Singapore—The Success of Planned Development

The story of Singapore tourism is a fascinating journey of the evolution of a city regarded only as a 'stop over', into one of the most popular destinations in the world. The city has exploited every aspect that may be of interest to a visitor to develop products that project different facets and appeal to different tastes.

Singapore has been popular for two of its iconic experiences—cuisine and shopping. The city provides a range of eating options for the visitor, the hawker areas teeming with outlets of Indian, Malaysian and Chinese dishes. Of late, Singapore has attracted an array of fine dining restaurants offering cuisines from across the world. Shopping remains the perennial favourite with visitors as Singapore offers an amazing mix of haute couture, upscale shopping malls with designer brands, trendy street labels and a variety of electronic goods.

Identifying the potential of MICE tourism very early, Singapore invested in modern conferencing and exhibition facilities, with the construction of Suntec Conference and Exhibition centre, and the establishment of several world class hotels. An important area was the development of attractions focused on the family holiday. Sentosa Island with a range of offerings for the young visitor and the Zoo and Night Safari became quite popular. In its quest to keep refreshing the product and to add new and exciting experiences, the Government has taken the lead in bringing in designers and architects to create unique structures. The Supertree Grove, a recent development featuring futuristic tree like structures and the Cloud Forest Dome with the world's tallest indoor waterfall are examples. 'City in the Garden' is an experience of ancient rainforests and wetlands, with wildlife and farmland providing a refreshing contrast to the bustle of the city. The markets and malls of Chinatown transport the visitor into the sights and smells of China; in the streets of Little India, one can savour the heady spices of the Indian subcontinent. Other regional precincts, like Arab Street, provide amazing glimpses of diverse cultures.

For the heritage lover, the Asian Civilizations Museum and the Peranakan Museum have important collections of art; Baba House is a fine example of a Peranakan heritage home. For the nature lover, the Bukit Timah nature reserves and Pulau Ubin provides an experience of undisturbed forests and rural countryside.

Marina Bay Sands is a new integrated resort built at the cost of US$ 8 billion, adding a new dimension to tourism in Singapore. It is regarded as the most expensive casino property in the world, which with the hotel with 2,500 rooms, a shopping mall, a convention centre, seven restaurants, a skating rink and the world's largest casino. The hotel has three towers of 55 floors each, which are topped by a 340 m sky Park and a 150 m infinity swimming pool.

(Continued ...)

This mammoth project is one of the two major projects initiated by Singapore to drive its tourism development for the future. The other is the 'Resorts World Sentosa' which has a Universal Studios theme park.

Singapore celebrates numerous festivals, both traditional and modern, which showcase the vibrant culture of the communities living in the city. Interactive illusionary art museums from Korea—Alive Museum and Trick Eye Museum—were opened recently, as was Madame Tussauds which opened in Sentosa. With its emphasis on improving and enhancing attractions, the Mandai area is being redeveloped to integrate with the Zoo, Night Safari and River Safari. For sports enthusiasts, the Formula 1 Singapore Grand Prix and the WTA finals featured the best in racing and women's tennis.

Singapore's oldest performing arts centres—the Victoria Theatre and Victoria Concert Hall have been reopened after extensive refurbishment. The new National Gallery is the largest visual arts institution in Singapore. The Singapore Pinacotheque de Paris, an expansion of the renowned private museum of Paris, opened its doors in Singapore recently.

The Singapore Tourism Board strives to ensure that tourism remains an important and vibrant economic pillar through long-term strategic planning and by forging partnerships, driving innovation and promoting excellence in the tourism sector. The Board aims to ensure that Singapore continues to offer compelling experiences to attract the increasingly well-travelled and sophisticated visitor.

Discussion Questions

1. List three initiatives of the Singapore Tourism Board that are aimed at adding new elements to the tourism experience at the destination.
2. 'Singapore is an example of controlled tourism, with the state using its powers and authority to decide the type and style of development'. Discuss.

The Indian Scenario

In a destination, the DMO is responsible for providing civic services such as sewerage, solid waste disposal and infrastructure such as roads, power and water. While municipal corporations are responsible for much of these functions, the regional or state governments have a major role to play in countries like India.

In the Indian context, the tourism departments in the state governments may be seen as charged with 'managing' destinations. This is a major point of difference from the Western models, where the city council or the municipal administration handles this responsibility, either directly or through special vehicles such as tourism boards. Broadly, tourism departments are responsible for the development of tourism circuits, which are clusters of tourist destinations and infrastructural development in destinations including the construction of tourist reception centres, budget accommodation units and wayside amenities. Works to improve tourism resources, such as monuments, are also taken up by these organizations. The tourism departments seek funding from the Union Tourism Ministry to take up such projects in destinations. Managing the assets created and operating services such as tour packages are responsibilities assigned to a 'Tourism Development Corporation', a public sector undertaking under the state department of tourism. This model creates a situation where the destination is managed by several agencies, and tourism agencies are charged with the responsibility to provide services and build infrastructure, without the authority to plan and regulate development or charge for the services.

In many Indian destinations, the absence of a coordinating mechanism and the dissipation of responsibilities into the hands of multifarious agencies have taken a toll on efficient management of the resources, leading to degradation of destinations. The over construction seen in most of our hill stations is a telling example of irresponsible management, where the authority which grants building permissions does not necessarily have the long term interest of tourism development in mind. Governance by municipal bodies in India is in a nascent stage, with very few having the professional expertise and financial resources to manage complex issues in tourist destinations. Another example is Ladakh, where a steep increase in tourism has given rise to major socioeconomic and environmental issues, which are elaborated in the case study. But the authorities do not appear to have understood the serious nature of the issue, or are turning a blind eye.

Case Study: Ladakh—The Changing Face of a Destination

When Ladakh was first opened to tourism in 1974, a total of 527 people visited. Of them, 500 were foreign tourists, 27 domestic. Since then, the trend of foreign dominance in tourist arrivals has remained. It has shaped the profile of Ladakh's tourism.

Slowly, trends changed. The official figures for 2010 pegged overall tourist arrivals at 77,800 of which foreigners were 22,115 and domestic 55,685. As of August, the 2011 arrivals stood at 148,588 with 29,856 foreigners and 118,732 domestic tourists.

As with any destination, Ladakh wants that tourist money. The problem? The spike in traffic and the changed mix in tourist arrivals can mould a destination differently. A major cause for the spurt in domestic arrivals was the cheap package trip sold by travel portals and airlines. Very competitive, package trips beat down prices. They attract traffic. Service providers stay busy. Yet, with tourist arrivals beating previous statistical predictions, the question is, what is Ladakh's carrying capacity? Is endless linear growth possible in a cold desert? According to the travel trade, Leh experiences water scarcity, and even as hotel/guest houses have increased in number, there is no modern town sewage system. Cars and Automated Teller Machines are more now, internet is still fragile, electricity fails, Leh's roads reek of generator fumes. This season, according to the trade, there were days when up to 500 taxis plied from Leh to environmentally sensitive locations such as Panggong Lake.

Ladakh's 270,000 people live in a vast physical expanse that is at time solitude incarnate. Will too many people make a Manali of Leh? Hence the argument in some sections of the tourist trade in Ladakh that instead of appealing to everyone, their region should be preserved as a high priced, modest volume destination, which also accommodates interested budget travellers.

Near Leh's Shanti Stupa, I met Shakeel Hussain, who has been a taxi driver for almost 30 years. He said the 2011 season had been terrific. His worry—besides farming and tourism—is what is there in Ladakh? What would happen to new hotels and mortgages should tourism falter, as it periodically does? Ladakh ponders (Menon, 2011).

Tourism's Impact: Paying the Price

The tourism economy is centred around Leh, and very little of the economic benefit accrues to more than 90% of Ladakhis who live outside this area. Within Leh, the handful of Ladakhis who own large hotels benefit disproportionately. Much of the money spent in Leh goes to tour operators and merchants who come to Ladakh just for the tourist season.

The problem goes beyond an uneven distribution of the benefits, however. Those not participating can become economically worse off simply by continuing to live as they always have. The reciprocal relations of mutual aid are broken down by the extension of the monetary economy, and the tourist's demands for scarce resources drive up the prices of local goods.

For example, pack animals in villages which were shared between one another are no longer available, as they are frequently often in the hills carrying tourist luggage. Villagers have begun selling traditional building materials in Leh, where a building boom induced by tourism supports far higher prices than what fellow villagers might offer.

(Continued ...)

Until recently, Ladakh had no waste problems; everything could be cycled back to the land. Many hotels have faultily designed water-based sewage systems that contaminate local streams. Cooling, heating, lighting and transportation needs have been provided primarily by fossil fuels trucked over the Himalayas, adding diesel fumes, coal smoke and spent oil to the list of Ladakh's environmental woes.

The social and cultural effects of tourism are more difficult to isolate. The openness and friendliness that the Ladakhis have traditionally shown to visitors has been eroded by the commercialization of their culture and their understandable resentment toward the invading crowds. Theft, virtually unknown in traditional Ladakh society, is now a common complaint among urban tourists and trekkers alike, and children now plague visitors for handouts.

Source: S.G. Menon, *Business Line.*

Discussion Questions

1. List the pros and cons of tourism development in Ladakh.
2. What are the measures that the authorities can adopt to ensure the sustainability of the destination?

The pattern of funding DMOs is one of the reasons why the DMOs have not been able to create much impact in India. In most of the states, the works carried out by these bodies are funded by the Union Government. The taxes that are generated by growth in tourism are not managed by the DMOs, and municipal taxation is negligible. The public sector character of the DMO ensures that the organization is not compelled to function professionally, nor be worried about fund cuts or finding alternative sources of revenue. The departmental structure also ensures that the stakeholders in a destination are not heard in the decision-making process.

Regional Tourism Organizations and National Tourism Organizations

Destination management is distinct from destination marketing, which may be one of the functions handled by a DMO. In many destinations, the tourism development-related functions, such as marketing, promotion, information dissemination and visitor management, are handled by a separate organization, often called the tourism board. Tourism boards can be at the regional level—regional tourism organizations (RTOs), or the national level—national tourism organizations (NTOs). These bodies are mostly in the public sector, but in some destinations they have been converted into private enterprises often funded jointly by the government and the private sector.

Destination Marketing

In the intensely competitive world of international tourism, destinations need to continuously evolve strategies to market their attractions and products. Marketing of destinations is a complex process, involving multiple stakeholders, often with conflicting interests. The funding of marketing campaigns is also a contentious issue.

Market research is a vital tool that enables destination marketing agencies to address different segments of tourists. Research provides important information on the desires and aspirations of each segment as well as the characteristics that are peculiar to any given segment. Based on these attributes that are identified through different forms of market research, destination managers are able to provide products and services tailor-made to certain markets, including product/service mixes that fulfil their requirements. Research also provides vital information on the likes and dislikes, preferences, period and reason of travel that are displayed by particular consumer markets. Another important role played by market research is the assessment of the branding strategy of the destination, which includes the evaluation and perceived attributes of the brand and the factors affecting the 'image' of the destination in the minds of the potential traveller. Market research helps in evaluating the effectiveness of marketing campaigns as also the reach and penetration of advertising. The various aspects related to destination marketing and market research are discussed in detail in the Chapter 10.

Impact of Tourism on Destinations

The impact of tourism on destinations and local population often evoke extreme and contradictory opinions. While tourism investors and destination managers insist that tourism has a positive effect on the local economy, many NGOs and academics point out that the negative impacts of tourism overshadow the benefits. In a destination, tourists spend their money on accommodation, food and beverage, entertainment, shopping, tour and travel services and gratuities. Most of this expenditure tends to remain within the economy, in the hands of local entrepreneurs and businesses. However, tourist spending has to be seen in the light of certain aspects that may affect its impact on the local economy. The expenditure made by tourists can stimulate more expenditure by its circulation in the local economy. This is called a 'cascade' effect. The direct economic effect of tourist expenditure is the amount paid by the tourist for goods and services, less the 'leakage', that is the amount spent to procure goods that are not produced by the local economy. Migration of local population from traditional occupation also creates impact on the destination.

The impacts in the social and cultural fronts brought into destination by the development of tourism need serious examination. There are many areas of contact and conflict in the cultural front. One of the most striking is the behaviour of the visitor in a destination. In beach destinations, large numbers of tourists descend on destinations with the sole aim of seeking pleasure, relaxation and entertainment. Very often, consumption of alcohol in large quantities, loud music, partying, drug use and sex are all involved in the celebrations. The tourists may not pay much regard to local customs and sensibilities.

Environment is another area of concern. Growth and development of tourism in a destination is closely followed by uncontrolled exploitation of resources—land, water, energy, creation of waste, pollution of air, water, noise, aesthetics, resulting in causing serious threat to environment and sustainable development. Tourism can also create positive impacts on environment by supporting conservation measures and adopting sustainable practices.

We will examine these and other impacts caused by tourism development in detail in Chapter 16.

Conclusion

We have seen that the term destination can be viewed from different perspectives, with 'supply' and 'demand' imperatives changing the way a destination can be defined. In order to be effective, destinations need to be a cohesive administrative unit. Different kinds of destinations attract different groups of tourists, or appeal to the same group during different periods. Destinations typically have a life cycle, the stages of which determine their attractiveness and have valuable lessons for their managers. DMOs are important entities, mostly in the public sector, tasked with managing the different stakeholders in a destination, with the ultimate objective of bringing benefits to the local population, while providing a memorable experience to the visitors. With increasing competition, DMO's have to adopt strategies of coordination to bring in competing stakeholders in marketing the destination together or in a coherent way. Increase in tourist arrivals, while bringing in economic benefits, also impacts the economic, social and cultural environment of the destinations.

Review Questions

1. What are the major components of a destination? How are these related to each other?
2. Discuss the relevance of destination life cycle in tourism business.
3. Examine the role of 'destination management' organizations in promoting sustainable business operations in tourism.

Activities

1. Arrange a quiz competition on the theme 'Golden Triangle'. The competition should focus on individual characteristics like attraction, accessibility and accommodation and administrative structure of Delhi, Agra and Jaipur.
2. Visit a tourism destination. Apply the 6As framework and list out in detail the components involved in each aspect.
3. Identify different types of destinations available in your state. Prepare a status paper of any two destinations using 6As framework.
4. Identify the core and periphery attractions in a destination and find out how far the periphery attractions strengthen the core attractions by enabling the tourist to stay/spend more in the destination. Also, find out potential areas to develop more periphery attractions and submit your findings to the DMO.
5. Select a tourism destination and examine the stage through which the destination is passing through, as per the Life cycle theory. Substantiate your findings by highlighting the characteristics of the identified present stage by empirical facts.
6. Arrange a focus group discussion with the stakeholders in a destination and find out the measures taken by the DMO to improve the quality of visit of tourists and life of local community.
7. Examine the linkage and leakage effects of a hotel in detail and suggest measures for plugging leakages and maximizing linkages with the objective of creating a sustainable model.

References

Books

Arnstein, Sherry R. 1969. 'A Ladder of Citizen participation'. *JAIP*, 35 (July, 4): 216-24.

Buhalis, D. 2000. 'Marketing the Competitive Destination of the Future'. *Tourism Management*, 21 (1): 97-116.

Butler, R.W. 1980. 'The Concept of a Tourist Area Cycle of Evolution: Implications for Management of Resources'. *Canadian Geographer*, 24(1): 5-12.

Cooper, C., J. Fletcher, D. Gilbert, R. Shepherd, and S. Wanhill. 1998. *Tourism Principles and Practice*, 2nd ed. Harlow: Longman.

Manente M. 2008. 'Destination Management and Economic Background: Defining and Monitoring Local Tourist Destinations'. Central Paper Session IV, Proceedings of the UNWTO international conference on Knowledge as Value Advantage of Tourist Destinations, Malaga (Spain), October 2008.

Web Resources

Cultural Survival. n.d. 'The Response to Tourism in Ladakh'. Cultural Survival. Available at: https://www.culturalsurvival.org/publications/cultural-survival-quarterly/india/response-tourism-ladakh
Menon, S.G. 2011. 'Two Sides to Ladakh Tourism'. *Business Line*. Available at: http://www.thehindubusinessline.com/news/variety/two-sides-to-ladakh-tourism/article2678113.ece

Suggested Readings

Books

Howie, F. 2003. *Managing the Tourism Destination*. London: Thomson Learning.
Morrison, A.M. 2013. *Marketing and Managing Tourism Destinations*. Oxon: Routledge.

Welcome at Haryana tourism's Surajkund fair
Image courtesy: Ministry of Tourism, Government of India.

CHAPTER 6

Attractions

Learning Objectives

By the end of this chapter, students will be able to:

- Define a tourist attraction and describe its characteristics.
- Categorize attractions based on different criteria and perspectives.
- List elements of successful attractions.
- Recognize the importance of visitor management strategies.
- Describe the roles and functions of agencies managing attractions.

Introduction

For many first time visitors to India, the main reason they chose the country as their holiday destination was their desire to see the 'poem in stone', the Taj Mahal. The Taj welcomes about 8 million (80 lakh) visitors every year, a tenth of which come from abroad. Even with its myriad destinations, India continues to be known in the tourism world as the land of the Taj.

The Taj Mahal is the main reason why visitors flock to the city of Agra. The destination Agra is known the world over as the city of the Taj. Like the Eiffel Tower for Paris, the Blue Mosque of Istanbul or the Pyramids of Giza, the Taj is the most iconic attraction of Agra, and indeed of destination India.

Beyond the thousands of visitors, a student of tourism is curious about many aspects relating to tourism in the Taj Mahal. Who owns and manages the Taj Mahal? Which authority is responsible for the upkeep and maintenance of the monument? Who is responsible for the management of visitor facilities? Is someone checking, if the large numbers of visitors are damaging the monument?

If the Taj Mahal is a popular attraction for tourists because of its beauty and historical value, the Ranthambore National Park in Rajasthan presents a different picture. Thousands of visitors come to Ranthambore, seeking to get a glimpse of the wildlife, particularly the tiger. A destination, with many hotels and tourist facilities, has come up close to the national park which is the only tourist attraction in the vicinity. What happens to the destination, if for some reason, the entry into the park is restricted or even prohibited? Which authority decides the number of tourists who can be given entry, without disturbing the fragile habitat?

In this chapter, we will examine these questions in some detail. An attraction, in its simplest definition, is 'something worth seeing', something that can persuade someone to travel away from their home (Yale, 2004).

Attractions create destinations, and often become the catalyst for tourism development in a region. In many cases, destinations are formed around a specific attraction or a group of attractions. Attractions are those aspects that are seen or experienced by visitors, forming the highlight or the main reason for the visit. The diversity of attractions, their significance to the tourism sector, and their interplay with other components of the destinations are important reasons why much attention is focused on the study of attractions.

The terms 'visitor' attraction and 'tourist' attraction are used regularly. As most of the attractions are visited by day visitors or excursionists in addition to tourists who stay overnight in the vicinity. 'The term Visitor Attraction is used in preference to Tourist Attraction, as this emphasizes the role of the day visitor market in the successful operation of attractions, rather than simply focusing on the overnight tourist' (Leask, 2010)).

Definitions

Leiper (1995) defines a tourist attraction as a system comprising three elements: a tourist or human element, a 'nucleus' or central element and a market or informative element. A tourist attraction comes into existence when the three elements are connected.

Primary nuclei are iconic attractions that tourists travel long distances to visit. The Taj Mahal is a good example. Secondary nuclei act as elements in the region of the primary attraction that are known to the tourist before the journey, but are not influential enough to warrant the journey on their own. The Agra Fort, which is a World Heritage monument in its own right, may be seen as a secondary nucleus. Tertiary nuclei are attractions that tourists discover while visiting a destination, or on the way to or from it. They are elements which were not known to the tourist before the trip. The Tomb of Itmad ud Daulah—a beautiful but little known monument on the banks of the Yamuna in Agra—is an example of a tertiary nucleus.

An interesting definition of a tourist attraction as agreed by the four national tourist organizations of the United Kingdom (Visit Britain) is as follows:

An attraction is where it is feasible to charge admission for the sole purpose of sightseeing. The attraction must be a permanently established excursion destination, a primary purpose of which is to allow access for entertainment, interest, or education; rather than being primarily a retail outlet or a venue for sporting, theatrical or film performances. It must be open to the public, without prior booking, for published periods each year, and should be capable of attracting day visitors or tourists as well as local residents. In addition, the attraction must be a single business, under a single management, so that it is capable of answering the economic questions on revenue, employment, etc.

This definition clearly excludes temporary attractions, such as festivals and events. It also excludes shopping areas and sporting venues. The main objective of defining an attraction in a very specific sense appears to be the collection of accurate data regarding visitation, revenue streams and organizational resources, which is an important input in management and marketing strategies.

While there is merit in the argument that accurate data is an important input from a management perspective, the definition of a tourist attraction has to keep in mind the iconic nature of many structures, which define visually the image of the destination in the mind of the visitor, and form the primary reason for the visit. Burj Khalifa of Dubai, Petronas towers of Kuala Lumpur and the Golden Gate bridge of San Francisco are visual symbols of those destinations.

Predominantly religious sites are generally not considered as 'tourist attractions', as the objective of travel to such a site is very different from that of a leisure traveller. Sites which have multiple businesses and operations are not included. Sports stadia, shopping malls and multiplexes are not considered attractions.

Categories of Tourist Attractions

Attractions can be grouped into types, based on their origin, location or use. Some studies classify sites as those with cultural and historical importance and natural landmarks. The commonest classification is into 'natural' attractions, such as forests, wildlife sanctuaries, national parks and areas of outstanding beauty or significance, and 'man-made' attractions which embrace a wide range, from monuments such as the Taj Mahal to modern construction masterpieces such as the London eye. 'Cultural' attractions are those highlighting and demonstrating the cultural heritage of the region. Cultural attractions can be further subdivided into 'tangible' cultural attractions such as archaeological sites, ancient monuments, museums and galleries. Examples of 'intangible' cultural attractions include fairs and festivals, parades and celebrations, music and dance and cultural practices (Figure 6.1).

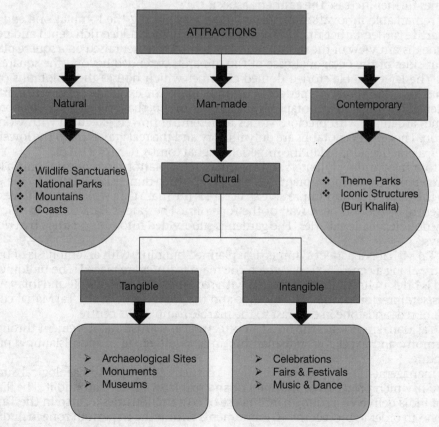

Figure 6.1   Classification of attractions
Source: Authors.

Case Study: Taj Mahal

An immense mausoleum of white marble, built in Agra between 1631 and 1648 by the order of the Mughal emperor Shah Jahan in memory of his favourite wife, the Taj Mahal is the jewel of Muslim art in India and one of the universally admired masterpieces of the world's heritage.

Outstanding Universal Value

The Taj Mahal is located on the right bank of the Yamuna River in a vast Mughal garden that encompasses nearly 17 ha, in Agra district in Uttar Pradesh. It was built by the Emperor in memory of his wife Mumtaz Mahal, with construction starting in 1632 and completed in 1648. The mosque, guesthouse and the main gateway to the south, the outer courtyard and its cloisters were added subsequently and completed in 1653. For its construction, masons, stone cutters, inlayers, carvers, painters, calligraphers, dome builders and other artisans were requisitioned from the whole of the empire and from Central Asia and Iran.

The Taj Mahal is considered to be the greatest architectural achievement in the whole range of Indo-Islamic architecture. Its recognized architectonic beauty has rhythmic combination of solids and voids, concave and convex and light shadows. Features such as arches and domes further increase the aesthetic aspect.

One remarkable innovation of the architect was placing the tomb at one end of the quadripartite garden rather than in the exact centre, which added rich depth and perspective to the distant view of the monument. The tomb is further raised on a square platform with four sides of the octagonal base of the minarets extended beyond the square at the corners. The large double storied domed chamber which houses the cenotaphs of Shah Jehan and Mumtaz Mahal is a perfect octagon in plan. The exquisite octagonal marble lattice screen encircling both cenotaphs is an example of superb workmanship. The borders of the frames are inlaid with precious stones representing flowers executed with wonderful perfection. The upper cenotaphs are only illusory and the real graves are in the lower tomb chamber, a practice adopted in the Imperial Mughal tombs. (UNESCO, n.d).

The four freestanding minarets at the corners of the platform provide not only a kind of spatial reference to the monument, but also give a three-dimensional effect to the edifice. Next to the tomb, the most impressive structure is the main gate which stands majestically in the centre of the southern wall of the forecourt. The gate is flanked on the Northern front by double arcade galleries. The garden is subdivided into four quarters by two main walkways.

The Taj Mahal is a perfect symmetrical planned building, with an emphasis of bilateral symmetry along a central axis on which the main features are placed. The building material used is brick in lime mortar veneered with red sandstone and marble and inlay work of precious/semiprecious stones. The mosque and the guest house in the Taj Mahal complex are built of red sandstone in contrast to the marble tomb in the centre.

The Taj Mahal represents the finest architectural and artistic achievement through perfect harmony and excellent craftsmanship in a whole range of Indo Islamic sepulchral architecture.

The management of Taj Mahal complex is carried out by the Archaeological Survey of India, (ASI), which protects the monument and regulates the area around it. The Supreme Court of India delivered a ruling banning use of coal in industries located in the Taj trapezium zone, in order to protect the 40 monuments within the trapezium zone including the three world heritage sites. The site is managed based on a Management Plan, which focuses on conserving the monument, and organizing the visitor movement in a planned way without causing damage to the complex.

(Continued ...)

Discussion Questions

1. Discuss the ways in which visitor management at the Taj can be improved.
2. What are the other major attractions for visitors in the city of Agra? How can these be combined to increase the duration of stay of visitors to the city? Discuss.

Several festivals, such as the boat races of Kerala and the Pushkar camel fair, have strong traditional links bringing the participation of the local population and the domestic visitor. Alongside, these festivals have been marketed effectively as authentic cultural attractions, with an inflow of large numbers of foreign visitors to view the events.

Further, attractions may be divided as permanent or temporary, as a celebration or event. From a management perspective, attractions can be divided as those in the public domain, managed by government agencies, and those which are privately owned and promoted.

Here is a list of categories (Figure 6.2):

1. **Cultural attractions**
   - Historical/archaeological site
   - Temple/mosque/church
   - Fort/castle
   - Palace/mansion
   - Museum/art gallery
   - Architecture/building
   - Interpretation/visitor/heritage centre
   - Village life
2. **Natural attractions**
   - Beaches
   - Backwaters
   - Hill stations
   - Deserts
   - Forests
3. **Nature-based attractions**
   - Wildlife sanctuary and national park
   - Zoo/safari
   - Botanical garden/park
   - Aquarium/sea life centre
4. **Others**
   - Amusement/theme park
   - Fair/festival
   - Parade/carnival

While the first three categories are self-explanatory, the fourth category comprises of attractions which have been purposely built for the entertainment of tourists, without depending on the natural or cultural assets of the destination and temporary celebrations such as fair, festivals and annual parades attracting residents and tourists alike for a limited period of time.

Another way of approaching attractions is from the perspective of what it aims to provide the visitor. Educational attractions are the ones that provide information and have educational value, such as an insight into heritage, art history and cultural practices. Entertainment

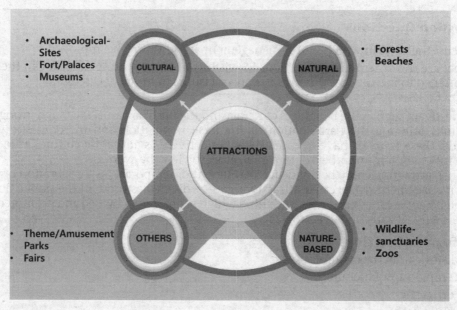

Figure 6.2   Categories of attractions
Source: Authors.

attractions are those which aim to give the visitor pleasure through options for entertainment. Theme parks and entertainment zones are examples of such attractions.

Attractions can also be divided from the perspective of the profile of the visitor–domestic attractions have a strong regional, ethnic or cultural flavour, attracting large numbers of domestic visitors. Sites with universal value, inscribed in world heritage list for example, appeal to all categories of visitors. The Kumbh Mela, which attracts millions of people's from all parts of the country, or the local temple festivals that occur in every part region of India are good examples of attractions that are predominantly domestic (Figure 6.2).

Management of Attractions

Most of the important attractions, natural or human made, are owned and managed by government or public bodies. Given the fact that these are enjoyed by the public, governments will continue to fund their upkeep. These are considered 'public goods', which means that the consumption of these goods cannot be restricted to a section of people, but are to be enjoyed by the public at large.

In India, the most significant attractions, both built and natural are under the Union Government or the state governments. Sites which are inscribed in the World Heritage List are the most significant attractions, which have outstanding universal value. India has 25 cultural and 7 natural sites in the List. Archaeological Survey of India (ASI) is the organization tasked with the protection of cultural heritage. The ASI manages most of the important sites, including the Taj Mahal. At the Taj, as in all major sites, the ASI personnel are involved in scientific conservation, repairs, upkeep of tourist facilities and monitoring impacts. We will look at the role of the ASI and other bodies in detail in Chapter 12 which discusses cultural heritage.

Natural sites in India are under the administrative control of the forest and wildlife departments of state governments, and the Union Ministry for Environment and Forests. A set of laws and rules lay down the conservation and protection strategy for the country, and wildlife and forest personnel in state governments work under their ambit to protect the parks and to provide tourists an educational experience during their visits. Natural attractions provide visitors with a wealth of activities and experiences. The highlight of the visit may be to get a sighting of the 'charismatic' species for which the attraction is famous, such as the Rhinoceros in Kaziranga. But most natural attractions have other activities, such as bird watching, and trekking, which provide education and enjoyment to the visitor.

Case Study: Kaziranga National Park

With an area of around 860 sq. km, Kaziranga is one of the largest protected areas in India and one of the most significant conserved forest areas on earth. Situated in the Golaghat and Nagaon districts in Assam, it has become an exceptional model of conservation and an example of the ongoing eco-biological processes within a floodplain ecosystem and the flora and fauna in it. It is also a symbol of the commitment of the people who work to protect this richly diverse biological heritage.

Kaziranga was declared as a proposed reserve forest in 1905 and a wildlife sanctuary in 1950. In 1974, Kaziranga was given the status of a national park and became a World Heritage Site of UNESCO in 1985.

Kaziranga has an expanse of grassland, giving a typical savannah look similar to the wilderness of Africa. There are numerous water bodies, recharged each year by the floodwaters of the river Brahmaputra. On the boundary, the hills are dominated by tropical moist mixed deciduous and semi evergreen forests. Kaziranga has the distinction of providing habitat to the world's largest population of the Great Indian One horned Rhinoceros, the population of which has reached around 1,600, thanks to careful conservation measures. It is also one of the places with the highest population density of the royal Bengal tiger, a good population of Asiatic elephant, swamp deer and the Asiatic wild buffalo. Over 500 species of birds can be found in the park, including many migratory birds.

Kaziranga welcomed 126,000 tourists, of which around 7,000 were foreign tourists. The park welcomes visitors between November and April. From May to October, the Park remains closed for visitors owing to the monsoon, during which time large sections of the

(Continued ...)

park are regularly flooded. Visitors are encouraged to observe wildlife by taking the guided tours on elephant or four wheelers. There are several observation towers for wildlife viewing. An interpretation centre provides information on flora and fauna and the conservation efforts.

Several tourist lodges are run by the Department of Forests around the park, and private resorts also provide accommodation. About 35 hotels and lodges are functioning on the outskirts of the park. Enterprising locals have started running home stays, providing the visitor an experience of local life in addition to wildlife viewing. The vehicles used to take visitors into the park are operated by members of the local community, with the people of adjoining areas employed as drivers and guides. Some souvenir shops, and performances of local art forms are other means of income. The inflow of tourists has led to the economic empowerment of people living on the fringes of the park.

Discussion Questions

1. List the important mammals that may be viewed at the Park. What accounts for their presence at Kaziranga?
2. Discuss the ways through which the local population can take advantage of a world class natural attraction such as Kaziranga.
3. Study the history and evolution of Kaziranga National Park, to gain an understanding on the changing trends in management of such sites.

Image courtesy: Ministry of Tourism, Government of India.

Many attractions of today were not built with the visitor in mind, and had a purpose and a clientele very different from the multitudes visiting their precincts. Good examples of these are the grand cathedrals of Europe, or the palaces of India. The potential to raise revenue from tourism is an irresistible draw, converting many such structures into tourist spots. In Europe, many houses of worship depend to the most part on tourism for their upkeep, rather than traditional sources such as donations and collections. Similarly, privately owned buildings such as the Mysore and Jaipur palaces provide a regular source of revenue from tourism.

Tourism is often referred to as a double edged sword (Bandarin, 2005), which 'on the one hand confers economic benefits through the sale of tickets and visitor spending… but on the other hand places stress on the fabric of destinations and the communities who live in them'. The managers of tourist attractions have to address this issue, appropriately termed the 'Tourist Attraction Management Paradox' by Johan Edelheim (2015), trying to balance the need to promote the attraction with the necessity to ensure its sustainability. We will examine the impacts of tourism on attractions, destinations and communities in detail in subsequent chapters.

Elements of Successful Tourism Attractions

Stephen Wanhill lists four elements that successful attractions have: entertainment, education, aesthetics and escapism (Wanhill, 2008). Entertainment and enjoyment are increasingly important to the visitor, as they seek to switch off from the tedium of everyday existence and work, and spend time with their family. It is a human need to be distracted and entertained, and attractions try to provide an experience that fulfils this requirement in myriad ways. Attractions that cleverly package education with entertainment are highly successful, as these appeal to a broad spectrum of visitors, providing the right ingredients to sections of visitors. Visits to a museum have changed beyond recognition in recent times, with museums investing heavily to engage with audiences and create new and attractive tools for interpretation. 'Edutainment'—education and entertainment—has established itself as a discipline, with the emphasis on creating compelling stories and narratives in an entertaining and fun-filled context. 'Escape' does not need much elaboration, as tourism is a definitive way of escaping from one's regular environment. The visitor seeks a temporary escape into another world or environment, to do things she does not normally do, to see new sights and to taste new flavours.

Visitor Management and Carrying Capacity

The cardinal duty of the managers of attractions is to ensure sustainability, which means that the attraction is protected from damage and passed on to future generations. This would mean careful management of visitors and their activities. It is here that the concept of carrying capacity becomes relevant. Carrying capacity is defined as 'the maximum number of persons that may visit a tourist destination at the same time, without causing destruction of the physical, economic, socio-cultural environment and an unacceptable decrease in the quality of visitors' satisfaction' (UNEP/, MAP/ and PAP, 1997). Other approaches, such as 'Limits of Acceptable Change' and 'Visitor Experience Resource Protection (VERP) are also used for the purpose of planning, particularly in protected areas.

Restricting visitor footfalls to a manageable level is the most common strategy employed by managers to restrict visitors to a site. Another strategy, particularly to limit pollution levels, is the 'park and ride' facility that keeps vehicles a safe distance away from a monument. This strategy is employed in the vicinity of the Taj Mahal, where visitors have to traverse the final kilometre to the monument using battery operated vehicles provided by the management, or by foot.

Case Study: Visitor Management in Nadgee Nature Reserve

The Nadgee Nature Reserve is a 20,671 hectare park on the far South coast of New South Wales. Most of the park is classified as wilderness. The Nadgee Wilderness is the only coastal wilderness in New South Wales and continues into Croajingalong National Park in Victoria, where it meets the Cape Howe wilderness area. These adjoining areas are the largest essentially unmodified coastal areas in South-east Australia and together are recognised internationally as the Croajingalong Biosphere Reserve.

In New South Wales, nature reserves are typically not designed to attract visitors because they generally contain significant natural values that high visitation could compromise. Nadgee Nature Reserve however, forms part of the Great South East Coastal Walk that extends for 140 kilometres along the coastline of Victoria and New South Wales. This walk is widely recognised as an outstanding coastal wilderness walk. While the walk offers a unique coastal experience for skilled hikers, its importance for recreation needs to be balanced with efforts to protect its wilderness values. To achieve this balance the National Parks and Wildlife Service (NPWS) and Parks Victoria have jointly adopted a permit system that applies from the northern end of Nadgee Nature Reserve right through to Sydenham Inlet in Victoria. Within the Nadgee-Howe section of the walk this permit system allows the NPWS and Parks Victoria to restrict the number of visitors allowed in the wilderness areas at any one time to 30 and limits the size of groups to eight people. These permits also restrict the number of consecutive nights that can be spent at a campsite to minimise any associated impacts.

The permit system for the Nadgee-Cape Howe wilderness areas allows the NPWS and Parks Victoria to collect information on the number of overnight visitors in the area. The application form for the permit also requests information on the intended itinerary for the trip, providing insight into the movement of visitors within the parks. In addition to the information collected through the permit system, the NPWS also uses vehicle and pedestrian counters, surveys and a sign-in book within the Nadgee Nature Reserve to monitor the number of day visitors to the park. All this information can be used to direct monitoring and management for visitor impacts within the park.

(Continued ...)

In 1995 and 1996, long-term monitoring was established at ten campsites within the wilderness area. This monitoring records a range of site attributes such as the vegetation type, canopy cover, understorey cover, tree damage, distance to freshwater, firewood source and availability, facilities (i.e., fire ring, constructed seating), number of fire scars, soil exposure and litter. A detailed site plan is drawn up for each campsite and photos are also taken of each site from fixed photo-points to assess changes in the area over time. This comprehensive monitoring system allows NPWS staff to assess the level of impact at each campsite and take action to protect camping areas if impacts exceed an acceptable level, thereby managing adverse visitor impacts within the park.

By monitoring the condition of campsites within Nadgee Nature Reserve, those showing signs of degradation can be closed and allowed to rehabilitate naturally. Park managers can also target education campaigns within the park to particular activities that might be having adverse impacts on park values. For example, the collection of firewood from within the wilderness area may reduce the available habitat for some reptiles and invertebrates. Targeted campaigns for campers to bring their own fuel stoves for cooking have assisted in reducing the impacts of this activity. The Nadgee Nature Reserve Plan of Management also lists locations where campfires will not be permitted, thereby protecting significant habitat from the risk of escaped campfires.

The role of national government, local self-government, service providers in tourism and civil society cannot be undermined in this context. A proper understanding of the possible diverse impacts on natural resource use for tourism should enable industry operators to develop and apply sustainable economic practice related to natural environment.

Source: http://www.environment.nsw.gov.au/sop04/sop04cs14.htm (accessed on 17 March 2017)

Discussion Questions

1. Why did authorities restrict entry into the reserve? What are the other ways by which entry can be controlled?
2. List the measures taken by the reserve authority to minimize environmental impact of tourist activities in the area.

Forests are ecologically fragile, and cannot tolerate large numbers of visitors. In such attractions, entry is strictly regulated, and detailed plans are made to manage visitors. Natural attractions place a heavy emphasis on low intensity development, keeping interventions to the minimum. The core areas of protected areas are kept undisturbed, and visitors are prohibited from entering such areas. In other areas, a limited number of visitors are allowed admission and a few activities are permitted. Beyond this zone are areas earmarked for tourism activities and recreation, where larger numbers of tourists are permitted entry, along with earmarked areas for campsites and interpretation centres.

Funding Strategies

Many natural attractions depend, to a degree, on tourism generated revenues for conservation. It follows that natural attractions will require management inputs and infrastructural development to make them suitable for the use of tourists. The management of a national park, for instance, may prepare a plan that includes numerous possibilities for tourism, such as hiking trails, cycling, camping, trekking, bird watching and angling. These activities bring in valuable funds which help conservation and preservation efforts.

Many human made attractions need considerable input of resources for maintenance and conservation, which is provided by tourism and adaptive reuse. Access to national treasures is considered the right of the citizens, so the admission is generally free or on the basis of a nominal charge. Such attractions charge a differential entry fee, so that tourists pay a higher admission charge that is seen as a kind of 'cross subsidy' for the local visitors.

Attractions such as museums, which are considered 'non-commercial' in nature, are increasingly under pressure to impose higher admission charges and to raise resources, in the backdrop of decreasing government support. Historic buildings and venues raise resources by multifarious means, including rentals, events and special exhibitions. Museums and galleries use methods such as merchandising, venue rentals, special shows and exhibitions and special education and outreach programmes to raise additional revenues.

Faced with the prospect of a gradual reduction in funding provided by the central government, many state government agencies which have fragile monuments and other attractions under their charge, are looking at alternative sources of revenue. One rather controversial route is adaptive re-use of buildings. Adaptive reuse is the adaption of a disused building for another purpose. Other avenues like approaching corporates for sponsoring conservation in return for advertising rights, tapping funds available under corporate social responsibility and transferring assets to the local community bodies are being tried.

Forts and palaces have of late become attractions, creating destinations and bringing in visitors. Chittorgarh and Kumbalgarh have become popular destinations mainly because of the magnificent forts. The forts of Jaisalmer and Amber are the main attractions of the region, acting as iconic symbols of these destinations. Relatively unknown outside the region, these towns have become popular destinations based on the popularity of the forts which brought in thousands of visitors interested in the awe inspiring built heritage. It is notable that the recognition of the forts by UNESCO came only recently, but tourism had brought visibility and attention to these wonderful monuments much earlier. As visitor attractions, these forts are great examples of the potential of a single attraction that becomes the nucleus for a tourism destination.

A panoramic view of Jaisalmer fort

Case Study: Hill Forts of Rajasthan

Rajasthan is known the world over for its forts and palaces. The forts of Rajasthan are a reminder of the power of the Rajputs, who ruled over large parts of the region for about a

(Continued ...)

thousand years. The princely states were controlled by powerful clans, who built magnificent forts for defence from attacks. Inside, the cities had palaces, market places, temples and residential areas. The forts were mostly built on hills, using the natural features that added to the fortifications. Structures for harvesting water were a common feature. The forts were also known for their patronage of art and culture. Mercantile centres and production centres were the sources of revenue for these forts. These were located at strategic points, controlling trade routes or strategic access points.

Of the numerous forts, six of the most majestic hill forts representing the best forms of architecture and ornamentation, have been listed as World heritage sites in a serial nomination in 2013. These are Jaisalmer, Kumbalgarh, Chittorgarh, Sawai Madhopur (Ranthambore), Amber (Jaipur) and Gagron (Jhalawar). ("8 Marvellous Hill Forts of Rajasthan." n.d.)

Chittorgarh, built over a long period by the Mauryans and later the Sisodiyas, is the largest fort in India, spanning around 700 acres in area. Chittorgarh, with its stories of Rani Padmini and Padmavati, is part of folklore and legends of the land. Kumbalgarh, built by Rana Kumbha in the fifteenth century, has a wall extending for 36 km. Jaisalmer fort is a 'living' fort, with a large part of the town's population still living inside the fort. Amber fort has some excellent examples of Rajput and Mughal architecture. Gagron fort is surrounded by water on three sides, and Ranthambore fort is protected by dense forest.

Source: Trans India Travels, n.d.
Image courtesy: Shutterstock.

Discussion Questions

1. All medieval forts and palaces must be converted to tourist accommodation. Discuss.
2. Discuss the importance of forts in building the brand image of Rajasthan as a tourist destination.

Entertainment Attractions

Attractions exclusively aiming at entertainment such as theme parks and dance shows are a relatively recent and an urban phenomenon. The Walt Disney theme park is an international example, and the numerous water-based theme parks in India attract the domestic visitor. A look at the most popular attractions in the world would go to show that 'iconic' attractions, such as museums and historic sites are losing out to attractions that offer family entertainment and fun. Theme parks have worldwide appeal, and 4 of the 20 most visited attractions in the world are Disney theme parks!

A form of entertainment that has seen brisk growth in recent years is the theme park based on popular films. Special parks and rides are designed based on wildly successful animation series such as Toy Story or Muppets, or globally acclaimed movies such as Star Wars and Pirates of the Caribbean. In India, the 'Bollywood' theme has been used to good effect to create a 'cultural entertainment' destination, the Kingdom of Dreams (KoD) (Table 6.1).

Table 6.1 Most visited attractions of the world

Sl. No.	Attractions	City	Numbers
1	Grand Bazaar	Istanbul	91,250,000
2	The Zocalo	Mexico City	85,000,000
3	Times Square	New York City	50,000,000
4	Central Park	New York City	40,000,000

Sl. No.	Attractions	City	Numbers
5	Union Station	Washington DC	40,000,000
6	The Strip	Las Vegas	30,500,000
7	Meiji Jingu Shrine	Tokyo	30,000,000
8	Sensoji Temple	Tokyo	30,000,000
9	Niagara Falls	Ontario	22,000,000
10	Grand Central Terminal	New York City	21,600,000
11	Basilica of our Lady of Guadalupe	Mexico City	20,000,000
12	Disney World's Magic Kingdom	Orlando Florida	18,588,000
13	Faneuil Hall Marketplace	Boston	18,000,000
14	Disney Land	Tokyo	17,214,000
15	Disneyland Park	Anaheim California	16,202,000
16	Forbidden City	Beijing	15,340,000
17	Golden Gate National Recreation Area	San Francisco	14,289,121
18	Tokyo DisneySea	Tokyo	14,084,000
19	Notre Dame Cathedral	Paris	14,000,000
20	Golden Gate Park	San Francisco	13,000,000

Source: Travel + Leisure, November 2014.

Case Study: Kingdom of Dreams

KoD is a unique visitor attraction, a cultural entertainment park, in Gurgaon, Haryana. KoD brings together a blend of India's culture, heritage, art, crafts, cuisine and performing arts buttressed with technological wizardry. KoD is a tourist destination, providing visitors a breathtaking, magical 'Indian experience'. Visitors get an experience of a selection of Indian cuisine, crafts, musicals, dramas, carnivals, street dances, mythological shows and more at a single location. KoD is a blend of Las Vegas style entertainment and Bollywood, a family entertainment zone with a potpourri of cultural attractions.

The centerpiece of KoD is Nautanki Mahal, the venue for Bollywood style musicals and theatre. Three musicals, *Zangoora*—the gypsy prince—*Jhumroo* and *Abhimanyu*, fastest feet are featured here with daily shows. *Zangoora*—the gypsy Prince is billed as India's answer to Broadway, and has been regularly performed here since 2010. It is the biggest and longest running Bollywood musical ever, combining storytelling and Bollywood style song and dance with stagecraft and technical wizardry. *Zangoora* brings together the best of Bollywood music strung together into a Bollywood potboiler storyline. (Kingdom of Dreams, n.d.)

Culture gully is an air conditioned boulevard, showcasing multifarious Indian cultures, culinary delights and shopping experiences. Cultural gully captures the features of India such as street performers, artisans, magicians, folk dancers, palm reading, tea sipping and much more. The boulevard offers a choice of cuisines from different parts of India.

(Continued ...)

Showshaa theatre presents Indian mythological shows, mock Indian weddings and special events. Lately, the space has changed into a nightclub, with a bar, elevated stage and lounges. The venue is available for product launches, dealers meet, award shows, incentive meets, conferences and other corporate programmes.

Discussion Questions

1. "Urban entertainment centres do not provide 'authentic' cultural experiences; they organize a sanitized version, shorn of natural flavour." Discuss.
2. Make a list of the possible attractions that KoD can add, as part of a strategy to increase visitor numbers.

In India, the most visited built attractions are amusement parks and water theme parks. Amusement parks are designed to offer wholesome entertainment and fun for the family. Most parks have a combination of shows, 'dry' rides, water rides and 'thrilling' rides, with separate sections for children featuring rides and shows aimed at the young visitor. These attractions have become popular day visits for families particularly those living in cities with limited scope for outdoor entertainment. Parks also provide a setting for incentive trips and 'bonding' trips for corporates, and for theme events like birthday or anniversary celebrations. India is yet to popularize theme parks, which are the biggest draws in the West. An exception is Chokhi Dhani, featured in our case study, which effectively used the charms of the village to provide a fun-filled experience.

Case Study: Chokhi Dhani

In 1990, two entrepreneurs set up a venture in Jaipur that was unique in conception and original in execution. Chokhi Dhani, the Rajasthani theme village, offered the visitor a glimpse of village life and culture, in a location just a few kilometres outside the bustling capital city of Rajasthan. The concept was to capture the vibrant spirit of Rajasthan into a 'perfect Rajasthani experience' to be savoured by inbound and domestic tourists.

The 'fair ground' is rich with images of Rajasthan. The walls are filled with *Bani Thani* art, Rajasthani handmade artefacts adorn the rooms and colourful hangings decorate the interiors. Guests are welcomed with fanfare by musicians and dancers dressed in ethnic finery.

Spread across 5 acres of landscaped grounds, Chokhi Dhani welcomes the visitor into a village ambience. Dotted with *machans* (a platform erected in a tree, used originally for hunting large animals and now for watching animals in wildlife reserves) and platforms, the area transforms itself into a festival venue, with folk artistes performing concurrently through the evening. Chokhi Dhani evokes the richness of the villages of Rajasthan, its colour and its rich cultural traditions.

There are rides on an elephant, a camel, a bullock cart or a horse drawn *tonga* (a two-wheeled cart drawn by a horse), which takes them on a round of the 'village'. There are custom made 'hang outs', like the Vaishno Devi temple, the Rathkhana with the traditional *raths* or chariots, a 'cave' for a mystic, the jungle *devta* (a male divine being), the temple for folk hero Veer Tejaji, and huts from Mewar, Registan and Jaisalmer with their unique features. To complete the village feel, there is the traditional water drawing system, the village blacksmith and the ancient method of extracting oil.

There is a rich collection of music, dance and entertainment by folk artistes. At the *Chaupal* (a community space or courtyard in a village), Kalbeliya artistes regale the guests with brisk music and fast body movements. *Bhopa-Bhopi* dancers relate a folk tale and Ghoomer and Bhavai dancers display their amazing talents. There are acrobats, hair masseurs and fire eaters, puppeteers and fortune tellers, an astrologer and a bioscope!.

(Continued ...)

For the children, there is a maze, a waterfall, a jungle themed zone and skill games. An area has been set apart for a display of art and culture of the states of India, complete with actors belonging to that state.

Chokhi Dhani is renowned for its authentic and tasty Rajasthani food, served in traditional style in four restaurants. In the tradition of *manuhaar*, mouth-watering delicacies are served on a leaf platter.

Expanding on the theme, the management opened a theme resort, the Chokhi Dhani village resort, offering modern amenities in a village environment. Rooms and cottages have ethnic designs, with traditional frescoes and wall paintings. There are conferencing and event facilities at the resort.

The village fair and restaurant concept has been taken to seven more cities under the Chokhi Dhani brand, where the core theme of Rajasthani culture and hospitality is retained. Every resort or dining establishment also has an outlet for Rajasthani arts and crafts, branded as Chokhi Dhani Kalagram. The venture has also gone online, with a website from where online purchases of jewellery, accessories, office décor, textiles and furnishings can be made.

Discussion Questions

1. "The concept of the village fair is an effective way to popularize ethnic cuisine and crafts." Discuss.
2. What are the pros and cons of the 'Chokhi Dhani model' of tourism product creation?

Events

Events are temporary attractions, and many events have come to define the destination experience. Most events are specific to a particular location, becoming part of the local culture and evolving into a popular, participative and evocative symbol of popular culture. Spectacular events such as the Carnival of Rio de Janeiro, the La Tomatina festival of Buñol, Spain; and the Pushkar festival in Rajasthan have become major international tourist attractions. There are mega-events such as the Olympics and the Commonwealth Games that move from city to city, attracting visitors to the destinations where they are held. By far the most impressive event is the Kumbh Mela, a staggering collection of humanity that takes place in four holy destinations by turn. Our case study indicates how the Mela is a conglomeration of different kinds of visitors.

Case Study: Kumbh Mela

There is nothing quite like the Kumbh Mela. Every three years, a multitude of people make a visit to a holy town, a pilgrimage that culminates in a dip in a river. The Kumbh Mela is an unparalleled spectacle, a congregation of visitors that move from one place to another, a sequence that has continued for millennia. Xuanzang (Hiuen Tsang), the Chinese monk and explorer, witnessed a Kumbh Mela and recorded it in his diary. The greatest spiritual festival ever held in the world, the world's most massive act of faith.

The 'Kumbh parva' is celebrated four times every 12 years, the site of the observance rotating between four pilgrimage places on four sacred rivers: at Haridwar on the Ganga, at Ujjain on the Shipra, at Nasik on the Godavari and at Prayag (Allahabad) at the confluence of the Ganga, Yamuna and the mythical Saraswati. There are several references to the importance of the Kumbh in ancient texts, which strengthens the belief in pilgrims that a dip in the holy river, at the appropriate time, has the power to cleanse one of all sins. People come from all walks of life, walking long distances and enduring hardship, to receive the benefit of taking a dip in the sacred river at the opportune time.

(Continued ...)

The Mela at Allahabad is considered the holiest, and is termed the 'Maha Kumbh'. Allahabad is considered the second oldest city in India, after Varanasi. It has a rich history dating back to the Mauryan times. The Maha Kumbh is regarded as the largest gathering of humanity on any occasion on earth.

The Kumbh Mela is a great religious and cultural festival as well, marked by a series of events and gatherings. Apart from the significance of the 'dates of the holy bath', the period of the Kumbh Mela is a time for the visitor to witness religious rituals, Vedic rites, the 'satsangs' or religious discourses, celebrations of music and dance and an audience with saints and leaders of holy orders.

On the most auspicious days of the Mela period, the 'Shahi Snan' is conducted, when a sea of humanity takes the holy dip. There is a procession of '*Akharas*', or holy orders, who march to the bathing *ghats* (steps leading to a river or water body, used to get to the water during ritual baths), led by their leaders and saints. On the days of 'Shahi Snan', a procession of different orders can be witnessed, with the saints and leaders of religious orders marching to the appointed bathing ghat, on elephants, horses, chariots, camels and palanquins, and accompanied by fanfare, music and dance.

Township of Tents

The Mela brings in a staggering number of visitors to the city of Allahabad, which calls for meticulous planning and years of preparation by the city administration. A tented city is set up on the banks of the Ganga with an area of around 2,000 ha. For the two months that the Mela lasted (in 2013), the Mela administration had to handle an estimated 90 million visitors, including about 30 million people gathered to take a dip in the water on the day of Mauni Amawasya (10 February 2013). A total of 750 special trains carried pilgrims to and from Allahabad. Nine pontoon bridges were built across the river. Twenty thousand policemen were deployed, and extensive arrangements made for accommodation, water supply, sewage disposal and transport. ("Kumbh Mela 2013," 2013).

The event is a major tourist attraction as well, drawing visitors from over the world. The Mela ground has a bewildering variety of activities. Chanting of Vedic hymns, classical dance and music concerts, display of physical prowess, discourses by religious leaders. A mélange of ornately decorated tents, austere mendicants, Naga sadhus, snake charmers and palm readers roam the tent city. Visitors stay in tents or camps on the banks of the Ganga. Many tour companies offer accommodation in deluxe and luxury tents, and transport guests to the main bathing areas by Jeep or boat. Private audiences with heads of the holy orders are arranged by some tour operators.

Discussion Questions

1. Discuss the advantages and disadvantages of tourism industry using events like the Kumbh Mela to bring in visitors to India.
2. "Casual visitors should not be allowed to visit mass congregations such as Kumbh Mela, as they are an unnecessary addition to the burden of civic authorities." Discuss.

Many destinations try to enhance the drawing power of the attractions by adding on events. These are called complementary attractions. The Konarak dance festival is a good example of an overlay of an event over an attraction. The event has created a brand identity in the market based on the location of the festival, and the marketing of the event has brought the historical site more visibility and attention.

Conclusion

In a dynamic and fast changing world of tourism, destinations have to keep 'reinventing' themselves in order to retain visitors and to attract new ones. Increasing the attractiveness of tourist sites is an important investment for destination managers. Tourist attractions need to be made more appealing by appropriate changes in technology, modification of offerings and enhancement of facilities. Ownership of attractions and involvement of the stakeholders in their management are important elements. Looking into the future, attractions that focus on family experiences in a convenient location will continue to be popular, as will theme parks and entertainment centres.

Review Questions

1. Examine the important features of natural and man-made attractions. Do you think that they need specific strategies for promoting sustainable business?
2. 'Visitor management is fundamental in promoting sustainable tourism'. Discuss.
3. Discuss the rules laid down for conservation and protection of natural sites in India.

Activities

1. Prepare a database of natural attractions in your state focusing on type, location, distance from airport, nearest railway station, facilities available and uniqueness, if any.
2. Make an assessment of cultural tourism in your state and organize a workshop to explore the possibilities of developing cultural tourism. Based on the outcome of the workshop, develop suitable packages.
3. Identify the rural evens that are regularly taking place in your state and suggest measures for linking them with tourism business.
4. Organize a quiz competition for college students on the tourism attractions of your state.
5. Conduct a painting competition on various natural attractions in your state inviting students from neighbouring colleges. Exhibit the same in the auditorium and explain each painting in detail from a tourism perspective to the visitors.
6. Visit an archaeological site and prepare a report on the measures taken by authorities for its conservation during the last ten years.

References

Books

Bandarin, F. (2005). Foreword. In D. Harrison & M. Hitchock (eds.). 'Foreword'. In *The Politics of World Heritage: Negotiating Tourism and Conservation*, edited by D. Harrison and M. Hitchock. Clevedon: Multilingual Matters.

Johan Edalheim, J. R. (2015). *Tourist Attractions: From Object to Narrative*. Canada: Channel View Publications.

Leask, A. (2010). 'Progress in Visitor Attraction Research: Towards more Effective Management'. *Tourism Management*, 31(2): 155–166.

Leiper, N. (1995). *Tourism Management* Tourism Management. Melbourne: RMIT Publishing.

UNEP, MAP, and PAP. 1997. 'Guidelines for Carrying Capacity Assessment for Tourism in the Mediterranean Coastal Areas'. Split.

Wanhill, S., A. Fyall, B. Garrod, and A. Leask. (2008). *Managing Visitor Attractions: New Directions*, 2nd Edition. Oxford: Butterworth-Heinemann.

Yale, P. (2004). *From Tourist Attractions to Heritage Tourism*. ELM Publications.

Web Resources

Kingdom of Dreams. (n.d.). Available at: http://www.kingdomofdreams.in/ (accessed on 18 June 2016).

Kumbh Mela (2013). Available at: http://kumbhmelaallahabad.gov.in/english/for_sanstha.html (accessed on 22 December 2016).

Taj Mahal. (n.d.). Available at: http://whc.unesco.org/en/list/252 (accessed on 22 December 2016).

Trans India Travels. n.d. '8 Marvellous Hill Forts of Rajasthan. (n.d.). Available at: http://www.transindiatravels.com/rajasthan/hill-forts (accessed on 22 December 2016).

Travel+Leisure. n.d. Available at: http://www.travelandleisure.com/slideshows/worlds-most-visited-tourist-attractions/22 (accessed on 12 June 2016).

Suggested Reading

Book

Richards, G. (2001). *Cultural Attractions and European Tourism*. Oxon: CABI.

The Golden Temple, Amritsar
Image courtesy: Ministry of Tourism, Government of India.

CHAPTER 7

Accommodation

Learning Objectives

By the end of this chapter, students will be able to:

- Distinguish between different types of accommodation.
- Clarify the business significance of accommodation.
- Illustrate the organizational structure of a hotel.
- List the job positions and functions in hotels.
- Categorise the operating models in the accommodation sector.
- Analyse the classification systems in hotels.

Introduction

In the picturesque town of Udaipur, a traveller is spoilt for choices when it comes to accommodation options. The Taj Lake Palace looks like it is floating in the Lake Pichola. On the banks of the lake are the Oberoi Udaivilas and the Leela Palace, two of the most luxurious hotels in the country. They are also extremely expensive—rooms and suites at these grand properties are priced at over ₹20,000 per night during the peak season. Just a stone's throw away, in the alleyways of the old city, a budget traveller can find a comfortable room for under ₹1,000. The city offers a wide range of accommodation to suit every pocket, attracting visitors ranging from price conscious back packers to the guest who is happy to pay a premium price if the experience is just right.

This is the accommodation sector, with a dizzying array of offerings, the largest component in the tourism system. The sector is characterized by its heterogeneity, as seen above—a variety of establishments different in type and size, all aiming to offer the tourist a place to rest and stay, while on holiday or on business.

In this chapter, we will seek an overview of the accommodation sector, the range of accommodation options available and the definitions of widely used technical terms. The issues related to the sector, such as classification of properties, management models and impacts on the economy will also be explored.

The development of a range of accommodation is one of the important strategies for development of destinations. Although the tourist may not choose to visit a destination in order to experience a particular hotel, the quality of the accommodation available will influence the decision of the visitor to choose the destination for her holiday. Accommodation is integral to the tourism product differentiation and plays an important role in bringing tangible economic benefits to the destination and the community.

Accommodation may be used as an interesting component by designing packages in destinations offering specific activities that are the main source of revenue. For example, in a hotel where the in-house casino is the main attraction, tourists may be offered accommodation at very low rates, in order to encourage them to spend their money at the casino.

Categories of Accommodation

One may come across with the different categories of accommodation discussed hereafter.

Commercial and Non-commercial Accommodation

If one stays at a friend's residence or with a relation at a destination, the accommodation is said to be non-commercial in nature, as no financial transaction for the stay takes place. In India, there are several familiar examples of non-commercial accommodation. Many organizations offer complimentary lodging facilities, popularly called *dharamsalas* (rest house for travellers), for visitors in pilgrimage destinations. Other examples of non-commercial accommodation are shelters for indigent persons, hostels and temporary dormitory accommodation for visiting student groups or student sports teams.

Any temporary accommodation arrangement that involves a commercial consideration and is done on an organized basis is termed commercial accommodation. This term encompasses a range of products and services.

Serviced Accommodation

Serviced accommodation implies that certain services, in addition to lodging, are provided by the accommodation provider. Accommodation arrangements, where housekeeping services such as room cleaning, bed-making and change of linen are provided by the business owner are included, come under service accommodation. A variety of additional services, such as room service, laundry, messaging, concierge and business centre may be available for the use of the customer within the establishment. Hotels, motels, bed-and-breakfast accommodation, guesthouses and inns come under serviced accommodation. This sector can be further subdivided into full service accommodation and partially serviced accommodation, depending on the range of services provided to guests.

Non-serviced Accommodation

In contrast to serviced accommodations, there are some commercial accommodation arrangements where the operator does not provide any services to the guest, other than providing the room for occupancy. Non-serviced accommodation is a form of accommodation where the customer uses a facility without the expectation of services as part of the price. Such accommodation units are also called self-catering accommodation. Cottages, apartments, rented homes and rented rooms in a family house are examples of this type. Some operators provide limited accommodation support, like sites used by campers, trailers and mobile home owners.

Types of Accommodation

Hotels

A simple definition of a hotel is that it is an establishment that provides travellers' overnight accommodation and guest services, such as meals and drinks, for a price. Hotels come in a great variety, depending on the amenities, location, size and quality. Hotels are classified into one, two, three, four and five stars by the official classification authority. According to the clientele, location and amenities, hotels are further divided as leisure hotels, business hotels, budget hotels, 'no frills' hotels, resorts and so on. While early days of hoteliering was dominated by small, family-run establishments, the market today is increasingly moving towards consolidation under big branded hotel groups who offer different products to market segments, and manage and market hotels using new models, as we will see later in the chapter.

Business hotel: Business hotels are located typically in the business district or close to business centres and cater to business travellers. These hotels provide facilities for conducting business, such as boardrooms, conference and meeting facilities, business centres with photocopy, fax, Wi-Fi and high-speed Internet access.

Design hotel, boutique hotel: Design hotels give emphasis on style, and have an overall design language, which is expressed in the spatial design, furniture, furnishings, colour and cuisine. Boutique hotels are also design-led small properties which offer luxurious and personalized service, emphasizing their distinction from larger branded properties. These hotels are oriented to attract young, fashionable guests who are willing to pay a premium for aesthetics, high levels of personalized service and attention to detail.

Resorts: While the original meaning of the word 'resort' is a destination, it has come to mean a hotel located in a leisure tourism destination offering extensive guest facilities, recreation and full service. In the Caribbean, many 'all inclusive' and 'destination' resorts became quite popular some time ago because they offered rooms, meals, drinks and activities for an inclusive price. These resorts aimed at providing the guests with all they needed within their premises, encouraging them to spend their entire vacation, and their money, within the resort itself.

Motels: The term motel originates from the words *mo*tor and ho*tel*. Motels are basic hotels typically situated on the sides of highways, with ample parking areas and facilities to sleep overnight. Motels were initially designed as simple buildings with the doors of the rooms facing a parking lot, ideal for motorists to park their cars and have an inexpensive overnight stay. Motels offering guest rooms and little else, were quite popular in the 1950s and 1960s, when a network of highways were built in the United States and private car ownership and long distance travel became popular. In many motels, the reception was placed outside the main building, so that the registration could be done when the motorist drove in, and the motel owner could keep an eye on the number of passengers in the car. Motels have become more sophisticated and added facilities like a diner, bar, gas station and swimming pool have become common.

Hostels: A hostel is a relatively inexpensive type of temporary accommodation, offering basic lodging and limited facilities. Popular with students, backpackers and budget travellers, hostels typically have shared bedrooms, common bathrooms and basic kitchenettes to do your own cooking. 'Youth hostels' were very popular in Europe, as it was customary for youngsters to travel widely after finishing high school. Hostels offer the opportunity for social encounters between guests and provide common areas to socialize and interact. Recently, hostels have started providing a degree of comfort that bring them into competition with budget hotels.

Bed and breakfast (B&B): B&Bs are small, family-run accommodation, with breakfast included in the price. Many B&Bs function like paying guest accommodation. A 'pension' is a type of B&B run by a family, offering lunch and dinner in addition to breakfast. B&Bs and pensions are popular with budget travellers, although the family atmosphere and the prospect of spending time with the host are becoming increasingly attractive to a segment of tourists looking for authenticity rather than comfort. Home stays, which are quite ubiquitous in some destinations like Goa and Kerala, offer the same kind of experience, with an opportunity to share the lifestyle of a local family.

Inns: An inn is a small establishment in a traditional setting, offering comfortable accommodation, food and drink to visitors. In Europe and Canada, inns are undergoing a makeover in line with market requirements. Inns in England have become popular tourist accommodation; thanks to smart market positioning and attractive offers. Inns come in different sizes and shapes—old coaching inns, thatched and timbered inns and country houses—and in different locales like the seaside or a market town, providing a taste of country hospitality in a setting rich in history.

Lodge: Although the word lodge is used for basic budget accommodation establishments, it originally referred to a house in a rural environment used seasonally by visitors with specific interests, like hunting, angling and skiing.

Mansion, Villa, Cottage, Chalet, Chateau: These are different kinds of houses that may be available for short stays to tourists in destinations. Most of these are offered to the guest on a self-catering basis. A mansion is a large house in a rural environment built in a typical architectural style. A cottage is a small house typically in a rural area. Chalets are wooden cottages in mountain and ski resorts. A villa is a luxurious country residence, but nowadays used to refer to a detached suburban house. A chateau is a French country house, usually in a vineyard. A manor is an English country house formerly owned by nobility.

Castles and palaces: A castle is a fortified building complex, built during the mediaeval period. Castles across Europe have been converted into luxurious accommodation for upmarket tourists. A palace is a residence of royalty, with grand furnishings and opulent settings. Some palaces have been transformed to luxury hotels, particularly in Italy and India.

A mansion in Dungarpur

Case Study: Historic Resort Hotels (HRH) Group of Hotels

HRH is a hotel group operating a chain of heritage properties. HRH is the only chain of heritage palace-hotels and resorts under private ownership. Headquartered in Udaipur, capital of

(Continued ...)

the erstwhile Mewar, the HRH group manages many palaces and properties of the Royal family of Mewar. Led by Sri Arvind Singh Mewar, Chairman and Managing Director of the group, HRH provides a 'seamless experience of heritage tourism, edutainment, adventure and spirituality' and experience of the living heritage of Rajasthan. Guests get an opportunity to enjoy the authentic and original heritage of Rajasthan while staying in the palaces and royal retreats of the HRH group of hotels.

The Fateh Prakash palace, built by the Maharana Fateh Singh (r. 1884–1930) as an exclusive venue for royal functions, is located on the eastern shores of the picturesque Pichola Lake, and is adorned with miniature paintings, portraits, royal artefacts and arms. The Shiv Niwas palace, built by the Maharana for visiting dignitaries and guests of the House of Mewar, has been converted to a hotel with a royal ambience, combing the elegance of the last century with modern twenty-first century amenities. The Jagmandir island palace is a historic seventeenth century structure redeveloped as a destination for ceremonial parties and mega events. Situated in the lake, the palace offers a restaurant, all day café, bar, spa and a museum. Shikarbadi, the royal hunting lodge, has been converted into a 'royal retreat' for guests to enjoy the wildlife and the rolling Aravalli hills. The Gajner palace, built by the Bikaner maharaja as a hunting resort during the British raj, was visited by many dignitaries, who partook in the Imperial Sand Grouse shoots during Christmas season. It is now a heritage hotel exuding the aura of a bygone age. Other properties include the 1940's art deco Karni Bhawan palace in Bikaner, the reconstructed Fateh Bagh at Ranakpur and the contemporary The Aodhi, Kumbalgarh and Gorbandh palace, Jaisalmer.

The HRH group arranges for 'regal experiences' for the MICE segment and 'regal weddings' in royal splendor. It also offers several attractions such as the Mewar light and sound show, the vintage and classic car museum, the crystal gallery, the City Palace museum, boat rides and boutique shops in Udaipur.

Discussion Questions

1. Give examples of heritage mansions in your town that have the potential to be converted as heritage properties.
2. 'Heritage properties do not provide an "authentic" experience of Rajasthan, but they aim to recreate a past that was feudal and elitist'. Discuss this statement.

Image courtesy: Department of Tourism, Government of Rajasthan.

Apartments: Apartments are self-contained accommodation units housed in multi-storied buildings having a number of such units. In tourist destinations, apartments are available for temporary accommodation, on serviced or non-serviced basis. Serviced apartments that are offered to travellers for extended periods are often called apart-hotels. A penthouse is an apartment on the highest floor of the building, usually stand-alone, having luxury fittings and amenities. Penthouses are available for temporary accommodation to upscale customers in some destinations.

Recreational vehicle (RV): RVs are outfitted with bathroom, sleeping facilities and kitchen, functioning as mobile houses. Recreational Vehicles, also called campers or caravans, are popular in the USA and Europe, where many travellers prefer to take a holiday on the road, and facilities for camping are conveniently available.

Time share: The classical time share scheme is that the customer purchases a period—typically a week or its multiples—in a property, retaining the right to use the unit annually, for a number of years. The 'owner' can split the number of days, gift the period or sell the entire time period, depending on the lease agreement signed. The owner is entitled to exchange his period with another person and take a holiday in any of the properties run by the time share company based on the agreed terms and conditions.

Mobile accommodation: We have already become familiar with RVs, which is preferred by people who love to be on the road. Many other forms of temporary accommodation which is mobile are found the world over. The most common are the cruise vessels and the house-boats. Cruises can be 'fly and cruise' where people fly into a departure port and board a cruise vessel for their holiday, or 'cruise and stay' where guests add a few days after the cruise is over to spend time at a destination of their choice. Many river cruises are quite popular, particularly in Europe and on the Nile River.

A Kerala homestay

Case Study: Homestays in Kerala

The Homestays of Kerala have introduced new dimensions for holidaying in Kerala, combining an authentic experience of the destination and an unorthodox form of accommodation. This modified form of bread and breakfast has been developed with the participation of the residents, who are willing to invite tourists to their homes, enabling them to share experiences related to the traditions and lifestyle of Kerala. The distinctive architectural style of the traditional houses—the *tharavads, manas* ([plural of *Mana*] are residences of the *Namboothiris*, a Brahmin caste in Kerala) *and illams*—is characterized by the *kettu* (portion), earmarked for specific purposes of the family. These large residences are being converted into accommodation units, opening avenues for tourists to experience the rich heritage of the villages, imbibing age-old customs in an ambience that was hitherto unavailable to the outsiders. Theme-based homestays focusing on traditional practices like Ayurveda, martial arts, performing arts and music are also emerging. Houses located on farms, outskirts of forests and scenic locations provide a homely platform for enjoying leisure holidays.

Olappamanna Mana located in Palakkad district is one of the oldest *namboothiri manas* in Kerala with a history of more than 300 years. This *mana* is renowned for its architectural design, and for its patronage of arts and letters such as Kathakali, classical music and Vedic

(Continued ...)

and Sanskrit learning. By maintaining its traditional style and typical Kerala ambience, the *mana* provides an accommodation milieu that is unparalleled.

Kandath Tharavadu, a homestay located in Thenkurussi Village in Palakkad district, is a stately house set amongst lush rice paddy fields. It is a two hundred year old gem of traditional architecture—*Ettukettu*—constructed primarily of mud and teak. Tourists enjoy their holiday amid a traditional agricultural homestead, with old household utensils, agricultural implements and ethnic food.

Olavipe homestay is situated in the backdrop of backwaters in Alappuzha district. Set in the middle of a working farm with a mixed produce and livestock ranging from coconuts, pepper, nutmeg, cinnamon, areca nut, flowers, vegetables, fruits, prawns, fish, cows and goats, this homestay shares traditional Christian values and heritage along with ethnic cuisine.

Philipkutty's farm located close to Kumarakom also has an ambience blended with agriculture, village life and scenic beauty. Here, the guests can try their hand in traditional farming practices, cooking classes on village dishes and producing organic farm products.

Ayesha Manzil in Kannur district has acquired fame for its mouth-watering Malabar cuisine featuring traditional Muslim delicacies. The hostess of the homestay, a culinary expert holds cooking lessons as part of the holiday package. The colonial style house with period furniture has great views of the Arabian Sea.

The success of the homestay concept in Kerala has spurred many entrepreneurs to convert their residences to accommodate visitors. Government of Kerala has set up an approval system for homestays with the specific objective of enabling the local community to become a part of the tourism growth story, while laying down quality standards that provide a benchmark for the tourism industry.

Image courtesy: Department of Tourism, Government of Kerala.

Discussion Questions

1. What are the reasons for the attractiveness of a homestay over comfortable hotel accommodation?
2. List the ways a homestay can market itself to tour operators and tourists.

Organizational Structure and Functions in Hotels

Let us look at the various activities of a hotel from the point of view of a guest. The hotel is where she stays for a short period of time, having arrived at the destination for business or pleasure. The hotel is central to the guests' stay in the destination, giving them a place to rest, relax and conduct their business. They may choose to meals at the hotel, either in the room or in a cafe or restaurant within the hotel. For business, they may work from their room or the business centre, conduct meetings and discussion or attend a conference or event at the hotel. While they stay in the hotel, the guest may want to visit the fitness centre or relax in the swimming pool or the spa. They may seek the guidance of the hotel staff to make reservations at a theatre or to manage their return flight bookings. In the privacy of the room, they may unwind with a hot bath or relax watching a movie on the entertainment system. The staff in the different divisions of the hotel attends to their needs, united in the objective of making the guests feel comfortable and relaxed during their stay.

A hotel is a complex organization, with multifarious operations involving many teams with different skill sets. While we need to get into detailed functioning of the hotel, as it is the domain of accommodation management, it is important for the student of tourism to have an overview of the operations in a hotel.

Functionally, the operations of a hotel can be divided into two—front of house and back of house. 'Front of house' operations involve those departments that come into direct contact and interaction with the guests and visitors to the hotel. The first point of contact is generally a member of the reservations team, who books a room for the guest before the arrival. Upon arrival, the guest is welcomed to the hotel by the reception team and the luggage transferred into the hotel. The front office is where the guest checks into the hotel and is allocated a room and issued a room key. The guest is led to the allocated room, which has been prepared by the housekeeping team, which will also ensure periodic cleaning of the room and refilling of the consumables. The concierge manages the luggage of the guests, takes messages and assists the guest with directions and making reservations. The room service team brings food and beverage (F&B) to the guest in the room, while the staffs in the restaurant and bar look after other needs in these areas. Guest's food and drink are prepared in the kitchen by the food production team.

As can be seen from the above, the 'front of house' operations encompass the following broad divisions:

1. Rooms division
   - Front office security
   - Concierge
   - Reservations
2. Food and beverage division
   - Kitchen
   - Restaurants
   - Room service
   - Bars and lounges
   - Banqueting
3. Sales and marketing division
4. Housekeeping division

'Back of house' operations refer to those divisions which do not come in direct contact with the guest. While these divisions perform vital operations, they serve to support the 'front of house' by ensuring and maintaining quality service delivery. The 'back of house' operations are as follows:

1. Engineering division
   - Electrical and electronics
   - Plumbing
   - Civil engineering
   - Horticulture
2. Human resources division
   - Recruitment
   - Training
   - Payroll and benefits
3. Accounting division

Front office: All activities taking place in the front of the guest is included under Front Office operations. These include meet and greet services, reception, luggage services, concierge, check-in and cash counters. The first people to meet the guests (check-in) and the last people to see them off (check-out) are from the front office operations, which is why this division is critical to the image of the hotel. Friendly and efficient front office staffs put the guest at ease and provide a positive experience at the beginning of the stay. From welcoming them to the hotel, checking them in to dealing with complaints, the front office performs a range of functions in close contact with the guests (see Table 7.1; Figure 7.1).

Food and beverage: The elaborate and sensitive activity of preparing food for the guests and visitors and its service through the outlets of the hotel or to the guest rooms comes under F&B. Generally, the processes of food production and F&B services are considered as part of the same activity. The division is responsible for sourcing raw materials and ingredients, food preparation, crockery and cutlery, bakery operations and presentation. Maintenance of hygiene standards in the kitchen and related areas is an important function. The outlets providing F&Bs are managed by the F&B service personnel. These include the restaurants, bars, coffee shops, bakery, cafe and lounges. The division is also responsible for catering and banqueting for the events and conferences in the hotel (Figure 7.2).

The sales and marketing: This division is responsible for revenue generation. The division works with tour operators, events' organizers and distribution systems in order to ensure maximum sales of the room inventory and confirmation of banquets and conferences which provide substantial revenues to the hotel. The sales team is responsible for yielding management, analysing various revenue streams and adopting diverse strategies to generate revenue and maintain growth.

Housekeeping division: This is responsible for the up-keeping of the rooms and fulfilling the requirements of guests in terms of linen, toiletries and in-room materials. The housekeeping also keeps an eye on all facilities within the rooms, such as electrical fittings, bathroom fittings, electronic appliances and supplies.

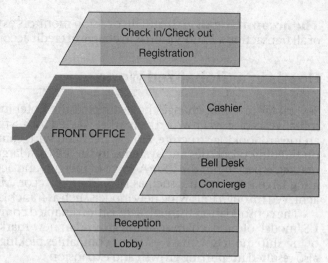

Figure 7.1 Front office division
Source: Authors.

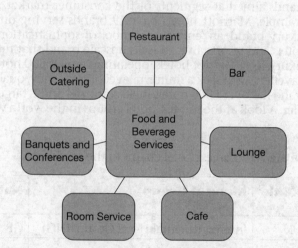

Figure 7.2 Food and beverages service division
Source: Authors.

The engineering division: It supervises all repairs and maintenance activities and is responsible for continuously inspecting and monitoring engineering elements in the hotel. The division also plans for periodic replacement and servicing of machines and equipment. All major renovation of the hotel is also the responsibility of the engineering division.

The human resource division: This division provides adequate staff to all operating divisions and is responsible for recruitment of staff at all levels. The HR division coordinates important staff related activities such as in-service training, career progression, payroll, incentives and performance assessment.

The accounting division: This division monitors expenditure and maintains the accounts of all transactions. The division is in charge of credit accounts, cash flow, loans and investments.

Hotels in a Globalized World

Several far reaching changes have affected the hotel industry in the last few decades. In the initial years of slow growth, the market was led by 3–5 firms, most of which had single brands, an inward looking structure, closely held and with cautious growth strategies concentrating on building properties and systems. In the 1980s, a large number of new players entered the market, especially in the USA. A wave of mergers and acquisitions took place in the 1990s, creating large hotel entities such as HFS, Choice, Accor, Marriott and Hilton. Rapid growth was achieved through following new models such as franchising, as will be explained subsequently.

The consolidation through acquisition enabled companies to expand worldwide, with the US 'model' of hotel chains gaining ground in new markets such as China and India. The new ownership models with investment companies picking up equity in traded hotel companies also resulted in spurring growth and expansion.

It is estimated that there are around 20 million rooms in the accommodation sector worldwide. A large part of this inventory is operated by branded hotel groups, which together manage about 8 million rooms. Major international groups operate hotels under different brands aimed at segments of the consumer market, with varying brand 'propositions'. For example, Marriott hotels have 19 brands serving different segments. The Ritz Carlton is a luxury brand, an 'enduring symbol of sophistication, style and legendary service', with 80 hotels and resorts. Bvlgari is an upscale brand that retains a 'distinctly Italian contemporary luxury feel'. Marriot hotels, operating in over 500 hotels across the world, are aimed at global travellers, who seek a uniform level of efficiency, quality service and comfort. The Courtyard brand has over 1,000 hotels in 40 countries and is targeted at the price conscious business traveller. A look at the top-ten hotel groups in the world will make this picture clear (Table 7.1).

Table 7.1 Largest hotel chains in the world

Rank	Name of Group	Nationality	Number of hotels	Number of rooms
1	Intercontinental Hotel Group (IHG)	GB	4,697	686,873
2	Hilton Worldwide	USA	4,115	678,630
3	Marriott International	USA	3,783	653,719
4	Wyndham Hotel Group	USA	7,485	645,423
5	Choice Hotels and Resorts	USA	6,303	502,663
6	Accor	France	3,576	461,719
7	Starwood Hotels and Resorts	USA	1,161	339,243
8	Best Western	USA	4,046	314,318
9	Home Inns	China	2,180	256,555
10	Carlson Rezidor Hotel Group	USA	1,079	168,927

Source: 2014 Global Hotel Rankings: The Leaders Grow Stronger, IHG Retain Top Spot (2014).

Marriott International recently acquired Starwood hotels and resorts worldwide. The companies announced that they have approved the merger arrangement which will create the world's largest hotel company. Combined, the company will operate or franchise more than 5,500 hotels with 1.1 million rooms worldwide. The new company will have a portfolio of 30 hotel brands in all segments. The merger of two of the largest hotel companies in the world is part of the trend of consolidation, mergers and acquisitions in the travel and hospitality industry.

Case Study: Marriott International

The story of Marriott is a saga of how a small outlet selling root beer grew into one of the biggest hotel companies in the world. The founder of the group J.W. Marriott and his wife Alice opened a root beer franchise in Washington DC in 1927, and later added hot food items in the menu. The newly branded 'Hot Shoppes' rapidly grew in number. In 1957, their first hotel was opened in Arlington, Virginia under the management of J.W. Marriott's son Bill. The group expanded cautiously, opening its first international hotel in Acapulco, Mexico in 1959 and the first Courtyard hotel in 1983. In the 1980s, Marriott began diversifying and creating more brands. It opened the first Fairfield Inn and Marriott Suites hotels, acquired Residence Inn and opened its 500th hotel in Warsaw, Poland in 1988. In 1995, Marriott acquired the historic brand the Ritz-Carlton, and doubled its presence overseas by acquiring the Renaissance Hotel group. This was followed by the rapid addition of many new brands by acquisition, such as the Gaylord Hotels and the Protea Hotels. In its latest mega acquisition, Marriott has announced the takeover of Sherwood hotels, one of the biggest hotel groups in the world, to form what will be the world's biggest hotel company (*New York Times*, 2015).

Marriott has over 4,100 properties in 85 countries, spread across a huge portfolio of 19 brands. Marriott International reported revenues of nearly $14 billion in 2014 (equal to ₹94,000 crores) and employs close to 200,000 people. Marriott Rewards Program, the guest loyalty program of the company has 54 million members, the largest in the world.

Marriott International operates and franchises hotels under the following brands:

Iconic Luxury	Entertainment/Destinations
• The Ritz-Carlton hotel company • Bvlgari Hotels and Resorts	• Gaylord Hotels
Luxury • JW Marriott Hotels	**Signature** • Marriott Hotels
Lifestyle/Collections • EDITION • Autograph collection • Renaissance Hotels • AC Hotels • Moxy Hotels	**Extended Stay** • Residence Inn by Marriott • TownePlace Suites • Marriott Executive Apartments
Modern Essentials • Courtyard by Marriott • SpringHill Suites by Marriott • Fairfield Inn and Suites By Marriott	**Vacation Clubs** • Marriott Vacation Club • Grand Residences by Marriott • The Ritz-Carlton Destination Club

The Ritz-Carlton Hotel Company, with 86 hotels worldwide in 29 countries and 35,000 employees, was purchased by the Marriott in 1983. The luxury brand has extensions into spa development, golf and the Ritz-Carlton destination club.

(Continued ...)

JW Marriott hotels and resorts is Marriott International's luxury brand consisting of 76 properties in gateway cities and resort locations. The attributes of the brand include dramatic and distinctive architectural and interior features, spacious guestrooms with luxurious appointments and amenities, fitness centres and spas with state-of-the-art equipment and a large complement of staff.

The Autograph Collection is a new brand of more than 60 independent hotels, comprising an array of properties ranging from a 15 room hunting lodge in the mountains of Colorado (Kessler Canyon) to a 3,000 room luxury casino on the Las Vegas strip (the Cosmopolitan). This collection of independent properties gets the benefit of the power of the global sales and marketing channels of Marriott, while the franchisees offer 'passionately independent' hotel experiences.

Renaissance Hotels is a Lifestyle brand with a motto of 'Live Life to Discover' and has nearly 170 hotels in 40 countries. Appealing to the business traveller who wants to discover something new, Renaissance announces its brand values as 'intriguing, indigenous and independent'.

Moxy Hotels is positioned to attract the millennial traveller, defined by attitude, lively and young at heart. With a multipurpose public space with a live Instagram wall, 24/7 café, music and cocktails in the evening, functional rooms and free Wi-Fi, the hotel aims to surprise budget conscious travellers with a thoughtful, spirited and fun guest experience.

Courtyard by Marriott is the 'upper moderate' tier brand of the group, with more than 950 hotels in 38 countries. The brand aims to attract the business travellers, who prefer a 'smart, dynamic hotel that helps them make the most of their time on the road'. The hotels have extensive features for conducting business, stylish public spaces, swimming pool and fitness centres.

Residence Inn by Marriott is a dominant brand in the extended stay hotel segment. Over 650 all suite properties serve the needs of the business travellers seeking apartment style accommodation for longer stays. Suites are larger than hotel rooms and come equipped with full kitchens with utensils, flatware and china, refrigerator, microwave, coffeemaker, dishwasher and cook top. Suites have separate work and sleeping areas, high speed Internet access and free Wi-Fi. There are useful services like self-serve F&B pantries and free grocery delivery.

Its e-commerce initiatives are remarkable, with Marriott.com having 44 million visitors per month, making it the world's largest lodging website. In 2013, approximately 45% of the gross sales of Marriott came through electronic channels. Mariette's proprietary global reservation system generated more than 100 million reservations. In nearly 500 Marriott hotels around the world, a guest can check-in and check-out on the mobile phone.

Discussion Questions

1. Why does Marriott International maintain so many brands? Discuss.
2. What are the advantages of taking the acquisition route, rather than building own hotels?
3. Discuss the pros and cons of big hotel groups vis-à-vis locally owned small accommodation units.

Operating Models in Accommodation

For business purpose, several operating models have been envisaged in the accommodation sector. The main operating models in the hotel sector are discussed below.

Owned/leased properties: Hotels are owned or leased by the hotel group and managed and marketed under one of their brands. This is the traditional model of running hotels, and all the established international hotel groups began operations by owning hotels and resorts. However, given the capital intensive nature of the model, companies are moving away from ownership and adopting 'lighter' models with little or no equity exposure. Among the large hotel chains, the Accor group is the only one which continues this model, with a large number of its properties owned or leased by the company.

Management contracts: This is a common model adopted by most branded hotel companies. A hotel owner, called the 'investor owner', gets into an agreement with a hotel company or 'operator' to run the hotel, based on a contract that sets out the details of the arrangement. It is common for investment companies like equity funds and institutional investors to invest in hotels, based on their assessment of the potential of such investments. These 'owners' do not have expertise to operate hotels, and prefer to bring in a professional companies with proven expertise and established sales and marketing channels to manage the hotel. Global brands have expanded operations in this space and get involved in hotel projects at the construction stage itself, providing inputs on prototype designs, interiors and design strategies and assisting in procurement. This involvement also enables brand integrity and improves efficiency. Typically, the management contract is signed for a period not less than 10 years and provide for fees to be paid to the operator such as a 'base' fee, a percentage of the gross revenue, and an 'incentive' fee which is based on exceeding agreed targets. The operator guarantees, assuring the owner of a fund flow or profit. Typically, the owner is responsible for maintenance of the asset and for major capital expenditure.

Franchise: The franchise model is when the hotel is managed by the owner under the umbrella of an established brand. The owner aims to obtain cost-effective access to clientele without entering the market on his own, and enters into a relationship with a known brand to operate the hotel under that brand. This is a popular model leveraging the strength of a well-known brand, giving the assurance of quality service experience and consistency, while retaining control of operations in the hands of the owner. The franchisee owns and operates the hotel, with the hotel group, or 'franchiser' looking after sales and marketing, staff training, standard operating procedures and management information and reservation systems. The franchisee pays a franchise fee, normally linked to the number of rooms in the hotel, to the franchiser for the use of the brand's logo and goodwill, and for the systems and marketing. The hotel group may insist on the hotel using materials such as towels, toiletries, stationery and brochures with the brand of the group, After the initial fee, the franchiser also collects continuing fees, such as a royalty, advertising fee and reservation fee. The group is also responsible for monitoring hotel quality, performance and customer feedback. A franchise model works in mature markets where the expertise to manage hotels is available outside the fold of hotel groups.

Many international hotel brands have powered their growth on the strength of the franchise model. IHG group operates 4,000 hotels, 85% of their total inventory, under franchise agreements. The group runs around 700 hotels (15%) on management contract basis and only own or lease 7 hotels (less than 1%). This 'asset light' approach is preferred by hotel groups as the arrangement leaves them to focus on building the brand and improving marketing.

The Accommodation Sector and the Economy

How does the accommodation sector impact the economy? Tourism, including the accommodation sector, contributes significantly to the economy of many countries. It provides employment to large numbers of persons and provides tax revenue to the government. The goods and services purchased by the sector are extensive and from many parts of the economy, and the payment for such goods and services pump more money into the local and regional economy. Purchases made by the employees from the incomes they obtain from the accommodation sector also benefit the economy. This is known as the cascade effect.

There are many channels through which hospitality industry impacts the economy.

Direct impacts: Direct employment, value added tax (VAT), excise and customs duties, income tax and corporate tax.

Indirect impacts: Employment created as a result of hotels and restaurants purchasing goods and services; manufacture of F&Bs; transporting goods to hospitality units.

Induced impacts: The employees spend their incomes purchasing goods and services, stimulating employment; consumption of consumer goods.

A 'multiplier effect' is the factor of indirect and induced effect created in the supply chain.

Employment Generation and Accommodation

The tourism sector is extremely labour intensive and is a major source of employment in destinations. Tourism is one sector that creates the maximum number of jobs, particularly at the skilled level, absorbing large numbers of young persons, women and migrant workers into its fold. Employment in the sector is quite diverse. Apart from direct employment in jobs that are in hotels—like food production, housekeeping, sales and marketing and front office—many jobs are indirectly dependent on the sector, such as taxi drivers, tourist guides and souvenir shop owners. Employment in the sector may be permanent, temporary, part-time or seasonal, depending on the type of accommodation, the destination and tourist arrivals. A large majority of employees in the sector are below 35 years and a good percentage is of women. Increasingly, jobs are being subcontracted or outsourced, leading to insecurity and diminished responsibility on the part of the employer. The irregular working hours, low wages and insecurity are major reasons for the large turnover rate in the sector, with estimates indicating that about 70% of hospitality graduates leave the industry within six years of graduation. A high attrition rate, in turn, leads to labour fluctuation, lack of skilled workers and aberrations in service quality.

Accommodation and Hospitality

Although the terms are often used interchangeably, these are two different sectors, with a large overlap. Hospitality industry includes:

- The provision of accommodation, meals and beverages (hotels and other accommodation).
- Restaurants—including coffee shops, cafeterias, takeaway food outlets, mobile food outlets, pubs, bars and clubs.
- Catering—including air catering, corporate catering, in house catering in establishments such as hospitals and college hostels.
- Event catering—for conferences and meetings.

The hospitality industry services tourists, excursionists and residents. But the impact of the industry is similar to that of the tourism sector. Often, economic data cannot distinguish between hospitality and tourism, another reason why these are considered together.

Classification of Hotels

Why do we have a classification system?

Hotel companies provide or claim to provide a wide range of facilities and services, confusing the customer on the reliability and authenticity of such claims. A classification system can provide

- an objective platform to differentiate hotels based on facilities and quality of service;
- the customer with accurate information;
- tourism agencies specific data that facilitate communication and marketing;
- the regulator a system based on which a graded taxation system could be implemented if necessary; and
- a transparent and measurable system by which hotels can benchmark themselves and work to improve services and facilities.

Different standards exist to classify hotels, but the most commonly used system is the star classification system. Star classification itself varies from country to country and there is no universal standard for rating hotels. Although the criteria and the standards may vary, the star classification system awards one to five stars to hotels based on the assessment made. The number of stars indicates the range of facilities; the more the number of stars, the more the facilities and services provided. While one-star hotels are typically small establishments with basic facilities, five-star hotels have the full range of facilities and amenities, from personalized service, luxury fittings to a choice of restaurants.

The star rating system depends on the establishment achieving a particular level of quality as laid down and the facilities provided. Assessment is done on the basis of quantifiable and measurable parameters. In assessing quality, the expectation of the consumer is the key element. Each establishment is assessed on the range of facilities, services and the quality. The assessment can be grouped into the different areas: bedrooms, bathrooms, food, overall cleanliness and level of service.

Overall cleanliness under which the condition, maintenance and monitoring of furnishings, fittings and fixtures are assessed. The standard of cleanliness of public areas, bathrooms, bed linen, towels, crockery and cutlery and furniture is scrutinized. The quality of the materials used is another important criterion.

Services provided, beginning with the reception, the efficiency, attitude and knowledge of key staff members, their turnout and social skills are all part of the assessment. Facilities such as reception services, porter, concierge, message taking service, city information, laundry and dry cleaning, complimentary newspaper, pressing service, shoe cleaning, booking of entertainment, valet parking are all services which are progressively provided, depending on the star rating that the hotel wishes to obtain.

Another important point of assessment is the dining arrangements at the hotel. Ranging from basic eating areas in a single-star hotel to full service formal dining restaurant in a five-star hotel, a range of dining options may be provided by hotels. The quality of cutlery and crockery, the F&B staff service and the quality and range of the courses of food for different meals form important considerations while rating hotels.

In some countries like India, a bar facility and the availability of alcoholic drinks are not a precondition to obtain a rating up to three-stars, whereas the minimum requirement for a single-star hotel in many countries is a provision of red and white wine, and alcoholic drinks to be available during meal times.

In bedrooms, some rating systems provide for a minimum area, which increases according to the star rating. A minimum number of lettable rooms is prescribed. The general quality of the room such as the condition of the furniture, flooring, fixtures and decor is checked. Air conditioning is an inevitable requirement, except for hotels in high altitudes. Daily cleaning of bedrooms and change of linen is a minimum requirement, as are daily making of beds, periodic change and washing of linen, in room glassware and crockery. Bed sizes are generally prescribed as are the number of pillows, sheets, blankets and bedspreads. In higher categories, the guest is offered a choice of pillows (pillow menu). In room communication and business services like telephones, direct dial facility, broadband connection, writing materials and stationery are generally prescribed. Wardrobe, safe, mini bar, writing desk and chair, sofa, house coat and slippers are provided, based on the category. Although a television has become one of the essential equipment in many systems, hotels provide a choice of radio and television channels and video on demand as entertainment options within the room.

In the case of bathrooms, too, the general quality of furnishings and fittings and overall decor is an important consideration. The provision for a washbasin, bathtub instead of a shower room, a choice of toiletries, running hot and cold water, heating and ventilation systems are all assessed as part of the rating process.

There are over 30 systems of classification and gradation of hotels in Europe. Classification is carried out either by government bodies or by professional organizations. Grading of hotels is based on government legislation or executive orders, when the system is managed by government agencies. In such environments, classification is considered obligatory and a necessary precondition for obtaining license of operation. Grading by professional bodies is done by hotel associations in many countries in Europe, and the rating system is detailed and service oriented. Some countries, particularly the Nordic countries, have resisted implementing a classification system in the interest of a free market environment.

Alternatives to Hotels

Serviced apartments aim to fill the gap between a short stay at the hotel and a longer stay in rented accommodation. As mentioned earlier, apartment hotels (aparthotels) are one of the long-stay options. Other options of longer stay accommodation in the organized sector are branded residences and corporate housing.

'Aparthotels' or extended stay hotels mainly provide the following facilities, apart from a bed: en suite bathroom, kitchenette, dining area and a working area with desk, table and Internet/telephone access. The additional services that are provided include reception desks, periodic—daily or weekly—cleaning and laundry service. Many hotel brands have come into the serviced accommodation sector, notably Adagio, a unit of Accor hotels, Staybridge Suites, BridgeStreet hospitality and Marriott executive Apartments (Accor Hotels, n.d.).

Capsule/Pod Hotels

Although there is no strict definition for the transit hotel, a temporary accommodation that is minimally sized, typically under 200 sq. ft., is considered a 'capsule' hotel room. Other terms which are used for similar accommodation are pod and transit hotels. These originated near airports and filled the need for guests who wanted to sleep or stretch themselves, while they waited for their flights. Capsule hotels have been quite popular in Japan but have not found much popularity outside that country. Some hotels make up for the limited bed space by providing luxury accommodation arrangements such as high-quality bed linen, bathroom fittings and rain showers, free Wi-Fi and automated check-in. Most of these types of hotels are located near major airports or in city centres where there is limited land availability. These typically offer short stays of around four hour duration at a reasonable rate. Many airports are offering the facility of a hotel 'pod' at an easy distance from the departure gates within the airport complex itself. At the Indira Gandhi International Airport in Delhi, 'Sams Snooze at my space' offers sleeping pods to passengers in the transit/departure area to sleep, relax or work in their comfort area, equipped with Wi-Fi, flat TV screens, DVD players, charging sockets and a working table.

Uncertainties in the Accommodation Sector

Tourism is a sensitive industry. Any disruptions in social, political, economic or environmental sphere can create disturbance and uncertainty in tourism business. The accommodation sector, an inevitable component of tourism is not an exception. Some areas of concern of accommodation sector are discussed below:

Competitive nature: The accommodation sector is highly competitive, with multiple players in all segments. Hotels try to distinguish themselves in the eyes of the customer in terms of value for money, quality and efficiency of service. The presence of multiple players and the continued entry of new players make it a volatile market.

Economic uncertainty: The fluctuations in the global economy have a direct bearing on the sector. The economic slowdown that affected markets across the world had a negative impact on the accommodation industry. Political instability in some countries or regions may affect business in related markets and cities.

Security concerns: National or regional political developments destabilizing the region or terrorism linked violence may have a direct and immediate impact on business. Travel advisories issued by governments disrupt travel and tourism significantly. A small news item is sufficient for many travellers to cancel their holiday plans, impacting business.

Taxation in the Accommodation Sector

The accommodation industry is subject to multiple taxations. Many states in India charge a 'luxury tax' on the room rent charged. The quantum of luxury tax varies from state to state, and the methodology of calculating the tax payable also differs widely. Generally, the tax is leviable on the actual rent charged on the customer, as this figure may be less than the advertised room rate (rack rate). VAT is another state tax applicable on restaurant charges. Service tax is a central tax, chargeable on all services provided, including room tariff, F&Bs, catering, restaurant bills and services such as laundry and telephone charges.

The multiplicity of taxes has a direct bearing on the prices and impacts the costs of tour packages. The composite tax burden is cited by industry bodies as a major impediment in the growth of the sector. Rationalization of the tax structure is one of the measures that is demanded to ensure that destinations remain competitive in a global environment.

Conclusion

Starting with its features and characteristics, we have explored the accommodation sector in a comprehensive manner. It can be seen that there is an amazing variety of accommodation types, and the global hotel industry has created types and brands suitable for each group of guests. Within the sector, there is again a complex hierarchy of professional and support positions, and it is no surprise that the accommodation industry is the biggest employer in tourism.

Accommodation plays a pivotal role in making destinations a second home to visitors. Accommodation in a family environment, opening avenues for close interaction with local community and their culture, in the form of homestays and B&B have become a common phenomenon today. Flexible, eco-friendly and utility-oriented accommodation facilities are also gaining importance in the tourism sector. Marketing strategies are also undergoing drastic changes for catering the requirements of specific segments of tourists like professionals and frequent travellers by offering customized facilities. While there are several challenges, the accommodation sector will see sustained growth, in line with new destinations opening up and increasing demand.

Review Questions

1. Give an account of different types of accommodation facilities available in India.
2. Explain the organizational structure and important functions of hotels.
3. Discuss different operating models in Hotel industry with suitable examples.

Activities

1. Collect details of accommodation units in your district, covering location, address, number of rooms, restaurant facilities and tariff, and categorize them according to the standard of services offered. Find out the different types of accommodation units that are not available in the area and discuss why investors are not venturing in these areas.
2. Conduct an organizational study of a hotel close to your institute, examining the departments, their duties and responsibilities and how various departments are integrated in the business.
3. Visit a hotel and identify the specific skills required for employees working in different departments for ensuring quality service delivery to tourist.
4. Make an assessment of the resource endowments in your family and surroundings and prepare a project report for starting a homestay business in your neighbourhood.

References

Web Resources

Accor Hotels, n.d. Our Brand Portfolio. Accor Hotels. Available at: http://www.accorhotels-group.com/en/franchise-and-management/our-brand-portfolio.html (accessed on 21 December 2016).
Global Hotel Rankings. 2014. 'The Leaders Grow Stronger, IHG Retain Top Spot'. Hotel Online. Available at: http://www.hotel-online.com/press_releases/release/global-hotel-rankings-the-leaders-grow-stronger-ihg-retains-top-spot (accessed on 21 December 2016).
New York Times. 2015. 'Marriott to buy Starwood Hotels, Creating World's largest Hotel Company'. The New York Times. Available at: http://www.nytimes.com/2015/11/17/business/marriott-to-buy-starwood-hotels.html?_r=1 (accessed on 21 December 2016).

Suggested Readings

Book

Barrows, C.W., T. Powers, and D. Reynolds. 2012. Introduction to Management in the Hospitality Industry, 10th edn. Wiley.

Web Resources

Bader, E., and A. Lababedi. 2007. 'Hotel Management Contracts in Europe'. HVS, London. Available at: http://www.hvs.com/StaticContent/Library/EuropeanHotelMgmtContracts/EuropeanHotel ManagementContracts.pdf

British Hospitality Association. 2015. 'The Economic contribution of UK hospitality Industry'. A Report Prepared by Oxford Economics for the British Hospitality Association. Available at: http://www.bha.org.uk/wordpress/wp-content/uploads/2015/09/Economic-contribution-of-the-UK-hospitality-industry.pdf

IHG. 2013. 'Our Business Model'. In IHG Annual Report and Form 20-F 2013. Available at: http://www.ihgplc.com/files/reports/ar2013/files/pdf/IHG-AR2013-business-model-preferred-brands.pdf

ILO. 2010. 'Developments and Challenges in the Hospitality and Tourism Sector'. Issues paper for discussion at the global Dialogue Forum for the Hotels, Catering, Tourism sector. Geneva, International Labour Organization. Available at: http://www.ilo.org/wcmsp5/groups/public/@ed_norm/@relconf/documents/meetingdocument/wcms_166938.pdf

LuxuryAccommodationsBlog. n.d. 'Understanding the Different Types of Accommodation in Tourism'. Luxury Accommodation Blog. Available at: http://www.luxuryaccommodationsblog.com/post/114961446726/different-types-accommodation-tourism

Marriott. 2012. 'Principles of Responsible Business'. In Marriott. Available at: https://c03ccb602f30 4983f586-6d2431fd9b6a841c5261996358a6ce31.ssl.cf2.rackcdn.com/content/uploads/Principles-Responsible-Business.pdf

McKenney, S., ed. 2015. 'Emerging Accommodation Segments 2015'. In *Hotel Alternatives*. Available at: http://hotelanalyst.co.uk/wp-content/uploads/sites/2/2015/01/hotel-alts-report-sample.pdf

NIOS. n.d. 'Tourist Accommodation'. National Institute of Open Schooling. Available at: http://oer.nios.ac.in/wiki/index.php/Tourist_Accommodation

The creation of a goddess idol
Image courtesy: Ministry of Tourism, Government of India.

CHAPTER 8

Travel and Tour Operations

Learning Objectives

By the end of this chapter, students will be able to:

- Distinguish between travel agencies and tour operators.
- Categorize tour operators according to their roles.
- List the steps involved in developing tour packages.
- Appreciate the operational aspects of MICE tourism.
- Enumerate new trends in travel agency business.
- Explain the role of IT in changing the tourism business.

Introduction

In this chapter, we focus attention on T&T operations, another significant activity in the tourism sector. While destinations may have many attractions for visitors to enjoy and hotels for their comfortable accommodation, it is the tour operator who puts it all together and ensures that the visitor gets to the destination. T&T operations span the entire gamut of travel intermediaries, and there are multiple channels that offer a variety of travel products to the potential traveller.

Simply put, this sector brings the buyer and seller together, creating packages combining two or more offerings and making holidays stress free and easy to purchase for the consumer. We examine the components of the tour operations process to gain an understanding of how tour packages are created and the different responsibilities undertaken by the different players in the field. The essential difference between a tour operator and travel agent is explained in depth, as this is an area where the nomenclature is not very specific on the business conducted. We will also look at online intermediaries, who have changed the tour business that was traditionally conducted and who will play a major role in the future of the tourism business.

The College Tour

To understand the world of tour operations, let us take an example we are all familiar with—the 'study tour'. This is a near universal aspect in colleges across India, giving an opportunity to the students to travel and learn about new places and regions. In most cases, student groups or representatives handle these tours. All students who have helped in organizing a 'study tour' or 'excursion' during college will recollect the multiple steps involved in this exciting operation. First, there are heated discussions on the destinations to be visited. Usually, the opinion of someone who has already gone on a similar tour is sought. Friends and classmates offer their views and share their experiences about destinations, itinerary options and reliable transportation providers. They may provide information about the attractions to be visited and those to be avoided. Opinions on restaurants, resting places and entertainment options are also freely given. This wealth of information, on the basis of first-hand experience, is usually the starting point of the structuring of a tour. On the basis of the information gathered, the inclination of the travelling group and other factors like the time and finance available, the outlines of the tour would emerge. There would be agreement on the basics—the destinations to be visited, the number of days and nights of the tour and the itinerary. The next step is to finalize the details of travel and accommodation. On the strength of 'reviews' provided by those who had gone on the tour earlier and information collected from sources such as the Internet accommodation options are shortlisted. The organizers visit the website of the destinations to ascertain the opening hours of the attractions they intend to visit and also to glean more information about possible excursions that can be undertaken from the base destination.

The stage is a set for a service provider to come into the project. The organizer makes contact with a local 'travels' or a 'tours' company, whose reliability has been endorsed by previous clients. The organizer contacts one or more such firms, providing them the outline of the itinerary and asking them to give suggestions regarding the possible accommodation options. The service providers may suggest alternatives, both in the routing of the itinerary and in accommodation. They make these suggestions on the basis of their knowledge of the destinations and the routes to be taken. They would also give a range of options for accommodation, listing the advantages and negatives of each suggested hotel. In a similar manner, transportation options are discussed—rates for each type of 'tourist bus' or van, railway connectivity and the arrangements for reception and local transport. Operators offer a 'quotation', a price for the whole tour. This figure encompasses the charges for all the services to be entrusted to them, which may consist all or most of the following components: train tickets, bus or van rentals, interstate tax, drivers allowance, accommodation, meals, the services of a local guide, entry tickets to monuments and attractions. After comparing rates and holding negotiations, the project is assigned to a selected tour operator, who takes over all the arrangements to be made. During the tour, representatives of the tour operator are at hand to ensure that all goes well. The operator sorts out problems and issues, using his experience and knowledge and has made the tour comfortable and safe.

The components of international tour operations are pretty much the same as those in our college tour example elaborated above. Travellers depend on many sources for information on destinations to be visited, word of mouth generally considered the most reliable. Depending on budgets and interests, a few destinations are shortlisted, after which a professional service provider is called in to provide advice and to finalize the arrangements. The views and preferences of group members often play an important role in determining the itinerary. Once the general outline of the holiday has become clearer in the minds of the visitor, the travel intermediary steps in and provides information and suggestions regarding accommodation, transport and the sites to be visited. Based on the budget of the traveller, the tour operator puts together a package that combines the preferences of the traveller with the practical solutions given by the operator. The tour operator has succeeded in providing a package that can be purchased by the consumer and will make all necessary arrangements along all destinations, ensuring that the tour is delivered without any glitch.

Whether it is a 'local' tour or an international holiday, the tour operator is an important service provider, putting the ingredients together, pricing the package and finally operating it. The tour operator plays a pivotal role in tourism and has grown and evolved with the growth in tourism worldwide.

The Tour Operator

What does a tour operator do?

A tour operator, as the term indicates, operates tours. The tour operator, in most cases, is involved in all steps of the tour, starting with the design of the itinerary. The tour operator creates the itinerary, confirms accommodation, ties up transportation arrangements, organizes excursions and provides guides. A package tour consists of a new 'tourism product' provided by a tour operator which is sold either directly to the customer or to travel agencies, in which travellers receive a combination of products associated with a trip. These are generally made of more than one of the following tourism services: accommodation, sightseeing, meals, transport services and entertainment. This package is then offered to the client, through a network of travel agents, either exclusively selling the products of that operator or which will feature the tour as one of their travel products. Once the travel agent sells a package tour, the responsibility shifts to the tour operator to operate the tour, including providing all the arrangements of the package (Figure 8.1).

The tour operator, apart from reaching out to the customer through the network of travel agents, often have direct sales operations also. Through sales offices or 'shops' directly owned

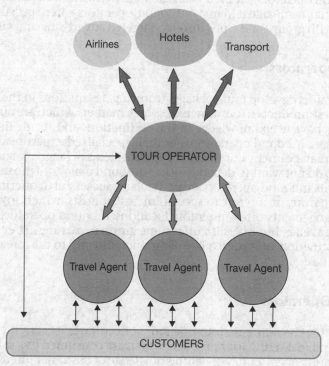

Figure 8.1   Tour operations
Source: Authors.

and operated by them, major tour operators connect directly with the customer. They sell travel products similar to the ones sold through the travel agent but also respond to customer enquiries, provide quotations for tailor-made tours and advise walk-in customers on their travel plans. Travel 'shops' have developed into important branding opportunities for tour companies, and are extensions of the brand image serving to engage with customers in a stylish and comfortable setting.

Types of Tour Operators

Operators may be categorized from the viewpoint of the customer: where they are from (source market) and where they plan a holiday (destination).

Outbound Tour Operators

Outbound tour operators create and market tour products featuring destinations outside the country, to be purchased by consumers within the country. Outbound operators may create their own tourism products, or may market tours made by partner companies in the destinations. Outbound operators will have a sound knowledge of the requirements and preferences of their customers. Most outbound operators offer group travel to well-known destinations, like Cox and Kings 'Duniya Dekho' packages. Customers are happy to travel with reliable brands familiar to them while undertaking long haul holidays in foreign lands. More and more outbound operators are offering customized tour products to customers who prefer to make their plans and need-specific destination-based support on certain components of their tour. Generally, outbound operators sell their packages directly to customers, investing in advertising and promotional campaigns. Many outbound operators offer special prices to regular clients, and work with groups and clubs through targeted advertising and sales programmes.

Inbound Tour Operators

Inbound tour operators develop tour packages featuring destinations in the country of operation, marketing these products to customers in source markets which are outside the country. Inbound operators have deep knowledge of the destinations and strong links with suppliers and service providers. Inbound operators offer their specialized expertise and local strengths to customers who may be uncomfortable to tackle problems of language and connectivity by themselves or who do not want to depend on an outbound operator who may not be familiar with the destination. Inbound operators are particularly successful in offering products which are specialized in nature, of interest to special interest tourists, which involve complicated itineraries and arrangements often in remote locations. Inbound operators mainly appeal to the independent traveller, but may also offer some group departures. They tend to specialize in a country or destination, offering a range of products directly to the foreign customer wishing to travel into the country.

Domestic Tour Operators

As the term indicates, the domestic tour operator concentrates its activities on the domestic market, creating and marketing tour products which are consumed by customers within the country. The domestic operator has in-depth knowledge of customer interests and trends and produces packages that appeal to different segments of the market. In complex and big countries like India, the domestic operator has a range of products that is sold in different target markets, taking customers to various destinations across the country. The diversity of markets and the range of destinations are important factors in domestic tourism.

Ground Operators (Ground Handlers)

Ground 'handlers' or ground 'operators' provide a range of services at destinations, which are together known as land arrangements. They market their services to outbound tour operators in source destinations, physically operating the tours in destinations on behalf of these operators. They also partner with operators in source markets in creating tours for independent travellers, creating itineraries and offering alternatives. Once a tour is booked, the ground operator will make arrangements and operate the tour on behalf of the tour operator. These companies are increasingly known as destination management companies (DMC). Given their importance, we will examine their activities in detail later in the chapter.

Mass Market and Specialist Operators

Tour operators may also be categorized as targeting the 'mass market', with large volumes of business and those aimed at the 'niche' markets, which are much smaller in number.

A mass market operator offers tour products which are affordable to the common man. These packages combine air passage, usually using a charter flight, with a holiday in a budget hotel in a popular tourist destination. The operator procures hotel rooms and airline seats in bulk at advantageous rates, and bundles the component costs into a highly competitive and attractive price for the customer resulting in the promotion of group inclusive tours (GITs). Typically, margins are very thin, and companies concentrate on large volumes to bring in profits. Mass market operators have dominated the market, particularly in 'sun, sea and sand' holidays offered to European customers during the winter months. Tour operators with millions of customers often acquire businesses to transform themselves into giant multinational entities, operating hotels, running airlines and cruise liners and providing travel products for all types of customers. Our case study provides a snapshot of Touristik Union International (TUI), the biggest operator, for the student to understand the scale of operation and the multiplicity of brands under the umbrella of one transnational company.

Case Study: Touristik Union International

TUI offers a range of holiday experiences and expertise for every conceivable type of traveller. TUI is an example of a 'global' business, with over 55,000 employees in 150 countries in all continents and over 220 brands. TUI Group is the world's leading tourism business, a global brand with an attractive hotel portfolio, a growing fleet of cruise ships and a modern and efficient leisure airline with direct access to 20 million customers. The broad portfolio consists of strong tour operators, 1,800 travel agencies and leading online portal, six airlines with more than 130 aircraft, over 300 hotels with 210,000 beds and 13 cruise liners. The turnover of the company was 18.5 billion euros (nearly ₹1.40 lakh crores), and the EBITA (earnings before interest, taxes and amortization) was 870 million euros (₹6,500 crores).

TUI business is grouped into three sectors:

- Mainstream brands take 20 million people on holiday every year.
- Accommodation and destinations brands sell over 25 million room nights per year.
- Specialist and activity—'The Moorings' has over 650 yachts for charter in 27 cruising destinations.

(Continued ...)

Mainstream: The companies under this group are active in the Western European source markets. TUI is the largest tour operator in Europe, with market leading brands in most countries. With a fleet of 138 aircraft and about 1,800 retail travel shops, TUI operates in all segments of the business.

Accommodation and Destinations Sector: Over 10,000 employees work in this sector, under many brands, selling products and services in over 150 countries. The online accommodation business includes the accommodation wholesaler and the online travel agent (OTA) businesses. Hotelbeds and Bedsonline are the major brands. Online accommodation sector is the fastest growing B2B segment, supplying accommodation to the leisure travel industry. The accommodation OTA business sells rooms directly to the end user. Laterooms.com (UK), Asiarooms.com (Asia Pacific) and MalaPronta.com (Brazil) are major brands. Their online database has over 60,000 hotels.

Inbound services include a global network of DMCs, a global cruise handling specialist and a meetings and events specialist. In destinations, TUI provides transfers, excursions and tours. Thirteen million customers in 51 countries were looked after by TUI owned DMCs. Worldcome, World of TUI and Destination Services are some of the major brands in this segment. Through its market leading brand, Intercruises, TUI provides ground handling and port agency services, catering to over 10,000 port calls at over 300 ports per year.

Specialist and Activity: This sector comprises of over 90 specialized travel businesses that service customers with a wide range of interests and passions. There are 1.4 million customers enjoying experiences like volunteering on community projects, sailing, skiing, cruising, trekking and watching the World Cup.

- *Adventure:* The adventure division is the world's largest adventure travel business. It consists of specialist adventure tour operators and DMCs.
- *Education:* Tours and packages for schools and universities, including educational tours, student ski trips, adventure and activity holidays and language education.
- *North American specialist:* Incorporating escorted tour and luxury adventure businesses across the US and major Canadian cities, the companies include Quark Expeditions and TCS, which is a private jet holiday business.
- *Sport:* This division offers supporter tours, match breaks to key events and corporate and hospitality programmes. Gullivers Sports Travel and Sportsworld are the leading brands.

Ski and luxury tailored holiday brands like Hayes & Jarvis, Crystal and Citalia; leading yachting and marine brands such as The Moorings and Sunsail; and Le Boat, the largest provider of self-drive boating holidays in Europe are other specialist brands.

TUI controls the end-to-end customer journey, from inspiration and advice to booking, flight, inbound services and accommodation. Having own hotels and cruise ships gives them the product differentiation and allows them to control quality and customer satisfaction, and can fulfil customer demand for destinations and experiences where content is scarce.

Discussion Questions

1. What are the advantages of creating such a large organization, involving itself in all aspects of travel and tourism?
2. List three possible reasons why TUI operates several brands in accommodation and travel sectors.

A Specialist tour operator offers specialized tourism products to a 'niche' clientele or market. For example, people with shared interests or hobbies, such as hiking, cycling, birding, adventure or visiting museums, will use the services of specialist tour operators who have the domain expertise to create and operate tours catering to these specific interests. Such tours very often involve detailed ground arrangements and logistics and require specialized expertise and deep knowledge. Unlike the mass market operators, specialized tour operators create customized tours for individuals and small groups, often charging high prices for their expertise and capabilities. Specialized operators offer personalized customer service, as against mass market companies which offer 'off the shelf' products. Snow Leopard Adventures, featured as a case study, is a specialist operator, providing highly specialized services to a niche clientele.

Case Study: Snow Leopard Adventures—A Specialist Tour Operator

Snow Leopard Adventures is one of the earliest specialist operators in India, focusing on adventure holidays. Founded in 1990 by Ajeet Bajaj, the intention of the company was to make available adventure holidays to the 'average person'. Ajeet Bajaj has rich experience in adventure travel. He is the first Indian to have completed the Polar Trilogy—skiing to the North Pole, South Pole and across the Greenland ice cap. Bajaj also has a wealth of experience in rafting and Kayaking, putting his knowledge to use in designing adventure tourism products.

Snow Leopard Adventures provides a range of adventure products, aimed at different segments of customers. The following are some of the activities offered:

- *Zip lining*. A high adrenaline activity of zipping on 400-m-long zip lines across the Ganga which flows 70 m below.
- *River rafting*. Rafting down the Ganga or Alaknanda in Uttarakhand or the Kundalika in Maharashtra, rafting and kayaking expeditions.
- *Trekking* in Uttarakhand (Gaja, Valley of Flowers and the origin of Ganga) and Ladakh (Markha valley).

(Continued ...)

- *Mountaineering* expeditions in Himachal Pradesh (Friendship peak), Ladakh (Stok Kangri) and Uttarakhand (Hanuman Peak).
- *Cycling and mountain biking* tours in the Himalayan foothills.
- *Rock climbing and rappelling.*
- *Horse safaris.*
- *Wildlife and jeep safaris.*

The company operates many camps for visitors, ranging from air conditioned huts to basic tents, which are used as base camps for adventure activities.

Snow Leopard Adventures offers a range of options to different target groups. Outdoor trips for schools are specially designed for young visitors combining nature education, community service and outdoor skills with adventure activities. The aim is to evoke student's interest in the natural and cultural heritage of India and make them sensitive global citizens.

The corporate adventure packages, aimed at the corporate sector, entail the use of soft adventure activities and management games to develop leadership skills, teamwork, communication skills and conflict management among groups of executives.

Family adventures are tailor-made tours aimed at families and small groups, interested in 'active vacations'. Soft adventure options are combined with sightseeing in scenic locations like Ladakh, Kerala and Rwanda.

For clients interested in adventure expeditions abroad, the company offers a range of tours in Bhutan, Nepal, Antarctica and Africa.

Image courtesy: Ministry of Tourism, Government of India.

Discussion Questions

1. 'The success of a special interest tour company depends on the professional knowledge of the owner/promoter'. Discuss.
2. Categorize the activities offered by the company into 'soft' and 'hard' adventure products.

Group Inclusive Tours and Free Independent Travel

Group Inclusive Tours (GITs)

GITs are the most popular form of mass tourism. The travel pages of newspapers offer many such tours—'10 Days in Europe' or 'The Magic of Thailand'. The details of a typical group tour can be found in every advertisement—the itinerary, dates of departures, inclusions and exclusions, hotels, optional tours and the tour price. The tour package generally consists of air passage, reception at the airport, coach or car transfers to the hotel, accommodation, meals, excursions and sightseeing trips, guide services and entertainment. Group sizes are generally large, and the departure dates are fixed. GIT operators normally set a minimum group size, without which the tour is not operated.

The biggest attraction of the 'package' tour is the price. Tour companies offering multiple group tours are able to buy accommodation and air passage at a discounted price, which is passed on to the customer as a competitive price. This allows for the budget traveller to choose a vacation based on the budget and reduces unforeseen expenditure at the destinations. Another important factor in favour of the group tour is that the responsibility of operating the tour lies with the operator. In other words, if there is any unexpected change in the tour such as a cancelled or diverted flight or a sudden disruption in traffic, the responsibility of solving the issue and continuing the tour rests with the operator, leaving the traveller with a peace of mind. Group tours generally are popular for the consistency in service quality, as tours are operated by experienced companies with huge volumes of business in different countries and destinations.

Many people, particularly the elderly, prefer group travelling for the opportunity to socialize and make friends. Travelling with a tour guide is seen as a benefit, as the guide provides authentic, in-depth information and makes all arrangements. This is particularly useful while travelling to destinations with unfamiliar language and customs. Other benefits of group inclusive travel are that it is hassle free, with arrangements made for transportation, entertainment and sightseeing. In many group tours, gratuity payments like tips are also included in the tour price, removing irritants from bothering the traveller. GIT packages are generally economical, with companies aiming for large volumes.

The general criticism of GITs is that their itineraries are generally packed, with very little personal time and little flexibility. Tours cover only the most well-known sites in destinations. Visits to shops and vendors are regulated, perhaps because of pre-existing tie-ups with the operator. Advance bookings are needed and departure dates are fixed, leaving no flexibility in the hands of the traveller. For travellers with special needs, such as dietary requirements, the group tour may not be advisable.

Group travel has rewritten the course of modern tourism. It has created tourists out of a wide spectrum of people who could not afford to travel. Mass tourism, with its emphasis on low prices and high volumes, has created destinations and brought prosperity to many regions. It is also accused of creating many problems in destinations, owing to the large numbers of visitors and the resulting social and environmental impacts.

Free Independent Travel (FIT)

FIT has many expansions—the most commonly used term is free independent travel or flexible independent travel. The FIT customer is a single unit, either a person or a small group of individuals, who prefer to travel by themselves, and not as a part of a larger group. They are 'free', which means that they choose the places they want to visit and the types of hotels they want to stay in. FIT travellers are also 'independent', not depending on any tour operator to provide them with all arrangements related to their trip. Generally speaking, FIT customers make their own travel arrangements and depend on the tour operator for making accommodation and local transport arrangements. FIT travellers tend to spend more on holidays and stay longer at destinations. Independent travellers prefer the freedom and adventure of the personalized trip to the regimented pattern of a group tour. While FIT travellers will depend on tour operators for organizing some of the components of the tour, they retain the flexibility and freedom to choose most of the ingredients and customize their holidays according to their liking. FIT customers generally spend more, visit far-flung destinations and spread their expenditure among the community, as opposed to the GIT, where the tour operator has included all components into the price of the tour.

It is the smaller tour operator who can afford to charge a higher markup for the package offered, based on the specificity of the tourism product and the quality of the offering. Smaller operators tend to have deeper knowledge of destinations and have niche offerings targeting clientele who are not very price conscious. Help tourism, featured in our case study, is one such operator. Help tourism has enabled visitors to gain an understanding of the Sunderbans by providing accommodation, tours and a sensitive and insightful portrayal of the local environment.

Bihu dancers, Assam

Case Study: Help Tourism

Help Tourism is a tour operator and destination management consultant specializing in east and northeast India. Help Tourism views tourism as a tool for sustainable development and conservation. In their words, 'the special taste of our tours and programmes originates from a meaningful combination of four local and home grown ingredients—heritage, environment, livelihood and people'. From 1991, help tourism has supported various communities in creating quality tourism destinations with a local flavour. Help tourism provides purposeful travel to natural areas to understand the cultural and natural history of the environment without concealing actual threats. It regularly conducts campaigns for sustainable development at local levels and encourages activities that confirm community development through tourism minus negative effects (Help Tourism, n.d.a).

The operator works with government agencies, local NGOs and community groups to create tourism products in a relatively lesser known part of India. With their emphasis on promotion of alternative livelihood avenues among communities which were dependent on natural resources in protected areas, help tourism has helped focus attention on the issues of ownership of natural resources, conservation and responsible tourism.

Sunderbans Jungle Camp: The Sunderbans National Park is a UNESCO world heritage site, a biosphere reserve and a tiger park located in the Sunderbans delta. Densely covered by mangrove forests, Sunderbans is one of the largest reserves for the Bengal tigers and home to numerous bird, reptile and invertebrate species. The project initiated by help tourism utilized the services of local youth who were poachers earlier, but turned into conservation volunteers. Eight cottages built on the island village of Bali provide the accommodation facility, which is managed by members of the local community. Food is simple and local and prepared by the villagers. The highlight of the tour programme is the boat cruise through the mangroves, giving an opportunity to sight the rich fauna of the region. Visitors are encouraged to explore the village and experience the local culture, including the performance based on 'Bonbibi', the popular myth in the area. Apart from Sunderbans, help tourism operates jungle camps in several other locations in Sikkim, West Bengal and Arunachal Pradesh, offering a glimpse of the rich cultural heritage of the communities and nature-based experiences such as guided safaris, nature walks, birding and trekking.

(Continued ...)

Birding tours: Help Tourism operates tours for special interest groups such as birders. Eastern India is home to 850 species of birds and is considered to be the richest birding area in India. The operator offers a range of birding tours in different parks of Sikkim, West Bengal, Meghalaya, Assam and Arunachal Pradesh, and also in Chilka Lake in Odisha, providing the services of experienced guides and birding experts. (Help Tourism, n.d.b)

Image courtesy: Ministry of Tourism, Government of India.

Discussion Questions

1. What are the features of help tourism that distinguish it from conventional tour companies?
2. Discuss the aspects of their tour products that enable community interaction and involvement.

The Tour Operation Process

We have seen how the role of the tour operator can differ according to the type of customers and their preferences. The tour business itself is a complex mix of companies, offering different types of products and services to the market. The orientation of the business itself may be varied—while most companies focus on the traveller, some companies market their products to other tour companies, a business to business (B2B) model. Then there are companies which aim to address the requirements of the corporate world, providing specialized services required by companies.

The development of a tour lies at the core of the tour business. It is a complex process involving multiple players, different sections of the tour company and quite often takes many months to years. As the stages of development reveal to us the different facets of the tour business, it is useful to study all the components that go into the development of a tour 'package'.

Development of Tour Packages

For the purpose of the discussion, the following assumptions are to be kept in mind: the tour company has been in operation in the market for some time and has a specialized staff structure. The company is looking for opportunities to expand operations, and is considering the introduction of a tour product featuring a new destination in a country to which the company is not offering any tours at present. The 'designer' will also take the feedback from experienced ground operators—DMCs. At the end of this exercise, the product manager has put together a tour with all components to go into the package. There is a choice of hotels in different categories which meet the standards of the operator.

Research

The operator conducts an extensive research of the market in order to ascertain interest levels and the feasibility of introducing the new destination as part of its portfolio. A good source for research is the feedback given by regular clients who have been patronizing the company. The travel agencies that have been selling the company products are also rich sources of market information. A key objective of this exercise is to identify demand, whether overt or latent, that can be converted into business through the introduction of the new package. Market trends are analysed closely—what kinds of holidays are being sold? Is there a change in preferences and aspirations among the target clientele? Products of competitors featuring the destination which is under consideration are studied carefully to understand the offerings and to identify aspects which can be improved. In-house inputs from the sales staff are valuable sources to gauge customer's interests and preferences.

Field Visit

Once the operator is reasonably confident that the new product has a chance of succeeding in the market, the stage is set for a field visit by specialized product managers. These are professionals having experience of creating similar products with good knowledge of the destination. The product managers test itineraries, interact with suppliers and service providers, check out hotels and attractions and make their independent assessment of the issues involved in designing the tour. The development of the tour itinerary is critical to the success of the product and calls for meticulous preparation backed with sound knowledge of the destination. The itinerary also takes into consideration local conditions, taxation and legal requirements. Potential partners are identified, and the possible dates of operation of group tours also arrived at.

Negotiations and Contracting

The itinerary, with all important components are ready to be firmed up, backed with legally binding contracts. The operator starts negotiations with 'suppliers'; suppliers could be airlines, travel agencies, hotels or transport companies, providing essential ingredients in the package. For air passage, the operator can negotiate a special price from the airline or partner with a travel agency holding inventory of seats.

After negotiations, the tour operator enters into a contract with the suppliers like accommodation establishments, based on a commitment to provide a minimum number of room bookings for the season. The system called the allotment or allocation system ensures that the accommodation provider gets a minimum guarantee on the number of room nights that will be underwritten by the tour operator. In other words, the tour operator commits to make payment for the minimum number of allotted rooms for the season, irrespective of whether the rooms are sold by the operator or not. This provides a cushion of comfort for the accommodation provider, although the tour operator may have contracted the rooms at a highly discounted rate. For the operator, a bulk allocation of rooms in a destination means that the operator can prepare an itinerary with the comfort that the room booking is already in place. While tour operators may make an advance payment, generally the system is that of pre-booking with the tour operator, retaining the flexibility of releasing the rooms of to a particular date called the lease period. In certain destinations where the supply is less, accommodation establishments insist on full commitments, without a release clause and with a substantial advance. Generally, both players tend to share the risk by having a mixture of these models.

The operator also negotiates with ground handlers—DMCs—to operate the tour at the destination. At the end of this convoluted exercise, legal contracts are signed, laying down the responsibilities and commitments of parties. The finance and legal department personnel are involved in this exercise.

After the complicated negotiations of contracting are completed and the contracts signed for the next year, tour operators engage in the next stage of the business, which is the pricing of the tour. This involves careful calculations of the amounts to be paid to the suppliers down the distribution channel, the commissions, taxes and surcharges to be paid and the product development and marketing expenses to be distributed. Based on these calculations, the cost of the tour package is arrived at.

Tour Costing and Pricing

Calculating the cost of the tour is an important factor that has implications on the tour pricing, and has to be done with precision and care. Several assumptions will have to be taken, based on experience and the 'gut' feeling on the product. The operator breaks the costs into two: fixed costs and variable costs. Fixed costs are those which have to be paid no matter how many tourists purchase the package. Examples of fixed costs are salaries, cost of permits, vehicle registration charges and business costs. The business costs or expenses are incurred on an annual basis and have to be shared by all business operations. Examples of business costs are loan payments, accounting and legal expenses, advertising budgets, promotion expenses, brochure publication, depreciation, stationery, mail charges, rent of business premises, interest payments, costs of business travel and stay, insurance, provident fund payments, communication charges for telephone and Internet, training and power and water charges. Variable costs are those which change according to the visitors purchasing the product. Costs for accommodation, travel, meals, sightseeing, wages and fuel are variable costs. While costing a tour product, an operator allocates a percentage of his total annual business costs to each operation. An important assumption is the expected number of tours to be sold during a season, as this has an impact on the final average cost that is worked out.

Pricing a tour product is the most risky and tricky element in the development of the tour product. There are several ways to price a product, but the commonest method is the markup—the percentage of the cost that is added as profit to the operator. For example, if x is the total cost arrived at after costing all the components, the final price may be $1.25x$, with the markup of 25% over the cost. There is no fixed percentage for markup; it depends on many factors, including how competitive the market is, the availability of similar products in the market, the demand for similar products and the promotional pricing strategy and discounts.

A simple markup works only if the product is sold directly to the consumer. However, as we have seen earlier, tour products are sold through several intermediaries. Travel agents form the main retail sales point, but tours are sold by online portals, visitor centres and tour wholesalers as well. The pricing strategy has to keep in mind the commission that is to be added, which is retained by the agent. Tour operators adopt several pricing strategies, such as skimming, penetrating, differential and backward pricing while devising a sales strategy.

Brochure Production and Distribution

The brochure continues to be the primary medium for marketing. Providing comprehensive information, often with colourful photographs of destinations, hotels and attractions; the brochure is a vital tool in the hands of the retail sales team. The tour operator produces brochures, incorporating the new tour product, giving important details such as departure dates, inclusions, exclusions, category of hotels and prices. Brochures are cost effective tools, helping the agent explain the tour product, leading to a sale.

Marketing

The tour package is marketed in several ways. Direct marketing techniques try to present the product directly to the consumer. A variety of promotional techniques are used, such as familiarization tours, sales team education, sales calls to agents, travel and tour marts, telemarketing and a host of advertising options. To support the travel agents, tour operators often conduct seminars and workshops to educate the agent about destinations and new packages that are being offered for the season. Representatives of the tour operator also support the efforts of the travel agent through sales visits and customer presentations.

The operation of the tour is the final leg of the tour operation process. Generally, the tour is operated by the tour operator through a local partner at the destination, the DMC. Representatives of the DMC receive clients at the port of entry, provide escorts to transfer them to the hotel, arrange for excursions and are available for troubleshooting. Feedback from the client is an essential part of the process, enabling the operator to improve service delivery.

Destination Management Company (DMC)

A DMC is a vital player in international tourism. Other terms to describe DMCs are ground handlers, ground operators and incoming tour operators. Generally speaking, tour operators align with a ground handling service provider, called DMC, which is responsible for providing all services at the destination end. It may be noted that destination management companies do not 'manage' destinations; they manage the operation of tours in destinations.

DMC is involved in all major components of the tour operation, except the sales. DMCs act as representatives of the tour operator, making arrangements such as hotel transfers, accommodation, sightseeing and events. On behalf of the tour operator, the DMC enters into contracts with certain suppliers and accompany the tour operator on product inspections. They handle all local complaints and emergencies on behalf of the tour operator.

DMC offers ideas for creation of new products and itineraries. They have extensive knowledge of destinations, which are constantly updated. Based on this, DMCs provide information on new products, service providers and suppliers.

Some DMCs offer integrated services, such as having in-house transportation facilities, offering guides and escort services and even providing accommodation. Generally, a DMC has an exclusive contract with the tour operator, preventing the DMC from accepting any business from a competing operator and the same source market. As they are not directly in control of the pricing, they work on slim commissions and margins and are at the mercy of the tour operator.

Charter Operations

The liberalization of international and domestic air transport rules and regulations has dramatically changed international aviation and tourism. In early days, the world of aviation was highly regulated, with restrictions on the number of flights, the number of airline companies permitted to operate, the pricing of tickets and the sales outlets for air tickets. Complex and restrictive regulations governed international air traffic. Deregulation of aviation business started in Europe in the 1950s and began with the introduction of charter flight operations.

A charter flight is permitted to operate between two airports, offering its seats only as part of a holiday package. The charter operator is not allowed to sell seats individually, as scheduled airlines do. Due to the limited facilities offered and lower overheads, charter companies could offer fares that are considerably lower than those on scheduled airlines to tour companies. Charter flights are generally operated from cheaper suburban airports where charges are lesser, offer minimal services and sell beverages and food on board. They focus on high capacity utilization or load factor, quick turnaround and competitive pricing. Charter operations enabled destinations to be opened up for tourism even while the countries continued with their highly regulated air traffic regimes. Charters brought in tourists and valuable foreign exchange earnings, without posing direct competition to the scheduled airlines. The advent of regular charter flight operations kick started international mass tourism, beginning with the holiday travel of thousands of Europeans to destinations in Spain and the Mediterranean. Gradually, long haul charters began operations, from Europe to destinations like Goa, Maldives and Bangkok, creating new destinations for leisure tourism like Pattaya and Goa. There was a quantum jump in the number of tour companies offering destinations in India coinciding with the introduction of regular charter flights from Gatwick, London to Goa and Kerala.

Charter operators operate on very fine margins. Given the high elasticity of demand and increasing competition, charter operators are constantly in the search of cheaper destinations. Often, charter operators have to achieve 90% capacity utilization to break into profits. This means that they will try to negotiate heavy discounts, often over 60% off the normal tariff, in tourist destinations served by charter airlines. Charter operations also tie the operator down with commitment contracts, where the risk of unsold seats is with the operator.

MICE Tourism

MICE is an acronym for meetings, incentives, conferences and exhibitions. MICE refers to a segment of tourism that is specialized in providing services for conducting a host of meetings and events. An array of service providers are involved in the MICE industry—tour operators, event planners, food and beverages providers, hotels, transportation and logistics specialists, conference centres, exhibition venues and tourism promotion organizations. In order to understand this segment better, it is necessary to examine each component separately.

Meetings and Conferences

Meetings and conferences are gatherings of a number of persons belonging to an organization, a company, a group with shared interests or a trade or professional association. Meetings may differ in size—the number of participants may not be very large for board meetings, seminars, symposia and workshops, but a large number of several thousands may congregate at a point for annual general meetings (AGMs) of companies and general assemblies of organizations. Meetings may also be classified into corporate or association meetings, depending on the type of organizer of the meeting. Meetings may also be of religious groups, political meetings and commercial meetings such as sales conferences.

Conferences are large meetings, particularly of international and national level professional associations and bodies, industry and trade organizations and academic associations. The largest segment among conferences is related to medical specialties. Conferences are generally spread across several days, and often have a trade show or exhibition organized as part of the event. International Congress and Convention Association, a global body on conventions, specifies that international meetings are those with a minimum attendance of 50 delegates, organized on a regular basis, and rotate among at least 3 countries.

It is estimated that there are around 14,000 events worldwide, with over 4,000 meetings (Ministry of Tourism, 2015). MICE tourism accounts for around 20% of all international arrivals. Of all segments of tourism, MICE sector is one of the fastest growing and is projected to grow annually at a rate of 10% for the next decade. While European cities like Vienna, Paris and London are the most popular venues for international conventions, the cities of Singapore, Seoul and Shanghai are growing in importance, which reflects a trend of a shift of conventions to Asia. Suntec Singapore is a good example of a major investment to create infrastructure that has paid rich dividends. The combination of a convenient urban location, world-class facilities with flexibility and quality, the proximity to good hotels and entertainment and shopping options have combined to create one of the most popular MICE venues.

Suntec Singapore Convention and Exhibition Centre
Suntec city is a multi-use development, housing offices, hotels, malls, restaurants and one of the best equipped convention centres in the world, offering all facilities in one integrated

(Continued ...)

campus. The Suntec Singapore Convention and Exhibition centre has 100,000 sq. m of event space which can be customized for different events. The exhibition halls are multi-purpose, transforming into conference hall, ball rooms or concert venues. The Suntec city mall has around 360 outlets spread over 82,500 sq. m of retail space, making it the largest shopping centre in Singapore. In the vicinity are major hotel brands offering around 5,000 upper category rooms. A full suite of facilities including extensive kitchens for huge banquets, theatres, interpretation, business centres and a team of professionals together provide service of the highest order, making Suntec Singapore one of the most popular convention centres in the world.

The key factors influencing the success of a convention destination are quality of facilities, accessibility, local support, accommodation offers and attractiveness of the destination.

Conferencing facilities: The availability of facilities of sufficient size, access of conferencing venue to accommodation facilities, ambience and costs, availability of services such as banqueting, translation and simultaneous interpretation are critical factors.

Accessibility: The flying time to the destination, relative expense for air passage, frequency and convenience of international air connections and ease of entry into the country and barriers such as visas and customs are important considerations.

Local support offered: The extent of assistance and backing offered by local association partner is critical for a favourable decision. Related aspects are the planning and logistical support available at the convention centre and the discounts and subsidies offered.

Accommodation: The availability of sufficient number of rooms, the relative costs of accommodation, safety and security and standards of service are very relevant when a destination is chosen.

Destination attractiveness: Entertainment options like bars, theatres, nightclubs, shopping options such as souks, malls with attractive prices, sightseeing options such as museums, galleries, monuments and local tours, and attractions are significant points that are taken into consideration.

General Features

One of the main functions of professional associations is to organize a yearly conference, giving members an opportunity to improve their knowledge, to network and to unwind. The destination of the conference/meeting will keep changing in order to retain the attractiveness of the event and to give members a chance to do some sightseeing on the side. Conferences will have trade shows, expositions and product launches taking advantage of the 'captive' audience. Pre- and post-conference tours, sightseeing options for spouses/partners and entertainment are part of the official programme. Owing to the large numbers of attendees and logistics involved, large conferences are firmed up many years in advance. The organizers of conferences and meetings depend on service providers to make all arrangements, such as venue selection, assistance with delegate ticketing and transportation, ground transfers, hotel bookings, sightseeing tours, conference planning and entertainment.

The Significance of MICE Market for Destinations

Meetings and conferences are extremely important for destinations for many reasons. For many urban destinations, the MICE market is of great importance, contributing a significant part of their yearly business. An international conference brings in a large number of delegates, who use top-end accommodation and fill up the rooms. The visit of large numbers of delegates brings in valuable business not only to the venue hotel but also to other hotels in the city and all major service providers such as car/taxi hire, coach rental companies, bars, souvenir shops, shopping areas and entertainment centres. Most conferences or exhibitions last for three days or more, which means that each major conference brings bulk bookings of thousands of room nights. Major conferences bring substantial business for other service providers such as transporters, event companies, guides and entertainers. Conferences also spur expenditure in entertainment zones, restaurants and bars. Shopping areas thrive on business generated during conventions. International conventions bring in foreign exchange as well. Many conferences offer pre- and post-tours to neighbouring attractions and destinations, encouraging more local spending. Destination marketers work with hotels to provide attractive deals for conference organizers, timing such offerings for the off season. As conferences are generally organized when leisure business is low, these are significant because of the business generated in a lean season time. Business visitors to conferences are a great source of word of mouth publicity and stimulate repeat visits to the destination.

The conference business is also changing, in response to the uncertainties of modern times and changing preferences of delegates. Organizers report that the trend is to organize smaller conferences for shorter durations, clearly a sign of the difficult economic times. At the same time, perhaps because of faster information dissemination and quicker travel options, conferences are organized in increased frequency—many biennial conferences have been converted to annual events that are shorter in duration. Conferences are organized with shorter lead times than previously, which is an indication that organizers are concerned about abrupt events and incidents that may have an impact on the conference, such as a terror attack or a sudden airport or airline strike. Safety concerns have taken primacy over other considerations, and destinations which can establish the efficacy of their systems providing safety to citizens and visitors are at an advantage.

Exhibitions

Exhibitions are huge events, attracting exhibitors and trade visitors in thousands. Exhibitions, such as industrial or manufacturing exhibitions, are important business platforms to evaluate products, conduct negotiations and finalize contracts. As mentioned earlier, some exhibitions are held along with conferences, while some exhibitions may have talk sessions on the sidelines. Exhibitions can be trade oriented or for the public, such as consumer goods exhibitions and trade shows. The International Tourism Bourse (ITB) in Berlin is the biggest tourism trade show with an area of over 150,000 sq. m. International exhibitions tend to remain at a site or city, building up a clientele who make regular visits. However, several exhibitions rotate venue cities, providing an opportunity to destination marketing organizations to make a bid to bring prominent exhibitions to their cities.

Incentive Travel

Incentive travel is defined as 'a global management tool that uses an exceptional travel experience to motivate and/or recognize participants for increased levels of performance in support of organizational goals'. Across the world, companies provide employees and business partners opportunities to travel and have interesting experiences at attractive destinations as a strategy to motivate them for their business performance or as a recognition for their achievements in improving business. Incentive travel does not have much to do with education or work-related experiences, but focuses on providing a fun-filled holiday experience. Incentive travel takes place in groups, and generally comprises of a package of air travel, transfers, accommodation and entertainment. As the intention is to motivate the participant, the effort is to make the incentive tour 'special', with unusual events and surprises. The basic premise of incentive travel is if the reward of a trip to a desirable destination is offered, employees will be motivated to work more and perform better, resulting in improved productivity. Businesses are interested in retaining high-performing employees and view incentive travel as a powerful and effective management tool. Incentive travel strengthens loyalty to the employer company, encourages social interaction and creates healthy competition amongst peers. Specialist tour operators work closely with corporate teams to create unique experiences. They organize travel and transfers, incorporate entertaining cultural shows and design inspiring excursions.

The Travel Agency

The term travel agent and tour operator are increasingly used interchangeably. Although the distinction between the travel agent and the tour operator has blurred, it is important to understand the specific roles they play in tourism. For a student of tourism, the two terms evoke separate but interlinked roles played by intermediaries in the business of tourism.

It may be kept in mind that the discussion in this chapter features the roles played by the travel agents and the tour operators largely in a Western context from the point of view of a source market. In countries like India, the tour operator has come to mean another very different connotation which we will explore as the discussion progresses.

What Does a Travel Agent Do?

Travel agencies have for long been seen as an enterprise which provides information on travel and tourism, makes impartial recommendations to the potential traveller and makes arrangements for travel and tourism. The agent, as the name indicates, acts as an agent or representative of different suppliers, such as airlines, hotels, cruise companies, transportation companies and attractions. The travel agency personnel has information on different holiday options for the leisure traveller and recommends destinations and products best suited to the tastes and requirements of the client. The agent also assists the traveller in obtaining travel documents such as passports, visas and travel insurance. Often, the travel agency is also an authorized money changer, providing currency and traveller's cheques. The various agency functions undertaken may be summarized as follows:

- **Airline tickets:** Approved by IATA, the agency has access to airline reservation systems and books tickets for retail customers.
- **Hotel reservations:** Using different electronic platforms, the agency arranges hotel bookings for customers.
- **Railway ticketing:** Accredited agents are authorized to book rail tickets on behalf of customers.
- **Bus tickets:** The agency assists the customer in getting seat reservation on bus/coach services.
- **Car rentals:** The agent arranges for car rentals from car renting companies and transportation providers.
- **Passport and visa services:** The travel agent assists the customer in applying for passport, visas and processing travel documents.
- **Travel insurance:** The travel agent offers a range of travel related insurance policies.
- **Foreign exchange:** The travel agent is an authorized money changer and helps the customer obtain foreign currencies, travellers cheques and international cards.

Passport and Visa Services

Passport

A Passport is an official document issued by a Government or competent authority to the citizens of the country. There are three types of passports issued by the GoI.

1. **Ordinary passport:** An ordinary passport has a navy blue cover and consists of 36 or 60 pages. It is valid for 10 years from the date of issue and can be renewed for another 10 years. It is issued to an Indian citizen and can be used for all travel. It is a 'Type P' passport, where P stands for personal.
2. **Diplomatic passport:** A diplomatic passport, with a maroon cover, is issued to designated members of the national government, judiciary, statutory authorities, diplomats, official public couriers and any other persons specifically authorized by the Government. It is a 'Type D' passport with D standing for diplomatic.
3. **Official passport:** The white cover official passport is issued to designated government servants or any other person specifically authorized by the government, deputed abroad on government business. It is a 'Type S' passport, S standing for service.

Visa

A visa is an entry in a passport or other travel document made by an official or government, indicating that the bearer has been granted authority to enter the country concerned. Normally, it indicates length of stay, period of validity and number of entries allowed during that period. A single entry visa will not be valid if it has been used once. A multiple entry visa can be used by the passenger for making multiple entries within the validity period.

GoI issues the following different types of visas:

Sl. No.	Type of Visa	Validity	Purpose
1	Business (B)	5 years	Business
2	Conference (C)		Attending conference and seminars
3	a. Diplomatic (D) b. Official (O) c. UN Official (UD)		Granted to diplomats, officials, and persons working in UN/international organizations located in India and their spouses/ children
4	Employment (E)	1 year	Employment for skilled and qualified personnel
5	Emergency		Travel on medical or humanitarian emergency
6	Entry (X)		Granted to a person of India origin, foreign spouse of Indian national and to spouse/ children of foreigners holding any type of visa other than tourist/transit visa

(Continued)

(Continued)

Sl. No.	Type of Visa	Validity	Purpose
7	Journalist (J)	6 months	Journalism, Travel writing
8	a. Medical (MED) b. Medical Attendant (MEDX)	1 year or the period of treatment whichever is less	Medical treatment
9	Missionaries (M)		Granted to foreign missionaries, other than those holding No objection to return to India
10	Research (R)	3 years or duration of research project	Research
11	Student (S)	5 years or duration of course whichever is less	Regular/full-time academic studies in recognized institutes
12	Tourist (T)		Tourism
13	Transit (TR)	Up to 15 days and up to 2 entries	Transit

Generally, the travel agency operations are divided into travel and tour operations. Travel professionals look after reservations, calculate fares, issue tickets, process applications for travel documentation and insurance and coordinate appointments for visas. On the tours side, tour counsellors provide information on destinations and tourism products, assist clients in choosing holiday packages of their choice, arrange for confirmation of bookings, provide vouchers and tour information and liaise with the tour operator for smooth operation of the tours.

Travel Management Company

Travel agencies are increasingly converting themselves into 'travel management companies', offering diverse travel related services under one roof. Travel management companies offer their services to large organizations, managing their travel related requirements like air transport, transfers, accommodation and car rentals. The term is also used to describe travel agencies which offer a range of services. They may represent many travel brands in a country, working to achieve the sales and marketing goals of that brand. Some of the activities that are taken up by such companies are listed below:

- **Airline sales:** The travel agency becomes the general sales agents (GSA) of airlines in a country, representing the airline, managing operations and looking after sales and marketing functions.
- **Hotels and resorts:** The travel agency acts as the representative of major hotel and resort chains, providing sales, marketing and reservation services.
- **Cruises:** The agency may conduct sales and marketing, public relations and operations on behalf of cruise companies.

- **Destinations:** The agency represents destinations, helping them to develop strategies for the market, conduct public relations campaigns, promotional events and direct marketing programmes.
- **Cargo:** The agency may offer warehousing facilities and function as cargo GSA for airlines.
- **Charters:** Chartering of aircraft, corporate jets, cargo charters, heli-sightseeing and emergency services.

What are the income streams of a travel agency?

- **Handling fee (cost plus):** A negotiated professional fee is charged for certain services.
- **Commission (rate minus):** A commission is built into the regular fare publicized by the supplier.
- **Markup (net plus):** Net fares are provided by the supplier to the travel agent, who sells the product to the customer after adding a 'markup'.
- **Production incentive:** Suppliers reward performers with financial incentives, if targets are met or exceeded.

The Travel Agent and the Tour Operator

The travel agent sells vacation packages, which have been prepared by tour operators. In effect, as the term indicates, the travel agency works as an agent of the tour operator. The travel agent can be regarded as an intermediary between the tour operator and the prospective client. Generally speaking, the travel agent will endeavour to match the client's interests, expectations and budgets with a suitable vacation solution. The travel agent may represent several tour operators, suggesting packages based on his understanding of the client's requirements and the feasibility of a sale. In other cases, the travel agent may be working exclusively for one tour operator, in which case the agency will offer the packages and holiday options offered by that particular tour operator only. The travel agent works on a commission basis. In other words, the agent adds an agency commission on the price of a tour, which is provided to him by the tour operator. Agents generally have shops which are easily accessible to the customer. Generally speaking, the travel agent works with a set of clients who have travelled with him previously, and trust his recommendations. Travel agents may not specialize in destinations but offer a variety of holiday options by displaying the brochures of different tour operators, widening the scope of their offering. Through personalized service, travel agents play an important role in helping the client to identify the optimal holiday option, suitable to his/her taste, budget and inclination. Providing accurate, authentic and reliable information about the tourism product is a key factor in ensuring a transaction.

The travel agent can be compared to a waiter in the restaurant, who advises the guest to choose a dish of his preference, by taking him through the menu card. The menu, in this analogy, is the variety of different packages that the agent has in his inventory, which has been prepared by the tour operator and provided to the travel agent. Extending the analogy, the tour operator is like the chef, who has taken the trouble of preparing the dish or the tour package, but is dependent on the waiter or agent to impact the sale.

Trends

With increasing use of the Internet, tour operators are shifting towards a business model of selling packages directly to the visitor, eliminating the travel agent. However, many travellers prefer to go to a travel agent known to and trusted by them, instead of an anonymous tour operator. This explains why, despite the ease of booking tours on the Internet, the travel agency system still continues to be in business.

Blurring of Lines

In recent times, the distinction between a travel agency and a tour operation has become less clear. Travel agents generally sell packages, along with providing other services like currency and travel insurance. Travel agencies also help book flight tickets and hotel accommodation over the Internet. A travel agent, or 'retailer', sells various types of travel services on behalf of suppliers, such as hotels, automobile rentals, tour operators and cruise lines. In other words, the travel agent is moving away from the passive role played earlier, and sells travel products other than tours to customers. In the UK, shops of travel agents are generally located on the 'high street'.

In Europe, in the face of increasing competition and dwindling traditional sources of revenue, travel agencies have evolved into consolidators, wherein they purchase large numbers of tickets from airlines and sell them on specific discounts, either separately or by bundling the tickets on the holiday products.

Horizontal Integration

When similar enterprises operating in similar or comparable environments collaborate with each other to bring in efficiencies, it is called horizontal integration. A good example of horizontal integration is the code-sharing arrangements that airlines employ. An example of horizontal integration in accommodation sector is the franchisee concept.

Vertical Integration

When enterprises operating at different points of distribution channel come together, for example through a merger, it is called vertical integration. Vertical integration is generally done to achieve better cost management, increase bargaining power and to strengthen the brand. Tour operators merging with airline companies, tour operators purchasing hotel companies and travel agencies bought over by tour operators are all examples of vertical integration. Tour operators often are vertically integrated. Several major operators own airlines and run charter operations into destinations, thereby offering relatively inexpensive transport as part of the package price.

Electronic Intermediaries and E-Commerce

The single biggest factor that has changed the dynamics of the tourism industry is the emergence and preponderance of electronic intermediaries. The development of e-commerce in the aviation industry has permanently changed the travel industry and has disrupted traditional systems and roles. Let us examine this phenomenon and understand the processes behind it.

Computerized Reservation Systems (CRS)

CRSs were created some decades ago by some of the biggest airline companies in the world, with an aim of distributing the sales of their tickets through travel agencies. Prior to this, booking flight tickets was a laborious process, involving manual labour. Agents would call up a booking office or a larger agency which was holding some ticket inventory. The rates had to be calculated manually and the passenger details entered by hand.

All these tasks were rendered redundant by the CRS. Earlier, terminals were placed with major agents that connected to the reservation system of an airline. Later, airlines came together to develop networks that would provide more powerful tools for reservations.

SABRE was the earliest platform, beginning its operations in the 1960s. Abacus, a GDS created by Cathay Pacific, Singapore Airlines, China Airlines, All Nippon Airlines and some other East Asian airlines, was purchased by Sabre in 2015. Travelport GDS is the entity that owns three of the major GDS platforms—Apollo, Galileo and Worldspan. Amadeus was founded in 1987, and became the number one CRS provider worldwide by 2003. Amadeus diversified its operations to go beyond sales and reservation and currently provides distribution activities such as an advanced IT network, providing technology solutions.

Global Distribution Systems (GDS)

CRS companies morphed into GDS and became independent of their founding airline companies. Airline companies, in their bid to encourage travellers to book directly with them, decreased the commissions to be paid to travel agencies. These agencies were serviced by the GDS companies not only for their reservations but also for all their back end computing needs. GDS empowered the travel agent to offer more products and services, such as hotels, cruises and car rentals. GDS also provides information about hotels to travel agents worldwide, enabling them to book rooms in hotels according to the customer's requirements. First, the hotel provides static information such as a description of the rooms, photographs and list of amenities. Thereafter, the hotel is given access into the system to include a certain number of rooms in the system and manage the room rates at which the GDS makes the room available to the agents. Hotels pay a fixed amount to the GDS operator for the facility and then make payments according to the reservations obtained. Hotels have the advantage of getting their information distributed worldwide, obtaining bookings from travel agents who are not directly connected to their sales systems.

Universal Internet access and powerful web-based programs have transformed the way the world operates. Internet has transformed the way travel is bought and sold. More travel products are sold online than any other product. Internet has created this vast virtual marketplace with a variety of sellers such as airlines and hotels, and different kinds of buyers such as travellers and travel agencies. Global distribution systems provide the platforms that link the buyers and the sellers and ensure that reservations and purchases are done smoothly and efficiently.

GDS connects travel providers with travel agencies both physical and online. They also provide services such as search, pricing, ticketing and inventory management, based on their technologies. GDS companies work with travel providers such as airlines, hotels, car rental companies, tour operators and cruise operators, taking their inventories and products to online travel agencies, physical travel agencies and travel management companies. These travel agencies in turn sell these products to travellers, with the back end computing power of the GDS providing the connectivity for easy bookings, reservations and ticketing (Figure 8.2).

Electronic intermediaries, thus, have disrupted the traditional distribution channels, resulting in reduced prices and better options for consumers, eliminating unnecessary middlemen and customising products. Another important way in which electronic intermediaries have changed the game is the flexibility brought in terms of pricing and the targeted promotions and campaigns that are possible. It is only because of the emergence and popularity of the global distribution systems that the relationship between airlines and travel agents has changed forever, resulting in reduced commissions. Recently, some airlines have gone in for a zero commission regime, shutting out the agent.

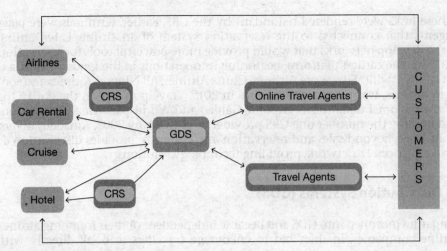

Figure 8.2   The global distribution system
Source: Authors.

Online Travel Agencies (OTAs)

Till a few years ago, a traveller used to book rooms in a hotel either by making a telephone call to the hotel or by visiting a travel agent in the neighbourhood who would then make a booking on the customer's behalf with the hotel. However, the advent of the Internet has radically changed the way business is conducted in all sectors, and the travel sector is no exception. An early innovation was the central reservation system which enabled hotel chains to book rooms in any of the group hotels using a computerized reservation system. Subsequently, major hotel chains started offering the facility of booking rooms from their websites, giving the customer an opportunity to collect more information about the property and the room and then making a purchase choice. Conventionally, a direct booking at the hotel's website or using a hotel's computer reservation system would offer the customer the best possible rate, as the transaction did not have any intermediaries.

The rules of the game have been radically altered in the recent past, with OTAs beginning operations and growing into a significant force. The first OTA that began operations was Expedia, launched by Microsoft in 1996. Priceline started operations in Europe around the same time and quickly expanded operations, offering the facility to book hotels and other components of holidays online. OTAs are increasing their market share substantially at the cost of traditional travel agents. OTAs are aggregators, collecting information from numerous suppliers and providing relevant information to the customer. Many OTAs have created separate business verticals to cater to different segments in the market. Using an OTA, the customer is empowered and informed, and can compare rates and obtain the best possible solution to his travel requirement.

There are two operating models for OTAs: Merchant model and Agency model. In the Merchant model, the OTA collects payment from the customer, keeps a fee for the transaction and makes payment to the hotel. In the Agency model, the customer makes payment to the hotel, including the commission or transaction fee payable to the OTA.

OTAs have of late started providing 'bundled' services, adding, for example, hotel rooms to flights offered. Other services that are bundled are car hire, travel insurance and sightseeing options.

An important aspect in the world of online travel intermediaries is the accuracy of recommendations made by the programme to the customer. Key to this is data analysis, driven by knowledge about the preferences and purchase behaviour of the customer. 'And, it is what may put Google in the driving seat for the future as it has the potential to assemble the most complete dataset of transactions, the competence to analyse it and push relevant offerings to customers' (Walsh, 2012).

In Europe, about 70% of hotel rooms are booked online platforms, while the corresponding figure for the USA is around 50%. It is estimated that online bookings of hotel rooms in India account for only 16% of the total bookings, but the figure is expected to grow to 25% by 2016 (ICRA, 2015).

In a dynamic online marketplace that is growing rapidly, there are certain disruptive strategies adopted by some OTAs. The basic revenue model for an OTA is the markup; it charges on the discounted rate given to be OTA by the hotel. However, some OTAs are offering heavy discounts, pricing rooms far below the rates given to them by the hotels. In the process, these OTAs incur heavy losses, but provide the customer with a windfall, obtaining rooms at throwaway prices. The objective behind this discount ward is to corner the market and kill off competition, although only time will tell if such a strategy will pay off in the long run.

Conclusion

Tour operators play a vital role in the business of tourism, connecting the traveller to the destination, providing the assurance of safe passage and the comfort of a hassle free holiday to the visitor. Tour operators or more accurately travel companies come in all sizes and shapes—the term actually encompasses the whole range of travel intermediaries, providing a variety of services. The sheer variety of travel intermediaries makes it difficult to generalize the steps in the tour process. With increased access and communication, tour companies are trying to come to terms with the changing requirements of travellers and the prospect of new players usurping established functions in the market. Traditional roles of travel agents have changed dramatically in recent times, and many established models of travel business are under threat of extinction. Add to this the disruptive influence of the Internet, which has changed the way the business is conducted; and you have a bewildering array of companies offering services of different hues, all aimed at the traveller.

Review Questions

1. Examine the role and functions of different types of tour operators.
2. Discuss the different steps involved in tour operation process.
3. Examine the significance of MICE market for destinations.
4. Explain the functions of a travel agency. Discuss how global distribution system (GDS) facilitates travel and tour operation business.
5. Write short notes on the following:
   - Online travel agency
   - Vertical integration
   - Tour costing
   - Travel itinerary

Activities

1. Select five destinations abroad which you would like to visit in future and identify major attractions and accommodation facilities available there. Present the details in your class and discuss the reasons why the destinations are popular.
2. Scan the print and electronic advertisement of five outbound operators in India and prioritize the target groups they focus. What are the avenues available to these companies to popularize their products in your town?
3. Arrange an interview with an inbound and an outbound operator and identify their linkages in tour operation business. What are the areas in which their operations differ?
4. Hold a discussion with a domestic tour operator to find out his focus areas and key markets.
5. Conduct an interview with a specialized tour operator after identifying his domain of expertise and find out the strategies adopted by him to maintain the USP.
6. Develop a tour package for a destination that is close to your institute/residence and design a brochure covering essential details.
7. Arrange a visit to a trade show near to your locality. Carefully observe the business and interact with the organizers focusing on planning, execution and management aspects.
8. Prepare a report on the tradeshow and present the same in a forum of youth who are interested to work in event management.

References

Web Resources

Help Tourism. n.d.a. Available at: http://www.helptourism.com/index.html (accessed on 21 December 2016).
——. b. 'Birding Tours in India: Eastern Himalaya and North East India'. In Help Tourism. Available at: http://www.helptourism.com/birding-ornithological-tours-india/birding-tours-india.html (accessed on 21 December 2016).
ICRA. 2015. 'Online Travel Agents: Boon or Bane?' ICRA Research Services. Available at: http://www.travelbizmonitor.com/images/Feature_Hotels_Online_travel_agents.pdf
Ministry of Tourism. 2015. 'India as a Global Conventions Destination Prospects and Strategies'. In IIMB–ICPB study for Ministry of Tourism. Available at: http://icpb.org/pdf/ICPB_Report_%20quantify_the_size_scope_and_economic_impact.pdf (accessed on 21 December 2016).
Walsh, J. 2012. The Ascent Of Online Travel Agents (OTAs) And Why Google Will Likely Be Planning Your Next Vacation. In IMD Real World Real Learning. Available at: https://www.imd.org/research/challenges/upload/TC078-12-THE-ASCENT-OF-ONLINE-TRAVEL-AGENTS.pdf (accessed on 21 December 2016).

Suggested Readings

Books

Buhalis, D., and E. Laws. 2011. *Tourism Distribution Channels: Practices, Issues and Transformations.* Cengage Learning EMEA.

Dwyer, L., and P. Forsyth, eds. 2007. *International Handbook on the Economics of Tourism.* Edward Elgar Publishing.

ICCA. 2013. *A Modern History of International Association Meetings.* International Congress and Convention Association.

ILO. 2013. *Toolkit on Poverty Reduction Through Tourism.* Geneva: International Labour Organization.

Lubbe, B. 2000. *Tourism Distribution: Managing the Travel Intermediary.* Kenwyn: Juta and Company Ltd.

National Skills Qualification Framework (NSQF). 2014. *Sector: Tourism and Travel.* Bhopal: PSS Central Institute of Vocational Education.

USAID. 2007. 'The Business of Inbound Tour Operators'. In *Tour Operators Manual.* USAID.

Web Resources

Barthel, J., and S. Perret. 2015. 'OTAs—A Hotel's Friend or Foe? How Reliant are Hotels on OTAs'. HVS. Available at: http://travelbizmonitor.com/images/HVS_OTAs_A_Hotels_Friend_Or_Foe.pdf

Chandra, K.K. 2014. 'Taking the Road Less Travelled'. Spectrum, *The Tribune.* Available at: http://www.tribuneindia.com/2014/20140504/spectrum/main1.htm

Cox & Kings. n.d. 'Duniya Dekho—Europe'. Cox & Kings. Available at: http://www.coxandkings.com/duniyadekho/europe/marvels_of_europe_-_winter/tourId/27805-213/

Hammock Holidays. n.d. 'About Hammock'. Available at: http://hammockholidays.com/holiday-planners/about_hammock

Le Passage to India. Available at: http://www.lepassagetoindia.com/main.aspx (accessed on 10 January 2016).

Snow Leopard Adventures Pvt. Ltd. (2013). Available at: http://www.snowleopardadventures.com/ (accessed on 21 December 2016).

SRIC Travels Pvt. Ltd. Available at: http://www.stictravel.com/stic/stic_html/htmlpages/air/Our Services.html

Travel Biz Monitor. 2016. 'Indians Leaning More towards 'Unbundled Packages' Instead of Set Travel Itineraries, Reveals Cleartrip'. Travel Biz Monitor.com. Available at: http://www.travelbizmonitor.com/Data-Analysis/indians-leaning-more-towards-unbundled-packages-instead-of-set-travel-itineraries-reveals-cleartrip-29465

Worldwide DMC. n.d. 'What is a Group Inclusive Tour or GIT?' A Blog for the Travel Trade. Available at: http://wwdmc.com/blog/what-is-a-group-inclusive-tour-or-git/

The Delhi metro
Image courtesy: Ministry of Tourism, Government of India.

CHAPTER 9

Transportation

By the end of this chapter, the student will be able to:

- Explain the role and importance of transportation systems in tourism.
- Recognize the business model of low cost carriers (LCCs).
- List the characteristics of LCCs.
- Enumerate the facilities at airports.
- Describe major civil aviation policies and regulations.
- Underline developments in rail transport and their linkages to tourism.
- Recall linkages between road transport and tourism in India.

Introduction

One of the most important prerequisites for the development of tourism is the availability of good transport systems. Investment in developing transportation networks of high standards have served destinations well, creating opportunities fuelled by demand for tourism services. On the other hand, many regions with the natural assets and resources to develop into major tourist destinations have remained undeveloped, mainly because of poor accessibility to tourist generating markets. The two sectors of tourism and transportation are interdependent and impact each other significantly. While developments in transportation have had a direct positive impact on tourism, the tourism industry, in turn, has spurred technological development in the transportation sector. The increased demand for more seats and more efficient and cheaper air travel is one of the main reasons for technological improvements in airline manufacture, as we will see in this chapter. We will explore all aspects of transportation—the different types of transport used in tourism, the impact of changing modes of transport on the development of tourism, the relationship between tourism demand and the level of accessibility.

The Evolution of Transport

In early days, the only modes of transportation available were water craft dependent on wind and manual labour and carts and carriages drawn by bullocks, mules and horses. Only the hardy and the religious undertook trips that were optional—pilgrims depended on whatever means were available and braved difficult conditions to fulfil their spiritual quests. In the West, the elite made use of carriages drawn by horses to travel to their destinations. The first significant change in transportation came with the advent of the steam engine. Steam power resulted in the development of massive nautical vessels that could traverse the oceans at considerable speed. The introduction of relatively comfortable and quick ships resulted in a spurt in travel between Europe and America, and also the beginning of the exploration of oriental destinations by a few Europeans. On land, vehicles powered by steam did not make a big impact on road transport. However, steam powered railways and the establishment of railway lines across Europe transformed tourism in the nineteenth century, offering an opportunity for thousands to travel for pleasure. The development of the internal combustion engine transformed road transport. Mass production of cars and the rapid development of roads stimulated tourism in an unprecedented manner. The advancement in the field of technology and consequent modernization is seen in all modes of transport—air, road, rail and water (Figure 9.1).

Aviation in Tourism

Travel in the modern era is defined by air travel. Whether travelling for business or pleasure, air travel has brought disparate parts of the world together and the biggest gainer has been the tourism industry. From short holidays at nearby destinations to travel to faraway countries on long haul routes, the speed, reliability and relatively reasonable pricing of air transportation has made it the pivotal component of tourism worldwide.

On an average, there are more than 100,000 flights being operated across the world every day, carrying more than 8 million passengers. Civil aviation is the most reliable means of mass transportation, and has transformed the world. Safe and reliable air transport is dependent on the adoption of rules, regulations and standards that cut across national boundaries.

As the sectors of aviation and tourism are closely interlinked, it is important to understand their interrelationship closely. While it has been noted that a liberalized aviation environment is directly beneficial to tourism development, liberalization and increased competition have led to very thin margins in the aviation sector, leading to the collapse of many airlines which could not survive outside controlled and sheltered environment.

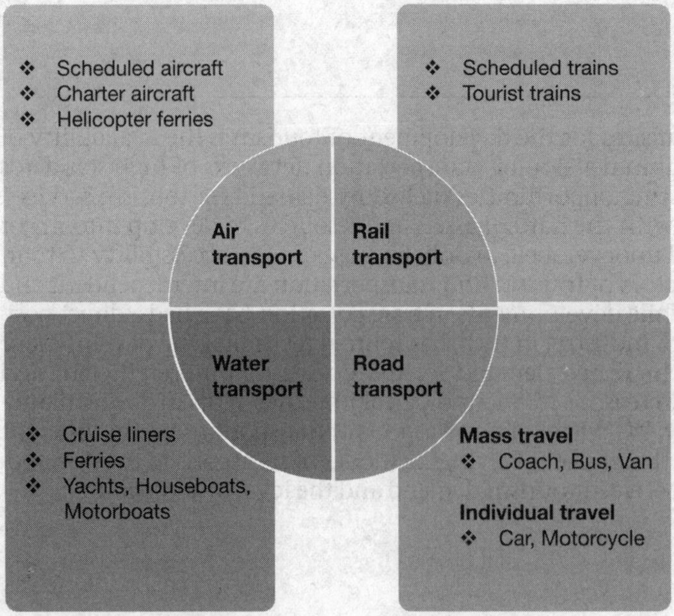

- ❖ Scheduled aircraft
- ❖ Charter aircraft
- ❖ Helicopter ferries

- ❖ Scheduled trains
- ❖ Tourist trains

Air transport

Rail transport

Water transport

Road transport

- ❖ Cruise liners
- ❖ Ferries
- ❖ Yachts, Houseboats, Motorboats

Mass travel
- ❖ Coach, Bus, Van

Individual travel
- ❖ Car, Motorcycle

Figure 9.1 Different types of transport
Source: Authors.

Civil aviation had previously functioned in a heavily regulated environment. Internationally, the numbers of airlines which could fly between two countries were usually limited to two, one from each country. The airfares were controlled, and minimum fares were prescribed. Most of the airlines that are owned by governments had a vested interest in continuing to operate in a controlled environment. The policy environment changed dramatically, owing to the demand for lower fares and the prospects for tourism development in destinations. Tourism was seen as an economic driver, bringing in foreign exchange, employment and other economic benefits. The cartelization practised by airlines was criticised as it bred inefficiency and was not friendly to consumer interests.

Simply put, the cheaper air travel became, the faster the development of tourism. A liberal environment meant the entry of more players in the market, increasing competition, improving customer service and bringing down fares. Liberalization also introduced the charter airline into the mix. Charter airlines offered seats at a fraction of the price charged by scheduled airlines, although these had to be bundled into a tour package and could not be purchased separately. The immediate impact of charter operations was that holidaymakers were able to go to destinations outside their countries even for short holidays, greatly enlarging the holiday market. Families, who would normally travel by road for their yearly holidays, opted to travel by air, bringing in new customers. Long haul charters, which commenced operations after the success of the short haul charters, brought far off destinations to the door steps of customers.

The Jet Age

The landmark technological advancement in transportation, which has eclipsed all previous developments in terms of its impact on travel, is the introduction of the jet propulsion engine in aircraft. Previously, air travel was restricted to a few, owing to the small numbers of passengers that could be carried by aircraft powered by propeller engines. Consequently, air fares remained high, and far beyond the common traveller. New aircraft powered by Jet engines, such as the Boeing 707 and the Douglas DC-8, changed commercial air travel, with their bigger capacity and speed. Airfares were brought down, and more destinations were connected, bringing in new passengers who travelled by air for business and for holidays. Subsequently, markets and destinations were connected using charter flights, resulting in a dramatic increase in the number of tourists. Recently, the introduction of wide-bodied jets brought in more efficiency.

The Boeing 747

If there is one commercial transport vehicle that can be credited with revolutionizing tourism, it is the Boeing 747. Before 1970, commonly used commercial aircraft carried around 150 passengers or less, resulting in high air fares, discouraging tourists from travelling by air. The Boeing 747 irrevocably changed air travel. The 'Jumbo Jet', as it was affectionately known, was the first wide-bodied aircraft produced. It had four engines and used a double deck configuration for a part of its length. The Boeing 747 could accommodate up to 660 passengers in a single class configuration, and 416 passengers in a typically 3-class layout. In other words, the 747 had a capacity that was 2½ times more than the largest commercial airliner in use at that time. The Boeing 747 remained the aircraft with the maximum passenger capacity for 37 years, till the Airbus A380 was put into service in 2007.

For the tourism industry, an important facet of the performance of the 747 was its long range. The aircraft was capable of flying over 13,000 km non-stop, which was enhanced to over 14,000 km for the 747-400ER series (Airliners.net, n.d.). This meant that far-flung destinations could be connected to major source markets. Long haul leisure tourism for the masses became a reality, thanks to the Boeing 747. Increased passenger capacity meant that the cost per seat was reduced substantially, resulting in lower fares which again directly contributed to increased tourism. From 1970 to 2007, more than 1,500 Boeing 747 aircraft were sold to all major airlines. The aircraft brought into prominence the 'hub and spoke' model, with smaller airlines ferrying passengers from secondary airports to major hubs, from where the 747 would transport them on intercontinental and trunk routes.

Airbus A380

The most recent technological innovation in air transportation is the introduction of the Airbus A380 into commercial service. It is the world's largest passenger airliner and entered the service in October 2007 for Singapore airlines. The most significant innovation of the A380 is that it is a full 'double-decker', meaning that the upper deck extends along the entire length of the aircraft. The Boeing 747 had an upper deck in the front section only. Due to this, the A380 can accommodate up to 853 passengers in an all economy class configuration! The A380 can fly non-stop for over 15,000 km, and currently services sectors such as Sydney (Australia) to Dallas (the USA).

Charter Operations

There are different kinds of charter operators. A 'time charter' is the one where a single tour operator contracts an aircraft for the season. A 'part charter' means that the tour operator has contracted a block of seats or a portion of the capacity of the aircraft. A 'back-to-back' charter is operated by tour operators as a series to a destination, with one set of passengers disembarking at the destination to begin their holiday and another set of passengers boarding the aircraft to return after their holiday. Only large operators with high volumes can manage this kind of operation on a continuous basis.

Low Cost Carriers (LLCs)

LCCs brought an entirely new dimension in civil aviation and profoundly influenced the development of tourism worldwide. Airline companies are divided into two, based on the services offered. The 'full service' carriers offer a range of services to the passenger, ranging from airport facilities, different classes of travel, a choice of meals, drinks and beverage services and onboard shopping. LCCs offered a very different flying experience, attracting passenger by low fares and offering very few services. The philosophy of the LCC operation is simple— people would fly a lot more if flying was made more affordable.

In the liberalized environment, LCCs started operations offering low fares to encourage people to travel by air. These 'no-frills' carriers, did not provide food and beverage service, charged separate fees for checked in baggage and operated on a slim staff strength. They do not offer services like executive lounges, frequent flyer programs or executive class travel. They encourage travellers to book directly, reducing intermediaries. They try to keep costs down by using secondary airports or by not using expensive airport infrastructure like aerobridges.

LCCs have redefined air travel, particularly in Europe and Asia. The biggest beneficiary of the introduction of LCCs has been the tourism industry. Because of competitive prices, a large new market interested in travelling for leisure has opened up. They demand new tourism products and create new destinations. Faced with the prospect of new markets, destination marketing companies and tourism service providers are offering new products with lesser known destinations, connected to big cities through short haul LCCs.

LCC concept was popularized in the US by Southwest Airlines. The success of the concept is evident from the fact that Southwest Airlines is the third largest airline in the world in terms of passenger traffic. Spurred by its success, LCCs started operations in other parts of the world.

LCCs have a 38% market share of the European passenger market and 30% of the US market. In Asia, although the penetration is only around 20%, LCCs are the fastest growing segment.

The LCC Business Model

Aircraft utilization and turnaround time: An airline makes money when the aircraft is flying, not when it is on the ground. Therefore, the effort is to keep aircraft flying as much as possible, with the first flight taking off early in the morning and the last flight ending its service by midnight. The 'turnaround' time is also an important factor. Before the aircraft can make a new trip, it has to be at the gate for the passengers to disembark and the baggage has to be unloaded. New passengers and their baggage have to come onboard, and the aircraft has to be cleaned and freshened up. The time needed for these activities is called the turnaround time. Typically, full-service carriers need about one hour of turnaround time, which has been reduced to less than half an hour by LCCs. Consequently, LCCs fly their aircraft for over 12 hours a day (in technical terms called the block time), compared to around 8 hours for full service carriers.

No-frills: The philosophy of an LCC is simple—get the passenger from point A to point B. Every other facility is considered to be a 'frill', which is chargeable. LCCs do not offer free food and beverages, but passengers have an option to either purchase food or drink from the website while purchasing the flight or from the cabin crew during the flight. Passengers cannot request for a specific seat on the aircraft. If they want to sit on a particular seat, this facility is available for a small fee. Seats with extra legroom are also charged a higher price. LCCs have shifted to ticketless travel and online check-in, reducing the deployment of personnel and usage of paper. LCCs generally do not offer refunds for missed flights.

Streamlined operations: LCCs generally use a single type of aircraft, which keeps down staff training costs, stock inventory and standby arrangements. The configuration is also standardized to a single economy class seating. LCCs operate point to point, which means that they do not make arrangements for connecting flights, transfers and luggage handling between flights.

Secondary airports: LCCs operate services to and from smaller airports (referred to as secondary airports), wherever available. Large, central airports are usually congested and more expensive, adding to costs and increasing turnaround time.

Sales and distribution: LCCs prefer direct sales through the airline website, keeping down distribution costs. Most are not integrated into global distribution systems, in view of the costs involved. LCCs generally avoid opening sales offices and discourage bookings through travel agents (Dwyer and Forsyth, 2006).

The success story of IndiGo is an indicator of the strength of the LCC model. In just a few years' time, the airline has overtaken the established giants and risen to the top! Our case study has more details.

Case Study: IndiGo

IndiGo is the most successful low-cost carrier in India. The brand message of IndiGo is 'low fares, on time flights and a hassle free experience'. IndiGo commenced operations in 2006 with a single aircraft. The fleet has grown to 97, with an average age of just 3.26 years (April 2015). Indigo operates with a single aircraft type, the Airbus A320-200, seating 180 passengers. Currently, it operates 649 flights to 34 Indian cities and five cities outside India.

(Continued ...)

IndiGo stresses on operational efficiency. All customers were booked on the IndiGo website will be automatically checked in the time of booking. Tickets can be booked online on the IndiGo website through the call centre, on the IndiGo mobile app and through online travel agents like MakeMyTrip. While booking the flight ticket, passengers have the option to book a specific seat, onboard meals and snacks, extra luggage weight, reserve a cab or a hotel room, lounge services and insurance. Handheld instruments ('Q busters') are used to reduce queues at check-in and passengers can opt for priority check-in for an extra fee.

IndiGo has carried 84 million passengers to date and has a market share of 36.5% (September 2015). IndiGo is the only profitable airline in India.

In 2012, IndiGo became the largest airline in India in terms of market share, surpassing Jet Airways just six years after commencement of operations. In 2014, IndiGo received its 100th aircraft, completing an order which it had placed in 2005 with Airbus. In August 2015, IndiGo placed an order of 250 Airbus A320 neo aircraft worth $27 billion, the largest single order in the history of Airbus.

IndiGo is owned by Inter Globe Aviation Ltd., which completed a ₹31.3 billion initial public offering (IPO). This means that the likely valuation of the airline is more than ₹265 billion!

Discussion Questions

1. List the possible reasons for the success of Indigo, especially in an environment where airline companies like Air India are struggling to remain profitable.
2. What are the ways in which Indigo earns revenues other than air fares?

Civil Aviation in India

The first air route was opened between Karachi and Delhi by the Indian state Air services in collaboration with the Imperial Airways, the UK. In 1932, Tata Sons started a regular airmail service between Karachi and Madras. In 1948, a joint sector company, Air India International Ltd was established by the GoI and Air India (earlier Tata Airlines), headed by J.R.D. Tata who had founded the first Indian airline in 1932, and he himself piloted its inaugural flight. In 1953, after Parliament passed the Air Corporations Act, Indian Airlines and Air India were set up after nationalization of the airline industry and the merger of the airlines operating during the time. In 1994, this Act was repealed, paving the way for the entry of private players to operate scheduled services. Moduluft, East West Airlines, Air Sahara, Damania Airways, NEPC Airlines and Jet Airways were early entrants into civil aviation. In 2003, Air Deccan began the era of low-cost carriers in the country.

Air India

Air India is the flag carrier, the national airline of India. A public sector unit owned by GoI, Air India is currently the third largest airline in terms of the number of passengers. Air India operates to 84 destinations, including 48 domestic and 36 international destinations, using a fleet of Boeing and Airbus aircraft. Air India operates two subsidiaries—Air India Express and Air India Regional—which fly to domestic and some Asian destinations. Air India is a member of Star Alliance, a worldwide alliance of 27 member airlines.

In 1953, GoI nationalized all Indian airlines, and created two airline entities. Indian Airlines operated to all domestic destinations and to neighbouring countries such as Pakistan, Nepal, Bangladesh and Sri Lanka. In 2007, Indian Airlines merged with Air India.

Directorate General of Civil Aviation (DGCA)

DGCA is the regulatory body governing the safety aspects of civil aviation in India. The following are the main functions of DGCA:

- Registration of civil aircraft
- Granting of air operator's certificates and regulation of air transport services, including clearance of scheduled and non-scheduled flights of operators
- Formulation of standards of airworthiness for civil aircraft
- Licensing of pilots, aircraft maintenance engineers, flight engineers and air traffic controllers
- Supervision of institutes engaged in flying training with a view to ensuring high quality
- Certification of aerodromes and communication, navigation and surveillance (CNS)/air traffic management (ATM) facilities
- Conducting investigation into incidents involving aircraft and taking accident prevention measures
- Safety oversight of all entities approved/certified/licensed under Aircraft Rules 1937.

Airports

In view of the critical role played by air travel in tourism, it is important for us to understand the functioning of airports, the various components that make airports work and the changing nature of airports worldwide. Airports are traditionally viewed as gateways, where aircraft deliver and pick up passengers. As the airports are very often the first touch point of destinations, the experience at an airport often determines the overall perception of the holiday and the destination. This is the reason why airports are regarded more than just gateways to a destination; they play a vital role in the overall holiday experience. Airports are seen as important infrastructure, not merely for tourism but for the economic development of the region. Countries, regions and cities invest heavily in building up and improving airport infrastructure, airport facilities and airport connectivity as an essential first step in a push for developing a region. An airline may take an operational decision to start a new service to a destination based on the quality of the airport. Destinations have to compete for the business provided by airlines, as the marketing and visibility brought to destinations by a new airline service is critical from the tourism and economic point of view.

Airports have been evolving over the years. From mere transit points, airports have become destinations by themselves. Some airports have grown into the most important part of the tourism experience. A good example is the Dubai International airport. The airport is the busiest airport by international passenger traffic, third busiest by international passenger traffic and the sixth busiest cargo airport in the world. The airport is the home base of the international airline Emirates and the regional airline Fly Dubai. It has been rapidly expanding and the Terminal 3 that was recently opened, which is the largest airport terminal in the world. The airport caters to about 8,000 weekly flights, operated by 140 airlines to over 270 destinations. However, what is important is that Dubai International Airport has become one of the most important parts of the economy of Dubai. The airport contributes 21% of the total employment and provides 27% of the GDP of Dubai.

Greenfield Airports

Greenfield airports are those which are developed at a new site or location. A greenfield airport project begins with a feasibility study to evaluate the viability of a new project to be built from scratch and the implications of such a project on the existing and projected air traffic. Identification and procurement of suitable land is another important component of a Greenfield project. There are several successful models of greenfield projects—the airports of Bengaluru and Hyderabad were greenfield projects built on a public–private partnership (PPP) basis, by Joint Venture companies in which government and a private developer consortium are partners.

Brownfield Airport Projects

When an existing airport undergoes significant redevelopment and expansion, such a project is called a 'brown' field airport project, to distinguish it from a 'green' field. Brownfield projects are undertaken when the owner or operator does not have the resources or expertise to modernize and expand the airport and brings in an experienced partner. The usual method adopted is the PPP route. The Delhi and Mumbai international airports are examples of brownfield airport projects that have become major successes. The PPP projects in India accounts for approximately 54% of the total passenger traffic in the country. Driven by their success, the Airports Authority of India intends to seek PPP concessionaires at four brownfield sites—Chennai, Kolkata, Ahmedabad and Jaipur—and two greenfield sites at Navi Mumbai and Goa Mopa.

Facilities and services: What are the facilities and services that are available at airports? What agencies function in an airport? What are the functions undertaken by different service providers for the passenger? It is important for us to gain an overall understanding of the way airports work, as each aspect of the functioning of an airport is interrelated with the passenger, thereby to the tourism industry. There will be more complex operations and facilities at an international airport compared to a domestic airport. This is because of the provision for formalities such as customs, immigration, public health and animal and plant quarantine.

Management: The overall management of the airport is entrusted to a specialized organization, headed by the airport managers. Among the key responsibilities that the organizations handle are air-traffic control, runway, taxiway and apron management, cargo management, security, passenger amenities and utilities. In an increasingly commercialized environment, airport managements are on the lookout for new avenues that increase customer satisfaction while providing durable revenue streams to the airport.

Check-in: When a passenger arrives at the airport with the intention of flying out, the most important point of contact is the check in counter. Check-in counters are located at the check-in concourse, which is the area close to the landside passenger entrance. At the check-in, the passenger obtains a boarding pass that specifies the airline, the time of departure and the assigned seat at the gate from which the airline is boarding.

Baggage handling services: At the time of check-in, the passengers there persists his bag to the airline staff, and obtains the receipt for the same. The baggage is taken to the sorting area, and sorted into flight loads by a specialized team of service providers, which ensures that these are the loaded onto the aircraft in which the passenger is travelling to his destination. On arrival, the baggage is delivered at the baggage reclaim area in the arrival concourse on conveyor belts. Baggage of passengers on connecting flights has to be transferred from one aircraft to another within a limited time. Baggage services also involve interline baggage, which are the baggage of passengers subject to transfer from the aircraft of one operator to the aircraft of another operator in the course of the passenger's journey.

Immigration services: Immigration services are manned by specialized officers who ensure that the passenger has the necessary travel documents to gain entry at the point of arrival. In most cases, it is the visa that is the most important travel document that permits entry into another country. At immigration, the identity of the passenger is also verified against databases to make sure that the passenger is entitled to travel abroad.

Security check: The passenger and his cabin baggage is subjected to a thorough check to ensure that prohibited material is not carried on board. Generally speaking, materials that are potential threats to the safety of the passengers and of the aircraft are prohibited from being carried on to the airport aircraft. Examples of prohibited materials and objects are guns, knives, inflammable material and liquids in large quantities.

Customs: Upon disembarking, the passengers go through customs area, where they are expected to declare objects in their possession that may attract customs duty. Requirements and prohibitions regarding items that can enter the country change from country to country, and it is the duty of customs operations to keep an eye on passengers and their luggage and confiscate contraband and prohibited items. Customs personnel also look after incoming cargo, examining documentation and verifying the admissibility of consignments.

Air traffic control: Management of airspace, implementation of modern air navigation infrastructure and adherence to international protocols and safety standards are among the vital aspects of air traffic control. It is the air traffic control that regulates traffic in and around an airport, ensuring that landings and takeoffs take place smoothly and in an orderly fashion.

Security: It is paramount to have an efficient security apparatus that is in charge for the entire airport campus. The security personnel watch the perimeter for any intrusions, control airport access to passengers and authorized personnel and inspect and screen baggage, as part of a comprehensive security protocol. Equipment such as CCTV cameras, baggage screening X-ray systems and handheld devices are used.

Passenger facilities: There is a wide range of passenger facilities that are provided at the airport. The most basic are flight information boards, passenger facilitation counters, airside waiting areas, passenger seating, toilet facilities and drinking water stations. With a view to improving the airport experience, many new facilities enabling a relaxed environment at the airport are being provided. Food and beverages outlets, ranging from basic coffee shops to fine-dining restaurants have become common. Airports offer a wide variety of shopping options, and most of the 'high street' fashion brands have a presence in the shopping area of major airports. A popular shopping area is the duty-free shop at international airports that allows the passenger to purchase goods without being charged the local duties or VAT.

Airport lounges: Airport lounges are offered by some airlines and a few airports for use by executive-class passengers and priority passengers such as those who are frequent flyers and commercially important persons (CIP). Lounges have facility for comfortable seating, food and drink and communication and entertainment. Some airlines have started providing arrangements for relaxation, such as shower rooms, massages and beds for day use.

Airport offices: Airlines flying into airports have offices on-site. Apart from selling tickets for flights, these offices also assist the passenger on any travel-related matter such as excess baggage, flight connections, lost and found baggage and special facilities.

Transport facilities: Airports cater to large numbers of passengers and have to provide proper infrastructure for smooth connections by rail and road. Many major airports have railway stations as well, offering a convenient connection to the suburban railway system. Bus stations offering transfers by bus to the city centre are quite common at airports. A range of options like prepaid taxi, rent a car and city taxi systems are available. An example is the airport express line, a train that connects the Delhi international airport to the city centre.

Cargo services: An important operation at the airport is the cargo services. Any property carried on an aircraft other than mail, stores and unaccompanied baggage is called cargo. Large contingents of cargo are handled and transported by specialized companies on passenger aircraft as well as on aircraft that carry only cargo. The cargo area has warehouses, vehicle parks, aprons and office buildings, which are generally separate from passenger terminals.

As brought out above, the modern airport is a complex organization, operated with the involvement and participation of multiple agencies, delivering seamless service to the thousands of passengers who pass through its doors. Our case study on the Delhi International Airport showcases an airport which has won international recognition for its quality of operation and world class facilities.

Rajpath, New Delhi

Case Study: Delhi International Airport Ltd

The Indira Gandhi International airport, Delhi, is the eighth largest airport in the world, and the busiest airport in India. The airport caters to 40.98 million passengers (2014–15), or more than 100,000 passengers per day. On an average, there are 950 airport movements a day at the airport. The Delhi International airport is a private airport constructed and managed by the Delhi International Airport Ltd (DIAL), a joint venture company between GMR consortium and Airport Authority of India. The Delhi airport won the best airport award for passenger service for 2014, under the category of airports handling 25–40 million passengers per annum.

There are three runways and two terminal buildings. The airport has an integrated terminal, from where domestic and international flights are operated. Terminal 3 is a nine-level building with two piers each 1.2 km long and has a total area of 5.4 million sq. ft. There are 168 check-in counters and 95 immigration counters. Seventy-eight passenger boarding bridges connect the terminal to aircraft for smooth embarkation and disembarkation. The car park can accommodate 4,300 cars, and has facility for 'park and fly' passengers. Within the airport is a 100 room transit hotel, sleeping pods and 20,000 sq. m of retail space. Shops in categories such as beauty and wellness, cafe bars, convenience travel and news, electronics, fashion and accessories, jewellery and gifting, liquor, perfumes and cosmetics and souvenirs are all available at the airport. There are special facilities for the disabled such as special parking facilities, wheelchair assistance and separate immigration desks. There are Foreign Exchange counters and automated teller machines in many parts of the airport. Inter terminal coaches have been provided for passengers to travel between terminals. The airport is connected to the city centre by an eight lane approach road. There is also a high-speed rail link to the city centre.

In 2004, the AAI invited expression of interest from experienced and qualified consortiums to run the airport. Based on a competitive bidding process, the GMR consortium was awarded the mandate to manage the airport, and a JV company was formed. DIAL appointed a management team with international experience, and worked on a phased plan of modernization, based on a master plan. On 3 April 2006, the management of the airport was transferred to DIAL. Within 2 years, a new runway was opened. A new domestic departure

(Continued ...)

terminal 1D was opened in 2009, and the new integrated passenger terminal T3 was inaugurated on 3 July 2010.

In the 8 years after DIAL took over the airport, it has made rapid strides in enhancing the service quality resulting in increased passenger satisfaction, world-class services and easy and comfortable arrival and departure.

Image courtesy: Ministry of Tourism, Government of India.

Discussion Questions

1. List the three areas in which a private airport provides better service to the customer as compared to an airport managed by Airports Authority of India.
2. 'All airports should be privatized, in view of the success of the DIAL model'. Discuss.

Regulation of Civil Aviation

Safe and reliable air transport is dependent on the adoption of rules, regulations and standards that cut across national boundaries. ICAO is the forum that creates these standards and agreements. ICAO is a specialized body of the United Nations, and currently has over 190 members. Its headquarters is at Montreal, Canada, and there are seven regional offices catering to specific geographic regions. We have become familiar with ICAO and its functioning in Chapter 4.

ICAO is engaged in creating standards and policies, undertaking studies and compliance audits and in assisting the aviation industry in myriad ways. ICAO is concerned with the following strategic objectives:

* Enhancing global civil aviation safety
* Increasing capacity and improving efficiency
* Enhancing global civil aviation security
* Developing a sound and viable aviation system
* Minimizing adverse environmental effects of aviation

Civil Aviation Policy

The national level Civil Aviation Authority exercises regulatory powers over the aviation sector, controlling and regulating all activities in the sector. The authority gives permissions for foreign airlines to start operations, the number of flights, the airports of operation and the code share arrangements with domestic airlines. The authority also licenses airline operators, thereby exerting control over the sectors on which airline companies can operate and the density of operation. In India, the MoCA and its organization, the Directorate General of Civil Aviation, exerts regulatory powers. One of the notable aspects of the regulatory regime in India is the '5/20' rule, which restricts international operations to only those airline companies which have been in operation for at least 5 years, with at least 20 operational aircraft. The policy also prescribes that airlines provide service on sectors with relatively lower passenger load in addition to the popular 'trunk' routes of heavy traffic. Issues like high air turbine fuel (ATF) fares and taxation are frequently raised by airline companies as obstacles to the growth of the sector.

Freedoms of the Air

The 'freedoms of the air' are a set of aviation rights regulating the entering and landing of aircraft of one country in the airspace of another country. These were formulated in the Chicago Convention on International Civil Aviation of 1944. Freedoms are the basic structures of international civil aviation. The first two freedoms deal with transit rights, and the next three with passenger and cargo. It may be noted that these 'freedoms' or 'rights' are not automatic, but flow from bilateral or multilateral agreements and treaties between countries. The box has the details of all the nine 'freedoms'.

Nine Freedoms of the Air

First freedom of the air: The right or privilege granted by one state to another state or states to fly across its territory without landing. For example, a flight from Dubai to Bangkok, overflying India, operated by a UAE carrier.

Second freedom of the air: The right or privilege granted by one state to another state or states to land in its territory for non-traffic purposes, for example, a flight from Dubai to Bangkok by a UAE carrier stopping to refuel at Chennai airport.

Third freedom of the air: The right or privilege granted by one state to another state to put down, in the territory of the first state, traffic coming from the home state of the carrier, for example, a flight from Dubai to Chennai operated by a UAE carrier.

Fourth freedom of the air: The right or privilege granted by one state to another state to take on, in the territory of the first state, traffic destined for the home state of the carrier, for example, a flight from Dubai to Chennai operated by Air India.

Fifth freedom of the air: The right or privilege granted by one state to another state to put down and to take on, in the territory of the first state, traffic coming from or destined to a third state, for example, a flight from Dubai to Bangkok to Kuala lump operated by a UAE carrier.

Sixth freedom of the air: The right or privilege of transporting, via the home state of the carrier, traffic moving between two other states, for example, a flight from Chennai to Dubai to Paris by a UAE carrier.

Seventh freedom of the air: The right or privilege granted by one state to another state of transporting traffic between the territory of the granting state and in a third state with no requirement to include on such operation any point in the territory of the recipient state, that is, the service need not be an extension of any service from the home state of the carrier, for example, a flight from Chennai to Paris by a UAE carrier.

Eighth freedom of the air: The right or privilege of transporting cabotage traffic between two points in the territory of the granting state on a service that originates or terminates in the home country of the foreign carrier outside the territory of the granting state, for example, a flight from Chicago to New York City to Toronto by a Canadian company.

Ninth freedom of the air: The right or privilege of transporting cabotage traffic of the granting state on a service performed entirely within the territory of the granting state, for example, a flight from Beijing to Shanghai by a Canadian company.

Source: Manual on the Regulation of International Air Transport.

Ministry of Civil Aviation (MoCA)

MoCA, GoI, is the apex regulator and policy-making body for civil aviation in the country. MoCA aims to promote the growth of the Indian aviation sector by implementing several measures that will increase connectivity, improve services and bring in a multiplier effect. MoCA proposes to take flying to the masses by making it affordable and to create an ecosystem that will enable safe, secure, affordable and sustainable air travel by enhancing regional connectivity, infrastructure development and deregulation. Currently, only 75 out of the 476 airstrips and airports have regular operations. MoCA plans to revive airstrips, converting them as 'no-frills' airports, providing fiscal incentives. MoCA plans to promote Scheduled Commuter Airlines (SCA), linking smaller towns and airstrips. There are also projects to create new airports as well as bring improvements to existing airports to enhance capacity and increase connectivity. To promote charter operators, MoCA has eased restrictions making it easier to begin operations to India.

From a tightly regulated and controlled sector, aviation in India has evolved into a more open and liberal environment, resulting in increased flights, operators and passengers. It is estimated that the civil aviation sector will grow at an annual rate of 20%. More deregulation is in the offing, enabling international partnerships and ease of doing business.

Rail Transportation

Rail travel is a mode of travel celebrating as much the experience of motion, the passengers aboard as well as the passing landscapes and peoples as it is about reaching the destination. This may well explain why heritage railways attract such a widespread and devoted following, whereas the fascination with propeller powered aviation prior to the introduction of jet propulsion, while vibrant, nostalgic and significant, has never reached the levels of interest in and commitment enjoyed by heritage railways. (Conlin and Prideaux, 2014)

Transportation by rail is the commonest and most popular mass-transport system in the world. In many countries like India and China, the bulk of domestic tourism movement takes place by rail, with great numbers using trains to return home for festivals and to take place in religious gatherings. Rail travel is popular primarily because it is relatively cheap, with the fares within the budget of all sections of the population. In many parts of the world, rail travel is the only option of long-distance travel available, as regions may not be connected by air. It is indisputable that rail travel enables the movement of very large numbers of travellers, as against air and road transport. The safety, dependability and relative comfort offered by long-distance trains are other factors that make rail travel popular. Railway stations are generally located in central areas of cities, providing easy accessibility and quick transfers. On the other hand, the railway system is not flexible—the travel times of trains are fixed, the stops are pre-determined and the routes determined by the tracks laid.

High speed trains connect cities and offer a more attractive alternative to air travel. The high speed trains have become part of the tourism experience in many destinations.

TGV (Train à Grande Vitesse)

The TGV or 'high speed train' is a high-speed rail service, connecting major cities of Europe. Initially started in France, the TGV expanded its network in all directions, connecting to Belgium, Germany, the Netherlands and the UK. For many years, the TGV held the record for the fastest conventional train service in the world.

The Shinkansen or the 'Bullet Train'

The Shinkansen is a network of high-speed railway lines in Japan, linking most major cities on the islands of Honshu and Kyushu. The original line, connecting the largest cities of Tokyo and Osaka, is the world's busiest high-speed railway line, carrying over 50 million passengers every year. In 50 years of its operation, Japan's Shinkansen network has transported over 10 billion passengers till date. Remarkably, it has not recorded a single passenger fatality due to derailment or collision during this period!

The Shinkansen is one of the top attractions of Japan tourism, with many travel packages developed by tour operators. The tourist attractions of Japan such as natural scenery, history, culture and entertainment have been combined with the railway network offering a new experience of visiting a destination.

The developments in rail travel of the previous few decades pale in comparison with the achievements of China in high speed rail travel. Our case study gives you the details and explains how the new system will transform travel in China and connect far flung cities.

Case Study: High Speed Rail Network of China

In terms of High Speed Rail (HSR) network length, no country comes close to China. The second ranked country in 2013 had an HSR network one quarter of the size of China's. By October 1, 2013, it had put in operation a passenger dedicated HSR network of 12,183 kilometres. By July 1, 2014, China Railways was running over 1,330 pairs of HSR trains a day on both this dedicated network and on upgraded conventional lines. Since the new generation of HSR lines only started operating in 2008, this represents a radical change in the provision of passenger services by China Railways in a very short time. As of October 1, 2014, over 2.9 billion passengers are estimated to have taken a trip in a China Rail High-Speed train (CRH services), a growth of about 39% per annum since 2008.

China is at a turning point in its urbanization, a strategic time to put in place the transportation backbone that will stimulate complementarity among its cities and their overall competitiveness. The 1,318 km JingHu (Beijing South-Shanghai Hongqiao) and 2,281 km JingGuang (Beijing West-Guangzhou South) passenger dedicated high speed lines became operational, connecting the three most vibrant economic clusters in China. The trip between Beijing and Shanghai (1,318 km) can be completed in four hours 48 minutes, for an average speed of 275 km/h (Ollivier, Bullock, Jin and Zhou, 2014).

Discussion Questions

1. Why did China build a high-speed railway network at high cost?
2. List three advantages that a rail network has over air connectivity.

Indian Railways

The rail network of India forms the spine of transportation across this vast country. The second largest railway system in the world, the Indian Railways covers 64,500 km of track on which 16,000 trains run every day stopping at around 7,000 railway stations. Indian Railways serves over 13 million passengers per day!

The first railway in the Indian subcontinent was a stretch of 21 miles from Bombay to Thane, a section of which was formally opened on 16 April 1853. On 15 August 1854, the first passenger train steamed out of Howrah station, travelling 24 miles to Hooghly. This was followed by a period of intense construction activity, when tracks were laid to create a network of railway lines all over the country. By 1880, the Indian railway system had route mileage of 9,000 miles!

Indian Railways and Tourism

Indian Railways has an array of facilities and tourism products catering to the requirements of tourists, both domestic and foreign. The International Tourist Bureaus located in important cities provide assistance to foreign tourists and Non-Resident Indians regarding enquiries, bookings, reservations and travel planning. The railways provide a separate foreign tourist quota in all major trains for the benefit of overseas tourists. Indrail passes provide excellent value for money and enables the traveller to explore the splendour of multifaceted India. Indrail passes are useful for those visitors who are on a budget, providing the facility of travel across the entire railway system without any restriction during the period of validity of the pass. The passes are available for periods ranging from half a day to 90 days, for all three classes. Passes can be purchased from general sales agents in some countries, Indian airlines sales offices and some travel agents within India.

The Railways, through its subsidiary organization Indian Railway Catering and Tourism Corporation Limited (IRCTC), operates many special trains and tour packages for the benefit of domestic and international tourists. The Buddhist circuit covers major destinations related to the life of Lord Buddha. The package is operated using a special train with air-conditioned coaches and also includes hotel stay and local sightseeing. In addition, IRCTC offers rail tour packages, which are all-inclusive packages that rail travel, transfers, accommodation, meals and sightseeing. These packages are offered to popular historical, pilgrimage and heritage tourist destinations. For a comprehensive view of the operations of IRCTC, please refer to the case study.

Case Study: Indian Railway Catering and Tourism Corporation Limited

IRCTC is a Public Sector Enterprise under Ministry of Railways. IRCTC was incorporated on 27 September 1999 as an extended arm of the Indian Railways to upgrade, professionalize and manage catering and hospitality services and to promote domestic and international tourism through the development of budget hotels, special tour packages, information and commercial publicity and global reservation systems. IRCTC has shown consistent growth, and the turnover has crossed ₹10 billion in 2014–15.

On an average, more than 500,000 tickets are sold daily from the website of IRCTC. The e-ticketing initiative of IRCTC has transformed the way tickets are purchased by travellers in India. It is an example of how technology and the power of Internet connectivity can bring convenience and satisfaction to a large segment of customers, increasing efficiencies and productivity.

IRCTC's main business activities are:

- on-board catering services;
- food Plazas, fast food units and outlets at railway stations;
- manufacture of packaged drinking water (Rail Neer) for passengers;
- online ticket reservations (e-ticketing);
- travel and tourism services—running of special trains, tour packages and travel services.

The travel and tourism segment of the business of IRCTC generated an income of ₹3.6237 billion. Its customized tour packages include Bharat Darshan tourist trains State Special tourist trains, Buddhist Circuit special trains, Maharajas Express luxury train, charter trains and coaches and online flight and hotel booking services.

IRCTC has recently launched the Pilgrims special tourist trains which have been received very well in the tourist market. IRCTC has a tourism portal www.irctctourism.com which is being developed as a one-stop travel shop offering various services such as online booking of tourist trains, special tourist trains and tour packages. Bharat Darshan tourist trains enable a budget traveller to travel across the country for a relatively small sum of ₹800 per day

Special tourist trains are being operated on religious routes like Sikh circuit, Buddhist Circuit, Char Dham Yatra and Jyotirlinga Yatra. The Buddhist Circuit Special Train offers 7 nights/8 days all-inclusive tour covering various destinations on the Buddhist circuit. IRCTC operates all-inclusive rail tour packages across the country, which includes confirmed rail travel, road transfers, accommodation, meals and sightseeing at reasonable rates.

(Continued ...)

The Maharajas Express, the luxury train operated by IRCTC, operates on five different itineraries, covering major tourist destinations in Rajasthan, Madhya Pradesh and Uttar Pradesh. IRCTC provides all-inclusive packages to the elderly people, through State Special trains covering various pilgrimage destinations such as Vaishno Devi, Ajmer, Shirdi, Tirupati, Rameshwaram, Dwarka, Somnath, Amritsar and Sravanabelagola.

Discussion Questions

1. What are the possible additional services that IRCTC can provide to rail travellers?
2. 'IRCTC should step aside and permit private operators to use the rail infrastructure to offer travel products'. Discuss.

Luxury Trains

The Palace on Wheels is an extraordinary tourism package offering a week-long stay in a specially designed train bringing alive the luxurious travel arrangements during the age of the Raj. Comfortable rooms with attached bathrooms, specialty restaurants, health spas, bars and lounges are some of the facilities offered on-board. The coaches are named after former Rajput states. Most of the travelling is done by night, leaving the days free for discovering and exploring the beautiful destinations covered by the itinerary.

A new luxury train called 'Royal Rajasthan on wheels' was launched covering other sectors in Rajasthan with added facilities. The 'Deccan Odyssey' covered a variety of destinations in central India, ranging from the beaches of Goa to the caves of Ajanta. The 'Golden Chariot' is another luxury train, covering destinations in Karnataka.

Heritage Train Tourism

People across the world have had a fascination with trains, particularly trains drawn by steam engines. Railway heritage has been transformed into tourism products and are successfully attracting thousands of visitors. Railway heritage encompasses locomotives, railway stations, railway museums, tramways and the experience of travelling. It appears as if the interest in steam engines is directly related to the phasing out of such engines by diesel and electrical propulsion.

Besides accessing far flung areas, railways often provide niche products to travellers interested in the history of rail travel, and who desire to relive such experiences. Heritage train enthusiasts are attracted by the history of early steam trains, particularly those which travel through mountainous and picturesque terrains. Many sections of track, which were lying unused, have resumed operations exclusively to cater to the requirements of the tourists and enthusiasts. The 'Fairy Queen' is a heritage train drawn by a steam locomotive that takes visitors on a journey from Delhi to Alwar.

Three mountain rail systems of India have been recognized as World Heritage Site—the Kalka–Simla line, the Darjeeling Mountain Railway and the Nilgiri Mountain Railway. Please see the box for more details on these internationally recognized lines that are a tourist's delight.

Mountain Railways of India

The mountain railways of India have been inscribed as World Heritage Sites by UNESCO. The mountain railways of India are outstanding examples of hill railways. Opened between 1881 and 1908, the three mountain railways are still fully operational, and are great examples of the engineering enterprise of the late nineteenth and early-twentieth centuries. The three

(Continued ...)

railways are the Darjeeling Mountain Railway in the foothills of the Himalayas in West Bengal, the Simla-Kalka railway in Himachal Pradesh and the Nilgiri Mountain Railway in Tamil Nadu. The Darjeeling Himalayan Railway was inscribed as a world Heritage site in 1999. Subsequently, in 2005 and 2008, the other two railways were added as extensions.

The Darjeeling Himalayan railway was the first example of a hill passenger railway. Across a mountainous terrain of great beauty, a link was established using ingenious engineering solutions, providing rail access to the residents of the hills. The Darjeeling Himalayan railway consists of 88.48 km of 2 feet gauge track that connects New Jalpaiguri with Darjeeling, and includes 6 zigzag reverses and three loops.

The Nilgiri Mountain railway was completed in 1908. The railway connects Mettupalayam and Udagamandalam (Ooty), over a distance of 45.88 km. This railway climbs from an altitude of 326 m to 2,203 m, using a rack and pinion traction arrangement.

The Kalka-Simla railway, built in the mid-nineteenth century, is 96.6 km long, and has long tunnels and at that time, the world's highest multi arc gallery bridge.

The mountain railways of India are examples of innovative transportation systems built over difficult terrain, which had great influence on the social and economic development of the region.

High Speed Trains

The Indian Railways has plans to increase the top speed of superfast trains plying across different sectors in the country. The Railway Ministry has announced that the first bullet train in India will run by 2023. It is expected that the bullet train would cover 508 km between Mumbai and Ahmedabad in about two hours, running at a maximum speed of 350 km/h and operating speed of 320 km/h (Prabhu, 2016). At present, the fastest train in India is the Gatiman Express with top speed of 160 km/h, running between New Delhi and Agra. The other major fast trains include Bhopal Shatabdi Express, Mumbai Rajdhani Express, Sealdah Duronto Express, Kanpur Reverse Shatabdi and the Howrah Rajdhani Express (Walk Through, n. d.).

Road Transportation

Road transportation is a vital and dominant aspect in tourism. Irrespective of the mode of travel adopted by tourists to arrive at a destination, they will travel by road around the destination or around it. Many tour itineraries are entirely by road, with tourists being taken from one destination to the next by a coach or a car. For independent travel, road is by far the most preferred mode of travel for holidays over short distances. In Europe and North America, different varieties of holidays by road have developed, ranging from biking to caravans and trailers. Increased ownership of cars, disposable incomes and leisure time all contribute to more holidays taken by road.

There are several reasons why road transport, particularly by car, is the perfect solution for a tourist's transport requirements. The car offers the convenience of 'door to door' transportation, without the hassles of changing vehicles. The traveller decides the departure time, the stops and the routes. Travelling with family members often involve large pieces of baggage, which can be accommodated without problems or extra charges in a car. Road travel offers unmatched flexibility in creating itineraries according to one's interests, travelling at one's own pace. Road travel is relatively cheap as compared to air or rail travel. Family vacations using the family car has become quite popular across continents, owing to the versatility it offers, of travelling in the privacy of a family car with the comfort of stopovers according to one's convenience and without bothering about too much of planning. It is estimated that more than 60% of all domestic holiday trips in Europe and the USA are made by car.

Tourists use the road to travel between destinations or to visit attractions around a destination. While the taxi or a chauffeur driven car is the preferred vehicle for those who can afford it, travelling by coach is by far the more common way to travel to, and around a destination. Long distance coaches, running on scheduled departures, are very popular among domestic tourists, as these offer cheap and convenient connections between cities. The night bus services between cities and tourist destinations enable the visitor to make the trip by night, which is convenient, comfortable and saves time.

Group tours generally offer transportation by coach, starting with transfers from the airport to hotels. Sightseeing trips at a destination are conducted using chartered coaches and travel to the next destination is also done by coach.

Many tour packages offer sightseeing trips on a 'seat in coach' basis. This means that the traveller occupies a seat within a coach which may have passengers from other groups as well. In destinations like Japan where road transportation is extremely expensive, most of the transfers from airports and tours are made on a seat in coach basis. In destinations where the road network is well-established and self-driving is the norm, car rental companies offer cars which may be driven around by the visitor. Other methods of getting around in a destination include scheduled buses, three wheeler taxis such as auto rickshaws, the 'motorcycle taxi' in some destinations like Goa and Bali, and the cycle rickshaw in certain parts of India.

Road Transport and Tourism in India

Road transport is a critical component of infrastructure that has great impact over the pace and pattern of economic development of a country or region. The road network in India is not well developed, with wide variations in the quality and extent of highways. However, over the last few years, the development of a modern highway network has been given top priority by the Central government.

National Highways Development Project

The National Highways Development Project (NHDP) is an ambitious programme undertaken by GoI to develop high quality roads to serve the needs of the nation. National Highways comprise about 2% of the total road length, yet carry over 40% of the traffic. NHDP comprises of the 'Golden Quadrilateral' and the North–South and East–West corridors. The Golden Quadrilateral, with a total length of 5,846 km connected the major cities of Delhi, Kolkata, Chennai and Mumbai. The North–South and East–West corridors (NS&EW) plans to link Kashmir to Kanyakumari (4,000 km) and Silchar to Porbandar (3,300 km). Apart from these signature projects, the National Highways Authority of India has embarked on a vigorous programme of upgrading National Highways to four or six lane, world class standard (Figure 9.2).

The construction of access controlled, multi-lane highways across the length and breadth of the country is gathering momentum, and large sections of highways have already been completed. Tourism sector is a beneficiary of this infrastructural development, as a modern road network provides great potential for a quantum jump in tourism. The development of safe, modern and comfortable road network has the potential to transform domestic tourism in India. Improved connectivity between destinations will lead to more tourism traffic and open up new source markets. Around the major cities of the country, taking a weekend break and short holidays will become increasingly popular, as more and more destinations become accessible and the travel experience becomes more and more comfortable. The boom in car sales and the entry of comfortable and fast cars in the market will also play a role in this scenario.

For interstate travel to become more comfortable and seamless, the barriers presently hampering the transport sector have to be brought down. Currently, the system of charging entry tax on commercial vehicles impedes interstate travel, particularly by contract carriages and 'tourist' coach services.

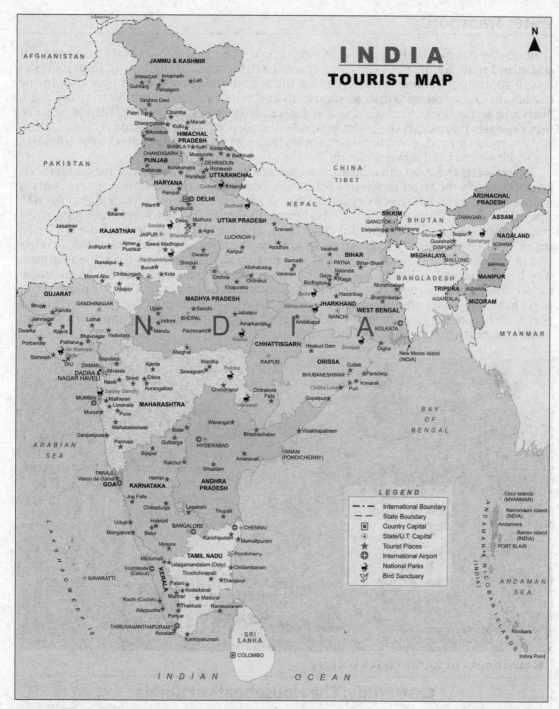

Figure 9.2   Map of national highways development project
Source: National Highways Development Project (2016).

Disclaimer: This figure has been redrawn by the authors and is not to scale. It does not represent any authentic national or international boundaries and is used for illustrative purposes only.

Water Transport

Water borne transport in the context of tourism can be divided into sea and ocean transport and inland water transport. Ocean going cruises have become one of the most important sectors in tourism, providing a major part of the revenue for many island countries in the Caribbean. Cruise tourism employs thousands and brings valuable business to many ports. Boats and ferries are extensively used in coastal destinations, connecting islands. In some regions, water transport is the preferred mode of transport owing to its convenience, access and low costs. Fast and convenient motorboats transport people and goods between islands in the Maldives and Lakshadweep islands.

Inland water transport offers an attractive alternative to road travel in some destinations. Ferries crisscross the water bodies in Kochi, with 'boat buses' popular among the residents as well as visitors to Kochi. The city cruises in the backwaters are a convenient and popular way to see the waterside attractions in the city. Visitors to Varanasi or Haridwar invariably go for a cruise on the Ganga, for the beautiful views of the ghats, and the experience of the *arti* (offering of light to the Gods in Hindu temples and holy places, usually with a lit lamp or a collection of lamps). In Europe, river cruises and 'hop on hop off' tour boats on the Seine are a great way to see the sights of Paris. Cruises on the Thames are popular, and so are the Amsterdam canal cruises. These journeys have become attractive tourism products rather than the means to get from one point to the other. The houseboats of Kerala, while not exactly means of transport, have become iconic symbols of the destination, capturing the beauty and tranquillity of water transport. Our case study provides more details.

Houseboats in Kerala backwaters

Case Study: The Houseboats of Kerala

Alumkadavu is where it all began. A sleepy little village on the banks of Kayamkulam Lake, Alumkadavu, is the birthplace of houseboat, the ubiquitous symbol of tourism in Kerala. The traditional Kettuvallam, built by boat-builders using local materials and time honoured

(Continued ...)

techniques, were the main freight carriers of the rivers of Kerala, and have close links with the local economy.

Initially conceived as a floating barge to carry heavy cargo such as paddy and coconut harvests from far flung fields, the Kettuvallam lost its usefulness as a network of roads were built connecting waterlogged lowlands to towns. Babu Varghese, an enterprising tour operator, invited some of his guests to travel in one of these watercrafts, building a makeshift roof to keep away the harsh sun. He went on to engage the skilled workers of Alumkadavu to fashion a room on a barge, using traditional material such as bamboo, coir and *panambu*, a reed commonly used for making mats. The transformation of traditional barges into houseboats triggered a rush for such craft, leading to the next stage in houseboat building, the commissioning of new boats in traditional style, made of Anjili wood, lashed with coir and glued with dark resin obtained from cashew. The manufacture of new craft gave an opportunity to create bigger and more comfortable boats, with multiple bedrooms, living spaces, modern toilets and even sun decks on the first floor. Add to this the prospect of lip smacking dishes cooked in traditional style by an onboard chef, and you have a tourism experience that had few parallels. The main difference lies in the mobility of these 'floating houses', offering cruises through palm fringed canals and lakes. Houseboats were ideal to view the spectacular backwaters of Kerala, a water world created by a network of rivers, canals and inland lakes. A relaxed cruise, followed by an overnight stay on a boat, miles away from the frenzy of the city, has caught the imagination of the global traveller.

Several companies offer a range of houseboats, from luxurious air-conditioned residences to basic rugged cruisers. Alappuzha remains the hub of houseboat tourism in Kerala, with over 500 boats based in the small town close to Kochi. The Department of Tourism, in a bid to maintain quality, has started a star classification system for houseboats.

The traditional kettuvallam, in its avatar as the houseboat, has emerged as the mascot of Kerala tourism, and a mandatory part of any tourist itinerary to the state.

Image courtesy: Department of Tourism, Government of Kerala.

Discussion Questions

1. Despite the success of the houseboats in Kerala, similar products have not been introduced in other water bodies of India. What could be the reasons for this?
2. Discuss the potential for establishing river cruises in India. Are there any working models?

Cruise Tourism

Although a relatively recent entrant, cruise tourism has become one of the most important forms of tourism. Cruise tourism involves taking a cruise through the ocean in a cruise ship, which is a vessel used for pleasure voyages. These are vessels with a large inventory of rooms across various categories and have several amenities such as swimming pools, restaurants and casinos. Cruise ships are destinations by themselves, offering accommodation, attractions, amenities and activities onboard. Cruise ships pick up passengers from designated points and travel to various destinations. Cruises may be ocean voyages, where the vessel traverses great distances across an ocean or destination/expedition cruises with several ports of call. Sightseeing excursions are conducted at each port of call, but the passengers return to the ship for night halts. The passengers aboard cruise ships are often called water tourists. Cruise tourism is estimated to account for 19 million passengers worldwide.

The largest type of cruise ships is called 'mainstream' class, with a capacity for 800–3000 passengers, with all the amenities offered. 'Mega' cruise ships have a capacity of over 5,000 passengers, and are examples of the sophistication achieved in ship design. Ocean going cruise ships are built to more exacting standards, and use more resistant materials to withstand the harsh and demanding conditions of ocean voyages. Small cruise ships take a few hundred passengers and offer a more limited set of services and amenities, without compromising on levels of comfort and basic facilities. The cruise industry is poised to grow strongly in Asia in the coming decade, as brought out in our case study.

Cruise Industry in Asia

The cruise industry in Asia is growing rapidly. In order to understand the trends, monitor guest source markets and the overall potential for cruise tourism growth, Cruise Lines International Association Southeast Asia commissioned CHART Management consultants to undertake an in-depth market analysis of Asia cruise trends. Some of the key findings are discussed below.

Cruise tourism in Asia is growing at double-digit rates, both in capacity deployed and as a passenger source market. Passenger capacity increased 20% between 2013 and 2015. There are more cruise visits to destinations in Asia, with 980 calls in 2015 and increase of 34% from 2013.

As a source market for cruise tourism worldwide, the volume of travellers sourced from Asia has nearly doubled since 2012. China leads with nearly 80% compound annual growth, followed by Hong Kong (74%), India (36%) and Japan (20%). The majority (91%) of Asian cruisers sailed within the region. A total of 981 cruises and 86 voyages have been scheduled, carrying more than 2 million passengers (2015).

The cruise industry will bring 7 million passenger destination days to the region, with nearly 4,000 port calls, touching 168 destinations across 19 markets. Singapore, Jeju island (South Korea) and Hong Kong are the most popular ports of call.

India would see 113 calls at Indian ports, with the potential to host 121,000 passenger destination days (2015). The most popular ports are Kochi, Mumbai and Mormugao in Goa (Cruise Lines international Association Southeast Asia, 2014).

Cruise holidays are generally offered on an all-inclusive price basis with accommodation, meals and sightseeing part of the package. Cruises offer many facilities on board such as fitness centre, casino, library, spa, swimming pool, cinema, gymnasium and specialty restaurants. Cruise lines charge for alcohol and soft drinks, specialty restaurants, facilities like spas and Internet access. The stakeholders in the cruise business are cruise liners, travel agents, port administrations, ground handlers, suppliers and destination managers.

Conclusion

The transportation sector is a vital ingredient in the tourism business, playing a pivotal role in connecting the traveller to the destination. There must be an effective partnership between tourism and transportation that is mutually beneficial. As we have seen in the chapter, there have been dramatic changes in transport vehicles in the last century, led by technological innovations. The tourism sector has immensely benefited from this leap forward, transforming the sector, bringing the world closer and creating destinations. The new challenges facing the world such as global warming and climate change may impact on the transportation sector in the future, which will have implications on the tourism business as well.

Review Questions

1. Give an account of low cost carriers business model.
2. Discuss the facilities and services available in an airport.
3. What are the nine freedoms of air?
4. Examine the latest development in rail transport and discuss how they support global tourism business.
5. Write short notes on the following:
   - IRCTC
   - House Boats
   - Cruise Tourism

Activities

1. Collect data on schedules, types of aircraft and seating capacity of flights flying to a destination from an airport close to you. Prepare a profile of a major tourism destination that can be accessed by an airline from this airport.
2. Prepare a chart of different types of aircraft with their general and technical specifications and features, and engage a class for school children on different types of aircrafts.
3. Conduct a quiz competition on airlines, airports and facilities of selected airports in India.
4. Arrange a poster exhibition, and explain in detail each poster to the visitor, on transport and tourism in your college giving focus on the following:
   - Shinkansen in Japan
   - Rail Tourism in India
   - Houseboat and backwaters in Kerala
   - Cruise Tourism
5. Prepare a summer vacation tour package for IRCTC that can be offered in your state.

References

Books

Conlin, M.V., and B. Prideaux. 2014. 'The Future of Railway Heritage Tourism? The West Coast Wilderness Railway, Tasmania'. In *Railway Heritage and Tourism: Global Perspectives*, edited by Michael V. Conlin, and G.R. Bird, 263-78. Bristol, UK: Channel View Publications.

Dwyer, L., and P. Forsyth, eds. 2006. *International Handbook on the Economics of Tourism*. Cheltenham: Edward Elgar Publishing Limited.

Web Resources

Airliners.net n.d. 'Aircraft Technical Data and Specifications'. Available at: http://www.airliners.net/aircraft-data/ (accessed on 14 April 2016).

Cruise Lines International Association Southeast Asia. 2014. 'Asia Cruise Trends'. Available at: http://www.cruising.org/docs/default-source/research/asiacruisetrends_2014_finalreport-4.pdf?sfvrsn=2 (accessed on 21 December 2016).

National Highways Development Project. 2016. National Highways Authority of India. Available at: http://www.nhai.org/nhdpmain_english.htm (accessed on 21 December 2016).

Ollivier, G., R. Bullock, Y. Jin, and N. Zhou. 2014. 'High Speed Railways in China: A Look at Traffic'. China Transport Topics No. 11. Available at: http://www-wds.worldbank.org/external/default/WDSContentServer/WDSP/IB/2014/12/16/000406484_20141216102415/Rendered/PDF/932270BRI0Box30ffic020140final000EN.pdf (accessed on 21 December 2016).

Prabhu, Suresh. 2016. 'First Bullet Train to Run in India by 2023'. *The Economic Times*. Available at: http://economictimes.indiatimes.com/industry/transportation/railways/first-bullet-train-to-run-in-india-by-2023-suresh-prabhu/articleshow/52453021.cms (accessed on 21 December 2016).

Walk Through. n.d. 'Top 5 Superfast and High Speed Trains of India'. Available at: http://www.walk-throughindia.com/walkthroughs/trains/top-5-super-fast-and-high-speed-trains-of-india/ (accessed on 21 December 2016).

Suggested Readings

Web Resources

AirAsia.com. n.d. 'What is low cost?' Available at: http://www.airasia.com/my/en/about-us/ir-what-is-lcc.page

Airliners.Net. n.d. 'Aircraft Technical Data and Specifications'. Available at: http://www.airliners.net/aircraft-data/

Boeing. n.d. '747 Commercial Transport/YAL-1: Historical Snapshot'. Available at: http://www.boeing.com/history/products/747.page

Boeing. n.d. 'Long Term Market: Airline Strategies and Business Models'. Available at: http://www.boeing.com/commercial/market/long-term-market/airline-strategies-and-business-models/

Flying 100 Years. 2014. '100 Years of Commercial Flight'. Available at: http://www.flying100years.com/stories/article/100-years-of-commercial-aviation

ICFAI. 2003. 'Ryanair: The "Southwest" of European Airlines'. ICFAI Centre for Management Research, Hyderabad, India. In ECCH Collection. Available at: http://www.staffs.ac.uk/schools/business/resits/postgrad/OperationsMgmtCaseStudy-Ryanir.pdf

Iorna. 2013. 'How Low Cost Airlines Dominated the Global Market'. BlueSky. In Airlines, *Ancillary Revenue, Asia, Featured on App, Investments, Low Cost Airlines, Middle East*. Available at: http://www.totalbluesky.com/2013/04/16/cost-airlines-dominated-global-market/

Johanson, M. 2014. 'How the Airline Industry has Evolved in 100 Years of Commercial Air Travel'. *International Business Times*. Available at: http://www.ibtimes.com/how-airline-industry-has-evolved-100-years-commercial-air-travel-1524238

Ministry of Railways. n.d. 'Annual Report and Accounts 2010–11'. Directorate of Statistics and Economics, Government of India, New Delhi. Available at: http://www.indianrailways.gov.in/railwayboard/uploads/directorate/stat_econ/Annualreport10-11/Annual_report_10-11_eng.pdf

MoT. 2005. 'Cruise Tourism: Potential and Strategy Study'. Ministry of Tourism. Available at: http://incredibleindia.org/lang/images/docs/trade-pdf/surveys-and-studies/study-reports/Cruise%20Tourism%20-%20Potential%20&%20Strategy%20Study.pdf

Reed, T. 2013. 'First Trans-Atlantic Commercial Flight Landed 75 Years Ago Sunday'. Forbes/Logistics and Transportation. Available at: http://www.forbes.com/sites/tedreed/2013/08/10/first-trans-at-lantic-commercial-flight-landed-75-years-ago-sunday/#7fa98e281164

The Economist. 2014. 'Low Cost Airlines: Making Laker's Dream Come True'. Available at: http://www.economist.com/news/business/21635001-low-cost-airlines-have-revolutionised-short-haul-flying-now-after-several-failed-attempts

A view of a travel mart
Image courtesy: Department of tourism, Government of Kerala.

CHAPTER 10

Marketing

Learning Objectives

By the end of this chapter, students will be able to:

- Define marketing.
- Distinguish between features of sales and marketing.
- Identify the ingredients of marketing mix, including its expanded versions.
- Isolate the differences in marketing of tourism services.
- Appreciate the dynamics of marketing environment and market research.
- List new dimensions in destination marketing.

Introduction

Marketing has become an integral part of any business. Creating and supplying products and services according to the customers' needs is the accepted strategy globally, and marketing provides the vital inputs that are needed to deliver this strategy. The tourism sector is no exception, and tourism marketing has become increasingly important for all stakeholders.

This chapter will give the reader an overview on the field of marketing, such a vital piece in the complex world of tourism. We will begin by getting to know marketing, which is a strategic tool in a business organization. We will seek to understand what marketing really means, moving from formal definitions of the term to its interpretation and extensions. The components that make up this challenging world of marketing and its relationships with other activities within an organization will be examined. In a dynamic environment, it is only natural that established paradigms are questioned and new postulates put forward. As a student of the business of tourism, it is necessary to have a clear idea of the role of marketing and how it operates in business. We will also try to understand the process of marketing destinations in some detail.

Defining Marketing

Theodore Levitt (1983), a noted Harvard professor, stated that the purpose of all business is to 'find and keep customers'. The dream of all businesses is to create a commitment in the minds of the consumer for their products, which leads them to repeatedly purchase products from them. This behaviour of the customer gives a competitive edge to the business, as compared to others in the market place. An effective marketing programme is the reason why customers behave in this manner, trusting a brand and purchasing products. Thus, marketing provides assistance in 'identifying, satisfying and retaining' customers.

The difficulty in defining marketing stems from the complexity of actions that are involved in the process. Marketing is more than selling, more than advertising, more than market research, and yet it is all these. As businesses move from the old simple 'build them and sell them' models to more complicated structures, marketing has evolved into a set of activities that addresses these new and dynamic requirements of organizations.

According to Chartered Institute of Marketing, marketing is 'a management process responsible for identifying, anticipating and satisfying customer requirements profitably'.

The American Marketing Association defines marketing as, 'Marketing is the process of planning and executing the conception, pricing, promotion and distribution of ideas, goods, and services to create exchanges that satisfy individual (customer) and organizational objectives'.

In simple terms, Marketing can be defined as a process through which products that can satisfy the needs and desires of customers can be provided, exchanged and obtained at a 'desired' price and place. Products can be goods, services or ideas.

The marketing process touches many parts of the organization. The needs and expectations of the customer need to be studied, and the strengths and weaknesses of competitors assessed. This information goes into the development or modification of the product, which is then promoted in the market to achieve the sales target.

Sales and Marketing

While this chapter will deal with various aspects of marketing, it will be interesting to understand the basic difference between sales and marketing. We will examine the classical models of sales and marketing, to understand the interrelationship between the two. It must be clear that there is no intrinsic contradiction between the two processes, although sales and marketing teams do have their internecine issues and problems.

Traditionally, marketing is seen as a wide ranging process involving various activities that provide an insight in to the needs and desires of the customers based on which products are created or modified. In simple terms, marketing communicates to an audience of potential consumers, telling the stories of the products and managing the brand identity. Marketing provides the trends and analyses that are going to product development. Marketing, in other words, begins with the customer. The focus is on building long-term relationships with customers, ensuring their loyalty to the brand. Marketing provides the prospects and leads for the sales team and makes the consumer aware of the brand and products. Thus, it can be said that marketing creates an environment in which sales can happen.

Sales is essentially a process by which a product is sold for a consideration. It is the touch point when a financial transaction is made. Sales is concerned about the entire transaction, which not only includes the price of a product but also other details of interest to the customer such as warranties, support, delivery timelines and training. Sales engage with the customer on a one-to-one basis, dealing with individuals and individual variations, converting interest levels into sales. Sales, therefore, has specific goals in terms of achieving targets or retaining or increasing the market share.

Sales is seen as a sub set of the marketing ecosystem, which takes all the efforts to fruition. It is the salesperson who brings in the revenue, and whose work can be measured in specific terms. Sales and marketing teams have to work in close coordination, sharing information and providing support to each other.

The Marketing Mix

What are the factors involved in the activity of marketing? The 'marketing mix', as it is known, is the set of elements that are relevant for marketing, consisting of '4 Ps'—product, price, promotion and place (distribution). McCarthy (1964) regrouped the elements of the marketing mix as postulated by Borden and proposed the four elements or 4 Ps. The marketing mix represents how the overall marketing strategy is translated into programmes for action.

1. Product

The product is the primary element, which is purchased by the customer. The product fulfils the wants and needs of the customer, and organizations are sensitive to the changing nature of these wants, altering and modifying products to increase their competitiveness. A variety of products are offered as part of the marketing effort, tailored towards segments of customers, trying to be closest to satisfying the desire of the customer.

A tourism product is a set of assets and services that are organized around one or more attractions to meet the needs of the visitors. The components of a product are presentation, basic design, service element, branding and image.

The tourism product consists of the following:

- *An attraction.* Attractions are the main reason for visitors to travel to the destination, as these are cultural or natural resources, places or events that have awakened the interest of visitors and motivated them to decide to travel.
- *Facilities and services.* These refer to the infrastructure, equipment and services that make tourism activities possible, the hotel that the visitors stays in, the tour operator service that arranges the visit and the restaurants and other services at the destination.
- *Accessibility.* Infrastructure, transport and communication services that facilitate the visit.

Tourism products can be categorized as follows:

- *Nature-based.* The main attraction is a natural resource, such as the forest, beach, mountain or a water body.
- *Cultural.* The cultural environment of the destination is the main attraction, such as music, dance, religious rituals, cultural events, ethnic lifestyle.
- *Historical.* Archaeological sites, historic buildings, monuments, museums and art galleries, art and history.
- *Wellness.* Relaxation, detoxification, rejuvenation, natural remedies and alternative treatments.
- *Faith.* Pilgrimages, religious gatherings, rituals and observances.
- *Sports and activities.* Trekking, kayaking, canoeing, angling and hunting.
- *Niche.* Special interests such as wine tours, butterflies, scientific pursuits.

Tourism product development aims at increasing business to tourism in the destination, bringing economic benefit to entrepreneurs, members of the community, investors and local government. Destination managers are concerned about developing sustainable tourism products, which are economically beneficial, socially acceptable and does not negatively impact the environment.

Every product, including tourism products, goes through a 'life-cycle', which is a series of stages or phases. Each stage has distinctive characteristics, challenges and opportunities. This requires very different marketing, financing and human resource strategies. Let us examine how to conceive the different stages of product life cycle in marketing:

- *Market introduction stage:* At this stage, the product needs to be distributed widely through all available channels, so that it can get the attention of more potential customers.

- *Growth stage:* Marketing efforts have to be intensified, to cater to the growing interest and consumption. The product may have to be modified and new products introduced to increase acceptance and to differentiate itself from competition.
- *Maturity stage:* New target segments have to be identified in order to retain appeal and bring in new business. More products have to be introduced to retain customer base, and some products may be repositioned to keep ahead of competition.
- *Saturation and decline growth:* Declining customer interest and sales are challenges, forcing the product to be re-launched.

2. Price

Price is a value fixed on the product by the provider, which the consumer is willing to pay anticipating a satisfactory experience. Pricing is based on three determinants—cost, competition and the satisfaction expected by the consumer. A rather long winded definition is as follows:

Price denotes 'the published or negotiated terms of the exchange transaction for a product, between a producer aiming to achieve predetermined sales volume and revenue objectives, and prospective customers seeking to maximize their perceptions of value for money in the choices they make between alternative products' (Middleton and Clarke, 2012).

As can be seen, the price of a product is based on the belief of the customer that they are getting fair value or 'value for money'. However good or advanced a product is, the customer may well judge it on the basis of the price tag. Price is also a 'competitive tool', as comparisons across products and organizations may be based on the price of a product.

Price is not always a function of the cost incurred by the provider. The economic value expressed in the price can be motivated by non-tangible factors such as image and prestige. Consumers may be ready to pay a higher price if they believe that the service they experience will be of better quality. The pricing strategy may vary based on different factors such as costs, expected profits, purchasing power of customers, fluctuations in demand and competitor strategies.

In tourism, there can be very different strategies adopted in pricing. A relatively unique experience can be priced very high. Strong competition can beat down prices, particularly when there is large supply. Intermediaries play an important role in determining prices. Many suppliers adopt a strategy of highly discounted prices close to the sales date.

In the case of a hotel product, there are different ways to price the hotel rooms. A rack rate is the rate provided in printed material which is announced and advertised. This is the maximum retail price that the hotel can charge on the room. Special rates such as 'privileged user' rates and corporate rates are given to regular and high-volume customers. To tour operators, the hotel provides a price that is not available to the direct customer. This price is not public, varies between one operator to the other, and is dependent on the volume of business that the tour operator provides to the hotel. The hotel may also offer discounted prices based on seasonality.

Similarly, airlines have an array of prices such as apex, standby and consolidated fares. Many LCCs periodically announce deep discounts on tickets for flight dates many months into the future. Such sales are helpful in raising cash for operation, and are also useful in bringing new customers to the airline. The 'yield management' strategy of every airline has a combination of seats offered at varying discounts for early bookings, and higher fares nearer to the date of the flight. During periods of high demand like peak holiday and festival seasons, the seats are priced very high.

3. Place (Distribution)

Once the product is ready to be sold, it has to be distributed to reach the customer. Organizations use a variety of distribution channels to get products across in the market. The types of distributors, their strengths and the perception of the customers about these channels are all important consideration for marketing managers. The simplest distribution channel is directly from the producer to the customer. Different levels of intermediaries are usually involved in the distribution process. However, the convenience of the customer is paramount when distribution channels are considered. The tourism product has to be marketed at the right place at the right time. Distribution is the method by which the tourism product reaches the potential customer, which can be direct or through travel distribution channels (Figure 10.1).

4. Promotion

Promotion is a set of activities that are undertaken by the provider to inform potential customers about the product. Promotion involves a basket of activities such as advertising, merchandising brochure production, public relations (PR) and sales promotion. Promotional strategies make prospective customers aware of the product, stimulate demand, provide information that helps decision-making and incentivizes the purchase. Channels for promotion include advertising—in the press, television, radio and Internet; direct mailing of brochures and promotional literature; events and exhibitions. Seminars and workshops are conducted to reach out to specific target groups. Distributors and intermediaries are provided with sales literature and induced with sales promotion incentives. Point-of-sale displays are traditional techniques to motivate the customer.

There are many promotion channels, some of which are linked to the distribution channels. Travel agencies are important channels through which the product is offered to the customer. Fairs and exhibitions offer a powerful channel to communicate to the buyer who may be an intermediary or a direct customer. PR activities are important, and are undertaken by businesses as part of the promotional strategy. Traditionally, press releases have been used to provide information on new products or to combat adverse or unfavourable news on products. Product launches before invited media are conducted to make new announcements. Media visits and familiarization tours are other significant activities for promoting products, particularly in tourism.

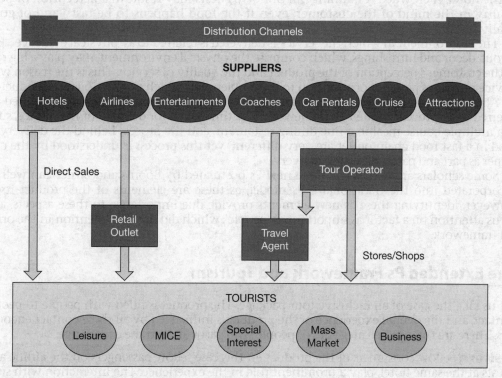

Figure 10.1 The distribution channels
Source: Authors.

The 7 Ps of Service Marketing

The marketing mix of 4 Ps has been criticized as being production oriented and not customer oriented. Critics say that the model regards the customers as passive recipients and does not take into account the human element in transactions.

The traditional model is handy and convenient, a simple mnemonic that is easy to remember. However, does it cover the requirements of a system as complex as marketing, particularly when marketing has moved to embrace activities in the service industry? Booms and Bitner (1981) argued that the 4 Ps paradigm is inadequate in the context of services marketing, and does not fully reflect the characteristics of the service industry. They added three more Ps—people, process and physical evidence—which according to them are important variables for success of any organization in the service sector.

In services marketing, the qualities of a service such as intangibility, perishability, heterogeneity and inseparability require a different kind of marketing mix, as the traditional model was derived from research on manufacturing companies.

Booms and Bitner suggested that 'participants' are all the human actors who play a part in service delivery, namely the employees of the firm and other customers. As the product is consumed at the point of production, personnel of the firm may influence the perceptions of the customers regarding the quality of the product. Therefore, they are part of the product, and product quality is inseparable from the quality of the service provider (Berry, 1984). Variability in service delivery can lead to fluctuations in the quality of the product, so it is important that aspects like training and monitoring of performance are given due importance. 'People' may also mean other customers. For instance, the experience of a hotel in the mind of a visitor may be coloured by the behaviour and type of other guests in the hotel. A crowded restaurant full of noisy guests may result in a perception of poor quality in the mind of the customer, even if the food happens to be tasty and of good quality.

The environment in which the service is delivered is referred to as 'physical evidence'. The layout, decor and furnishings, which comprise the physical environment, may play a big role in the customer's perception of the product and the quality of service. This is the reason why service providers pay a lot of attention to the ambience in which transactions are conducted.

All the procedures, mechanisms and flow of activities by which the service is acquired are referred to as 'process' in the 7 Ps framework. The time taken for delivery of the service, such as a multiple course meal in a fine-dining restaurant, and the process behind the delivery of food in a fast food chain outlet are very different, yet this process is understood by the customer as part and parcel of service delivery.

Some scholars argue that the three new Ps postulated by Booms and Bitner can well be incorporated into the traditional 4 Ps model, as these are elements of the product itself. However, identifying these as new elements provide due importance to these aspects, and focus attention on a factor as important as 'people', which did not find mention in the original framework.

The Extended Ps Framework and Tourism

Let us take the case of an inclusive tour package. The product is filled with people-to-people contact, and the overall experience of the product is influenced by all these contact encounters. There are three main categories of people who participate in the experience:

Visitors: Fellow consumers of the product, in this case fellow passengers on the airline and guests at the same hotel, play a prominent role in the experience. The interaction with such people will play a role in the perception of the product in the mind of the customer.

Employees: The staff of each service provider plays a role in the product—the salesperson who sells the product, the taxi driver, the ground handling staff at the airport, the on-board airline crew, the reception staff at the hotel, the escorts and guides of the ground handler, the waiter at the restaurant and the bar. It is entirely accurate to say that 'employees physically embody the product and are walking billboards from a promotional standpoint' (Zeithaml and Bitner, 1996).

Community: The interaction with members of the local community, the souvenir shop-keeper or the person on the street can influence the perception of the visitor about the value of the product. Many of the community may not be part of the tourism ecosystem, and yet an instance of timely assistance on the street or an unfriendly gesture may be the key memory of a holiday.

It follows that organizations should concentrate on the elements that can be controlled, such as the design of the holiday product and the knowledge and attitude and skills of the staff of all the service providers involved. In the case of other visitors, a targeted delivery of the product to segments of customers with similar interests may, to an extent, mitigate the risk of conflict between fellow consumers. Although the marketer has very little control over the community and its interaction with the customer, a good knowledge of the destination and providing accurate information about the destination and the community may encourage a healthy and fruitful interaction.

From 4 Ps to 4 Cs?

The traditional approach of 4 Ps is being revisited in the light of rapid developments in technology and changing aspirations of consumers. Of late, researchers have been postulating new approaches focused on the consumer, rather than the seller. A popular formula is to replace each 'P' with a 'C', bringing attention to the element from the consumer point of view.

Consumer wants and needs (product): The focus must be on what the consumers need, and what they want to purchase. It is not about what product the seller has that can be bought by the consumer. The consumer orientation challenges the marketer to study the wants and needs of the consumer in more detail, so that individualized products can be created. In a sense, this is a move away from 'mass market' to a 'niche market' approach. For a tourism product, this may mean all the components that go into a package created by the tour operator, as the customer may want an inclusive product, or a 'do it yourself' product where the customers get to customize the package according to their desires. In another case, customers may need to have the product 'delivered' to them by a knowledgeable person, clarifying their doubts and providing the assurance of quality. This brings into focus the service—or 'people' element into the product.

Cost to satisfy (price): The new approach is to devalue the importance of price. The principle of cost colours many aspects, such as the cost of travelling to make the purchase, the emotional and mental cost involved in consuming the product (the 'guilt' of the customer) and other complex psychological aspects that determine the consumer's evaluation of the product. The customer may consider the cost to change or implement a new product or service, or the cost of not selecting a product or service from a competitor. In short, there are different correct solutions, changing according to the cost of satisfying an individual customer, rather than a clear winner based on price alone.

Convenience to buy (place): Changing preferences of customers, new devices and technology are disrupting traditional distribution channels. All the points of sale from where a customer can purchase a product based on her convenience have to be kept in mind. It is time to look beyond the clear-cut direct versus indirect channel, instead to focus on the convenience of the customer and the distribution channel to reach the customer through the channel most convenient to her.

Communication (promotion): The difference between communication and promotion is that communication moves away from the 'manipulative' nature of advertising and promotion, to start creating a dialogue with the consumer, which is cooperative and interactive. Personalized communication is getting more importance in a world where the consumer demands more information. Internet-based marketing lays emphasis on the interaction between customers and companies, aimed at delivering products preferred by consumers and providing value to them.

The Environment and Marketing

While the marketing mix is within the control of marketing organizations, there are several factors in the environment that is not under their influence. These environmental factors play a critical role in the marketing process, modifying products and distribution channels and changing the way organizations communicate with consumer segments.

Demography

Trends in the target population are important factors that influence marketing. The size, growth rate, age distribution and educational levels are some of the demographic factors that force marketing agencies to adapt their products. In countries like India, the majority of the population is below 35. Typically, the segment consists of young couples and families with small children. What kind of products would interest the segment? What other facilities and attractions that are important to this age group?

Another important segment from a demographic perspective is the 'empty nest'. The growing number of people over 60 years is a formidable segment for the tourism industry. These are potential travellers who have time and money on their hands and are interested in taking long holidays. The marketing teams of tour companies strive to create products that will appeal to this demographic segment.

Asian Millennium Traveller

Millennials, or 'Generation Y', are loosely defined as the generation born between 1981 and 1995. The Millennials are entering their most productive and affluent phase, and offer unprecedented volumes in the economic sectors. 60% of the world's millennials reside in Asia, with China and India accounting for a third of the total. The expenditure of the Asian Millennials on international travel is expected to reach US$ 340 billion by 2020. More travellers mean more opportunities for business and leisure tourism, which translates to a need to be better equipped to take advantage of the coming boom.

Tourism in Asia

Asia is driving international tourism growth, with the strongest growth in international tourist arrivals. Arrivals to the region are expected to increase twice as quickly compared to those in advanced economies. China and India will power this growth. Southeast Asia will be the strongest among Asian sub-regions, with 9% growth. Dynamic economies, rising middle class, good existing infrastructure, excellent intraregional connectivity are some of the reasons.

The emergence of the Asian millennial travellers (AMT) represents growth opportunities. To successfully capture the next wave of consumer demand powered by AMTs, professionals will need to acquire an in-depth understanding of this key consumer group.

(Continued ...)

Key insights into AMTs:

- AMTs differ between regions, with diverse travel and spending preferences.
- AMTs depend on different sources of information. Even while using their knowledge and awareness to check online sources, they still rely on traditional information sources such as newspapers and travel agents.
- AMT desire greater control over their travel experience, seeking out extensive information from online sources such as travel reviews, blogs and social media.
- AMTs have low brand loyalty, and are focused on price and convenience. (Singapore Tourism Board, 2013).

Strategy for the AMTs

To capture this opportunity, a different strategy needs to be adopted. These are some 'thought starters':

Know your audience. Different markets will need different approaches, channels and partners. A market that depends heavily on social media platforms necessitates a strategy with activities on such sites, rather than online intermediaries.

Facilitate customized travel. Tools that allow AMTs to craft their own personalized experience should be created and sold. A model popularized by low cost carriers, this means 'unbundling' packages and favouring a basic offering, which the customer can enhance using 'add-ons' according to her preferences.

Build trust. Creating consumer-led marketing campaigns and more platforms for engagement is critical, and companies should be prepared to receive positive and negative feedback.

Create next generation loyalty programmes. Companies will have to find ways of creating continuity and engaging the consumer, through refining loyalty programmes to meet the needs of the millennial generation.

Differentiate or disappear. Companies need to develop a unique and differentiated offering that resonates with their target segment, appeal to their attitude, aspirations, ideals and preferences (YourSingapore.Com, 2013).

Social: Several social and cultural forces impact marketing efforts, forcing companies to create and modify products. Socio-cultural values change from place to place, and differences in language, attitude towards work, food and visitor behaviour are all important considerations. For example, fast food chains do not serve beef products in India or pork products in the Middle East, in deference to the food taboos prevalent in major parts of those regions. Socially conservative communities may not approve of beach tourism, apprehending behaviour unacceptable according to their norms, and destination marketers are sensitive to such signals.

Political: The political environment plays an important role in marketing. States and regions may enact laws to provide preferential treatment for persons of the local community in employment. A law restricting alcohol usage and shutting down of places of alcohol consumption will have a direct effect on tourism, forcing marketers to move products to other destinations. The regulations of transport industry such as aviation are other important examples. In India, that was an explosion of growth in tourism which is closely linked with the deregulation of civil aviation and the opening up of Indian skies.

Technology: Rapid changes in technology and the increasing use of online transactions have changed the way marketing is conducted in all sectors; travel and tourism sector is no exception. Marketing channels and distribution networks have undergone a dramatic trans-formation in recent times, thanks to the advances in technology and the way people use devices to make purchases. The mobile phone is increasingly replacing many gadgets, and marketing strategists have to change with this trend and provide solutions which the con-sumer can access on cell phones.

Market Research

The above discussion shows the need for a specific marketing strategy for every organization. The first step in the creation of a marketing plan or strategy is market research.

Market research is a vital tool that enables destination marketing agencies to address differ-ent segments of tourists. Research provides important information on the desires and aspira-tions of each segment, as well as the characteristics that are peculiar to any given segment. Based on the attributes that are identified through different forms of market research, the destination managers are able to provide products and services tailor-made to certain markets, including product/service mixes that fulfil their requirements. Research also provides vital information on the likes and dislikes, preferences, period and reason of travel that are dis-played by particular consumer markets. Another important role played by market research is the assessment of the branding strategy of the destination, which includes the evaluation and perceived attributes of the brand and the factors affecting the 'image' of the destination in the minds of the potential traveller. Market research helps in evaluating the effectiveness of mar-keting campaigns as also the reach and penetration of advertising.

Market research involves collecting information from current customers and potential cus-tomers. Information from public sources can provide insights into the market and competi-tion. The two main aspects of market research are desk research and surveys. Information can be gathered by desk research, through a review of secondary sources such as journals, publica-tions, official statistics and trade reports. Targeted surveys provides valuable information to find out the views of the customer about the product or service, information about the cus-tomers, information about the effectiveness of the marketing strategies, market trends and information on competition. Quantitative surveys provide statistical information, while qual-itative surveys provide information on opinions and attitudes and likes and dislikes. Data can be collected through questionnaires distributed in important aggregation points like airports, railway stations, festival venues and hotel lobbies. Effective destinations make accurate use of the information generated through statistics collection and market research agencies in order to constantly fine tune their products and services and to improve the delivery of their mar-keting campaigns along with issues related to seasonality. Surveys can be done directly from customers, and also from staff members who deal with customers. The data gathered through research is then analysed for arriving conclusions or assessments. This information is used by different divisions in an organization for planning and strategy formulation (Figure 10.2).

An organization depends on market research for many purposes like assessment of demand, supply and carrying out self-assessment, mentioned below:

Demand assessment

- To learn about the consumer population—the types, groups, demographic trends.
- To clearly identify the needs and aspirations of the consumer.
- To gain an understanding about the attitudes, behavioural patterns and values of the consumer.

Supply assessment

- To accurately know of competing products presently in the market.
- To be informed of the activities of competitors, their sales trends and distribution channels.

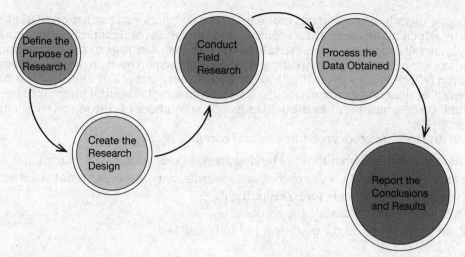

Figure 10.2 The market research process
Source: Authors.

Self-assessment

- To assess and measure the effectiveness of promotional activities.
- To understand the reception of the consumer to new products or modifications in existing products.
- To learn about customer perception and satisfaction levels.

For a tourism entrepreneur, conducting market research is vital, as a deep knowledge of the market is the starting point in creating a business plan. Extensive study of the target population and existing services will reveal the area or segment whose needs are not fully met. This is done by profiling the population (of potential tourists) and by analysing the existing products and services. This potential space can be exploited by creating or formulating a product or service that is unique or distinct and which can be placed in the market.

Destination Marketing

Destinations are considered to be a defined geographical region which is understood by its visitors as a unique entity, with the political and legislative framework for tourism marketing and planning. An 'image' about the destination is created in the mind of the traveller, which is based on research, advertising, word-of-mouth publicity and media exposure. This image is tested against the actual experience at the destination, which is a composite of interactions with the local population, attractions, cuisine and the overall holiday experience provided by the travel intermediary.

Destination marketing refers to the management process through which national tourism organizations (NTOs) and tourism enterprises identify their target visitors, communicate with them to ascertain and influence their wishes, needs and motivations and formulate and adapt tourism products accordingly with a view to achieving optimal tourist satisfaction, thereby fulfilling their objectives (ILO, 2012).

Destination marketing is an activity undertaken by DMOs, NTOs or tourism enterprises in identified markets for potential customers. This requires a study of their interests, needs and motivations and the formulation of products that will appeal to the identified customers, for encouraging them to travel and take holidays in the destinations. Destination marketing is a process by which destinations attract tourists, and the success of their destination marketing strategy, generally speaking, is the increase in the number of visitors to the destination. This demands a clear perspective on marketing. A marketing perspective is an overall management orientation reflecting corporate attitudes that, in the case of travel and tourism, must balance the interests of shareholders/owners with the long term environmental interests of the destination and at the same time meet the demands and expectations of customers (Middleton and Hawkins, 1998).

Marketing tourism products is intricate and complex because:

- Customers do not see what they are buying and take a decision based on trust.
- They may not get what they expected, as standardization of product is not possible.
- They pay for the product before consuming it.
- They cannot try out or sample the product.
- And, they cannot return the product if not fully satisfied.

The Destination As a Brand

In a crowded marketplace, it is important for destinations to create a distinctive and memorable identity. The development and communication of this identity is known as branding. A brand represents a source of value to the consumer, keeping the destination on 'top of the mind' of the potential traveller as and when a travel decision is contemplated. The brand also reflects the core strengths of the destination product. The brand identity of a destination has to reflect the essence of the offering of the destination that resonates well with the products offered by the suppliers in the destination, as well as be in harmony with the image that the local community wants to project about the destination.

A strong and dynamic brand will help a destination to stand out and obtain attention. Building and maintaining a brand with a distinctive attributes and values have become the central concern of any marketing organization. 'Brand management' has implications on several aspects of a destination, such as investment inflows, tourist arrivals and policy. In many ways, the management of the brand is increasingly seen as the most important activity to be undertaken by destination marketing organizations.

It may be recollected that tourism is a business where the product is purchased by the consumer without actually seeing or testing it. In other words, it is the image of the destination and the expectation of fulfilment that drives the consumer to make a purchase decision.

There is a complex relationship between the local stakeholders in the destination. Often, stakeholder interests may be conflicting, with the common resources of the community (zero priced public good) being viewed differently by different interest groups. These local resources may be central to the tourism experience and the importance they play in the purchase decision is getting more prominence.

As we have seen above, the overall experience of a tourist involves numerous encounters with people of the destination, ranging from service providers to local community members with no direct stake in the business of tourism. Destination marketers need to take this into account while preparing the marketing strategy for the destination. A simplistic plan to raise visitor arrivals without looking at the complex interplay between stakeholders and between the community and the visitor may not yield the desired results, and will be counterproductive.

Many destinations have devised strategies to manage large numbers of visitor arrivals which may not be conducive to the overall strategic objective set by the destination. This may include discouraging certain segments of tourists from visiting the destination through indirect measures, such as increased parking charges (Cambridge) and discouraging charters

(Mauritius; Buhalis, 2000). Marketing strategies of such destinations will reflect the policies adopted by the destination management organizations.

Leisure Market

Certain characteristics of the leisure market have major implications on the marketing plans of destinations. Leisure travellers choose a convenient time to travel, and this seasonality depends on many factors such as weather in the source market, family constraints such as examination 'season' for children, annual holidays and festivals. Leisure travellers are generally price sensitive, and those who travel to escape extreme weather may not be particular about the attributes of the destination so long as the weather is pleasant. Newer trends such as responsible travel and avoiding over-exploited destinations also complicate marketing strategies of destinations.

Business Travel Market

For the business traveller, the destination is fixed for business reasons and cannot be altered. However many destinations which have the infrastructure that is needed to attract business travel, particularly the MICE segment, compete with each other. Business travel is inflexible and price inelastic. It is also highly seasonal. The availability of good convenient air connections, large inventory of high quality rooms, promotion of business spaces such as exhibition halls and convention centres are all prerequisites for this nations being marketed to the segment (Figure 10.3).

Role of Stakeholders in Marketing

Traditionally, destination marketing is one of the core functions of DMO and NTO. However, tourism enterprises devise their marketing plans in order to gain more business and make profits. These plans and strategies are independent and competitive, as enterprises are fighting

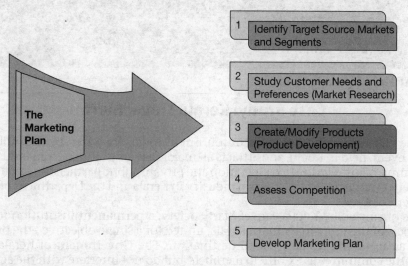

Figure 10.3   The marketing plan
Source: Authors.

for the attention of the same target segment in source markets. The overall brand identity of the destination may also be diluted by these competing efforts, blunting the marketing strategy of the destination as a whole. The harmonization of the marketing activities of individual businesses to strengthen and synergize the efforts of the DMO is a challenge faced by most DMOs. There are interesting examples of synergy. The Kerala Travel Mart (KTM), created and supported by the DMO (Kerala Tourism), is run by an organization formed by the tourism enterprises of that state (see case study). Competing players of the same destination have come together to create a biennial event that showcases all the products and services of the destination, attracting buyers from all major markets. The strategy of joint marketing has created a powerful business platform which benefits all the players, increases market penetration and strengthens the brand.

Buyers at Kerala travel mart

Case Study: Kerala Travel Mart

KTM is the biggest buyer-seller event in tourism in India, organized by the industry. It is a biennial event, held in Kochi, and attracts all major players in the tourism industry. It is a stellar example of intra-industry cooperation and private public partnership, a collaborative venture between the travel and tourism industry in Kerala and the Department of Tourism, Government of Kerala.

KTM is organized by Kerala Travel Mart Society, a permanent institution formed by the members of the tourism sector of Kerala, united for a single objective—the promotion of Kerala as an international tourism destination. The Government of Kerala is represented on the committee as ex-officio members, but do not interfere with the activities of the mart. The Department of Tourism provides a grant for the conduct of the Mart.

(Continued ...)

The Mart is owned by the industry, and managed by an elected managing committee, consisting of business owners of Kerala elected by majority vote by all eligible members. A secretariat headed by a Chief Executive Officer assists the committee. Members of the society are drafted in to work on various aspects of mart management, through committees for accommodation, airlines, transportation, buyers, coordination, exhibition, finance, media, FAM tours, programmes and cultural events, sellers, reception and workshops.

The membership of the society is open to any licensed tourism service provider in Kerala—adventure tour operators, Ayurveda centres, airlines, homestays, hotels, tour operators, cultural and art centres, transporters, travel agents and event managers. There are currently 667 members in KTM society. The members are also given the opportunity to purchase space in the mart venue, as sellers (exhibitors). Stalls are allotted either through draw of lots or through an online booking system.

Potential buyers from across the world are invited to attend the mart, drawing from databases and through the active participation of India tourism offices worldwide. Although the bulk of the buyers are tour operators or travel agents, a good number of airline representatives, travel writers, event organizers attended the marts. There is a spurt in participation of buyers from within India, in line with the burgeoning interest in Kerala for the domestic traveller.

Selected buyers are provided complimentary accommodation, local transfers and mart entry, and also offered complimentary post-mart familiarization tours. A part of their travel expenses are reimbursed if they completed all their pre-fixed appointments with the sellers.

The popularity of the Mart may be gauged from the following table:

Number of Buyers Attending KTM			
KTM year	**Total**	**Domestic**	**International**
2000	**570**	320	250
2002	**788**	318	470
2004	**1166**	421	745
2006	**1261**	742	519
2008	**1550**	980	570
2010	**1450**	1100	350
2012	**2398**	1890	508
2014	**2853**	2207	646

KTM has become a success only because of the full-scale participation of the tourism industry of Kerala. The major member hotels around Kochi contribute approximately 800 rooms for accommodating the hosted buyers, and many others contribute rooms for the familiarization tours. Members volunteer their time and energy to complete all tasks relating to the Mart.

The demand for stalls at KTM remains very high, indicating that the Mart is successful in attracting business. All the 253 stalls at KTM 2016 were sold out within 20 minutes!

Image courtesy: Department of Tourism, Government of Kerala.

Discussion Questions

1. List the possible factors that resulted in a successful partnership like KTM in Kerala.
2. What are the advantages and disadvantages of an industry-led business event, as compared to a mart that is organized by professional event managers?

Destinations with a stake in tourism would have a marketing organization entrusted with this specialized responsibility. But what about funding marketing campaigns? Is this the exclusive responsibility of the government, whether local, state or central? The model adopted by most developed destinations is that the local and regional governments market destinations creating their campaigns, as they have a direct stake in ensuring that tourism flows to their destinations. The federal or central government concentrates on developing a brand image for the country that complements the efforts of the destinations. A good analogy is the international marketing campaigns carried out by states like Karnataka and Kerala, even while the 'Incredible India' campaign is driven by the MoT. But finding funds for costly international campaigns are increasingly becoming a challenge for governments. Some destinations have already moved into a cost sharing model, with stakeholders like hotels contributing to the overall marketing budget through a 'per bed' charge levied on them. Some destinations raise specific marketing charges from all service providers as a means to fund marketing programmes.

All destinations have a common objective—to market their products with a view to maximizing profits, and bring benefits to the region. However, with increasing awareness of the negative impacts of uncontrolled tourism, destination managers are increasingly adopting strategies that are more complex, with the emphasis shifting to the long term sustainability of tourism as an economic activity without drastically affecting the environment and natural resources. This calls for a move away from the simple 'less price more business' to strategies that aims at higher profits with lower volumes. How can this be done? Many destinations are concentrating on incentivizing innovation, creating new and diversified products, limiting supply through taxation and better environmental management. DMOs work with local businesses and suppliers to maintain competitiveness of the destination. On the marketing front, innovative products that maintain a distinct identity of the destination are invaluable to create a distinct image for the destination in the minds of the visitor. An example for this phenomenon is the case of Kerala. During the early years of its establishment as a destination, Kerala was projected as a 'sun and sea' destination, with marketing campaigns focusing on the beaches of Kerala. Another campaign was to position Kerala as a destination offering a range of experiences, from beaches to forests. Both these campaigns made way for an intensive campaign which moved away from these 'generic' positions, and concentrated on the backwaters of Kerala, and the houseboat product, as a differentiator. This projection of a product unique to the region, in a setting that was also peculiar to the destination, provided a powerful and compelling marketing proposition. Generally, DMOs carry out the activities discussed hereafter.

Marketing and Promotion

As noted above, marketing of destinations is a complex exercise which necessitates a clear understanding of the market, its social and economic environment, demographics, attitudes and preferences. Market oriented businesses like tourism depend on market research in order to produce or modify tourism products in line with the attitudes and expectations of customers. DMOs conduct surveys and studies on consumers to ascertain their interests, apprehensions, preferences and attitudes. The information gathered through such penetrating consumer research is an important input in formulating marketing plans tailored to the particular market. It offers a clear idea of the market perception and analyses the factors that come into play in the mind of the consumer while making a decision to choose a holiday destination.

An active programme to increase awareness, aimed at suppliers and sellers, is an essential part of the marketing process. While marketing campaigns are usually done by the DMOs, a range of promotional programmes are featured in any promotion strategy, and involves wide participation of the stakeholders. Apart from 'above-the-line' activities like advertising, promotion involves 'below-the-line' projects, such as attending travel fairs, creation and distribution of promotional material such as brochures and posters, dissemination of electronic material such as email newsletters and the organization of familiarization tours and media trips. Many of these activities require a partnership and coordination with hoteliers and service providers at the destination.

Case Study: Tourism Malaysia

Malaysia received 27.4 million tourists in 2014, with an annual growth rate of 6.7% over the previous year. The growth in arrivals is attributed to Malaysia's strong participation in international tourism trade and consumer events, better connectivity and increased flight frequencies from selected markets, sound partnerships with industry members, effective advertising and promotions campaigns.

The functions of the Malaysia Tourism Promotion Board (Tourism Malaysia) are as follows:

- Stimulate and promote tourism to and within Malaysia.
- Invigorate, develop and market Malaysia internationally and domestically as a tourist focal point.
- Coordinate all marketing or promotional activities relating to tourism conducted by any organization, government or non-governmental agency.
- Recommend measures and programmes that stimulate development and promotion of the Malaysian tourism industry.

A total of 890 promotional programmes comprising sales missions, exhibitions and expositions, seminars and workshops and local promotions were organized abroad by Tourism Malaysia in 2014. The international promotion is overseen by several offices, divided into separate markets. The marketing efforts in all markets are segmented into sales missions, international tourism exhibitions and expositions, seminars and workshops, and tactical, digital and online advertising campaigns.

There are seven overseas offices for the Southeast Asia market, and three marketing representative offices.

For the North and East Asia market, there are eight Tourism Malaysia offices and a representative office. A CEO Mega FAM Programme for 10 major tour operators from Northern China was organized, aimed to introduce new products such as fly and drive, cycling tourism and ecotourism.

In the South and West Asia and Africa markets, special events such as F1 Petronas Malaysia Grand Prix, 1 Malaysia GP sale and Malaysia international shoe festival were promoted.

In the Americas, Europe and Oceania (AERO) markets, Tourism Malaysia participated in a total of 14 international tourism exhibitions and expositions, including BIT Milan, ITB Berlin, MITT Moscow, TUR Gothenburg, Top Resa Paris and WTM London.

Tourism Malaysia is active within the country as well, working through its 14 state offices to encourage domestic travel. Community based tourism, Touch 'n Go Karnival Fuyooh 2014, Art of Speed Asia, Southeast Asia augmented reality hunt, Homestay Carnival and Pahang River Rafting Challenge are some of the events and programmes created for the domestic market.

For the Visit Malaysia Year (VMY 2014), a brochure with 1,030 domestic tourism packages was launched, in collaboration with 297 domestic travel agencies. VMY was promoted through numerous advertising campaigns for the international and domestic markets. The campaigns were delivered through selected television channels and tactical advertising campaigns in partnership with airlines and travel agents. Aggressive digital advertising campaigns on popular digital platforms such as Google search, Yahoo and YouTube were carried out. A total of 1,381 guests from 59 countries were invited to participate in 19 Mega FAM familiarization trips. A total of 622 articles published in overseas print media, as well as 361 documentaries and electronic media broadcasts resulted from this initiative.

(Continued ...)

In order to obtain information on visitor demographics, spending and travelling patterns, Tourism Malaysia conducts many surveys, interviewing 50,000 respondents annually. Hotel occupancy rates survey, hotel facilities survey and studies are also carried out (Tourism Malaysia, 2014).

Discussion Questions

1. List the three most important channels of promotion used by Malaysia to popularize their destinations and products? In your view, will these strategies work well in India as well?
2. Discuss the significance of PR strategies in promotion, in the light of the experience of Malaysia.

Media and Public Relations

One of the key areas of activity of any destination marketing initiative is the management of media and the rolling out of a PR strategy. It is important for any destination to remain visible in the media space, so that the consumer gets many opportunities to understand and become familiar with the destination and be attracted to the offerings and attractions. Destinations invest in publicity campaigns in key markets, devoting a sizeable portion of their marketing budgets to this exercise. Publicity campaigns have several components such as advertising campaign, TV commercials, commercials on FM radio, promotion and websites, and downloadable ring tones apps and services, celebrity ambassadors, radio and TV events, and commissioning advertorials.

The PR strategy focuses on increasing exposure to the brand in mass media. Features and articles are effective ways to reach out to the reader, providing information and stoking interest in the destination. In order to get these pieces in print, professional PR agencies are called into action. These agencies have extensive links in the media houses, with journalists and management, which are leveraged to provide space for articles featuring the destination. Articles are perceived as more trustworthy than advertisements, and have more value in influencing the reader as compared to paid advertising.

Media tours: The PR agency arranges for select journalists, columnists and writers to travel to the destination and experience the products first hand. These complimentary trips are often carried out during the lean season to rope in the hotel owners and other service providers into the project.

Media persons are constantly bombarded with information, and cannot be expected to undertake the research needed to understand a destination properly and to prepare articles based on the destination. This is where these tours and exposure visits become relevant. The media persons are handpicked from friendly and popular media vehicles such as newspapers, travel and general interest print and online magazines and blogs. Some DMOs offer tours of the major destinations to large groups of media persons to develop goodwill and to get them familiarized with the cultural offerings and heritage of the destination. Another common way of supporting media programs is by partnering with TV channels and media houses to create travel shows and TV episodes set in specific destinations.

Media interaction and meetings: The top brass of the media are invited to attend special events in the destination. If any important dignitary from the destination is in town, the PR agency organizes one-to-one meetings and press interactions, so that the presence of the dignitary can be leveraged for bringing more visibility in the media for the destination. The PR agency, on behalf of the DMO, continually feeds the media with press releases, article outlines, images and videos in order to create media products that may be featured in a publication.

Advertising: Creating and launching an advertising campaign is an essential part of the mandate of the destination marketing organization. An advertising campaign is created by professional agency, which undertakes a detailed study of the products and potential of the destination to identify the attributes of the brand that will serve as effective symbols of the destination. The agency also examines the consumer research findings of the source market. Based on their understanding of the brief, the agency prepares a campaign with an aim to attract the attention of the reader/viewer leading to increased travel from the market to the destination. The campaign may have many components built into it such as print, television, radio, collaterals, online advertising and 'out of home' advertising. Media planning is the next step in the delivery of an advertising campaign. A media plan is a document that details the media properties to be used, the frequency of exposure of different advertising elements in the media and the time frame within which the campaign is delivered. Specialized agencies are involved in media buying which may include negotiating with media groups for the best possible price package. The campaign is then rolled out based on the approved advertising plan and budget. While the campaign is on, consumer research agencies are engaged to obtain feedback in on the effectiveness of the campaign. A successful example of a destination implementing a creative and effective advertising campaign is Madhya Pradesh. Extensive market research led the DMO to creating a marketing plan focusing on the domestic market, rather than go international. To appeal to the intrinsic cultural ethos of the source markets, the advertisements had a rustic and earthy feel to them, suggesting familiarity and friendship. The campaign succeeded beyond expectations, transforming the destination into one of the front runners in the national scenario.

The Stupa at Sanchi

Case Study: Television Commercials of Madhya Pradesh

Madhya Pradesh (MP) has all the ingredients of becoming the premier tourism destination in India. The caves of Bhimbetka, the Stupa of Sanchi and the temples of Khajuraho are some of

(Continued ...)

the magnificent examples of its rich and varied cultural heritage. The state has some of the most richly endowed national parks, with the highest population of tiger and other wild-life. Many of its ancient towns are acclaimed pilgrimage places. Its strategic location, in the centre of the country, makes the destinations of the state accessible from all parts of India. And yet, Madhya Pradesh was not known as a popular tourist destination, attracting just a small number of visitors, mainly foreign tourists to Khajuraho.

As a significant step to create a strong brand equity, MP Tourism engaged Ogilvy and Mather to create a campaign that will position the state as an attractive destination. The first campaign '*Hindustan ka Dil Dekho*' (*See the Heart of India*) was instantly popular on television, as it introduced a destination in a very different and interesting way. Using the bioscope, an instrument familiar to Indian minds, the TVC ran a series of images of promi-nent destinations before the viewer. The catchy and folksy song as voice over had simple lyrics that egged the viewer to go see the attractions of MP.

Til dekho
Tar dekho
Aankhen phaad phaad dekho…
Bandhavgarh ki jhaadi dekho
Ujjain ke sant dekho
Khajuraho shilpkari dekho
Bhimbetka kalakari dekho…
Dharmon ki mehfil dekho
Hindustan ka dil dekho.

[Meaning: see the oilseed, see the mark, see with wide open eyes, see the forests of Bandhavgarh, see the holy men of Ujjain, see the sculptures of Khajuraho, see the artwork of Bhimbetka, see the symphony of faiths, see the heart of India]

The TVC was followed by a print campaign that took the message further, using the comic strip format.

In 2009, the agency took the idea forward, creating a TVC that depicted a person who has seen the splendours of the state and was overwhelmed. 'Hindustan ka dil Dekha' is com-municated through a pair of expressive eyes, and comes with an equally attractive jingle:

Bandar dekha, haathi dekha
barasingha aur cheetal dekha
Mandu ka jahaz mahal, aur marble ka pahad dekha
Sanchi ki shanti mein, kudke aandhar jhaak ke dekha
Hindustan ka dil dekha!

[Meaning: I saw a monkey, an elephant, I saw the swamp deer and spotted deer, I saw the ship-like mansion in Mandu, and the hills of marble, in the peaceful environment of Sanchi, I had a vision of myself, I saw the heart of India]

The two campaigns also highlighted the tag line 'The Heart of Incredible India', neatly tying the campaign with the hugely popular Incredible India campaigns launched by the MoT.

In 2010, Ogilvy created the third TVC for MP Tourism, this time using shadowgraphy to bring the state alive. Shadowgraphy, or shadow theatre, is an art form creating landscapes, animals and people using shadows formed by human hands. This time too, the approach is deliberately 'non tourist' that provides a distinctly different communication route that is memorable. Some of the most beautiful landmarks of the state are recreated in black and white in a stark and simple manner. The song accompanying the visuals is a haunting melody sung by Raghuvir Yadav, the noted actor, singing '*MP ajab hain, sabse gajab hain*' (*Madhya Pradesh is unique, and the best*).

In 2013 came the fourth TVC in the series. This time, the theme is the play with colours that India is renowned for. Colours of different hues enveloped visitors, forming into the key

(Continued ...)

attractions of MP. Entitled '*Sau tarah ke rang*', (Colours of a hundred hues) the ad combines graphics with slow motion camera work to create a dream like sequence.

The series of compelling television advertisements, complemented by campaigns in print, radio and online transformed MP into one of the most popular domestic tourism destinations in India. Around 53 million tourists visited MP in 2012, up from 11 million in 2006.

Image courtesy: Department of Tourism, Government of Madhya Pradesh.

Discussion Questions

1. What are the possible reasons for the state's poor performance in tourism before the campaign was launched?
2. In your opinion, will a creative campaign alone drive tourist traffic? What are the essential ingredients that should accompany an aggressive marketing strategy?

Internet advertising: Advertising on the Internet has developed into a separate discipline, with DMOs placing a separate advertising budget for the purpose. Online campaigns including online media campaigns have become an essential part of any marketing initiative. But with the public increasingly using and consuming online media, it is imperative for any destination to be present and visible on popular online platforms. The creation of interesting, and often intrusive advertisements is another important element.

There are several ways to advertise online:

- Pay per click advertising
- Keyword optimization strategy
- Blog posting
- Video marketing
- Viral marketing
- Article marketing
- Social networking and forum marketing

Blogs are influential and popular in creating a favourable impression about destinations. Several travel bloggers have dedicated followers, and their opinions about destinations are seen as authentic and reliable. Consequently, marketing organizations take an active effort in influencing bloggers by offering familiarization tours, product information and incentives.

Social media platforms are becoming more and more important for these to shape the opinion of the potential traveller regarding destinations. Online review forums are also seen as authentic sources. Most marketing organizations have a social media strategy by which destinations or famous attractions have their own pages on popular media platforms like Facebook and Twitter, and engage with the audience on an active basis by providing information, clearing doubts and providing interesting opportunities to network.

As important as being present on social media is to monitor activities and opinions on the Internet. With its wide reach, social media can spread information, particularly negative information, about a destination instantly and the strength of the media is that it cannot be controlled or stopped. DMOs are quite aware of the dangers posed by this kind of development, and engage companies to continuously monitor online news feeds and social platforms, with a view to respond immediately to any incident or news item that has the potential to blow up into a crisis.

Collaterals and emails: DMOs need to be in constant touch with their associates, partners and agents in the market of operation. One of the time-tested vehicles for engagement is a newsletter. The newsletter is a periodical which provides information and news on the destinations and the developments that have happened in the recent past. The newsletter becomes an information document that can be archived and used as reference material by the trade.

The newsletter is also useful in communicating new offers, incentives, trade trips and visits being organized to the destination. Currently, paper newsletters are increasingly being replaced by online newsletters delivered by email. These have the flexibility of offering links to sites that will deliver more information, video clips and interactive tools. DMOs also make use of collaterals such as brochures, CD-ROMs and gifts to continue the relationship with the trade.

Enhancement of distribution channels and servicing the travel trade is an essential part of the business of destination marketing. This involves conducting workshops, training sessions and educational modules for the travel trade, creating online tutorial programmes, the supply of correct information about the products and services in the destination and services such as chat or telephone support.

Events: DMOs often conduct events in key cities in source markets to promote destinations. Events also offer an opportunity for other promotional activities such as photo opportunities, write-ups and media networking. Events may be entirely cultural, such as concerts and dance events showcasing a facet of the cultural heritage. Some events combine a cultural component with a business session, such as a presentation or travel trade meet. Cultural events are more preferred in informal settings, where the music, dance and other cultural elements of the destination are showcased and presented before an invited audience. NTOs, through the marketing offices, representative offices or agents, bring in performers and artists, who conduct performances and recitals in key cities. Travel agents, media and other key partners and associates are invited to such events, which may also include a meal featuring the traditional cuisine of the destination.

Product launches: DMOs may prepare or market specific products tailored to the individual source markets, based on the consumer research findings. These products are fine tuned to meet the requirements of the market and are normally sold through the distribution channels established by the marketing offices. These products are launched in special promotional events to which important partners and agents are invited to familiarize themselves with the products. Product launches are also effective from a PR point of view.

Alliances: Marketing offices often form strategic alliances in order to penetrate the market better for marketing purposes and to offer more attractive products. The most commonly seen alliance is that of the destination and an airline, usually the national airline of the country or destination. The airline provides complimentary air tickets that are utilized by the DMOs to create familiarization tours for travel agents, media visits for journalists and prizes in trade shows. When complimentary visits are organized, the national or regional destination marketing organization takes the responsibility of organising the rest of the trip, by involving hotels and service providers directly.

Perceived Value

The perceived value of the product by the customers plays a decisive role in ensuring repeat visit and promoting word of mouth publicity. To understand the concept of perceived value, let us take the example of a train running between two cities. This train has different classes—1AC, 2AC, 3AC and sleeper class. A traveller chooses to travel in a class of his choice, and is willing to pay much more for travelling in a higher class as compared to the sleeper class, for instance. Why does the traveller do so, particularly when he knows that everyone on the train will arrive at the destination at the same time? The traveller is taking the decision based on the perceived value of the service he is purchasing that is the experience provided to him while travelling on the train. He chooses to spend more in order to obtain more privacy, a bigger personal space and better quality of service. In his mind, the extra amount paid by him is justified.

(Continued ...)

In the case of goods, the perception of value is in its quality. A consumer may be willing to pay a high price for a product of a particular brand, as he feels that the brand gives him a sense of comfort about the quality of the product. The 'non-monetary' costs such as time and effort expended to find and purchase the product are important considerations in the perception of value.

These concepts of value and quality are not easily defined when it comes to the tourism sector, as most of the products in tourism are services which defy standardization. Moreover, tourism involves interaction between the consumer, the service provider and the environment which provides a dynamic and complex setting.

The quality of a service is determined by several factors. Parasuraman, Zeithaml and Berry (1985) have created a conceptual model of service quality, suggesting that there are five factors determining quality of service. *Tangibles* are those aspects which can be seen or felt—the materials or equipment used, the appearance of personnel and the support facilities. *Responsiveness* is the attitude displayed by the service personnel, their response to customer needs and willingness to serve. *Reliability* indicates the performance of the service consistently at the same level of efficiency. *Assurance* is the feeling of trust and faith that customers have on the abilities, skills and knowledge of the service personnel. *Empathy* is the extra care and sensitivity displayed by service personnel, anticipating an understanding needs and providing solutions. It is the feeling of being made to 'feel special', over and above expected levels of service.

The model postulates that the customer forms certain expectations regarding a service, based on past experience, word of mouth and information gathered. When the service is delivered and experienced by the customer, the experience is compared to the expected service, and this comparison determines the level of satisfaction felt by the customer. Naturally, if the actual service is perceived to be less than the expected level of service, the customer will not be satisfied. While meeting the expectations of a customer is adequate, the customer is not really excited or pleased by the service experienced. Such a customer is always open to trying out the service offered by a different service provider the next time, as he has no compelling reason to remain with the company which provided the first service. This is why organizations always trying to *exceed expectations* of the customer, to deliver an experience that will surprise and please him. A delighted customer will have no reason to switch service providers and will be happy to retain the services of the existing provider.

Conclusion

Beginning with the basics, we have explored the concept of marketing. In a fast changing world, the practical applications of marketing have undergone major changes, in keeping with emerging trends. The changes in the market place have stimulated a major change from a product oriented sales approach to a customer oriented marketing approach. Marketing as a discipline has evolved through the years, from a relatively simple 4 Ps framework to a paradigm that is complex and interconnected, bringing various factors into consideration. Marketing of tourism products faces special challenges due to the peculiarity of the service product. Destinations are giving more emphasis for more accurate and tailored marketing, using new channels such as the Internet to reach out to the customer and have a lasting engagement. New combinations and alliances are emerging, with the stakeholders cooperating with each other to create new marketing strategies.

Review Questions

1. Explain the 7 Ps of service marketing.
2. Discuss the logic of switch over from 4 Ps and 4 Cs in tourism marketing.
3. What is destination marketing? Discuss the role of stakeholders in tourism marketing?
4. Examine how destination management agencies can support marketing initiatives.

Activities

1. Prepare a list of goods and services traded in your locality and classify them under different types of markets—local, regional or national. Also prepare a power point presentation of the distinguishing features of each type of market and strengthen your understanding on the dynamics of different types of markets. Arrange a discussion on niche tourism products and markets. With the knowledge acquired, conduct a field study in your locality and identify the potential for developing niche tourism products.
2. Prepare a list of various tourism products of your state and classify them under different categories (see product section under marketing mix). Examine the current status of each category of product in the light of product lifecycle and suggest suitable marketing strategies for a sustainable business.
3. Identify a tourism destination of your choice and prepare a demographic profile of the tourists visiting the destination. Using the information collected, give your suggestions for developing an appropriate marketing strategy for the destination.
4. Arrange a visit to a travel/tour company or a classified hotel having minimum 3-star classification. Prepare a general profile and business status of the organization. Discuss with the manager the issues faced by the organization in marketing its products. Conduct a market research and give your suggestions for improving the business of the organization.
5. Visit a tourism destination and list out the major stakeholders in tourism business. Identify the role of each stakeholder in business and find out the major problems faced by the destination. Give your suggestions for strengthening the destination management organizations
6. Conduct a field survey among randomly selected tourists in a destination and identify the gap between their expectation and real experience of the destination.

References

Books

Berry, L.L. 1984. The Employee as Customer. In *Services Marketing*, edited by C.H. Lovelock. Englewoods Cliffs.

Booms, B.H., and M.J. Bitner. 1981. 'Marketing Strategies and Organization Structures for Service Firms'. In *Marketing of Services, Conference Proceedings: American Marketing Association*, edited by J.H. Donnelly and W.R. George. Chicago, IL.

Buhalis, D. 2000. 'Marketing the Competitive Destination of the Future'. *Tourism Management*, 21(1): 97–116.

McCarthy, Jerome E. 1964. *Basic Marketing: A Managerial Approach*. Homewood, IL: Irwin.

Middleton, V.T.C., and J.R. Clarke. 2012. *Marketing in Travel and Tourism*, 3rd edn. Oxford: Butterworth Heinmann.

Middleton, V.T.C., and R. Hawkins. 1998. *Sustainable Tourism: A Marketing Perspective*. Oxford: Butterworth Heinmann.

Parasuraman, A., V.A. Zeithaml, L.L. Berry. 1985. 'A Conceptual Model of Service Quality and Its Implications for Future Research'. *Journal of Marketing*, 49(4): 41–50.

Zeithaml, V.A., and M.J. Bitner. 1996. *Services Marketing*. New York: McGraw-Hill.

———. 2000. *Services Marketing: Integrating Customer Focus Across the Firm*, 2nd edn. Boston, London: Irwin/McGraw-Hill.

Web Resources

ILO. 2012. 'Toolkit on Poverty Reduction through Tourism'. Available at: http://www.ilo.org/wcmsp5/groups/public/—ed_dialogue/—sector/documents/instructionalmaterial/wcms_218329.pdf (accessed on 22 December 2016).

Singapore Tourism Board. 2013. 'Navigating the Next Phase of Asia's Tourism'. Travel Rave, Singapore Tourism Board. Available at: http://origin-www.yoursingapore.com/content/dam/travelrave/resources/TravelRave2013-Highlights-Report_NavigatingthenextwavinAsiasTourism.pdf?intcmp=TravelRave2013-Highlights-Report_NavigatingthenextwavinAsiasTourism-Downloadlink (accessed on 18 April 2016).

Tourism Malaysia. 2014. 'Laporan Tahunan 2014 Annual Report'. Available at: http://www.tourism.gov.my/pdf/uploads/activities/Tourism_AR2014_FA.pdf (accessed on 22 December 2016).

YourSingapore.Com. 2013. 'Capturing the Asian Millennial Traveller'. Available at: http://www.yoursingapore.com/content/dam/travelrave/resources/Capturing-the-Asian-Millennial-Traveller.pdf?intcmp=Capturing-the-Asian-Millennial-Traveller-Downloadlink (accessed on 22 December 2016).

Suggested Readings

Books

Burnett, J.J. 2003. *Core Concepts of Marketing*, 2nd edn. New Jersey: Wiley.

———. 2007. *Non Profit Marketing Best Practices*. Hoboken, New Jersey: John Wiley & Sons Inc.

Hunt, S.D. 2015. *Marketing Theory: Foundations, Controversy, Strategy, Resource Advantage Theory*. New York: Routledge.

Mamoun, N., M.N. Akroush. 2011. 'The 7Ps Classification of the Services Marketing Mix Revisited'. *Jordan Journal of Business Administration*, 7 (1): 116–147.

Mc Carthy, E.J. 1964. *Basic Marketing: A Managerial Approach*. Homewood, Il: R.D. Irwin.

Middleton V.T.C., A. Fyall, M. Morgan, A. Ashok Ranchhod. 2009. *Marketing in Travel and Tourism*, 4th edn. Oxford: Routledge.

Palmer, D.E. 2010. *Ethical Issues in e-Business: Models and Frameworks*. Hershey: New York.

Pride, W.M., and O.C. Ferrel. 2014. *Marketing*. South Western: Cengage Learning.

Web Resources

Afshar, V., and M. Gupta. 2015. 'The 5 Cs of Digital Marketing'. Available at: http://www.huffingtonpost.com/entry/the-5-cs-of-digital-marke_b_8104090.html?section=india (accessed on 22 December 2016).

Choudhury, S. 2007. 'Hindustan Ka Dil Dekho'. Cutting the Chai. Available at: http://www.cuttingthechai.com/2007/04/297/hindustan-ka-dil-dekho/ (accessed on 22 December 2016).

Goi, C.L. 2009. 'A Review of Marketing Mix: 4 Ps or More?' *International Journal of Marketing Studies*, 1 (1). Available at: http://www.ccsenet.org/journal/index.php/ijms/article/viewFile/97/1552%3Forigin%3Dpublication_detail (accessed on 22 December 2016).

Kerala Travel Mart. 2016. Available at: http://www.keralatravelmart.org/ (accessed on 22 December 2016).

Levitt, T. 1983. 'The Globalization of Markets'. *Harvard Business Review*, May. Available at: https://hbr.org/1983/05/the-globalization-of-markets (accessed on 16 April 2016).

Learning and Teaching Scotland. 2005. 'Marketing in Tourism: An introduction'. Available at: http://www.educationscotland.gov.uk/Images/Marketing%20inTT_tcm4-252713.pdf (accessed on 22 December 2016).

Rafiq, M., and P.K. Ahmed. 1995. 'Using the 7Ps as a Generic Marketing Mix: An Exploratory Survey of UK and European Marketing Academics'. *Marketing Intelligence and Planning*, 13 (9): 4–15. Available at: https://www.researchgate.net/publication/247624673_Using_the_7Ps_as_a_generic_marketing_mix_An_exploratory_survey_of_UK_and_European_marketing_academics (accessed on 17 April 2016).

Sanib, N.I.R., Y.A. Aziz, Z. Samdin, K.A. Rahim. 2013. 'Comparison of Marketing Mix Dimensions between Local and International Hotels Customers in Malaysia'. *International Journal of Economics and Management*, 7 (2): 297–313. Available at: http://econ.upm.edu.my/ijem/vol7no2/bab06.pdf (accessed on 22 December 2016).

The Tomb of Sher Shah Suri, Sasaram, Bihar
Image courtesy: Amit Kumar

Section C: Tourism in India

This section examines the extent and scope of tourism in India. As a relatively recent phenomenon in the country, tourism is on a growth trajectory and several indicators suggest that India will continue to register robust growth in the near future. Students must be well grounded in matters relating to the sector, and this section, with its focus exclusively on India, provides a framework in which the student acquires in-depth knowledge of the business of tourism and the tourism products of the country.

Chapter 11 begins with an overview, which provides a snapshot of the tourism sector in India. Drawing a connection with travels of the ancient and medieval worlds, students are drawn into tourism in the modern sense that came to India in the last few decades. The miniscule portion of the international tourist traffic that India currently attracts still contributes a healthy 6.8% to the country's GDP. The scope of tourism to provide employment and to expand into a much larger economic sector is brought out. Domestic tourism is gaining momentum, and the humungous number of tourists that will holiday within the country has the potential to drive the sector at a brisk pace. The chapter introduces to the student several issues connected with tourism development, such as the coordination between ministries, regulation by the MoT, federalism and community participation.

Every Indian student of tourism should strive to gain knowledge about the vast cultural heritage of India, which is the raison d'être of tourism in the country. Chapter 12 on cultural heritage aims to provide an essence of this vast area of knowledge. Beginning with a discussion on culture and what it signifies, students enter the world of cultural tourism, exploring its various facets. The division into tangible and intangible heritage and the elements of cultural resources are explained. The chapter then takes a review of the world heritage sites in India and sketches the role of the Archaeological Survey of India (ASI) as the custodian of built heritage. There is a brief roundup of the management of heritage and the agencies involved in the effort, with relevant case studies of different models adopted. The importance of museums as repositories of material culture is stressed, as is their significance as prominent tourist attractions. Moving on, students are given information on the major performing art forms, forms of internationally recognized intangible heritage and the wealth of Indian fine arts.

With its amazing diversity of climate types, forests and natural formations, India has an impressive array of natural heritage resources that are crucial to tourism. Chapter 13 on natural heritage aims to provide students the basic information needed to gain an appreciation of this resource. Students and practitioners of tourism have to be concerned with and involved in issues concerning natural heritage, as this fragile asset is under threat from many recent developments. The chapter takes students through some of the major biodiversity areas such as the Himalaya and the Western Ghats, while getting into grips with the notion of diversity in flora and fauna. Moving on, the legal entities in natural heritage like national parks, wildlife sanctuaries and biosphere reserves are explained, as these are frequently misunderstood. The important issues concerning conservation in protected areas are discussed, with a view to provide a framework to analyse the present situation prevailing in the country that affects tourism and visitation.

Chapter 14 examines the organized business sectors in Indian tourism, particularly the accommodation and tour segments, in some detail. For students who have familiarized themselves with the segments of the industry in Section B, this is an opportunity to get into grips with the dynamic Indian situation. From a brief history of the beginnings and growth of the accommodation sector, the chapter analyses the distribution of hotels in the country both in terms of the range and geographical distribution. Apart from providing basic information on major hotel chains, there is a discussion on emerging trends in the accommodation sector, with a case study of an international chain establishing its footprint in the country. The attention shifts to the tour business in India. A typical large tour business is profiled, to enable the student to get insights into the operations side of the industry. The process of creating tour packages is also detailed out. The growth of the segment catering to the domestic tourist is discussed with several case studies. The chapter ends by giving an overview of the outbound tour business segment, which will be the mainstay of tour business in the future.

Chapter 15 surveys the changing roles of government agencies in shaping Indian tourism. Beginning with the command economy model in the 1980s, where the tourism policy prescribed the growth of the sector through public investment, the approach of government changed to acknowledge the primacy of the private sector, a change that is captured in the initial section which scans official documents across the last four decades. A discussion on planning follows, teasing out the steps in the process and demonstrating the application of a process to create a master plan in a fragile destination. The roles of the national, state and local governments are discussed at length to enable the student get into grips with the different agencies that regulate or coordinate tourism activities. There is also a reference to the structures of public sector entities such as India Tourism Development Corporation (ITDC) and state corporations, leaving the question of their relevance as a point of discussion.

Red Fort, Delhi
Image courtesy: Invis Multimedia.

CHAPTER 11

Tourism Sector in India

By the end of this chapter, students will be able to:

- Locate India's position in international tourism.
- List the most important markets and purpose of visit.
- Describe the significance of tourism to India's economy.
- List the ministries related to tourism.
- Enumerate the factors that will affect the outlook for tourism in India.

Introduction

As a tourist destination, India is a composite of hundreds of micro destinations, offering a bouquet of experiences that can hardly be matched by any other country. The mainstay of Indian tourism is undoubtedly its multifaceted culture and cultural expressions. From a dazzling range of monuments, buildings and archaeological sites and remains, the built heritage that is scattered in all parts of India are tangible indicators of the rich past of India, and leaves visitors wonderstruck with its beauty and magnificence. The natural heritage of the country is no less impressive—India has a wide array of climate types, geographical features, forests and natural formations which has a wealth of flora and fauna of all conceivable categories. The rich tapestry of customs, traditions, music and dance is another valuable asset that attracts visitors to its shores.

History

The Indian subcontinent has a rich history of contact with regions around the world. As early as the Harappan civilization, there was trade contact with Mesopotamian cities, of goods such as ivory, pearls and copper. There was regular trade between Indian ports and those of the Greco-Roman world, particularly of spices. From great cities like Alexandria, India welcomed visitors and settlers. All around the coast, ports like Barbarikon, Muziris and Kaveripattanam had thriving business relations with Roman and Arab merchants. India exported textiles in great bulk to the West from the early days of the Common Era. Indian vessels also established connections to the East, with Kalinga, Chola and Vijayanagara kingdoms active in the maritime world. Later, the Portuguese, Dutch, French and English merchant vessels came to trade in spices.

Accounts of travellers have several references to Indian cities and kingdoms. Faxian, the Buddhist monk who travelled to Indian from China in the fifth century, recorded his journeys through India. He visited sites related to the Buddha's life in the plains and then sailed to what is now Sri Lanka. Xuanzang, monk and scholar, also spent much time in India in the seventh century, visiting prominent Buddhist locations and monasteries.

While leisure travel would come very late, tourism—in the exact sense as defined in modern terms—was quite commonplace from ancient times. Our history is replete with stories of travellers—wandering ascetics, singing bards, pilgrims, monks, traders, craftsmen, travelling through the expanses of India. For the last many centuries, thousands have been travelling great distances for spiritual reasons—the Kumbh melas, a visit to the holy city of Varanasi, the Char Dham yatra. Many of the ingredients of modern day tourism were part of this great travel history of India. Service providers were abundant, serving the 'tourist', providing accommodation, food and refreshment, assisting him to conduct his religious rituals. Transportation before the age of mass transportation was still vibrant and effective. Horse, bullock and camel carts would have provided transport. For the affluent, there would have been mules or horses or palanquins. From time immemorial, tourism has been active in India, perhaps not in an organized form as we know it today, but as an efficient business process, involving thousands of professionals engaged in parts of the vast movement endeavour.

The continuous connections with the outside world would go to show that India had always been an open land, welcoming visitors and traders, encouraging them to settle down and conduct their business and providing shelter to those in need. Indeed, the ports of India were known to be highly cosmopolitan, with numerous international visitors, sailors, traders and missionaries. Inbound tourism to India dates back to Harappan times!

India in International Tourism

Although India has been a late entrant into international tourism, the tourism sector today represents one of the most important economic sectors in the country and among the fastest-growing areas of the Indian economy. GoI regards tourism both as a growth engine and a generator of employment. Tourism has the capacity to provide avenues of employment both direct and indirect, jobs which range from highly specialized ones to unskilled employment. UNWTO estimates that about 6-7% of the total jobs in the world are generated in the T&T sector. Tourism is also important for the Indian economy as it is the third most important earner of foreign exchange.

The development of tourism in India has been steady. A National Tourism Policy was announced in 1982, followed by an Action Plan in 1992 and a National Strategy for Promotion of Tourism in 1996. In 1997, a Tourism Policy was announced. In the early days, tourism development was sought to be done through the efforts of the public sector unit ITDC, formed in 1966. In 1989, the Tourism Finance Corporation of India (TFCI) was established to provide easier financing options to tourism enterprises. In the public sector, hotel management institutions and Food Craft Institutes (FCIs) were also established.

Arrivals

It is important to understand where we stand in the international arena. With all its wealth of attractions and experiences, India managed to attract only 0.68% of the international tourist arrivals, ranking 41st in the world. Of the total 1,135 million international tourist arrivals, only 7.7 million tourists came to India (2014 figures). This was an improvement of 10.2% over the arrivals in 2013. Of all the visitors, 91% came by air and landed in one of the major airports of the

Table 11.1   Foreign tourist arrivals in India, 1999–2014

Year	Foreign Tourist Arrivals	Annual Growth (%)
1999	2,481,928	5.20
2000	2,649,378	6.70
2001	2,537,282	–4.20
2002	2,384,364	–6
2003	2,726,214	14.30
2004	3,457,477	26.80
2005	3,918,610	13.30
2006	4,447,167	13.50
2007	5,081,504	14.30
2008	5,282,603	4
2009	5,167,699	–2.20
2010	5,775,692	11.80
2011	6,309,222	9.20
2012	6,577,745	4.30
2013	6,967,601	5.90
2014	7,679,099	10.20

Source: India Tourism Statistics, MoT, 2014.

country. Delhi saw the largest number of arrivals (33%), followed by Mumbai (20%) and Chennai (10%). As can be seen from Table 11.1, there has been a steady growth in foreign tourist arrivals.

The top 10 source markets for foreign tourist arrivals to India in 2013 were USA, UK, Bangladesh, Sri Lanka, Russian Federation, Canada, Germany, France, Malaysia and Japan. The top-15 markets accounted for 70.72% of the total foreign arrivals. An analysis of the foreign tourist arrivals would show that the majority of international tourists visit India in the period from October to March, with December recording the highest arrivals. The USA is the biggest source country for foreign tourists, with a share of 15.58% of the total arrivals, followed by UK, Bangladesh, Sri Lanka and Russia (see Table 11.2 and Chart 11.1).

Eastern Europe registered the highest rate of growth (29.5%), followed by West Asia (17.9%) and Australasia (7.8%). Western Europe contributed the highest share of arrivals (26.64%), followed by North America (19.24%) and South Asia (17.44%).

Purpose of Visit

Every inbound traveller arriving in India fills in a disembarkation card, which is received at the Immigration counter. This card provides valuable information about the visitor. One of the most important pieces of information obtained from an analysis of the data provided is the purpose of visit to India. In 2013, 30.3% of the foreign tourists arriving in India came for

Table 11.2   Foreign tourist arrivals, top-10 markets

Rank	Country/Market	Share (%)	FTAs (millions)
1	USA	15.58	1.085
2	UK	11.62	0.809
3	Bangladesh	7.53	0.525
4	Sri Lanka	3.77	0.262
5	Russian Federation	3.72	0.259
6	Canada	3.66	0.255
7	Germany	3.62	0.252
8	France	3.56	0.248
9	Malaysia	3.48	0.243
10	Japan	3.16	0.22

Source: MoT Statistics (2014).

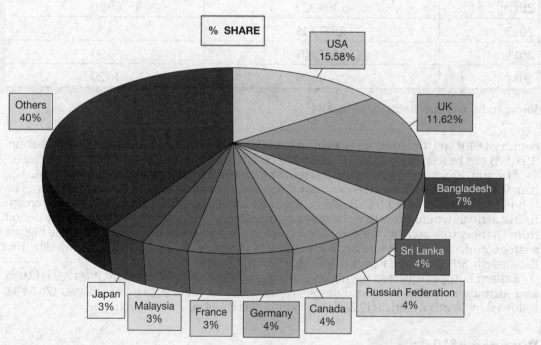

Chart 11.1   Foreign tourist arrivals: market share
Source: Authors.

'leisure, holidays and recreation'; 25.9% listed 'visiting friends and relatives' as purpose of visit, while 20.9% came for 'business and professional' reasons (Table 11.3 and Chart 11.2).

Further analysis of data throws up some interesting information, which has implications on our marketing strategies. In the biggest source market, the USA, 46.2% of visitors came to India to visit friends and relatives and 19.6% came on business. Leisure and holiday visitors were only 16.8% of the total number. Similarly, data from the UK visitors indicate that only 27.9% were leisure visitors, with 38.4% coming to India to visit friends and relatives. A conclusion that can be drawn from this data is that a large part of the foreign tourists from the USA and the UK may be persons of Indian origin (PIO's), who have acquired citizenship of those countries but maintain family links with India. The data also indicates that we have a long way to go in attracting substantial numbers of the outbound leisure visitor population from these two large markets.

Foreign Exchange Earnings

In 2014, India earned an estimated ₹1.2 trillion of foreign exchange from tourism ($19.66 billion), which is 1.58% of the total international tourism receipts of $1,245 billion.

Table 11.3 Purpose of visit

Year	FTA (Numbers)	Business and Professional	Leisure, Holiday and Recreation	Visiting Friends and Relatives	Medical Treatment	Education	Others
2009	5,167,699	15.1	57.5	17.6	2.2	–	7.6
2010	5,775,692	18.6	24	27.5	2.7	–	27.2
2011	6,309,222	22.5	26	24.9	2.2	–	24.3
2012	6,577,745	22.5	27.1	27.2	2.6	–	20.6
2013	6,967,601	20.9	30.3	25.9	3.4	1.9	17.6

Source: Indian Tourism Statistics 2014, Market Research Division, MoT, GoI.

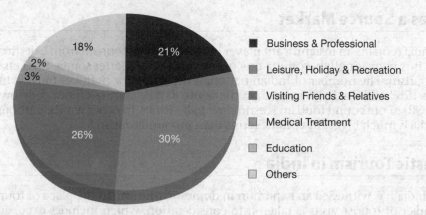

Chart 11.2 Purpose of visit
Source: Authors.

Contribution to Economy

The contribution of T&T to the global economy rose to 9.5% of global GDP (US$ 7 trillion). The development of the tourism sector in India is important, considering the economic impact and contribution of domestic and international tourism to the economy of the country, and its contribution to the GDP and employment. The investment in the sector is estimated to be ₹1.63 trillion, which is 7.2% of the total investment in the country.

As per the second TSA data, tourism GDP accounted for 3.7% of GDP in terms of direct impact and 6.8% of GDP when indirect effects are included.

The WTTC India estimates that T&T contributed 8.6% of the GDP, translating to US$ 117.9 billion (₹5.53 trillion) in 2010. This includes a direct impact of ₹1.97 trillion, equivalent to 3.1% of total GDP of India and the rest as the indirect effect on all sectors of the economy. This figure is projected to rise to US$ 330.1 billion (₹18.54 trillion) by 2020 (World Travel and Tourism Council, 2010).

Domestic travel spending generated 80.7% of direct T&T GDP in 2013. This figure is projected to rise by 6.7% annually to ₹9.65 trillion by 2024.

In India, tourism is estimated to be growing at an annual rate of 8.1%, which is higher than the overall rate of growth of the Indian economy. By 2020, India will need to build an additional 180,000 rooms to cater to the demand. This works out to an investment of US$ 25.5 billion (₹1.66 trillion).

Employment

Directly and indirectly, travel and tourism sector supported 266 million jobs, or one in 11 jobs worldwide. The sector is expected to generate around 347 million jobs by 2024, growing at around 4% annually. T&T directly employs more people than the communication services, automotive manufacturing and mining sectors.

In India, the T&T economy has created about 18.6 million jobs, representing 3.8% of total employment. However, if the indirect impacts are also calculated, the estimated employment rises to around 50 million jobs, which is 10% of the total employment in India.

Another study conducted by KPMG estimates that T&T sector directly supported 25 million jobs in 2012, 4.9% of the total employment in India. This figure is expected to rise to 31 million by 2023. Applying the multiplier effect (of 0.6 additional jobs per direct job created) the total employment supported by the sector is 40 million, 7.7% of the country (KPMG, 2013).

India as a Source Market

While India remains an insignificant player in international tourism from a destination point of view, it is increasingly becoming one of the most sought after source markets in international tourism. The number of Indian nationals departing for holidays outside India during 2013 was 16.63 million, 11.4% more than the figure in 2012. The compounded annual growth rate (CAGR) of outbound tourism is estimated to be 10.3%. In other words, outbound tourism from India is much bigger in volume terms than inbound tourism!

Domestic Tourism in India

Of late, India has witnessed an explosion in domestic tourism. In the place of tourist arrivals, the number of tourist visits is taken into consideration, which includes excursions as well. MoT estimates that the number of domestic tourist visits in India during 2014 was to the tune of 1.29 billion!

The collection of domestic tourism statistics in India is not very accurate or regular. Data sent by the Departments of tourism of states and UT administrations are compiled in MoT. This data is often based on monthly returns collected from accommodation establishments. This data is supplemented by surveys commissioned by MoT. It may be noted that the statistics presented for domestic tourism are in terms of tourist visits and not tourist arrivals. According to the data released by MoT, the top five states in terms of domestic tourist visits are Maharashtra, Tamil Nadu, Delhi, Uttar Pradesh and Rajasthan.

ASI provides accurate data on the number of visitors to the major monuments of the country ('ticketed' monuments), which are termed centrally protected monuments/sites. According to this data, a total of 48.2 million persons visited these monuments in 2014, which included 45.4 million domestic visitors and 2.8 million foreign visitors. The 10 most popular monuments for domestic and foreign visitors in 2014 may be seen in Table 11.4.

Recognized Tourism Industry Units

MoT grants recognition to inbound tour operators, travel agents, tourist transport operators, adventure tour operators and domestic tour operators in the country, based on certain guidelines and conditions. At present, there are 168 inbound tour operators, 107 travel agents 54 tourist transport operators, 6 adventure tour operators and 14 domestic tour operators which are registered with the ministry. However, a much larger number of operators continue to operate their businesses serving the sector, without the formal recognition or classification of the ministry.

Tour Guides

A guide is a person hired by the traveller to lead the way, pointing out objects of interest, educating the visitor and providing information that enriches the visit. Guides play an important role in shaping the visitor's experience of a site or destination—a knowledgeable, friendly and enthusiastic guide will convert a routine visit into an unforgettable episode filled with fascinating insights, but an ill-informed, rude and pushy guide will turn the visit into a forgettable and uncomfortable incident.

In India, there are three tiers of guides approved by the authority. Local guides are approved and licensed by the local government and are authorized to function within a particular site/monument or city. State level guides are approved by the state governments and operate within a specific state. Regional level guides are licensed to operate within a specific region which may include several states. Certain qualifications are prescribed by the licensing authority, which also provides training to selected guides (Prakash and Chowdhary, 2010).

Hotels Sector

Rising affluence, a burgeoning and aspirational middle class and poor penetration of investment are some reasons for India to be considered one of the most lucrative hotel markets in the world. Consequently, a large number of hotel projects optimistic about the growth of the hotel industry in India in the long run are in the pipeline. A recent trend is the arrival of major players in the hotel industry into India and the introduction of global brands. Of the top 20 global brands, 18 have already established a presence in India. The general trend that is seen in India is that global brands enter the country through a Joint Venture with an Indian partner or developer. This arrangement works well for both partners—for the Indian developer, an early tie up with an international brand provides vital inputs regarding room specifications, global standards and parameters at the planning stage of the project. It is estimated that India will add more than 60,000 quality rooms in the next five years (ICRA, 2012).

Table 11.4 Domestic and foreign tourists visiting monuments

10 Most Popular Centrally Protected Ticketed Monuments for Domestic Visitors (2014)

Rank	Name of Monument	No. of Domestic Visitors	Percentage Share
1	Taj Mahal, Agra	5,139,640	11.9
2	Qutub Minar, Delhi	2,980,710	6.9
3	Red Fort, Delhi	2,736,699	6.4
4	Sun Temple, Konark	2,334,556	5.4
5	Agra Fort, Agra	1,794,737	4.2
6	Golconda Fort, Hyderabad	1,471,232	3.4
7	Charminar, Hyderabad	1,397,000	3.2
8	Ellora Caves, Aurangabad	1,276,206	3.1
9	Bibi-Ka-Maqbara, Aurangabad	1,064,265	2.5
10	Gol-Gumbaz, Bijapur	1,064,265	2.5
	Others	21,488,586	50
	Total	**43,019,998**	**100**

10 Most Popular Centrally Protected Ticketed Monuments for Foreign Visitors (2014)

Rank	Name of Monuments	No. of Foreign Visitors	Percentage Share
1	Taj Mahal, Agra	695,702	23.2
2	Agra Fort, Agra	363,823	12.1
3	Qutub Minar, Delhi	307,043	10.2
4	Humayun's Tomb, Delhi	276,641	9.2
5	Fatehpur Sikri, Agra	255,129	8.5
6	Red Fort, Delhi	141,498	4.7
7	Mattancherry Palace Museum, Kochi	104,717	3.5
8	Western Group of Temples, Khajuraho	89,511	3
9	Excavated Site, Sarnath	85,991	2.9
10	Group of Monuments, Mamallapuram	70,840	2.4
	Others	604,957	20.2
	Total	**2,995,852**	**100**

Source: Indian Tourism Statistics 2014, Market Research Division, MoT, GoI.

Government-owned Hotels

Historically, hotels in many states have been established and operated by public sector enterprises owned and promoted by the government. In the initial phases of tourism development, when private investment was not forthcoming, the state governments set up hotels in locations and destinations of tourist importance. MoT also supported such initiatives, providing grants for developing tourist accommodation such as 'Yatri Nivas' in destinations. State governments set up the state tourism development corporations (TDC's) to run such hotels and resorts.

Hotel Classification System

India has adopted a star classification system for the classification of hotels and accommodation establishments. There are also systems for approving other categories of hotels and accommodation units such as heritage hotels, B&B establishments and guest houses. As of 2014, there are 1,233 approved hotels and accommodation establishments in India, with a total of 79,567 rooms (including those pending classification). The number of unapproved hotels and rooms will be several times higher than this number. The number of hotels classified under the star categories may be seen in Charts 11.3–11.5.

Federalism and Tourism

Tourism sector does not find a mention in the Constitution of India. By the nature of the sector, it can be seen that tourism needs interventions at the local and regional levels, rather than at the national level. According to the federal principles enshrined in the Constitution,

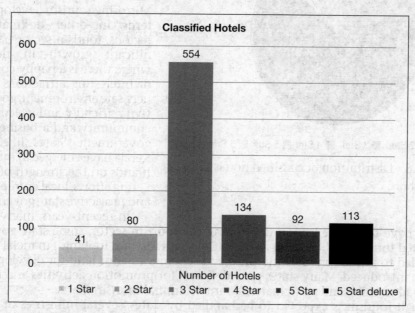

Chart 11.3 Classified hotels
Source: Authors.

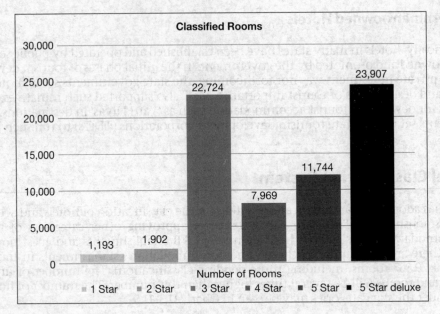

Chart 11.4   Classified rooms
Source: Authors.

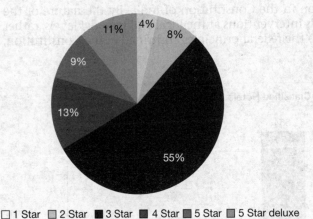

Chart 11.5   Distribution of classified hotels
Source: Authors.

the tourism sector is treated as a state subject, with the primary responsibility of developing tourism resting with the state governments. Mirroring tourism development patterns in other destinations and regions, tourism sector has seen significant growth in destinations where there is a happy combination of interesting attractions and products, safe environment, good connectivity, friendly and welcoming local community and a business friendly government. States like Goa and Kerala have emerged as international brands on the strength of slick marketing efforts, local entrepreneurship and pro-active state governments.

In recent years, many state governments have taken the lead in developing the tourism sector. Some state governments have created tourism policies that are ambitious and forward looking. Financial incentives are provided to attract private enterprise and schemes to allot land for developing hotels have been introduced. Many states provide funds for promotion activities and marketing, including advertising and participation in international tourism marts.

Although tourism is expected to be handled by states, several ministries of the Union Government have prominent roles to play in the tourism environment and have a great impact on the trajectory of inbound tourism. The visa offices of the Ministry of External

Affairs issue visas permitting entry into the country. A large majority of tourists enter the country through the international airports which are under the administrative control of the Ministry of Civil Aviation. Air connectivity, including the operation of foreign carriers and the domestic airline regime, is governed by the legislations and orders of the Civil Aviation ministry. The vast hinterland of India is best accessed by rail, with the ministry of railways looking after its functioning including special activities and initiatives for tourists. The policy directives of the ministry of finance regarding foreign direct investment (FDI), fiscal policy and interest rates have a direct bearing on private investment in tourism projects. The restrictions placed on visiting certain areas of the country, such as the Inner Line Permit, have profound implications on tourism development in such regions. In many parts of India, central police forces play an important role in maintaining law and order.

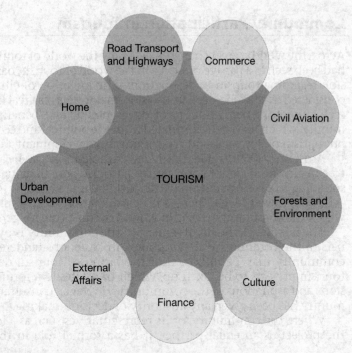

Figure 11.1 Ministries related to tourism sector
Source: Authors.

A large majority of the cultural and natural assets of the country, which are the main resources generating tourism, are owned and managed by the agencies of the union government. ASI is the custodian of the most important monuments and sites and also exercises control over construction in the surrounding region. The activities in and around wildlife sanctuaries and natural parks are governed by Central Acts, under the oversight of the ministry of environment and forests. The coastal areas of the country have been placed under the coastal regulation zone, with restriction on activities and developments. It is clear that the GoI, and its agencies, have a vital part to perform for ensuring the growth of the tourism sector (Figure 11.1).

The role of MoT is limited to undertaking marketing and promotion at a national level and providing funds to the states to assist in the creation and development of infrastructure at destinations. However, the reality is very different. Many cash strapped state governments do not provide budgetary funds for the development of infrastructure or connectivity that are essential for tourism to develop and seek the assistance of the union government. Central financial assistance to state governments is under schemes framed by MoT. The ministry controls investment into the sector by linking its financial incentives to project approvals and monitoring. The classification system operated by the ministry and the systems of accreditation and recognition of service providers are other ways through which the ministry is involved in the sector. MoT periodically announces the tourism policy, which lays down the framework for developing tourism circuits and destinations, the incentives provided by the ministry to the sector and the regulatory environment.

Community Participation in Tourism

Across the world, a great change is sweeping the world of tourism. The local community, which had been seen as a passive presence in the world of tourists, has come to be central in any discussion regarding tourism in destinations. The inclusion of citizens and groups which were not considered as 'stakeholders' in decision-making has far reaching implications for the tourism sector, upsetting many notions of 'development' and 'benefit' to local communities. The community, which had been eliminated from the political and economic processes, will now decide on tourism policy, scale and type of tourism development, taxation and resource allocation.

Arnstein's (1969) 'Ladder of Citizen Participation' can be adopted in the context of tourism to explain the stages of community participation. Imagine a 'ladder', with each rung corresponding to a level of citizen participation (Figure 11.2).

In the lowest levels, there is no participation, but 'manipulation' and 'therapy', through which the community is manipulated as a substitute for genuine participation.

The next level, the involvement of the community is by way of 'tokenism', where members of the community are employed in basic jobs tendered by tourism development. The community may be informed of the proposed tourism development or 'consulted' about tourism projects to be taken up, which translates to a forum for airing the views, apprehensions and aspirations of the community. However, consultation does not mean that the community has been given any authority of decision-making.

Where the community, or its representatives such as a local government, collaborates in the project as an equal partner, it has a formal role in the decision-making process. This means that the community takes an informed decision to start a tourism project and also takes responsibility on its impacts. At the highest level of involvement, the community owns the enterprise, taking full responsibility for the nature, form and stakeholders of the enterprise.

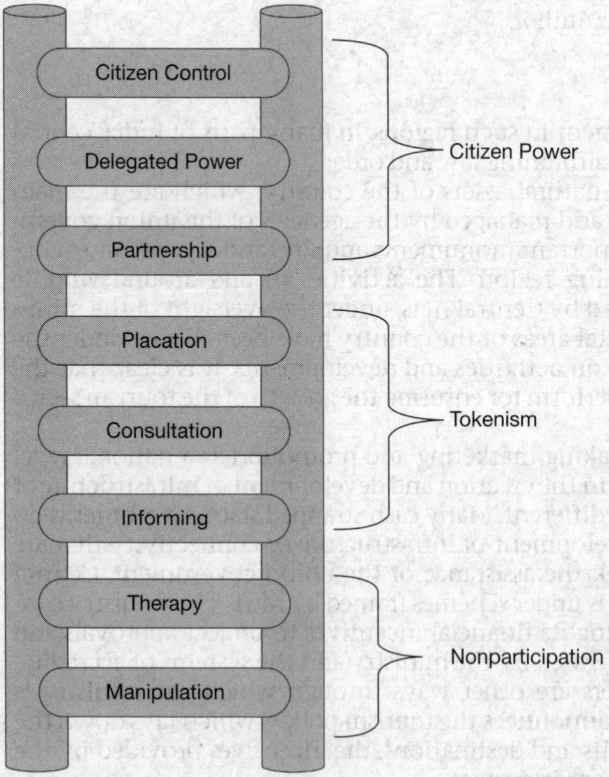

Tourism development in India has characteristics similar to the above model. Government agencies went ahead with tourism projects, acquired land and prevented access to public resources in relatively undisturbed areas of the country without consulting the local communities. Large tracts of land were acquired after displacing residents to be sold off to private developers, in the name of developing destinations. Tourism, being a private sector-led activity, is particularly sensitive in managing the conflict between development projects and the apprehensions of the community.

It took time for the local community to realize that they have to get their voice heard and take active control of the scale of development of tourism. The biggest constraint

Figure 11.2 Ladder of citizen participation
Source: Arnstein (1969).

that stood in the way of the empowerment of the community was the lack of legitimate power and authority.

Local Governments and Tourism

In India, administrative functions have been discharged primarily by the Union and state governments. Although a Panchayat system had been practised in the villages of many parts of India from the olden times, it was not representative and was dominated by caste and traditionally dominant groups. The traditional formations in the community did not have authority to collect taxes or to regulate activities and served only as a meeting place to discuss social issues. With the advent of independence, the issue of strengthening local governance gained popularity. The 73rd amendment introduced a three tier system, providing constitutional status to the Panchayati Raj institutions (PRIs). The 73rd and 74th Amendment of the Constitution of India provide for local self-government and participative decision-making at the grassroots level. The empowerment of the local governments have provided an administrative framework based on which local governments take significant decisions on matters concerning the community.

The devolution of decision-making powers to local government has not been implemented completely in most of the states. Major approvals for tourism projects like hotels and resorts, including critical ones like plan approvals, have to be obtained from the state government. Clearances from the environment angle for major projects have to be obtained from the GoI. The role of the local self-government is reduced to providing 'no objection certificate' to projects.

However, there is steady progress in the process of empowering PRIs. The institutions in many states are being provided with powers and responsibilities to prepare plans for economic development and social justice and to implement schemes for economic development. Existing laws are being modified in some states to enable the PRIs to levy, collect and appropriate taxes, duties, tolls and fees.

Across the world, the central pillar of the government that affects the tourism sector is the local government. It is the local government that is responsible for the basic infrastructure in the destination. Local government is responsible for critical tasks such as keeping the destination clean, providing good connectivity, safety and security and in some places, the provision of utilities such as power. The local government is also concerned with stimulating investment and regulating economic activity. Lastly, the local government is the authority charged with regional planning. It is only natural, therefore, that it is the local government that pilots the complex interrelationships between the tourism industry on the one hand and the local community on the other.

In India, it is early days, the devolution of powers to local governments has not been completed in many states. But where the local governments have become stronger, financially independent and administratively powerful, they have started engaging with all sectors actively, including the tourism sector. The local body is exercising more attention before approving proposals of tourism projects. More community dialogue and consultation is taking place. In states like Kerala, the local bodies have taken decisions against issue of foreign liquor licenses even to tourism establishments. It is clear that the local self-government institutions in India will involve more deeply in economic issues and be invested with important decision-making powers that will have great impact on sectors like tourism.

Tourism Education

To meet the requirement of human resources for the travel and tourism industry, MoT has created institutional and academic infrastructure in the form of Indian Institute of Tourism and Travel Management (IITTM), Institutes of Hotel Management (IHM) and FCI. IITTM offers postgraduate diploma programmes in travel and tourism and related fields. It is estimated that around 80 universities have colleges offering degree or postgraduate courses in hospitality and tourism.

Hotel Management

We have seen earlier that the hospitality industry is at the cusp of a leap forward, with a quantum jump in the number of hotels to be opened in the near future and the consequent increase in the requirement of trained and competent staff. In keeping with the burgeoning demand for trained personnel, tourism and hospitality education courses have become quite popular in India.

The beginning of hospitality education in the country was the establishment of IHMs and Institute of Hotel Management Catering technology and Applied Nutrition. For imparting training in hospitality related craft disciplines, FCIs were also set up. MoT established the National Council for Hotel Management and Catering Technology (NCHMCT) to supervise and regulate the development of hotel management and catering education. Currently, there are 21 central government sponsored IHMs, 21 state government institutes and 15 privately run institutes offering graduate level courses.

The New Visa Policy

The cumbersome and time-consuming visa application and processing system was seen as a big impediment in the growth of tourism in India. The issue of simplifying the procedures has been raised regularly by tour operators before the GoI. Indeed, it can be said that the single biggest bottleneck in increasing tourism business to India was the antiquated and unresponsive visa processing system in the Indian missions abroad.

There had been a series of inter-ministerial consultations in the matter. Recently, there has been a breakthrough, and a new visa regime has replaced the old system. Currently, India has put in place the electronic travel authorization (ETA) facility, known as the e-Tourist Visa or 'e-TV'. The e-TV facility is available to citizens of more than 115 countries, and this figure is likely to go up. A simple application process, which can be completed in the comfort of one's home, has been introduced. Visitors intending to travel to India for sightseeing, tourism, visiting friends and family, short duration medical treatment or business visits can now apply online, with a few simple documents to be uploaded. An application has to be made at least four days in advance of the date of arrival. The payment of visa fees can be made electronically. Upon processing and approval, a travel authorization will be issued electronically to the applicant, a copy of which must be carried at the time of travel. Upon arrival, the biometric details of the applicant will be captured at the airport. The e-TV is valid for entry through 16 designated airports. The popularity of the new scheme is evident from the fact that over 200,000 visas were issued in eight months of introduction of the scheme.

Prospects for Employment Generation

The umbrella sector of travel, tourism and hospitality generates employment in a gamut of sub-sectors. Employment in the tourism environment includes jobs in tour operations, both domestic and inbound, tourist transport operations and travel agencies. In the hospitality sector, food production, front office, F&B and housekeeping departments offer the most openings. The restaurant sector is booming, with a spectrum of offerings with great potential for absorbing manpower.

It is estimated that the restaurant sector employs 66% of the workforce in the sector, followed by hotels (27%) and the travel and tourism services (17%).

With the tourism sector poised to register an annual growth rate of around 10% in the coming years, there will be a continuous requirement of trained manpower to fill these positions. Industry reports indicate that there is already a shortfall of around 500,000 persons in the hospitality sector alone (2011-12), which will widen to 1.1 million by 2022. Add to this the forecasted requirement of about 7 million jobs by 2022, and it is clear that urgent steps are needed to ensure that the full benefit of the growth is utilized and these jobs are filled with the right people.

Matching demand and supply is a tricky exercise, as there can be wide variations in the kind of manpower that is needed. However, the most important fact that emerges is that a large majority of vacancies is likely to arise in non-managerial positions. The tourism sector is a skill-heavy sector, with manpower possessing a wide variety of skills needed in every establishment. Managerial positions account for only 16% in the hospitality sector and 21% in the travel and trade sector (Report of the National Skill Development Council).

Data collected from industry sources on the educational qualifications required for the sector reveals the following:

- Higher secondary: 62%
- Graduate: 15%
- Vocational/diploma: 12%
- Up to secondary: 6%
- Postgraduation and above: 5%

Employers believe that the quality of manpower is not up to the mark in terms of expectations of the industry. Thus, given the need for retraining of incoming manpower supplies at the entry-level, employers do not attach a premium to recruitment of skilled workforce. There is a mismatch between the capability of the manpower and expectations of the industry, perhaps owing to the dated curriculum being followed by educational institutions.

The industry offers relatively lower remuneration at entry-level and employees are expected to put in long hours with fewer holidays and hard physical work. Students are hesitant to take up such entry-level jobs, and there is also high attrition at the lower levels. There is a trend showing that young employees leave entry level jobs in the T&T sector for jobs in other sectors such as retail, banking and entertainment that offer better pay. It is important to manage the expectations of students regarding pay structure, career progression and working environment, so that students have a realistic idea of the sector before a course in travel and tourism, or during the course of their education.

To increase employability, it may be useful for students to obtain certification in specific skills even while they pursue their academic education. As the sector is oriented towards service, training in soft skills such as communication, interpersonal skills, etiquette and grooming is important.

Studies have indicated that a large part of the employees currently employed in the sector have not been fully trained for the jobs they are performing. A combination of formal in-house training, on-the-job training and more courses offering skill training appeared to be the need of the day. The existing training infrastructure has to be augmented by adding training institutes and increasing the capacity of the existing ones. A good number of employees are not permanent, but work on a temporary or casual basis. There is a need to improve their skills as well, particularly relating to cleanliness, personal hygiene, etiquette and basic manners, basic cooking, garbage disposal, basic tourism awareness and behavioural skills (KPMG, 2013).

Outlook for Tourism

There are several pointers that indicate that tourism will continue to enjoy robust growth in India. The important ones are outlined below:

Rise in middle class population: The number of households in the middle class is expected to increase to around 115 million households by 2025, widening the market of travellers. The migration of people and capital to urban centres also brings in more people with a desire to travel.

Demographic profile: A total of 65% of the Indian population is below 40 years, an age group influenced by global attitudes and new forms of relaxation and enjoyment like tourism.

Rising Income levels: There is more 'disposable' income thanks to increased wages and salaries. There is greater aspiration for leisure travel, thanks to more information and wider exposure. The number of working women has dramatically increased in India. Double income households have led to an increase in disposable incomes. There is an increased propensity to spend among the middle-class.

Consumerism and consumption: In tier 2 and 3 cities and towns of India, there is increased consumerism, which has a positive impact on travel and tourism.

Government initiatives: Government has given infrastructure status to large capital intensive hotel projects. This will enable these projects to obtain loans at lower rates of interest, with longer repayment periods. Financial incentives like the opening up of the hotel sector for 100% FDI and sops like tax holidays for hotel projects in certain regions are expected to spur more investment in the sector. Up to 49% of domestic airline companies can be owned by foreign airline brands, thanks to the new FDI regime.

Simplification of visa procedures: For inbound tourism, this is very significant, as travel to India, without advance planning, is now possible, and tiresome procedures like visiting the mission to obtain a visa have been removed. This is expected to bring in more volumes in the aviation sector, including opening new sectors overseas.

Diversity of products: To cater to this huge emerging market, more product offerings are hitting the market, appealing to every possible segment. The variety and diversity of products and increased choice are helping potential travellers to find the appropriate holiday for themselves. More service providers and convenience have led to a dramatic increase in eating out and ordering in, directly benefiting the restaurant and hospitality sector.

Easy credit: Many banks are offering financing options to fund family holidays. The Indian middle-class is increasingly getting comfortable with a 'credit culture', taking loans to fulfil their ambitions and paying through EMI's.

Conclusion

Tourism sector in India has of late witnessed robust growth. It has made its mark through the economic contribution to the economy and from the employment generated directly and indirectly. The much awaited easing of visa restrictions will spur a growth in inbound arrivals. Domestic and outbound tourism are also showing brisk growth. All these developments will bring in increased investments into the sector, stimulating the creation of jobs at the skilled and managerial levels. Management of tourism destinations will increasingly engage governments, particularly at the state and local levels.

Review Questions

1. Discuss the diverse roles played by government in promoting tourism.
2. Explain how tourism promotes local economic development.
3. Examine the case for promoting tourism development in India.

Activities

1. Collect the Scheme and guidelines of MoT, GoI for granting recognition to inbound tour operators, travel agents, tourist transport operators, adventure tour operators and domestic tour operators. Organize an awareness programme in a tourism destination for unregistered organizations/potential entrepreneurs and extend support service for enabling them to register their units.
2. Prepare a list of tour guides in a destination. Through observation and informal discussion with them find out the following:

   a. How many of them possess valid guide license?
   b. How many of them possess the required guiding skills?

   How will you assist them in improving their skills?
3. Prepare a document indicating the role and specific intervention made by different central ministries and state governments during the last 10 years in promoting tourism in your state. Organize a workshop and discuss areas that need immediate attention.
4. The PRIs can play a pro-active role in strengthening community involvement in tourism business. Organize a focus group discussion involving elected representatives, community leaders and tourism industry stakeholders to explore potential areas for community intervention in tourism.
5. Conduct a survey among tourism establishments in a destination and identify the human resource requirements of each organization with specific skills required.

References

Web Resources

Arnstein, S.R. 1969. 'A Ladder of Citizen Participation'. *JAIP*, 35 (July, 4): 216–24. Available at: http://lithgow-schmidt.dk/sherry-arnstein/ladder-of-citizen-participation_en.pdf (accessed on 22 December 2016).

ICRA. 2012. 'Consumer Confidence Low: Revival Contingent on Global Environment'. *Indian Hotels Industry, Quarterly Review*, (March). Available at: http://www.icra.in/Files/ticker/Indian%20Hotels%20Industry%2030032012.pdf (accessed on 22 December 2016).

KPMG. 2013. 'Travel and Tourism Sector: Potential Opportunities and Enabling Framework for Sustainable Growth'. KPMG. Available at: http://www.kpmg.com/IN/en/IssuesAndInsights/ArticlesPublications/Documents/KPMG-CII-Travel-Tourism-sector-Report.pdf (accessed on 22 December 2016).

Prakash, M., and N. Chowdhary. 2010. 'What are We Training Tour Guides For? (India). *Turizam*, 14 (2): 53-65. Available at: http://www.dgt.uns.ac.rs/turizam/arhiva/vol_1402_nimit.pdf (accessed on 22 December 2016).
World Travel and Tourism Council. 2010. 'Travel and Tourism Economic Impacts—India'. World Travel and Tourism Council. Available at: http://www.wttcii.org/pdf/india_tsa_2010.pdf

Suggested Readings

Web Resources

Ministry of Home Affairs. 2011. 'Area and Population'. Office of the Registrar General and Census Commissioner, Government of India. Available at: http://censusindia.gov.in/Census_And_You/area_and_population.aspx
MoT. 2014. 'India Tourism Statistics at a Glance'. Market Research Division, Government of India. Available at: http://tourism.nic.in/writereaddata/CMSPagePicture/file/marketresearch/statisti-calsurveys/India%20Tourism%20Statistics%20at%20a%20Glance%202014.pdf
Statistics and Tourism Satellite Account. n.d. 'Historical Background'. Available at: http://statistics.unwto.org/en/content/historical-background

Beside the statue of Gommateshwara, Shravanabelagola, Karnataka
Image courtesy: STARK World.

CHAPTER 12

Cultural Heritage of India

Learning Objectives

By the end of this chapter, students will be able to:

- Distinguish between the basic terms related to culture and heritage.
- Understand the term cultural tourism and its manifestations.
- List the measures taken to protect culture at national and international levels.
- Gain an insight into the operational aspects of culture and heritage in tourism.
- Explain the basic features of important performing arts and cultural forms of India.

Introduction

For centuries, pilgrims from across the Indian subcontinent made their way through difficult routes, braving dangers and obstacles, to visit the four 'dhams' or religious seats. The ancient spiritual city of Kashi held a fascination for travellers who spoke a different language and practised a different way of life. The thread that brought such disparate people together was termed the cultural fabric of India. Even while they spoke in different tongues, dressed differently and ate different kinds of food, these travellers were united by some shared beliefs transmitted to them by their forefathers.

Case Study: Varanasi—A Destination of Living Culture

Varanasi, alternatively known as Kashi and Benares, is undoubtedly one of the most fascinating places on earth. Varanasi is one of the oldest continually living cities in the world, with a history going back, at least, 2,500 years. Kashi, according to Hindu mythology, is the centre of the universe, the city of Lord Shiva. As the celebrated author Mark Twain wrote, 'Benares is older than history, older than tradition, older even than legend and looks twice as old as all of them put together'. Because of the belief that Varanasi offers 'moksha', liberation from the cycle of rebirth, pilgrims have been thronging the city from time immemorial.

One of the most enduring sights of Varanasi is the riverside. On the banks of the Ganga, about a hundred 'ghats' or bathing steps have been built, which are used by the devout for their ablutions, where the dead are cremated and the diverse residents of the city are found. The Dasaswamedha ghat witnesses a colourful and somewhat 'touristy' ceremony of Ganga Aarti, a tribute to the holy river. The old city has many temples, including the celebrated Kashi Vishwanath and Sankat Mochan temples. A traveller is mesmerized by the rituals, offerings and practices that are happening around the river. Manikarnika Ghat is considered the most auspicious place for cremation. Many ghats and shrines have places with connections to epics, myths and legends. Kashi had attracted saints, philosophers and poets through the centuries and continues to inspire art and literature.

Varanasi is renowned for its sumptuous cuisine, particularly the roadside eateries in the *galis* or narrow alleyways of the old city. Food is part of the culture of the city, with a variety of *kachoris* served with a variety of *dal-sabzi* (dish of vegetables and lentils), *chaats* (a savoury snack, usually prepared by roadside vendors) and delicacies such as *littis* (a deep fried snack, made of vegetables and cereals) filled with *sattu* (a flour made of pulses and cereals). The dairy products and sweets come in an array of tastes and flavours—the amazing *lassi* (refreshing drink made of thick yogurt, mixed with salt, sugar, spices or vegetables) served in earthen cups with cream and rose-water, *thandai* (a milk-based refreshing cold drink, popular in Varanasi) laced with spices and bhang, and *peda* (a sweetmeat made of milk solids), *gulab jamun*s (a sweet consisting of a ball of deep-fried cottage cheese in thick sugar syrup) and *kalakand* (a traditional sweet made of thickened milk and cottage cheese [paneer])as dessert. Every meal deserves to end with the famed Banarsi paan that comes in many flavours.

(Continued ...)

Varanasi has a musical tradition that goes back many centuries. Because of its fame as a city of knowledge and the arts, Benaras attracted musicians both vocal and instrumental, establishing its own music and dance tradition. The Benarsi Gharana has a distinctive style in playing the tabla. Several luminaries of music, including Ustad Bismillah Khan lived and performed in Varanasi.

Varanasi has a flourishing tradition of silk weaving. The Benaras silk is renowned worldwide for its fine work and intricate designs. Varanasi is also known for its metalwork such as brassware and copperware, glass bangle work, carpets, musical instruments and jewellery. Varanasi is also sacred to Buddhism. Gautama Buddha delivered his first sermon, laying the foundation for the Sangha, at Sarnath, close to the city.

Image courtesy: Amit Kumar.

Discussion Questions

1. Make a list of things and activities of Varanasi that can be grouped under the term 'living culture'.
2. 'Spiritual tourism' offers great scope for India because of its ancient roots. Discuss.
3. How can destination Varanasi attract the visitor who is not very much interested in 'living culture'?

In this chapter, we explore this further, to gain an insight of Indian culture and its manifestations. Tourism is heavily dependent on the culture and its expressions, so it is of utmost significance that we have deep knowledge and a clear understanding of commonly used terms, the heritage that our culture has provided us and the issues connected to such heritage.

There are several other terms—cultural heritage, tradition, values, customs—which are used while talking about the Indian experience in the context of tourism. Amongst this multiplicity of terms, it may be useful for us to have a clear understanding of the term 'culture' when used in the context of tourism.

We will discuss how cultural heritage is protected and the international and national organizations involved in this endeavour. We will also examine the major heritage sites in India that have such an important role to play in tourism.

Culture

We do not need to concern ourselves with the specific definition of culture—indeed there is a confusing range of definitions available, which explore different facets of this complex word ("What is Culture?" n.d.). From a practical point of view, culture may be seen as a way of life of an ethnic or social group of people, an accumulated set of beliefs, values and behaviours acquired through generations and shared by members of that group. Culture is transmitted from one generation to another and may indicate ideas, skills, attitudes and societal roles. Culture is expressed in different forms—our behaviours, music and dance, literature, religious rituals and practices are all forms of cultural expression ("Culture". n.d.). When one talks about a common culture, it is the sharing of certain values, attitudes and practices and following certain beliefs and ideas that leads to the growth of a specific identity. Tradition indicates beliefs that are derived from history and selected through the ages, passed on as ideas and values with special significance. The manifestation of culture may be seen in many dimensions—from social habits, music and dance, language, cuisine and religion.

Indian culture, as it is manifested now, has been shaped by a variety of influences over centuries, with its origins in the agrarian lifestyle many millennia ago and evolved through the impacts of the great religions of the land. India is known for its multiculturalism, a term that denotes the peaceful coexistence of different cultures within the same geographical region.

Cultural Tourism

For a large majority of visitors, the fascination that India holds is its ancient culture. Many surveys have shown that Western travellers to India are attracted for its 'cultural values', 'cultural heritage' or 'cultural traditions'. Indeed, 'culture' may be one of the most ubiquitous words used in contemporary Indian tourism, finding place in promotional literature, sales pitches, academic articles and everyday usage. When we say 'Namaste' to our guest, we explain the term and the gesture of putting our palms together as the proper way to greet a guest according to Indian culture. Our culture, the tour guide may well say, teaches us to respect elders, dress conservatively or welcome a guest as God. In India, the word is used very frequently and in different contexts. New habits and mannerisms of the younger generation are said to be due to the influence of 'western culture'.

Visitors to India are often categorized as 'cultural tourists', and the bulk of Indian tourism is designated as 'cultural tourism'. While there are problems about such sweeping generalizations, it is sufficient for our discussion to understand what the terms stands for. Cultural tourism includes many activities such as visiting historical sites, monuments, architectural landmarks, artworks, galleries and museums and religious structures and sites. The term also includes experiencing the lifestyle of the destination in its myriad forms and manifestations such as music, visual and performing arts, practices, rituals, celebrations, traditions and events. A visit to a village or a market is cultural tourism, so is partaking a traditional meal. If the visit exposes the visitor to any facet of the historical context or cultural identity of the population, it becomes part of cultural tourism. Cultural expression and creative industries, the commercialization of cultural skills and knowledge, are driving tourism in many destinations. India is naturally blessed with a plethora of cultural expressions, and can rightfully be called one of the world's greatest cultural destinations.

Heritage

How does one define Heritage? A simple definition is: Heritage is that which you have received from the previous generations and which you will pass on to the coming generations. Heritage is something that we inherit from our families, our predecessors and our forefathers. The words attached to your name are your heritage: it could be the name of your father or mother, or the family or caste name, or the name of the village or region from where your family comes. The monuments in our towns are our heritage, so are the traditions in our villages and the stories we heard from our grandmothers.

Tangible and Intangible Heritage

It follows that heritage need not necessarily be 'tangible', that can be seen and felt as physical objects and things. 'Intangible heritage', which is not physical in nature, is also part of our inheritance. Heritage is 'a source of identity and cohesion for communities (UNESCO, n.d.a). We will deal with these in some detail, as tourism is in many ways crucially dependent on heritage in all its manifestations.

UNESCO and Heritage

UNESCO, a specialized agency of the United Nations, works for international cooperation in the field of culture, as part of its mandate. The General Conference of UNESCO in 1972, discussed the pressing need to protect and preserve heritage of outstanding universal value and agreed on a convention concerning the protection of the world cultural and natural heritage. According to the convention, heritage has two components (Figure 12.1):

- Cultural heritage, including monuments, buildings and archaeological sites, as well as cave paintings, monumental sculptures and inscriptions.
- Natural heritage includes natural sites, geological and physiographical formations and natural sites and features with outstanding universal value from the historical, aesthetic, ethnological or anthropological point of view (UNESCO, n.d.b).

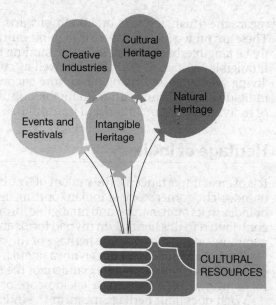

World Heritage Lists

The convention on the protection of the World Cultural and Natural Heritage is more popularly known as the World Heritage Convention. The convention linked together the concepts of nature conservation and the preservation of cultural properties. It defines the kind of sites that can be considered for inscription on the World Heritage List (WHL) and sets out the duties and responsibilities of states parties in protecting and preserving

Figure 12.1 Cultural resources
Source: Authors.

such sites. It also explains how international financial assistance under the aegis of World Heritage Fund will be used and managed. In addition, UNESCO maintains a List of World Heritage in Danger, in order to focus attention on the threatened sites.

Inscription of a heritage property on the WHL signifies that the world heritage committee has deemed that the property has cultural or natural values that can be considered on outstanding universal value. It places the responsibility on each state party to protect, manage and preserve the cultural heritage that has been inscribed.

Cultural heritage is defined by the World Heritage Committee as 'monuments, groups of buildings and sites', including urban centres, archaeological sites, industrial heritage, cultural landscapes and heritage routes.

Natural heritage consists of natural sites of outstanding universal value from the point of view of science, conservation or natural beauty, natural features and geological and physiographical formations.

The convention also established the World Heritage Committee, charged with the publishing of the WHL, a list of properties forming part of the cultural heritage and natural heritage of outstanding universal value. When a site is approved by the World Heritage Committee, it is said to be a World Heritage Site (WHS). The List has around 1031 sites, comprising 802 cultural sites, 197 natural sites and 32 mixed sites (WHLUNESCO, n.d.c). Some of these sites are transnational, with elements in different countries.

International Convention on Intangible Heritage

Keeping in view the universal will and concern in safeguarding the intangible cultural heritage of humanity and considering the impact and progress in protecting cultural heritage through the instrument of the 1972 convention, UNESCO in their conference in 2003, adopted the convention for the safeguarding of intangible cultural heritage. Intangible heritage is defined as 'practices, expressions, representations, knowledge and skills that communities, groups and individuals recognize as part of their cultural heritage (UNESCO, n.d.d).

While natural and cultural heritage were included in the 1972 convention, the general understanding of the term cultural heritage has changed along the years. Heritage today means the rituals, festivals, oral traditions, arts, traditional knowledge and skills and practices. These are understood today as 'intangible cultural heritage'—heritage that need not necessarily be tangible, but are vital in understanding the traditions and knowledge of communities. Intangible heritage is traditional as well as contemporary, which means that the culture is 'living' and evolving. Intangible culture encourages a sense of identity and responsibility for individuals and communities. Intangible culture has to be recognized as such by communities or individuals that maintain and transmit it.

Heritage of India

It is of great importance for the student of tourism to have a clear understanding of the heritage of India. The corner stone of Indian tourism, upon which the entire sector rests, is the heritage of India, in its built, natural and intangible forms. The culture of India has manifested from and contributed to this heritage. In myriad forms and ways, tourism professional needs to interpret, communicate and analyse the heritage of the country as part of his practice and profession.

The Indian tourism product is not a singular entity—it is the amalgamation of a multiplicity of experiences, combining the grandeur of the built heritage with the authenticity of a colourful living heritage, producing a kaleidoscope of sensory inputs that is unique in the world.

What does built heritage mean, in the Indian context. We can proceed from the grandest and internationally renowned to the local, and through this journey, gain an insight into the wealth of tangible heritage around us, much of which has not been appreciated or interpreted for the visitor.

World Heritage Sites in India

The most prestigious list of global heritage sites is the one maintained by UNESCO, called the WHL. The WHL was a result of the 1972 convention for the protection of the World cultural and natural heritage. Over the years, there have been efforts at UNESCO to ensure that the WHL becomes a comprehensive, representative and credible listing of all heritage properties of the world of outstanding universal value. India boasts of 35 WHSs, 27 cultural sites 7 natural sites and 1 mixed site (UNESCO, n.d.e).

The greatest and grandest of our temples and monuments figure in this list. The first sites to be inscribed in the list were the Ajanta and Ellora caves in 1983. Delhi boasts of three sites—Qutub Minar and its monuments, Humayun's tomb and the Red Fort complex. Agra and its neighbouring region has three cultural sites—the Taj Mahal, Agra Fort and Fatehpur Sikri The great living Chola temples of Thanjavur, Gangaikondacholapuram and Darasuram are inscribed, as is the Mahabalipuram temple complex. From Karnataka, the great monuments of Hampi and Pattadakkal figure in the list. From Madhya Pradesh, the Stupa at Sanchi and the Rock shelters of Bhimbetka are on the list. The brilliant craftsmanship of the Khajuraho monuments and the Sun temple at Konarak are recognized and are entered on the list. The Hill forts of Rajasthan, consisting of the Jaisalmer, Chittorgarh, Kumbalgarh, Ranthambhore and Amber and Gargon forts are a recent entry, along with the Jantar Mantar of Jaipur. Rani ki Vav and the Champaner Pavagadh group of monuments from Gujarat are also listed. Mumbai has two sites in its vicinity—the Elephanta caves and the youngest site of all, the Chhatrapati Shivaji Terminus (former Victoria terminus). The churches and convents of Goa are inscribed and also the Mahabodhi temple complex of Bodh Gaya. The architectural work of Le Corbusier, an outstanding contribution to the modern movement, Capitol Complex at Chandigarh and Nalanda Mahavihara (Nalanda University) at Nalanda, Bihar, are the new additions to the list in 2016.

The natural sites range from the Western Ghats spanning the coastal states to the Great Himalayan and Nanda Devi National Parks of the Himalayas. Two of Assam's National Parks, Manas and Kaziranga have been inscribed. The Sundarbans National Park in West Bengal and Keoladeo National Park in Rajasthan are also entered in the list. Khangchendzonga National

Park became the first mixed site from India in the WHL in 2016 owing to its natural and cultural significance.

The list of sites is completed by an interesting entry, which is not a 'site' in the strict sense: the three hill trains of India—Darjeeling, Simla-Kalka and Nilgiri have been inscribed as world heritage, considering their unique nature.

Although the WHL has some of the most renowned examples of built heritage of India, it is but a small fraction of the wonderful wealth of monuments and sites that is scattered across the country (Table 12.1). A glimpse of this treasure can be had by understanding the work of the ASI.

Archaeological Survey of India (ASI)

ASI is the premier organization of the GoI tasked with the protection of the cultural heritage of the nation and to conduct archaeological research. Students of tourism are concerned with the former mandate, which means that the ASI is the custodian of the sites and monuments which form a major part of the tourism product of India.

ASI protects 3,650 ancient monuments and sites of national importance (ASI, n.d.a). These monuments are from different historical periods and include temples, mosques, churches,

Table 12.1   List of world heritage sites in India

Cultural (27)	
Agra Fort (1983)	Hill Forts of Rajasthan (2013)
Ajanta Caves (1983)	Humayun's Tomb, Delhi (1993)
Buddhist Monuments at Sanchi (1989)	Khajuraho Group of Monuments (1986)
Champaner–Pavagadh Archaeological Park (2004)	Mahabodhi Temple Complex at Bodh Gaya (2002)
Chhatrapati Shivaji Terminus (formerly Victoria Terminus, 2004)	Mountain Railways of India (1999)
Churches and Convents of Goa (1986)	Qutub Minar and its Monuments, Delhi (1993)
Elephanta Caves (1987)	Rani-ki-Vav (the Queen's Stepwell) at Patan, Gujarat (2014)
Ellora Caves (1983)	Red Fort Complex (2007)
Fatehpur Sikri (1986)	Rock Shelters of Bhimbetka (2003)
Great Living Chola Temples (1987)	Sun Temple, Konârak (1984)
Group of Monuments at Hampi (1986)	Taj Mahal (1983)
Group of Monuments at Mahabalipuram (1984)	The Jantar Mantar, Jaipur (2010)
Group of Monuments at Pattadakal (1987)	Capitol Complex, Chandigarh (2016)
Nalanda Mahavihara (2016)	
Natural (7)	
Great Himalayan National Park Conservation Area (2014)	Nanda Devi and Valley of Flowers National Parks (1988)
Kaziranga National Park (1985)	Sundarbans National Park (1987)
Keoladeo National Park (1985)	Western Ghats (2012)
Manas National Park (1985)	
Mixed (1)	
Khangchendzonga National Park (2016)	

Source: World Heritage Centre, UNESCO (http://whc.unesco.org/en/statesparties/in)

tombs, cemeteries, palaces, stepwells, rock cut caves and ancient mounds and sites. The officials of the ASI are involved in the maintenance, conservation and preservation of these structures and also conduct research activities. Although some of these sites are already visited by tourists, a large majority of them are yet to be explored and exposed to visitors, offering an important resource that can be exploited by tourism professionals.

Tentative List

Another significant list, which is an effort of a countrywide campaign led by ASI, is the tentative list. A tentative list is an inventory of those properties which each country intends to consider for nomination as a WHS before UNESCO. The tentative list for India was prepared after wide consultations with stakeholders like regional and state governments, local communities, heritage groups, tourism bodies and NGO's. Put differently, the tentative list will have properties which may, in the future, be listed as a WHS (UNESCO, n.d.f).

Prominent monuments which are on the tentative list are the Buddhist sites of Sarnath and Nalanda, the Harappan sites of Lothal and Dholavira, the temples of Bishnupur, Srirangam, Aihole, Badami, Belur and Warangal, the Qutb Shahi monuments of Charminar and Golconda fort and those of Deccan sultanates, the majestic Harmandir Sahib in Amritsar, the Mattanchery and Padmanabhapuram palaces of Kerala and the Mandu monuments. The Moidam mounds of Assam and the Apatani cultural landscape are also featured on the tentative list. The list also has many historic cities like Bhubaneshwar, Chettinad, Ahmedabad, Mumbai and Delhi, and the relatively modern entries like the Baha'i temple, Santiniketan and the Cellular Jail.

Several examples of natural heritage find place, from the Mughal gardens of Kashmir to the river island of Majuli, several national parks and the Chilika Lake.

State Monuments and Sites

Structures and monuments of a relatively lesser importance—from the national perspective—are looked after by the state governments, mostly by the Departments of Archaeology. Many of such sites are also significant, both from the historical and tourism points of view. Each state government maintains a register of such monuments and makes plans for their protection and conservation.

Privately Owned Heritage

Lastly, there are several monuments and sites which are under private ownership and management, which are important for tourism. Several forts and palaces fall into this category.

Heritage Assets and Tourism Development

Cultural heritage sites are by far the most important tourism attractions in India today. Hundreds of thousands of tourists visit these sites and museums every year, bringing in economic benefits to the destinations.

There is an increasing realization that growing numbers of tourists also pose a danger to the monuments in multiple ways. In sensitive sites, the movement of so many people through aged precincts pose a danger to certain parts of the structure. Body heat and breath may be hazardous to extremely sensitive locations, such as fragile paintings in Ajanta.

The aim is to achieve a level of sustainability, where tourists do not pose a threat to the heritage site. This calls for decisive interventions in managing destinations and well thought out strategies. Early intervention and partnerships between various stakeholders will help in minimizing negative impacts. Sustainable tourism management in destinations is an essential requirement. This calls for assessing impacts of proposed developments, particularly those for tourism use in sites and periodic monitoring. Interventions need to be planned after careful analysis of the requirement, an exploration of alternatives and the checks and balances that should be built in. Since the benefits of tourism development should be fully utilized by the local stakeholders, it is important to develop capacity through training and education projects. Good practices in similar sites should be shared and disseminated. Stakeholders have to be fully aware of the value of the heritage asset and the need to preserve it. Incentive mechanisms such as financial incentives and, recognition have to be introduced to encourage responsible actions and the creation of sustainable tourism products and services.

There are several international funding initiatives aimed at assisting destination management organizations in their conservation efforts. A good example of international collaboration for conservation and development of tourism at a heritage site is the Ajanta Caves conservation project.

Here, the aim was to use increased tourist arrivals as a tool to revive the local economy and provide more employment to the community. Japan International Cooperation Agency (JICA) extended loans for the project, which has multiple stakeholders. The plan had several components, ranging from improvements to the airport to civic infrastructure, the conservation of the paintings and construction of visitor amenities.

A view of a cave at Ajanta

Case Study: Ajanta and Ellora Conservation and Tourism Development Project

The Ajanta caves were among the first to be registered as WHSs, in 1983. Even while the number of visitors visiting the Ajanta caves space was increasing, the state of preservation of the site and the conservation of the paintings is a source of concern to heritage professionals. The challenge before the managers of the site of the Ajanta and Ellora caves was to attract more tourists to the heritage site, cater to the increasing demand of tourists and use this development for the revival and revitalization of the local economy, leading to the production of employment opportunities and entrepreneurship in the local community.

(Continued ...)

JICA agreed to provide loans for the preservation of these heritage monuments and for educating the visitors, under the Overseas Development Assistance program. This culminated in the Ajanta and Ellora Conservation and Tourism Development project, where JICA has been working with the MoT, Maharashtra Tourism Development Corporation (MTDC), ASI and Airport Authority of India, along with other state agencies for the implementation of the project. The objective of Ajanta caves conservation project is to promote tourism to conservation of the site, improvement of the environment and development of infrastructure around the temples. The ultimate aim was to revitalize the local economy through tourism and to increase the awareness about the site among domestic and foreign travellers. The loan disbursed for Phase I was 3,362 million Yen. A loan agreement for 7,331 million yen was signed with JICA on 31 March, 2003 to undertake the Ajanta and Ellora development conservation project (phase 2).

The project is a good example of funding from an external source being channelized by the GoI into a project that has multiple stakeholders. While the ASI, which manages the site, took up civil construction and conservation works, MTDC was involved in creating tourist related infrastructure. Airport Authority was involved in upgradation of the Aurangabad airport, and state bodies took up other works like water supply and road development. Besides conservation works, the access to these tourism attractions were improved by developing the road connection from Aurangabad, expanding the water supply system in the area, construction of a new terminal building at the airport and the preparation and implementation of a site management plan.

An important component of the plan was to reduce air pollution around the heritage site which was resulting in the accelerated deterioration of the cave paintings. The main components of the project are the monument conservation, improvement of Aurangabad airport, afforestation, construction of tourist complexes and water supply at tourist attractions, public awareness activities, human resource development and computerization of tourist information. In 2013, the world-class tourist visitor centres at Ajanta and Ellora were commissioned. The Ajanta visitor centre is spread across 18,000 m². The replicas of four main caves—1, 2, 16 and 17—have been created here using simulated stone technology. The centre also houses audio-visual presentations, a library, cafeteria, amphitheatre and ample parking space.

Ellora visitor centre has been constructed in around 12,000 m² with similar facilities. A real-life replica of the Kailasa temple in a reduced proportion has been constructed. The total investment under the programme is around ₹3.8 billion.

Under the project, the ASI undertook several significant projects that improved the visitor experience as well as helped in conservation and better preservation of the paintings. Construction of a proper parking space and relocation of vehicle parking away from the caves have significantly reduced air pollution. The painted caves—numbers 1, 2, 16, 17 and 19—have been provided with high quality fibre-optic lighting. Footbridges and pathways have been built for better visitor traffic management. Extensive conservation works were undertaken in many of the caves. Drainage facilities have been improved in order to prevent seepage and leakage into the caves.

Apart from the Ajanta Ellora project, JICA is also involved in the funding of the development of Uttar Pradesh Buddhist circuit project, for the improvement of the roads, public utilities, site development and support programs at different sites related to the life of the Buddha which are located in Uttar Pradesh.

Image courtesy: Department of Tourism, Government of Maharashtra.

Discussion Questions

1. 'In sensitive sites, it may be necessary to prevent tourists from entering areas which are very fragile. Instead, replicas of these areas may be viewed by the visitors instead of the original sites'. Discuss.

(Continued ...)

2. This project is an example of a comprehensive vision for the destination. Discuss the various interventions that substantiate this statement.

Conservation, Tourism and the Community

It must be kept in mind that cultural heritage sites, in many instances, mean different things to different stakeholders. While the tourism professional sees a monument as interesting attraction suitable for a visit for his client, the community may value the monument as an enduring symbol of a great past, and the destination manager may view it as vital for his strategy to bring in more tourists. Cultural tourism is one of the largest and fastest growing segments in the international tourism market. Culture and creative industries are essential components of a destination to increase its attractiveness and competitiveness, and most destinations endowed with such resources try to develop these assets forgetting comparative advantage in a competitive market place.

Projects to regenerate heritage sites may offer good opportunities for community participation leading to renewal initiatives that benefits the entire community, not confined to a few who get employment. The Humayun's Tomb Conservation Project is an excellent example of stakeholders working together for the conservation of a monument and renewal of an urban precinct.

The project brought in funds and expertise provided by the Aga Khan Trust for Culture, a transnational organization focusing on physical, social, cultural and economic revitalization of historic urban environments. In consultation with the local community, the project combines the conservation project at a WHS with the renewal of the historic precinct of Nizamuddin, improving the quality of life, providing livelihood options and reviving the 'living culture' of the area.

Humayun's tomb, Delhi

Case Study: The Humayun's Tomb Conservation Project—An Example of Public Private Partnership

The city of Delhi houses some of the most important sites and monuments from the Mughal period. The magnificent tomb of Humayun, son of Babur, is one of the earliest and combines Persian and indigenous elements of architecture. Located in the heart of New Delhi,

(Continued ...)

Nizamuddin heritage precinct comprises the area of Hazrat Nizamuddin Basti, Sunder Nursery and the WHS of Humayun's Tomb. The Humayun's tomb complex has been the venue for a unique project that enhanced the tourism value of the site and undertook valuable conservation work of the medieval monument.

The first project in the Humayun's tomb complex that was taken up under the Public Private Partnership model was the restoration of the Mughal gardens in 2003. The Aga Khan Trust for Culture supported the restoration of the gardens, supplementing the efforts of the ASI. The fountains, pathways, waterways and other elements in the gardens were studied and restored. These activities were backed up with support for research that informed the conservation and restoration process and the development of educational materials useful to visitors, architecture and heritage students. As part of the implementation process, a management plan was established to ensure proper long term maintenance.

Recognizing that this model was a success, the Nizamuddin Urban Renewal Project was devised, taking the same model to a broader area. The project commenced with the signing of a MoU. The different players involved in the project are the ASI, the owner and custodian of the property; the Central Public Works Department which manages the Sunder nursery; the Municipal Corporation of Delhi; the Aga Khan foundation and the Aga Khan Trust for Culture. The project will unify the two zones into an urban conservation area of cultural significance while improving the quality of life for resident population. The project integrates conservation, social economic development and environmental development objectives in consultation with local communities and relevant stakeholders. Since its inception, the project has attracted additional partners and received funding from numerous non-governmental funds. Heritage Conservation works now being undertaken at the mausoleum of the Mughal emperor and associated buildings are based on exhaustive archival research and the highest standards of documentation. Master craftsman, using traditional tools, craft techniques and building materials are in charge of the works. Regular training programs and workshops for conservation professionals and craftsmen from across India are also being held.

Socioeconomic Initiatives

Apart from the conservation initiatives, the project envisages several initiatives in the social and economic front. At Hasrat Nizamuddin Basti, efforts are being made for a community centred, collaborative approach that will result in socioeconomic development of the area. The objective is to provide better employment conditions and strengthen urban services, particularly in education, health and sanitation. The primary school in the vicinity has been refurbished. There is more emphasis on arts education, greater parent interaction and improved school management. The polyclinic has been improved to ensure better diagnosis and treatment. Street improvement plans have been prepared and will be implemented by the Municipal Corporation of Delhi.

Cultural Revival Initiative

The endeavour is to sensitize the residents of the unique 'living culture' of the area that encompasses performing arts, classical music, poetry and traditional arts. Steps are being taken to revive and revitalize these components by making them viable in a contemporary milieu. Several projects have been started aimed at improving family incomes through sales of products based on traditional skills, thereby bringing the benefits of tourism development to the locals.

Image courtesy: Ministry of Tourism, Government of India.

Discussion Questions

1. What are the possible reasons for a private foundation such as the Aga Khan Trust for Culture to fund such a project? Discuss.
2. List the stakeholders involved in this complex exercise.

Management of Cultural Heritage

As heritage is a priceless, perishable asset vital for tourism, it is in our interest to gain knowledge of the management of heritage properties. In many parts of the world, tourism businesses and organizations are playing an increasingly important role in contributing to the management of heritage and new structures of partnerships are being formed. In India too, there is a change in approach towards heritage management.

Across the years, there has been a change in the way heritage has been managed. Heritage structures were placed under the 'protection' of government bodies, primarily to ensure that these are conserved well, that these are not destroyed or defaced by human intervention and that visits to such sites take place in highly controlled environment. Almost all such initiatives were led by the Central Government, without any regard to the aspirations and involvement of local populations and implemented by officials using exclusively government funding. In a sense, the management approach was against people, with government assuming the role of protecting sites for posterity. While this approach had its merits in the days when local communities were not aware of the importance of this precious legacy, this paternalistic and insulated mind had to change with the times. The emphasis is shifting to involving more stakeholders in managing heritage; respecting the cultural values and preferences of the local communities; and recognizing that these sites are important in an economic sense. Funds for heritage conservation are coming from more sources rather than just government finances, individuals and organizations are getting involved in the professional management and maintenance of some monuments and there is a conscious shift to an integrated approach that coordinates between different agencies and community groups.

Why is this important? It is absolutely clear that governmental funding will not be sufficient for the proper maintenance of our monuments. Given the importance of heritage as an important ingredient in the tourism experience, it is necessary that tourism businesses give more attention to contributing to the local management of our built heritage. This will not only ensure that we play a role in preserving such structures but also create durable tourism assets in more regions and destinations. The involvement of tourism players can take many forms, such as funding conservation projects, helping structure and operate adaptive use projects, increasing local awareness on heritage conservation, inviting contributions from visitors by building interest in local heritage and culture and assisting local governments to manage their assets better.

Of late, Corporate Social Responsibility funds are being channelized towards conservation of heritage and construction of tourist facilities. Indian Oil Foundation (IOF), a non-profit trust formed by Indian Oil Ltd, has embarked on an ambitious programme for upgrading some notable heritage sites to world class standards under their CSR strategy.

Case Study: Indian Oil Foundation—Corporate Social Responsibility (CSR) for Heritage Preservation

With the objective of protecting, preserving and promoting the glorious past of India, Indian Oil created a non-profit trust in 2000, the IOF in collaboration with ASI and the National Culture Fund of Ministry of Culture, GoI. With an initial corpus of ₹250 million and an annual contribution of ₹100 million, the IOF will adopt at least one heritage site in every state. IOF is currently developing tourist and public infrastructure facilities at the following heritage sites:

1. Konark Sun Temple, Odisha
2. Khajuraho Group of Temples, Madhya Pradesh
3. Kolhua, near Vaishali, Bihar

(Continued ...)

4. Kanheri Caves, Maharashtra
5. Bhoganandishwara temple, Karnataka

Konark Sun Temple

This ornately sculpted temple was built to worship Surya, the sun god. Ornately sculpted, this thirteenth century Hindu place of worship depicts the vast chariot of sun God, Surya. The temple was conceived as a gigantic solar chariot with twelve pairs of exquisitely ornamented wheels dragged by seven rearing horses. The temple comprises a sanctum with a lofty shikhara, a *jagamohana* (an assembly hall, usually close to the centre, found in Hindu temples) and a detached *nata mandira* (a dance hall, found in Hindu temples), besides numerous subsidiary shrines. Over time, the sanctum and the nata mandira have lost their roof. The nata mandira exhibits a more balanced architectural design than that of other Odishan temples. The sanctum displays superb images of the sun god in the three projections, which are treated as miniature shrines.

The following facilities for the benefit of tourists are being developed by IOF:

* Main avenue—landscaped, street-scaped avenue from outer ring road to entry gate for straight access and better view of the iconic temple.
* Interpretation centre—four display galleries, audiovisual centre, VIP lounge, admin office, souvenir counter, snacks counter, toilet block and ticket counter.
* Landscaping in the remaining area.
* Main parking and drop off point—facilities for adequate parking about 60 buses, toilet block, waiting lounge, water points, snacks counter and landscaping.

Discussion Questions

1. "With funds available with corporates under CSR, monuments which receive little attention and funding for conservation can now be preserved and maintained as tourist attractions". Discuss.
2. What are the facilities which are lacking in many of our heritage sites? Who is responsible for providing these facilities? Discuss.

From the point of view of the tourism industry, these initiatives are invaluable in that these help the custodians of the site to develop facilities such as interpretation centres, reception, cloak rooms and toilets of high standards and create infrastructure that can cater to the increasing tourist traffic. Given the very large number of heritage structures that are crying out for conservation and preservation, all possible avenues of funding and partnership should be explored to bring funds and expertise for this important work.

Museums as Cultural Products

Museums
Nothing replaces the authenticity of the object presented with passionate scholarship. Bringing people face-to-face with objects is a way of bringing them face-to-face with people across time, across space, whose lives may have been different from our own but who, like us, have hopes and dreams, frustrations and achievements in their lives. —Thomas Campbell, Director, Metropolitan Museum of Art, New York

Museums are great institutions reflecting the pride and grandeur of nations and communities. Museums historically were great academic institutions, particularly in colonial countries, engaging in collecting and study of art objects. Museums are centres of education, research and public outreach and entertainment. Museums provide an opportunity to see objects that have been usually seen only in newspapers, books or television. Young visitors get an opportunity to understand many things about the history and culture of the region which they would be studying in the textbooks. Artefacts tell stories in many layers, connecting the contemporary with a historical context. Museums also provide communities with a sense of collective heritage. Museums foster creativity and curiosity and are great places for family outings. Museums encourage better appreciation and understanding of collective heritage and foster dialogue and self-reflection.

All major cities have museums as a proud reminder of a glorious past and as important cultural centres. Increasingly, tourists are flocking to museums, which have become important attractions to be included in itineraries. The importance of museums can be gauged from the fact that more and more destinations are using museums as part of their destination marketing strategies. For instance, Visit Britain, the marketing body for Great Britain, has used the British Museum as an important component of their recent campaign—'Culture is Great'. Promotional campaigns that feature increase visitor arrivals to the museums also help in deepening the understanding of the visitor on the culture of the destination. Museums are more than storehouses of artefacts, kept in iconic buildings. Through their collections, exhibitions and events, museums have become sources of information, education and inspiration. Museums have become iconic elements that present before the visitor the cultures of the land, inspiring the visitor to explore the destination in more depth and encouraging her to return to the destination. Museums also engage visitors and point them to areas of their individual interests. Today, museums have become destinations in their own right, drawing millions of visitors and evolving to be one of the most visited attractions in cities. Increasingly, museums depend on the revenue generated by visitors and constantly strive to improve the offering to the visitors in order to spur more visits and sustain their engagement. Museums attempt to maximize revenue generation through special exhibitions, events, merchandizing and outreach programs.

How are museums important to tourism? As tourists become more sophisticated, they gravitate towards cultural experiences in a destination. Museums contribute to cultural tourism as they are valuable assets of heritage and provide an insight into the different facets of the culture of a destination. Museums evoke a sense of respect in the destination and provide insights into the culture, art forms and practices of the land.

It is clear that museums have multiple obligations, duties and functions. Although museums are important knowledge centres, their central role is to work as cultural institutions. Through history, museums have grown to become the central and fundamental public institutions of culture. However, in recent times, the orientation of the museums has undergone drastic change. While earlier, the objective of a museum was to function as a repository of collections and a centre for research and study, museums have reoriented themselves to become responsive to visitors and constantly strive to provide interesting and memorable experiences to the visitor. Museums have also started developing strategies to bring in more visitors and to make the visitors spend more within its walls.

The British Museum in London is the most popular tourist attraction in the United Kingdom and attracted around 6.7 million tourists in 2014, which is close to the total number of inbound tourists visiting India!

Several significant museums are located in the main cities of India. The Indian Museum in Kolkata is the oldest museum in Asia and was established in 1814.

Indian Museum: The Oldest Museum in India

Founded in 1814, Indian Museum is the earliest museum not only in the Indian subcontinent but also in the Asia Pacific region. Its origin lies in the Asiatic Society, a learning centre for the development and study of the knowledge of Asia, founded by Sir William Jones in 1784. The members of the Asiatic Society of Bengal decided to establish a museum in its premises, and a museum was established on 2 February 1814 with Dr Nathaniel Wallich, a Danish botanist, as Honorary Curator. The museum grew with donations, and a memorial was submitted to the GoI for the establishment of an Imperial Museum. After protracted negotiations, the idea was accepted, and a fine site on Chowringhee was identified for a new building. On 1 April 1878, the Archaeology gallery and bird gallery of the Zoological section were opened in the present building. Later, it was transformed into a multipurpose institution displaying objects of Art, Archaeology, Anthropology, Zoology, Geology and Botany.

The museum movement in India originated on the foundation of the Indian Museum, and the establishment of the museum also give a stimulus to the study of arts and culture of the subcontinent.

The collection at the Indian Museum is the largest among all museums of India. Among the significant collections are the remains of the magnificent Stupa of Bharhut, in present day Madhya Pradesh, belonging to the Shunga period (second century). The Gandhara gallery has a rich collection of sculptures of the Gandhara style. The long archaeology gallery displays objects from the Kushana, Gupta, Chandela, Pala, Hoysala, Chola and Pallava periods. A modest collection of Egyptian antiquities are on display, including a mummy, which is a star attraction of the museum!

The Indian museum also houses collections other than art and archaeology, owing to its peculiar origin and early days. The geological collection is from the Geological Survey of India and displays, fossils, rocks, minerals and meteorites. The zoological section, from the Zoological Survey of India, has on display galleries of insects, fish, reptiles, birds and mammals. The botany section has many interesting displays, one of which is the 37 different varieties of opium! (Ministry of Culture, n.d).

The National Museum, New Delhi, is the premier museum of India, housing collections that are representative of the rich and diverse culture of the Indian subcontinent. ASI established 44 site museums in many locations across the country. Various exploratory investigations led by the officials of the ASI resulted in the establishment of these site museums. Prominent site museums are located in Sarnath, Agra, Delhi Fort, Sanchi, Ajmer, Nalanda and Bijapur (ASI, n.d.).

Sarnath is the oldest site museum of the ASI, and the present building was completed in 1910. The antiquities and the Museum range from the third century BC to twelfth century BC. The most important object on display is the lion capital which has become the national emblem of India. A range of Buddhist deities, scenes from the blood curse life, railings of the Chandra period, Brahmanical deities are other major objects on display.

The ASI museum at Nagarjunakonda is situated in an island in the Nagarjunasagar dam, accessible only by boat. The museum houses the antiquities retrieved from the excavations, with exquisite objects of the Ikshvaku period. Objects depicting the life of the Buddha, as well as medieval sculptures are other treasures of the museum.

The Chhatrapati Shivaji Maharaj Vastu Sangrahalaya (CSMVS) is the premier museum of Mumbai. The museum, formerly known as the Prince of Wales Museum, is housed in a splendid period building which is a good example of the Indo-Saracenic style of architecture. The museum has a vast collection of art from India and abroad, and it also has a natural history section. Ancient Indian art comprises of sculptures, particularly from Elephanta and other sites in Western India. There is a rich collection of Indian miniatures, coins and decorative art objects.

The Salar Jung Museum in Hyderabad is unique, in that it represents the collection of a single individual, Nawab Mir Yusuf Ali Khan, popularly known as Salar Jung III. He was the Prime Minister to the seventh Nizam of Hyderabad and spent a large part of his life and income in collecting art objects. The museum was opened in 1951 and was subsequently taken over by the government. Presently, it is housed in a vast new building displaying artworks from India, the Middle East, Far East and European art. The 'veiled Rebecca' is one of the highlight objects. A rich collection of decorative arts, miniatures, manuscripts and arms also adorn the museum galleries.

Several new museums and art galleries are coming up, funded by public and private sources. Virasat-e-Khalsa, which was opened recently in Anandpur Sahib, is unique in that it uses state of the art technology in design, display and interpretation to convey the narrative. The Museum has proven to be one of the most popular draws, attracting over 3 million visitors within 2 years of its opening.

Virasat-e-Khalsa: A Unique Museum

The Khalsa Heritage Complex and Museum (Virasat-e-Khalsa, Anandapur Sahib) is a new museum that has been established at Anandapur Sahib, to celebrate 500 years of Sikh history and 300 years of the formation of the Khalsa Panth. It is meant to be a tribute to the heroic saga of the Sikhs. The Museum offers a fascinating insight into the Sikh faith and its history.

This is a 'narrative museum that endeavours to tell a story that is deeply spiritual and filled with stirring emotion. In this case, the simple use of objects and artifacts will not capture the narrative and its contexts, nor will the images and text'. A new design approach was adopted, with the creation of unique scenographic environments that effectively engage multiple media to present an immersive experience, where the spoken word will play a greater significance over the written one. Audio guides which are triggered by the visitor serves as an overlay on the scenographic exhibit environments. The museum has 14 galleries and numerous installations (Virasat-e-Khalsa, n.d.). The complex was designed by acclaimed Israeli/Canadian/American architect and urban designer Moshe Safdie.

The museum, which breaks new ground in the aesthetics of display, received 34 lakh visitors in the first 22 months.

Handicrafts

As the word indicates, handicrafts are creative products made by the skill of the hand without the help of modern machinery and equipment. Centuries of traditions and rich cultural heritage of India are best manifested by the huge variety of handicrafts manufactured all over the country. Through the ages, handicrafts were seen as a mirror of the cultural identity of the people. Indian handicrafts are a timeless reminder of the unbroken continuity of skilled traditions, expressed in multifarious ways, along the length and breadth of India. Each region of India has got its own distinct cultural and traditional identity, which are manifested through various forms of art.

India has been considered the treasure house of crafts from ancient times. Along the silk route, handcrafted objects from India were exported to Africa, West Asia and Europe and also to the East. Examples of handicrafts can be seen in the artefacts of the Harappan civilization. The Rig Veda refers to a variety of pottery made from clay and wood used in rituals. The cultural traditions of India found expression during the Mauryan age. The sculptures from Bharhut, Mathura, Sanchi and Amravati are indicators of the rich ornament and jewellery making traditions prevalent during the time. There are many designs inspired by these ornaments which are in use in India today. Rich and inventive traditions of sculptures, textiles, leather products and metalwork continued in India, assimilating new knowledge that came from contact with foreign artisans, but adapted to the local conditions and requirements. In the South, bronze sculpture, silk textiles and intricate temple sculptures flourished during the Chola and Vijayanagara empires. The Mughals brought with them a rich heritage of handicrafts, among them inlay work, enamelling, glass engraving carpet weaving and textiles (Cultural India, n.d.)

Broadly, Indian handicrafts can be divided into three—folk, religious and commercial crafts. Folk crafts are those which are made for everyday use in the community. Among such objects, those that are modified according to the demands of the market and marketed are regarded as commercial crafts. A wide spectrum of handicrafts is made to be used in rites and rituals.

It is estimated that one out of every 200 Indians is an artisan. Crafts form the second largest employment sector in India, second only to agriculture. Indian crafts and the millions of practising craftspeople are huge and important resources of traditional knowledge and indigenous technologies.

The study of crafts, and the understanding of its context within culture, aesthetics and impact on the economy is important to every tourism student or professional. In a rapidly changing world, the world is increasingly turning uniform and technology driven. For the visitor, the world of handicrafts is important and interesting presentation of our cultural assets, traditions and values. We have to be aware of the extraordinary richness of craft traditions and the custodians of such traditions, as these are unique assets of the country, giving individuality and identity.

Indian handicrafts must be regarded as a lively, experiential and contemporary practice, not as a revivalist lip service to the past. Paradoxically, while craft traditions are a unique means of earning a livelihood for rural artisans, they also carry the stigma of inferiority and backwardness. Crafts are unfortunately considered as decorative, peripheral and elitist. Craftspeople are usually seen as picturesque exhibits of the past, rather than dynamic entrepreneurs for the present and future (NCERT, 2006). Tourism too has played a role in this portrayal, with displays and demonstrations by artisans in artificial settings like hotel lobbies and the sale of trinkets by artisans in traditional gear. The sector has a huge responsibility in respecting these traditions and providing the artisans with remunerative prices for their works. One of the interesting ways to do this is to develop rural tourism products, where the traveller has to go to the villages and dwellings of craftsmen, to watch them create their beautiful products and to purchase authentic, high value products at remunerative prices. Raghurajpur, in Odisha, is a good example of such an initiative.

The folk arts of India, because of their traditional aesthetic sensibility and authenticity, have captured the interest of the international market. Religious and mystical motifs adorn the folk paintings, ornaments, pottery and textiles and many have become quite popular with tourists. It is all the more important that the true value of this cultural asset be recognized, and tourism does its bit to ensure that the communities who are the custodians and producers of this invaluable heritage are supported and respected.

A shop in craft village

Case Study: Raghurajpur, The Craft Village

Raghurajpur, a small village in Puri district, occupies a unique place in the cultural map of India. The village is inhabited by artisans producing sheer poetry on pieces of treated cloth, dried palm leaf or paper.

Situated on the southern bank of River Bhargavi and surrounded by coconut, palm, mango, jackfruit groves and other tropical trees, Raghurajpur has an idyllic setting. A number of betel vines dot the nearby paddy fields. The village runs from East to West with houses arranged into neat rows, facing each other. At the centre, runs a line of small temples and the lone Bhagavat Tungi, the community meeting place of the villagers.

To reach Raghurajpur, one has to get down at Chandanpur bus stop, which is about 10 km from Puri and 50 km from Bhubaneswar, on the National Highway NH 203 connecting Puri and Bhubaneswar, two important tourist destinations of the state of Odisha. From there, one has to take her cycle rickshaw or walk on a scenic road to reach this village.

This coconut palm shaded village is quite different from other villages of the state. It has its own identity. What is unusual is the number of outsiders, including foreigners, visiting the village round the year. These people don't come here to see a typical Odishan village from close quarters, but to see and enjoy the rich traditions of Odishian arts and crafts at one place. The village has a community of artisans, who produce different varieties of handicrafts such as *patta* paintings, palm leaf engravings, papier mache toys and masks, wood

(Continued ...)

carvings, wooden toys, cow dung toys and tusser paintings. Perhaps nowhere else in India one finds such a congregation of so many arts at one place. This is also the only village in India where each family is engaged in one craft or another. There are 102 households, having 311 artisans, in the village. Some of them are winners of national awards. One comes across the best tradition of Odishian paintings and some of the finest pieces of work in this village.

The tradition of Pata painting in Odisha is very old. There are several centres of this art: Puri, Parlakhemundi, Champamal, Athgarh and Dinabandhupur. Usually, the lane in which these painters or *Chitrakaras* live is called *Chitrakar Sahi*. Although there are several centres of Pata painting Odisha, it is Raghurajpur which is famous for this unique art.

Chitrakaras are involved with the ritual performed in the temple of Lord Jagannatha on the occasion of *Snana Purnima* in the lunar month of *Jyestha*. During the period of *anasara,* the fortnight following the full moon day, three *patas* painted by *Chitrakaras* are placed on the *Singhasana* inside the main temple. The *Chitrakaras* are also called to execute colourful paintings on the chariots for the car festival. Apart from taking part in the rituals, they also produce paintings which they sell at Bedha Mahal inside the temple premises and Chakada Mahal outside the main gate.

The art received a new lease of life in the mid-twentieth century. Ileana Citaristi, an Italian lady who has done extensive research on Odisha art and culture, observes,

[B]y the late fifties, only a few old men among the 90 odd families of Raghurajpur were still painting, whereas all the youth had deserted the profession; it was only around the year 1953 that, with the intervention of an American lady, Mrs Halina Zealey, a new future opened up and the artists once again took out their brushes and colours.

Besides producing these unique works of art, this village has a living tradition of performing art known as *Gotipua*, the earlier form of Odissi. A worthy son of Odisha Guru Kelu Charan Mohapatra, an exponent of Odissi dance, was born in this village and had his early training in Gotipua tradition here. Now a Gotipua Gurukul, namely Maa Dasabhuja Gotipua dance school, has been established here under the guidance of Guru Maguni Charan Das. The trainees of the school present their performances in different cultural events in India and abroad.

INTACH selected this village to revive the ancient wall paintings of Odisha. The work has already been completed and now the village looks like a living museum of paintings.

To give this village its rightful place bought in the cultural and tourist maps of the country, Odisha tourism and Ministry of Tourism, Government of India have identified this village for development of rural tourism. After visiting Raghurajpur on June 27, 2002, Shri Jagmohan, Hon'ble Union Minister of tourism and culture, declared that this village would be developed as a model for rural tourism in India. Basic tourist amenities such as road, drinking water, sanitation, interpretation centre and rest house would come up soon. Once the rural tourism project is completed, Raghurajpur will come in the national travel circuit of the Government of India.

Acknowledgement: P. K. Jena, Tourism Department, Odisha, Bhubaneswar.

Source: Orissa Review (2004).

Image courtesy: Amit Kumar.

Discussion Questions

1. Compare Raghurajpur with Hodka (Case Study 2.2). What are the similarities?
2. From published statistics, find out the tourist arrivals in Odisha in the last five years. Do you think the developments in Raghurajpur have played a role in increasing tourist arrivals? Analyse the reasons.

Intangible Heritage of India

Intangible cultural heritage is a term that includes,

> [P]ractices, representations, expressions, as well as the knowledge and skills ... that communities and groups ... recognize as part of their cultural heritage. It is sometimes called living cultural heritage and is manifested... as oral traditions and expressions, performing arts, social practices, rituals and festive events, knowledge and practices concerning nature and the universe and traditional craftsmanship. (UNESCO n.d.g)

Expressions of intangible heritage provide us our identities and are examples of our diversity and creativity. It is no surprise, then, that these expressions of India are vital aspects of the tourism resources of India. As no visitor, domestic or foreign, is left untouched by some aspect of our intangible heritage, it is important for tourism professionals to have basic knowledge of some of our most noteworthy expressions of art. Several of our festivals have become significant tourism events as well because these provide many opportunities for visitors to glimpse our traditions, arts and crafts. The Hornbill festival is a brilliant example of a festival of recent origin evolving into a celebration of the diversity of the Northeast and a treat to every visitor.

Case Study: The Hornbill Festival

The state of Nagaland came into being in 1963, as the 16th state of the Indian union. The state is inhabited by 16 major tribes, each of which is distinct in character in terms of customs, language and dress. It is a land of folklore passed down the generations through word of mouth. Music is an integral part of life, from folk songs eulogizing ancestors, the brave deeds of warriors and traditional heroes, poetic love songs immortalizing ancient tragic love stories, to gospel songs that touch your soul or modern tunes!

Each tribe is distinguished by the traditional ceremonial attire, colourful and intricately designed costumes, jewellery and beads that adorn the people. The ceremonial dress is an awe inspiring sight to behold, the multi-coloured spears and *daos* (axes) decorated with dyed goat's hair, the headgear made of finely woven bamboo interlaced with orchid stems, adorned with boar's teeth and hornbill feathers and elephant tusk armlets.

Festivals are occasions for offering thanks, celebrating jungle and village spirits, fertility of mother earth, social bonding among communities and purification and rejuvenation. Each tribe celebrates its myriad festivals revolving around the agrarian calendar that makes Nagaland a land of festivals. The Hornbill festival has been called the 'festival of festivals', aimed at bringing together the colour and vibrant elements of all the tribal festivities and providing a glimpse of Naga life. A local heritage event has evolved into a notable attraction in the travel itinerary of both domestic and international travellers.

In 2000, the state government decided to project the cultural assets of Nagaland through a week-long festival, to coincide with the celebration of the Nagaland statehood day on 1st of December. The festival was named after the Hornbill in collective reverence to the bird enshrined in the cultural ethos of the Nagas, to espouse the spirit of unity in diversity. The annual festival is held for ten days, from 1 to 10 December, with participation from all the tribes and sub tribes, in a medley of cultural performances, indigenous games, a craft bazaar, music events, fashion show, motor sports, floral galleria, food courts, film festival, beauty pageant and competitions. The cultural programmes feature art forms from all tribes— Angami, Rengma, Zeliang, Kuki, Ao, Kachari, Chakhesang, Pochury, Chang, Konyak, Phom, Khiamniungam, Yimchungru, Sangtam, Lotha and Sumi.

The venue is Kisama, situated about 10 km from Kohima, the capital. Kisama is a term derived from two villages—Kigwema (Ki), Phesama (Sa) and 'Ma' which means village. The Naga heritage village was established by the government on the land of these two villages,

(Continued ...)

to protect and preserve all ethnic cultural heritages and to uphold and sustain the distinct identity of dialects, customs and traditions of all ethnic groups of Nagaland. The heritage complex consists of the imposing tribal Morungs, youth dormitories that are resplendent specimens of vernacular architecture. Some of the Morungs have the majestic log drums beaten by male members in different tempos and arrangements, in olden times used to send out messages (Nagaland Tourism, n.d.).

One of the star attractions of the festival is the Hornbill International Rock contest, bringing overseas bands and the best groups of India, who vie for the 'highest prize money' in India given to a band! The remarkable aspect of the festival is the wide participation of the local populations, the spirit of camaraderie and celebration and the authenticity of the celebrations. The Hornbill festival 2015 saw a remarkable rise in the number of visitors to 243,000, as compared to 172,000 in 2014 (Vero, 2015).

Discussion Questions

1. What are the necessary ingredients to ensure the success of a created event like this festival?
2. 'If events can kick start destinations, all states should organize festivals of a grand scale'. Discuss the pros and cons of this argument.

Dances of India

Music and dance, which constitute a major segment of intangible heritage in India, are elemental art forms, expressing a gamut of human emotions and experiences. Ceremonies of all kinds and mundane everyday matters all have their own music and dance traditions. The turn of the seasons, the agricultural calendar, important festivals and events and celebrations such as births and marriages have provided fertile themes for a variety of folk music and dance forms. Folk dance forms of neighbouring regions contribute to and learn from each other. The *Ghoomar* dance of Rajasthan and the *Garba* of Gujarat are beautiful expressions of grace and colour, as is the *Lavani* dance of Maharashtra. The *Dandiya* ras performed by men is acrobatic and graceful. Several forms of folk theatre such as *Nautanki, Bhavai, Tamasha Jatra* and *Yakshagana* narrate the legends of heroes and deities. *Chhau, Kalripayattu* and *Lazim* are examples of highly physical forms of folk art.

Classical dances are the best examples of the continuing performing arts traditions that have flourished in different parts of India. In a sense, these dance forms are links between our past and the present, exemplifying the interaction between ritual, entertainment and customary practice. Classical dances evolved based on the patronage of royalty and the temples. The structure and idiom of the forms were guided by detailed treatises like the *Natyashastra* and the *Abhinaya darpana* and drew inspiration from myths, legends and classical poetry. Most classical arts also continued a mutually enriching dialogue with folk and tribal forms.

There are eight major classical dance styles in India—Bharatanatyam from Tamil Nadu, Kuchipudi from Andhra Pradesh, Kathakali and Mohiniyattam from Kerala, Odissi from Odisha, Kathak from North India, Manipuri from Manipur and Sattriya from Assam.

Bharatanatyam

Bharatanatyam takes inspiration from temple dance forms that were prevalent for more than a thousand years. The *Natya Shastra* and *Abhinaya Darpana* provide much of the theoretical material. Generally, Bharatanatyam is performed by a single dancer, with a regular and accepted pattern of performance, which expresses the full repertoire form. After an invocation song, there will be *Alarippu*, an abstract piece of pure dance. The next item, the *Jatiswaram*, is a short pure dance piece set to a raga in the Carnatic style and composed of *Adavus*, which are dance sequences without any lyrics. The Varnam provides the dancer to express herself using *Nritta* (pure or abstract dance) and *Nritya* (a combination of Nritta and Abhinaya (see below) to illustrate a poetic piece), where the words are explained using movement and mime. The dancer may perform more items displaying her expertise in *abhinaya* (expressional dance; acting or emoting), expressing different *bhavas* (emotions or moods conveyed by the performer) or *rasas* (sentiments [as in the 'nine sentiments']). *Keertanam, Kritis, padam* and *Javali* are the usual pieces performed. The concert ends with a *tillana*, which is a fast paced number performed to the accompaniment of musical syllables and a *mangalam* (a short dance piece at the end of a concert, praising the Gods and invoking blessings) invoking the blessings of the Gods.

Kuchipudi

Kuchipudi originated in the village of the same name in Andhra Pradesh. The dance form was initially performed only by boys, who would enact *Bhaamaakalaapam*, a dance drama about Krishna and Satyabhama. The tradition of the dance drama form continues, but now solo performances are also common. The movements of Kuchipudi dance are comparatively faster and the dancer presents her dexterity in footwork and balance by demonstrating techniques such as *tarangam*, dancing on the rim of a vessel or with a pitcher of water on the head. The dance form is performed to both Carnatic and Hindustani classical music and the songs accompanying the dance are mainly taken from *Krishna Leela Tarangini*, a text which depicts the life and events of Lord Krishna. The instruments mainly used in the dance form include mridangam, violin, veena, flute and cymbals (Das, 2012).

Kathakali

Kathakali owes its roots to several theatrical forms popular in the region from ancient times. *Koodiyattam, Chakiarkoothu, Ramanattam* and *Krishnanattam* are some forms that have influenced Kathakali. Kathakali blends music, dance and acting to relate stories from the epics in an elaborate and stylized way. Kathakali is known for its elaborate headgear, face painting styles (Chutti) and elaborate abhinaya. The *Aharya*, costume and make up, are clearly defined into types to depict categories of characters such as *Pacha* for the heroic and *Kathi* for the anti-heroes. The actors undergo a strict training regimen for many years to obtain the flexibility and control needed for the gruelling performance. The entire body, including facial muscles, fingers, eyes, eye brows are brought into expression.

A Kathakali performance begins with *Kelikottu*, an introductory announcement of the performance that brings the audience to attention and the *todayam*, a devotional piece invoking blessings. The main scene to be enacted is performed with the musicians singing the lyrics in the traditional Kerala ritual singing style of *sopana sangeetham*.

Although there are several schools teaching and practicing Kathakali, the Kerala Kalamandalam in central Kerala is the most-well-known. Visitors to the centre can have a glimpse of the classes in different styles of music and dance in the campus.

Mohiniyattam

Mohiniyattam is a classical dance form of Kerala derived from the words 'Mohini' (beautiful women) and 'attam' (dance), which literally means 'dance of the enchantress'. The dance form is of feminine style with swaying movements of the upper body. The dance form developed in the tradition of Devadasi system later grew and developed into classical status. Although the reference on Mohiniyattam is found in eighteenth century texts, the dance form became popular in the period of Maharaja Swati Thirunal, a nineteenth century ruler of Travancore who was a patron of dance and music (Das, 2012).

Mohiniyattam is a solo dance with Carnatic Music compositions and rhythmic swaying of body in white and gold costume with jewellery including necklaces, bangles, waistband and anklets. The hair of the dancer is tied in a bun and decorated with jasmine flowers. The musical instruments used in the performance mainly include *Edakka* (a percussion instrument of Kerala), Violin, Veena and Mridangam. Mohiniyattam belongs to the lasya style which is feminine, tender and graceful and theme of the dance is usually 'sringara' or love. The foot work is rendered softly and importance is given to hand gestures and mukabhinaya (subtle facial expressions). The hand gestures, which are 24 in number, are mainly adopted from *Hastalakshana Deepika*, a text followed by Kathakali (Centre for Cultural Resources and Training, n.d.a).

Odissi

Odissi is an ancient and complex dance form, focusing on the relationship between the divine and the human, with links to early traditions of dance of the region. Dance was considered divine and the imposing temples built in Odisha have dance halls and sculptures of dancers. Odissi is based on the treatises of *Natyashastra and Abhinaya Darpana* and depends on the *Gita Govinda* of Jayadeva for most of its compositions. The body movements are built around the *chowk*, a squarish masculine stance, and the *tribhanga,* the feminine, three angled stance. The performance starts with a *mangalacharan* or offering, followed by an invocation to a deity, usually Ganesha. The *batu*, a piece of nritta, is in praise of Lord Shiva, with the next piece, the *pallavi*, an elaborate representation of a musical composition set in a raga. The main piece is usually from the *Ashtapadi*, with emphasis on abhinaya (Centre for Cultural Resources and Training, n.d.b).

Kathak

Derived from the word *katha* (story), the original performers were called *kathakars* or story tellers who narrated and enacted stories from the epics. This simple style evolved into a lyrical and expressive dance form which adapted to the requirements of royal courts during the Mughal period. The form acquired sophistication and rhythmic virtuosity under the patronage of the Oudh Nawab, and *gharanas* were established in Lucknow, Jaipur and Benaras.

The dance form depends on an intricate system of footwork, with complex rhythmic patterns demonstrated by the artiste performing pure dance. Combinations of body movements and sequences of pirouettes are featured with a 'conversation' between the *pakhawaj* or *tabla* with the dancer. The nritya or abhinaya portions are presented with the music compositions of *tumri* (a popular semi-classical vocal music form), *bhajan* (a form of folk or semi-classical music, usually devotional in nature) or *dadra* (a crisp and compact musical form, similar to the Tumri, but sung at a faster rhythm). The virtuosity of the dancer is in the interpretation and improvization of the melodic and the poetic lines. Kathak is the only form of classical dance set to the Hindustani style of music and is regarded as a synthesis of Muslim and Hindu genius in performing arts.

Manipuri

As the word indicates, this is the dance of the state of Manipur, associated with the festivals and rituals of the region. With the arrival of Vaishnavism, the popular folk dance form was infused with themes of Radha and Krishna. The *Ras leela* forms the mainstay of the dance, with characters playing Krishna, Radha and the *gopi*s (female cowherds). The costume of richly embroidered stiff skirt, a dark blouse in velvet and a fine veil over the face is characteristic of the form. There are five principal *Ras* dances, four of which are linked to the seasons. *Sankirtana* (a form of devotional chants) singing accompanies the dance. The male dancers play the traditional drum or *pung* while dances. *Choloms* are the masculine aspect of dance, which is also performed during festivals.

Sattriya

The Sattriya dance form was introduced in the fifteenth century AD by the Vaishnava saint poet of Assam, Mahapurusha Sankaradeva to bring harmony to the region and as a powerful medium for propagation of the Vaishnava faith. The dance form evolved and expanded as a distinctive style of dance, sharing all the characteristics of a classical dance form. The Vaishnava monasteries in Assam are called Sattras and the name of the dance form was derived from its religious character and association with the Sattras. Ojapali is one of the traditional dance forms prevalent in Assam which includes the Sukananni or Maroi Goa Ojah of Sakti cult and Vyah Goa Ojah of Vaishnavite cult. Sankaradeva included Vyah Goa Ojah into his daily rituals in Sattra, and thus has become part of the rituals of Sattras in Assam (Centre for Cultural Resources and Training, n.d.c).

Sattriya dances are usually performed in the *namghar,* the prayer hall of the Sattra. The dancers wear white costumes with turbans and head gears made out of a type of silk produced in Assam, woven with intricate local motifs. The ornaments are also based on traditional Assamese designs (Das, 2012). The dance form is governed strictly by the principles in respect of *hastamudra*s (hand gestures), foot works, *aharya*s (costumes worn by performers) and music. The instruments used in Sattriya includes are khol (drum), boratal (cymbals) and violin. Sattriya dance has currently two separate streams. The first one is the *bhaona* (a type of rural entertainment, combining music and dance)-related range starting from the Gayan-Bhayanar Nach to the Kharmanar Nach, and the second one include independent dance form such as Chali, Rajagharia Chali, Jhumura and Nadu Bhangi.

Representative List of the Intangible Cultural Heritage of Humanity

UNESCO maintains a list of intangible heritage to demonstrate the diversity of this heritage and raise awareness about its importance. A total of 314 elements have been inscribed in the list (2014), out of which 10 are from India. An overview of the art forms, festivals and crafts from India that have been approved to be on this prestigious list will be useful to the student of tourism.

Kutiyattam

Kutiyattam, a form of Sanskrit theatre practised in Kerala, is one of world's oldest theatrical art forms, dating back 2000 years. In its stylized and codified theatrical language, *netra abhinaya* (eye expression) and *hasta abhinaya* (the language of gestures) are prominent. It is traditionally performed inside the Hindu temple theatres, called *Koothambalams*, in Kerala. There are two or more characters on stage at the same time, with the *Chakkiars* providing the male cast and the *Nangiars* playing the female roles. The *Nangiars* beat the cymbals and recite verses in Sanskrit, while in the background *Nambiars* play the *Mizhavu,* a large copper drum. Access to performances was originally restricted owing to their sacred nature, but the plays have progressively opened up to larger audiences. Nevertheless, the actor's role retains a sacred dimension, as attested by purification rituals and the placing of an oil lamp on stage during the performance symbolizing a divine presence.

Vedic Chanting

The Vedas, regarded by Hindus as the primary source of knowledge and the sacred foundation of their religion, represent one of the oldest unbroken oral traditions in existence. Composed over 3,500 years ago, it comprises a vast amount of Sanskrit poetry, philosophical dialogue, myth and ritual incantations. The Vedic heritage embraces a multitude of texts and interpretations collected in the four Vedas—*Rig, Sama, Yajur* and *Atharva*. The Vedas also offer insight into the history of Hinduism and the early development of several artistic, scientific and philosophical concepts, such as the concept of zero. The verses of the Vedas, derived from classical Sanskrit, were traditionally chanted during sacred rituals and recited daily in Vedic communities. The value of this tradition lies not only in the rich content of its oral literature but also in the ingenious techniques adopted by the Brahmin priests in preserving the texts intact over hundreds of years.

Ramlila

Ramlila, literally 'Rama's play', is a performance of epic Ramayana in a series of scenes that include song, narration, recital and dialogue. It is performed across Northern India during the festival of Dussehra, held each year according to the ritual calendar in autumn. This staging of the Ramayana is based on the *Ramacharitmanas*, composed by Tulsidas in the sixteenth century in a form of Hindi so as to make the common classes understand the *Ramkatha*. The most representative Ramlilas are those of Ayodhya, Ramnagar and Benares, Vrindavan, Almora, Sattna and Madhubani. Ramlila recalls the battle between Rama and Ravana and consists of a series of dialogues between gods, sages and the faithful. Festivals are organized in hundreds of settlements, towns and villages during the Dussehra festival season celebrating Rama's return from exile. The audience is invited to sing and take part in the narration. The Ramlila brings the whole population together, without distinction of caste, religion or age.

Novruz

The day accepted as the New Year's Day by the Turks living in Central Asia, Anatolian Turks and Iranians is called Novruz. It is a combination of the Persian words *nov* (new) and *ruz* (day). It corresponds to 22 March according to the Western calendar and 9 March according to the Moslem one, when the day and the night are of equal length. Although it has been claimed that Novruz was a Persian conception, it marks the New Year and the beginning of spring across a vast geographical area covering, inter alia, Azerbaijan, India, Iran, Kyrgyzstan, Pakistan, Turkey and Uzbekistan. Novruz is associated with various local traditions, such as the evocation of *Jamshid*, a mythological king of Iran, and numerous tales and legends. The rites that accompany the festivity vary from place to place, ranging from leaping over fires and streams in Iran to tightrope walking, leaving lit candles at house doors, traditional games such as horse racing or the traditional wrestling practised in Kyrgyzstan. Songs and dances are common to almost all the regions, as are semi-sacred family or public meals. Novruz promotes the values of peace and solidarity between generations and within families, as well as reconciliation and neighbourliness, thus contributing to cultural diversity and friendship among peoples and various communities.

Chhau Dance

Chhau dance is a tradition from Eastern India. There are three major forms of Chhau hailing from the regions of Seraikella, Purulia and Mayurbhanj. Chhau dance is intimately connected to regional festivals, notably the spring festival *Chaitra Parva*. Chhau is an integral part of the culture of the communities in these regions. It binds together people from different social strata and ethnic background with diverse social practices, beliefs, professions and languages. Its origin is traceable to indigenous forms of dance and martial practices. Its mode of movement includes mock combat techniques, stylized gaits of birds and animals and movements modelled on the chores of village housewives. Chhau is taught to male dancers from families of traditional artists or from local communities. The dance is performed at night in an open space to traditional and folk melodies, played on the reed pipes *mohuri* and *shehnai*. The reverberating drumbeats of a variety of drums dominate the accompanying music ensemble.

Ramman

Ramman is a religious festival and ritual theatre of the Garhwal region in the State of Uttarakhand. The festival and the eponymous art form are conducted as an offering to the village deity, Bhumiyal Devta, in the courtyard of the village temple. The Ramman is unique to the village and is neither replicated nor performed anywhere else in the Himalayan region. This event is made up of highly complex rituals: the recitation of a version of the epic of Ramayana and various legends and the performance of songs and masked dances. All households, irrespective of caste and community, offer prayers and perform rituals to the main deities of the Ramman. Talented youth and elders selected by village heads are the performers at Ramman. The family that hosts Bhumiyal Devta during the year must adhere to a strict daily routine. Combining theatre, music, historical reconstructions and traditional oral and written tales, the Ramman is a multiform cultural event that reflects the environmental, spiritual and cultural concept of the community, recounting its founding myths and strengthening its sense of self-worth.

Buddhist Chanting

A chant is a form of musical verse or prayer. In the monasteries and villages of the Ladakh region, Buddhist lamas (priests) chant sacred texts representing the spirit, philosophy and teachings of the Buddha. Two forms of Buddhism are practised in Ladakh—Mahayana and Vajrayana. Each sect has several forms of chanting, practised during life-cycle rituals and on important days in the Buddhist and agrarian calendars. It is undertaken for the spiritual and moral well-being of the people, for purification and peace of mind. The chanting is performed in groups, either sitting indoors or accompanied by dance in monastery courtyards or private houses. The monks wear special costumes and make hand gestures (*mudras*) representing the divine Buddha, and instruments such as bells, drums, cymbals and trumpets are used during the chants. Chants are practiced every day in the monastic assembly hall as a prayer to the deities for world peace and for the personal growth of the practitioners.

Kalbelia

Kalbelia Dance, performed by the Kalbelia tribe, is a folk dance form of Rajasthan. Dancers dress traditional black swirling skirts during the dance accompanied by music. The dancers wear traditional tattoo designs, jewellery and garments richly embroidered with small mirrors and silver thread. Kalbelia songs disseminate mythological knowledge through stories, while special traditional dances are performed during Holi, the festival of colours. The songs also demonstrate the poetic acumen of the Kalbelia, who are reputed to compose lyrics spontaneously and improvise songs during performances. Songs and dances are an expression of the Kalbelia community's traditional way of life. Once professional snake handlers, Kalbelia today evoke their former occupation in music and dance that is evolving in new and creative ways. Transmitted from generation to generation, the songs and dances form part of an oral tradition for which no texts or training manuals exist. Songs and dance are a matter of pride for the Kalbelia community and a marker of their identity at a time when their traditional travelling lifestyle and role in rural society are diminishing. They demonstrate their community's attempt to revitalize its cultural heritage and adapt it to changing socioeconomic conditions.

Mudiyettu

Mudiyettu is a ritual dance drama from Kerala based on the mythological tale of the battle between the goddess *Kali* and the demon *Darika*. Mudiyettu performers purify themselves through fasting and prayer then draw a huge image of goddess Kali, called as *kalam*, on the temple floor with coloured powders, wherein the spirit of the goddess is invoked. This prepares the ground for the lively enactment to follow. The immensely powerful and arrogant Darika, the demon who received a boon from Brahma which granted that he would never be defeated by any man living in any of the fourteen worlds as per Hindu mythology, went on to conquer the whole world. Lord Shiva incarnates as goddess *Bhadrakali* and kills Darika. Mudiyettu is performed annually in '*Bhagavati Kavus*', the temples of the goddess, in different villages along the rivers Chalakkudy, Periyar and Moovattupuzha. Mudiyettu serves as an important cultural site for transmission of traditional values, ethics, moral codes and aesthetic norms of the community to the next generation, thereby ensuring its continuity and relevance in present times.

Sankirtana

Sankirtana comprises an array of arts - singing, drumming and dancing-performed to mark religious occasions and life-cycle of the Vaishnava people of the Manipur plains. Sankirtana practices are usually centred on the temple and is often visualized as manifestations of God. Usually, two drummers and about ten singer-dancers narrate the lives and deeds of Krishna through song and dance. Sankirtana has been able to bring together people of the community as this being a festive as well as a ritual event for them. The social support the art form gets is reflected from the fact that the whole community is involved in its safeguarding by traditionally transferring the skills from mentor to disciple.

Visual Arts of India

Architecture

The Treasures of India as artistic traditions have been fascinating to visitors to India, as well as to any person interested in art and aesthetics. Indian architecture showcases the national genius and many of the great monuments are cloaked with sculptures of outstanding beauty. Sculptures formed part and parcel of the structure of temperance and was intimately connected to the architecture. The hallmark of Indian cultural traditions is the transmission of the spiritual contents into plastic forms embodying the high ideals and common beliefs. Gods and goddesses they had visualized in idealized figures of man and woman. Indian art is set to be a blend of symbolism and reality, spirituality and sensuality. Indian art is a treasure trove of the customs and manners and beliefs of the life of that age, holding a mirror to contemporary society.

Sculpture

The bearded man, dancing girl and the beautiful terracotta figures are fine examples of the artistry of the Harappan age. The dancing girl is on display at the National Museum, New Delhi. The Mauryan age had sculptures of remarkable polish and finish, exemplified by the magnificent lion capital housed now in the Sarnath museum, which has been adopted as the Emblem of GoI. The Yakshi (Didarganj Yakshi) is a striking example of not only the exceptional skill of the sculptor but also the jewellery and clothing styles of the era. This beautiful sculpture can be seen in the Patna museum. The remnants of the Stupa of Bharhut, with exquisite images of celestial beauties and other scenes, can be viewed at the Indian Museum. The Stupa at Sanchi is a tribute to the monuments built by the Satavahanas, with richly carved gateways.

The zenith of Indian sculptural art was during the Gupta period, when the techniques were perfected, the iconographic canons established and a highly evolved aesthetic sense combined to produce works that are timeless in their beauty. The images of the Buddha in red sandstone (Sarnath and Mathura) and Vishnu (National Museum) are wonderful specimens that speak to the visitor about this magnificent heritage of India.

Painting

The Ajanta caves have painted picture galleries, where paintings on Buddhist themes were created over a period of about eight centuries. The Rajarajeshwara and Brihadeshwara temples of Tanjore have some important wall paintings, as do the Lepakshi temple. The murals of Kerala are a later style, seen on some temple walls and at the Dutch Palace in Kochi.

The earliest examples of painting in India are the illustrations on Buddhist and Jain religious texts. With the establishment of the Mughal Empire, the Mughal School of painting took root in the country. In the Deccan, sophisticated schools of painting flourished in Golconda, Ahmednagar and Bijapur and contributed to the development of the Mughal style.

Unlike Mughal painting which is primarily secular, the art of painting in Rajasthan, Pahari region and central India took inspiration from religious texts, folk lore and Indian epics. Miniature painting flourished in different areas within the Pahari region, leading to development of individual styles such as Kulu—Mandi, Basohli, Guler and Kangra. The Rajasthani schools were patronized by Rajput rulers following the Mughal style, leading to development of several local styles such as Malwa, Mewar, Bundi—Kota, Bikaner, Kishangarh and Marwar.

Conclusion

India, with its diverse natural and cultural heritage, offers a fertile ground for the promotion of heritage tourism, which still remains in its infancy. The tangible and intangible heritage comprising age old constructions and performing arts add diversity, colour and educational value to heritage tourism. The increasing role of local community in the management of cultural heritage will not only strengthen the segment but also promote tourism on responsible lines. Development of museums as cultural products will add value to tourism in India.

The range and diversity of cultural expressions that can be found in India makes it a country without parallel. The imprints of a variety of external influences and the peaceful coexistence of divergent faiths and beliefs, have created a cultural tapestry that is so rich and multilayered that it takes a lifetime to imbibe it. It is no wonder, then, that India is viewed by the world as a unique cultural destination. The challenge for tourism students and professionals is to gain working knowledge of this vast body of knowledge, to enrich tourist experiences, create new ways of inquiry and exploration and to serve as authentic and sensitive ambassadors of this wonderful heritage.

Review Questions

1. Distinguish between culture and heritage. Discuss the scope for developing heritage tourism in India.
2. Give a detailed account of any one of the WHSs in India from tourism perspective.
3. Discuss the role of museums in promoting cultural tourism.
4. What is intangible heritage? Briefly discuss the major classical dances of India.
5. Evaluate the role of handicrafts in tourism business.

Activities

1. Make a list of buildings and centres of worship in your locality having more than 50-years old and prepare a status paper of five oldest constructions. Present the details in your class and discuss the need for conservation of these sites.
2. Visit any one heritage site listed by the Central/State Government and identify the heritage value that attracted you the most. Also, make a presentation in the class on the current status of the site along with the measures taken for its conserving.
3. Prepare a dossier on built/natural heritage of India after scanning leading newspapers/periodicals for a period of one year.
4. Identify 10 old traditional houses in your locality and collect details of antiques available with these families. Take photographs and identify the purpose for which they were used after discussing with the members of the family.
5. Prepare a proposal for conserving a heritage site availing financial support from a company under its CSR Programme.
6. Identify the cultural and heritage uniqueness of any one locality and prepare a resource map that can be used for setting up a local museum.
7. Form a group of five members in your class and arrange an interview with a craftsman. Prepare his socioeconomic background and develop a status paper on his business. Suggest measures for business development linking his activity with tourism. Present the findings and suggestions before a selected audience for comments.
8. The tour operators and hotel owners in a tourism destination have decided to organize a classical dance fest for five days. Design and develop a brochure highlighting the theme and uniqueness of different dance forms proposed to include in the fest.
9. Organize a painting competition on the theme 'Natural and Cultural Heritage of my State'. Prepare a write up on all selected entries. Arrange an exhibition of the same in your institution.

References

Books

Citaristi, Eleana. 2001. *The Making of a Guru: Kelu Charan Mohapatra, His Life and Times.* Delhi: Manohar.

Orissa Review. 2002. 'A Destination in the Making'. Orissa Review. Information & Public Relations Department, Government of Odisha, Bhubaneswar.

Web Resources

2013. 'Ajanta–Ellora Set to Give Boost to Foreign Tourist Arrivals in India'. Available at: http://www.sarkaritel.com/ajanta-ellora-set-to-give-boost-to-foreign-tourist-arrivals-in-india-30999/ (accessed on 23 December 2016).

ASI. n.d.a. 'Alphabetical List of Monuments'. Archaeological Survey of India. Available at: http://asi.nic.in/asi_monu_alphalist.asp (accessed on 23 December 2016).

——. b. 'Museums'. Archaeological Survey of India. Available at: http://asi.nic.in/asi_museums.asp

Centre for Cultural Resources and Training. n.d.a. 'Mohiniyattam Dance'. Available at: http://ccrtindia.gov.in/mohiniyattam.php (accessed on 23 December 2016).

——. n.d.b. 'Performing Arts'. Available at: http://ccrtindia.gov.in/performingart.php (accessed on 23 December 2016).

——. n.d.c. 'Sattriya Dance'. Available at: http://ccrtindia.gov.in/sattriya.php (accessed on 23 December 2016).

Cultural India. n.d. 'Indian Crafts'. Available at: http://www.culturalindia.net/indian-crafts (accessed on 23 December 2016).

'Culture'. n.d. Available at: https://www.tamu.edu/faculty/choudhury/culture.html (accessed on 23 December 2016).

Das, A. 2012. 'The 8 classical Dance Styles of India!' GAS. Available at: https://georgandreassuhr.wordpress.com/2012/12/16/the-8-classical-dance-styles-of-india/ (accessed on 23 December 2016).

Ministry of Culture. n.d. 'History of Indian Museum'. The Indian Museum, Government of India. Available at: http://indianmuseumkolkata.org/history.php (accessed on 23 December 2016).

Nagaland Tourism. n.d. Available at: http://tourismnagaland.com/?page_id=77

NCERT. 2006. 'Position Paper: National Focus Group on Heritage Craft'. New Delhi, NCERT. Available at: http://www.ncert.nic.in/new_ncert/ncert/rightside/links/pdf/focus_group/heritage_craft.pdf (accessed on 23 December 2016).

'What is Culture?' n.d. University of Minnesota. Available at: http://www.carla.umn.edu/culture/definitions.html (accessed on 23 December 2016).

UNESCO. n.d.a. 'Protecting Our Heritage and Fostering Creativity'. UNESCO. Available at: http://en.unesco.org/themes/protecting-our-heritage-and-fostering-creativity (accessed on 23 December 2016).

——. n.d.b. 'Convention Concerning the Protection of the World Cultural and Natural Heritage'. UNESCO. Available at: http://whc.unesco.org/en/conventiontext

——. n.d.c. 'World Heritage List'. UNESCO. Available at: http://whc.unesco.org/en/list (accessed on 23 December 2016).

——. n.d.d. 'Text of the Convention for the Safeguarding of the Intangible Heritage'. UNESCO. Available at: http://www.unesco.org/culture/ich/index.php?lg=EN&pg=00022 (accessed on 23 December 2016).

——. n.d.e. 'India'. UNESCO. Available at: http://whc.unesco.org/en/statesparties/in (accessed on 23 December 2016).

——. n.d.f. 'Tentative Lists'. UNESCO. Available at: http://whc.unesco.org/en/tentativelists/state=in (accessed on 23 December 2016).

——. n.d.g. 'Definition of Intangible Heritage'. UNESCO. Available at: http://www.unesco.org/services/documentation/archives/multimedia/?id_page=13 (accessed on 23 December 2016).

Vero, C. 2015. 'Hornbill Festival 2015 Concludes'. *Morung Express.* Retrieved from http://morungexpress.com/hornbill-festival-2015-concludes/ (accessed on 23 December 2016).

Virasat-e-Khalsa Museum. n.d. Available at: http://virasat-e-khalsa.net/ (accessed on 23 December 2016).

Visalam. n.d. 'CGH Earth'. Available at: http://www.cghearth.com/visalam (accessed on 23 December 2016).

Suggested Readings

Web Resources

ASI. n.d. 'Conservation and Preservation—Aurangabad Circle'. Archaeological Survey of India Aurangabad Circle. Available at: http://www.asiaurangabad.in/index/conservation_and_preservation.aspx (accessed on 23 December 2016).

Bendiktsson, G. 2004. 'Museums and Tourism: Stakeholders, Resource and Sustainable Development. Goteborg University. Available at: http://gu.se/digitalAssets/1176/1176849_Dissertation_Gudbrandur_Benediktsson.pdf (accessed on 23 December 2016).

CCRT. n.d. 'Performing Arts'. Centre for Cultural Resources and Training. Available at: http://ccrtindia.gov.in/performingart.php

Chettinad, Village Clusters of the Tamil Merchants. n.d. In UNESCO. Available at: http://whc.unesco.org/en/tentativelists/5920/ (accessed on 23 December 2016).

CSMVS. n.d. 'About the Museum'. Chhatrapati Shivaji Maharaj Vastu Sangrahalaya. Available at: http://csmvs.in/about-us.html

Development Commissioner. 2010. *A Treasure of Handicraft Clusters from India*. New Delhi: Development Commissioner of Handicrafts.

Gopalakrishnan, S. 2011. 'Kutiyattam: UNESCO Proclamation and the Change in Institutional Model and Patronage'. Indian Folklife. Available at: http://indianfolklore.org/journals/index.php/IFL/article/viewFile/1004/1259 (accessed on 23 December 2016).

Ivanovic, M. 2008. *Cultural Tourism*. Cape Town: Juta and Co. Ltd.

Malde, S. 2013. 'Museums Connecting Cultural Tourists: More Substance Over Style Pleas'. *The Guardian*. Available at: http://www.theguardian.com/culture-professionals-network/culture-professionals-blog/2013/apr/02/museums-cultural-tourists-digital-content

Mohanty, B. 1984. *Pata-Paintings of Orissa*. New Delhi: Publications Division, Government of India.

Nagaland Tourism. n.d. http://tourismnagaland.com/?page_id=77 (accessed on 23 December 2016).

Nature and Characteristics of Cultural Tourism. n.d. 'Cultural Tourism in the Regions of Montana-Vidin–Dolj'. Retrieved from http://www.montana-vidin-dolj.com/en/publications/?NewsId=3

Ranjan, A., and M.P. Ranjan, eds. 2007. *Handmade in India*. New Delhi: Council of Handicraft Development Corporations. 'Raghurajpur, the Craft Village'. 2004. Orissa Review. Available at: http://odisha.gov.in/e-magazine/Orissareview/nov2004/englishPdf/raghurajpur-craftvillage.pdf (accessed on 23 December 2016).

UNESCO. n.d. 'Kutiyattam Sanskrit Theatre'. UNESCO. Available at: http://www.unesco.org/archives/multimedia/?s=films_details&pg=33&id=1746

Wood, C. 2014. '21 Reasons Why Museums are Great'. *The Telegraph Travel*. Available at: http://www.telegraph.co.uk/travel/destinations/europe/united-kingdom/articles/21-reasons-why-museums-are-great/

Tiger in Bandhavgarh sanctuary
Image courtesy: Ministry of Tourism, Government of India.

Natural Heritage of India

By the end of this chapter, students will be able to:

- Appreciate the variety of natural heritage of India.
- Identify the major national parks and wildlife sanctuaries of India.
- Describe the importance of biodiversity from a tourism point of view.
- Distinguish between types of protected areas.
- Understand the significance of conservation and proper management for tourism.
- List the steps to be taken by tourism enterprises to contribute to conservation.

Introduction

In the previous chapter, we have discussed in some detail about the range of cultural heritage that India possesses. As we have seen, the amazing diversity of our art and culture, the magnificence of all monuments, the intricate and beautiful art forms, the bewildering variety of handicrafts, the wonderful depth of intangible heritage handed down from generation to generation—the visitor experience in India is rich, multi-layered and complex and offers a seemingly unlimited variety of options and experiences that the visitor can enjoy and savour while touring India.

In this chapter, we will explore another equally impressive resource that India has, which forms a veritable treasure trove for the visitor and offers great opportunities for tourism service providers. The natural heritage of India is vast and varied and each region has its characteristic landforms, forest types and flora and fauna. Because of its sheer size and geographical location, India presents limitless opportunities for the visitor interested in taking a holiday in a natural setting. India has a beautiful coastline running for many thousands of kilometres.

While all this treasure is all around us, it is a matter of concern that nature-based tourism has been reduced to a visit to a prominent wildlife sanctuary (WLS) in search for a glimpse of the tiger. Let us examine this phenomenon and the impacts such large-scale tourism developments have made on parks and sanctuaries.

India: A Land of Biodiversity

India occupies 2.4% of the world's land area, in which 16.7% of the world's human population live. Add to this figure, 18% of the world's livestock, and one can imagine the pressure on the lack of available land area in the country. And yet, India has 8% of the global biodiversity. What exactly is 'biodiversity'? The IUCN (n.d.) defines 'biological diversity—or biodiversity—as a term we use to describe the variety of life on Earth. It refers to the wide variety of ecosystems and living organisms: animals, plants, their habitats and their genes' (Figure 13.1).

While there are multifarious ways in which our biodiversity wealth is important for all of us, it provides a powerful backdrop to many tourism products and activities. India is a megadiverse country with over 45,000 species of plants and 91,000 species of animals. Of the 34 global biodiversity hotspots, 4 are present in India, represented by the Himalaya, the Western Ghats, the Northeast and the Nicobar Islands. Our forests cover 21.05% of the geographical area of the country, with 3% of the total area under tree cover.

The forests and sanctuaries of India are home to many endangered species. The world's largest tiger population resides in India. Globally important endangered species, like Asiatic elephant, Asiatic lion, one-horned Rhinoceros, snow leopard, the great Indian Bustard and the lion-tailed macaque, they all call this land home. Many of these 'charismatic' animals captivate the minds of visitors, drawing them in thousands to our wildlife sanctuaries and national parks (NPs).

The Himalayas

The sudden rise of the Himalayan mountains from less than 500 m to more than 8,000 m results in a diversity of ecosystems, from alluvial grasslands and subtropical broadleaf

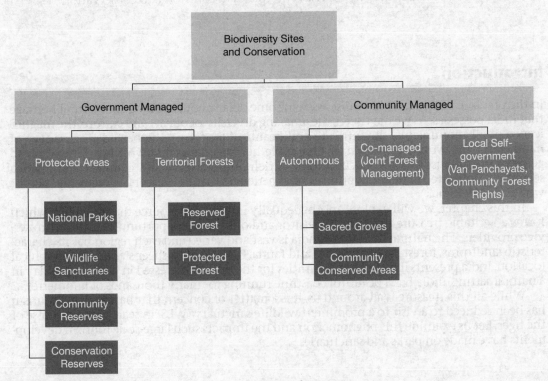

Figure 13.1 Biodiversity sites and conservation
Source: Authors.

forests along the foothills to temperate broadleaf forests in the middle elevations, mixed conifer and conifer forests in the higher hills and alpine meadows above the tree line. This enormous mountain range, which extends over nearly 750,000 sq km, lies in two separate regions of India, namely the Eastern Himalaya and the Western Himalaya. Charismatic large mammals such as the tiger and elephant are found in the foothills and Terai region. The snow leopard, musk deer, Himalayan tahr, blue sheep, black bear, Chir pheasant, Himalayan monal and Western Tragopan are some of the characteristic fauna of the mountains. The Eastern Himalaya is exceptionally rich in diversity and a rich centre of avian diversity—more than 60% of the bird species found in India have been recorded in the Northeast.

Western Ghats

The Western Ghats run roughly in a North-south direction for about 1,500 km parallel to the coast bordering the Arabian Sea. The importance of the Western ghats in terms of their biodiversity can be seen from the known inventory of their plant and animal groups. There are over 7,000 species of flowering plants, 330 butterfly species, over 500 bird species and 120 mammal species. The largest global populations of the Asian elephant and a variety of other mammals such as the tiger, dhole and gaur are found in plenty in this region (Pande and Arora 2014).

Protected Areas

A total of 5.07% of the country's area, covering 167,000 sq. km, is under a network of Protected Areas (PAs). There are 726 PAs in India (Pande and Arora 2014). A Protected Area is defined by the IUCN as follows:

> [A] clearly defined geographical space, recognized, dedicated and managed, through legal or other effective means, to achieve the long term conservation of nature with associated ecosystem services and cultural values.

PAs are formed in order to minimize the exploitation of resources and human intervention, with the objective of conserving biodiversity. PAs are also created to protect endangered species and help maintain natural processes without intervention. PAs can be designated for particular conservation uses such as plant diversity, wilderness species management, natural resources and wildlife conservation.

India has designated 726 PAs, extending over 167,000 sq km. These have been divided into the following:

- National Parks: 103
- Wildlife Sanctuaries: 531
- Conservation Reserves: 66
- Community Reserves: 26

In addition, there are 25 Marine PAs in peninsular India and 106 in the islands (Choudhary, 2016).

National Parks

An NP is 'a large natural area set aside to protect large-scale ecological processes, which also provide a foundation for environmentally and culturally compatible spiritual, scientific, educational, recreational and visitor opportunities' (Dudley, 2006). An NP, according to the Wildlife Protection Act, 1972, is an area which has ecological, faunal, floral, geomorphological or zoological association or importance and is declared as an NP to protect and develop its environment or wildlife in it. NPs have severe restrictions on non-forest related activities within the territory and activities undertaken by people living inside the area. For instance, grazing of livestock will never be permitted within an NP. The spectacular Namdapha National Park in Meghalaya is one of the richest regions in terms of floral and faunal diversity and is yet to be surveyed and studied.

Snow Leopard

Case Study: Namdapha National Park

Namdapha NP is located within the most North-eastern part of India, in Changlang district in the state of Arunachal Pradesh. It is the third largest park in India (1,985 sq km) and has one of the richest collections of biodiversity. Among the last great remote wilderness areas of Asia, Namdapha and its adjoining areas is flanked by the Patkai hills to the south and by the Himalaya in the north. The area lies close to the Indo-Myanmar-China tri-junction. The entire area is mountainous and comprises the catchment of the Noa-Dihing river, a tributary of the Brahmaputra which flows westwards through the middle of Namdapha. The park, declared as a Tiger Reserve in 1983, spans a wide altitudinal range from 200 m to 4,571 m. The terrain is steep and inaccessible. Interior and higher areas have not been explored, except by hunters and local communities.

There is extensive diversity of flora and fauna in this belt, with evergreen, moist deciduous, sub-tropical, temperate and alpine forests to be found. In the tropical rainforests, there are over 1,000 plant and 500 bird species.

The park is home to four types of big cat species: Tiger (*Panthera Tigris*), Leopard (*Panthera Pardus*), Snow Leopard (*Panthera Uncia*) and Clouded Leopard (*Neofelis Nebulosa*), as well as several species of lesser cats. A number of primate species such as Assamese macaque, pig-tailed macaque and stump-tailed macaque are seen in the park. Hoolock Gibbon, the only representative of the ape family in India, dwells in this impenetrable virgin forest. There is abundant bird life here, with over 500 species, notably five varieties of hornbills, the endangered white winged wood duck, jungle fowl and pheasants.

(Continued ...)

A trek through this remote region of the Himalayas is a once in a lifetime experience. It takes the visitor through rainforest and spectacular forest terrains, with an opportunity to view rare wildlife, learn survival skills and get acquainted with the lifestyle of the Lisu and Chakma tribes.

Image courtesy: Ministry of Tourism, Government of India.

Discussion Questions

1. Discuss the potential of Namdapha National Park from a tourism point of view. What are the main constraints that stand in the way of development?
2. List five possible activities that can be offered to visitors at the Park.

Wildlife Sanctuaries

A sanctuary is an area which is of adequate ecological, faunal, floral, geomorphological, natural or zoological significance. A WLS is declared for the purpose of protecting, propagating or developing wildlife on its environment. Certain rights of people living inside the sanctuary, such as grazing rights, may be allowed to be continued, even after the area has been declared as a WLS. Some sanctuaries have been recognized as 'reserves' under special national programmes. There are 48 tiger reserves and 32 elephant reserves in the country, where special programs for the protection and propagation of these endangered species are carried out (Choudhary, 2016).

Conservation Reserves

Conservation reserves are areas generally adjacent to NPs and sanctuaries, or those areas which link one protected area to another. Conservation reserves are declared as such by state governments, after consulting the local communities, for protecting landscapes, seascapes, flora and fauna and their habitat. The rights of people living inside a conservation reserve are not affected. Conservation reserves are typically buffer zones and migration corridors between NPs and WLSs and such areas are administered under the provisions of Wildlife Protection Act, 1972.

Community Reserves

Community Reserves can be declared by the state government in community or private lands, where individuals or the community has volunteered to conserve wildlife and its habitat (Ministry of Environment, Forest and Climate Change, n.d.a).

Biosphere Reserves

Biosphere Reserves are parts of landscapes extending over large areas of terrestrial or coastal ecosystems and representative examples of biogeographic zones. Biosphere reserves are established to conserve the diversity and integrity of plants and animals to safeguard genetic diversity of species and to ensure sustainable use of natural resources.

A biosphere reserve must contain an effectively protected and minimally disturbed core area of value of nature conservation, typical of a biogeographic unit and large enough to sustain viable populations representing all trophic levels in the ecosystem. The idea for biosphere reserve was introduced to minimize conflict between development and conservation. These were first introduced under the man and biosphere (MAB) programme of UNESCO. Each bio-sphere reserve will have a core zone containing suitable habitat for numerous plan and animal species, including higher order predators. The core area may be a NP or sanctuary, and the buffer zone adjoining the core zone may permit activities such as tourism, limited recreation, fishing and grazing. The Transition zone is the outermost part of the biosphere reserve. This is a zone of cooperation where conservation knowledge and management skills are applied. This includes settlements, croplands, managed forests and area of recreation and other economic uses (Ministry of Environment, Forest and Climate Change, n.d.b).

Natural World Heritage Sites

Natural World Heritage sites are some of the more significant places in terms of biodiversity, ecology or scenery. Several of India's PAs have been listed as world heritage sites by UNESCO in the natural category. Inclusion in this prestigious list implies that these places have out-standing universal value (OUV). OUV implies that the site is of importance for the present and future generations of all humanity and transcends national boundaries (Table 13.1).

People within Protected Areas

A large part of our PAs have significant human habitation, estimated to around 4 million. The conflict between protectors of the parks and the people who live in and around them is one of the key issues in conservation. The villagers graze their cattle in the lands within the PA and collect firewood for their daily use from the forest. Many communities depend on the major and minor forest produce for their livelihoods. According to the Wildlife Protection Act, 1972, the rights of people who live within a protected area have to be settled before the area can be notified as a NP or WLS. While this has not been carried out, there have been several attempts to relocate villages to areas outside the sensitive areas. The intention is to relocate villages within PAs to land earmarked for their resettlement outside the PAs. There are increasing incidences of human–animal conflict, sometimes leading to violent confrontations. More enforcement measures by Park authorities for protection of the PA resulted in increased conflict with the villagers. There is a problem of growing alienation and marginalization of communities living within and around our PAs, driven to destitution and poverty due to low agricultural productivity,

Table 13.1   Natural heritage properties of India inscribed on the world heritage list

Sl. No.	Name	Year Inscribed
1	Great Himalayan National Park Conservation Area	2014
2	Kaziranga National Park	1985
3	Keoladeo National Park	1985
4	Manas National Park	1985
5	Nanda Devi and Valley of Flowers National Parks	1988
6	Sundarbans National Park	1987
7	Western Ghats	2012

Source: World Heritage Centre, UNESCO (http://whc.unesco.org/en/statesparties/in)

overgrazing and limited economic opportunities. It is no coincidence that these areas have many things in common—high levels of poverty, mineral wealth, forests and tribal population!

In the context of the declining population of the tiger, Tiger Task Force examined this issue in detail and made many recommendations (GoI, 2005). It is important to design policies and actions focusing on earmarking inviolate spaces for endangered species like the tiger, even while involving local communities in conservation activities and rebuilding forest economies. It must be remembered that some of the poorest populations of India share their habitats and resources with the tiger. It follows that the tiger conservation has to keep in mind the forest dependent population in these areas. The tragedy of communities living within NPs is that the villages are denied access to basic needs, they do not have legal livelihood options and development works such as medical facilities and schools are not established in the villages. The need of the hour is careful and sensitive relocation and resettlement of villagers living in the core areas to alternative areas with irrigation and grazing opportunities, protecting their customary way of life and enabling them to continue their traditional bonds with the land.

Management of Protected Areas

The management of PAs is of vital interest to key stakeholders like tourism businesses. Currently, wildlife conservation and management of PAs face many challenges which are complex and intricate in nature such as commercial interests like mining and road construction, local human activities like fuel wood and forest produce collection, grazing and hunting. Increasing population of humans and livestock in the communities that live in or around PAs results in habitat loss and fragmentation of areas. Due to the proximity there is always a threat of human-wildlife conflicts. Dependence on forest produce encourages over use of resources and depletion of plants and herbs. There is the ever looming threat of poaching of wildlife, due to a flourishing illegal international trade in animal parts. Tourism practices may often willingly or inadvertently have severe impacts on wildlife in the area.

Protected Areas and Wildlife Tourism

India has some of the most varied wildlife, particularly of large mammals, many of which are endangered species. Many NPs and WLSs have been established for the specific conservation and protection of endangered animals. Some key examples are the Gir National Park in Gujarat for the Asiatic Lion, Kaziranga National Park in Assam for the One-horned Rhinoceros, the Dachigam National Park in Kashmir for the Hangul or Kashmir Stag, the Ranthambhore National Park, Rajasthan, for the Asiatic Tiger and the Sundarbans National Park for the Royal Bengal Tiger. As many of these PAs offer spectacular natural scenery and various opportunities for undertaking nature-based activities as well, these have become major tourist destinations attracting tens of thousands of domestic and foreign visitors. It follows that wildlife are a precious natural resource vital for tourism and it is in the interest of tourism that steps are taken for the conservation of the environment and wildlife and such steps are supported by the tourism industry. The tourism industry has a responsibility to ensure that tourism takes place in a sustainable manner. We shall look at this particular aspect of sustainability in subsequent chapters.

At present, a large part of the total income from wildlife tourism comes from the entry fees, which means that the greater the number of visitors, the higher the earnings for the Forest Department. Such a situation does not provide incentives to create an ecotourism environment, but encourages actions to increase visitation to the fragile PA. This calls for creation of ecotourism products in PAs that can be priced higher and can bring new revenue streams that are different from gate collections.

Nature Tourism: Boon or Bane?

Studies have shown that there is an increase in the number of visitors to PAs in developing countries, contrasting with a decreasing trend in wealthy countries (Balmford et al., 2009). There are many factors that have contributed to increased tourism to PAs:

- Sustained marketing leading to increased awareness
- Improved accessibility to cities and urban centres
- Establishment of comfortable hotels and resorts
- Curiosity about charismatic species such as elephant and tiger

Benefits

The benefits for conservation from nature-based tourism and the economic benefits to local population are matters that have been debated for the long. The employment generated by tourist facilities near PAs, to a large part, goes to the members of the local communities. To a large extent, the jobs are unskilled positions, whereas for higher and skilled positions, personnel from outside are recruited. However, the development of ecotourism experiences, utilizing the expertise of the local population, can provide the visitors with memorable encounters with nature and bring in regular income streams to local community members. The eco-development project undertaken in Periyar Tiger Reserve, where former poachers and forest produce collectors were brought together to create trekking packages for tourists within the reserve, is one example of the potential that exists for such projects.

Harmful Effects

Developments that can be directly attributed to tourism on the fringes of PAs are of great concern. Many hotels add to the stress on the local environment by drawing large amounts of groundwater, disposing of solid and liquid waste irresponsibly and encroaching on the grazing lands of villagers. Tourism businesses are accused of not contributing enough to conservation and of taking away the economic benefits that have accrued from the natural resources of the area. Many hotels and resorts close to PAs did not have any concern for local environmental issues. Swimming pools and water fountains using precious groundwater in areas of acute water shortage point to the irresponsible actions taken by resort owners.

Several negative impacts due to overdevelopment of tourism in fragile areas have been documented:

- Resource extraction
- Hunting
- Harassment of animals
- Over harvesting of water
- Water pollution
- Fire hazards

'Tiger-centric' Tourism

With our vast wilderness areas, India can offer multifarious experiences to the visitor interested in nature. A visit to a NP can be for a range of reasons—to relax amidst the serenity of nature, to enjoy the pristine and unpolluted air of the countryside, to understand the wealth of our forests, to view majestic wildlife in their natural habitat and to test one's endurance and physical fitness in adventure activities.

However, for a large number of visitors to natural areas in India, the visit had only one purpose–to get a glimpse of the tiger. This 'tiger-centric' tourism, at the cost of the other experiences that are available, has created huge stress on our tiger reserves (Sinha, 2010). We should be aware that the tiger population in India had dipped down to alarming levels and conservationists were of the view that the tiger was at the verge of extinction. In response to this situation, many sanctuaries were designated as tiger reserves and a series of management and conservation measures were undertaken. Thanks to these initiatives, the tiger was saved from extinction, but the situation continues to be grave. Recent reports have given rise to some optimism, with the population rising to 2,226 tigers in the country—up from 1,706 four years ago.

Status of Tigers in India

By virtue of being the top predator, the tiger functions as an umbrella species for the conservation of biodiversity, ecosystem functions, goods and services in forest systems of Asia. The 'Project Tiger', a pioneering conservation initiative of the GoI, aims to harness this role of the tiger along with the tigers' charisma to garner resources and public support for conserving representative intact ecosystems. Tigers are a conservation dependent species. Major threats to tigers are poaching that is driven by an illegal international demand for tiger parts and products, depletion of tiger prey caused by illegal bush meat consumption and habitat loss because of the ever increasing demand for forested lands.

India is unique in having a significant number of tigers in the wild, in spite of growing population and resource extraction pressures on their habitat. The latest estimate of tigers in various landscapes published by the Ministry of Environment and Forests claims an appreciable rise in numbers of the big cat. That there could be as many as 2,226 tigers in the country—up from 1,706 four years ago—in nature reserves ranging from the hills in the Northeast to central Indian forests and the Western Ghats, besides the mangrove-rich Sundarbans delta, gives India a special place on the global conservation map (*The Hindu*, 2015). Karnataka has the largest tiger population of 406, followed by Uttarakhand (340), Madhya Pradesh (308), Tamil Nadu (229) and Assam (167).

The Western Ghats landscape showed a substantial increase in tiger population. The Mudumalai-Bandipur-Nagarhole-Wayanad complex, falling in the three states of Karnataka, Tamil Nadu and Kerala, holds the world's largest tiger population currently estimated over 570 tigers (Jhala, Qureshi and Gopal, 2015). The two NPs of Bandipur and Nagarhole in Karnataka, together with the Mudumalai National Park in Tamil Nadu and the Wayanad Wildlife Sanctuary in Kerala, form the largest protected area in southern India, with the largest habitat of wild elephants in South Asia.

The experience of some of our prominent tiger reserves such as Ranthambhore indicate that uncontrolled and unregulated tourism development focused on the tiger is unsustainable and may lead to grave conservation and environment problems. Demands of the tourists must never take precedence over conservation as the tourism business is entirely dependent on the success of conservation and the health of charismatic species like the tiger. Park managements must be empowered to manage tourism activities within reserves professionally and within the carrying capacity of the area. Tourism carrying capacity is defined as the maximum number of people that may visit a tourist destination at the same time, without causing destruction of the physical, economic, socio-cultural environment and an unacceptable decrease in the quality of visitors' satisfaction (UNWTO, 1981). The tendency to create luxury tourism focused on sighting of the tiger needs to be discouraged.

Management of Tourism in PAs

Tourism in PAs has to be managed sensitively to ensure that it does not damage the habitat of wildlife or the environment. To this end, each protected area must develop its own tourism plan, earmarking an area outside the core for tourism activities. There should be a ceiling on the number of visitors allowed to enter a given part of the reserve at a time that is arrived at keeping in mind the carrying capacity of the habitat and the availability of facilities, transport and guides.

Tourists' expectations of sighting charismatic species will need to be managed, along with concerns about particular species and individual parks, to design more effective conservation strategies. Park managers in India have an important role to play in managing the growth in wildlife tourism and educating tourists (Karanth et al., 2012).

The traffic within the sanctuary needs to be regulated to manageable levels. In the interest of the safety of tourists and protection of wildlife, guidelines have been framed regarding the type of vehicles to be used, the minimum distance between vehicles, the competence levels of the guides and the timing for undertaking excursions.

Strategy for Managing Tourism in Protected Areas

With a view to ensure effective management, the National Wildlife Action Plan has outlined a strategy for tourism in PAs:

> Regulated, low impact tourism has the potential to be a vital conservation tool as it helps win public support for wildlife conservation. However, in recent years, the mushrooming of tourist visitation and tourist facilities has led to overuse, disturbance and serious management problems for PA managers.

> In case of conflict between tourism and conservation interests of a PA, the paradigms for decision must be that *tourism exists for the parks and not parks for tourism* and that tourism demands must be subservient to and in consonance with the conservation interests of PA and all wildlife. While revenues from tourism can help the management of the PA, maximization of income must never become the main goal of tourism, which should remain essentially to impart education and respect for nature.

> The objective of wildlife tourism should be to inculcate amongst the visitors empathy for nature, both animate and inanimate, and to provide a communion with nature rather than to merely ensure sightings of a maximum number of animal populations and species. Students of all levels must be encouraged to visit PAs and to participate in conservation action therein, and concessions and park interpretations must facilitate these educative processes. (The National Wildlife Action Plan, n.d.)

What Should Be Done?

Park managers need to take nature-based tourism as one of the important revenue streams to realize the full benefit, channelizing the funds into conservation and the creation of livelihood options for local people. At least a portion of the gate collection of reserves should be ploughed back into conservation and to provide economic opportunities to local people. Balancing PA management, tourism growth, local community needs and rapid ongoing land use changes around the PAs requires attention and cooperation between government agencies, private enterprises and local communities (Karanth and Defries, 2011).

Hotels and Tour Operators

Protection of wildlife and conservation are best left to experts and park managers. As per Sinha (2010), the least that tourism businesses should be doing are the following:

- Comply with all statutory requirements
- Adopt responsible practices—minimize water and energy consumption, minimize waste generation and manage waste responsibly
- Educate visitors on responsible behaviour and importance of conservation
- Employ local community members in as many levels as possible
- Contribute to park management initiatives for conservation
- Spread awareness about illegal trade and habitat restoration

Communities and Ecotourism

In Chapter 2, we have discussed the term ecotourism and its various definitions. While there may be differences in precisely defining the term, there is a broad agreement that ecotourism should be tourism that consumes less, encourages local participation, ownership and business opportunities, benefit indigenous communities, contribute to biodiversity conservation and mandates responsible behaviour on the part of tourists and the tourism industry.

The role of the community in ecotourism initiatives differs widely from one setting to the other. There are some excellent examples of how the community can be fully involved in creating and operating tourism enterprises, such as homestays, tour operations and souvenir manufacture, involving themselves fully in all the steps of decision-making. Such initiatives result in new jobs, provide additional supplementary sources of livelihood and increase awareness and appreciation of the region's natural and cultural heritage.

On the other hand, many so-called ecotourism projects have been accused of displacement of Adivasis, increased energy and water consumption and objectification of the indigenous communities. In any ecotourism project, elements such as the role of the community, process for eliciting community involvement, support to this process through relevant capacity building, benefit sharing between stakeholders and regulatory mechanisms that impose stringent control on developments have to be spelt out (Equations, 2010). Local communities must be encouraged to start tourism enterprises, bringing the benefits of tourism development to those households.

Nature-based Tourism

Nature-based tourism implies that tourism is based on dependent upon natural attractions. Tourists would travel to regions already to the attractiveness of the natural resources available in that region. In other words, the primary reason for travel to such an area would be the natural environment of that site. The experiences that the tourist obtains from the natural setting could be of a wide variety. For instance, bird watching is an activity that is possible exclusively in a natural setting which could be as diverse as forest grassland or a water body. Other activities have a more direct dependence on the setting—hiking, camping, kayaking, rock climbing, and fishing are examples of activities to be undertaken in natural areas. Nature-based tourism is important in that it becomes a powerful reason to conserve wildlife habitats and to preserve natural environments. The quality of the environment is a vital ingredient of this tourism activity.

Nature-based tourism is recognized as an important 'ecosystem service', capable of generating substantial resources for local economic development and conservation. Wildlife viewing and outdoor recreation centred on PAs is reportedly one of the fastest-growing sectors in tourism. (Goodwin, 1996) The rapid growth in nature-based tourism, particularly to PAs, has implications for managing strategies for these areas. The intrinsic value of tourism to a protected area needs to be converted into sustainable opportunities that provide avenues for economic development for the local population, as well as contribute funds for development projects within PAs.

Nature-based Activities

The most popular nature-based activity is of course visiting the beach and the associated activities like surfing, snorkelling, diving, boat cruises and fishing trips. Inland water bodies are used for several activities like canoeing, kayaking, scenic cruises and angling.

Beach Tourism

In many ways, beach tourism has come to define recreational and leisure tourism all over the world. Beach tourism forms the biggest segment of leisure tourism in most established tourism destinations. Historically, beach tourism originated in Europe as a result of annual holidays given to the working-class in the nineteenth century, coinciding with the annual repair of machinery in manufacturing units. Beach destinations developed, which offered water-based activities, an environment of relaxation and recreation and warm weather. Beach tourists, to a large extent, stay in beach destinations for a relaxed holiday, the emphasis on imbibing the warmth of the coastal area and the natural beauty of the seaside setting. The craze for taking annual beach holidays spread to the USA and Australia. With the advent of cheap air travel, the number of tourists interested in beach holidays increased significantly and more beach destinations opened up, particularly in Spain and along the Mediterranean coast. Today a country with a coastline has one of the most important natural resources that form a vital asset for a tourism destination.

With almost 7,500 km of coastline, India has the potential to become a major beach tourism destination of the world. However, except for Goa, Kovalam, Puri and Diu, India, do not boast of many beach destinations. Poor access and connectivity, inadequate infrastructure and the absence of a 'permissive' culture are all cited as reasons why beach tourism did not become popular across the beaches of India.

Lakes and Backwaters

Lakes, backwaters and other water bodies are also important and attractive natural settings attracting tourists. For example, the central attraction of Jammu and Kashmir continues to be Dal Lake. The backwaters of Kerala have become one of the most iconic tourism experiences of the state. The Chilika Lake is one of the most important destinations in the state of Odisha. Water bodies, besides presenting a beautiful natural setting for creating accommodation, offer numerous options for activities such as kayaking, houseboats and cruises.

Mountains

The majestic Himalayas are priceless natural assets for tourism. As mentioned earlier, the foothills of the Himalaya Mountains have many hill stations, which attract thousands of tourists.

The Hill Station
The geomorphology of the Indian subcontinent has resulted in several natural features that have been useful for tourism. The extremely hot summer of the North Indian plains and the Deccan Plateau resulted in the colonial rulers seeking more salubrious locations to escape the heat. The foothills of the Himalayas and the Nilgiri hills in the south, provided a solution—guest houses were built on hillsides that gave refuge from the heat. Another reason for the establishment of the hill station was as a place for convalescence for European

(Continued ...)

invalids who were recuperating from tropical illnesses. Hill stations are destinations which are peculiar to the topically countries, particularly where those which had seen colonial rule. Most of the hill stations well-established in the early nineteenth century and became favourite haunts for the ruling elite to escape the stifling heat of the summer. The most important attributes needed for a hill station were an agreeable cool climate, beautiful scenery and accessibility. The tendency of migrating to a hill station during summer months became a part of the official calendar—Shimla became the summer capital of colonial India. Cantonments and military offices were built, schools were established and English cottages were built. The hill stations evoked memories of a distant homeland and provided the comforting setting and social environment that the plains lacked (Kennedy, 1996). Other prominent hill stations that developed before independence were Dalhousie, Nainital, Mussorie and Darjeeling in the north and Ooty (Udhagamandalam) and Coonoor in the south.

After the advent of mass tourism in India, these hill stations became extremely popular and remain prominent tourism destinations, particularly amongst domestic tourists. Most major hill stations have seen widespread development, bringing infrastructural growth, hotels and tourist facilities and employment to the region. However, most hill stations today face severe problems because of unplanned development, inadequate infrastructure, waste disposal issues and environmental degradation.

Further up, many of the most sacred pilgrimage places of India are located in the mountains and continue to attract pilgrims and visitors from all over the world. The mountains offer great locations for myriad activities, drawing a segment of holidaymakers. Walking, trekking, cycling are options available in these locations. Apart from these, for the adventure tourist, the mountains are settings for paragliding, rock climbing, river rafting and skiing expeditions. There are several wonderful treks in Ladakh, but the Chadar trek is one of the most magnificent in the world.

Confluence of Indus and Zanskar rivers

Case Study: Trekking in Ladakh

Ladakh, the land of the high passes, is one of the most remote areas of India, situated in the Tibetan plateau, north of the Himalaya and to the south of the Karakoram mountains. Ladakh is part of Jammu and Kashmir and has two districts, Leh and Kargil, administered by the Ladakh autonomous Hill Development Council.

(Continued ...)

Ladakh, owing to its location on the rain shadow region of the Himalayas, is a high altitude desert with sparse vegetation. Because of its unique geographical features, climate and culture, Ladakh has become a popular tourist destination in recent years.

Ladakh is known for its range of trekking options, which include light, family-oriented treks through the villages of the Indus and Nubra valleys, to extreme treks through Zanskar and the high valleys of Ripchar and Suru. Companies such as Rimo Expeditions offer a range of options, from fixed departure tours and customized trips to mountaineering, mountain biking, white water rafting and family adventures. The company has 16 different trekking, rafting and biking options in Ladakh, including the Markha, Ripchar and Nubra valley treks and biking across the Hindustan Tibet road. Run by Chewang Motup and Yangdu Goba, both hailing from the mountains, Rimo Expeditions combines personal knowledge and direct operations with high safety standards and quality equipment. However, the trek that caught the imagination of adventure lovers across the world is the trek on the frozen Zanskar River.

The Chadar Trek

The Chadar trek has been regarded as one of the biggest challenges for the adventure lover. Every winter, the muddy Zanskar River, which is one of the tributaries of the Indus, turns into ice, frozen over in the extreme subzero temperatures. The residents of the scattered villages of the Zanskar valley used to walk on the frozen river to reach the outside world, when the road to Zanskar is cut off by snowfall. Of late, some adventure tour companies have been offering this trek, which involves walking about 50 km on ice.

The trek for the most part is on the frozen sheet of ice, the 'chadar', occasionally involving rappelling across rock surfaces in areas where the river has melted. The walk takes the traveller alongside frozen waterfalls and to camping in caves on the mountainside. Crossing glaciers and traversing passes are part of the experience. The temperature may go down to -35° C.

The Chadar trek is possible only during a short period in the winter, normally between mid-January and mid-February. An all-weather road will soon link Zanskar to Leh and the trek may soon lose its allure.

Source: Tripathi (2011).
Image courtesy: Ministry of Tourism, Government of India.

Discussion Questions

1. List five extreme adventure experiences that travellers can enjoy in India. Discuss the ways through which these can attract more visitors.
2. Tourism in Ladakh has made good use of the resources provided by natural heritage in the region. Discuss.

Diving in India

India has a long coastline and several islands, a rich repository of natural beauty and marine diversity. Off the mainland, many spots in Goa have been developed for diving. The Lakshadweep archipelago has numerous atolls and lagoons with colourful coral reefs and overhangs. The islands of Andaman and Nicobar are rich in underwater marine life, much of which is undisturbed. Commonly visible species are turtles, moray eels, manta rays and sting rays.

Conclusion

Nature-based tourism, particularly in WLSs and NPs, has the potential to increase awareness on conservation, bring revenues to PAs and empower local communities. But, as we have seen in the chapter, there is a massive problem of unregulated tourism development both within and on the fringes of PAs, which pose challenges to the sustainability of such models. One of the main challenges for biodiversity conservation is to build awareness about its importance and increase knowledge about natural environments, so that there is a bigger stake within the community for caring for PAs. Encouraging nature enthusiasts to visit natural areas is a great way of building up a constituency of concerned citizens who are involved in conservation matters. It is of vital importance that the tourism sector engages with park managers to develop management guidelines and best practices for better management of these precious resources.

Review Questions

1. Examine the significance of biodiversity from tourism perspective.
2. Examine how tourism is managed in PAs.

Activities

1. Arrange a poster exhibition, collecting all relevant details including flora and fauna of India's Natural Heritage that included in the World Heritage List.
2. Organize a seminar on nature and nature-based tourism attractions in your state and prepare packages that suit the requirements of different demographic segments of tourists.
3. Design and develop measures for supporting conservation efforts of PAs through tourism in your state by involving local community. Suggest livelihood generation programme to local community members through tourism.
4. Arrange a debate on 'Wildlife Tourism—A boon or bane' and suggest measures for sustainable development of wildlife tourism.
5. Design eco-friendly awareness programme for visitors using different media on dos and don'ts in PAs and celebrate Wildlife Week in any one wildlife tourism destination.

References

Books

Balmford, A., J. Beresford, J. Green, R. Naidoo, M. Walpole and A. Manica, A. 2009. 'A Global Perspective on Trends in Nature-Based Tourism'. *PLOS Biology*, 7 (6): e1000144. doi:10.1371/journal.pbio.1000144

Goodwin, H. 1996. *Pursuit of Ecotourism, Biodiversity and Conservation*, Volume 5, issue 4, pp. 277–291. Springer.

GoI. 2005. 'Joining The Dots'. The Report of the Tiger Task Force, Ministry of Environment and Forests.

Karanth, K.K. and R. DeFries. 2011. 'Nature-based Tourism in Indian Protected Areas: New challenges for Park Management'. *Conservation Letters*, 4: 137–49. doi: 10.1111/j.1755-263X.2010.00154.x

Karanth, K.K., R. Defries, A. Srivathsa, and V. Sankaraman. 2012. 'Wildlife Tourists in India's Emerging Economy: Potential for a Conservation Constituency?' *Fauna and Flora International, Oryx*, 46 (3): 382–90.

Kennedy, D. 1996. *The Magic Mountains: Hill Stations and the British Raj.* Berkeley: University of California Press.

UNWTO. 1981. 'Saturation of Tourist Destinations'. Report of the Secretary General, Madrid.

Web Resources

Choudhary, V. 2016. 'Abhinav Nature Conservation'. Available at: http://natureconservation.in/category/environmental-science/environmental-education-and-policy/ (accessed on 22 December 2016).

Dudley, N., ed. 2006. 'Guidelines for Applying Protected Area Management Categories'. IUCN, Switzerland. Available at: https://portals.iucn.org/library/efiles/html/paps-016/2.%20Definition%20and%20categories.html (accessed on 3 April 2016).

Equations. 2010. 'Community Involvement in Ecotourism in Madhya Pradesh'. EQUATIONS. Available at: http://www.equitabletourism.org/readfull.php?AID=1226 (accessed on 22 December 2016).

GoI. 'Annual Report 2013-14'. Forests and Climate Change, Ministry of Environment.

GoI. 2005. 'Joining The Dots'. The Report of the Tiger Task Force, Ministry of Environment and Forests. Available at: http://projecttiger.nic.in/WriteReadData/PublicationFile/full_report.pdf (accessed on 22 December 2016).

IUCN. n.d. 'About Biodiversity'. IUCN Available at: http://iucn.org/iyb/about/ (accessed on 3 April 2016).

Jhala, Y.V., Q. Qureshi, and R. Gopal. eds. 2015. 'The Status of Tigers in India 2014'. National Tiger Conservation Authority, New Delhi, and The Wildlife Institute of India, Dehradun. Available at: http://www.indiaenvironmentportal.org.in/files/file/Tiger%20Status%20booklet.pdf (accessed on 22 December 2016).

Ministry of Environment, Forest and Climate Change. n.d.a. 'Protected Area Network in India'. GoI. Available at: http://envfor.nic.in/public-information/protected-area-network (accessed on 4 April 2016).

———. n.d.b. 'Biosphere Reserves'. GoI. Available at: http://envfor.nic.in/division/biosphere-reserves (accessed on 22 December 2016).

Namdapha National Park. n.d. UNESCO. Available at: http://whc.unesco.org/en/tentativelists/2104/ (accessed on 22 December 2016).

Pande, H.K., and S. Arora, eds. 2014. *India's Fifth National Report to Convention on Biological Diversity.* New Delhi: Ministry of Environment and Forests, GoI. Available at: https://www.cbd.int/doc/world/in/in-nr-05-en.pdf (accessed on 4 April 2016).

Sinha, S. 2010. 'Asian Animal Protection Forum'. Available at: https://groups.yahoo.com/neo/groups/aapn/conversations/messages/18851 (accessed on 22 December 2016).

The National Wildlife Action Plan. n.d. Available at: http://forest.and.nic.in/ActsNRules%5CNational%20Wild%20life%20Action%20Plan%20-%202002.pdf (accessed on 22 December 2016).

The Hindu. 2015. 'The Science of Saving Tigers'. *The Hindu.* Available at: http://www.thehindu.com/opinion/editorial/editorial-the-science-of-saving-tigers/article6812248.ece?ref=relatedNews (accessed on 22 December 2016).

Tripathi, S. 2011. 'On Thin Ice'. *Lonely Planet India Magazine.* Available at: http://www.shikhasgreen-diary.com/magazine%20articles/Zanskar%20Frozen%20River%20trek.pdf (accessed on 22 December 2016).

Suggested Readings

Book

Liu, W., C.A. Vogt, J. Luo, G. He, K.A. Frank, and J. Liu. 2012. 'Drivers and Socioeconomic Impacts of Tourism Participation in Protected Areas'. *PLOS ONE,* 7 (4): e35420. doi:10.1371/journal.pone.0035420

Web Resources

Kaziranga Park administration. n.d. 'Management and Administration: Tourism'. Kaziranga National Park. Available at: http://assamforest.in/knp-osc/linkpages.php?u=ma&sm=tr

Leave No trace. n.d. 'Get involved'. Center for Outdoor Ethics. Available at: https://lnt.org/get-involved

Ministry of Environment and Forests. n.d. 'Chapter IV'. In *Wildlife Conservation Act, 1972*. Ministry of Environment and Forests, GoI. Available at: http://envfor.nic.in/legis/wildlife/wildlife1c4.html

National Forest Foundation. n.d. 'It's All Yours'. National Forest Foundation. Available at: https://www.nationalforests.org/our-forests/its-all-yours - It's all yours;

US Forest Service. n.d. 'Know Before You Go'. National Forests, US Forest Service. Available at: http://www.fs.fed.us/visit/know-before-you-go

A temple in Khajuraho
Image courtesy: Ministry of Tourism, Government of India.

CHAPTER 14

Tourism Business in India

By the end of this chapter, students will be able to:

- List the major hotel groups of India.
- Enumerate the distribution of approved hotel rooms in India.
- Understand the trends in accommodation sector.
- Learn of the 'Indian' innovations in accommodation.
- Gain an overview of tour operation business in India.
- Describe the features of outbound operations.
- Understand the contributory factors of growing outbound market.

Introduction

In the opening chapter of this section, we have seen the important role that the travel and tourism sector has come to play in the Indian economy. We have also noted the potential of the sector in bringing in precious foreign exchange, providing employment and bringing benefits to vast numbers of persons. The winds of change that are blowing through the country will benefit the sector immensely, and the signs are already visible. Improved infrastructure, an 'open skies' policy and simplified procedures have all combined to make travel to India easier, cheaper and more comfortable. The burgeoning domestic economy and the ever-increasing numbers of the Indian middle class offer fertile ground for growth of domestic tourism, which will remain the mainstay of tourism in the future.

In this chapter, we will take a close look at the tourism business in India, tracing its development and evolution and understanding the operations of the sectors that comprise the tourism business in the country. The accommodation and tour sectors understandably take centre stage in our discussion, although the developments in related sectors such as transportation and aviation cannot be ignored.

Hotel Industry

The Indian Hotel industry is dominated by home grown, Indian owned hotel chains, with international chains only recently entering the country. Hotel development was concentrated in the big cities in view of the international business traffic and in established tourist destinations such as Goa, Jaipur and Agra. In keeping with the burgeoning growth of cities, such as Hyderabad, Bengaluru, Pune and Gurgaon (now Gurugram), many upscale hotels have been opened, often managed and operated by international brands. Indian hotel chains have carved a niche for themselves in the market and are known and respected for their professionalism and high standards of service delivery.

Major Hotel Chains

The Indian Hotels Company Ltd. (IHCL), collectively known as Taj Hotels Resorts and Palaces is one of the largest groups in Asia. Beginning with the iconic Taj Mahal Palace hotel, Bombay in 1903, the group currently runs 93 hotels in 55 locations in India and additional 16 hotels overseas. The group operates across the spectrum, with the *Taj* brand representing luxury and unique experiences, *Taj Exotica* the luxury resort and Spa brand, *Taj Safaris* for wildlife lodges, *Vivanta by Taj* as the 'cool luxury' brand, *Gateway* hotels as an upscale brand for the modern 'nomad' and *Ginger* at the economy end of the spectrum.

The Oberoi group, founded in 1934, operates 30 hotels in 6 countries, a Nile cruiser and a vessel in the Kerala backwaters. The Oberoi brand is renowned for a blend of service, luxury and quiet efficiency—the *'Vilas'* properties in Agra, Jaipur, Udaipur and Ranthambhore are fine examples of their philosophy. The *Trident* is a brand of 5-star hotels offering quality and value.

ITC hotels, launched in 1975, are known for the concept of 'Responsible Luxury', integrating green practices with luxury hotels. ITC hotels are classified under four brands: *ITC Hotels— Luxury Collection* at the deluxe category, *WelcomHotel* for 5-star global traveller, *Fortune* Hotels in the mid-market segment and *WelcomHeritage* operating palaces, forts and havelis.

Hotels and Rooms Inventory

It is difficult to accurately state the number of hotels or rooms in India. There is no national registry of hotels or a central regulatory body that controls hotel operations. Statutory permissions to open and operate a hotel are given at the State or municipal levels. Most of the hotels are not part of any industry body or take part in industry surveys.

The MoT is the authoritative body to provide information on the hotel sector of India. An analysis of the data that is available in the Annual Statistics Report of the ministry is very informative and provides a snapshot of the hotel industry.

As per the Report of 2014, there are 1,233 hotels which are approved or classified by the MoT (this figure includes 117 hotels which are awaiting classification or reclassification). There are 79,567 rooms in these hotels. It may be noted that 42 heritage hotels approved by the ministry are also included in the total figure, as are a few B&B establishments.

The breakup of the hotels into different star categories is provided in Table 14.1.

Beyond the Statistics

The total inventory of approved rooms in the country is extremely low, when compared to the figure of 8 million foreign tourist arrivals and domestic tourists whose numbers are many times this figure. To understand this further, we need to go deeper into the data to look for indications that will inform our analysis.

Table 14.1   Approved hotels and rooms

Category	Number of Hotels	Percentage	Number of Rooms	Percentage
1-Star	41	4.04	1,193	1.72
2-Star	80	7.89	1,902	2.74
3-Star	554	54.64	22,724	32.73
4-Star	134	13.21	7,969	11.48
5-Star	92	9.07	11,744	16.91
5-Star Deluxe	113	11.14	23,907	34.43
Total	1,014		69,439	

Source: Indian Tourism Statistics 2014, Market Research Division, MoT, GoI.

The hotels may be grouped into three, based on the market segment these cater to—premium (5-star and 5-star deluxe)—luxury resorts, deluxe properties and upper end business hotels; mid-market (4- and 3-star) aimed at the mid segment business and leisure traveller and budget (2-star and below).

Premium

It is seen that 205 hotels are in the luxury/premium segment, with a total inventory of 35,651 rooms. About 45% of the total rooms in the country are to be found in this segment. This segment consists of the large business and conference hotels, with hundreds of rooms, as well as the luxury resorts in destinations. Not surprisingly, Delhi and Maharashtra (predominantly Mumbai) lead the way, with many premium properties located in these metropolises.

Mid-market

Coming to the mid-market segment, it is seen that there are 688 hotels with a total of 30,693 rooms, forming 39% of the total inventory. The global trend is that the most number of hotels and rooms are found in the mid-market segment, owing to its popularity with the middle-class travellers. In India, it is a little atypical that the number of rooms is lower than that in the premium segment. We will discuss this further later in the analysis.

Budget

The most revealing part of the analysis is that less than 4% of rooms (3,095) are in the budget category. It is fairly evident that all over the country, there are vast numbers of hotels catering to the budget traveller, and the official figure cannot reflect the real position of the segment. This leads to the inescapable conclusion that at a large majority of budget hotels are not included in the official statistics. Even if we assume that the number of 'unclassified' rooms in this category is, at least, equal to the number in the mid-market category, the total number of rooms in the country will be over 110,000. It is clear that at the lower end of the spectrum, hotels do not find any value in getting themselves classified, which has resulted in such a low number of 'classified' hotels in official figures.

Distribution of Hotels

The ministry data also provides information on the distribution of hotels across the states of India. An examination of this data throws light on several interesting aspects of the hotel sector and offers insights on future trends.

Table 14.2 is an excerpt of the data of classified hotels in each state. For convenience, only the top-12 states have been included in this table.

Data shows that Maharashtra leads the field in the number of 'classified' rooms (14,483). However, Kerala is in the second position (11,936) followed by Delhi, Andhra Pradesh (presumably including Hyderabad) and Tamil Nadu. A large part of the data of Maharashtra can be safely assumed to be of Mumbai. It is seen that Maharashtra has the highest number of premium/luxury hotels (32) and rooms. While 54% of the total rooms are in the premium segment, 32% fall in the mid-market segment.

In Kerala, the picture is different. Although there are 22 premium properties, the rooms in this segment total to around 2,000 only, indicating that most of the premium properties in this state are small in size. The most surprising aspect about Kerala is that 67% of the rooms are in the mid-market category, spread across a large number of hotels (339). The state laws laying down minimum standards for permitting liquor (bar) licence may be a reason for this anomalous growth.

Delhi offers another peculiar picture. More than 70% of the total room inventories are in the premium segment, with less than 10% in the mid-market. One of the reasons for the skewed and highly unusual development is the exorbitant real estate prices within the city and non-availability of land. Given the astronomical prices, developers can hope to recoup their investments only by constructing premium properties and charging high room rates. Karnataka and Uttar Pradesh are two other states having a similar picture.

Goa received 3.545 million domestic and 514,000 foreign visitors (2014). It is renowned the world over as one of the foremost destinations in India. However, Goa has only 43 hotels and 4,254 rooms in the classified categories. Any visitor to Goa would have been struck by the large number of hotels and boarding establishments, particularly close to the popular beaches. This leads to the conclusion that a large number of Goa's hotels have not been classified by the ministry.

Trends in the Accommodation Industry

The hotel industry has been able to maintain a relatively high average room rate (ARR), thanks to increasing demand and the demand–supply gap. Industry estimates for the year 2013-14 show that the average room rate was recorded at ₹4,729 (Khanna, Thapar and Das, 2015). Although the industry cyclically goes through ups and downs, it is a safe presumption that the hotel industry will see significant investment in the long term. It has been estimated that the country needs to add 60,000 rooms in the next five years. As the data shows us, there is very poor penetration of high quality hotels into tier 2 and 3 cities of India. This uneven growth and the demand–supply gap has roused the interest of many groups who see the hotel sector as a growth area with great potential. The entry of major hotel companies into the country, while not investing directly in projects, will also bring in investors. These groups have already started establishing a presence, entering into joint ventures or management contracts with local developers. This arrangement works well for both partners—for the Indian developer, an early tie up with an international brand provides vital inputs regarding room specifications, global standards and parameters at the planning stage of the project.

Table 14.2 Analysis of star hotels

State	5* Deluxe		5*		4*		3*		2*		1*		Heritage		Total		Ranking		Total Rooms in Segment		
	H	R	H	R	H	R	H	R	H	R	H	R	H	R	H	R	H	R	P	M	B
Andhra Pradesh	8	1802	9	1500	7	891	34	2763	0	0	0	0	0	0	59	7026	5	4	47.00	52.01	0.00
Delhi	15	4094	6	1231	6	558	7	192	4	184	0	0	0	0	47	7506	6	3	70.94	9.99	2.45
Goa	9	1633	10	820	3	434	12	797	1	10	0	0	0	0	43	4254	9	7	57.66	28.94	0.24
Gujarat	1	170	10	1100	4	236	21	1188	1	16	0	0	0	0	47	3463	6	11	36.67	41.12	0.46
Haryana	4	1108	1	285	5	504	28	1486	1	24	0	0	0	0	44	4102	8	8	33.96	48.51	0.59
Karnataka	9	1892	5	738	1	29	11	675	0	0	2	68	0	0	39	4527	10	6	58.10	15.55	1.50
Kerala	8	883	14	1256	76	2160	263	5898	30	469	0	0	0	0	446	11936	1	2	17.92	67.51	3.93
Maharashtra	19	6424	13	1458	15	1762	44	2883	11	393	5	142	0	0	162	14483	2	1	54.42	32.07	3.69
Rajasthan	11	1184	6	662	2	143	12	615	3	67	0	0	19	719	60	3965	4	9	46.56	19.12	1.69
Tamil Nadu	6	1316	3	429	4	465	36	2382	11	334	34	983	0	0	100	5982	3	5	29.17	47.59	22.02
Uttar Pradesh	9	1598	7	1185	2	130	13	677	2	69	0	0	0	0	37	3876	11	10	71.80	20.82	1.78
West Bengal	3	617	3	423	3	340	10	474	2	66	0	0	0	0	32	2482	12	12	41.90	32.80	2.66
INDIA	113	23907	92	11744	134	7969	554	22724	80	1902	41	1193	42	1237	1233	79567					

Source: Adapted from official statistics of MoT (Indian Tourism Statistics 2014, Market Research Division, MoT, GoI).

Case Study: AccorHotels in India

AccorHotels is one of the world's biggest hotel groups. Operating nearly 3,800 hotels and 500,000 rooms in 92 countries, the group employs about 180,000 persons. 1,336 hotels are owned or leased units, through Hotelinvest, an aligned business which is a property owner and investor. The group has 17 brands, in the entire range from luxury to economy. The brand portfolio is extensive: luxury and upscale brands are Sofitel, Pullman, MGallery, Grand Mercure and The Sebel. Midscale brands are Novotel, Suite Novotel, Mercure, Mama Shelter and Adadio, ibis, ibis Styles, ibis budget, hotelF1 and adagio access form the economy brands (Accor Hotels Group, 2015). A total 15% of the inventory is luxury and upscale, 38% midscale and 47% economy and low cost; 37% of the hotels are owned/leased hotels of affiliates, 34% are on management contract and 29% on franchise contract.

AccorHotels has 31 hotels with 5,965 rooms in India at present (2015)—1 Sofitel, 2 Grand Mercure, 10 Novotel, 11 Ibis and 6 Hotel Formule1. There are 1,431 employees in these hotels, which are owned, leased and managed hotels (Accor Hotels Group, n.d.). The group has recently opened two more hotels, a Pullman and a Novotel in New Delhi Aerocity in December 2015, adding 670 rooms to their profile in India. In India, the Accor Hotels group is the only international operator to have invested significantly in the country: a unique strategy that allows AccorHotels to understand the challenges and the opportunities attached with developing hotels in the region. The group also has many projects in the management contract business model, with the physical asset owned by the owner while AccorHotels offers an appropriate brand from its portfolio and also manages day to day operations of the hotel, supported by a best in class distribution network and award winning loyalty programme.

According to the Chairman and Chief Executive Officer Sebastien Bazin, Accor Hotels plans to have around 80 hotels by the end of 2020, and India is a major commitment in terms of development capacity and pool of talent. Out of the new hotels that the company is planning to open, around 10 will be under Ibis brand, 10 will be Novotel while the rest will be a combination of other brands. According to him, India needs greater number of midscale and economy brands and the Accor Hotels group, while continuing with their upscale and luxury brands, sees the economy and midscale segment as one with main growth capacity (*The Economic Times*, 2015).

Discussion Questions

1. From online sources, examine the mid-range portfolio of AccorHotels, and prepare a chart showing the differences between the brands.
2. What may be the reasons behind the optimistic outlook that AccorHotels has about the accommodation industry in India?

The continuing rise in domestic demand is one of the reassuring factors for the industry, as the highly volatile international situation has resulted in uneven demand from foreign visitors. The unstable economic scenario and depressed oil prices may have an adverse impact on demand, particularly from oil dependent markets such as Russia. On the other hand, easing of visa processes is expected to spur more inbound movement.

The Federation of Hotel and Restaurant Associations of India

The Federation of Hotel and Restaurant Associations of India, known by its acronym FHRAI, is the apex body of the four regional associations representing the hotel industry. FHRAI represents the interests of the hotel and restaurant industry and works to create an interface

(Continued ...)

between political leadership and policy-makers and the industry stakeholders. Founded in 1955, FHRAI has 3,876 members comprising of 2,557 hotels, 1,216 restaurants, FHRAI claims to be the voice of the hospitality industry.

One of the demands of the industry is to lower the threshold figure of ₹2 billion set for eligibility under Infrastructure Lending List for hotel projects to ₹500 million so that hotel projects catering to diverse market segments can leverage benefits out of it. FHRAI urges government to permit selected term lending financial institutions to float industry specific tax free bonds, to mobilize funds and deploy these to help asset creation. Rationalization of the tax structure to improve competitiveness is another demand of the sector.

The Hotel Industry Survey commissioned by FHRAI assesses the performance of hotels in major cities, on financial and operating metrics such as occupancy, average room rates and revenue per available room. The survey brings out that India is unable to convert its inherent comparative advantages into a sustainable competitive advantage for our hospitality and tourism sector. It is estimated that the industry needs to add 120,000 rooms in the budget and mid-market category, which envisages a capital investment of ₹500 billion. FHRAI believes that India can be made competitive with neighbouring destinations such as South East Asia by rationalizing the multiple tax structures, improving the visa regime and reviving investor confidence by access to lower cost funding and single window project clearances. Although there has been a steep increase in the number of hotels and quality rooms in India in the last 20 years, the growth has mainly been concentrated in the major cities. In tier 2 and tier 3 cities, there is acute need for quality accommodation.

Hotels in Public Sector

Historically, hotels in many states have been established and operated by public sector enterprises owned and promoted by the government. In the initial phases of tourism development, when private investment was not forthcoming, the state governments set up hotels in locations and destinations of tourist importance. MoT also supported such initiatives, providing grants for developing tourist accommodation such as 'Yatri Nivas' in destinations. Another reason for hotels being established in the public sector was that several buildings belonging to governments were transformed into hotels. These included royal mansions, palaces and lodges, colonial residences and buildings that were taken over by governments from local rulers. Again, several hunting lodges and guest houses built during the British period became the property of the Forest department, which were converted to resorts and other tourist accommodation and operated by state government entities. State governments set up the state TDCs to run such hotels and resorts. Over time, these public sector enterprises have pursued different trajectories, with some TDCs adapting to the modern challenges and commercial requirements and running profitably and professionally, while many properties under some TDCs are in a state of poor maintenance and in dire need of professional management. Some states have created policies enabling the handing over of such properties on lease to private players.

Indian Innovations: Palaces

Mention must be made of the innovations which have been successful in the hotel sector. A distinguishing feature of the Indian hotel industry is the Palace Hotel. In the early days of tourism promotion, India was marketed as an 'exotic' land and the imagery that was popular was of Maharajas, royal lifestyles and riches. Several palaces and royal mansions were converted into hotels and resorts during this period, thanks to alliances formed between erstwhile rulers who owned these properties and hotel companies like the Taj Group of Hotels who had the professional expertise to manage and market such properties. These 'palace hotels' became very popular and commercially successful triggering numerous projects, particularly in Rajasthan which had an abundance of grand mansions and was an early success in tourism.

Case Study: Falaknuma Palace

The Falaknuma (meaning 'mirror in the sky') palace was built by a Hyderabad nobleman in the latter part of the nineteenth century, and at a point of time was the residence of the Nizam of Hyderabad. Later, it was used as a guest house for visiting dignitaries. It lay unused and neglected for many decades, until the Taj group took the baroque palace on lease. The palace has been sensitively restored by experts over a period of ten years and opened as the Taj Falaknuma Palace in 2010. Set in 34 acres of land 2,000 feet above the city of Hyderabad, the palace has gardens set in Rajasthani, Mughal and Japanese styles. The interior revels in opulence, with its large Venetian chandeliers, grand marble staircases, stained glass windows and fountains. The palace is grandly built and furnished, using Italian marble, the best fittings and ornate furnishings. There is a priceless collection of objects d'art, murals, crystal and rare furniture.

The Royal family leased the residence to the Taj group of hotels, resorts and palaces and the family members personally supervised part of the refurbishment. In a beautiful example of adaptive reuse, the crumbling building has been converted into a palace hotel, with 60 luxurious guestrooms categorized into luxury rooms, palace rooms, historical suites, royal suites, Grand royal suites and the Grand Presidential suite. Billiard and smoking rooms, a dining table to seat 101 persons (the world's largest), a library, stables, terraces and a garage filled with vintage cars, the hotel transports the guest into a royal ambience of the Nizams (Taj Falaknuma Palace Hyderabad, n.d.)

The hotel has been recently declared the best Palace hotel in the world by TripAdvisor (2015), based on reviews from discerning travellers (Taj Hotels and Resorts, 2015).

Discussion Questions

1. How do opulent palace hotels like Taj Falaknuma Palace differentiate themselves from modern 5-star deluxe hotels? Attempt to identify what kind of clientele would be interested in such properties.
2. What are the possible ways through which such a hotel can increase revenues?

Heritage Hotels

Building on the success of the palaces that were converted to luxury hotels, several heritage properties notably in Rajasthan opened their doors to visitors. These 'heritage hotels' are palaces, castles or stately mansions of erstwhile royalty or aristocracy. Many of them have been lovingly restored to their past glory, with the addition of comforts and conveniences expected by the modern traveller. Some of these have their owners in residence, which adds a personal touch to the hospitality provided. The conversion of these havelis, lodges and palaces into heritage hotels have several effects, In Neemrana, the restoration work on a dilapidated fort and palace and its conversion into a 'non hotel' created a new destination, bringing new economic activities to the village. Many similar projects have brought tourists into far flung rural areas, creating new circuits and itineraries.

The economic value in transforming the buildings into hotels has resulted in the conservation and preservation of many heritage structures, focusing more attention to the economic value for old buildings and precincts. The prospect of enjoying the luxuries and majesty of a bygone era has added a new dimension to Indian tourism and tempted thousands of visitors.

For the owners, heritage tourism is a charming reminder of bygone period of gracious living and pomp, as well as a lucrative new enterprise.

Kerala entrepreneurs took a different route in heritage tourism. Many wooden mansions were painstakingly dismantled and reassembled in tourist destinations, to be used as accommodation for tourists. These 'transplanted' mansions were carefully restored by master craftsmen skilled in woodwork and metalwork and presented as luxury villas to the traveller. Coconut Lagoon, of the CGH group, was the flag bearer of this endeavour.

Gradually, the 'royal' ambience was supplemented by buildings of some antiquity—colonial era bungalows in hill stations and near wildlife sanctuaries, underused residences such as in Chettinad and residences and guest houses in plantations such as in Coorg and Assam. Other innovations that have provided a unique touch to the hotels in India are the houseboats of Kashmir and Kerala and the 'tree houses' in the Western Ghats.

A mansion in Chettinad

Case Study: Chettinad—Villages of Grand Mansions

In the districts of Sivaganga and Pudukkottai, there is a region known as Chettinad, comprising of many villages and a couple of small towns. The 'Nattukottai Chettiars' hailed from Chettinad, and have left some amazing reminders of their wealth and influence in these villages. In the second half of nineteenth and early-twentieth century, the Chettiars, who belong to a powerful banking and trading community, made enormous fortunes by financing and trading in many businesses spread over Southeast Asia.

At the height of their wealth, many Chettiars built palatial mansions in their villages, bringing material from the countries with which they were commercially connected—teak wood was imported from Burma, satin wood from Ceylon (now Sri Lanka), steel from Great Britain, marble from Italy and Belgium, tiles from Japan, Germany and France, and crystal

(Continued ...)

and chandeliers from Belgium and Italy. Most of the houses are built in traditional style, with art deco elements incorporated.

The buildings typically was built on an east-west axis, as a long series of courtyards, connected to opulent halls and pavilions. Every aspect of the architecture was conceived and made to display the wealth of the owner: from the huge development in plan, to the monumental façade, the height of which was enhanced by adding multiple levels of balustrades and the use of elements such as doubled colonnades and loggias (Chettinad: Village Clusters of the Tamil Merchants, n.d.). The mansions reflect the lifecycle rituals and living traditions of the Chettiar community, with specific spaces for rituals and functions. The elaborate kitchens indicate the culinary traditions of Chettinad.

Heritage Accommodation: Adaptive Reuse

Many of the elaborate houses have been pulled down; however, the villages of Kanadukathan, Pallathur and Kothamangalam still have some outstanding specimens. Some have been converted into accommodation units for tourists. 'Visalam' is a property operated by CGH Earth Group of hotels. The group has sensitively restored a mansion, provided modern conveniences, yet retained the charm and ambience of the building. The hotel has 15 rooms of quiet elegance, restored from the capacious halls of the mansion. A swimming pool has been added. Visitors are encouraged to tour the village, to marvel at the majestic buildings, from the comfort of a bullock cart. Stately villas view with colonial style bungalows and rambling ruins. The markets have silversmiths, stone and wood carvers and jewellers. The hotel celebrates the famous Chettinad cuisine and guests are encouraged to try their hand at making some local dishes (Visalam, n.d.).

Chidambara Vilas, at Ramachandrapuram in Kadiapatti, is another luxury heritage hotel that has opened its doors to visitors. Other heritage properties in the vicinity are Chettinadu Mansion and The Bangala.

Image courtesy: Ministry of Tourism, Government of India.

Discussion Questions

1. Is there a mohalla or precinct in your city/town which has special characteristics that may be of interest to visitors? How can such an area be developed for tourism?
2. Is there a possibility to convert some rooms in a heritage building in the vicinity of such a neighbourhood to accommodate visitors? What interventions are needed to make this idea work?

The Travel and Tour Sector

We have noted that the tourism and hospitality industry is seen as one of the key drivers for growth in the country. In this section, we will examine the travel and tour sector in some detail, understanding its origins, evolution and mode of operations. This dynamic part of the tourism industry plays a key role, marketing the products of the country, creating new products and services and providing logistics and other support.

History

One of the earliest entrants into the sector was Jeena and Co., established in 1900, concentrating on shipping and freight business and later venturing into travel business. During the early fifties, there was virtually no inbound tourism and the firms in the sector were all ticketing agents, selling tickets of Air India, Pan Am, KLM, TWA and BOAC which were the only carriers that operated international flights from Bombay and Calcutta. Travel Corporation of India (TCI), established in 1961, was one of the earliest travel companies and became a major destination management company of India. SITA world travel, later SITA India, was begun in 1963 and played a major role in inbound tourism. Stalwarts like the late Nariman Katgara, Adi Katgara, Gautam Khanna, Jimmy Guzder and Inder Sharma played a stellar role in laying the foundation for a durable travel and tourism industry in India.

With the opening up of the economy, India witnessed a boom in tourism, with new destinations welcoming visitors by the setting up of hotels and tourist facilities. There was a significant improvement in international connectivity also, with a liberalized regime permitting the operation of all major airlines into India. New airports were built and many airports expanded to cater to the new generation airplanes. The domestic airline market was transformed with the advent of private carriers which offered connectivity and convenience. With the essential ingredients of accessibility and accommodation in place, tour operators began offering packages which explored the variety and diversity of Indian destinations. MoT started investing in marketing campaigns and conducted promotional programmes inviting tour operators and media to undertaken familiarization tours. To cater to the increased demand for ground arrangements, many DMCs started operations, entering into operational tie ups with tour operators of Europe. This period also saw the beginning of charter operations to Goa, bringing a sharp increase in tourist arrivals and triggering a rush to construct hotels and resorts.

Travel Agents Association of India and Indian Association of Tour Operators

Travel Agents Association of India

The Travel Agents Association of India (TAAI) was established in 1951 by a group of travel agents, inspired by the success of the ASTA. Over the years, TAAI has grown into a major voice of the travel and tourism industry of India, taking up issues and problems on behalf of the members. TAAI strives to raise the professionalism of its members and help promoting and stimulating the growth of travel and tourism in India. TAAI has around 2500 members, who meet regularly at the chapter or region level and at the annual conference (TAAI, n.d.).

Indian Association of Tour Operators

The Indian Association of Tour Operators (IATO) was formed in 1982 as a forum of tour operators of the country. IATO presently has around 4,000 members and works to articulate issues concerning the tour operators before government and other fora. IATO claims to have members across the travel and tourism sector, including government organizations, transport operators and educational institutions (IATO, n.d.).

Emerging Trends in Destination Management

Conventionally, the product managers (PMs) of the foreign tour operators (FTO) have good knowledge of the destinations and the role of the DMC is limited to providing the components of the itinerary based on the directions of the PM, who is responsible for the creation of the product.

However, PMs are increasingly taking up more and more products under their responsibility and have become less familiar of destinations. A good example is India as a destination. Earlier, itineraries used to be restricted to the Golden Triangle, with a few extensions like Goa. However, there is a full array of different itineraries crisscrossing the country on offer to the inbound customer, making it virtually impossible for a PM of a FTO to be entirely familiar to the destinations and products offered.

The trend is to provide in-depth information to customers, forcing companies to invest in creating and nurturing 'destination specialists'. The DMC is constantly on the lookout for adding new products and integrating new experiences into itineraries. DMCs have taken over this responsibility and have invested in collecting and providing deep knowledge of destinations.

Profile of a Tour Business

In order to gain a broad understanding of the tour business in India, it may be interesting to profile a tour company operating in the country, its structure, business divisions and responsibilities. We will outline the structure and functions of one of the larger companies in the business, to understand in some detail the hierarchies and working methods.

Our Company is primarily into destination management. In other words, its business processes are oriented towards providing services as a DMC. In an earlier chapter, we have familiarized ourselves with how a DMC works; noting that while we loosely use the term tour operator to cover such businesses, a DMC essentially provides support to an inbound tour operator.

Management Level

The Company is headed by a Chief Executive Officer (CEO). The CEO is assisted by the Chief Operating Officers (COO) and the Chief Financial Officer (CFO). Below these top management positions, there are Heads of business divisions and general managers. The above executives collectively comprise the management of the company.

The Heads of Business divisions are responsible for certain markets or business areas such as conferences. Some Heads may look after specific segments and products. For example, our company may have business divisions such as

- UK
- Western Europe
- USA
- Charters
- High Value FIT products
- MICE

The structure of the Management team is described in Figure 14.1.

Professional Level

The professional level comprises of deputy general managers, managers, deputy managers, team leaders, team consultants, team associates, management trainees and executive trainees. Some of these executives are allocated to each business division.

Some work in Operations offices, which look after specific market segments. The staff in operations is involved in handling bookings, preparing itineraries and despatching vouchers.

Service and Operations

Service offices: A large part of the professional staff is located in service offices in the field. The service offices are situated in airports and major destinations, where the bulk of the guests would be arriving, visiting or staying.

Airport transfers: One of the most important operating points for a DMC operation is the port of entry, usually the International airport. As a big majority of guests arrive at the Delhi or Mumbai international airports, all DMC's have a substantial deployment of field executives and supervisors aimed at airport operations. The airport representatives work shifts and ensure that there is the presence of the company 24/7 at the airport. They are key members of the logistics team and are involved in 'meet and greet' at the airport and organizing transportation arrangements.

(Continued ...)

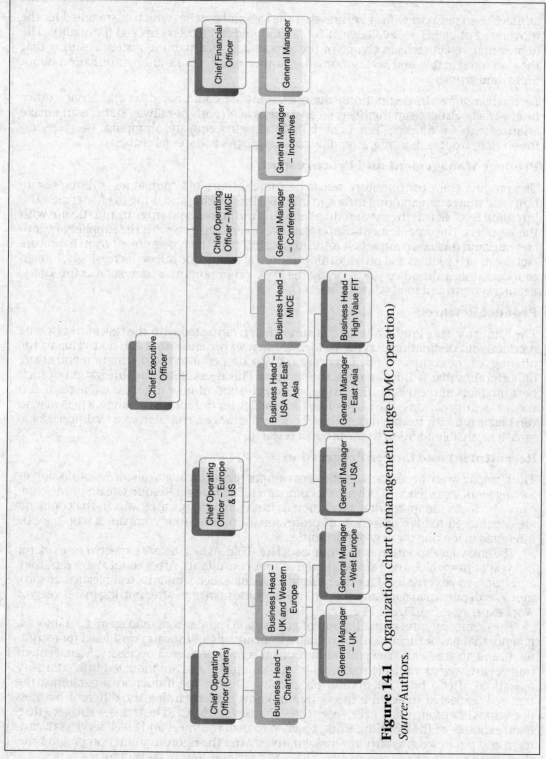

Figure 14.1 Organization chart of management (large DMC operation)

Source: Authors.

(Continued ...)

Officers: The Transport Officer ensures that the cars and coaches which are required for the movement of guests are available at the airport and have been checked for quality. The Representative Officer is in charge of the airport staff, maintaining rosters, ensuring that they are presentable and well groomed. Another officer looks after information about flights and arrivals.

Destination offices: In destinations, the operations are coordinated by the Service office heads. The Logistics team members receive guests at airports or railway stations and make arrangements for transfers, hotel check in, local sightseeing and shopping. They are also involved in trouble shooting, attending to emergencies and special requests.

Product Management and Procurement

The product team continuously researches hotels, transport companies, airlines, restaurants and museums exploring means to improve the offering and bring in efficiencies. The intention is to identifying new products entering the market and entering into tie-ups with the suppliers. The procurement team then takes over, connects with the suppliers, negotiates rates and finalizes contracts. It is the responsibility of the procurement team to prepare fact sheets on products and provide information on health and safety. Increasingly, foreign tour operators insist on certification by the DMC on important aspects such as fire safety, heating systems and food safety issues.

Product Research

The company has a Product Research team which is entrusted with the task of researching products and destinations, trying to identify new experiences that can add value to the offerings of the company. The intention is to go 'deeper' into the destination and create opportunities that will make itineraries unique. This necessitates the integration of such new products into existing itineraries, or even creation of new itineraries. The team also tries to identify persons who can deliver the product, for instance, in Varanasi, a person who can organize a visit to an old neighbourhood and arrange a recital from a traditional 'gharana' is a valuable addition to the product research.

Recruitment and Career Progression

The Company recruits executives through campus recruitment and also hires professionals having work experience in other tour companies. The Human Resource team of the company also looks for appropriate professionals from job portals. Employers in the company are encouraged to give references of professionals in other tour companies who may be interested in looking for new opportunities.

The entry level position is the tour associate. Tour Associates are expected to work for 2–3 years, after which they are promoted as tour consultants. After about two years, they are eligible to be considered for the position of team leader. Similarly, team leaders are promoted as deputy managers, and they in turn become managers after putting in 2–3 years of work experience (see Figure 14.2).

The Company hires a small group of graduate/PG students as management trainees, a practice that has begun recently. Graduates from any disciplines are considered for recruitment, and an academic background in tourism is not considered necessary. Management trainees are seen as valuable resources by the company, and are inducted into company operations after a brief orientation programme. During the induction programme, the trainee is expected to acquire the skills and knowledge regarding the different business operations like group tours, FIT's, incentives, charters and MICE. The trainees also get a first-hand exposure of the frontline work, assigned to man the 'meet and greet' services department and put in work as airport representatives. After the rigorous induction programme, the trainee is then placed as tour associate, and continues as tour consultant.

(Continued ...)

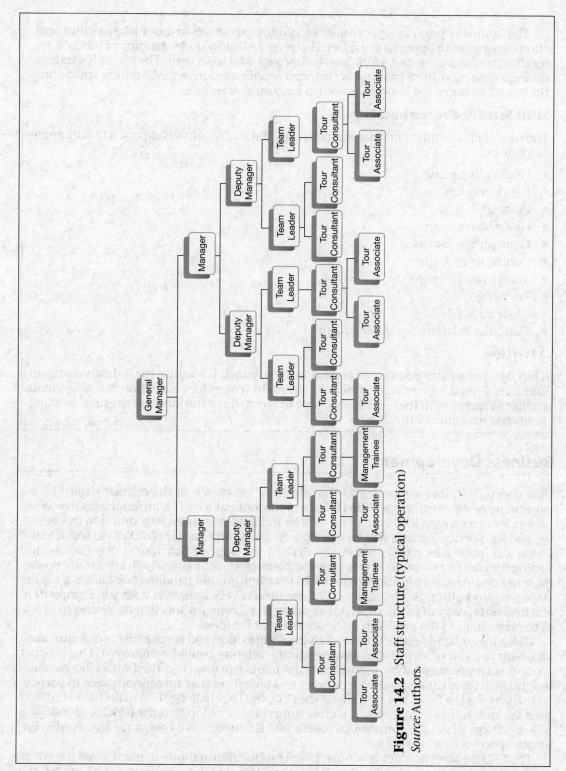

Figure 14.2 Staff structure (typical operation)

Source: Authors.

(Continued ...)

The Company provides opportunities to young executives to move laterally into operations whenever an opportunity arises. This requires a clear understanding of business segregation, business processes, workflow, technology and tools used. The executive trainees undergo nine months of training as customer service executive (CSE), during which time the executive learns the basic skills needed for customer service.

Skill Sets for Professionals

The basic skill sets and functional competencies that an executive is expected to acquire are as follows:

- Product Knowledge
- File Operations
- Costing
- Guide Management
- Contracting—Hotels
- Contracting—Airlines
- Tariff Management
- Branding
- Trade Shows
- Customer Relationship Management

Attrition

The DMC has an attrition rate of around 15-20%, which is roughly the industry standard and hires several new recruits annually. The main reason for resignation is a desire for a change in career, with the employee unable to reconcile to the long and irregular working hours and hardships of the field.

Business Development

How does a DMC increase business? The 'pie' must get bigger, or the company must grab a larger share of the existing 'pie'. The DMC is on the lookout for FTOs introducing a new destination; for instance, an FTO who plans to offer Indian destinations in addition to their existing portfolio of destinations will be seeking a credible and experienced DMC in India. Many DMCs will make sales pitches before the FTO, in the hope of concluding negotiations and signing the contract with the FTO to provide ground services. FTOs, which are already operating into a destination, may also be convinced to switch ground handling companies, if a more attractive proposition is offered. The DMC business is very dynamic, with stiff competition and frequent change of partners. SITA is a leading DMC, bringing together the strengths of one of the early Indian DMCs with an international tour business.

DMCs invest considerable time in studying competition and conducting competitor analysis, with the aim of identifying areas where the offering could be improved. This product analysis is complemented by inputs from the market manager in the DMC, who provides insights into the attitudes, preferences, tastes and prejudices that are generally seen in particular markets. For the DMC, the customer is the FTO, and the challenge is to make the FTO divert their business from a competitor. It is clear from this discussion that the DMC is essentially a B2B operation, where the commercial transaction is between two companies involved in different aspects of tour operation.

The FTO prepares product brochures based on the information—in many cases the entire text—prepared and provided by the DMCs. For FTOs which operate on a B2C model, the brochure is launched with considerable investment in publicity and marketing. For B2B operations, the FTO sends the brochures to retail sellers. Many FTOs provide training programs to retailers, improving their knowledge about destinations and itineraries. In some cases, the DMC is required to assist the FTO marketing programs by travelling with the sales team in educating agents on destinations.

Looking to the Future

The inbound tour business is undergoing a great transformation. Till the turn of the twentieth century, 70% of the inbound business was GIT, where sales were made by retail agents from brochures supplied by tour operators. Around 30% business was FIT, concentrating on tailor made tours. Tour operators agree that this ratio has been reversed, with a majority of the present business coming from independent travellers visiting destinations on tailor-made itineraries. Group tours based on brochures have shrunk considerably.

Earlier, tourists visiting India preferred the comfort and assurance of travelling in escorted groups with no 'loose ends'. Owing to the reputation of India being a 'difficult' destination, tourists wanted the reassurance that logistics and arrangements were being looked after by competent companies. Information about destinations was comparatively difficult to find, and it was virtually impossible to make own arrangements due to the difficulties in communication.

The inclination of tourists to travel at their own pace to destinations of their choice has developed over time. One of the major reasons for this is the ready access to information about destinations and the spread of the Internet which brought the world of traveller reviews, choice of destinations and the comfort of personal research within the reach of everyone interested in travel. Many travellers have an opportunity to arrive at a more informed and nuanced view of destinations and to form their own conclusions, rather than be controlled by the often superficial information provided by brochures.

In the present 'information' ecosystem, tour operators have started providing destination information in depth, through books with attractive photographs, highlighting iconic attractions. FTOs also provide itineraries in an outline or skeletal form, enabling the visitor to build on the basic itinerary by choosing accommodation, excursions and visits of their own choice. This fulfils the aspiration of the visitor to prepare an itinerary of her own choice, instead of choosing a readymade one. At the same time, the presence of a tour operator offers her the comfort and assurance of quality service.

The trend for the future is that group tours will dwindle to an insignificant part of the inbound business. In this highly dynamic environment, it is clear that DMCs will play a very different role, focusing on depth and spread of knowledge of destinations. This calls for higher quality manpower in the companies, very different from the 'street smart' operating personnel involved in logistics at present.

Domestic Tourism

The most significant development that has happened in recent years in the Indian tourism sector is the burgeoning growth in the number of domestic tourists. Although the statistics released by the MoT cannot be held to be entirely accurate, the sheer numbers of domestic tourist visits as given in the statistics go to show that domestic tourism is far more important for the tourism sector of the country than inbound tourism. This necessitates a radical rethinking of the entire tourism paradigm. For the last 40 years, service providers, particularly tour operators, have been geared to providing ground services to the inbound visitor. Product development, packaging, competitive pricing and sales were not given very high priority owing to the fact that the Indian operators were involved in the tourism process as a DMC, offering destination based ground services, rather than as a full-fledged tour operator. However, in recent years, many DMCs have also started direct tour business, attempting to sell packages directly to potential visitors online, or through sales offices.

The rapid rise in domestic tourists, coupled with the increasing spending power of the middle class, has given rise to a whole new market, which is just about beginning to discover its feet. Several factors have contributed to this explosion in domestic tourism. In a liberalized environment, millions of Indians have benefited from increased affluence and find themselves with more disposable incomes. Access to television and the Internet have provided this middle-class aspirations and lifestyle choices, with leisure travel becoming an accepted expenditure in the family budget. Infrastructure has improved radically. Better abroad and rail connections and faster trains and public transport have shortened distances between source markets and destinations. An array of airlines offering discounted tickets and attractive packages to remote corners of the country also contributed to the large number of tourists who choose to fly. Our case study profile Intersight Tours and Travels, a company that specialized in domestic tour operations as its mainstay and which has put in place a distribution network very similar to an international tour operation, but within the country.

Case Study: Intersight Tours and Travels—Domestic Tourism Specialist

In the mid-nineties, Kerala was slowly getting to be known as a destination that offered experiences other than the Kovalam beach. Prominent Indian Destination Management companies, centred in Delhi and focusing on the Golden Triangle, were looking for partners to offer services in South India, in order to provide ground services to European tour operators, who were interested in expanding the product offering. Kerala based tour operators started operations, offering local transportation arrangements to their principals in the North.

In 1995, Intersight Tours and Travels began operations, promoting Kerala as their specialized product. From his experience, Abraham George, who founded the company, realized that the inbound market was dominated by bigger players with more resources and networks and decided to move into a new market, which was hitherto unexplored and untested. Intersight decided to concentrate on marketing Kerala to the Indian domestic tourist market, concentrating on Mumbai and Delhi. Intersight worked meticulously in creating products in different price points, adapted to Indian customers, particularly the mid segment customers. In doing so, the company virtually created a new destination in the minds of middle class travellers.

In 2000, Intersight introduced Rail Tourism, becoming one of the first operators to tie up with the Railways to provide transportation on the rail network exclusively for its customers. They chartered rail coaches which brought in their customers to Kerala from Mumbai, Ahmedabad and Hyderabad. They were supported by Kerala Tourism, which understood the potential of this innovative operation. The Rail Tourism product brought in large numbers of middle class tourists to Kerala, where the company provided high quality services based on their relationship with hotels and local service providers. With the advent of 'no frills' carriers, their packages became even more popular.

Expanding to new markets in Gujarat and north Indian states, Intersight embarked on an exercise to create partnerships with travel agents spread across India. These agents sold the Kerala packages created by Intersight to their clients, depending on local marketing efforts and personal contacts. Intersight was careful to maintain this relationship, depending entirely on the travel agent route to bring business and protecting the commissions of the agents. Currently, Intersight has a continuing and mutually beneficial partnership with about 2,000 agents in tier 2 and tier 3 cities. They could build confidence among the agents

(Continued ...)

based on their local knowledge and expertise on Kerala and educate them on the destination and its potentials. Their 200 employees and 14 sales offices provide support to the agents and serve as a link between them and the ground handling services provided by the company.

The operations of Intersight have grown to handling almost 100,000 clients every year. With a turnover of ₹1 billion and a network of 500 hotels and suppliers, Intersight has created a strong brand based on the strengths of domestic tourism in the Indian market. Lately, the company has expanded operations, offering holidays to all major Indian destinations.

Discussion Questions

1. What are the advantages and disadvantages of including rail transport as part of tourism products?
2. Why is it that certain destinations in India have become very popular in the Indian market, while some others struggle to find visitors?

Domestic tourists also display specific segmentations akin to developed markets. There is a huge demand for weekend getaways and short holidays for the residents of metropolitan cities. The MICE market within the country is getting stronger by the day, with even smaller companies offering incentives to distributors and business associates. More conferences and business meetings are being organized. Corporate travel has become sustained and shows a healthy growth year on year. Multi-destination leisure holidays lasting several days have become quite common for the domestic visitor.

There are several advantages that domestic tourism offers as compared to inbound tourism. Domestic tourism is more durable, in that the tourist is less averse to changing holiday plans in the event of an unforeseen incident. The domestic visitor has access to more accurate information regarding the law and order situations and is not influenced by alarmist news and rumours. Domestic tourism is immune to a large extent to foreign exchange fluctuations and international upheavals. More and more domestic tourists are travelling to attend family functions and to visit friends and relations, activities which are not dependent on extraneous factors. Variety, affordability and connectivity will determine the nature of domestic tourism. Hammock Holidays is a good example of a tour operator catering to the evolving requirements of the young corporate holidaymaker.

Case Study: Hammock Holidays—Shaping Bengaluru's Leisure Market

Hammock Holidays has helped shape the leisure markets for young professionals, especially in Bengaluru and in the process, contributed to the development of many distinctive holiday products such as homestays, farm holidays, spiritual journeys and authentic experiences.

Started in 1996, before the Internet and Google became so prevalent, Hammock Holidays offered a shift in focus from the existing pattern of travelling to just places of historical interest, pilgrimage tours or the standard foreign tours with the motto 'India for Indians'. To serve this end, Hammock identified unique and special holiday options and experiences, often building customized holiday programmes for Bengaluru's growing bands of young professionals. The programmes were structured to give a *'total travel experience'* by going to the extent of giving route maps specifying petrol bunk locations, bathroom stops, restaurants, road conditions and even interesting points on the way for a photograph or a beautiful view.

(Continued ...)

Customized travel plans also encouraged the youth to self-drive to locations within a 5–7 hour driving distance from Bengaluru. Soon other agents were replicating the format and this led to a huge surge in the weekend traffic out of Bengaluru. But, the youth market is a demanding tribe and quite well-informed and organized too; you have to give them something new every time.

Hammock scouted for new destinations and supported opening up these to the customer. One such was the opening up of Wayanad in Kerala to the Bengaluru travellers. Hammock pro-actively worked with the few resorts which started in Vythiri and Kalpetta and Lakkidi in Wayanad right from the requirements in the room layout to pricing and marketing. Today Wayanad is a much loved get-away for Bengalureans.

Coorg, about 5-hours drive from Bengaluru, is a case in point with its special cuisine, customs and traditions very different from the rest of Karnataka. Despite the great beauty of the place and the unmatched hospitality of its people, Coorg did not have any quality hotels. Coorg had many traditional homes which had become empty nests as children left the old lifestyle for cities, leaving behind a rich tradition and culture. Hammock stepped in to support the identification, development and growth of homestays not merely by providing them with guests, but by educating the guests about the culture and heritage of Coorg. The first ever homestay in Coorg—Alath Cad Estate Bungalow started by Mrs and Mr Muddaiah were initiated and supported by Hammock Holidays. This has now practically become a resort with 11 rooms!

Along with rising disposable incomes of the young, their tendency was to opt for an overseas holiday. Hammock Holidays converted a large number of their clients who wanted the easily available Far East and Middle East travel options (Dubai, Singapore and Bangkok being the most favoured), to try out the extraordinary Indian destinations as against the overseas ones.

In the early 1990s, when the IT industry used to offer cash or material things as incentives, Hammock brought in the shift of offering the employee a holiday which would in turn help to rejuvenate and allow the person to spend quality time with loved ones. This was welcomed by many corporates. The biggest company Hammock works with in this fashion is Wipro Technologies and the business has been ongoing since 2000.

Despite information on destinations being readily available, Hammock still caters to a large number of holiday makers who prefer to work with a known face and who are happy to pay a service fee for the authentic and reliable travel advice offered by the company.

Image courtesy: Cox & Kings.

Discussion Questions

1. What are the possible reasons why customers prefer to work with an 'offline' tour company rather than buy tourism products online? Do you think this is a sustainable model?
2. Make a list of some destinations that can be marketed as weekend 'getaways' from your city.

More and more Indians are taking advantage of the amazing cultural and geographical variety that the Indian subcontinent has, providing holidays that are very much like holidays in a foreign land. Indians are increasingly travelling long distances to explore the country, enriching themselves with cross-cultural interaction and spreading the benefit of tourism to the far corners of the country.

Many states have realized the economic importance of domestic tourism and have framed specific strategies to attract the domestic visitor. Marketing campaigns targeting specific segments of the domestic are also being deployed by companies. The 'Bharat Dekho' campaign of Cox and Kings Ltd (CKL) is an example of a sustained marketing campaign offering products exclusively designed for the domestic visitor.

Bharat Dekho Ad of Cox & Kings

(Continued ...)

Case Study: Cox and Kings Ltd

CKL is the longest established travel company in the world, with its beginnings in 1758. Headquartered in India, it is the leading holidays and education travel group that operates in 26 countries across four continents. In India, CKL has 168 offices located across the country.

A premium brand in all travel-related services, the business can be broadly categorized as leisure travel, corporate travel, education and activity travel, MICE, trade fairs, visa processing and foreign exchange.

CKL is among the largest travel-related services players, with a wide range of specialist options. Innovative packaging, pricing and marketing have been the hallmarks of its success over the years. In India, the company has robust domestic business under the brand name 'Bharat Dekho' and is a leading MICE operator out of India. CKL is among the major providers of foreign exchange in the country. The outbound tours are segregated into escorted tours (Duniya Dekho), customized tours (Flexihols), unique and luxurious travel (luxury escapades) and NRI business.

In 1758, the company was appointed as general agents to the Regiment of Foot Guards in India. By 1878, CKL was an agent for most British regiments posted overseas. The Royal Navy was next and in 1912, the Royal Air Force came under its wings. CKL employs over 5,000 trained professionals. Headquartered in Mumbai, with 12 sales offices in India and six international offices, the company has appointed over 150 franchisees across 20 states covering 70 cities. The company's extensive network of 600 GSA's and PSA's, covering all major towns and cities of India, enhances its reach.

CKL has subsidiaries in the UK, Japan, Australia, New Zealand, UAE, USA, Singapore, Hong Kong, Greece and Germany and representative offices in seven countries. In 2011, CKL acquired Holidaybreak, an education and activity travel group that has more than 15 long established and widely recognized brands. Holidaybreak provides educational and activity trips for schoolchildren, worldwide adventure holidays, short breaks in the UK and Europe and mobile home and camping holidays throughout Europe. The company also owns Tempo Holidays, Australia; East India Travel Company, North America; ETN, UK; MyPlanet Australia and Bentours International, Australia.

CKL is among the first travel organizations to brand domestic holidays. Under the brand 'Bharat Dekho', several products that range from religious and pilgrimage tours, educational tours, weekend breaks, activity holidays, spa holidays, budget holidays, summer and beach retreats, train vacations, coaching and touring holidays are marketed.

The Company provides destination management services in inbound tour operators. Specialized services to foreign participants visiting India for international meetings, conferences, incentives and exhibitions are also provided. The company is also involved in ground related services to international cruise companies touching Indian shores.

Under the flagship 'Duniya Dekho' brand are escorted tours designed and marketed by the company to Indian travellers who prefer to travel in groups. These escorted group tours cover many important destinations in Europe, Australia, New Zealand, USA, Middle East, South Africa and Mauritius and are designed for the 'value traveller'. The brand has also launched a series of premium group holidays, called 'luxury escapades', featuring the finest luxury hotels and the most exclusive entertainment avenues of the world.

'FlexiHol' is a brand that is targeted at the FIT market. After identifying the interest of the traveller, the company suggests destinations and customizes the holiday itinerary.

Image courtesy: Cox & Kings.

Discussion Questions

1. Prepare a paper on the destinations covered by Bharat Dekho campaign and examine any one itinerary in depth to understand the tour programme.

2. Based on the above discussion, prepare a tour product that does not find a place in the campaign. Prepare a pitch on the product, indicating its advantages.

Although a large number of domestic tourists prefer to stay in budget accommodation, hotels at the top end are reporting that the domestic visitor enjoys luxury just as much as a foreign visitor and is willing to pay for it. It is clear that the vast middle class of the country has begun to accept leisure travel as a desirable lifestyle choice. What this means for the tourism sector is the opening up of a market that is far bigger than the present markets. This disruptive development has the potential to contribute to the intensive development of tourism in India, the contours of which are only emerging in the last decade. If connectivity, particularly by road, can be improved significantly, this will directly benefit the movement of domestic tourists and bring in social economic benefits to destinations. Many tourism products and destinations may have to be repackaged and offered from a different perspective to the domestic visitor.

MICE Tourism in India

India's share of the global MICE market is miniscule, ranking 36th in the world. India has a market share of below 1% of the world convention market. It is estimated that the business generates about 50 billion annually.

India Convention Promotion Bureau (ICPB) is an industry-led organization established to promote India as a preferred MICE destination. ICPB undertakes a continuing programme of creating awareness, marketing programmes and advisory functions to develop MICE market in the country. ICPB helps event planners and organizations during the bidding process by providing information and support services, guidance for obtaining government incentives and participating in road shows and marketing visits.

Although most cities may have some conferencing facilities, it has to be understood that there are few facilities that can accommodate very large international conventions and exhibitions. New Delhi is by far the most preferred destination for meetings and conventions. The Indira Gandhi airport is connected with major international capital cities and with most important national cities. With three world heritage sites and multifarious attractions, it has several sightseeing and shopping options to offer. The main convention venues are Pragati Maidan, the NSIC complex, Vigyan Bhawan for government events and India Expo Centre, Noida. The city has a capacity of over 10,000 rooms in the upper categories and several smaller size convention centres and meeting halls.

Mumbai has the busiest international airport in the country, with extensive international connections. There are several world class convention venues and a plethora of high quality hotels and banqueting venues.

Recently, Hyderabad with Hyderabad International Trade Expo (HITEX) and Hyderabad International Convention Centre and Jaipur with Jaipur Exhibition and Convention Centre (JECC) have become popular venues for conferences and exhibitions because of the good infrastructure, availability of world class accommodation and the attractiveness of the cities as tourist destinations.

India is yet to develop a comprehensive ecosystem conducive to the convention business. The important ingredients are excellent connectivity, well developed public transport network, safe, clean and secure environment, easy availability of a range of hotels rooms and professional services. Our public transport systems are not well developed and where present, crowded and perceived as unsafe. Seamless connectivity between airports to city centres is still not built. The bidding and marketing campaigns need to be supported by government agencies such as diplomatic missions, tourism boards and ICPB. A multiplicity of taxes and high prices may make our destinations less competitive when compared to Colombo, Bangkok or Kuala Lumpur.

The India Outbound Travel Market

The Indian outbound travel market is estimated to be growing at an average annual rate of around 16% from 2004 (UNWTO, 2009). According to the UNWTO, the Indian outbound tourists will grow to about 50 million by the year 2020. Another study indicated that the expenditure by Indians while travelling abroad will be over US$ 28 billion by the same time.

Trends in Outbound Travel

According to the MoT, the number of Indians travelling outside its boundaries rose from 1.94 million in 1991 to 18.33 million in 2014, with a CAGR of 10.25%. As can be seen from the table, the increase has been steady for the entire period, with a dip around 2011–12 perhaps because of the economic slowdown. The number of outbound Indians in 2014 registered a growth of 10.3% over 2013 (see Tables 14.3 and 14.4).

The Bureau of Immigration, GoI, collects figures for outbound travel by Indians, from travellers at the time of departure. The official figures released by MoT provide the data of destinations visited by outbound Indians. A large number of Indians travel abroad for employment, particularly to countries in West Asia such as Saudi Arabia, Kuwait and the UAE. The table has a list of the top 15 destinations to which Indians travelled during 2008–12. (Data on prominent destinations such as France, Spain and Germany were not available in the report of the Ministry and therefore do not find a place in the list. Countries from West Asia have been eliminated from this list.)

It is clear that Indians are choosing to travel to foreign destinations in the vicinity, perhaps because of low airfares, attractive packages and familiarity. Thailand has seen amazing growth over the last five years, which appears to be stabilising. Singapore, the perennial favourite for Indians, seems to have lost ground, but still attracts more than 933,000 Indian visitors annually. Malaysia remains popular with Indians and is growing at a healthy level. Sri Lanka and Nepal shows very high growth in recent years, perhaps because both countries are on a path

Table 14.3 Trends in outbound travel

Year	Number	Percentage Growth
2005	7,184,501	15.6
2006	8,339,614	16.1
2007	9,783,232	17.3
2008	10,867,999	11.1
2009	11,066,072	1.8
2010	12,988,001	17.4
2011	13,994,002	7.7
2012	14,924,755	6.7
2013	16,626,316	11.4
2014	18,332,319	10.3

Source: India Tourism Statistics, MoT, 2014.

Table 14.4 Top outbound destinations

Rank	Country	2008	2009	2010	2011	2012	2013	Percentage Growth (2013 over 2012)
1	Thailand	497,022	596,529	746,214	891,748	985,883	1,028,414	4.31
2	Singapore	778,303	725,624	828,994	868,991	894,993	933,553	4.31
3	USA	598,971	549,474	650,935	663,465	724,433	859,156	18.60
4	China	436,625	448,942	549,321	606,474	610,914	676,682	10.77
5	Malaysia	550,738	589,838	690,849	693,056	691,271	650,989	-5.83
6	Hong Kong	350,674	366,646	530,910	498,063	414,158	434,648	4.95
7	UK	359,237	272,754	371,000	356,000	339,400	375,000	10.49
8	Indonesia	155,391	156,545	159,373	181,791	196,983	231,266	17.40
9	Switzerland	132,107	136,322	165,999	200,624	217,863	212,960	-2.25
10	Sri Lanka	85,238	83,634	126,882	171,374	176,340	208,795	18.40
11	Italy	135,517	139,094	182,552	188,408	251,361	199,253	-20.73
12	Nepal	84,073	91,994	108,077	147,037	165,139	180,974	9.59
13	Australia	116,001	124,888	138,705	148,191	159,279	168,800	5.98
14	Macau	82,369	107,513	169,096	169,660	150,825	160,019	6.10
15	Canada	110,890	107,959	127,619	139,213	146,652	147,099	0.30

Source: Indian Tourism Statistics 2014, Market Research Division, MoT, GoI.

of recovery after difficult times, when tourism was severely affected. (The data is up to 2012 and therefore does not reflect the impact of the 2015 earthquake in Nepal).

Among the Western countries, the USA continues to dominate, although this figure may include some persons travelling to take up employment in that country. In Europe, the UK and Switzerland continue to be attractive to Indians, followed by Italy.

Dubai: The Most Popular Destination

According to the figures of Dubai's Department of Tourism and Commerce Marketing (Dubai Tourism), India is the top international source market for Dubai, with over 1.6 million visitors to the emirate. With a year on year growth of 26%, India was the second fastest growing source market for Dubai Tourism in 2015 (*The Economic Times*, 2016).

China is growing at a healthy 10.77%. Hong Kong and Macau are also recording a good number of Indian arrivals, indicating the growth in the segments of travellers visiting destinations offering incentives and entertainment options such as casinos.

The number of Indians holding passports is around 50 million which is expected to double by 2020. Because of the vastness of the country, the market is also complex and varied. The Indian travel trade estimates that about 65% of outbound travel is from the markets of Western and Northern India. South India accounts for 25% of the market and the balance is from the East. A total of 40% of all visits abroad are conducted for business, while VFR and leisure account for 20% each of the total number.

According to the industry, the main factors that influence the selection of a holiday destination among Indians are:

- Safety and security
- Variety of things to see and do
- Overall image of holiday destination
- Good tourist facilities and infrastructure
- Ease of obtaining visas

Reasons for Increase in Outbound Travel

India is seen as a major outbound market. The reasons are discussed below:

- **Large population:** emerging middle class of approximately 350 million, growing annually by 50 million
- **Expanding economy:** India is the third largest economy in the world on the basis of purchasing power parity and the 10th largest on the basis of nominal GDP (Economic Outlook, International Monetary Fund, 2014). The Indian economy is doing well despite global uncertainties. There are more people working, salaries are higher and most international brands across categories are available to the Indian consumer.
- **Liberalizing travel and aviation environment:** liberalization of the civil aviation policy regime and the 'open skies' approach has brought in more air connections to major destinations of the world.
- **Changing lifestyles:** India is witnessing a change in the lifestyles and buying patterns of consumers because of increased disposable incomes, attractive discounts and offers, availability of loans, credit cards, rising aspiration levels, increased literacy and brand consciousness.
- **'Value for money' choices:** At times, it is costlier to holiday within India than to take a short break at an international destination. Low-cost domestic and international airlines have brought international travel closer to the average Indian holiday maker.
- **Creating new reasons for travel:** Indian weddings abroad, exploring destinations featured in Bollywood hit movies and family reunions on foreign shores are some of the new reasons for Indians to travel abroad. The exposure and awareness due to traditional media, social media, the workplace, friends and family has ignited the desire to travel abroad.

Destination Marketing in India

Advent of NTOs in India from many major and unique destinations, the offers and incentives, timely partnerships with airlines—all have contributed to the increase in outbound traffic. NTOs are attracting Bollywood film producers and TV program producers to shoot in their country to create mass awareness.

Outlook for the Outbound Market

The Indian travel market is already showing signs of 'maturing', with higher levels of repeat travel and an interest in high-quality niche destinations. As superficial sightseeing metamorphoses into in-depth exploration and experience, Indians will spend more time and money in each destination. Indians are increasingly experimental, holidaying to off-beat destinations. There will be a shift from seeing the sights to experiencing the destinations. Cruise holidays will gain popularity, particularly with the older segment. Within the leisure category, new motives for travel are being added day by day. Special occasion travel—for honeymoon, wedding anniversaries, birthdays, family reunions, get-together of batch-mates—is all set to boom. Educational tours to destinations are on the increase. Business travellers are increasingly adding a leisure component to their business trips. Youth in urban centres with disposable incomes are increasingly teaming up to travel. Though multi-destination trips seem to be the norm, the habit of slow, immersive travel will see an increase, with travellers opting for single destination trips that are experience-oriented. The 'one main holiday a year' will be supplemented with weekend breaks to short-haul destinations.

Breaking a long-haul flight by visiting the hub city of the international airline is an increasing trend. Gulf carriers are most preferred for their excellent connectivity, cost-effectiveness, quality service, brand recall and young carriers with new fleets and feature-rich aircrafts. An increasing number of FITs and luxury travellers will contribute to the revenues of the destination, especially for unique experiences and quality service.

Shopping is quite popular among Indians; and interestingly, many of them are shifting from cheap goods to high-value branded goods. Indians are comfortable with the idea of train travel while on holiday and see this as an opportunity to understand the lay of the land. Growth of segments like the young, independent traveller and young couples indicate the increasing youth and FIT market. Multi-generational travel is increasing and older retirees are travelling more independently. Travel by female groups and DINKS (Double Income No Kids) is on the rise.

The New Attitude to Travel

The Indian youth traveller wants to discover offbeat destinations and activities. Short-haul destinations with easy visa access and out of the box, activity-oriented short duration packages will attract a large number of takers. There is a shift in the Indian traveller mindset—in his quest for new experiences, he is now willing to move out of his comfort zone and even pay more—this is especially true of youth and FITs.

The Evolving Role of the Tour Operator

Indians are becoming savvier with using the Internet. Though online bookings are done by Indian travellers, traditional travel agents continue to play an important role thanks to their expertise in handling visas, creating and managing multi-sector itineraries, the presence of a support team at holiday destinations and efficient crisis management. Many travellers continue to depend on one to one discussions with an agent before committing on an expensive holiday.

OTA fares have strengthened the price-sensitive Indian traveller's bargaining power with traditional agents. OTAs and traditional agents are now attempting to imbibe the strong qualities of each other—OTAs have started franchisee networks and leading traditional agents have started online portals. This mix, if handled effectively, could augur well for both the trade and the traveller.

Conclusion

We have taken a comprehensive look at the main sectors in the Indian tourism business. The hospitality and tourism sectors are seen as key drivers of growth, contributing to the gross domestic product and providing employment. With its potential, the sector will witness robust growth, setting up more businesses, bringing foreign investment and stimulating domestic entrepreneurship. The hotel sector is set to witness interesting times, with the entry of transnational companies and the expansion of quality hotels in tier 2 and tier 3 cities. Technology is set to play a disruptive role in hospitality and tour sectors, with more customers shifting to online travel agents and aggregators for their requirements.

Review Questions

1. Give an account of the latest trends in accommodation sector in India.
2. What are the major features of India outbound tourism?
3. Examine the reason for the growth of outbound tourism market in India.
4. Write short notes on:
   • MICE tourism in India
   • Indian innovations in accommodation
   • Emerging trends in destination management.

Activities

1. Conduct a study of the hotels in a district. How many of them are approved or classified? If the number is low, discuss the possible reasons why they do not prefer to be classified.
2. Survey 10 travel agencies/tour operators in your state and find out top-10 outbound destinations preferred by tourists.
3. Visiting their websites, make a profile of two online travel agents based out of India. How are their products different from conventional agencies?

References

Web Resources

Accor Hotels Group. 2015. 'Accor Hotels Overview'. Available at: http://www.accorhotels-group.com/fileadmin/user_upload/Contenus_Accor/Franchise_Management/Documents_utiles/General_information/MAJ_2015/panorama_uk.pdf (accessed on 24 December 2016).

Accor Hotels. n.d. 'Accor Hotels Worldwide: India'. Available at: http://www.accorhotels-group.com/en/group/accorhotels-worldwide.html#/area:AS/country:IND/ (accessed on 24 December 2016).

Chettinad: Village Clusters of the Tamil Merchants. (n.d.). UNESCO. Available at: http://whc.unesco.org/fr/listesindicatives/5920/ (accessed on 24 December 2016).

HRH Group of Hotels. n.d. Available at: http://www.hrhhotels.com/Index.aspx (accessed on 24 December 2016).

IATO. n.d. 'IATO: Profile, History and Objective'. Indian Association of Tour Operators. Available at: http://iato.in/WhyIATO.aspx (accessed on 24 December 2016).

Khanna, A., R. Thapar, and T. Das. 2015. 'FHRAI Indian Hotel Industry Survey 2013–14'. HVS. Available at: http://www.hvs.com/article/7197/fhrai-indian-hotel-industry-survey-2013-2014/ (accessed on 24 December 2016).

Kuoni Destination Management. 2016. Available at: http://www.kuoni-meetings-events.com/#.VqchV1N96Rs (accessed on 24 December 2016).

SITA. n.d. 'Corporate Profile'. SITA. Available at: http://sita.in/world-of-sita/corporate-profile (accessed on 4 April 2016).

TAAI. n.d. 'A Brief history of TAAI and Its Growth'. Travel Agents Association of India. Available at: http://www.travelagentsofindia.com/history.php (accessed on 24 December 2016).

Taj Falaknuma Palace Hyderabad. n.d. Available at: https://taj.tajhotels.com/en-in/taj-falaknuma-palace-hyderabad/signature-experiences/ (accessed on 14 March 2016).

Taj Hotels and Resorts. 2015. 'Taj Falaknuma Palace, Hyderabad Recognized as Number One Palace Hotel in the World'. Available at: https://www.tajhotels.com/en-in/about-taj-group/press-and-media/press-releases/press-releases/2015/taj-falaknuma-palace–hyderabad-recognized-as-number-one-palace-/ (accessed on 3 April 2016).

The Economic Times. 2015. 'Accor Hotels to Have Around 80 Hotels in India by Around 2020'. *The Economic Times*. Available at: http://articles.economictimes.indiatimes.com/2015-11-04/news/68017013_1_34-hotels-accor-hotels-midscale (accessed on 24 December 2016).

——. 2016. 'India is Dubai's Number One Source Market for Tourists'. *The Economic Times*. Available at: http://articles.economictimes.indiatimes.com/2016-01-29/news/70178013_1_cent-growth-economic-growth-tourists (accessed on 24 December 2016).

UNWTO. 2009. 'The Indian Outbound Travel Market with Special Insight into the Image of Europe as a Destination'. World Tourism Organization and European Travel Commission. Available at: http://publications.unwto.org/sites/all/files/pdf/090616_indian_outbound_travel_excerpt.pdf (accessed on 24 December 2016).

Visalam. (n.d.). CGH Earth. Available at: http://www.cghearth.com/visalam (accessed on 24 December 2016).

World Economic Outlook: Legacies, Clouds, Uncertainties. (2014). International Monetary Fund. Available at: https://www.imf.org/external/pubs/ft/weo/2014/02/pdf/text.pdf (accessed on 24 December 2016).

Suggested Readings

Books

Bentley, C. 2011. *A Guide to the Palace Hotels of India*. USA: Hunter Publishing.

Yeoman, I., Rebecca, T. L. Y., and Wouters, M. 2012. *2050 – Tomorrow's Tourism*. Bristol: Channel View Publications.

Chhatrapati Shivaji terminus
Image courtesy: Tourism India.

CHAPTER 15

Government Bodies in Indian Tourism

Learning Objectives

By the end of the chapter, students will be able to:

- Gain an overview of the tourism policies and approaches adopted by Government over the years.
- Recognize the need for planning and list the different steps involved in the process.
- Appreciate the role of government in tourism and roles and responsibilities of public sector units in national and state levels.
- List the initiatives of central and state governments for promoting tourism education for quality human resource delivery.

Introduction

Enthused by the prospects of embarking on a profitable career, a young entrepreneur decides to start a B&B unit, converting a family building into a tourism enterprise. As she contemplates the investment needed, she wonders if she will be eligible for an incentive or financial assistance. Which agency will help her? Before she starts the business, does she have to take a licence? Should the unit be registered under any authority? What tax is attracted on the room rate, and how is the payment to be made to the tax authority? Will the Destination marketing authority assist her marketing efforts? The answers to these questions lie in our understanding of the levels of governments that control economic activities, the separate roles played by government agencies and their impacts on the tourism sector. Our federal polity has given India a complex and multi-layered governance system, creating an environment that is interlinked and dynamic.

In India, the government in its many avatars is involved in tourism in a central and pivotal manner. This chapter will explore the various ways in which government agencies and organizations engage with the tourism sector, and how this involvement has changed over the years. We will analyse the pros and cons of government participation in the tourism business and examine the vital contribution that governments have to make for the development of the sector. We will also examine the ways in which destinations need to prepare themselves for the increase in demand on infrastructure and services to tourism and the process of tourism planning, as it is an important ingredient in the overall tourism development framework, for destinations in particular, but also for the country in general.

History of Policy Making in Tourism

The growth of tourism in India happened without a particular design and without policy-makers paying any attention to the sector. Even during the time of limited air connectivity and difficult ground conditions, there were many adventurous tourists who came with their backpacks and visited many destinations of the country. They stayed in certain destinations where the local community was welcoming and friendly, creating enclaves for their accommodation and recreation. During this time, tourism was not seen as a priority sector and did not find mention in policy documents.

Tourism Policy of 1982

The first tourism policy of India was framed in 1982. The aim was to develop tourism circuits, which connected destinations that collectively would make an attractive package of interest to the visitor and to provide assistance for the construction of infrastructure in these chosen destinations. The policy emphasized the central role to be played by government, which would acquire land and provide areas for specific tourism projects. The policy was formulated in an environment of a closed economy with rigid licensing procedures prevalent at the time. The policy did not emphasize the role of private sector, and foreign investment was not envisaged. The responsibility of promoting international tourism was assigned to the central government and domestic tourism to the state governments.

Tourism was given the status of an 'industry' in 1986 and became eligible for several incentives and facilities including tax incentives, subsidies, priorities in the sanctioning of loans by the state financial institutions and preferences in providing electricity and water connections. In 1991, tourism was made a priority sector for foreign direct investment making it eligible for automatic approvals up to 51% of the equity. A National Strategy for Tourism development was evolved in 1996, which advocated the strengthening of an institutional set up in human resource development, setting up an Advisory Board of Tourism Industry and Trade, the integrated development of tourist destinations and the promotion of private sector in tourism development.

National Tourism Action Plan

Although the tourism policy was not translated into concrete action, tourism continued to grow, particularly in the favourable climate of a modernizing India. The National Tourism Action Plan of 1992 again called for integrated tourism development and the development of circuits. There was also mention of marketing and human resource development programmes to be undertaken by the central government as part of tourism development. The action plan also flagged the importance of the domestic visitor and urged state governments to formulate strategies to attract domestic tourism. Tourism was granted 'export house' status in 1998 making hotels, travel agents, tour operators and tourist transport operators eligible for such recognition, entitling them to various incentives (GoI, n.d.).

National Tourism Policy of 2002

In 2002, a new tourism policy was announced. Tourism was seen as an engine of growth, generating foreign exchange, providing employment and bringing economic prosperity. Tourism was now depicted as a development tool that could transform lives, particularly in backward areas. The National Tourism Development Policy laid down the objective of positioning tourism as a major engine of economic growth and to harness its direct and multiplier effects for employment and poverty eradication in an environmentally sustainable manner. Tourism development, according to the policy, should be 'government led, private sector driven and community welfare oriented'. The policy puts sustainability as the 'guiding star'. Over exploitation of natural resources should not be permitted, nor the carrying capacity of the site ignored. There would be greater emphasis on ecotourism.

Tourism was seen to be a priority sector because it was able to maximize the productivity of India's natural, human, cultural and technical resources. Tourism was labour intensive and cottage or small industry based, 'providing employment that is of a high quality thus contributing to higher quality of life'.

The policy also listed the issues that had prevented the sector from realizing its potential. It was unable to effectively link its role in relation to national development priorities, undue focus was laid on the international market at the expense of domestic tourism, the poor quality of the environment surrounding many of the India's main tourist sites, the security scenario in the region that affected the perception of India as a safe and secure destination, the quality of facilities and services, the quality of transportation service, the multiplicity and high levels of taxation, limited availability of tourist information in source markets, limited scope, lack of accurate and reliable market data and poor community participation leading to, in some cases, hostility to tourism were all cited as reasons for this situation.

The policy set out the following key objectives:

- **Positioning and maintaining tourism development as a national priority activity:** This aims to include tourism in the concurrent list of the Constitution of India and to provide effective linkages and Close coordination between departments.
- **Enhancing and maintaining the competitiveness of India as a tourism destination:** The aim is to implement a system of visa on arrival and improve the air capacity by opening out India's skies.
- **Improving India's existing tourism products and expanding these to meet new market requirements:** This includes developing beach and coastal tourism resort products, leasing sites for the development of beach resorts by the private sector, development of international cruise destinations and developing village tourism and adventure tourism.
- **Creation of world class infrastructure:** Including development of roads, railways waterways.
- **Developing sustained and effective marketing plans and programmes:** Including creating an India tourism brand position that captures the essence of the tourism product (MoT, 2002).

The Approach Paper to the 12th Plan

As we know, the three main sectors of the Indian economy are agriculture, industry and services. According to the approach paper prepared by the Planning Commission for the 12th Five Year Plan, the principal goal of the Plan is to increase the pace of inclusion of much larger numbers of people in the process of growth through creation of more jobs and more enterprises.

The service sector is the principal generator of employment in India. Although there has been significant growth in the Information Technology Enabled Services (ITES) sector, it contributed only 12% of the total growth in GDP in the services sector. Sub-sectors in services such as tourism and hospitality are potentially important sources of employment growth.

The world T&T industry accounts for US$7,340 billion of global economic activity, which is forecasted to grow to US$14,382 billion by 2019. The industry accounts for approximately 7.6% of global employment. T&T accounts for about 8% of total employment in India. It is capable of providing employment to a wide spectrum of jobseekers, from the unskilled to the specialized, even in remote parts of the country. Compared to other modern sectors, a higher proportion of tourism benefits accrue to women. Internationally, women account for 70% of the workforce in the T&T industry, making it more inclusive than other sectors.

The broad scope of economic activities involved in tourism enables wide participation in its growth, including the participation of the informal sector, because the skill requirements for most of the jobs are modest and can be relatively easily acquired. Furthermore, tourism is highly dependent upon natural capital and culture, assets that some of the poor have, even if they have no financial resources. The interaction of tourists, business suppliers, host governments and host communities in the process of attracting and hosting the tourists and other visitors gives rise to the demand for, and supply of, a wide range of tourism-related goods and services. Therefore, tourism has good potential to stimulate overall economic growth. A marginal shift in investment to the tourism sector has the potential to propel India to a faster growth trajectory.

The main constraints identified in the Approach Paper include inadequate transportation—including airports—infrastructure, lack of hotel facilities, multiple and high taxation, inadequate financial resources for enterprises and skills, inadequate safety and hygiene conditions around tourist attractions and convergence of actions by multiple agencies. The challenges are further magnified in the context of a federal structure where the responsibilities of policy-making and implementation are fragmented across levels of government.

There should be strategies to enhance non-cash livelihood benefits to the locals, such as:

- Capacity building, training and empowerment.
- Mitigating of the environmental impact of tourism on the poor and management of competing demands for access to natural resources between tourism and local people.
- Improving social and cultural impacts of tourism.
- Improving access to services and infrastructure like health care, security, water supplies, transport and waste disposal (Planning Commission, 2011).

Tourism in the 12th Five Year Plan Document

In the 12th Five Year Plan document, the tourism sector has been identified as a major player to promote faster, sustainable and more inclusive economic growth. Tourism was seen as having better prospects for promoting pro-poor growth as it involves collection of activities, services and industries comprising transportation, accommodation, eating and drinking establishments, retail shops, entertainment businesses and other hospitality services, all of which enable wide participation, including by the informal sector. The challenges in the tourism sector lie in successfully preserving the natural endowments in their original forms and making them accessible to the domestic and international travellers, leading to more sustainable growth. The plan document noted that the global ranking of the level of tourism infrastructure in India was 68th in 2010. (The ranking has since improved to the 52nd position in the 2015 T&T competitiveness index.)

The strategy advised in the plan document was that tourism development should be reoriented to eliminate poverty. It emphasizes the need to adopt a pro-poor approach and ensure that tourism contributes to poverty reduction. Pro-poor tourism is essentially about the distribution of resources and opportunities and not just the creation of a new tourism product. Authorities have the responsibility to advocate for and promote the interests of the poor and marginalized communities. Increased economic benefits to the poor can be achieved through the expansion of business opportunities by enabling them to set up small enterprises. Main activities in this area should be enterprise support, expansion of markets and development of complementary tourism enterprises such as craft initiatives and cultural displays.

Employment opportunities should be expanded by ensuring that the investors and operators in the formal tourism sector are committed to source employment locally while being focused on skill development for enabling the local community to take up skilled jobs which may be created. Further, collective benefits should be enhanced through levies on tourists and operators, equity partnerships in which the community has a stake, lease fees paid by private operators and donations from tourists.

The focus must be on promoting participation, bringing the private sector in the formal tourism sector into business partnerships with small local entrepreneurs and building a more supportive policy and planning framework. Participation can be promoted by enhancing the participation of the local community in decision-making, perhaps by integrating tourism into the participatory district planning process.

Planned Tourism Development

All of us who have visited a hill station recently would have experienced some inconvenience in the midst of all the happy experiences of the holiday. A traffic jam, air pollution, haphazard construction or piles of solid waste on the road sides are not uncommon in our hill stations, which were once known for their pristine atmosphere and beauty.

Overdevelopment

All our major destinations are facing serious problems of overdevelopment and stretched civic services, which are a direct result of the changes brought to these destinations by the growth of the tourism sector. Increased arrival of tourists in a destination would lead to increased demand for goods and services, bringing in more investments. Unplanned and unregulated development would often follow, adding room inventories and temporarily catering to the increased demand from the tourism sector. However, infrastructure in the destination would not keep pace with increased numbers of residents, visitors and vehicles, leading to an extremely undesirable situation, wherein the value of the destination itself is eroded by these developments. Several destinations have also experienced a dip in numbers, with visitors moving elsewhere, having heard from various sources about the degraded quality of the destination. Stretched infrastructure continues to be a problem in all destinations.

In this scenario, it is relevant to understand how planners anticipate future demand and put in place a mechanism by which the demand can be met. For instance, all projections have shown that India faces an acute shortage of rooms and the supply is not keeping up with the demand generated. How do governments ensure that private investment is guided into the accommodation sector? Similarly, how do planners work towards increasing tourism arrivals and tapping new markets?

The Case for Planned Tourism Development

Overcrowded destinations lead to undesirable developments, resulting in degradation of the quality of life, alienation of the local community from the tourism development in the region, giving rise to social tensions, protests and even violence. There may be severe cultural challenges that upset the social and cultural milieu, resulting in increased crime rates and the rise of negative impacts on the population. The degradation to the environment can be catastrophic with deforestation, pollution of aquifers and groundwater sources, degradation of air quality, increase in communicable diseases and widespread visual pollution. All of these impact tourist arrivals, affecting the local economy. Such impacts may not be reversible, and the damage to the destination in terms of its image may be long lasting.

Planned tourism can prevent many of these undesirable impacts. Tourism, if properly planned and implemented, can ensure the optimal deployment of resources in the destination. Tourism can generate employment, spur entrepreneurship and bring other economic benefits to the community. Tourism has helped to revive and revitalize regions and bring lasting economic prosperity. Tourism can often become the catalyst to spur infrastructural development, the benefits of which are enjoyed by the larger community and not merely by the tourists.

What Is Planning?

Planning embraces various factors that are relevant in its process—social, political, economic, technological and cultural. In simple terms, planning is a process that involves setting certain goals and outlining strategies and tasks that will help accomplish the goals. There are different kinds of planning at different levels. Economists and development specialists make plans for improving the economy and for bringing socioeconomic development. Infrastructure planners prepare plans for creating and maintaining infrastructure. Urban and regional planners are concerned with spatial plans for the region or for the city. Land use and resource planners concentrate on zoning and the environmental aspects of planning. Similarly, tourism planners aim to make plans that will develop tourism in the region or will modulate the effects of tourism.

A planned approach is necessary in tourism in order to ensure that the resources available are used in an optimal and sustainable manner. Planning also creates an environment in which the community is integrated into the tourism development process and benefits from it. A planned approach ensures that the economic benefits that accrue out of tourism are maximized and available to members of the local community. It keeps the interest of the visitors central to the planning process, ensuring a better experience and high satisfaction levels.

Planning at the National Level

At the national level, tourism planning is articulated through the tourism policy which is announced periodically. Through the policy, MoT addresses issues that affect tourism at the national level and suggest solutions and plans to drive tourism forward. Tourism policy sets targets and goals, particularly in terms of the tourist arrivals and foreign exchange earnings. The policy addresses problems affecting tourism, such as the visa regime, safety and security of tourists and airport infrastructure. Based upon research and projections, as well as after consultations with stakeholders, the policy put forward a strategy to achieve the objectives set.

Planning at the State Level

At the regional or state level, attention is focused more on destinations. Issues of access and infrastructure availability, land-use planning, zoning and carrying capacity are aspects of regional level planning. States also formulate plans for marketing destinations within the country and abroad. Ensuring sustainability and preventing the degradation of natural resources are high priorities in the planning process at the regional level. This calls for a high level of integration and interdisciplinary approaches.

Steps of Planning Process

The steps of tourism planning process are discussed below (Figure 15.1).

- **Study preparation:** Study preparation consists of a pre-feasibility study, which evaluates the availability of local resources. A team of physical planning experts like architects and environmental planners, financial and marketing analysts, sociologists, engineers are included in the project team for preparing the study.
- **Determination of development objectives:** Development objectives are determined with the participation of the community and local government keeping local imperatives in mind.
- **Survey and evaluation:** The existing and potential tourist resources are assessed. Infrastructure and superstructure existing in the area, such as transportation, water supply, power and waste management, are evaluated. Existing and potential tourist markets and trends are also examined.
- **Analysis and synthesis:** The data obtained through surveys and evaluations is analysed to establish specific targets, projecting requirements and demand. Carrying capacity analysis to determine the optimal level of development has to be carried out. The economic, social cultural and environmental impacts have to be specifically analysed. A useful tool is to conduct a SWOT analysis.
- **Policy and plan formulation:** On the basis of the information and knowledge gathered through the previous steps, an action plan is formulated.

Steps of the planning process may vary with the destination, in keeping with the terms of reference and scope of the exercise. For instance, many planning processes will incorporate market analysis, competition study and product opportunity evaluation.

An example of a Master Plan for a fragile destination may be seen in the Master Plan for Valley of Flowers (VoF). The various steps undertaken by the planners may be seen from the case study, leading to recommendations and implementation.

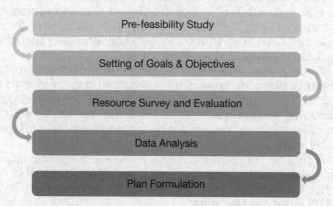

Figure 15.1   Steps of planning process
Source: Authors.

Landscape, Uttarakhand

Case Study: Master Plan for the Valley of Flowers—Hemkunt Sahib Area

Situated in the Chamoli district of the state of Uttaranchal, VoF and Hemkunt are part of the Nanda Devi Biosphere Reserve (NDBR). MoT, GoI, engaged Tata Consultancy Services to prepare the master plan for the development of ecotourism in the VoF—Hemkunt area.

The Government of Uttar Pradesh, (Chamoli district was in UP at that time) created the 'Valley of Flowers (VoF) National Park' in 1982, recognizing its importance as a fragile eco-system. The sacred shrine of Hemkunt Sahib was discovered in 1934. It is believed that the 10th Guru, Guru Gobind Singh meditated on the banks of the Hemkunt Lake. The site is held to very sacred by Sikh pilgrims, who make their way to the shrine. Located at an altitude of 4,329 m, Hemkunt Sahib is one of the highest shrines in India. It attracts around 400,000 visitors annually. Both these are accessed by the same route—the nearest road head is the village of Govind Ghat after which there is a trail that later branches, with one path proceeding to VoF and the other to Hemkunt Sahib.

Participative planning approach: Before preparation of the project report, the consultants adopted a participative planning approach involving all stakeholders in the process, most importantly the local community. Participative consultations included group discussions and surveys, interacting with people of all walks of life. The draft report was presented to the Departments of Forests and Tourism for review and feedback and the master plan discussed before stakeholders.

Scope of the study: The Terms of Reference included, inter alia, an assessment of the impact of tourism, identification of growth centres and involvement of local community, the design of a site management plan specifying the carrying capacity, design of waste management and detailed land use plan.

Situational analysis: The first step was a detailed analysis of the present state of infra-structure, services and facilities. The analysis included climate, accessibility, an inventory

(Continued ...)

of the flora and fauna, a study of the local settlements and activities and the state of infrastructure used by the tourists. The access to the areas was along the trek path route starting from Govind Ghat, the settlement accessible by road, and going to the village settlements of Pulna, Bhyundar and Ghangharia in the upper valley. VoF is accessible by a trail and lies at a distance of 3 km from Ghangharia. The path to Hemkunt Sahib is at a distance of 6 km from Ghangharia. Private taxis and buses ply till Govind Ghat, after which one has to trek or take a mule. Mules are not permitted into the VoF. The Eco Development Committee (EDC) Bhyundar, under the aegis of the Department of Forests was created to regulate the growth of private commercial establishments started by the local community persons en route. The EDC collects an 'eco-fee' from the hotels, lodges and restaurants at Ghangharia to support its efforts in managing the trek path and keeping it clean. Some EDC members are also trained guides, supplementing their incomes through nature interpretation services. The mules are brought to the region by non-locals, who pay a fee to the EDC to conduct their operations. As there is demand for services during the tourist season, the local population, particularly the younger generation, has shifted from marginal farming and rearing livestock to tourism based income activities. As the path to Hemkunt Sahib and the VoF is the same to a large part, the majority of the visitors to the area are pilgrims visiting the shrine (389,000 in 2003). Visitors to the VoF were 6,321 only.

For accommodation, a few basic lodges were available at Govind Ghat. 73% of the land of the Park was perpetually under snow and glaciers, 21% of land was alpine meadows and 6% under forests. The little land available at Ghangharia had been developed in a haphazard fashion, along the trek path. The Gurudwara provides free accommodation and food to visitors. While electricity is available at Govind Ghat, transit points further up did not have power supply and are dependent on generators. Local streams provided water supply and there are no treatment facilities. Sewerage was disposed of in soak pits. There are open drains which drained into the streams polluting them. One of the major pollutants was the urine and dung of mules on the trek path and at transit points. The EDC staff was responsible for the collection of non-biodegradable solid waste, which was brought down to Govind Ghat from the trek route. There was no system of disposal, and the collected waste used to pile up. There was more waste dumped en route, which found its way into the streams.

Environmental impact of tourism: The study focused on the impacts of tourism activity on the ecology of the region. The different stresses on the environment were examined separately. The uniqueness and fragility of the biodiversity of the area, abundance of rare medicinal plants and steepness of slopes were natural stress areas. Areas of concern due to disturbances due to tourism were the disposal of solid and liquid waste, pollution of water bodies, sanitation concerns and animal waste. The study emphasized on the need to prepare a hazard mitigation plan and suggest safety measures.

Ecotourism development strategy: The Ecotourism development strategy examined the potential of developing ecotourism, the development considerations and the framework to develop tourism in a sustainable manner that will contribute to the overall development of the region. The Limits of Acceptable Change model was adopted to recommend the ecotourism development strategy by the consultants. The strategy identified the area concerns and issues, and prepared an inventory of selected resources and social conditions for which standards were specified. After an analysis of alternatives, a set of actions was suggested for implementation and a monitoring mechanism was advised to be set up.

Environmental management plan (EMP): An important component was EMP. A hierarchy of environmentally sensitive and development-oriented sub-regions was identified and environment management measures suggested specific to each sub-region. EMP for spatial development includes separate plans for land management, waste management, built up areas, products and services, sanitation, energy, air and noise pollution, environmental orientation and monitoring. The aim of EMP is to set out the mitigation measures and environmental

(Continued ...)

specifications required to be implemented for all phases of the project so that the extent of impacts can be minimized and managed. The plan will work towards reducing output and managing waste, usage of environmentally friendly products, reducing water use, lowering energy consumption and providing environmental education to visitors. EMP laid down an array of recommendations, among which are: ban all future permanent construction in the valley, effective storm water drainage measures to reduce erosion, ban on plastic rain-coats and bags, provision of boiled water to reduce consumption of bottled water, collection and removal of waste from fragile area to a management facility like vermin composting for mule excreta, separation of collected waste, restriction of construction of toilets to selected locations only, laying of a more efficient power line and extensive sensitization and orientation plan for environmental education to the locals and visitors.

Carrying capacity: The development plan was based on the carrying capacity of the area, which determined the optimum number of visitors to the Valley. Various options like fluid and fixed carrying capacities were considered. The criteria which were used to arrive at the optimum number are use levels, transportation facilities, recreation opportunities, desired resource conditions and the acceptable level of impact. The study recommended that given the fragile nature of the region and the normal load impact per person, the number of persons visiting the valley at any given point of time must be limited to 150. Excess load of visitors will have to be controlled at the entrance gate and diverted to nearby areas which are more resilient, such as the shadow garden and demonstration nursery. What is more important is the sensitization of the visitor on the behaviour expected of them during the visit to the valley. The most impact to the environment was due to the behavioural patterns of the visitors, not the number of visitors. This means that the sensitization of the visitors and the local community, coupled with planned management measures within the limits of acceptable change framework will minimize the impacts in the valley. The study envisaged the establishment of a Germplasm bank of endangered species of the valley, with an educational garden, which will serve to absorb the excess visitors to the region.

Development plan: Within the valley, the plan proposed the improvement of the trek path and trail and the development of four vista points, with temporary structures offering rain shelter and rest. Warnings and directional and interpretation signages have to be established to enhance the visitor experience. The park will function on the basis of 'visitor carries waste' principle, with an 'eco deposit' and declaration of the plastic items in the visitor's possession. The deposit will be returned when the visitor while exiting can show that the waste is being carried back and has not been deposited in the park.

Implementation plan: The Implementation Plan proposes a series of projects that should be implemented in a phased manner. The implementation plan divides the work according to the agencies which will be implementing individual projects and proposes the estimated costs of these projects. The plan estimates that works for a total of ₹255.3 million have to be undertaken in the area. The plan addresses the issues relating to the roles and responsibilities of the main institutional stakeholders such as EDC, the traders association, the Mahila Mandal, the Forest Council, the Village council or Gram Sabha, the Zila Panchayat and government departments, such as forests, tourism, public works, jal nigam, electricity, health and revenue. The plan advocates the establishment of a Visitor Management System (VMS) for promotion, hospitality and marketing. The promotional activities under the system include the preparation of self-guiding brochures, advertising in select media, public relations programmes and a web-based management system with information on the area and attractions and a mechanism to continue the engagement with the visitor.

Source: MoT (2005).

Image courtesy: Ministry of Tourism, Government of India.

(Continued ...)

Discussion Questions

1. Prepare a list of stakeholders in the area and identify their roles.
2. What are the aspects of the Plan that are likely to create conflicts when the plan is executed?

Destination Planning

We know that tourism development, while bringing prosperity and economic progress to destinations, can also be detrimental to the region and the community. Destination planning is important because planned development ensures that the scale and type of tourism that develops in a location is in accordance with its social and environmental character and does not leave a negative impact. Planning is a continuous process, addressing the direction of future development, analysing trends and making course corrections, wherever necessary.

Any planning exercise starts with an analysis of the situation existing in the destination. This includes the review of the resources and infrastructure, the factors that might influence the developments, present impacts of tourism, the challenges and opportunities facing the destination, the aspirations and attitudes of the community and the social and economic conditions. The analysis must also examine the products, visitor trends and target markets.

In developed countries, planning for tourism development and the preparation of tourism development strategies are the functions of the local governments. This is the ideal situation, given the fact that local governments are most knowledgeable about the resources a city or region has, and have the biggest stake in the economic development of their neighbourhood. The city/town council which is a representative body is in the best position to assess the need for an activity like tourism, its potential benefits vis-à-vis the impacts on the community and the environment and take decisions based on their wisdom, the aspirations and attitudes of the citizens and with full local participation and approval. Planning in this 'decentralized' system ensures equity, accuracy and the participation of those affected by decisions.

However, in many developing countries like India, planning remains an exercise conducted at the state or national levels. There are many reasons for this, but the most important is the relative inexperience of local governments and the reluctance on the part of the state governments to part with their powers. As we shall see, the local governments are rapidly getting empowered with funds, functions and staff, and will soon be in a position to play a more active and dynamic role in local level planning (Figure 15.2).

Planning and the Ministry of Tourism

Planning for tourism development has been pursued at national level by MoT. Based on the national objectives and policies framed, the ministry prepares plans for the development of certain sectors in tourism on priority. An example of this approach is the emphasis given on developing integrated tourism circuits. States are encouraged to identify clusters of destinations that could be integrated into specific circuits, providing the visitors an experience that is multi-dimensional. This approach was pursued on the understanding that uneven development of facilities in some destinations may not be sufficient to attract sustained tourism arrivals and that specific circuits connecting destinations and offering a bouquet of experiences are better positioned to attract tourism and to be sold as packages. While there are divergent views as to whether this approach has resulted in measurable increase in tourist arrivals, it is indisputable that the integrated tourism circuit approach resulted in the development of tourist facilities and infrastructure in lesser known destinations and also helped in focused attention on many areas of outstanding tourism value hitherto undiscovered by the tourism industry.

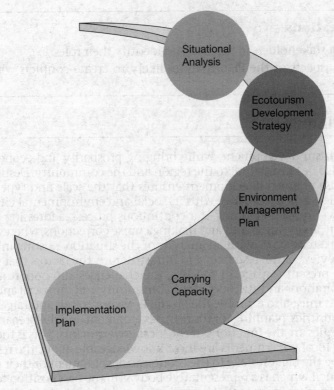

Figure 15.2 Steps for master plan development of a destination
Source: Authors.

Some initiatives of the central government, spurred by the national level planning approach, are heavily dependent on the participation and initiative of the state governments. An example is the scheme to establish 'special tourism zones' that was undertaken in the 1990s under the leadership of the ministry. A study was commissioned by the ministry to identify locations that could be developed into new beach tourism destinations. The thinking behind this approach was that new beach destinations were needed to be established in India to meet emerging demand, and planned destinations could be created on a public private partnership basis. A few locations were identified, and states were required to acquire the land necessary for establishing these 'special tourism zones'. Central government would ensure that the hotels established in these zones would be given special incentives, on the lines of the special economic zones. While some state governments enthusiastically invested in the idea, acquiring land and building infrastructure, the scheme did not take off, partly because the incentives were not provided as envisaged and the private sector did not display much enthusiasm. Bekal in Kerala was the only location where major hotels were established on land provided by the state government, while in some other locations, land was allotted to hotel groups but the construction was not taken up. The failure of this centralized planning approach drives home the point that planning for tourism development is more effectively done at the regional or local level.

Planning for tourism development, in the Indian context, has often been interpreted in a narrow sense, with governments acquiring private lands, which would subsequently be made available to hotel groups, generally on a leasehold basis, to set up hotels. This model has not been found attractive and has in many places resulted in local communities resisting tourism.

There are some exceptions, where state governments have involved the local communities in planning and decision-making processes. However, planned tourism development remains in a very preliminary level in the country. There are signs of change—the Responsible Tourism initiative of Kerala is a fine example of destination level planning to ensure that tourism development brings economic benefits to the community, respects local culture and is environmentally sustainable.

Planning for Sensitive Destinations

In certain regions, there is no alternative to planned and monitored tourism, where government agencies must play the most critical regulatory role. Unplanned tourism development around wildlife sanctuaries has created numerous problems and even affected populations of endangered species. The large numbers of visitors have resulted in severe stress on the environment, waste disposal issues and pollution. Fragile environments such as islands, coral reefs also need careful planning to control tourism over development. On the coast, unregulated development has shown to lead to the 'demise' of destinations, with tourists abandoning such over-developed destinations for better places. In India, the Coastal Regulation Zone (CRZ) framework brought in a system which put specific mechanisms in place for the approval of hotels and other businesses in coastal areas. To an extent, this mechanism has created an environment of planned development, although there are many in the tourism industry who feel that the CRZ regime in India is too harsh and discourages investment.

National, State and Local Governments

In India, there are three levels of governments. Central government is responsible for matters at the federal level, tackling issues that affect the entire country. It is responsible for subjects which are in the central list under the Constitution of India and also legislates on matters in the concurrent list. The second level of governance is the state government, which looks after affairs at the state level. The third level of governance is the local government. Local self-government institutions such as municipalities, corporations and panchayats fall into this category. It is important for us to understand the three levels of government, as agencies under these governments play very different but significant roles affecting the tourism sector.

Before we get into specific aspects of government involvement, it will be useful for us to look at the various ways in which government intervenes in the tourism sector. Government, in a broad sense, provides the legal and financial framework that is needed by the tourism sector to conduct its business in an orderly and stable manner. The role of government is seen in the facets further discussed in the chapter.

Government and the Tourism Product

Government owns and operates many tourism sites and products, which are central to the tourism experience of many destinations in India. Our monuments, museums and archaeological sites are owned, protected and maintained by government. Our wildlife sanctuaries and national parks, likewise, are in the hands of government agencies. Government is involved not only in maintaining the product but also in product development, using the resources under its command. In certain cases, government prepares a plan for targeted intervention in key locations, considering their strategic importance. The recent initiative—National Mission on Pilgrimage Rejuvenation and Spiritual Augmentation Drive (PRASAD)—is an example of planned investment in selected spiritual destinations.

Case Study: National Mission on Pilgrimage Rejuvenation and Spiritual Augmentation Drive (PRASAD)

As we have understood, pilgrimage tourism forms the major part of domestic tourism movement in India. A quest of religious identity, spiritual upliftment and a visit to holy shrines are all motivations to travel, particularly in India, where a large majority of the population are religious followers of one faith or another. With major religions having many pilgrimage centres, there is a huge number of visitors thronging such places, putting the infrastructure under strain and creating problems in managing civic services. MoT decided to launch a scheme, PRASAD, to ameliorate the conditions at major pilgrimage centres. The aim was to identify core deficiencies, facilitate provision of products and services and address all related issues to pave the way to development of religious tourism in India.

Among the major issues to be tackled are the inadequate infrastructure, connectivity, hygiene and cleanliness, solid waste management, the safety and security of pilgrims and the need to develop a code of religious etiquette. The vision statement of the scheme lays down the vision, that is, to position tourism as a major engine of economic growth and job creation, promote sustainable pilgrimage tourism, bridge infrastructural gaps at pilgrimage destinations and create employment through active involvement of local communities with pro-poor approach through development of a 'Responsible Tourism' initiative. Among the Mission objectives are to harness pilgrimage tourism for its direct and multiplier effects on employment generation and economic development, create awareness among the local community about the importance of tourism and to promote local arts, culture handicrafts and cuisine.

The strategy is to identify and prioritize projects that need to be taken up through dedicated public funding and to leverage to the extent feasible additional resources from sources such as CSR of central public sector undertakings (PSUs) and the corporate sector.

This scheme is to be implemented as a 'central sector' scheme, which means that all the funding for projects under the scheme will be provided by the central government. The National Steering Committee headed by the tourism minister will approve destinations to be taken up and provide the overall guidance to the scheme. The Central Sanctioning and Monitoring Committee (CSMC) will be responsible for sanction of projects and monitoring the implementation. The scheme will be implemented by the mission directorate, which will work through a project management consultant (PMC). PMC will prepare a detailed perspective plan for identified destinations, identifying infrastructural gaps, assessing fund requirement, preparation of project reports, stakeholder consultations and project structuring. Project reports will be prepared for components admissible for financial assistance, such as development and upgradation of passenger terminals, improvement of last mile connectivity, tourism information and interpretation centres, wayside amenities, infrastructural development, such as water supply, sewerage and electricity and restoration and conservation of heritage structures. Courses to address skill gaps will be conducted to empower the local community to take advantage of the employment opportunities. The operation and maintenance of the facilities created or upgraded will be maintained and operated by the state governments, directly or through local bodies or private partners.

The outcome of the integrated development of pilgrimage centres on a mission mode will be measured on the basis of parameters like increase in tourist traffic, employment generation, enhancement of awareness and development of skills and increase in private sector participation.

Initially, the following pilgrimage centres have been selected for development under the PRASAD scheme: Ajmer, Mathura, Kedarnath, Amritsar, Varanasi, Gaya, Kamakhya, Puri, Amaravati, Kanchipuram, Velankanni and Dwaraka (MoT, n.d.). A sum of ₹1 billion has been provided for the scheme in 2015-16 (MoT, 2015).

(Continued ...)

> **Discussion Questions**
> 1. What are the five main bottlenecks that most religious centres face? Who is responsible for these issues?
> 2. While investment to upgrade infrastructure is important, does the scheme envisage steps to motivate visitors to adopt a more responsible behaviour? What are the steps that can be taken to encourage this change?

Government as Regulator

Government regulates virtually all activities related to tourism. Visas, which permit inbound visitors to enter the country, are issued by government. The ports of entry are controlled by government. Government gives permissions for hotel construction and for running a tour company. Restaurants, bars and other tourism facilities can operate only after securing the necessary permissions from government.

Government and Infrastructure

All the vital infrastructure that is used by tourism is owned and operated by government. Major airports, the railway system and the road network are all controlled by government. Utilities like power distribution, water, sanitation and waste disposal are operated by government agencies.

Government and Quality Control

Government runs approval and classification schemes which provide tourism players an assurance of quality. Government also develops systems by which quality of experience is monitored and grievances are redressed. Government issues guidelines and advisories on quality of services to be provided and to set benchmarks.

Government as Facilitator

Government encourages investment by providing incentives to the industry, like concessional land parcels and tax breaks. Government coordinates with the tourism industry in promoting destinations and runs marketing campaigns to attract visitors. Research and analysis projects of the government help the industry understand the markets better, contributing to better marketing initiatives.

Government and Human Resource Development

Government is involved in assessing the human resource needs of the industry. Government runs academic institutions, training students in hotel management and tour operations. Government also runs skill development programmes and short-term courses to ramp up skilled manpower needed for the sector.

Each level of government has a different role to play in tourism. The central government, through MoT, coordinates with other ministries on matters related to the tourism sector and is involved in funding state governments for developing infrastructure relevant to tourism. We had noted that in many destinations in India, projects useful for tourism, such as reception centres, wayside amenities and budget accommodation, are being built by state government agencies using central funds. The central government also conducts large scale marketing campaigns in inbound markets. We will examine the functions of the ministry in some detail later.

The state government, in many ways, has the most important and pivotal role to play in tourism. State governments build tourism-related infrastructure, maintain vital public infrastructure like roads and power distribution, decide on the level of taxation, provide incentives for investment facilitation and invest in marketing and promotion. State taxes, such as sales tax, property tax and licensing of alcohol vending, are some of the aspects of state control connected to tourism. In some states, tourism establishments have to register with the tourism department before beginning operations.

The local governments are in an early stage of their evolution. In mature environments, the local governments perform significant functions like giving building approval for projects, establishing controls such as carrying capacity levels, involve local communities in decision-making and decide on the priority that tourism should have in the local economy. Food and beverage establishments and lodging units—like the one at the beginning of this chapter—will have to obtain a license from the local corporations, municipalities or panchayats before beginning commercial operations.

Ministry of Tourism

MoT in the Union government is the main body that formulates policies and implements programs related to tourism in the country. The ministry coordinates with sister ministries in the central government to remove obstacles and solve problems that will result in an increase in visitor arrivals and enhancing the contribution of the tourism sector to the national economy. The ministry also has a field division, the offices of which are involved in implementation of the programmes of the ministry. The ministry has 20 offices within India and 14 offices abroad, which are involved in promoting India as a destination and marketing tourism products of India. It engages itself in developing tourism-related infrastructure by providing funds to state governments and by taking up the development of tourism circuits. It works closely with the tourism sector, providing incentives for marketing and investment, classifying hotel, preparing guidelines and standards and taking up promotion programs. It plays a major role in human resource development, directly running Institutes of Hotel Management (IHM) and the Indian Institute of Travel and Tourism Management (IITTM). The market research division of the ministry conducts surveys and commissions studies on aspects of tourism in the country.

MoT has been consistently advocating the easing of the visa regime of India, in order to ensure that tourists can travel to India without hassles. Thanks to the strong lobbying and advocacy efforts of the ministry, India has introduced the e-TV system. E-TV enables the traveller to enter the country at 16 selected ports, with a copy of the electronic travel authorization (ETA) sent over email. The e-TV is now available for nationals of over hundred countries, enabling visitors intending to visit India for visiting friends and relatives, recreation, leisure, short-duration treatment or casual business, an easy option to apply for a visa online, without the hassle of visiting the office of the service provider. The electronic visa system has cut down the processing time also, and it is expected to dramatically improve visitor figures. Thus, a long pending demand of the tourism sector has now been fulfilled.

India Tourism Development Corporation (ITDC)

ITDC is a PSU under MoT, mandated to undertake multifarious activities in the tourism sector. Set up in 1966, ITDC grew to be the visible symbol of tourism in the country, operating hotels and conducting tour operations. ITDC provided a range of services, establishing a range of hotels from resorts to traveller's lodges, running duty-free shops in airports, conducting money changing business, operating a fleet of coaches and taxi services, setting-up and operating sound and light shows in monuments, handling tours and promotional and marketing functions.

The role of ITDC changed dramatically in the last few years. As part of the disinvestment initiative, government decided to dispose hotels owned by ITDC.

After the first round of disinvestment, ITDC now owns eight hotels, three of which are in Delhi. ITDC operates six more hotels under joint venture arrangements with some state governments. Presently, ITDC has a turnover of ₹5.0419 billion, the bulk of which came from the hotels and tours divisions. ITDC is a well-established brand in Indian tourism, with some properties like the Ashok Hotel, Delhi, at prime locations. However, ITDC is increasingly dependent on business generated from government clients. Its properties require significant upgradation and renovation, and the long and cumbersome government procedures prevent the organization from responding quickly and effectively to issues and problems (ITDC Ltd, n.d.).

Disinvestment of ITDC Properties

Based on the recommendations of the Disinvestment Commission, the GoI approved a disinvestment structure. Nineteen hotel properties of ITDC were disinvested and one property given on long-term lease cum management contract. Employees in these hotels were given the option of opting for the Voluntary Retirement Scheme (VRS) introduced in the company. The total upfront realization for GoI and its agencies from the sale of these properties was ₹4.4418 billion. A detailed look at the disinvestment process is given in Box 15.1.

India Tourism Development Corporation

ITDC came into existence in October 1966 and has been the prime mover in the progressive development, promotion and expansion of tourism in the country. The corporation is running hotels, restaurants at various places for tourists, besides providing transport facilities. Over the years, ITDC expanded across the country, opening hotels which brought in quality accommodation to lesser known destinations, introducing new destinations before the tourism sector. However, with the advent of private investment into the sector and the opening of hotels in the private sector in popular destinations, the performance of ITDC hotels started to decline and the financial health of the company became a matter of concern. ITDC ran into heavy losses. Among the many reasons advanced for this decline were heavy employment costs, rise in availability of room supply compared to demand and problems in management and leadership.

Disinvestment Strategy of GoI

In the 1990s, GoI moved away from a command economy approach and embarked on a programme of decontrol and deregulation, both of which are known as the process of liberalization. The major elements in this policy were to restructure and revive potentially viable Central Public Sector Enterprises (CPSEs), close down CPSEs which cannot be revive, bring down government shareholding in all non-strategic CPSEs to 26% or lower.

One of the early steps taken was the disinvestment process, offering shares of the public sector enterprises to the public at large and to investors. Another approach was the strategic sale of assets, which was adopted in the case of some PSUs, including ITDC.

At present, ITDC has a network of eight 'Ashok' hotels, five joint venture hotels, one restaurant, eleven transport units, one tourist service station, seven duty-free shops at airports and seaports and two light and sound shows. ITDC is a listed company, with an issued and subscribed equity capital of ₹857.7 million, out of which GoI holds 92.11%.

In 2001-02, GoI was successful in selling eight hotels and long-term leasing one hotel from the ITDC portfolio, yielding ₹1.7956 billion. The hotels are:

1. Agra Ashok
2. Bodhgaya Ashok

(Continued ...)

3. Hassan Ashok
4. Madurai Ashok
5. Temple Bay Ashok Mamallapuram
6. Qutub Hotel, New Delhi
7. Lodi Hotel, New Delhi
8. Laxmi Vilas Hotel, Udaipur
9. Bangalore Ashok (lease)

In 2002–2003, the disinvestment of 10 hotels of ITDC realized proceeds, totalling ₹2.7281 billion (Union Budget, n.d.). Ministry of Finance (2007) lists following hotels:

1. Airport Ashok Kolkata
2. Kovalam Ashok
3. Aurangabad Ashok
4. Manali Ashok
5. Khajuraho Ashok
6. Varanasi Ashok
7. Hotel Ranjit, New Delhi
8. Hotel Kanishka, New Delhi
9. Hotel Indraprastha, New Delhi
10. Chandigarh Project (Punjab Hotels Ltd)

Government has now (February 2016) identified five more ITDC hotels for privatization as part of its plan to disinvest eight such loss making properties. These include Hotel Janpath, New Delhi, Patliputra Ashok, Bharatpur Ashok and property at Kosi, Hotel Donyi Polo Ashok and Pondicherry Ashok (*The Economic Times*, 2016).

Tourism Education

Indian Institute of Tourism and Travel Management (IITTM)

IITTM was created in 1983 by the Tourism Ministry, out of a realization that the tourism sector needed the services of professionals with adequate education and training in the tourism and travel sectors. The institute is mandated to provide avenues for higher education in tourism and to serve as a research and resource centre for all tourism-related subjects. Over the years, it has played a major role in the propagation and professionalization of tourism education. It is committed to developing quality human resources for tourism and allied services, aiming for managerial excellence and professional competence. The institute is currently offering post-graduate programmes in tourism, international business, cargo management and logistics management. It also offers many short-duration programmes. The headquarters of IITTM is in Gwalior, and it has centres in Bhubaneshwar, Goa, Delhi and Nellore.

Hospitality Education

The National Council of Hotel Management and Catering Technology (NCHMCT), set up in 1982, is an autonomous body under MoT, for coordinating the development of hospitality education in India. NCHMCT regulates academic activities in the field of hospitality education and training, overseeing the activities of 21 central government-sponsored IHMs, 21 state government institutes, 15 private sector institutes and 7 FCIs. These institutes offer certificate, diploma, degree and masters programmes in different aspects of hospitality education.

NCHMCT conducts the Joint Entrance Examination for admission to the degree programmes—BSc. Hospitality and Hotel Administration, filling the 7,500 seats available across the country. NCHMCT also grants affiliation to institutes to run courses in hospitality (NCHMCT, n.d.).

Institute of Hotel Management and Catering Technology

IHMCTs were established by MoT over the years to develop trained manpower in the supervisory and executive levels for the hospitality industry. The initial diploma programme has now been converted to a BSc. Programme in hospitality and hotel administration. Students are given intensive training in food production, F&B service, front office operations and housekeeping services. Till recently, government run IHMCTs were the only institutions offering courses in hospitality. However, in view of the increasing demand for skilled professionals, IHMCTs have been started by state governments and some private entrepreneurs. Complementing the efforts of these institutes, the ministry has started programmes like 'Hunar se Rozgar Tak' (HSRT) (From Skills to Employment), aimed at providing short-term courses to develop skills related to the sector.

Hunar Se Rozgar Tak

HSRT is an initiative of the GoI, MoT. It was launched as a special initiative in the year 2009-10 for the creation of employable skills specific to hospitality and tourism sector amongst youth. This initiative has since grown manifold in magnitude and size. The objectives underlying this initiative are two-fold primarily:

1. To reduce the skill gap that afflicts the sector.
2. To work towards the accrual to the poor the economic benefit of growing tourism.

While the initiative is in the nature of an umbrella programme to cover training areas and trades in the sector on a sweep, the actualization so far has been largely relating to four hospitality trades namely food production, F&B services, housekeeping and bakery. The implementation of this initiative is in the hands of an assorted institutional base, comprising MoT-sponsored IHMFC institutes, institutes under the aegis of the state governments and the union territory administrations, the State Tourism Development Corporations and the star–classified hotels. A decision has been taken to also allow the government ITIs, colleges and universities which have brought up sector specific training facilities with MoT's assistance to implement HSRT.

Source: MoT (2014).

State Governments and Tourism

We have noted that state governments have a central role to play in tourism development in India. The Tourism department acts as a catalyst and facilitator, encourages investment, lays down policy and builds infrastructure. The department is the nodal point to provide last mile connectivity and undertaking domestic and international marketing campaigns. The department maintains offices and information centres, assisting visitors with information and services. The Policy framework prepared by the State Tourism department is the most important initiative that spells out the vision of the state in the tourism sector, the trajectory of growth to be pursued, the incentives that the state offers to attract investment and the investments that the state intends to make to boost tourism. An example of a state government which aims to influence the pace of tourism development through forward looking policy pronouncements is Andhra Pradesh.

Case Study: Andhra Pradesh Tourism Policy

Government of Andhra Pradesh (GoAP) firmly believes that tourism sector can be a major growth engine for economic development, employment, generation and eradication of poverty. GoAP has envisaged a mission-based approach to firmly set Andhra Pradesh on the path of sustainable development and growth. The tourism sub-mission will focus on two key aspects: theme-based development to develop tourism projects under themes of beach, ecotourism, Buddhist, religious, heritage, MICE, recreation/adventure, spiritual/wellness and medical; and destination-based development through hub and spoke model to develop five important tourism hubs—Visakhapatnam, Vijayawada, Tirupati, Rajahmundry-Kakinada and Srisailam-Nagarjunasagar—by 2020.

A tourism policy 2015–20 has been formulated, with the following targets:

1. To be the most preferred state in India for domestic tourist arrivals and among top 12 states for international tourist arrivals.
2. To facilitate investments in the tourism sector to the tune of ₹100 billion and contribute 7% to the state GDP by 2020.
3. To facilitate creation of 500,000 additional jobs in the tourism sector.

Five Policy instruments have been identified to achieve these targets:

- Enabling a conducive environment for setting up and operating tourism infrastructure projects and services.
- Incentives to encourage and promote private investments.
- Industry status for tourism infrastructure projects for specified purposes.
- Comprehensive skill development and capacity building in the tourism sector.
- Marketing and branding of the 'Sunrise state' as a globally recognized tourist destination and facilitating investments through a dedicated Investment Promotion team.

Fiscal incentives, ranging from 55% to 15% of the total investment, are to be given to tourism infrastructure projects such as hotels, resorts, amusement parks, MICE centres, golf courses, training institutes, wayside amenities and museums. Similar incentives are offered for tourism services such as water sports, cruises, adventure services, ropeways, tour operations, souvenir shops and so on at destinations.

In order to ensure ease of doing business, a State Tourism Promotion Board will be set up, responsible for approving projects, incentives, policies and monitoring project implementation. There will be a state tourism promotion committee to evaluate, monitor and execute projects and to address multi-departmental issues.

The Policy intends to promote Andhra Pradesh as a tourism education hub, with the establishment of a tourism university with international technical collaboration (GoAP, 2015).

Discussion Questions

1. Make a presentation of the Policy outlining key points not covered in the summary above. Another person may present the policy of another state. Compare the two policies on investment, product development and promotion.
2. Have a discussion on the statement: 'financial incentives cannot be a substitute for accurate project report preparation based on field data'.

State Tourism Development Corporation

In most of the states, the work related to the tourism department is conducted through the PSUs under the department – the state tourism development corporation.

There are STDCs in all the states of India, involved in all aspects of the tourism business. These provide accommodation facilities at far flung tourism destinations. Many STDCs run package tours opening up the state's treasures before the visitor. Often, these organizations have vehicles and coaches, providing transportation links to destinations and vehicles on hire. Some like Karnataka Tourism, operate luxury trains like The Golden Chariot. Many STDCs also operate in niche areas like ecotourism and adventure tourism, providing interesting options to the visitor in natural settings. The STDCs also take on the work of production of publicity and information materials, including maps, brochures, CD's and websites. A major area of operation is promotion and marketing. STDCs maintain sales and marketing offices in major cities of the country and organize promotional events and programmes. Some STDCs invest in large scale marketing campaigns which include print, television and Internet advertising, participation in international tourism marts like ITB and WTM and organizing familiarization tours and press visits. The STDCs are the channels for utilizing the funds provided by MoT, creating properties for accommodation, wayside facilities and tourism infrastructure. Tamil Nadu Tourism Development Corporation (TTDC) is one of the public sector units which have been recording a net profit, with operations spread across accommodation and tour operations.

Brihadeeshwara temple, Thanjavur

Case Study: Tamil Nadu Tourism

Tamil Nadu Tourism comprises Tourism Department in the Secretariat and a Commissionerate of Tourism functioning to formulate policies and implement programmes for the development of the tourism sector in the state. TTDC is a state-owned PSU to initiate novel ventures and innovate new schemes for providing demonstration effect.

(Continued ...)

As the nodal agency for development of tourism in the state, the department plays a crucial role in catalysing private investment, strengthening promotional and marketing efforts and providing trained manpower resources in the sector. All policy matters including development policies, incentives and manpower development and growth strategies are looked after by the department. The department is responsible for infrastructure and product development with central and state funds as well as research and monitoring functions. The department prepares the media plan and formulates strategies for marketing and promotion.

TTDC was incorporated in 1971 with the main object of promoting tourism by building tourism-related infrastructure on commercial basis. The corporation has the distinction of owning the largest chain of hotels in South India, with 54 hotels under the TTDC brand. Out of these, TTDC directly operates 23 hotels and 21 hotels have been leased to private hoteliers (Tamil Nadu Tourism, n.d.). TTDC has a fleet of 17 coaches and offers a wide range of package tours covering all South Indian states. The tour division operates rail-cum-road tour packages from major cities to Tamil Nadu.

In 2013–14, TTDC had a turnover of ₹1.0876 billion, with a net profit of ₹119.5 million (Department of Tourism, 2014).

Organizational Structure of Tamil Nadu Tourism

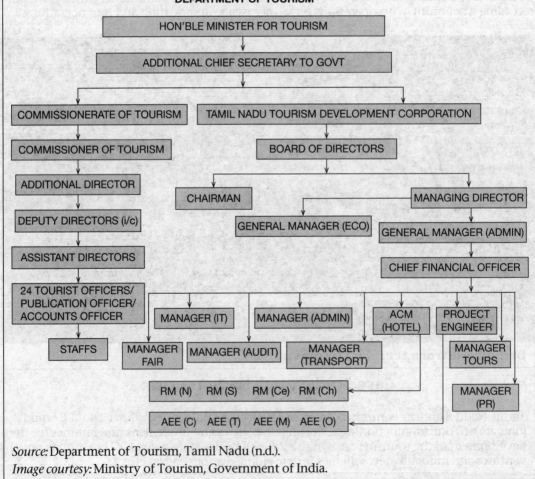

Source: Department of Tourism, Tamil Nadu (n.d.).
Image courtesy: Ministry of Tourism, Government of India.

(Continued ...)

Discussion Questions

1. Study the pattern of lease arrangement that Tamil Nadu tourism has adopted to bring in private sector to manage hotels. Have a discussion on whether this model can be followed by other public sector units.
2. From the website of TTDC, list out the packages offered by the PSU. Discuss the reason why TTDC is making a profit, in the face of competition by private sector units.

The STDCs were seen as the main vehicles for providing facilities for tourists in destinations, like the ITDC was seen as the primary hotelier providing world class facilities at the national level. This model was appropriate for a time when the regulatory environment was not conducive for private investment, and government investment in business was the norm. This public sector-oriented model has become outmoded in the present context of liberalization, international engagement and the flowering of private enterprise. It is abundantly clear that PSUs cannot effectively provide services in a sector like tourism with its emphasis on customer satisfaction and intense competition. This is one of the reasons why most public sector units, like STDCs, are facing losses and are unable to consistently maintain a high standard of service delivery. There are exceptions, of course, to this analysis, but it can safely be concluded that state governments need to look at new models of managing assets under their ownership, with a view to providing the best possible service to visitors. It must not be forgotten that the public sector has been entrusted with the best of public assets, which will be impossible to replicate by the private sector. However, it is in the best interest of tourism development that such assets are leveraged to obtain optimal results. Many STDCs have started considering disinvestment or alternative management models to involve the private sector. The success of Chhattisgarh Tourism Board in leasing out their properties is a case in point.

Another interesting question that emerges is whether it is right on the part of government to play the role of the regulator as well as operator. Many of the operations of the PSU are monopolistic in nature, meaning that the private sector is denied an opportunity to start operations, while the public sector unit is permitted to do so. Resorts within wildlife sanctuaries run by government agencies are examples of such a disparity. Similarly, STDCs using government funds to promote its properties while ignoring the properties established by the private sector also appear to be misuse of public funds, preventing a level playing field. Kerala has put in place a clear distinction between the STDC and the directorate, ensuring that opportunities for promotion and marketing are available to the private players who are at the same footing as the PSU.

Conclusion

Government plays myriad roles in tourism, all of which are important for the development of the sector. As tourism is still in early stages in India, there is duplication and intermingling of roles among governmental agencies and also between government and the private sector. This is only to be expected, as in the early days of our foray into tourism, government had to take on the role of the operator now in the hands of the private sector, entering into direct operations of running hotels and conducting tours. In developed countries too, this model was adopted in the past, to kick start tourism in many destinations. Once the initial investments were made and tourism activities stabilized, government agencies would exit direct operations, leaving these in the hands of the private sector. It is clear from international experience that the tourism industry has a lead role in developing and operating tourism products. The role of government is to support and steward such efforts, through strategic interventions. The tourism department works with the industry for review of policies and regimes, for instance, taxation and incentives, defining industry strategy and identifying significant infrastructure projects. Government has to work in close tandem with the industry in defining and reinforcing the brand and in conducting research and analysis studies. The primary role of government is to build and maintain core infrastructure, such as roads, water and waste water systems, power and also maintain amenities and products under the control of government agencies. The general industry view is that government must not take up activities that compete with private sector activities, and have a business friendly and transparent regulatory practice that facilitates development of tourism businesses.

Review Questions

1. Critically examine the policy measures adopted by GoI for tourism development.
2. Examine the case for plant tourism development in India.
3. Discuss in detail the various steps involved in tourism planning.

Activities

1. Visit a tourism destination of your choice. Make a table of positive and negative developments in the locality that can be attributed to the growth in tourism.
2. Organize a debate on planned tourism development in your state and prepare an outline of a project that can help in accelerating tourism development.
3. Visit a beach or a hill station and list out the impacts of unplanned development of tourism in natural attractions.
4. Hold a discussion and list five interventions made by the state government in your state as a facilitator that has contributed to tourism development during the last two decades.
5. Prepare a status paper on tourism education in your state giving emphasis to public sector, private sector, courses, curriculum and placement.
6. Arrange a visit to the office of STDC and find out its specific role in promoting tourism business.

References

Web Resources

Department of Tourism. 2014. 'Tourism: Demand No. 29'. Policy Note 2014–15, Culture and Religious Endowments, Tamil Nadu. Available at: http://www.tamilnadutourism.org/pdf/tour_e_pn_2014_15.pdf
——. n.d. 'Tourism an Overview—Organizational Chart'. Department of Tourism, Tamil Nadu. Available at: http://www.tamilnadutourism.org/organi-chart.html (accessed on 23 December 2016).
GoAP. 2015. 'Andhra Pradesh Tourism Policy 2015–20'. Available at: http://www.ap.gov.in/wp-content/uploads/2015/10/12062015YATC_MS9.pdf (accessed on 23 December 2016).
GoI. n.d. 'Tourism'. Planning Commission, GoI. Available at: http://planningcommission.nic.in/plans/mta/mta-9702/mta-ch23.pdf (accessed on 23 December 2016).

ITDC Ltd. n.d. 'The Ashok Group'. Available at: http://www.theashokgroup.com/images/investors/20150904_174344.pdf (accessed on 23 December 2016).

Ministry of Finance. 2007. 'White Paper on Disinvestment of Central Public Sector Enterprises'. Department of Disinvestment, Ministry of Finance, GoI. Available at: http://www.divest.nic.in/white%20paper.pdf

MoT. 2002. 'National Tourism Policy'. GoI. Available at: http://tourism.gov.in/sites/default/files/policy/National%20Tourism%20Policy%202002.pdf (accessed on 23 December 2016).

———. 2005. 'Master Plan for Ecotourism in Valley of Flowers—Hemkunt Belt'. GoI. Available at: http://incredibleindia.org/lang/images/docs/trade-pdf/surveys-and-studies/study-reports/Master%20Plan%20For%20Valley%20of%20Flowers%20-%20Hemkund%20in%20Chamoli%20District.pdf (accessed on 23 December 2016).

———. 2014. 'Hunar Se Rozgar Tak'. GoI. Available at: http://tourism.nic.in/writereaddata/Uploaded/Guideline/122620141103194.pdf (accessed on 24 December 2016).

———. 2015. 'Swadesh Darshan and Prasad Schemes'. Press Information Bureau, GoI. Available at: http://pib.nic.in/newsite/PrintRelease.aspx?relid=123582 (accessed on 23 December 2016).

———. n.d. 'PRASAD'. GoI. Available at: http://tourism.gov.in/sites/default/files/Scheme%20Guidelines_8.pdf (accessed on 23 December 2016).

NCHMCT. n.d. 'Annual Report'. National Council for Hotel Management and Catering Technology. Available at: http://www.nchm.nic.in/annualreports (accessed on 23 December 2016).

Planning Commission. 2011. 'Faster, Sustainable and More Inclusive Growth: An Approach to the 12th Five Year Plan'. Planning Commission, GoI, New Delhi. Available at: http://planningcommission.gov.in/plans/planrel/12appdrft/approach_12plan.pdf (accessed on 23 December 2016).

Swadesh Darshan and Prasad Schemes. (2015). In Press Information Bureau. Ministry of Tourism. Government of India. Retrieved from http://pib.nic.in/newsite/PrintRelease.aspx?relid=123582 (accessed on 10 January 2016).

Tamil Nadu Tourism (n.d.). Retrieved from http://www.tamilnadutourism.org/about-ttdc.html (accessed on 10 January 2016).

Tourism (n.d.). In Planning Commission. Government of India. Retrieved from http://planningcommission.nic.in/plans/mta/mta-9702/mta-ch23.pdf (accessed on 10 January 2016).

Tourism an Overview—Organisational Chart. (n.d.). In Department of Tourism, Tamil Nadu Retrieved from http://www.tamilnadutourism.org/organi-chart.html

Tourism: Demand No. 29. (2014). In Policy Note 2014-15. Department of Tourism, Culture and Religious Endowments. Tamil Nadu. Retrieved from http://www.tamilnadutourism.org/pdf/tour_e_pn_2014_15.pdf (accessed on 23 December 2016).

The Economic Times. 2016. 'ITDC identifies five hotels for disinvestment'. *The Economic Times*. Available at: http://articles.economictimes.indiatimes.com/2016-02-12/news/70568934_1_india-tourism-development-corporation-itdc-hotel-janpath (accessed on 23 December 2016).

Union Budget. n.d. 'Privatisation'. Available at: http://indiabudget.nic.in/es2002-03/chapt2003/chap710.pdf (accessed on 23 December 2016).

White Paper on Disinvestment of Central Public Sector Enterprises. (2007). In Department of Disinvestment. Ministry of Finance. Government of India. Retrieved from http://www.divest.nic.in/white%20paper.pdf (accessed on 4 April 2016).

Suggested Readings

Books

Gunn, C.A., and T. Var. 2002. *Tourism Planning: Basics, Concepts, Cases.* New York: Routledge.

Hall, C.M. 2007. *Tourism Planning: Policies, Processes and Relationships*, 2nd edn. Harlow: Prentice Hall.

Web Resource

MoT. 2015. 'Draft National Tourism Policy'. GoI. Available at: http://www.tourism.nic.in/writere-addata/CMSPagePicture/file/Events/Draft_National_Tourism_Policy_2015.pdf

The temples at Mahabalipuram
Image courtesy: Amit Kumar

Section D: Towards the Future

In this final section, we focus attention on a few issues that are currently important to tourism worldwide, but will assume such importance in the future that every person in the sector will be affected by the changes that will take place in their wake. In the future, there will be significant changes in tour packaging and pricing, the modes of travel, preferences of tourists, attractions and popular destinations.

Chapter 16 examines the different types of impacts that tourism development has had on destinations and local communities. Tourism is not an 'isolated' industry; its existence is dependent on a vibrant interaction with the local environment and people. While bringing the fruits of development, such as increased incomes and better quality of life, tourism may also cause great damage to the cultural fabric and pristine environments. The chapter also looks at strategies that may be adopted to minimize the negative impacts and achieve sustainable levels of tourism.

The aspect of 'sustainability', which has popped up in several contexts, occupies centre stage in Chapter 17. Tracing the history of the sustainable development paradigm, students are taken through the more important international initiatives and the principles that emerged through these deliberations. More and more businesses are turning towards sustainable practices and systems, and processes are changing to incorporate these principles. Certification systems will increasingly play a role in providing reliable information to the consumer.

Chapter 18 on climate change describes a grim scenario—the effects of global warming caused by increased temperatures across the world. Experts predict that the world will witness rising sea levels, desertification and deforestation. Tourism is both a victim and contributor to climate change, and the chapter will look at both these aspects at length. The adaptation and mitigation strategies are also explained in detail.

The final chapter, Chapter 19, of the book bears the same name as the section—Towards the Future. Some of the major developments that will shape the tourism business are explored in the chapter. E-business has transformed the travel sector, and information and communications technology (ICT) will exert great influence on the sector in the future, changing the way travel products are created, marketed and sold. Shifts in demographics, such as increased lifespan and falling birth rate will also affect the design and positioning of tourism products. New source markets will dramatically change destination marketing strategies, with China and India poised to see the highest growth rates in outbound traffic. Tourism in the twenty-first century will be very different from the previous century, and all of us will need to change and adapt to be part of this exciting future.

Section D: Towards the Future

Village life experience tour
Image courtesy: Department of Tourism, Government of Kerala.

CHAPTER 16

Impacts of Tourism

By the end of this chapter, students will be able to:

- Grasp the ways in which tourism influences the society, economy and environment.
- List the negative impacts of tourism in socio-cultural and environment spheres.
- Gain insights into the need for minimizing negative impacts for ensuring sustainable development.
- Delineate the impacts of tourism on various ecosystems.

Introduction

Destinations are the theatres in which tourism products and services are produced and consumed. The changes that happen in destinations depend on the kind of tourism that takes place, the type of tourists visiting the destination and the preferences and choices they exercise during their stay.

What are the different types of impacts of tourism on destinations? This question is of critical importance to any student of tourism. The universal acceptance of tourism as an economic activity is attributed to its labour-intensive nature resulting in the creation of employment, income and support to development process. Being a multi-faceted industry, tourism interacts with existing socioeconomic and environmental aspects of the destination, creating benefits and sometimes undesirable effects. Tourism may bring economic benefits and the fruits of development; it may also leave harmful effects on destination communities.

It is important to understand these impacts in specific, measurable terms. This chapter will focus attention on the economic, social, cultural and environmental impacts that tourism can bring to a destination. For policy-makers and development planners, the sector of tourism has to be seen as an integrated whole, with its positive and negative effects assessed in respect of all these three areas.

Economic Impacts

Tourism as an economic activity cuts across various productive sectors in the economy. The positive economic impact of tourism is seen in the generation of income, increase in employment avenues, influx of foreign exchange and local development. For a destination, the structure of the local economy needs to be understood to gain insights on its capacity to derive benefits out of tourism development. The level of dependence of a destination on the tourism sector is another significant aspect that has great implications for future growth of the sector.

Governments have struggled to objectively assess the economic benefits that tourism brings to a destination. However, recent models such as TSA, which we discussed in Chapter 2, have created robust frameworks to measure the impacts of tourism.

Generation of Income

Governments and the local communities are the main beneficiaries of income generation brought by tourism activities. Government revenues can be *direct*, such as income tax from jobs created by tourism, corporate taxes on tourism-related businesses and levies like departure taxes; or indirect, such as value added tax, sales tax, service tax and excise duties levied on goods and services consumed by the tourists.

Tourism business takes place in destinations, with local community members and non-local entrepreneurs take part in tourism commercial activities. While business establishments directly deal with the tourists and supply goods and services, many members of the local community earn their livelihoods based on tourism, either through direct employment in the sector or through the supply of farm produce and foodstuff for hotels and restaurants. Sources of income generation to the local community include salaries, rentals from leasing out of land and buildings and profits from businesses. In many destinations, the local community is involved in the production and sale of souvenirs, local guiding, local transport, entertainment and recreation options.

Employment

Tourism is a labour intensive industry, with some estimates claiming that one in every eleven jobs created in the world is contributed by T&T. Studies have shown that the sector produces more employment for unit of capital invested, compared to manufacturing or agriculture. Employment generated by tourism can be broadly classified as direct, indirect and induced and construction related. Employment in hotels, travel and tour companies, airlines and other tourism establishments can be considered as direct employment. Indirect employment includes all activities that can be connected to tourism business but are not directly linked with tourists. This include supply of farm produce and other inputs to hotels and restaurants, outsourcing services like laundry, gardening, local transport and cargo movement. Incomes from tourism may induce people to undertake other economic activities resulting in the generation of employment, which is termed induced employment. Hiring of staff by a new fuel station in a destination to cater to the increased number of vehicles purchased by residents employed in the tourism sector is an example of induced employment. A large number of skilled and unskilled labours would be involved in the construction of hotels, resorts, restaurants, parks and amenities in a developing tourist destination. Once the construction work is over and the business starts functioning, these establishments need periodical maintenance, repair and upkeep. Hence, destinations open an avenue for construction-related employment.

Foreign Exchange Earnings

Many countries have an adverse balance of payments situation, which means that the payments made on imports of goods are more than the value of exported goods. Due to the dependence of critical imports like oil, these countries try to increase exports or encourage activities that bring in foreign exchange. Inbound tourism brings in foreign currency, which is why it is called an 'invisible' export. This earning in foreign exchange contributes to improving the balance of payments situation, and hence tourism is seen as an attractive economic sector.

Import Substitution

Domestic tourism may be regarded as a form of 'import substitution', as the expenditure incurred by domestic tourists remain within the country and does not flow outside the country, which would have been the case if these tourists had decided to take a holiday abroad.

Cascade Effect of Tourism Expenditure

Just as tourism sector generates employment which is direct and indirect, there is a cascade effect triggered by expenditure in the sector that flows through the local economy. The direct effects are the value of goods and services directly purchased by the tourists, less the costs incurred in importing those materials not locally produced. The establishments that receive this direct expenditure, such as hotels and restaurants, purchase goods and services in order to run their businesses. These include rentals paid, salaries, food and beverages supplies, payment for utilities like water and electricity. These suppliers in turn purchase goods and services from the local economy which is another round of expenditure. This system of cascading rounds of expenditure is called the indirect effect of tourism. There are also induced effects, the goods and services purchased by those earning incomes from the sector.

Local Development

The development of tourism in a destination brings with it investments made by governments to facilitate access and to provide high-quality services. These investments result in improved infrastructure facilities like road, transport, energy, water and communication which are beneficial to the local residents.

The Multiplier Effect

The magnitude of positive economic impact is largely decided by the multiplier effect on income and employment. Every rupee spent by the tourist can create connected economic activities which can ultimately augment the process of economic development in that area. This interdependence of sectors within an economy creates the multiplier effect—an increase in demand for a particular good or service will positively affect not only the units producing the good/service but also those units supplying these 'frontline' establishments.

This largely depends upon the existence of linkage effect of tourism industry. If a destination has a network of facilities that can meet the related requirements of the tourism business, the opportunity to redeploy the income generated can be utilized to the maximum extent, so that the benefit of the multiplier effect can be reaped by the destination. In other words, how

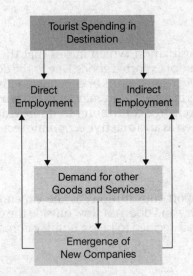

Figure 16.1   Multiplier effect in tourism
Source: Authors.

the initial expenditure on tourism circulates within the destination through various economic activities decides the value of the multiplier effect on income and employment. This effect plays a decisive role in determining the magnitude of economic impact of tourism in a destination. Multiplier effect is normally expressed as a ratio between the increase in output or income to the increase in tourist expenditure (Figure 16.1).

Leakages

The size of the multiplier largely depends on the chances of ensuring economic linkages in the local economy and effectively plugging the 'leakages' that take away money from the economy. For example, if the establishments in a destination meet a substantial part of their requirements from outside the destination or even outside the country, a large part of the income generated by tourist consumption leaves the destination, reducing the value of the multiplier effect. Leakages occur due to demand-side factors, such as the desire of some tourists to consume international brands and imported goods, or supply-side issues, such as the limited capacity within a destination to supply goods consumed by tourists. Minimizing leakages and maximizing linkages will largely decide the success of the economic impact of tourism in a destination.

Inflation

A situation of general rise in prices, bringing down the value of money, is called inflation. Tourist destinations are often subjected to localized inflation. Generally, prices of commodities may rise due to increased demand and limited supply. Abnormal increases in land prices result in the local community moving away from the preferred areas in destinations, urbanization and the influx of real estate businesses.

Over Dependence

The dependence of the economy on tourism receipts has been studied carefully because of the impact it has on destinations. Tourism earnings, expressed as a percentage of total exports, provide an accurate picture of the level of dependence of the economy on tourism. The growth of tourism in a destination may result in a drop in employment in traditional occupations and economic activities. For example, traditional fishing activity in a coastal area may be affected as a result of the development of a beach resort with its consequent disturbances. Overdependence on tourism may create a precarious economic situation, as the fate of the destination becomes dependent on the socioeconomic conditions of tourism generating regions. For example, if the source market of a destination is affected by economic depression, the number of visitors taking a holiday will come down, affecting the business and economic situation of the destination. Apart from economic downswings, tourism is vulnerable to socioeconomic and environmental phenomena happening in other parts of the world, such as terrorist attacks, natural calamities and political upheavals, leading to uncertainties in the tourism business.

Enclavization

Enclavization happens when the tourists are provided all their requirements at a single location or resort, which discourages any expenditure outside this location or any contact with the local community during their tour. In such cases, the community at the destination fails to get any opportunity to generate income through tourism. This situation is more explicit in cruise tourism, 'all-inclusive' resorts and islands that are hired by tourism companies.

Sustainable economic development of tourism presupposes an inclusive growth strategy, so that the benefits remain within the community and is shared by large sections of society. Research on business development in the backdrop of the existing socioeconomic condition should be promoted to supplement innovative practices which can contribute towards product development and promote linkages. Projects that can be operated by the local community through micro, small and medium enterprises should be supplemented by adequate capacity-building and skill-oriented training programmes which will enable unemployed and under employed youth to engage in productive activities through tourism.

Social Impacts

Tourism is necessarily a 'people industry', with the visitor interacting with people of a different culture, lifestyle or ethnicity, in the alien environment of a destination. This interaction is what makes tourism unique—the consumer travels to the destination to consume the product. The contact between the 'host' and the 'visitor' brings with it the potential for change, both positive and negative, not merely for the local community but even for the visitor. Compared to economic impacts, socio-cultural impacts are not quantifiable and hence difficult to measure. Socio-cultural impacts can be experienced in the destination over a period of time.

The socio-cultural impacts produced by tourism activity in a destination depend on many factors. Predominant among these is the kind of tourism, and the nature of the tourist, that travels to the destination. In a previous chapter, we examined the different typologies of tourists. The type of tourism product will determine the type of tourists that are attracted to a destination, which in turn may determine the socio-cultural changes brought into the destination. Other important determinants of the impacts of tourism are the pace of tourism development in a destination, the geographic spread of such tourism development and the kind of developers that spearhead these changes.

Socio-cultural impacts can also be classified into direct and indirect changes. The changes in behaviour and attitude in those persons who come in direct contact with the visitor may be termed as direct impacts. They, in turn, may influence members of the community by their changed behaviour, which may lead to changes in their behaviour patterns, an example of indirect impact of contact with the visitor.

Preservation of Culture and Traditions

Apart from enabling social development through employment creation, income distribution and reduction of poverty, tourism helps to promote protection of culture, heritage, cultural diversity, peace and harmony. In a globalizing world, traditional practices, customs and cultural forms are under threat, with the present generation disinclined to follow in the footsteps of their elders. Tourism brings respect and value to these activities, as visitors are eager to learn about cultural contexts different from what are familiar to them. Visible symbols of culture and tradition, such as art forms, skills and practices, have been supported and preserved because of the interest of visitors in these and the prospect of financial benefits for the practitioners. Accordingly, places known for culture and tradition are now preserving these assets, which are being marketed as tourism products. This enables not only the preservation of culture and heritage but also brings more employment to the destination. It also fosters a sense of pride in the traditions and practices. It must be noted that these so-called positive impacts may not be seen as beneficial by some in the community, who may prefer to keep away from tourists.

Civic Pride

The advent of tourism may instil a sense of pride in the resident and an increased awareness of the natural and cultural heritage of the destination. Interest of the visitor in cultural symbols may trigger an increased sense of ownership and an urge to preserve and protect local crafts and customs.

Cultural Commodification and Loss of Authenticity

Commodification is converting anything into an object for commercial use. Cultural commodification refers to the alteration of cultural forms and crafts to create commodities that have a ready market. Traditional craftsmen often change the designs, raw materials and method of production to produce souvenirs that may attract the tourist and result in sales. In the process, they may abandon the time consuming traditional practices, losing these skills permanently while they try to cater to a new market. Performing art forms are often presented out of context and in curtailed forms before the visitor, distorting the cultural context. A Kathakali performance, which traditionally lasts for many hours, is transformed into a 'capsule' form to be performed to tourists within an hour, devoid of its intricacies and nuances.

The phenomenon called 'staged authenticity', the recreation of events and rituals for the benefit of the visitor, is another concern for cultural destinations. The sanctity and cultural moorings associated with an art form is destroyed when it is performed, for instance, in a hotel environment. A good example is the tendency to stage 'Theyyam', an ancient ritual in which an individual is possessed with divinity, before tourists in an alien environment. Theyyam, performed with ritualistic fervour in the sacred groves of the villages is also performed on the streets in front of tourists as part of showcasing the 'culture' of Kerala. These distortions may result in a situation where even the local community fails to distinguish between the authentic and the 'touristy' forms.

Standardization

It is common belief within the tourism industry in destinations that products or services offered to tourists must not be too 'strange' to them. Mass tourism is the reason why such beliefs have become entrenched in the minds of service providers that tourists at a new destination would search for items they are familiar with, such as F&Bs and international brands in accommodation facilities. Although this may not be possible to be provided in all destinations, service providers in the industry attempt to standardize products and services, losing in the process the unique qualities and experiences that destinations may be able to offer.

Strained Kinship and Family Relations

An alarming development with sociological implications is strained kinship and family relationships in destinations. It is reported that schools located near tourist destinations face dropouts during tourism season, as children find an opportunity to earn money through petty trade. Although such activities bring a degree of financial empowerment, there is also the tendency to disobey their parents and question them. This leads to tensions within families and the rupture of family relations and roles.

Inbound and Outbound Migration

Tourism brings inbound and outbound migration at the destination. Inbound migration happens when the local community does not have the skills required for the tourism industry, attracting non-local labour which migrates to the destination in search of employment. Local community members involved in traditional livelihood activities at the destination may lose their livelihoods with new tourism development because of displacement, loss of access to common property, pollution or changed regulations. This may result in outward migration, as local community members move out of the destination in search of livelihood. Sometimes, a large quantum of land is acquired for tourism projects which results in forced displacement of local community from the destination.

Resentment and Friction

Employment of non-local persons in higher and skilled positions in tourism enterprises leads to resentment amongst the local population. The jobs generally occupied by the local community members are unskilled positions at the lowest level of the pyramid, such as cleaning staff, gardeners and maintenance personnel. The disparity in status and incomes may result in a building up of social tension between the local community and business owners. Denial of access to certain parts of the destination—fenced off areas on beaches, casinos, clubs and marinas—may also lead to pressure and conflict.

Demonstration Effect

The local community may try to imitate the lifestyle, dress and other behavioural aspects of tourists. This 'demonstration effect' is a common negative impact that occurs in destinations where the local cultural norms are drastically altered by behaviour of the local community directly influenced by tourists. It may be kept in mind that the behaviour of the tourists and their dress 'style' in a tourist destination may be very different from what they would adopt in their home environments. Many studies have shown that tourists tend to adopt a lifestyle very different from their regular lifestyle while on holiday, with changes in patterns of behaviour, alcohol consumption and sexual activity. This may create a cultural conflict within the minds of the impressionable members of the local community, particularly the young generation. The 'hippie' culture which became popular in certain sections of the community in some Goa villages at a point of its development as an international destination is an unfortunate example of this demonstration effect.

Intrusion into Local Customs and Private Space

Many tourists visiting regions with conservative values and lifestyles do not display due sensitivity and respect while interacting with the local population or visiting public spaces used by the community. Photographing community members without permission, entering taboo places such as sacred and religious spots, wearing inappropriate dress are common causes for resentment.

In Kumarakom and other backwater villages of Kerala, the streams and canals are traditionally used for many household activities, such as bathing, washing their clothes and utensils and for evening conversation between neighbours. The plying of house boats and tourist boats through these water bodies has resulted in loss of privacy and the intrusive presence of tourists in their 'backyards' have led to great resentment, for the communities have lost the private space they have been enjoying for long years.

Increase in Crime

Tourism development often results in urbanization and overcrowding in the destination. There are regular reports of burglary and theft of valuables, with gangs descending on destinations to loot the tourists. Criminal activities, like drug use and gambling, are also reported from destinations. This aggravates social tensions within the destination as the local community members will also start involving in these illegal and unethical activities.

Exploitation of Women

It is seen that over 40% of the workforce in the organized sector of tourism comprises of women. They are usually relegated to relatively low skilled and low paying jobs like cleaning, housekeeping and laundry services. Women usually get part time or temporary jobs in the sector and there are complaints of discrimination in the wages paid, compared to their male counterparts. In the case of self-enterprises like homestays, it is the women who may face the additional burden of housework to cater to the guests who come to their home.

In tourism marketing, women are often used as the 'face' of a destination, with images of womens set in natural locales or cultural sites quite popular in destination brochures and publicity material. Women have been objectified and depicted as pleasure providers, and their portrayal in marketing campaigns is often patronizing and misleading.

Child Abuses

One of the most horrendous impacts of unbridled tourism growth in poor destinations is the exploitation of children. The exploitation and abuse of children span a range of activities and situations. Children are hired as low-paid labour in tourism enterprises, brought from far off villages by agents. They are used by vendors on beaches and tourist areas to sell trinkets, exploiting the sympathy generated among visitors. The most shameful of all is the commercial sexual exploitation of the children. Tourism may not be the only cause of the exploitation, but it provides easy access for it. Children are exposed to the globalized world and are attracted by the new pattern of consumerism. Lured by the prospects of owning 'modern' and fashionable accessories, such as mobile phones, laptops and bikes, youngsters fall into the trap of the sex trade. Sometimes children are trafficked to brothels near the tourism destinations frequented by paedophiles and forced to engage in sexual activities. In some places, an organized crime syndicate supported by networks of pimps, taxi drivers, hotel staff, brothel owners, entertainment establishments and tour operators offers tour packages exclusively for sexual fulfilment, with underage sex workers.

Child Abuse in Tourism

Salim began as a kitchen hand at a beachside restaurant in Goa for INR 10 a day. Six months later he was earning five times the amount peddling pineapple to tourists. Now nine years old, he is a self-styled entertainer. 'I sing, dance and run errands for the *firangi*s (foreigners). Sometimes they even ask for massage in their rooms'. However, prod further and the boy's eye go blank and he says he finds it embarrassing to talk about abusive situations he may have faced. When asked in which hotel he was taken to, he pointed towards the... (a prominent five-star hotel). The enterprise brings him about INR 150, a day, more than Salim used to make in an entire fortnight.

Source: EQUATIONS (2003).

Conflicts Arising Out of Resource Use

With more number of tourists coming to a destination, there would be stress on usage of natural resources like water and energy, which may lead to increased infrastructure costs for the local community like higher taxes for water supply, sanitation or energy facilities.

Use of Common Property Resources

Tourism resorts near the coast or water bodies prevent the use of these common property resources by the local community, preventing them from accessing these for their livelihoods as well as for recreation. There have been instances where the resort groups privatize the common property area, building walls and fences and restricting entry to the general public. In certain cases, they place umbrellas and benches on the beach area accompanied by security personnel. Restriction on usage of common property resources result in community-industry conflicts and it is usually seen that the local community ends up on the losing side.

Vandalism and Destruction of Sites

In certain cases, it is seen that there are damages to heritage sites from vandalism, spoiling, pilferage and illegal removal of cultural heritage items. Sometimes, dilapidation of cultural sites may occur when historic sites buildings and monuments are unprotected. In certain heritage areas, it is found that the newly constructed buildings do not match with the existing architecture, and sometimes traditional buildings are replaced with new structures as part of tourism development. This loss of 'visual integrity' reduces the value of the heritage site and the gradual loss of popularity of the destination.

Tourism is an activity that takes place in a socio-cultural environment where social institutions, relationship, customs, traditions and other aspects related to the social facets of life play a decisive role. Planners, destination managers and tourism businesses and of course the tourists should bear in mind that any alteration of the existing social systems will create uncompensated loss to tourism as well as the local community. Any attempt to superimpose external values and social systems in the destination society will ultimately result in the destruction of the original system and the social USP of the destination will be lost forever. It is important to keep in mind that the community has every right to live in their place of origin in a style and pattern of their own, and any intrusive activity like tourism should respect the primacy of the community on their rights to use common property resources, nurture their customs, traditions and continue their way of living. A keen awareness on the social environment and an understanding on the need to preserve it should be given prime importance while planning and developing tourism in a destination. A proper management solution for sustainable social system demands the role of community as a watchdog. Strategies need be evolved to preserve and enrich the existing social system and the heritage of a destination, side by side with strategies for tourism development. DMOs should develop codes of conduct pertaining to child abuse, women, labour exploitation and commodification of art and culture with the full participation of the community, and these should be implemented through civil society organizations, such as NGOs, elected bodies and social leaders. Tourism enterprises must be willing participants in such initiatives as these are essential for sustaining the business at the destination.

Environmental Impacts

The environment of a destination is a primary component of the tourism experience. All aspects of the physical environment—land, water, air, flora, fauna and the built environment—are ingredients of tourism and are affected in some way by its growth. Tourism has undoubtedly created major problems to the environment in destinations which witnessed large numbers of arrivals, but tourism even in small numbers can severely stress certain sensitive environments. With tourism development, there is increased construction of roads, airports, hotels and urban facilities. The waste generated by tourists becomes the burden of destinations and creates health hazards and affects livelihoods. Irresponsible actions by tourists have brought about grave problems such as destruction of coral reefs, forest fires and hunting of endangered wildlife. In many cases, it is the population of the destination that suffers the effects of the degradation to the environment.

For many years, these issues have been studied and documented, and it can be said that the days of wanton destruction of the environment, in the name of tourism, are gone. Several conferences have thrown light on the problem and suggested solutions. However, it cannot be said that tourism development is being carried out on the basis of sustainability principles.

Physical Impacts

Physical impacts of tourism can be of two types—physical impacts of tourism development and physical impacts from tourism activities.

Physical Impacts of Tourism Development

Construction and Infrastructure Development

Tourism-related facilities are often preferred on attractive landscape sites like coasts, primarily sandy beaches and dunes, in proximity to lakes and rivers, near forest areas and on exposed mountain tops. Large-scale construction in such sensitive sites creates irreversible changes in the ecosystem, like the destruction of sand dunes and natural formations, soil erosion and removal of natural flora. The construction of high rise buildings close to popular beaches creates environmental stress and visual pollution. Agricultural land is diverted for construction of tourism facilities, creating distortion in land use patterns that affect long term land usage, water flows and traditional agricultural practices.

Due to the establishment of tourism-related infrastructures and facilities, many species like the Oliver Ridley turtles are under severe threat.

Transformation of nesting habitat comes from the construction of new aquaculture ponds, fishing harbours and tourist facilities, as well as growth of existing coastal villages which are increasing in many parts of the world within the range of the Olive Ridley, particularly along the East coast of India (Pandav and Choudhury, 1999) and in some zones in coastal México to Central America. (Cornelius et al., 2007)

Deforestation and Unsustainable Use of Land

In regions which have lax forest laws and where private persons own forests, tourism is one of the main culprits for deforestation, with natural forests cut down to make room for 'eco-lodges' and luxury accommodation ('glamping'—glamour and camping!). Some coastal wetlands have been drained and filled up in the name of tourism for the construction of buildings, roads and other tourism-related establishments. The cutting down of natural flora such as mangroves in some backwater destinations in Kerala resulted in depletion of fish population in the water bodies, as the mangroves were the rich breeding grounds of local fish species. In some cases, trees and mangroves were removed only to provide unrestrained views of the lake for tourists!

Reclamation of Lake for Endogenous Tourism Project at Kumbalanghi

One of the main components of the Endogenous Tourism Project at Kumbalanghi, a backwater destination in Ernakulam district of Kerala was construction of a 4-acre Kalagramam or an Artist's Village in the middle of the backwater at Kallencheri in the panchayat (Local self-government). According to the proposal, the village was to house a handicrafts centre, a museum to preserve and exhibit traditional fishing equipment, an ethnic food court and an open-air theatre. The Artist's Village will also have a one-kilometre-long walkway along the banks of the backwater. This new land was to be created using sand dredged out of the backwater spread over 14 acres.

Source: Haridas (2006).

Physical Impacts from Tourism Activities

Marine Activities

Tourism can cause both direct and indirect impacts on sensitive marine ecosystems such as coral reefs. Snorkelling, diving and boating can cause direct physical damage to reefs, and fishing and collecting can contribute to over-exploitation of reef species and threaten local survival of endangered species. Indirect impacts relate to the development, construction and operation of tourism structures such as resorts, marinas, ports and airports. 'There are 109 countries with coral reefs. Reefs in 90 of them are being damaged by cruise ship anchors and sewage, by tourists breaking off chunks of coral, and by commercial harvesting for sale to tourists' (Responsible Travel, n.d.).

The impacts of tourism-related marine activities and its actual/potential impacts are depicted in Table 16.1.

Table 16.1 Marine activities and impacts

Activities with Direct Impacts	Actual and/or Potential Impacts
Snorkelling	Physical damage (breakage, lesions) Kicking up sediment
Scuba diving	Physical damage (breakage, lesions)
Motor boating and yachting	Physical damage from anchoring Physical damage from boat groundings
Fishing	Contribute to over exploitation of reef fish stocks Compete with local fishers
Collecting (shells, lobsters, conch, coral)	Threatening local survival of rare species Contributing to over exploitation and competing with local fishers
Activities with indirect impacts	Actual and/or potential impacts
Resort development and construction	Increased sedimentation
Resort operation — Sewage disposal fertilizer run off Irrigation	Nutrient enrichment
Resort operation — Solid waste disposal	Leaching of toxic substances from inappropriate waste disposal litter (especially, plastics)
Seafood consumption	Over exploitation of high priced resource species (snapper, grouper, spiny lobster, conch)
Demand for marine curiosities	Exploitation of rare/endangered/ vulnerable species such as shells, black coral, turtles
Construction of artificial beaches and beach replenishment	Increased sedimentation from sand removal or Beach instability
Airport construction or extension	Increased sedimentation from dredging and infilling
Marina construction Marina operation	Increased Sedimentation from dredging Pollution from inappropriate disposal of oils and paint residues
Motor boating and yachting	Pollution from fuelling Nutrient enrichment from sewage disposal Pollution from fuelling
Cruise ships	Nutrient enrichment from illegal sewage disposal litter from illegal or accidental solid waste disposal

Source: Tourism's impact on reef. Available at: http://www.unep.org/resourceefficiency/Business/SectoralActivities/Tourism/Activities/WorkThematicAreas/EcosystemManagement/CoralReefs/TourismsImpactonReefs/tabid/78799/Default.aspx (accessed on 24 December 2016).

Table 16.2 Impacts of trampling

Trampling Impacts on Vegetation	Trampling Impacts on Soil
Breakage and bruising of stems	Loss of organic matter
Reduced plant vigour	Reduction in soil macro porosity
Reduced regeneration	Decrease in air and water permeability
Loss of ground cover	Increase in run off
Change in species composition	Accelerated erosion

Source: Environmental Impacts of Tourism. Available at: https://www.gdrc.org/uem/eco-tour/envi/one.html (accessed on 24 December 2016).

Trampling

Tourists using the same path over and over again tramples the vegetation and soil, eventually causing damage that can lead to loss of biodiversity and other impacts. Such damage can be even more extensive when visitors frequently wander away from established trails. It is estimated that every year in the Indian Himalaya, more than 250,000 pilgrims, 25,000 trekkers and 75 mountaineering expeditions climb to the sacred source of the Ganges River, the Gangotri Glacier. They deplete local forests for firewood, trample riparian vegetation and litter. Studies conducted by University of Idaho have shown that the impacts of trampling can be on vegetation as well as soil. This is depicted in Table 16.2.

Changes in Habitat and Animal Behaviour

Tourism leisure activities can result in the degradation of habitat. Wildlife viewing can bring about stress for the animals and alter their natural behaviour when tourists come too close. Safaris and wildlife watching activities have a degrading effect on habitat as they often are accompanied by the noise and chaos created by tourists as they chase wild animals. This puts high pressure on animal habits and behaviour and tends to bring about behavioural changes. It has been observed that animals change their regular route of travel, sometimes get affected on the mating practices or neglect their young ones. In some places, live animals are used as bait to attract predators, in order to ensure sighting for tourists.

Depletion of Natural Resources

Tourism development can put pressure on natural resources when it increases consumption in areas where resources are already scarce.

Water Resources

Water consumption by tourists and tourism facilities amounts to many times, (sometimes up to 10 times) the minimum domestic requirement. Only a miniscule portion of this amount is taken up for drinking or cooking. Water is mainly used in baths (bathtubs), swimming pools and to maintain gardens. Major water consumers are golf courses and water theme parks. It is estimated that an 18-hole golf course consumes 5 million litres of water while a water theme park consumes 1 million litres of water daily. This can result in water shortages and degradation of water supplies as well as generate large volumes of waste water. The problem primarily occurs in arid climates and on small islands with limited water supply, but even in many destinations with more plentiful precipitation, which are frequented by tourists during the dry season. Because of the hot climate and the tendency of tourists to consume more water when on holiday than they do at home, the amount used up by an individual tourist can be as high as 440 litres a day! This results in severe water shortages, depletion of water table, drying out of wetlands and intrusion of salt water into near-coastal freshwater biotopes. In destinations where piped water supply is not available, most tourist establishments tap into ground water sources for their requirements. The large quantities pumped up by these units drain ground water, lowering the water table, depriving local populations of water for their consumption and for agricultural use.

Local Resources

Tourism can create great pressure on local resources that may already be short in supply at the destination like energy, food and other raw materials. Because of the seasonal nature of the tourism industry, many destinations have more inhabitants in the peak season compared to the low season. A high demand is placed upon these resources to meet the high expectations tourists often have. Increased construction of tourism and recreational facilities has increased the pressure on land resources like minerals, fossil fuels, fertile soil, forests, wetland and wildlife and on scenic landscapes. Greater extraction and transport of these resources aggravate the physical impacts associated with their exploitation. Building resources are often removed from ecosystems for tourism-related constructions, like hotels and roads, in non-sustainable manner as in the case of extracting fine sand of beaches. This increases the danger of erosion of the beaches, so that in some cases sand is pumped onshore and coastal protection steps have to be taken.

Pollution

Tourism causes the same forms of pollution as any other industry like air emissions, noise, solid waste and littering, releases of sewage, oil and chemicals, architectural/visual and even light pollution.

Air Pollution

Air pollution in tourism is generally associated with the transportation sector. Transport by air, road and rail is continuously increasing day by day in response to the rising number of tourists. 'Air travel is the world's fastest growing source of greenhouse gases like carbon dioxide, which cause climate change. Globally the world's 16,000 commercial jet aircraft generate more than 600 million tonnes of carbon dioxide (CO_2), the world's major greenhouse gas, per year' (Friends of the Earth, n.d.). Lodging properties can produce toxic air pollutants and ozone depleting substances. Cleaning supplies, synthetic materials, paints and pesticides can release toxic air pollutants and volatile organic compounds (VOC). 'Ozone-depleting substances such as chlorofluorocarbons may be released by improperly maintained heating, ventilation and air conditioning (HVAC) units, refrigeration units and fire extinguishers' (United States Environmental Protection Agency, 2005). Sometimes air pollution is directly caused by tourism activity—tour buses often leave their motors running for hours while the tourists go out for an excursion because they want to return to a comfortably air-conditioned bus.

Solid Waste Pollution

Solid waste is another major problem, especially in developing countries where there are hardly any capacities for regulated disposal. In tourism destinations, waste disposal is a serious problem and improper disposal can be a major threat to the natural environment especially, rivers, backwaters, valleys and forest areas. It is estimated that cruise ships in the Caribbean produce more than 70,000 tons of waste each year. Solid waste and littering can cause visual impacts of the natural environment and cause death to animals, both terrestrial and marine. Trekking tourists in Nepal on expedition leave behind their garbage, oxygen cylinders and even camping equipment. In February 2014, 'a 40-year old female elephant was found dead with about two kg of plastic waste in its bowels in a forest near the holy hill Sabarimala' (Press Trust of India, 2014) resulting from the leftovers of the two month long pilgrimage.

Water Pollution

The pollution of water mainly occurs due to the discharge of untreated water, inorganic and organic wastes and sewage. Tourism industry contributes to water pollution mainly by discharge of fuel by the water transport or by dumping of organic and inorganic wastes from the accommodation sector. The other main source of water pollution is by high usage of fertilizers for golf courses which finally results in groundwater contamination. Sewage pollution can affect the ecological balance of an area, resulting in a conspicuous decline of species diversity.

Noise Pollution

Noise pollution in tourism is generally associated with the sound generated from transportation systems like airplanes, cars and buses as well as recreational vehicles such as ropeways, cable cars. It is reported from Nilgiris that 'many of hawkers from the plains trading in a variety of items including cheap musical instruments, add to the noise pollution' (Radhakrishnan, 2013). During the tourist season, the pristine environment of Manali and Ladakh is spoilt by the noise of all the cars and vehicles that crowd into these destinations. The noise pollution results in causing irritation and stress for the humans and wildlife, especially in sensitive areas.

Light Pollution

Tourism is one of the major culprits in light pollution all over the world.

> The effects of light pollution on plants and animals in the environment are numerous and are becoming more known. In general, the most common action is that light pollution alters and interferes with the timing of necessary biological activities. But for approximately half of all life, those nocturnal species that begins its daily activities at sun fall, our artificial lights at night seriously constrain their lives, exposing them to predators and reducing the time they have to find food, shelter, or mates and reproduce. (Light pollution harms the environment, n.d.)

Illuminations from beach side resorts pose problems for sea turtle nesting. Night safaris with powerful lights disturb natural hunting patterns. The powerful lights used by the vehicles in the night causes night blindness to animals resulting in collisions.

Aesthetic Pollution

Quite often tourism-related constructions fail to integrate with the natural features and indigenous architecture of the destination and look out of place. This happens mainly because of lack of proper land use plans and building regulation or its violations. This has resulted in rambling developments along coasts and other scenic routes.

Environmental Impact Assessment (EIA)

While there has been extensive documentation on the issues faced by destinations which may have been caused by tourism, an objective framework to assess the environmental impact needs to be in place. EIA is undertaken before a proposed development project is given permission to begin work, as a planning tool.

EIA can help the planner to understand the impact of a project on an aspect of the environment, or will be able to project in monetary terms the environmental costs that the project may entail. This will help an analysis of the usefulness of the project and its net benefits. Development projects can be modified or better systems incorporated at the initial stage itself, if the EIA is conducted professionally.

Positive Impacts of Tourism

It may also be noted that alternative forms of tourism emerged in the 1980s focused on a perfect synergy between tourism and environment and models have been developed for protecting the environment through tourism. The widespread acceptance of ecotourism can be attributed to this. Let us briefly discuss how tourism has contributed positively to environmental conservation

Raising Environmental Awareness

Alternative models of tourism have the potential to build public awareness on the importance of environment conservation as well as on the possible impacts of tourism on the environment. One of the major components of ecotourism is education and interpretation by which the tourists are educated on the importance of the nature, ecosystems and the biodiversity within it. The newly developed sustainable tourism criteria like GSTC build awareness for the tourism industry operators on sustainable practices that need to be incorporated while practicing tourism.

Contributions to Conservation

While practicing tourism in protected areas, entrance fees are collected from the tourists. These fees are used for the conservation of protected areas in many places. Some governments collect money in the form of user fees, taxes, sales or rental of recreation equipment and service charges, which are used to manage natural resources. The draft Guidelines for Ecotourism in and around Protected Areas, 2011 issued by Ministry of Environment and Forests, GoI, states that

> [A]s part of the state-level Ecotourism strategy, the State government should levy a "*local conservation cess*" as a percentage of turn-over, on all privately run tourist facilities within 5 km of the boundary of a Protected Area. The rate of cess should be determined by the state government, and the monies thus collected should be earmarked to fund Protected Area management, conservation and local livelihood development.

Although this has not been implemented in India, a cess is collected from service providers to fund conservation activities in certain destinations.

Conclusion

The dual impact of tourism is spread over positives as well as negatives. The growing environmental awareness and realization of the need for protecting the environment has been recognized as a boon to tourism industry. Today, planners, policy-makers and businessmen are focusing on environmental protection, promotion and even product development based on conservation measures. Efforts to promote and ensure sustainable development of tourism give prime focus to environmental aspects. Notwithstanding the prevalence of green washing in the tourism industry, some earnest attempts to protect the environment are being taken through community-based tourism activities and particularly through Responsible Tourism initiatives. The emphasis given to environment in Global Sustainable Tourism Criteria and the Responsible Tourism Classification System developed for Kerala should be an eye-opener to policy-makers and practitioners. Issues like waste management in tourism have to be addressed by integrating with the general waste management system adopted in the destination by local governments or the state government. It is high time that proper and scientific EIA and carrying capacity studies are carried out before major investments are made and certainly for popular destinations which continue to grow. The results of such exercises will enable planners to take appropriate decisions regarding the scale and type of tourism development.

The need of the hour is to have a harmonious blending of tourism with the socioeconomic environment of the destination resulting in the mutual benefit of tourist, community and the environment at large. To accomplish this, it is imperative to have an understanding on the positive and negative impacts of tourism on social, economic and environmental spheres. This will enable us to think and act rationally so as to use tourism as an effective tool for ensuring sustainable development bringing benefits to the present generation without depriving future generations of this potential. The endeavour is to minimize the negatives and maximize the positives to bring out the potential of the tourism sector as a growth engine of the economy.

Review Questions

1. Discuss the importance of tourism on society, economy and environment.
2. Examine the physical impacts of tourism activities on marine ecosystem.

Activities

1. Conduct a survey among hotels in a city which is close to you and examine the areas of operations through which the establishments are linked to local economy. Also find out the leakages of hotel business that could have been used for strengthening local economic development.
2. Divide the class into four groups and make a situational analysis of employment in a tourism destination focusing on direct, indirect and induced effects. Prepare an interview schedule covering qualification, experience, skill, working condition, salary and

perks, nature of employment, its impact on family and collect the required data. Organize a seminar on labour and employment in tourism and present your findings.

3. Following observation method, find out the demonstration effect of tourism in any one of the destinations and arrange a poster exhibition in your institute on the theme to create awareness on the impacts of demonstration effect.

4. Organize a focus group discussion of local community members in a tourism destination and identify the physical impacts of tourism development and physical impacts from tourism activities.

5. Development of tourism is closely followed by increased demand for natural resources and public goods in a destination. Conduct a study among the resident population in a destination and find out the magnitude of pressure on natural resources and public goods due to tourism development.

References

Books

Cornelius, S.E., R. Arauz, J. Fretey, M.H. Godfrey, R. Márquez-M., and K. Shanker. 2007. 'Effect of Land Based Harvest of Lepidochelys'. In *Biology and Conservation of Ridley Sea Turtles*, edited by P.T. Plotkin. Baltimore, MD: Johns Hopkins University Press.

EQUATIONS. 2003. 'Weighing the GATS on a Development Scale: The Case of Tourism in Goa, India'. EQUATIONS, India.

Pandav, B., and B.C. Choudhury. 1999. 'An Update on Mortality of Olive Ridley Sea Turtle in Orissa, India'. *Marine Turtle Newsletter* (83): 10–12.

Web Resources

Friends of the Earth. n.d. 'Aviation and Global Climate Change'. Friends of the Earth. Available at: https://www.foe.co.uk/sites/default/files/downloads/aviation_climate_change.pdf (accessed on 24 November 2016).

Haridas, A. 2006. 'Artist's Village yet to take off'. *The Hindu*, Kochi. Available at: http://www.the-hindu.com/todays-paper/tp-national/tp-kerala/artists-village-yet-to-take-off/article3235258.ece (accessed on 24 November 2016).

'Light Pollution Harms the Environment'. n.d. Available at: http://physics.fau.edu/observatory/lightpol-environ.html (accessed on 24 November 2016).

Press Trust of India. 2014. 'Plastic Waste from Sabarimala Devotees Kills Wild Elephant in Kerala Forest'. *Indian Express*. Available at: http://indianexpress.com/article/india/india-others/plastic-waste-from-sabarimala-devotees-kills-wild-elephant-in-kerala-forest/ (accessed on 24 November 2016).

Radhakrishnan, D. 2013. 'Tourists Cause Pollution Problems in Nilgiris dt'. *The Hindu*. Available at: http://www.thehindu.com/todays-paper/tp-national/tp-tamilnadu/tourists-cause-pollution-problems-in-nilgiris-dt/article4682459.ece (accessed on 24 November 2016).

Responsible Travel. n.d. 'How Responsible are Cruise Liners?' Responsible Travel. Available at: http://www.responsibletravel.com/copy/how-responsible-are-cruise-liners (accessed on 24 November 2016).

United States Environmental Protection Agency. 2005. 'Reducing Air Pollution from: The Hospitality Industry'. Owner/Operator Information Sheet, National Service Centre for Environmental Publication. Available at: http://nepis.epa.gov/Exe/ZyPURL.cgi?Dockey=P100BVZA.TXT (accessed on 24 November 2016).

Suggested Readings

Books

Hall, C.M., and A.A. Lew. 2009. *Understanding and Managing Tourism Impacts: An Integrated Approach.* Oxon: Routledge.

Mason, P. 2016. *Tourism Impacts, Planning and Management*, 3rd edn. Oxon: Routledge.

Rath Yatra, Puri, Odisha
Image courtesy: Ministry of Tourism, Government of India.

CHAPTER 17

Sustainable Development of Tourism

Learning Objectives

By the end of this chapter, students will be able to:

- Specify the origins and basic concepts of sustainable development.
- Trace the relationship between sustainable tourism as a subset of sustainable development.
- Familiarize themselves with major international initiatives and campaigns on sustainable tourism.
- Gain insights into global sustainable tourism criteria for hotels, tour operators and destinations.
- Explain the basic principles of responsible tourism drawing lessons from Kerala's experience.

Introduction

We have encountered the term 'sustainability' in several previous chapters. It is getting increasingly evident that the tourism business of the future, in whatever form and size, whether in source markets or destinations, will have to consider aspects of sustainability as integral to its existence. Issues related to sustainability are already part of any discussions about the prospects of tourism and will dominate any discourse on the future of tourism.

This chapter will approach sustainability by explaining recent initiatives at the global level that will take centre stage in the coming years. Every practitioner of tourism will be involved in some aspect of the activities that these initiatives are laying down, and it is important for us to be fully aware of the direction and nature of discussions that are currently taking place.

What Is Development?

The term 'development' has different connotations which change according to contexts and populations. Development can mean increase in material aspects such as wealth, quantity of production, infrastructure and GDP. It can also mean an improvement in employment, quality of life, social security and overall happiness of the population. It is a matter of perception, and our understanding of the term has evolved over the years. The Industrial Revolution is a landmark in the development history of the world as it set the background for urbanization, leading to a structural change in the socioeconomic fabric of the world. The model of mass production promoted by entrepreneurs such as Henry Ford gave impetus to ever-increasing production and the accumulation of wealth by exploiting natural resources, using technological advancements. On the agricultural front, vast stretches of forests and grasslands were converted to cultivation, with continuous use of pesticides and fertilizer. Rapid urbanization resulted in exploitation of water sources, profound changes in land use, killing of wildlife and waste disposal into water bodies. Disasters such as the Santa Barbara oil spill and movies like *Silent Spring* brought the environmental damage wrought by 'development' into the attention of society. More evidence was brought to the public domain about the problems of unbridled industrialization and the reckless use of chemicals for agriculture. While the advanced, 'developed' world went in for legislation to curb this menace, the developing part of the world continued its push for industrialization to cope with the demand for an improved quality of life for its citizens.

It is in this context that the United Nations Conference on the Human Environment was held in Stockholm, Sweden, in 1972. The idea of 'sustainable development' was born out of the efforts to find out a solution on the 'right' approach to development, keeping in view the need to have a healthy and productive environment. The concept, evolved following the Stockholm Conference, was further fine-tuned in 1992 in the first United Nations Conference on Environment and Development (UNCED), popularly known as Earth Summit, held in Rio de Janeiro, Brazil, resulting in the adoption of 'Agenda 21', which 'recognized each nation's right to pursue social and economic progress and assigned to States the responsibility of adopting a model of sustainable development'. During this period, the world witnessed several serious deliberations on resource use and conservation. The World Conservation Strategy by the International Union for Conservation of Natural Resources in 1980, the formation of World Commission on Environment and Development (WCED) in 1983 and its report on *Our Common Future* in 1987 need special mention. A programme for further implementation of Agenda 21 (Rio+5) was formulated by the United Nations in 1997 at New York and the World Summit on Sustainable Development (Rio+10) held in Johannesburg, South Africa, in 2002 followed by United Nations Conference on Sustainable Development (Rio+20)) at Rio de Janeiro, Brazil, in 2012. A close examination of these summits reveals the progressive initiatives adopted on sustainable development. For example, the Rio+20 gave emphasis on seven areas which include decent jobs, energy, sustainable cities, food security and sustainable agriculture, water, oceans and disaster readiness (UNCSD, n.d.).

World leaders assembled at the Millennium Summit in 2000 and adopted the United Nations Millennium Declaration with a view to reduce extreme poverty and setting out a series of time bound target of 2015 for addressing income poverty, hunger, disease, lack of adequate shelter while promoting gender equality, education and environmental sustainability. The 15-year efforts have been remarkably successful with reduction in number of people with extreme poverty, under nourishment, maternal mortality, under five mortality and increase in number of primary school enrolment rate especially girls, notable achievements in fight against HIV/AIDS, malaria and tuberculosis as well as improvement to access of sources of water. On New Year's Day of 2016, global leaders gathered at the United Nations Summit and adopted 17 SDGs of the 2030 Agenda for Sustainable Development to build on the success of MDGs. The idea for SDG was born in the Rio+20 Conference. SDGs mainly focus on addressing the root causes of poverty and also the universal need for sustainable development.

Millennium Development Goals and Sustainable Development Goals

MDGs:

1. Eradicate extreme poverty and hunger
2. Achieve universal primary education
3. Promote gender equality and empower women
4. Reduce child mortality
5. Improve maternal health
6. Combat HIV/AIDS, malaria and other diseases
7. Ensure environmental sustainability
8. Develop a global partnership for development

SDGs:

1. No poverty
2. Zero hunger
3. Good health and well-being
4. Quality education
5. Gender equality
6. Clean water and sanitation
7. Affordable and clean energy
8. Decent work and economic growth
9. Industry, innovation and infrastructure
10. Reduced inequalities
11. Sustainable cities and communities
12. Responsible consumption and production
13. Climate action
14. Life below water
15. Life on land
16. Peace, justice and strong institutions
17. Partnerships for the goals

Sustainable Development in Tourism

A perusal of the various conventions, conferences and declarations on sustainable development would reveal that tourism can play a significant role in augmenting sustainable practices across the world as it establishes a close linkage with society, economy and environment. This has necessitated the development of separate action programmes for tourism based on the international initiatives on sustainable development. This section attempts to familiarize major international initiatives on sustainable tourism—the Charter for Sustainable Tourism, Agenda 21 for the T&T industry, International Year of Ecotourism and Quebec Declaration.

Charter for Sustainable Tourism

The Charter for Sustainable Tourism was formulated by the participants of World Conference on Sustainable Tourism at Lanzarote, Spain, in 1995. The basic objective was to prepare guidelines which will appeal to the international community, including governments, public authorities, decision-makers and professionals in tourism, to work for the ultimate objective of achieving sustainable tourism development. The main principles and objectives of the declaration included following:

1. In the long run, tourism must be ecologically bearable, economically viable and socially equitable.
2. Tourism development should integrate natural, cultural and human environment giving due respect to the fragile ecosystems.
3. Local culture, community and their identity should be safeguarded while formulating strategies for tourism development.
4. Sustainable tourism development presupposes solidarity and mutual respect among all stakeholders in tourism.
5. Tourism must be based on the diversity of local economy and opportunities should be integrated for local economic development.
6. Tourism should preserve the quality of life of people and promote socio-cultural enrichment in destinations.
7. With the participation of NGOs and local communities, authorities should take action to integrate planning of tourism for sustainable development.
8. Special priority should be given to environmentally and culturally vulnerable areas, particularly in technical and financial aid to promote sustainable development.
9. A framework for positive and preventive actions to secure sustainable tourism development has to be developed by travel industry in conjunction with agencies/NGOs.
10. The environmental repercussions of transport in tourism should be given adequate attention.
11. A code of conduct for stakeholders should be adopted and implemented, particularly by the industry, for promoting sustainable tourism.

Agenda 21 for Travel & Tourism

Agenda 21 for the T&T industry is another major initiative which draws heavily from Agenda 21 for sustainable development. The initiative was launched by the major international organizations—the UNWTO, WTTC and the Earth Council for promoting tourism along environmentally sustainable lines. The primary focus was to create awareness on sustainable development among all stakeholders in tourism and to adapt programmes for local implementation. Accordingly, governments, trade organizations and national tourism agencies have to establish systems and mechanisms to incorporate sustainable development principles at the core of the decision-making process. Training, education, awareness, community participation, skill development, resource management, conservation, waste management, transport, health, partnership for sustainable development are given emphasis in Agenda 21 while developing and implementing systems for operation.

The United Nations declared 2002 as the International Year of Ecotourism (IYE) with a view to encourage the efforts taken by governments and various international organizations to achieve the aims of Agenda 21 in promoting development and protection of the environment. The activities around the IYE were designed with the objectives of generating awareness among public and private sectors, the civil society and the consumers on the capacity of ecotourism as an approach for sustainable local economic development. It focuses on contribution to conservation of natural and cultural heritages and improvement of living standards of people in those areas, disseminating methods and techniques for the planning, management, regulation and monitoring of ecotourism to ensure long-term sustainability and for promoting exchange of experiences in the field of ecotourism. The main event of the IYE was the

WES, which took place in Quebec City, Canada. The key purpose of the summit was to bring together various stakeholders of ecotourism and to enable them to learn from each other and identify the agreed principles of ecotourism as well as the priorities for future development and management of ecotourism. The significant outcome of the summit was the Quebec Declaration on Ecotourism, which produced a series of recommendations to governments, the private sector, NGOs, community-based associations, academic and research institutions, inter-governmental organizations, international financial institutions, development assistance agencies and indigenous and local communities.

The MDGs also place on record due emphasis to the role of tourism in eradicating extreme poverty and hunger, promoting gender equality and empowering women, ensuring environmental sustainability and developing a global partnership for development. Considering the multifaceted nature of tourism industry and close relation with economy, society and environment, we may find that all aspects envisaged in SDGs have practical significance in the tourism sector.

In the backdrop of these initiatives, efforts were taken periodically to promote specific initiatives to promote sustainable development of tourism at international and national levels. In this section, we will examine the major global efforts taken for sustainable development of tourism.

Major Sustainable Tourism Initiatives

Global Code of Ethics for Tourism

The Global Code of Ethics for Tourism (GCET) is a set of 10-point Articles to guide stakeholders in tourism including national and local governments, local communities, tourism industry and tourists in tourism development. The call for the code was mooted in a resolution of the UNWTO General Assembly in 1997. The draft code was prepared in 1999 and the final official recognition for the code was given on 21 December 2001 (UNWTO, n.d.a). The 10 articles conceived in the GCET are given below:

- Tourism's contribution to mutual understanding and respect between peoples and societies.
- Tourism as a vehicle for individual and collective fulfilment.
- Tourism, a factor of sustainable development.
- Tourism, a user of the cultural heritage of mankind and a contributor to its enhancement.
- Tourism, a beneficial activity for host countries and communities.
- Obligations of stakeholders in tourism development.
- Right to Tourism.
- Liberty of tourist movements.
- Rights of the workers and entrepreneurs in the tourism industry.
- Implementation of the principles of the GCET.

Although the Code is not a legal binding document, it offers a voluntary mechanism by which the stakeholders are encouraged to use the document.

Sustainable Tourism Eliminating Poverty

The sustainable tourism eliminating poverty (ST-EP) initiative was launched by UNWTO as a response to one of the MDGs set by United Nations to eradicate extreme poverty. The initiative promotes poverty alleviation by giving assistance to organizations that promote sustainable tourism projects with activities that specifically alleviate poverty, deliver development and create jobs for people living on less than a dollar a day. The ST-EP foundation was established in 2004 at Seoul, Republic of Korea, to take forward the initiative to different regions. ST-EP projects have been funded initially by a grant of the Korea Government, but augmented by international donors and through partnerships with organizations, like SNV, the Netherlands Development Organization. The project has rapidly increased since then and now includes more than 100 projects in 34 developing countries. The ST-EP initiative is based on seven mechanisms which focuses on employment of the poor in tourism enterprises, supply of goods and services to tourism enterprises by the poor or by enterprises employing the poor, direct sales of goods and services to visitors by the poor, establishment and running of small, micro or community-based tourism enterprises or joint ventures by the poor, redistribution of proceeds from tax or charge on tourists for the benefit of the poor, voluntary support by tourists or tourism enterprises to the poor and investment in infrastructure stimulated by tourism benefiting the poor (UNWTO, n.d.b).

Green Passport Campaign

The 'Green Passport' is a campaign launched to improve the tourism sector's efforts to communicate with tourists on sustainable tourism through campaigns on sustainability issues. The campaign developed within the framework of the International Task Force on Sustainable Tourism Development (ITF-STD) aims to raise tourists' awareness of their potential to contribute to sustainable development by making responsible holiday choices. The campaign takes the triple bottom line approach of responsible tourism, thereby ensuring respect for environment and culture, triggering economic benefits and social development for the local communities. A green passport website (http://www.unep.fr/greenpassport/) has been developed in English, French, German, Chinese and Greek which provides communication materials such as postcards, leaflets and brochures on sustainable tourism practices (UNEP, n.d.).

Green Passport

The Green Passport consists five sections for travellers, which include planning the trip, getting there, getting around, before going back and after the trip, giving a clear understanding on the various aspects involved so as to enable the stakeholders to behave in an environment friendly manner.

The campaign was launched jointly by United Nations Environment Programme (UNEP), the French Ministry of Ecology, Energy, Sustainable Development and Sea, the Brazilian Ministries of Environment and Tourism and other partners at the Berlin Tourism Fair in March 2008. Paraty, a city in Brazil, was chosen as the first tourism destination to implement the Green Passport Campaign at the local level, considering its natural and cultural features as well as the commitment of the local community for sustainable tourism development. The 'Green Passport' is an international campaign and is available for national adaptation by any country.

AITO Sustainable Tourism Guidelines

How to Travel Sustainably and Responsibly
Here are some simple, but effective, tips designed to help you support our objectives:

Before You Go...
Global warming
One of the biggest environmental costs when travelling is the carbon footprint created when you fly. For example, on a trip to India each passenger is responsible for releasing nearly two tonnes of the global warming gas carbon dioxide into the atmosphere. AITO operators support carbon-balancing initiatives, whereby the amount of CO_2 generated on a flight is calculated and the traveller pays to offset these emissions by investing in projects which lower CO_2 levels in the atmosphere. Examples include reforestation programmes, providing low-energy light bulbs to poor households so they burn less wood, developing community-based hydroelectricity and backing the development of cleaner cooking fuels.

We encourage you to follow suit and fly 'climate neutral'.

Language
'Hello', 'thank you' and 'goodbye', attempting to master a few words of the local language is a great way to bring down barriers. It also shows cultural respect.

Local customs
It is important to familiarize yourself with the local dress code, cultural etiquette and perhaps any pertinent political information too. Remember, you are the visitor and by showing respect you will be respected and appreciated.

Packing
Keep your packing to a minimum and avoid disposable goods. Waste-disposal facilities can be limited in some destinations and recycling is often non-existent in many parts of the world.

On Holiday...
Eat with the locals
Support local businesses and preserve traditional cuisine by dining in local restaurants.

Souvenirs and shopping
Wherever possible buy your souvenirs from local shops. Avoid buying souvenirs that exploit wildlife or threaten endangered species.

Plant and shells
Avoid picking or collecting plants and shells.

Wildlife and animal welfare
Avoid disturbing wildlife and damaging their natural habitat; do not feed animals or fishes.

(Continued ...)

Begging
Don't give out sweets or money, especially to children. Giving will only teach them that begging is rewarding and can undermine parental authority.

Litter
To state the obvious, the world is full of it—don't add to it!

Photos: Think before you click
People in colourful local dress always make good subjects for photographs, but ask before you snap.

Water: Pollution and usage
If it is necessary to wash in streams or rivers, do not use detergents or other chemicals; it may be someone's drinking water further downstream.

Once Back Home...
Continuing support
Many tour operators support a wide variety of charitable initiatives, or advise you where to direct your support, so that you can 'give something back' to the destination of your choice.

Source: AITO (n.d.)

Green Hiker Campaign

The Green Hiker Campaign is an initiative of World Wide Fund for Nature (WWF) to inspire tourists and tour operators in the Himalayan region to opt for sustainable model of tourism (WWF India, n.d.). The human activity in Himalayas, especially tourism activities like hiking, has resulted in severe threat of the pristine ecosystem. There have been damages to the high altitude wetlands in the region and the fauna, especially the birds and mammals, find it difficult to breed and bourgeon as they used to do earlier. Tourists leave a lot of litter while they make their visit, and this has been the major cause for environmental degradation. The campaign by WWF is to raise awareness about environmental issues and thereby encouraging tour operators and tourists to decrease their impact on the local environment. The campaign in India was launched in June 2010 in association with MoT, GoI, with the slogan 'nature leaves a mark on you, don't leave one behind' (Hi-Tec, 2010). The campaign was later extended to other countries like Bhutan and Nepal which borders the Himalayas.

Case Study: They're Our Mountains, After All

My first Goecha La trek has been my most memorable trek till date, with the Himalaya at their astounding best and Kanchenjunga, the icing on the cake! The entire trek took us from September 29 to October 8, 2012. With the strong motivation to contribute to the conservation of this untouched beauty, my team and I signed up for the Green Hiker campaign. Under the campaign, we took the following initiatives on our trek: Our first mantra was 'have legs, will walk'. During the eight days it took from the base camp at Yuksom to the summit at Goecha La, and then back to Yuksom, we only walked. Not only was it a thrilling experience to get up close and personal with nature, but it was also reassuring to know that we weren't causing any air pollution. From Day 1, we carried out a cleanliness drive throughout the trek, collecting any garbage found on the way and stuffing it into our daypacks. The majority of this waste was left behind by trekkers and other tourists who passed by that route. To make the drive more efficient, I assigned each team member with one kind of garbage to collect, that is, one would pick up plastic plates and glasses, while another would pick up food wrappers and so on. The garbage we collected every day was dumped into the bin of the nearest trekker's hut or a makeshift dustbin. We ensured that no plastic waste was left behind. We reused water bottles that we collected on the way. This way, the use of plastic was curtailed as we no longer purchased or used new plastic bottles. Before stepping into a stream, we made sure to remove our footwear and bags, especially since the stream water is the main water source not only for trekkers but also local people and animals. We sought accommodation only in home stays and trekker huts which not only minimized resource consumption but also benefitted the local economy. None of these trekker huts had electricity; nevertheless, they were great places to bond with fellow trekkers after a long day's walk.

In places where trekker huts were not available, we set up tents at an optimum distance from water bodies to avoid any kind of disturbance. We did not even camp at Samiti Lake (one of the most scenic places in the trek) to help preserve its purity and beauty. Majority of the trekker huts had decent toilet facilities which consisted of pits dug deep into the ground. In places without toilet facilities, we choose to dig small pits and covered the same with mud once done. For this, we chose spots away from water bodies to prevent pollution. We used only headlamps and torches for light and lit no campfires to avoid air pollution or the danger of accidental forest fires. Our food was cooked on traditional kerosene stoves and our tour operator ensured that minimum forest resources were utilised. In addition, we carried packed lunches and protein bars to prevent unnecessary consumption of fuel for cooking. We felt a lot of emotions during our trek. There was joy on reaching Goecha La summit after 10 gruelling days of climbing, sadness on realising that the trek was drawing to a close, frustration at missing out on some gorgeous views due to fog. But more importantly, we felt a sense of responsibility towards the Himalaya—to protect, to conserve and to respect. More than the trekking, the fact that we did our bit to protect these majestic mountains gives me utmost happiness and motivates me to trek again.

I'd like to thank the Green Hiker team for starting such a wonderful initiative, my trek mates who worked together as a team and our tour operator for ensuring that we trekked responsibly. All in all, I've had a great experience as a green hiker and I hope to implement these sustainable measures in my future treks as well.

Discussion Questions

1. Examine how responsible tourism can be practised with stakeholder's participation in mountain ecosystem.
2. Discuss how tourist can engage themselves in conservation activities during trekking.

Source: Krishnamachary (2013).

Hotel Energy Solutions

Hotel Energy Solutions (HES) is a project created to increase energy efficiency in European small and medium hotels in response to the contribution of tourism industry to climate change especially the accommodation sector. It is estimated that tourism industry contributes to 5% of the world's CO_2 emissions, out of which the accommodation sector contributes to 2%. The project aims to increase energy efficiency in small and medium European hotels by 20% and their use of renewable energy sources by 10%. The project initiated by UNWTO was done with the support of Intelligent Energy Europe in close partnership with UNEP, International Hotel and Restaurants Association (IH&RA), European Renewable Energy Council (EREC) and French Environment and Energy Management Agency (ADEME). The project delivers information, technical support and training to help small and medium enterprises (SMEs) in the tourism and accommodation sector across the EU-27 to increase their energy efficiency and renewable energy usage as well as developing policies to increase sustainability.

The energy toolkit provided by HES helps the accommodation sector to develop strategies to reduce energy consumption, energy bills and environmental impact. The energy benchmarking tool and the decision-support sequence provided in the tool helps in evaluating carbon emissions and provide mitigation techniques for energy efficiency options. The energy-related report provided by the HES gives an indication of the overall electricity consumption and the usage of renewable energy in the hotel while assessing the possibilities of reduction in energy consumption. The Carbon Foot Print Report of HES provides an estimate of the quantity of CO_2 emitted in relation to hotel energy consumption. The Carbon Footprint calculator associated with it provides data on the hotel's consumption of electricity, fossil fuel, biomass and renewable energy. The return on investment calculator provides the hotelier the best investment choice in relation to technology solutions for energy management.

Case Study: Energy Savings at Hotel Chateau Montagne, Bulgaria

Chateau Montagne Hotel is a new hotel, opened in the beginning of 2007. It is located in the central part of the Troyan town. The hotel is a three-star category family hotel and has a total number of 60 beds. It has a restaurant, lobby bar, fitness centre, sauna and massage hall. Chateau Montagne offers room service, tourist information and free parking for its customers. The hotel is also suitable for business tourism with its convenient conference hall.

The hotel was assessed under the cleaner production (CP) methodology as a part of the Programme for Sustainable Development of Enterprises in Bulgaria. The following energy efficiency options have been identified in 2008:

CP Options	Environmental Benefits	Economic Savings
System for change of sheets and towels in the rooms upon visitors request and put signs for visitors for the availability of such an option.	25% reduction of changing of sheets and towels—Reduction of water, detergents and energy for washing the towels and sheet.	Investment—Printing materials (paper, toner)=80 BGN/year 30 working hours per year Savings—518 EUR/y (1013 BGN)
Switch off the mini bars, when the rooms are not in use.	Reduction of consummation of electricity by 29,946 kWh per year	Investment—40 working hours per year Savings—759 EUR/y (1484 BGN)

The hotel management implemented the proposed options for direct implementation in 2009. At the same time the management started a monitoring-program, which will provide regularly data for energy monitoring and evaluation of the proposed measures. What is more important is that the process of option generation, evaluation and continuous improvement of the processes is accepted and in practice at the hotel. The benchmarking indicator total energy consumption, kWh/Guest night has been reduced from 44.55 kWh/guest night in 2008 to 22.29 in 2009 while the EU reference value for the category is 34.2 kWh/guest night. For 2009 the savings achieved are more than 7,690 EUR, also by introducing energy efficient lighting.

Discussion Questions

1. Identify the major energy saving measures that can be adopted by a resort with minimum investment.
2. Discuss how GHG emissions can be controlled by adopting energy saving mechanisms in hotel sector.

Source: UNWTO (n.d.c).

Hotel Carbon Measurement Initiative

The Hotel Carbon Measurement Initiative (HCMI) is a voluntary and free framework developed by the International Tourism Partnership, WTTC, KPMG and a working group of 23 global hotel companies by which hotels can measure and report their carbon footprint (Business in the Community, n.d.). Many corporate clients who spend time in hotels for meetings, events or stays have started demanding to give a feedback on the carbon footprint they make as part of their activities. HCMI was created as a solution to this situation with the aim of aligning the hotel sector on how it reports carbon emissions in a uniform manner which could be easily understood by the customers. In order to standardize the process, the boundaries of what hotels should include in their GHG reporting have been defined.

Hotels are to report on all GHG emissions resulting from activities within their premises including restaurants, meeting spaces, shops, casinos, golf courses, spas, garden space, fitness centres, back of house—kitchen, offices, employees' locker rooms, storage rooms and in-house laundry facilities—and any other amenities that are located within the hotel's premises. Since laundry associated emissions can make up a significant portion of a hotel's overall emissions, the methodology suggests including the GHG emissions from outsourced laundry also in the calculations. GHG emissions from private space—areas which are not accessible to hotel guests or conference attendees (e.g., private apartments) or not related to the hotel (e.g., the hotel leases a floor to a third party) and on-site staff accommodation are excluded from the calculations. Other emissions coming from activities such as travel (guests' travel to and from the hotel and employees' business travel), production of purchased materials and consumables in the hotel, waste disposal, product use and other outsourced activities (except laundry) are excluded from the calculations. Calculations are to be performed once a year and the total GHG emissions should be calculated using a 12-month dataset. The data period can be defined by each hotel or company internally. The methodology was tested at numerous diverse properties ranging from boutique hotels, resorts, casinos and major conference hotels. A range of industry experts were also consulted during the preparation of HCMI and the first version was launched on 12 June 2012. Currently, over 21,000 hotels are using this methodology globally.

Global Sustainable Tourism Council Criteria

In the light of growing consumer awareness and demand, there are several programmes that offer certification of sustainable practices adopted by operators and businesses. Many governments have started initiatives that encourage sustainable practices in destinations, hoping to attract 'responsible' visitors. A casual survey would reveal that the marketplace is crowded with many companies claiming to offer sustainable products and services. How can such claims be measured and demonstrated and how can false claims be fought? These questions have led to a new global initiative, supported by a range of tour operators and international organizations.

The Global Sustainable Tourism Council (GSTC) Criteria acts as the global baseline standards to have a common understanding for sustainability in T&T. The Criteria can be considered as the minimum requirements organizations should aim at while practising sustainable tourism. The criteria have been prepared looking closely at the positive and negative impacts of tourism and have been organized into four pillars—sustainable management, socioeconomic impacts, cultural impacts and environmental impacts. While designing the criteria, efforts were made to take into account the numerous guidelines and standards for sustainable tourism which were prepared earlier globally and to undertake wide range of consultations across the world in both developed and developing countries. Since the culture, environment, customs and laws of destinations vary, the criteria have been developed in such a way that these are adaptable to local conditions. Special attention was given while developing criteria that the process matches with the ISO codes of conduct and the standards-setting code of the

ISEAL Alliance, a global agency in providing guidance for the development and management of sustainability for all sectors.

One of the aims is to evaluate sustainable tourism standards to ensure that these contain the elements of the GSTC criteria. This process is called 'GSTC-Recognition'. 'GSTC-Approval' is a process applied to sustainable tourism certification programmes that use a GSTC-recognized standard and follow internationally accepted procedures for third party certification. 'GSTC-Accredited' certification bodies use a GSTC-recognized standard and award certification to businesses, entitling them to use the GSTC certified mark that ensures confidence and worldwide acceptance.

At present, two sets of GSTC criteria have been developed, one for the hotels and tour operators and the other for the destinations (GSTC, n.d).

GSTC Criteria for Hotels and Tour Operators

The GSTC criteria for hotels and tour operators were launched with a true collaboration between tourism organizations, stake-holders and individuals. The expected uses of the criteria are enlisted below:

- Serve as basic guidelines for businesses of all sizes to become more sustainable and help businesses choose sustainable tourism programs that fulfil these global criteria.
- Serve as guidance for travel agencies in choosing suppliers and sustainable tourism programs.
- Help consumers identify sound sustainable tourism programs and businesses serve as a common denominator for information media to recognize sustainable tourism providers.
- Help certification and other voluntary programs ensure that their standards meet a broadly-accepted baseline.
- Offer governmental, non-governmental and private sector programs a starting point for developing sustainable tourism requirements.
- Serve as basic guidelines for education and training bodies, such as hotel schools and universities.

The criteria are broadly divided into four major sections and sub-sections.

In the first section, 'demonstrating effective sustainable management', there are criteria indicating the establishment of a sustainable management strategy that addresses environmental, social, cultural, economic, quality, health and safety issues. It asks for a scrutiny whether the organization complies with all legislations and regulations at local, national and international level to implement a sustainable management system. It also checks whether the staff of the organization receive periodic guidance and training regarding their roles and responsibilities in order to operate the system sustainably. It calls for measuring customer satisfaction, checking the accuracy of promotional materials of the organization and its products, providing information and interpretation of natural and cultural heritage sites and ensuring usage of common property resources comply with legislations and community rights. The section has a criterion to evaluate whether the designing and planning of construction-related activities comply with the existing laws in relation to protected areas and heritage conservation, meet the zoning requirements, respect the natural and cultural heritage, use locally appropriate materials and sustainable technologies and gives special attention to ensure access for persons with special needs.

The second section on 'maximizing social and economic benefits to the local community and minimizing negative impacts' speaks of supporting initiatives for local infrastructure and social community development including education, training, health and sanitation. It also calls for giving equal opportunities for employment to women and local minorities including managerial positions and ensuring provision of a living wage. The section has a criterion that examines the organizational policies to purchase local services and goods, ensure support to small local entrepreneurs to develop and sell products like souvenirs, cuisine and agricultural products, develop code of conduct for activities in indigenous and local communities and implement mechanisms to combat exploitation of local communities especially children, women and other minorities. The section also stresses that the activities of the organization do not adversely affect provision of basic facilities like food, water energy, health care, sanitation and access of livelihood, transport and housing of local communities.

The third section on 'maximizing benefits to cultural heritage and minimizing negative impacts' has criteria that look at the efforts of the organization to establish a code of conduct for tourists who visit culturally or historically sensitive sites. A criterion evaluates the steps taken to ensure that the historical and archaeological artefacts are not sold unless it is permitted by local to international law. Another criterion assesses the organization's efforts to include elements of local art, architecture or cultural heritage in its operations as well as contributing to the preservation of the cultural heritage.

The final section 'maximize benefits to the environment and minimize negative impacts' lays down that the organization has put in place purchasing policies favouring locally appropriate and ecologically sustainable products including building materials, capital goods, food, beverages and consumables and evaluates the usage of disposable and consumable goods. A criterion examines the sources of energy and water, their consumption pattern and measures adopted for reducing their usage. It also calls for controlling greenhouse gas emissions, treatment of grey water, management of waste, minimizing pollution, reduced usage of harmful substances including pesticides, avoiding introduction of alien species, captivity and harvesting of wildlife species.

GSTC Criteria for Destinations

The GSTC Criteria for Destinations (GSTC C-D) and the related performance indicators are developed with an interdisciplinary, holistic and integrative approach and are designed in such a way to be used by all types and scales of destinations. This set of criteria focuses on sustainable destination management, maximizing socioeconomic and environmental benefits to the local community and minimizing negative impacts.

Demonstrate Effective Sustainable Management

The section on sustainable destination management lays down that the destination will have a destination management organization responsible for a coordinated approach to sustainable tourism. The destination has established a comprehensive destination strategy developed with public participation which addresses issues related to environmental, economic, social, cultural, quality, health and safety and aesthetics. There is a multi-stakeholder committee in tourism for sustainable management of the destination. The destination has in place a tourism resource mapping system, a mechanism that monitors visitor satisfaction, crime and safety of the destination, checks on issues related to climate change, addresses the concerns of people with disabilities, ensures that laws and regulations are properly implemented, promotes sustainable standards and has in place a crisis management plan that is communicated to residents, visitors and enterprises in case of emergencies at the destination.

Maximizing Economic Benefits to the Host Community

The section, 'maximizing economic benefits to the host community and minimizing negative impacts', highlights the situation in the destination that provides benefit to the residents. The direct and indirect economic contribution of tourism to the destination's economy is monitored and publicly reported at least annually. There is a system that supports local entre-preneurs to develop local sustainable products, promotes public participation in destination planning, addresses local communities' aspirations, concerns and satisfaction with destination management, supports local small and medium-sized enterprises in tourism and encourages tourists, public as well as organizations to contribute to sustainable tourism initiatives. The destination has laws and practices to combat exploitation in any form particularly of children, women and minorities.

Maximize Benefits to Communities, Visitors and Culture

This section outlines the steps taken by the destination in the cultural front. The destination has a system to evaluate and conserve natural and cultural sites and laws governing sale, display and gifting of historical and archaeological artefacts. There is a visitor management system that protects cultural and natural assets, guidelines for proper visitor behaviour and provision for accurate and appropriate interpretive information at the sites.

Maximize Benefits to the Environment

This section lays down the steps taken by the destination to protect the environment. The destination has a system to monitor the environmental impact of tourism, monitoring water resources, water quality and management of waste water. Enterprises are encouraged to conserve water, monitor and reduce energy consumption and greenhouse gas emissions and solid waste.

The GSTC movement was initiated by a partnership of tourism organization and businesses aiming to recognize and reward genuine practitioners of sustainable tourism, which in turn builds confidence and credibility with customers. There are sustained efforts to raise awareness about the 'GSTC Certified' brand, so that sustainable tourism products and services that have been through the GSTC process are popularized in the market place, bringing benefits to businesses and raising confidence in the minds of customers.

Protect Children Campaign

Source: UNWTO (n.d.d).

Tourism is a sector that has witnessed the exploitation of children either as cheap substitutes for manual labour or their sexual abuse by paedophiles and situational offenders (Wolfe, 2014). According to the ILO, it is estimated that around 218 million children are engaged in labour worldwide, while around 2 million are vulnerable to sexual exploitation and abuse. Children from deprived backgrounds are trafficked to tourist destinations by organized prostitution gangs and offered to tourists, some of whom are emboldened by their anonymity at a loosely monitored destination to commit such shameful acts.

The Protect Children Campaign coordinated by UNWTO and the Task Force to Protect Children in Tourism has been launched with the intention to eradicate child labour and sexual exploitation in the global travel industry. The campaign highlights that it is undesirable for the industry as well as the tourists to tolerate exploitation of children in all its forms. Article 2, Section 3 of the UNWTO Global Code of Ethics states that

> [T]he exploitation of human beings in any form, particularly sexual, especially when applied to children, conflicts with the fundamental aims of tourism and is the negation of tourism; as such, in accordance with international law, it should be energetically combated with the cooperation of all the States concerned and penalized without concession by the national legislation of both the countries visited and the countries of the perpetrators of these acts, even when they are carried out abroad.

UNWTO has launched the campaign to encourage the industry to enforce the Global Code of Ethics for Tourism, and thereby protecting the rights of children.

The Protect Children campaign was formally launched at the 23rd meeting of the International Task Force to protect Children on 10 November 2008 at the World Travel Market (WTM), London, and globally on 20 November, the Universal Children's Day. The campaign has already attained great support from various stakeholders of tourism industry including several national governments, United Nations agencies, tourism boards and from the public and private sectors (UNWTO, n.d.d).

UNWTO World Tourism Network on Child Protection

The World Tourism Network on Child Protection is an open-ended network of a range of tourism stakeholders, from governments, international organizations and NGOs to tourism industry groups and media associations to prevent all forms of youth exploitation in the tourism sector. Originally formed in 1997 at the ITB Berlin Tourism Fair in Germany as the Task Force for the Protection of Children in Tourism, the official name of the body was changed to World Tourism Network on Child Protection on the occasion of its 26th meeting in 2011.

The First World Congress against Commercial Sexual Exploitation of Children held at Stockholm in August 1996 introduced its Agenda for Action, which urged all participants to mobilize the business sector, including the tourism industry, against the use of its networks and establishments for the commercial sexual exploitation of children. The Agenda also urged to promote better co-operation and encourage the establishment of national and international coalition to this effect and to foster action and interaction among the business sector, including tourist agencies and the WTO, employers and trade unions along with communities, families, NGOs, computer and technology industry, the mass media, professional associations and service providers to monitor and report cases to the authorities and to adopt voluntary ethical codes of conduct. As a protective measure, the Agenda urged to develop or strengthen and implement laws to criminalize the acts of the nationals of the countries of origin when committed against children in the countries of destination (extra-territorial criminal laws) in the case of sex tourism and to promote extradition and other arrangements to ensure that a person who exploits a child for sexual purposes in another country (the destination country) is prosecuted either in the country of origin or the destination country. For this, the Agenda advised to strengthen laws and law enforcement, including confiscation and seizure of assets and profits and other sanctions, against those who commit sexual crimes against children in destination countries. The Task Force for the Protection of Children in Tourism was formed as a follow-up to the Stockholm Congress against the Commercial Sexual Exploitation of Children held in 1996. Immediately after its formation, the Task Force launched an international campaign, 'NO Child Sex Tourism', to combat the commercial sexual abuse of children in tourism by raising awareness among the tourism stakeholders.

The mission of the World Tourism Network on Child Protection is to support efforts to protect children from all forms of exploitation in tourism. Although its main focus is the protection of minors against sexual exploitation, it encompasses the issues of child labour and the trafficking of minors. The focus of the body till 2007 was on the prevention of sexual exploitation of children in tourism. In March 2007, the 20th meeting of the Task Force decided to extend its mandate to cover all forms of exploitation of minors in tourism, including child labour and child trafficking (UNWTO, n.d.e).

Responsible Tourism

We have, in Chapter 2, familiarized ourselves with the concept of responsible tourism. It is an approach to manage tourism in destinations, with an aim to maximize economic, social and environmental benefits while minimizing costs to destinations. We have noted that responsible tourism goes beyond nature-based tourism and ecotourism, and gives prominence to issues related to the local community along with environmental matters. Responsible tourism focuses on empirical evidence—tangible and measurable signs of how benefits reach the local people and how environmental impacts are reduced.

Every stakeholder in the tourism ecosystem—visitor, hotelier, local business, travel intermediary, resident, local government—have to act in a responsible manner with the final objective of achieving the goal of sustainable tourism. Visitors to a destination respect local culture, acknowledge local beliefs and traditions and give their custom to local enterprises. Hotels adopt responsible practices in their premises, ranging from installing environment friendly measures, recycling and treating waste, hiring locals and sourcing from local farmers. The local community is involved in important decisions, derives economic benefits from tourism and ensures that the visitor has a safe and enjoyable stay at the destination.

Several market studies have demonstrated that there is great interest among consumers in responsible tourism products and services. A total of 93% of *Conde Nast Traveller* readers surveyed in 2011 said that travel companies should be responsible for protecting the environment, and 58% said their hotel choice is influenced by the support the hotel gives to the local community. The 'TUI Travel Sustainability Survey 2010' of almost 4,000 holidaymakers in 7 European countries and the USA found that 'the most interesting sustainability issues" are: pollution (71%), biodiversity (64%), climate change (62%) and social and community issues (61%). More than 90% of US travellers surveyed by the online travel publisher *TravelZoo* in 2010 said that they would choose a 'green', environmentally conscious hotel if the price and amenities were comparable to those at a non-sustainable, non-green hotel (Center for Responsible Travel, n.d.).

There are many 'versions' of responsible practices in the tourism industry, depending on the stakeholders' perspective. Tour operators have produced policies that spell out their commitment to reducing carbon footprint, conserving the assets of a destination and contributing to the local economy. Many operators provide guidelines to their customers regarding appropriate behaviour, responsible consumption and purchasing local goods and services. Airlines and operators offer programmes by which travellers can 'offset' or balance their carbon footprint in several ways. Hotels publicize their efforts to recycle water, reduce power consumption and provide employment to local residents and source from local producers. These 'fair trade' holidays ensure that money spent by the visitor remains in the local economy as a fair price for the privilege of temporarily using the resources and environment of the destination.

In source markets like the UK, there is strong support for responsible tourism and visitors are urged to travel with operators who have demonstrated their commitment to the principles of responsible tourism. Some simple questions that can be asked of a tour operator are:

- Do you have a written policy regarding adopting responsible practices?
- Have you measured the positive contribution your company has made in a destination?
- Are there specific projects in the local community that you are involved in?
- Do you check beforehand if the hotels you use for your clients employ local people, including managerial positions?
- Do you insist that your hotel partners adopt sound environmental practices?
- Do you provide accurate information about local cultures to your clients?

Guiding Principles of Responsible Tourism

The first International Declaration on Responsible Tourism took place at Cape Town, South Africa known as Cape Town Declaration in 2002, which was conducted as a side event preceding the World Summit on Sustainable Development. The deliberations in the Conference concluded with recommendations for implementing responsible tourism focusing on triple bottom line approach. Accordingly, guiding principles for economic, social and environmental responsibilities were developed.

Guiding principles for economic responsibility

- Assess economic impacts before developing tourism and exercise preference for those forms of development that benefit local communities and minimize negative impacts on local livelihoods (for example through loss of access to resources), recognizing that tourism may not always be the most appropriate form of local economic development.
- Maximize local economic benefits by increasing linkages and reducing leakages, by ensuring that communities are involved in, and benefit from, tourism. Wherever possible use tourism to assist in poverty reduction by adopting pro-poor strategies.
- Develop quality products that reflect, complement and enhance the destination.
- Market tourism in ways which reflect the natural, cultural and social integrity of the destination and which encourage appropriate forms of tourism.
- Adopt equitable business practises, pay and charge fair prices and build partnerships in ways in which risk is minimized and shared, and recruit and employ staff recognizing international labour standards.
- Provide appropriate and sufficient support to small, medium and micro enterprises to ensure tourism-related enterprises thrive and are sustainable.

Guiding principles for social responsibility

- Actively involve the local community in planning and decision-making and provide capacity building to make this a reality.
- Assess social impacts throughout the life cycle of the operation—including the planning and design phases of projects—in order to minimize negative impacts and maximize positive ones.
- Endeavour to make tourism an inclusive social experience and to ensure that there is access for all, in particular vulnerable and disadvantaged communities and individuals.
- Combat the sexual exploitation of human beings, particularly the exploitation of children.
- Be sensitive to the host culture, maintaining and encouraging social and cultural diversity.
- Endeavour to ensure that tourism contributes to improvements in health and education.

Guiding principles for environmental responsibility

- Assess environmental impacts throughout the life cycle of tourist establishments and operations—including the planning and design phase—and ensure that negative impacts are reduced to the minimum and maximizing positive ones.
- Use resources sustainably and reduce waste and over-consumption.
- Manage natural diversity sustainably and where appropriate restore it; and consider the volume and type of tourism that the environment can support and respect the integrity of vulnerable ecosystems and protected areas.
- Promote education and awareness for sustainable development—for all stakeholders.
- Raise the capacity of all stakeholders and ensure that best practice is followed, for this purpose consult with environmental and conservation experts.

Kerala Declaration

In order to take stock the global progress of responsible tourism Movement and to give clear directions on how to move forward, another conference was held at Kochi, Kerala in 2008. The conference attended by various stakeholders in tourism including representatives of governments at international, national and local levels pledged to take forward the concept of responsible tourism into practice, focusing on local economy, well-being, local culture and environment. The outcome of the conference was the Kerala Declaration on Responsible Tourism. Some of the key resolutions and suggestions that were adopted as part of the declaration are summarized below:

- Recognized that responsible tourism can only be achieved by government, local communities and businesses cooperating on practical initiatives in destinations through stable local level 'partnerships', based on transparency, mutual respect and shared risk taking and ensuring clarity about roles and expectations.
- Reiterated the need for 'monitoring, measurement and reporting' of key local social, economic and environmental issues through locally agreed indicators. It also emphasized that transparent and auditable reporting is essential to the integrity and credibility and for establishing benchmarks and targets which enable individual consumers and businesses to make informed choices.
- Recognized that 'governance' is a major challenge often central to all the stakeholders to achieve change. It demanded for the local governments to take overall responsibility to bring together the efforts of destination stakeholders through dialogue in multi-stakeholder forums to establish responsible destinations rather than pockets of responsibility in destinations.
- Recognized the importance of 'empowerment' and strengthening the role of local communities in decision-making about tourism development through their existing civil society structures and local governance processes.
- Highlighted the importance of 'taking responsibility for sustainable local social and economic development' demanded for the conservation of natural and cultural heritage, providing employment opportunities at community level, change in the procurement practices of government and tourism enterprises to support local entrepreneurs, ensuring market access for micro and small enterprises and providing opportunities for tourists to support communities in a meaningful and dignified way.
- Recognized the need for co-operation and competition between different groups in the informal sector and demanded for 'multi-stakeholder processes' and co-operation within a shared undertaking to take and exercise responsibility.

- Highlighted on 'disability and inclusion' and demanded ensuring access to built and natural environments, provide information and interpretation in ways accessible to those with physical or cognitive disabilities and create opportunities for employment by those with disabilities in the tourism industry.
- Urged the 'media' to communicate the ideas of responsible tourism and to exercise more responsibility in the way in which they portray tourism destinations to avoid raising false expectations and to provide balanced and fair reporting.

Case Study: Kerala—Pioneer in Responsible Tourism

The Kerala Government, realizing the role of tourism in deciding the growth momentum focusing on sustainability, took efforts to enable the community members to take an active role in tourism development. A public debate in this direction was mooted in 2007, involving elected representatives, NGOs, policy-makers, industry practitioners, community leaders, social activists, environmentalist, media persons and academicians, which decided to promote Responsible Tourism (RT) in Kerala giving due emphasis to triple bottom line approach—economic, social and environmental aspects. The Government of Kerala also decided to launch RT initiatives in the state on a pilot basis in May 2007 in four destinations that are known for their tourism attractions. The destinations selected were Kovalam (beach), Kumarakom (back water) Thekkady (forest) and Wayanad (hill).

The RT initiative in Kerala has adopted a 'trial and error' mechanism where learning by doing was given prominence. The project has succeeded in creating visible benefit to the local community on economic, social and environmental fronts as the stakeholders in these pilot destinations were placed in the forefront of RT initiatives.

Economic Benefits

Efforts have been taken to promote local production, micro enterprises and value-added products that could be linked with the tourism industry so that the community at large can derive economic benefit out of it. A production system has been designed and implemented which ensures regular supply of products that are daily demanded by the hotels, resorts and other accommodation units in the RT destinations. For this, new production groups have been formed in addition to the existing Kudumbashree (State Poverty Alleviation Mission) groups. Karshaka samithis (farmers groups) were newly formed and encouraged for homestead farming. Micro enterprises have been started to supply various products, like curry powders, flour, meat, fish, candles and pappadams, which could be supplied to hotels which ultimately bring benefits to the local community. In order to ensure timely supply of vegetables to hotels, supply groups have been constituted under the leadership of panchayat called 'Samrudhi'. The Samrudhi supply system collects products from farmers and homes and supply to hotels ensuring regularity of supply to hotels. Institutional mechanisms like Price Committee and Quality Assurance Committee were constituted under the leadership of the President of Gram Panchayat, representatives from hotel and resorts, Kudumbashree Mission and Department of Tourism for fixing the price and ensuring quality of the products supplied.

Social Benefits

While developing tourism, it is imperative that utmost care has to be taken to conserve the social and cultural aspects of the destination. Steps have been taken to ensure conservation of art and culture as well as providing skill-development programmes for the local community members which would finally result in social uplift and economic benefits for them. A detailed study has been conducted to identify the local art and culture of the destinations.

(Continued ...)

Meetings were conducted with the women and children to form cultural groups. They were given training and women cultural groups were established to perform traditional art forms like 'Thiruvathira' and 'Kolkali' and a Children's group was formed to perform the 'Singari Melam'. These groups are linked to hotels for performing art forms and the participants are remunerated. Skilled handicraft makers were identified from the destinations and skill development programmes were conducted to develop local souvenirs. Souvenirs made out of different materials like wood, coconut shell, paper, coir, clay have been developed as part of the project. Village Life Experience an innovative package has been developed to showcase the rural life and sustain the traditional occupations of the destination. Under this initiative, tourists are taken around villages to have a real experience of the village life where they can enjoy a visit to a fish farm, vegetables and fruits farm, paddy fields and can also learn a bit about coconut leaf weaving, broom stick making, screw pine weaving and the traditional fishing techniques like bow and arrow fishing and net fishing. The package cost is equally divided among the villagers who participate in the tour. In order to develop the package, training was given to local community members, who are part of the initiative on the new products, manners and etiquette to be followed while dealing with tourists. The local community members were identified and given training to escort the tourists as guides for the package. As part of the initiative, the ethnic food items of Kumarakom were identified and an Ethnic Food restaurant has been established, managed by the Kudumbashree women. Training was given to Kudumbashree members on micro enterprise development and preparation of food. This has become a major eating point for tourists at a reasonable price. A labour directory has been prepared to identify the skilled and unskilled labours of the destination. This provides a detailed list of unemployed professionals in the destination. The labour directory has given a good chance for the local community to attain related jobs in the tourism sector, thereby ensuring economic benefits to the local community. In order to enhance the capacity of local community to link with various jobs as well as to develop as tourism entrepreneurs, a number of training programmes have been conducted for the local community members. The training given include manners and etiquettes for auto, taxi and boat drivers, food production, candle making, pappad making, glass painting, life guarding, escorting, guiding and souvenir making.

Environmental Benefits

One of the major issues that arise out of tourism in destinations is the environmental problems like waste management, land use change, pollution and threat to flora and fauna. Awareness campaign for public and other stakeholders have been conducted on proper waste treatment and disposal. Household and Industry surveys have been conducted to identify the average waste generated daily. Based on the survey, biogas plants and pipe composts are being supplied to households and industry on subsidize rates. In order to address the issue of plastic waste, awareness campaigns have been conducted for general public along with Gram Panchayat and Kudumbashree members. Collection mechanisms for non-bio degradable wastes are in place at certain destinations. Steps have been taken to promote alternative materials like paper and cloth bags, products out of areca nut, bamboo and screw pine by giving training to local community members. Mangroves play an important role in the protection of Ecosystem in Kumarakom. But unfortunately many stretches of mangroves were destroyed by tourism and related activities. Awareness campaigns were conducted in various platforms of RT and 1600 seeds of mangrove have been distributed to resort owners and local community members to plant near the backwater frontage for planting them at public places near the water bodies. Similarly planting of local species of trees like mango, jackfruit tree are in progress at various destinations. Although the traditional occupation of the local community is farming, many land owners have been keeping the land as fallow for selling it for tourism development. Data was

(Continued ...)

collected on the available fallow lands of the destination. With the help of Kudumbashree units at Kumarakom, 55 acres of fallow land was converted into a good harvested Paddy field and another fallow land of 30 acres under the ownership of a church was reconverted into Kudumbashree group's vegetable cultivation land.

The RT Classification Scheme for accommodation units adopting the principles of GSTC has been launched to ensure that the sector upholds responsible tourism practices. The RT project initiated on pilot basis is now being broad based to the entire state of Kerala. The project has so far achieved nine national/international awards in the last eight years including the UNWTO Ulysses Award for Innovations in Public Governance in 2013, and leads as a Pioneer destination in successful implementation of responsible tourism globally.

Discussion Questions

1. List three activities undertaken in destinations of Kerala that conform to the guidelines for economic responsibility.
2. What are the government bodies that are involved in responsible tourism movement of Kerala? Do you think the local governments of your state will support such a movement? If not, what are the reasons?

Conclusion

Sustainability has moved from the margins to the centre, dominating any discussion on development. Sustainable tourism development as a theme has evolved over the last three decades, enriched by the deliberations of several conferences and deliberations. We have seen that tourism is a potent tool for bringing benefits to communities, and there is strong evidence that responsible tourism makes economic sense as well. There is increasing recognition among large sections of travellers and travel professionals of the importance of responsible tourism, which maximizes economic benefits to the residents of the destination, respects and conserves local culture and minimizes negative environmental impacts. International tourism is seeing a definite shift towards 'greener' vacations, with more customers willing to pay a little more to mitigate the impact of their holiday and choosing to use the services of those who are conscientious and responsible in their business practices. Companies that have adopted policies of sustainability will out-perform competitors, creating distinct brand identities that will attract the discerning traveller. More destinations will adopt responsible tourism as an approach to destination management.

Review Questions

1. Trace how sustainable development and sustainable tourism are related.
2. Give an account of major international initiatives and campaigns on sustainable tourism.
3. Critically examine the GSTC criteria for hotels and tour operations.
4. What is responsible tourism? Critically examine the social, environmental and economical responsibility principles.

Activities

1. Study the websites of three prominent tour operators and identify their initiatives towards sustainable tourism. Discuss if these are significant change makers, or are examples of 'greenwashing'.
2. Collect more details on Green Passport Campaign and organize a campaign in a destination of your choice for creating awareness among stakeholders.
3. Conduct a study on energy consumption by any one hotel near to you and prepare a status paper on various types of electrical gadgets used. Also identify the scope of developing alternative sources for conventional energy.
4. Examine the GSTC criteria for hotels and suggest measures for implementing the same in a destination near to you. Also, delineate items that are not applicable to the hotel and suggest reasons for the same.

References

Web Resources

AITO. n.d. 'Sustainable Tourism Guidelines'. Available at: https://www.aito.com/sustainable-tourism/guidelines (accessed on 25 November 2016).

Business in the Community. n.d. 'Hotel Carbon Measurement Initiative'. Business in the Community. Available at: http://www.bitc.org.uk/programmes/hotel-carbon-measurement-initiative (accessed on 25 November 2016).

Center for Responsible Travel. n.d. 'The Case for Responsible Travel: Trends and Statistics'. Washington DC, CREST. Available at: http://www.responsibletravel.org/news/Fact_sheets/Crest_RTI_TrendStats_print_1_4%20(3).pdf (accessed on 25 November 2016).

GSTC. n.d. 'What We Do'. Available at: https://www.gstcouncil.org/en/about/gstc-overview/welcome-to-sustainable-tourism.html (25 November 2016).

Hi-Tec. 2010. 'Green Hikers Campaign-Advice for Himalayan Hikers'. Hi-Tec, Inspired by Life. Available at: http://www.hi-tec.com/in/blog/19/green-hikers-campaign-advice-for-himalayan-hikers/ (accessed on 25 November 2016).

Krishnamachary, A. 2013. 'They're Our Mountains, After All. Green Hiker, World Wide Fund for Nature. Available at: http://greenhikercampaign.blogspot.in/2013/01/theyre-our-mountains-after-all.html (accessed on 25 November 2016).

UNCSD. n.d. 'Rio+20 United Nations Conference on Sustainable Development'. Available at: http://www.uncsd2012.org/about.html (accessed on 25 November 2016).

UNEP. n.d. 'Green Passport'. United Nations Environment Programme. Available at: http://www.unep.org/resourceefficiency/Business/SectoralActivities/Tourism/Activities/GreenPassport/tabid/78823/Default.aspx (accessed on 25 November 2016).

UNWTO. n.d.a. 'Background of the Global Code of Ethics for Tourism'. Ethics and Social Responsibility, UNWTO. Available at: http://ethics.unwto.org/en/content/background-global-code-ethics-tourism (25 November 2016).

———. n.d.b. 'Overview of ST-EP activities'. Tourism and Poverty Alleviation, United Nations World Tourism Organization. Available at: http://step.unwto.org/content/overview-st-ep-activities-0 (accessed on 25 November 2016).

———. n.d.c. 'Energy Savings at Hotel Chateau Montagne, Bulgaria'. Hotel Energy Solutions, UNWTO. Available at: http://www.hes-unwto.org/hes_root_asp/files/CS-Bulgaria_EN.pdf (accessed on 25 November 2016).

UNWTO. n.d.d. 'Protect Children Campaign'. Ethics and Social Responsibility, UNWTO. Available at: http://ethics.unwto.org/en/content/protect-children-campaign (accessed on 25 November 2016).

———. n.d.e. 'World Tourism Network on Child Protection'. Ethics and Social Responsibility, UNWTO. Availabe at: http://ethics.unwto.org/content/world-tourism-network-child-protection (accessed on 25 November 2016).

Wolfe, D. 2014. 'Most Child Sex Tourists are Situational Offenders'. *Huffpost Living,* Canada. Available at: http://www.huffingtonpost.ca/debbie-wolfe/sex-offenders-_b_5574933.html (accessed on 25 November 2016).

WWF India. n.d. 'Green Hiker'. World Wide Fund for Nature. Available at: http://www.wwfindia.org/about_wwf/critical_regions/high_altitude_wetlands/green_hiker/ (accessed on 25 November 2016).

Suggested Readings

Books

Leslie, D., ed. 2012. *Responsible Tourism: Concepts, Theory and Practice.* Oxfordshire: CAB International.

Middleton, V.T.C., and R. Hawkins. 1998. *Sustainable Tourism: A Marketing Perspective.* Oxford: Butterworth-Heinemann.

Spenceley, A., ed. 2008. *Responsible Tourism: Critical Issues for Conservation and Development.* London: Earth Scan.

Swarbrooke, J. 1999. *Sustainable Tourism Management.* Oxon: CABI Publishing.

Responsible tourism
Image courtesy: Department of Tourism, Government of Kerala.

CHAPTER 18

Climate Change and Tourism

Learning Objectives

By the end of this chapter, students will be able to:

- Grasp the essential aspects of climate change.
- Distinguish between terminologies used in climate change.
- Know the ways by which tourism is affected by and contributes to climate change.
- Illustrate the adaptation measures that can be used to mitigate effects of climate change.

Introduction

In this chapter, we delve into climate change, a subject that has profound implications for the entire planet. We gain a specific understanding of the terms used, and keep abreast of the latest findings and projections on the changes that will occur due to changes in climatic patterns. Tourism is both a victim and a contributor, and the various aspects of the involvement of the sector will be discussed at length. Attention will be paid on the mitigation strategies that seem to be the only route to avert great cataclysmic events that may occur in the future, if steps are not taken now.

Weather

'Weather' is the state of the atmosphere at a moment in time, as determined by the simultaneous occurrence of several meteorological variables like temperature, wind, cloud cover, precipitation at a specific geographical location. Common weather phenomena include rain, wind, cloud or snow. We may talk about the weather on a particular day, or how the weather has changed from sunny to rainy during the day.

Climate

'Climate' refers to the composite or generally prevailing weather conditions of a place or region, throughout the year, averaged over a series of years. The patterns of variations in temperature, rainfall, humidity, wind and other meteorological variables are assessed over a long period of time, usually over 30 years. India has a variety of climate types, ranging from the humid tropical climate of the Western Ghats and parts of Assam to the mountain climate of Himalayan regions and the sub-tropical arid climate of Western Rajasthan.

Climate Change

Climate change is a long term change in earth's climate, especially a change due to an increase in the average atmospheric temperature. Climate change is defined as the changes in the earth's weather, including changes in temperature, wind patterns and rainfall, especially increase in the temperature of the earth's atmosphere.

The global mean temperature has increased approximately 0.76 degree Celsius in the last century. The pace of this change is likely to increase over the twenty-first century and scientists project that an increase between 1.8 and 4.0 degrees Celsius may occur by 2100. Global warming, as this phenomenon is known, has become the defining challenge of our age. Human activities such as industrialization have contributed to the increase in 'greenhouse' gases such as carbon dioxide in the atmosphere. The greenhouse effect in the atmosphere has caused rise in temperatures, resulting in major changes, such as melting of ice caps and glaciers, warming of oceans and change in temperature and wind patterns. A direct result of these phenomena is the rise in sea levels, which was approximately 3.1 mm per year from 1993 to 2003. The biological response to this continued warming and sea level rise has already started, and will continue for centuries.

The Inter-Governmental Panel on Climate Change has projected that it is very likely that the manifestations of climate change will be different across regions of the world. It is very likely that heat waves and heavy precipitation events will be more frequent, tropical cyclones will be more intense and wind, precipitation and temperature patterns will shift. Snow cover is projected to reduce substantially.

This has become one of the serious threats to the society and environment globally in the recent years. The economic and environmental consequences of climate change that may occur in this century are considerable and may impede the ability of many nations to achieve sustainable development by mid-century.

No sector will be left unaffected and climate change will be a pivotal issue affecting sectors such as agriculture, energy, transportation and fisheries. With its close links to natural regions and the environment, tourism is a 'climate-sensitive' sector, with the variations in the climate bringing major changes. Tourism is one of the sectors which are already feeling the effects of this phenomenon with the changes evident in many destinations already.

In many destinations, tourism activities are linked to the natural environment and changes in climatic conditions would have a critical impact on major tourism resources like snowfall, water and biodiversity of the destination. The impact of climate change varies with regions and the Caribbean, Small Island Developing States (SIDS), Southeast Asia and Africa are at considerable danger.

Studies have shown that while some destinations face danger, climate change would result in a shift of attractive climatic conditions for tourism, particularly in the higher altitudes. This may cause a shift in preference of destinations by the tourists. Changes in climate may influence the length of stay as well as the activities of the tourist season. This, in turn, would have an impact on the operating costs such as heating, cooling, irrigation, food, water supply and insurance costs. Climate change can also create chaos for tourists with changes in water availability, biodiversity loss, altered agricultural production, increased natural hazards and increasing incidence of vector borne diseases at the destination.

Tourists have the flexibility to avoid destinations affected by climate change or to shift their travel times to avoid adverse climate conditions. There may be seasonal and geographic redistribution of tourist demand in the century, with shift in preferred destinations to higher latitudes and higher elevations. European tourists may take vacations closer to their home countries, taking advantage of the favourable climates in the vicinity.

Increased awareness of the potential impacts of air travel and the mitigation policies that would increase cost of air travel are other factors that will have implications on tourist demand. Other trends, such as fuel prices, advances in transportation technology, economic fluctuations and health concerns, may also play a significant role in determining the demand.

Tourism as a Contributor

On the one side tourism and travel sector is affected by climate change, it also contributes to global carbon dioxide and greenhouse emissions. It is estimated that the sector accounts for approximately 5% of global carbon dioxide emissions (in 2005), which is projected to experience a growth of 130% by 2035. In tourism, the major culprit is the emissions from the aviation. Long-haul travel by air, representing 2.7% of all tourism trips, contribute to 17% to global tourism-related carbon dioxide emissions, while tourist trips by coach and rail, representing 34% of trips, contribute only 13% of carbon dioxide emissions. It is observed that the tourism-related emissions are projected to continue to grow if the current business pattern exists. This calls for mitigation initiatives in the tourism sector if considerable reduction in carbon dioxide is to be achieved.

Mitigation Measures

The aim of the global initiative to combat climate change is to reduce GHG emissions to well below half of the levels in 2000 by mid-century. Strategies for climate mitigation could be a combination of voluntary, economic and regulatory instruments at various stakeholders of tourism including transportation, accommodation, tour operators, tourists as well as destination mangers. Four major mitigation strategies are adopted for addressing greenhouse gas emissions in tourism. They are: (a) reduction in energy use, (b) improvement in energy efficiency, (c) increased use of renewable energy and (d) sequestering carbon through sinks. These strategies can be achieved by the following means:

- Eliminating greenhouse gas emission by keeping away from activities that can be evaded without considerable changes to the tourism product or service quality.
- Reducing greenhouse gas emission by focusing on energy efficiency practices in specific activities.
- Substituting practices that are liable for large amount of greenhouse gas emissions with options that have lower carbon footprint.
- Offsetting emissions to achieve full carbon neutrality.

The above strategies could be applied in the internal operations of the organization, the operations of the supply chain partners of the company and the activity space of the tourists. The organization would have to then take decisions internally, make choices to advocate with their supply chain members and the tourists on the practical measures to eliminate, reduce, substitute or offset their carbon footprint.

Transport

In 2005, transport generated 75% of the emissions caused by global tourism, with approximately 40% caused by air transport. Air transport is estimated to contribute over 500 metric tonnes of carbon dioxide emissions (2005 figures). It is estimated that a passenger travelling more than 500 km by air contributes an average of 0.15 kg of carbon dioxide (Simpson et al., 2008). The airline sector can adopt the following measures to mitigate the greenhouse gas emission:

- Maintaining a young fleet of airlines by replacing old aircraft technology with new technology.
- Increasing the average passenger load factor to, at least, 80% by increasing the seat density and cooperating with other airlines flying in the same sector.
- Decreasing the non-passenger aircraft as less weight reduces fuel consumption.
- Adopting more flights with less stopovers in the schedule for long hauls as the energy consumption during take offs are comparatively high.

Cars are another widely used means of transport for tourism. It is estimated that a small car contributes to 0.09 kilograms of carbon dioxide per passenger kilometre. The sector could promote use of low emission cars by replacing old cars with new technology. The industry could educate the tourists on the mission for reduced emissions as well as adopting suitable price strategies for tourists preferring energy efficient vehicles.

The railways and coaches are the other means of transportation used by tourists which contribute to only a very small percentage of greenhouse gas emissions. The rail sector could think about replacing diesel engines with electric ones and adopting usage of renewable energy sources in its operations. If the sector gives priority on good quality of service to tourists, more tourists could be attracted to use this mode of public transport.

Accommodation

Accommodation is responsible for an estimated 21% of greenhouse gas emissions in global tourism industry. The sector could adopt considerable options for reducing their emissions as listed below:

- **Reduction of usage of energy in relation to room temperature, lighting, restaurant, showers, pools.** This involves setting of room temperature of air-conditioners to an average temperature of 25°C, which is usually comfortable for the tourists. Appropriate building designs including position, usage of proper materials and insulation would help in maintaining acceptable temperatures. Adopting technical options like usage of thermostats, mechanisms for switching off air-conditioners when doors or windows are open could also help in energy-saving. Hotels could use energy efficient bulbs instead of conventional bulbs for lighting. Design of rooms could be such that it helps to use the day light to the maximum possible extent. Usage of energy saving entrance key cards that automatically turn the power off and on could be introduced. In restaurants, fans, condensers and compressors of refrigerators and freezers should be regularly checked and cleaned. One has to ensure that the doors are intact and refrigerator closes properly. The refrigerators should never be over-filled to ensure proper air circulation for best cooling and energy saving. Hot food should be allowed to cool before placing in the refrigerators. In the case of showers, pools and laundry operations, the water temperature could be maintained at 57°C, the lowest temperature at which no bacteria can occur. In order to reduce the overall amount of water used and heated, the flow systems in showers have to be reduced. Dependency on renewable energy sources like solar energy should be used for heating water in pools and rooms.

- Measures may be taken for the **reduction of waste and promotion of recycling of waste generated**. Hotels can choose appropriate materials in packing like dispensers instead of soap containers and avoiding sachet packing for butter and jams and discourage the use of small bottles for mineral water.
- Restaurants can opt out for locally produced food, **reducing the use of imported food products** that may be transported by air.

Tour Operation

Tour operators can play a major role in mitigation of greenhouse gas emissions, as they develop packages which involve travel, accommodation and activities, all of which are generators of emissions. They can play their role in reducing GHG emissions by offering energy efficient transportation systems in the destination, avoiding long haul destinations and working with hotel partners adopting mitigation measures. They could also think of developing low-carbon packages that include mostly train travel.

The Role of Tourists

Although the tourism industry come up with effective measures for mitigating greenhouse gas emissions, it is the tourists who finally make the decisions. Tourists have the best capacity to adapt, as they have control over key resources such as money, time and knowledge. They have to make critical decisions, such as choice of destinations, mode of transportation, type of accommodation and use of resources at the destination. Tourists can put pressure on the tourism industry for products that are eco-friendly. By opting not to travel or travelling less frequently, staying longer at destinations, minimizing air travel, favouring tour operators promoting eco-friendly practices and staying in environmentally certified hotels, they can actively contribute to reducing the impact of their holiday on the climate. They can also support projects that offset emissions, which cannot be reduced directly.

Destinations

There is an urgent need for all societies to adapt to the changes in climate, and destinations can adopt strategies for reduction of risks and mitigation of climate change. They should officially take a position to adopt sustainable tourism practices in the destination. This involves development of systems for local procurement of daily requirements of tourism industry, adopting renewable source of energy for street lights and garden lamps, providing low-carbon public transportation system at the destination and develop campaigns and initiatives for tourists to practice sustainable tourism.

Resolution on Tourism and Climate Change adopted by UNWTO General Assembly, 17th Session

The General Assembly,
   Having taken cognizance of the document relative to climate change and tourism and of the report of the Secretary-General.

(Continued ...)

Taking into account that the effects of climate change have already a serious impact on several tourism destinations; that certain activities relating to the tourism sector generate only a small proportion of the total greenhouse gas emissions; that there is scientific evidence that global warming will continue to increase at an alarming rate if substantial remedial actions are not taken.

1. *Expresses* its appreciation for the active engagement of the UNWTO Secretariat to analyse the complex issues deriving from the inter-relations between climate change and tourism with a view to taking effective measures of adaptation and mitigation, through transfer of advanced clean technologies, to combat the effects of warming on the tourism sector.

2. *Expresses* its appreciation to the Secretary-General for having organized the Djerba Conference on 9–11 April 2003, the Davos Conference on 1–3 October 2007 and the London Ministerial Summit on 13 November 2007, which generated meaningful discussions on climate change and tourism.

3. *Takes note* with satisfaction of the participation in these two events of the tourism authorities of a broad number of countries and of a wide spectrum of tourism stakeholders from the public and private sector and welcome the exchange of views on the problems and the actions to be undertaken.

4. *Takes note* of the main elements of the Davos Declaration issued on 3 October 2007 and of the conclusions reached at the London Ministerial Summit on 13 November and emphasizes that the recommendations emanating from these forums should not discriminate against developing countries by creating obstacles to their economic development and in particular of those developing countries located at long distance from tourists generating markets.

5. *Recognizes* the urgent need for the tourism sector to adapt to climate change conditions; to mitigate greenhouse gas emissions in line with the principle of common but differentiated responsibilities included in the United Nations Framework Convention on Climate Change (UNFCCC); to help the transfer of new technologies, especially through the clean development mechanism; to make efforts to secure financial resources to assist developing countries which are especially vulnerable to climate change; and *calls* on governments, international organizations, professionals of the tourism sector, media and other actors to engage in the response to one of the greatest challenges of our times.

6. *Reiterates* the importance for the tourism sector to identify consensus measures to address climate change but without losing sight of all other priorities, especially poverty alleviation and tourism contribution to MDGs.

7. *Takes note* with interest of the preliminary findings of the technical study on climate change and tourism undertaken by a group of experts under the supervision of UNWTO in cooperation with the UNEP and the World Meteorological Organization (WMO) and *welcomes* comments from the state members after the final report has been circulated by the Secretary-General.

8. *Welcomes* the close cooperation established by UNWTO with other relevant agencies of the United Nations system and in particular with UNEP and WMO, in view of the forthcoming climate change summit to be held in Bali in December 2007 and of the future actions to be taken within the United Nations framework and *urges* UNWTO to work in close consultation with the UNFCCC, which is the appropriate mechanism within the United Nations system to address issues relating to climate change.

Source: Climate Change and Tourism: Responding to Global Challenges. 2008. UNWTO Available at: http://sdt.unwto.org/sites/all/files/docpdf/climate2008.pdf (accessed on 24 December 2016) Cartagena de Indias, Colombia, 23–29 November 2007.

Adaptation Measures

While we have discussed the mitigation mechanisms in tourism, it is important to understand how adaptation measures for climate change could be incorporated in the tourism sector. Adaptation is a process by which strategies aiming to moderate, cope with and take advantage of the consequences of climate events are enhanced, developed and implemented (Lim and Spanger-Siegfried, 2004). UNDP has developed a framework which provides four guiding principles for adaptation that are relevant for tourism sector.

The UNDP Framework

1. Place adaptation in a development context.
2. Build on current adaptive experience to cope with future climate variability.
3. Recognize that adaptation occurs at different levels in particular, at the local level.
4. Recognize that adaptation is an ongoing process.

It has been recognized that the impacts of climate change negatively affect the whole of the country or the destination, including its water resources, energy, health, agriculture and biodiversity which are closely linked to tourism. Therefore, adaptation measures are to be taken in a holistic way, rather than in isolation, for the sustainable development of the destination. Tourism sector already has experience in dealing with adaptation in climate change, and it would be appropriate to take the views of various stakeholders of tourism who have expertise in adaptation. It needs to be understood that while adaptation strategies are finalized at the national level, implementation often takes place at the local level. As climatic conditions continue to evolve, adaptation will be an ongoing process of implementing and evaluating strategies.

Towards a Framework for Adaptation

'A Framework for Climate Change Adaptation in the Tourism Sector', has been developed as an integration of the common recommended components from the frameworks developed by Simpson et al. (2008)), Lim and Spanger-Siegfried (2004) and USAID (2007) and knowledge gained from the AIACC project (2007) which have each been applied in several developing nations and in several economic sectors, but not explicitly focusing on the tourism sector. This involves a seven-step process as identified in Figure 18.1. The sequence is not a linear one, but an iterative cycle of problem definition, adaptation implementation and evaluation of outcomes, that has feedbacks between the steps as identified.

Step 1: Getting the Right People Involved in a Participatory Process

The framework emphasizes that it is important to involve the right people through a participative manner for the success of adaptation process. Tourism is a multidisciplinary sector and involves a number of stakeholders who are directly linked to tourism or whose livelihoods are affected by tourism. They include local, national and international government ministries, tourism industry representatives, local community members and local businesses; those in sectors that are affected by tourism adaptations like transportation, energy and agriculture; those sectors the adaptations of which affect the tourism sector such as insurance and health; and sectors that have relevant expertise like universities and NGOs. Usually, all the identified stakeholders may not want to engage in the adaptation process and one should proceed to

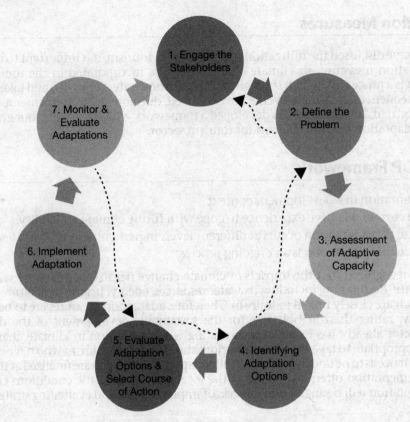

Figure 18.1   Sequence of steps in adaptation process
Source: Climate Change Adaptation and Mitigation in the Tourism Sector Frameworks, Tools and Practices (2008).

Step 2 only with the stakeholders who are willing to participate. The stakeholders through a consultative process need to develop protocols for communication and decision-making within the adaptation process.

Step 2: Screening for Vulnerability: Identifying Current and Potential Risks

The next step is to understand how climate change may affect the studied destination as well as the tourism sector. This include the assessment of physical risks to tourism resources like biodiversity, water supply and infrastructure like coastal resorts, business and regulatory risks, including changes in insurance coverage and market risks that would emerge with changes in international competitiveness through transportation costs. It would be good to analyse the information from existing national or regional climate change to understand recent and projected climate changes and the implications for natural and human systems that are highly relevant to tourism. Since tourism was not given priority in many of the earlier climate change assessments, it is recommended to do a scoping assessment of the range of tourism specific risks to supplement existing information. The result of the Step 2 process could be communicated to the key stakeholders and this would be an effective strategy for generating public and stakeholder interest and getting support for future adaptation programmes. This might help in bringing back stakeholders who were unwilling to participate in the adaptation process in the first stage.

Step 3: Assessment of Adaptive Capacity

Adaptive capacity refers to the potential, capability, or ability of a system to adapt to climate change stimuli or their effects or impacts. Adaptive capacity greatly influences the vulnerability of communities and regions to climate change effects and hazards (Bohle, Downing, and Watts, 1994; Downing et al., 1999; Kates, 2000; Kelly and Adger, 1999; Mileti, 1999). Augmenting adaptive capacity requires the design and implementation of adaptation strategies and responses in order to either reduce the likelihood of adverse events or lessen the negative scale. Also adaptation requires the capacity to learn from past experience in order to cope with current or future events, both known and unknown. Adaptive capacity cannot be measured directly, but the social, educational, institutional, place-specific and other factors which determine adaptive capacity can be assessed. This assessment of adaptive capacity requires the identification of both the systems and the hazards involved (Brooks, Adger and Kelly, 2005). The IPCC (2001) has identified eight determinants of adaptive capacity, namely:

1. Available technological options
2. Resources
3. The structure of critical institution and decision-making authorities
4. The stock of human capital
5. The stock of social capital including the definition of property rights
6. The system's access to risk-spreading processes
7. Information management and the credibility of information supplied by decision makers
8. The public's perceptions of risks and exposure

The research conducted in destinations based on the IPCC determinants lead to a selection of key factors that could be assessed in this step of the process. These factors listed below would vary from destination to destination.

- Any new technology relevant to tourism and climate change like coastal defence.
- Level of available resources including money, human-skills, population and time.
- Natural resources available relevant to assist in adaptation strategies like beach sand, and fresh water.
- Levels of biodiversity and resilience of biodiversity to environmental change.
- Number and structure of local and regional authorities and record of successfully developing, implementing and regulating relevant policies like EIA.
- Social structures—number of community groups and NGOs and their profile.
- The destination's record in responding to crises like floods, cyclones, storm surge.
- Existence of disaster response plan and report on its effectiveness.
- Awareness and knowledge within the destination and its stakeholders of the different risks and opportunities posed by climate change.

Step 4: Identifying Adaptation Options

In this stage a list of alternative technologies, management practices or policies would be compiled to enable them to handle the anticipated impacts of climate change. This involves preparatory and participatory activities. These preparatory activities help to identify the existing adaptation strategies and policies that address current climate related risks. A review of the climate change reports of other regions and communities would help in identifying additional adaptation mechanisms needed for the destinations. A review of national assessment documents and pilot project reports of major donor organizations could also be completed. The participatory activities include holding discussions with stakeholders. This could be in the mode of workshops, focus group discussions, field discussions or by using Delphi techniques with the stakeholders. The opinion of national and international experts in climate change risk assessment and adaptation should also be taken to get information and experience from other nations and to help identify any potential gaps in the stakeholder generated adaptation portfolio.

Step 5: Evaluate Adaptation Options and Select Course of Action

Analysis of the whole list of potential adaptations identified in the building stage would be difficult with limited timeframes and budgets. Hence a second round of stakeholder consultation is recommended to present the full initial list of stakeholder identified adaptations to finalize the portfolio of adaptations to be considered for implementation and also to determine the criteria to evaluate the adaptations. It is suggested that a weightage is given for each criterion for rating the level of importance. Since this process is highly transparent, the stakeholders would own the process of evaluation and selecting adaptation options to implement.

Step 6: Implementation

The roles of implementing stakeholders, the resource requirement and timelines are to be precisely defined for the proper implementation of adoption process. It is suggested that an implementation plan be developed with the following components:

- Strategic plan outlining actions and timelines of involved stakeholders
- Capacity building needs assessment and training plan
- Financial/business plan covering expenditure needs and revenue sources
- Outreach/communication plan
- Sustainability plan
- Plan for monitoring the performance of adaptations

The evaluation criteria and related indicators are to be finalized by stakeholders in this step for the monitoring and performance plan.

Step 7: Monitor and Evaluate Adaptations

The final step in the process is to continuously evaluate the effectiveness of the implemented adaptations. Complete evaluation of the criteria may be difficult as the long-term risks posed by climate change may not be realized for many years. Once the evaluation of the implemented adaptation strategies are done, it would help in refining the strategies that was done in the earlier stages if needed.

Conclusion

Climate change is no more a myth and it is important for all societies around the world to adapt to unavoidable changes in climate. The mitigation and adaptation strategies adopted by the tourism sector would definitely have impacts on the tourist destinations. The strategies and policies adopted at national and international level is likely to make an impact on tourist flows as they would lead to increase in transportation costs. The policies could adversely affect countries that heavily depend on tourism as their main source of economy. But on the other hand, opportunities may arise for carbon emission transport modes like coach and rail and new technologies that are useful for tourism may emerge. Irrespective of the nature and dimension of climate change impacts, the tourism industry and destinations have to adapt to climate change in order to minimize associated risks and capitalize upon new opportunities in a responsible and sustainable manner.

Review Questions

1. 'Tourism is a climate sensitive sector.' Discuss.
2. Examine how different components of tourism contribute towards climate change.
3. Elucidate on the mitigation strategies adopted for addressing Greenhouse gas emissions in tourism.
4. Discuss a framework for for climate change adaptation in tourism sector.

Activities

1. Organize a discussion on developing alternative transport system for a destination which create minimum pollution but at the same time add value to the experience of tourists.
2. Identify details of flights (number, capacity and destination) in an airport near to you and suggest whether any rearrangement of the existing system will help in nullifying greenhouse gas emissions.

References

Books

Simpson, M.C., S. Gossling, D. Scott, C.M. Hall, and E. Gladin, E. 2008. 'Climate Change Adaptation and Mitigation in the Tourism Sector: Frameworks, Tools and Practices'. UNWTO, UNEP and WMO.

Bohle, H.G., T.E. Downing, and M.J. Watts. 1994. 'Climate Change and Social Vulnerability: Toward a Sociology and Geography of Food Insecurity'. Global Environmental Change.

Brooks, N., W.N. Adger, P.M. Kelly. 2005. 'The Determinants of Vulnerability and Adaptive Capacity at the National Level and the Implications for Adaptation'. Global Environmental Change.

Downing, T.E., M.J. Gawaith, A.A. Olsthoorn, R.S.J. Tol, and P. Vellinga. 1999. 'Introduction'. In *Climate Change and Risk*, edited by T.E. Downing, A.A. Olsthoorn, and R.S.J. Tol. London: Routledge.

IPCC. 2001. 'Climate Change 2001: Impacts, Adaptation and Vulnerability'. Contribution of Working Group II to the Third Assessment Report of the Intergovernmental Panel on Climate

Change, edited by J.J. McCarthy, O.F. Canziani, N.A. Leary, D.J. Dokken, and K.S. White. Cambridge University Press.

Kates, R.W. 2000. 'Cautionary Tales: Adaptation and the Global Poor'. Climatic Change.

Kelly, P.M., and W.N. Adger. 1999. 'Social Vulnerability to Climate Change and the Architecture of Entitlements'. *Mitigation and Adaptation Strategies for Global Change*, 4 (3, pp. 253–266.).

Lim, B., and E. Spanger-Siegfried, eds. 2004. *Adaptation Policy Frameworks for Climate Change: Developing Strategies, Policies and Measures.* New York: United Nations Development Programme, and Cambridge: Cambridge University Press.

Mileti, D.S. 1999. *Disasters by Design: A Reassessment of Natural Hazards in the United States.* Washington D.C.: Joseph Henry Press.

Web Resource

USAID. 2007. *Adapting to Climate Variability and Change: A Guidance Manual for Development Planning.* Washington, D.C.: USAID. Available at: http://pdf.usaid.gov/pdf_docs/Pnadj990.pdf (accessed on 25 November 2016).

Suggested Readings

Books

UNWTO. 2008. *Climate Change and Tourism: Responding to Global Challenges.* UNWTO.

——. 2009. 'From Davos to Copenhagen and Beyond: Advancing Tourism's Response to Climate Change'. UNWTO Background Paper, UNWTO.

——. 2009. *Adaptation to Climate Change in the Tourism Sector.* UNWTO.

Web Resource

Ensaa.eu. 2011. 'Defining Climate Change'. Available at: http://www.ensaa.eu/index.php/climate-change/97-defining-climate-change.html (25 November 2011).

Towards the future
Image courtesy: Amit Kumar.

CHAPTER 19

Towards the Future

By the end of this chapter, students will be able to:

- Describe the growing significance of ICT and e-business in tourism.
- Identify major barriers for adoption of technological innovations in tourism.
- Gain insights into the role of social media in knowledge sharing and tourism promotion.
- List new trends and segments that can influence tourism markets.
- Recognize the need for promoting accessibility in tourism from a planning perspective.

Introduction

In this chapter, we examine a few major developments that will play a major role in shaping the future of the tourism business. There is no doubt that climate change and its implications will be central to the changes in tourism, given its impacts on long haul travel. Tourism will also be impacted by the new perspectives brought in by an understanding of its environmental and socio-cultural impacts.

In this century, the tourism sector has been drastically transformed by the changes brought about by the widespread use of e-business applications. While the use of technological innovations such as global distribution systems has become widespread in the business, its dominance has been established with the universal access to the Internet, enabling businesses to bypass intermediaries and to place their products before the consumer. We explore the latest developments in ICT that will shake up the tourism business in the coming decades. Another aspect that is of great importance is the changing demographics of the tourists and their concerns about safety and security in the light of threats and attacks.

ICT and E-business

ICT is an increasingly popular term used to describe the integration of telecommunication and computer networks to provide users with the capacity to store and manipulate information and technological developments that enable them to electronically communicate with the world. ICT applications have a wide range of uses in improving business activities and functions, turning traditional enterprises into e-businesses. In order to fully utilize the benefits of these changes, enterprises have had to change the way they did business, undergoing 'business process re-engineering' to adapt to the new business environment. Amongst the sweeping changes brought in, the most significant is the access to information, knowledge and the marketplace that the Internet has opened up, both for the buyer and the seller.

The global tourism environment is driven by ICT, which has revolutionized the way tourism is practised. From product creation to consumption to feedback, the potential of ICT to reach out to a global audience has changed every process in tourism. All the components of the tourism value chain, from creation of products to their marketing, distribution and sale, have undergone a transformation under the relentless progress of the ICT sector.

As tourism is an activity which is heavily dependent on information, its generation, processing and communication are of critical importance. The use of ICT brings in several benefits to tourism businesses, particularly in reduced distribution costs, disintermediation and customer relations. While sectors such as aviation and hotel chains have integrated electronic channels into their business systems, there are several smaller entities which have not done so. In the future, the transformation of enterprises into e-businesses will become a necessity for survival, as the large majority of transactions will move into the online space. ICT applications will become universal, with all businesses using these to conduct a range of business operations, from information dissemination to marketing to sales and customer feedback.

In developed countries of Western Europe, Internet penetration is over 70%. Around 50% web users buy at least one service related to their travel online. In the USA, this figure rises to 70%, and 52% purchase all or most of their personal travel products online. The global traveller has better transport facilities to explore new destinations, and the Internet has brought far-flung destinations closer to source markets and travellers. It provides avenues for direct communications, lowering distribution costs and bypassing offline and online intermediaries.

Electronic intermediaries will become more sophisticated, feeding into customer databases and offering personalized and customized products and services based on preferences and interests. Marketing strategies will depend heavily on online electronic channels, tailoring delivery based on user traffic data.

Barriers to Adoption

Studies have established that there are barriers to adoption of technological innovations. These are grouped under technological, organizational and environmental contextual factors (Tornatzky and Fleischer, 1990). The organizational context includes the size and level of the organization, leadership structures and the financial resources under its command. Technology adoption by competitors and business partners may force an organization to go in for innovations, which are termed as the environmental context.

The extended e-business impact model introduced by Zhu and Kraemer (2005) moves this forward, examining the usage levels (e-business intensity) and value creation brought by e-business applications (e-business impact). The adoption of e-business practices can have impacts on sales, efficiency, business relationships and customer satisfaction. There is unprecedented potential for e-business to reach out to potential customers transcending geographical barriers. Businesses can bring in substantial savings by saving on transaction related expenses such as commissions by dealing directly with customers. Direct communication with the customer means quicker reaction times, mid-course corrections and better quality of customer relationships. Organizations without an electronic customer relationship management system (e-CRM) will find it difficult to compete in an environment where each business entity is empowered by more and more information on what the customers are looking for and what they need. In short, e-business applications will become indispensable for all tourism enterprises to remain competitive in the future.

The Digital Divide in Tourism

Digital divide is defined as 'the gap between individuals, households, businesses and geographic areas at different socioeconomic levels with regard both to their opportunities to access ICT and to their use of the Internet for a wide variety of activities' (OECD, 2001).

Access to ICT and its use by tourists is ever increasing. Destinations who have adopted ICT are in a better position to compete in the global marketplace. Even if there is Internet access and the hardware to access the Internet, there are discrepancies in the skills possessed, the services that can be provided and the willingness and ability to utilize the potential profitably. Telecommunication infrastructure, connectivity, access policy and regulations, income and skill levels are all factors that affect the usage of ICT by enterprises and destinations.

Destinations vary in the use of ICT, based on their location, structure, stakeholder involvement and expertise. One of the significant developments that have overtaken tourism is disintermediation, reducing prices through the reduction or abolition of intermediary agencies. Destinations with online platforms enable distribution of products through multiple channels directly to consumers. Destinations having excellent Internet penetration and widespread use of online platforms by local businesses are best placed to exploit the potential of a global marketplace. Destinations are in a position to develop customized web applications, linking all stakeholders, providing potential travellers with relevant information, customizable options, e-commerce facilities enabling seamless transaction opportunities and integration into social media platforms that provide them interesting possibilities to stand out in a crowded and competitive environment.

Social Media and Tourism

Although a recent phenomenon, social media has revolutionized the way we communicate with each other. This new method of reaching out has implications for almost all sectors. Tourism sector has been on the forefront of the change brought about by social media. In the tourism industry, social media platforms have revolutionized communication, interaction and feedback.

Knowledge Sharing and Social Media

Tourism is a knowledge-based industry, involving information being shared between buyers and sellers and between potential buyers and customers. Knowledge sharing on the social media has only begun and this is a sector that is going to see great developments in the coming years. ICT applications enable users to generate, store and share knowledge. The distribution of travel-related information has shifted from unidirectional sources such as websites to communicative and interactive platforms such as those available on social media. Based on particular interests, people will communicate with each other, exchanging

information on all aspects relating to travel. This creates a knowledge universe which is not dependent on the information provided by suppliers, destination managers or sellers. This transformed level of communication increases trust and provides authenticity; the future will see more and more consumers rely on such platforms seeking information relating to their travel plans.

There is a universal desire to share one's travel experience with others. Social media sites that allow uploading of personal information, photographs and videos are the best platforms to be used by people who want the world to know all about their holidays and their opinions about the products and services. The electronic 'word of mouth' through social media influences the process of travel planning.

Internet has provided a potent platform for people with common interests to get together in the virtual world. Specific social networks are formed which become an exchange for ideas, information and knowledge. In the tourism sector, this kind of knowledge sharing will also include information about tourism products, feedback on specific experiences and offerings and useful tips about destinations. This becomes a valuable source for anybody was planning to take a vacation in that particular destination.

Conventional mechanisms of feedback and customer reviews have been rendered obsolete because customers prefer real-time feedback and sharing of that experience to a wider audience. Micro-blogging sites such as Twitter provide a platform for instant feedback and experience sharing on a real-time basis. This digitized word of mouth communication has become a powerful tool in the hands of the consumer.

In the pre-trip stage, social media has emerged as a reliable medium to search for and gather information that contributes to planning the travel. The shared information strongly influences travellers' decision-making process. During the trip, the traveller logs into the social media networks to optimize his/her experience at the destination, looking for in-depth knowledge that enhances the quality of the holiday by enabling him/her to explore more areas, taste the best cuisine from recommended restaurants and shop for the most authentic crafts. During the holiday and afterwards, the traveller shifts from knowledge gatherer to a knowledge provider, adding media related to the destination, drawing from personal experiences and sharing the newly acquired information over social media platforms that may be useful to the next traveller.

Content generated by travellers, while having several advantages, also has the potential to be coloured by individual memories and experiences. A small incident may result in a highly negative review of a destination, hotel or restaurant. To get around this bias, many sites provide access to several reviews or put in place a rating system that ranks products and services on the basis of feedback.

The tourism industry of the future will be acutely sensitive to the potential of social media to build, or break, their business. By understanding consumer demand in a highly personalized form and harvesting information from online communities and forums, the industry can continue to improve their offerings according to the changes in preferences, interests and desires.

Data Tracking and Personalization

All online platforms try to reach out and interact with the user. The travel industry provides great scope for improving interactivity. Social media data about individuals can be mined to create personal profiles that provide useful information to travel companies to offer suitable and attractive travel products.

People are eager to share their locations, details of their holidays and friends and acquaintances with whom they spend their leisure time. Numerous sites keep track of all this online information, building up formidable databases on people. Search engines like Google are already keeping track of our search patterns and the time we spend on websites, and use this information to serve up advertisements and suggestions that may be useful to us. Similarly, Facebook provides information on the sites we visit, if we are on their Facebook Connect platform. What does all this add up to? The vast data that can be obtained about a person active online may be used to build up a 'persona', which will enable advertisers to offer accurate, tailored and timely advertisements according to his buying patterns, holiday preferences and interests.

With the traveller in the centre, several smaller entrants into the online travel space are coming out with new offerings that are personalized according to the preferences or unmet requirements of the user. Recognizing that the user will search around for better deals, many companies have adopted this customer habit into their programs and provide 'curated' options, giving suggestions on the best deals available.

The balance of power has shifted in favour of the user and the traveller. The early model was of tourism service providers such as tour companies creating packages and products, combining the parts of a tour into a bundle available to the customer at a price. Depending on factors, such as affordability and preference, products were chosen and consumed. The future belongs to the users, who will demand information according to their personal set of requirements, based on which they will make a decision to travel or take a holiday. Technology will provide such personalized solutions, providing information and content directly to the consumer, through a variety of devices.

ICT and India

Reports indicate that India has overtaken the USA to have the second-largest population of Internet users in the world. Over 400 million Indians will have access to Internet, second only to China which has about 650 million users. The peculiarity about the Indian usage is that a large majority of this number—over 270 million—will enter the Internet age through their cell phones. The introduction of affordably priced smart phones and inexpensive data packages has resulted in this boom in usage. It may be recollected that Internet penetration in India remains very low, particularly in rural areas where it is only 10%. Poor quality access and expensive broadband connections were the prime reasons, but equally important is the fact that digital information available in Hindi and other Indian languages was very limited and continues to be so. A striking development is the establishment of high speed fibre optic network providing data connectivity to far-flung areas and villages, bringing millions of new users online. However, the smartphone will be the device of choice for Internet access, and this huge new customer universe will leapfrog traditional distribution and sales channels and log into the possibilities offered by online companies.

Tourism in India stands to be one of the major gainers of this new digital world opening up before hundreds of millions of new users. As we have seen in a previous chapter, the vast marketplace of domestic tourism is in the initial stages of opening up and the future will see the dominance of this market in all tourism marketing programmes. The availability of information in digital form in Indian languages will be the key in attracting new customers and potential travellers, as destinations and services providers look beyond the English speaking audience in cities, which in numerical terms is a small fraction of the vast middle-class of the country which will look at online sources to plan their holidays. Some destinations like Kerala have already seen the potential and have large sections of their websites in Hindi and other languages.

Hindi Page of www.keralatourism.org

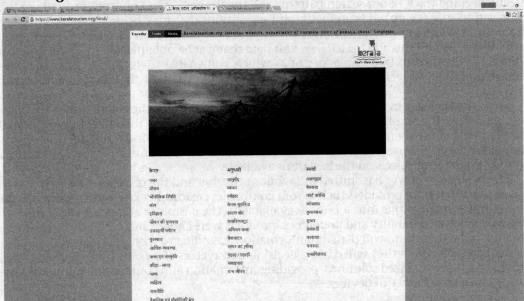

Image courtesy: Department of Tourism, Government of Kerala.

It is therefore imperative for tourism professionals and students to realize the transformation of the industry that is imminent and be prepared to adopt and upgrade their skills and expertise to fully utilize the potential of this new and exciting disruption in the T&T business.

Demographic Shift

There is an inexorable shift in the demographics of the world. Lifespan is increasing and people are living longer. Developments in healthcare and preventive health, better lifestyles and food habits have all contributed to the advancing age of society, resulting in increase in populations. The identification of demographic trends and a closer study of consumer behaviour amongst the growing segments of potential travellers will concern tourism researchers in the future.

The Senior Citizen Market

In developed countries, an increase in life expectancy, coupled with falling birth rates, will result in an ageing population. For example, in 2001, 20.9% of the German population was below 20 years and 24.1% over 60. By 2050, only 16.1% will be below 20 and 36.7% will be over 60-years of age. While there are widespread implications to this change in demographics, it is agreed that there will be profound changes in social costs, pressure on governments because of the higher expenditure on healthcare and pensions, and bleak prospects for the younger generation who will be faced with declining growth in economic sectors. People may choose to take shorter vacations closer home. More affluent sections may continue to take vacations to long haul destinations. The senior citizen market will become the biggest contributor to tourism in destinations having a strong cultural component. Senior citizens may be financially secure and have substantial purchasing power. They are on the lookout for interesting experiences by travelling to new places, as a means to keep mentally and physically active and fit.

They are happy to pay extra, provided the service meets their expectations. The present population of middle-aged travellers from affluent societies are well travelled and have overcome linguistic and cultural barriers. They are technologically competent, having familiarity with the Internet and online resources. In the future, they will make a formidable group of senior travellers, venturing into new territories and destinations, albeit in more comfortable environments and without the pressure of strenuous physical activity.

For destinations in the future, the senior citizen market is a bonanza waiting to be captured. But there are several requirements to be met to fully utilize the surge in traffic of this age group. First, the concerns of such a segment need to be addressed. Ease of access, availability of high-quality healthcare back up, security, comfort and access to rest rooms are some of the requirements of senior citizens. Tourist products may need to be redesigned in view of the special requirements of the segment. For example, in popular destinations and sites, some mechanism may need to be introduced to provide fast track access, without the hassle of queues and waiting in extreme weather. The introduction of sightseeing tours exclusively for the segment, with plenty of rests and short walks, is another innovation that will be appreciated by this segment.

Another aspect that will assume importance in the future is a more careful analysis of this segment and its further break up into sub-segments. For instance, the generalization that all senior citizens from Europe visiting India will be affluent may not hold well once the numbers increase dramatically. Destinations will need to split this once-homogenous segment to provide offerings that are different and address differing requirements. A detailed study of their motivations, lifestyles and preferences will be needed, which calls for in-depth research.

Health-related tourism would hold a lot of promise. Destinations will need to tweak their offerings to have health packages as adjuncts and not the main offering, as leisure clientele will be turned away if the marketing pitch is based on the destinations offering confined to health packages. While respecting the wish of the elderly to have a holiday away from their routine check-ups and ailments, it is important for destinations to present their health-related offerings in an indirect or incidental way that may arouse the interest of a leisure traveller.

Youth Travel

Youth travellers, who traverse the world of tourism with their backpacks, are sometimes seen as a nuisance who do not contribute substantially to a destination. This assessment cannot be farther from the truth. Youth travellers are potent ambassadors of destinations, but can also be extremely effective reporters of accurate updates about destinations, with the potential to create positive and negative perceptions about regions and countries.

Globally, the youth travel market accounts for about 20% of arrivals. With increased accessibility, rising incomes and more information, the youth travel market in developing economies like India is poised for continuous growth in the near future. Youth travel is price sensitive, which also means that the market can be attracted during off-peak periods bringing in revenues to destinations without competing with the general leisure market. The youth market generally tends to stay in budget hotels, guest houses and hostels, bringing in incomes to the local community. They disperse their expenditure widely within the destination, by eating, shopping and spending at local shops and establishments. They are explorers, wandering into nooks and crannies of destinations, discovering new things to see and do.

This segment does not understand borders and share their views with a community that is truly universal. They are the trend setters, creating itineraries, highlighting issues and exchanging ideas, all of which herald exciting changes in the way tourism takes place. Their energy, sense of adventure and outreach through electronic media will ensure that they will open up destinations, reject old models of service delivery and push the boundaries of tourism. Most importantly, they take memories of the destination back to return in another avatar as more affluent visitors with their families sometime in the future.

The youth traveller desires to be more than a passive recipient of sensory inputs and looks beyond the shallow 'sun, sand and sea' holiday. It is a need for a more active participation that drives the young traveller, a personal journey of learning, exploration and sharing. This is the stimulation to move away from the prescribed, packaged and 'safe' itineraries, staking out on their own on a trip of self-discovery. The quest for an 'immersive' experience takes them to programmes offering a different view of destinations—responsible tourism products, volunteering opportunities and active holidays.

The youth market needs careful study by service providers and destination managers, in order to build and maintain their appeal to this effervescent group. Destinations offering avenues for close and authentic interaction with the local community on level terms as against the patron—host relationship of the past—will be preferred by the youth of tomorrow. Heritage to the youth means looking beyond the tangible beauty of a monument; it signifies a continuum that lives on as living culture. Music, art and dance as symbols of cultural continuation and assimilation are powerful cultural voices that will attract the market. Arts to them are not the 'antiseptic' festivals organized as showcases for a musical or dance heritage of the region, a local celebration and festival will hold more authenticity and attraction.

The Future of 'Family' Holidays

Family holidays will continue to be a favourite form of leisure travel. In the modern world, when time is at a premium, a family holiday is a way to spend quality time with each other in the family, away from the stress of work.

Besides the time honoured meaning of the term, 'family' may come to include the new structures that have come into vogue. Single parent households, children living with grandparents, step-parents and step-children, partners and their children and same sex partners with adopted children are some of the new versions of the traditional family, and these family units also see holidays as a way of bonding and connecting.

The features of family holidays will continue to remain more or less the same, the emphasis being on relaxation, outdoor activities, shopping and entertainment. Family milestones such as anniversaries, birthdays and weddings will bring families together on holiday. There will be more intergenerational interaction, with grandparents living longer and travelling. Family holidays create lasting memories and work as a strong integrating influence.

In the future, families from China and India will form a large part of the inbound tourism to Europe. Travelling in family units or groups of families, these holidaymakers will be wooed by destination managers with specialized and customized offerings such as familiar cuisine, specific shopping trips and value for money packages. The emergence of a new aspirational middle-class, which prefers to travel with their families, will force destinations and service providers to compete with domestic destinations within these countries. The increased diversity within the family segment will throw up opportunities and challenges before the tourism sector. Service providers will attempt to create campaigns focusing on safety, hassle-free travel and immigration and 'fun-filled' packages to attract this diverse and important segment.

Accessibility in Tourism

Accessible Tourism is a form of tourism that involves collaborative processes between stakeholders that enables people with access requirements, including mobility, vision, hearing and cognitive dimensions of access, to function independently and with equity and dignity through the delivery of universally designed tourism products, services and environments. (Buhalis and Darcy, 2011; Darcy and Dickson, 2009)

Accessible tourism is an evolving multidisciplinary field in tourism focused on the issues relating to disability and access in tourism. According to the Convention on the Rights of Persons with Disabilities, tourists with disabilities have rights to access transport, built environment and tourism goods and services. It is not a person's impairment that 'disables' someone from participating in tourism activities, but the barriers that create a 'disabling' environment. An approach to disability should keep in mind the importance for individual autonomy, independence and the freedom to make one's own choices; respect for the differences among persons with disabilities and the need for equality of opportunity and inclusion.

It is here that the principles of universal design (UD) are relevant, incorporating the accessibility requirements with the widest possible range of abilities, creating environments that enable access to all people to the widest extent possible.

In destinations such as those in India with many heritage sites, there are several challenges as interventions may not be possible or unacceptable. The approach in such locations will be a combination of improving physical access and movement and 'perceived accessibility' by interpretation and a deeper understanding of the environment. Needless to say, this calls for highly specialized and individualized interventions and site interpretation techniques.

Planners have to address the need of providing accessible tourism as part of an overarching objective of sustainable tourism. This necessitates a reorientation of practices and approaches, from one that stressed the removal of barriers of exclusion to a rights-based approach in the context of practicing responsible tourism. There is a need for extensive stakeholder involvement and collaboration so that destinations can work towards improving accessibility to a range of attractions, transportation and facilities. In the future, destinations will be judged by visitors, increasingly based on principles of sustainability, which include accessibility and responsible tourism practices. In previous chapters, we have stressed that tourism will be seen as a driver of economic growth and prosperity. Equally, tourism will be regarded as a sector that promotes inclusion, equity and understanding, and accessible tourism will be seen as a key component.

Crises and Insecurity

In the future, conflicts may become common in many parts of the world, severely impacting tourism. International terrorist acts, internecine conflicts and epidemics may become more common than they are today. In a previous chapter, we have seen that climate change may trigger extreme weather conditions that may appear periodically. Tourism is a fragile sector, often the first affected when an incident breaks out. However, the sector also has a history of quick recovery, particularly after a natural disaster or calamity. Visitors may need a greater degree of comfort and security in the light of such developments.

The recent spike in international terrorism poses a credible threat to tourism. There have been many attacks focused on tourists and directed against them. Hotels and public facilities like railway stations used by tourists are frequently made targets for terrorist attacks. The terrorist outfits use these attacks to attract global attention through international media. Terrorism of late is directed against tourism as a means to hit the economy of regions and destinations. The perceived 'security' at a destination will affect the image of a destination. In the future, countries significantly dependent on tourism will have to invest considerable resources to strengthen their anti-terrorism infrastructure and put in place a visible and understandable level of security to reassure the potential traveller about the effectiveness of the machinery that is handling threats from terror outfits. A range of preventive measures, already being adopted in the wake of 9/11, will have to be put in place by airlines and hotels, as part of a preventive security strategy.

Conclusion

Tourism in the twenty-first century will be very different from the previous century in many ways. Technological developments will disrupt the way the Industry functions, creating new challenges and offering new ways of doing business. We have gained an understanding of the user-centric innovations that will redefine how we share information and what sources we will depend on to make our choices. Breakthroughs in technology will bring vast populations of potential travellers to the tourism fold, opening up unprecedented opportunities. The demographics of a changing population will engage tourism planners more and more, as consumers will continue to demand customized and personalized products and services. Issues such as accessibility will be seen as yardsticks with which destinations are judged, as rights and equity occupy centre stage.

Review Questions

1. 'Today ICT has become an indispensable component of tourism businesses'. Discuss.
2. Examine the role of social media in shaping the future of tourism industry.
3. What is accessible tourism? Examine possible measures that can be taken to make a destination accessible for different segments of tourists.
4. In the back drop of current tourism business and emerging trends, give your perspective on future trends in tourism business.

Activities

1. Conduct an interview among 20 tourists in a destination using an interview schedule to examine the following:

   a. The influence of social media in taking travel decision.
   b. The use of ICT in facilitating their travel and stay.
   c. The demographic composition of the tourist and delineate their preferences for attractions, accommodation and activities in the destination.

2. Visit a tourism destination and list out the following:

   a. Minimum essential facilities required for making the destination accessible to differently-abled people.
   b. Identify the safety and security issues that demand immediate attention after interacting with tourists and business operators at the destination.

References

Books

Buhalis, D., and S. Darcy, eds. 2011. *Accessible Tourism: Concepts and Issues.* Bristol: Channel View Publications.
Darcy, S., and T. Dickson, 2009. 'A Whole-of-Life Approach to Tourism: The Case for Accessible Tourism Experiences'. *Journal of Hospitality and Tourism Management,* 16 (1): 32–44.
OECD. 2001. 'Understanding the Digital Divide'. Paris: OECD Publications.

Tornatzky, L., and M. Fleischer. 1990. *The Process of Technology Innovation.* Lexington, MA: Lexington Books.

Zhu, K., and K.L. Kraemer. 2005. 'Post-adoption Variations in Usage and Value of e-Business by Organizations: Cross-country Evidence from the Retail Industry. *Information Systems Research,* 16 (1): 61–84.

Suggested Readings

Books

Buhalis, D., and S. Darcy, eds. 2011. *Accessible Tourism: Concepts and Issues.* Bristol: Channel View Publications.

Gahlen, K. 2011. *Sustainable Youth Tourism.* LAP Lambert Acad. Pub.

Pick, J.B., and A. Sarkar. 2015. *The Global Digital Divides: Explaining Change.* London: Springer.

Glossary

Accessible Tourism: Accessible Tourism is a form of tourism that involves collaborative processes between stakeholders that enables people with access requirements, including mobility, vision, hearing and cognitive dimensions of access, to function independently and with equity and dignity through the delivery of universally designed tourism products, services and environments.

Adaptive Reuse: Adaptive reuse is the adaption of a disused building for another purpose.

Agri-Tourism: Agri-tourism is where tourists get the opportunity to visit farms, ranches, wineries and agricultural industries.

Apartments: Apartments are self-contained accommodation units housed in multi-storied buildings having a number of such units.

Architecture Tourism: Architecture tourism involves tour packages designed connecting architectural monuments.

Avi Tourism: Avi-tourism or bird watching tourism is a specialized sector of nature based tourism which focuses exclusively on watching birds and their activities.

Back-to-Back Charter: A back-to-back charter is operated by tour operators as a series to a destination, with one set of passengers disembarking at the destination to begin their holiday and another set of passengers boarding the aircraft to return after their holiday.

Backward Pricing: Backward pricing is a method of pricing in which prices are set by determining what consumers are willing to pay; then, costs are deducted to see if the profit margin is adequate.

Base Destinations: Base destinations are used by tourists as hubs from where a variety of products can be experienced through excursions.

Biking: Biking or Bicycle tourism is self-contained cycling trips for pleasure, adventure and autonomy rather than sport, commuting or exercise.

Biodiversity: Biodiversity refers to the wide variety of ecosystems and living organisms: animals, plants, their habitats and their genes.

Biosphere Reserves: Biosphere Reserves are areas established to conserve the diversity and integrity of plants and animals, to safeguard genetic diversity of species and to ensure sustainable use of natural resources.

Boutique Hotels: Boutique hotels are design led, small properties which offer luxurious and personalized service, emphasising their distinction from larger branded properties.

Brand Loyalty: The more a consumer trusts a brand resulting in more the chances of re-purchase is known as brand loyalty.

Bread and Breakfast: Bread and Breakfast are small, family run accommodation, with breakfast included in the price.

Brownfield Airport Project: When an existing airport undergoes significant redevelopment and expansion, often undertaken on PPP model, such a project is called a 'brown' field airport project.

Business Costs: Business costs are those incurred on an annual basis, and has to be shared by all business operations.

Business Hotels: Business hotels are those that cater to business travellers which provide facilities for conducting business, such as boardrooms, conference and meeting facilities, business centres with photocopy, fax, Wi-Fi and high-speed Internet access.

Castle: A castle is a fortified building complex, built during the mediaeval period.

Cemetery Tourism: Cemetery tourism is tourism that falls under the category of 'dark' tourism associated with tourists visiting places related to death and disaster.

Central Destinations: Central destinations are those where the attractions are bunched around a central area, such as the city centre.

Chalets: Chalets are wooden cottages in mountain and ski resorts.

Chateau: A chateau is a French country house, usually in a vineyard.

Climate Change: Climate change is defined as the changes in the earth's weather, including changes in temperature, wind patterns and rainfall, especially increase in the temperature of the earth's atmosphere.

Climate: Climate refers to the composite or generally prevailing weather conditions of a place or region, throughout the year, averaged over a series of years.

Club Spa: Club Spa, whose primary purpose is fitness, offers a variety of professionally administered spa services on a day-use basis.

Community Reserves: Community reserves are areas declared by the state government in community or private lands, where individuals or the community has volunteered to conserve wildlife and its habitat.

Conservation Reserves: Conservation reserves are areas generally adjacent to national parks and sanctuaries, or those areas which link one protected area to another.

Core Attractions: Core attractions are those by which the destination is known to outside world and form the base or nuclei of tourism in the destination.

Cottage: A cottage is a small house typically in a rural area.

Cruise Tourism: Cruise tourism involves taking a cruise through the ocean in a cruise ship, which is a vessel used for pleasure voyages.

Cultural Commodification: Cultural commodification refers to the alteration of cultural forms and crafts to create commodities that have a ready market, devoid of its intricacies and nuances.

Cultural Destinations: Cultural destinations are those featuring cultural products, such as monuments, museums or performing arts and festivals.

Cultural Heritage: Cultural heritage is defined as 'monuments, groups of buildings and sites', including urban centres, archaeological sites, industrial heritage, cultural landscapes and heritage routes.

Day Spa: Day spa offers a variety of professional administered spa services to clients on a day-use basis.

Decrease in Demand: Decrease in demand takes place when consumers demand less at the same price or are willing to pay a lower price for the original quantity.

Demand Forecasting: Demand forecasting is an attempt to predict the future so as to enable the organization to plan and execute programmes to lead the business to success.

Demonstration Effect: The Demonstration Effect takes place when the local community tries to imitate the lifestyle, dress and other behavioural aspects of tourists.

Design Hotel: Design hotels are those which give emphasis on style, and have an overall design language, which is expressed in the spatial design, furniture, furnishings, colour and cuisine.

Destination Spa: Destination spa provides a comprehensive program that includes spa services, physical fitness activities, wellness education, healthful cuisine and special interest programming.

Destination: Destination is a distinct geographical location which a visitor calls, and where there is a feature or a set of features that the visitor experiences.

Differential Pricing: Differential pricing is the strategy of selling the same product to different customers at different prices.

Digital Divide: The gap between individuals, households, businesses and geographic areas at different socioeconomic levels with regard both to their opportunities to access ICT and to their use of the Internet for a wide variety of activities.

Diplomatic Passport: A diplomatic passport, with a maroon cover, is issued to designated members of the national government, judiciary, statutory authorities, diplomats, official public couriers and any other persons specifically authorized by the government.

Domestic Tour Operators: Domestic tour operators are those who concentrate its activities on the domestic market, creating and marketing tour products which are consumed by customers within the country.

Domestic Tourism: Domestic tourism is tourism that takes place within the country.

Domestic Tourist: A domestic tourist is a resident visitor within the country of reference as part of a domestic tourism trip.

Drifter: Drifter is a tourist interested in experiencing and enjoying the environment in its authentic form by immersing himself in the lifestyle and culture of the destination.

Ecotourism: Ecotourism is environmentally responsible travel and visitation to relatively undisturbed natural areas, in order to enjoy and appreciate nature (and any accompanying cultural features—both past and present) that promotes conservation, has low negative visitor impact, and provides for beneficially active socioeconomic involvement of local populations.

Enclavization: Enclavization happens when the tourists are provided all their requirements at a single location which discourages any expenditure outside this location or any contact with the local community during their tour.

Excursionist: A visitor whose trip does not include an overnight stay.

Explorer: The explorer is a tourist who prefers to arrange his trips independently and tries to go somewhere new, and do something unusual and different.

Film Tourism: Film tourism can be defined as a branch of cultural tourism that refers to the growing interest and demand for locations which became popular due to their appearance in films and television series.

Fixed Costs: Fixed costs are those which do not vary with the level of output.

Franchise: The franchise model is when the hotel is managed by the owner under the umbrella of an established brand.

Free Independent Traveller: The free independent traveller is a single unit, either a person or a small group of individuals, who prefer to travel by themselves and not as part of a larger group.

Freedoms of the Air: The 'Freedoms of the Air' are a set of aviation rights regulating the entering and landing of aircraft of one country in the airspace of another country.

Full Service Carrier: A Full Service carrier is that offer a range of services to the passenger, ranging from airport facilities, different classes of travel, a choice of meals, drinks and beverage services and onboard shopping.

Global Code of Ethics for Tourism: The Global Code of Ethics for Tourism is a set of 10 point articles to guide stakeholders in tourism including national and local governments, local communities, tourism industry and tourists in tourism development.

Golden Triangle: Golden Triangle denotes a particular set of tourism products that is experienced by the tourist in three places in India—Delhi, Agra and Jaipur.

Goods: Goods are products which are visible and tangible objects that can be transferred from a seller to a buyer.

Green Hiker Campaign: The Green Hiker Campaign is an initiative of World Wide Fund for Nature to inspire tourists and tour operators in the Himalayan region to opt for sustainable model of tourism.

Green Passport Campaign: The 'Green Passport' is a campaign launched to improve the tourism sector's efforts to communicate with tourists on sustainable tourism through campaigns on sustainability issues.

Greenfield Airports: Greenfield airports are those which are developed at a new site or location.

Greenwashing: When a company or organization spends more time and money claiming to be 'green' through advertising and marketing than actually implementing business practices that minimize environmental impact.

Gross Travel Propensity: It gives the total number of tourism trips taken as a percentage of the population.

Ground Operator: Ground operator is one who provides a range of services at destinations, which are together known as land arrangements.

Group Inclusive Tour: A group inclusive tour is tour to a destination or event for a group of people, usually with some common affiliation and organized through a travel operator and escorted by a tour guide.

Handicrafts: Handicrafts are creative products made by the skill of the hand without the help of modern machinery and equipment.

Heritage: Heritage is something which we inherit, from our families, our predecessors and our forefathers and passed on to the coming generations.

Horizontal Integration: When similar enterprises operating in similar or comparable environments collaborate with each other to bring in efficiencies, it is called horizontal integration.

Hostel: A hostel is a relatively inexpensive type of temporary accommodation, offering basic lodging and limited facilities.

Hotel Carbon Measurement Initiative: The Hotel Carbon Measurement Initiative is a voluntary and free framework developed by the International Tourism Partnership, World Travel and Tourism Council, KPMG and a working group of 23 global hotel companies by which hotels can measure and report their carbon footprint.

Hotel Energy Solutions: Hotel Energy Solutions is a project created to increase energy efficiency in European small and medium hotels in response to the contribution of tourism industry to climate change especially the accommodation sector.

Hotel: Hotel is an establishment that provides travellers' overnight accommodation and guest services, such as meals and drinks, for a price.

Inbound Tour Operators: Inbound tour operators are those who develop tour packages featuring destinations in the country of operation, marketing these products to customers in source markets which are outside the country.

Inbound Tourism: Inbound tourism relates to tourism of non-resident visitors within the country.

Incentive Travel: Incentive travel is defined as a global management tool that uses an exceptional travel experience to motivate and/or recognize participants for increased levels of performance in support of organizational goals.

Increase in Demand: Increase in demand takes place when consumers demand more quantities of a product at the same price or they are willing to pay a higher price for the same quantity.

Individual Mass Tourist: The individual mass tourist is a traveller with similar tastes and requirements as the organized mass tourist, with the exception that the tour is not entirely fixed, and some flexibility is built into the package.

Inflation: A situation of general rise in prices bringing down the value of money.

Inn: An inn is a small establishment in a traditional setting, offering comfortable accommodation, food and drink to visitors.

Intangible Heritage: Intangible heritage is defined as 'practices, expressions, representations, knowledge and skills that communities, groups and individuals recognize as part of their cultural heritage'.

Internal Tourism: Internal tourism is a combination of domestic and inbound tourism, that is, the tourism of resident and non-resident visitors within the country of reference as part of domestic or international tourism trip.

International Tourism: International tourism comprises inbound and outbound tourism that is the total of tourism across countries.

Leisure: Leisure time refers to the free and discretionary time available to an individual, after meeting basic and essential needs, during which the individual may or may not undertake activities without external compulsion for pleasure or otherwise.

Lodge: Lodge is a basic budget accommodation establishment.

Manor: A manor is an English country house formerly owned by nobility.

Mansion: A mansion is a large house in a rural environment built in a typical architectural style.

Marketing: Marketing can be defined as a process through which products that can satisfy the needs and desires of customers can be provided, exchanged and obtained at a *desired* price and place.

Mass Market Operator: A Mass market operator is one who offers tour products which are affordable to the common man.

Media Plan: Media plan is a document that details the media properties to be used, the frequency of exposure of different advertising elements in the media and the time frame within which the campaign is delivered.

Medical Spa: Medical Spa is a facility that has a full-time licensed health care professional on-site, which is further defined as a health professional with a degree in Medicine.

Military Tourism: Military Tourism can be defined as visits made to a destination that has military background and history.

Mineral Springs Spa: Mineral springs spa offers an on-site source of natural mineral, thermal or seawater used in hydrotherapy treatments.

Motels: Motels are basic hotels typically situated on the sides of highways, with ample parking areas and facilities to sleep overnight.

National Park: National park is a large natural area set aside to protect large-scale ecological processes, which also provide a foundation for environmentally and culturally compatible spiritual, scientific, educational, recreational and visitor opportunities.

National Tourism: National tourism comprises domestic tourism and outbound tourism, that is, the tourism of resident visitors within and outside the country of reference.

Natural Heritage: Natural heritage consists of natural sites of outstanding universal value from the point of view of science, conservation or natural beauty, natural features and geological and physiographical formations.

Nature-based Destinations: Nature-based destinations depend on the natural resources and scenic beauty of the area, like wildlife sanctuaries, hill stations and coastal destinations.

Net Travel Propensity: It specifies the percentage of total population that takes at least one trip over a specific time period, usually one year.

Official Passport: The white cover official passport is issued to designated Indian government servants or any other person specifically authorized by the Government, deputed abroad on government business.

Ordinary Passport: An ordinary passport has a navy blue cover, and is issued to an Indian citizen for all travel.

Organized Mass Tourists: Tourists who prefer to enjoy facilities at the destination to which they are accustomed, in their resident environments.

Outbound Tour Operators: Outbound tour operators are those who create and market tour products featuring destinations outside the country, to be purchased by consumers within the country.

Outbound Tourism: Outbound tourism refers to tourism of people visiting destinations in other countries.

Palace: A palace is a residence of royalty, with grand furnishings and opulent settings.

Part Charter: A part charter means that the tour operator has contracted a block of seats or a portion of the capacity of the aircraft.

Passport: A passport is an official document issued by a government or competent authority to the citizens of the country.

Penetrating: Penetrating is the practice of offering a low price for a new product or service during its initial offering in order to lure customers away from competitors.

Periphery Attractions: Periphery attractions are secondary nuclei to core attractions and are optional to tourists.

Photography Tourism: Photography tourism is defined as a combined passion for travel and photography.

Price: Price is a value fixed on the product by the provider, which the consumer is willing to pay in anticipation of a satisfying experience.

Protected Areas: Protected areas are clearly defined geographical space, recognized, dedicated and managed, through legal or other effective means, to achieve the long term conservation of nature with associated ecosystem services and cultural values.

Rack Rate: Rack rate is the rate provided in printed material which is announced and advertised.

Recreational Vehicles: Recreational vehicles are vehicles outfitted with bathroom, sleeping facilities and kitchen, functioning as mobile houses.

Resort/Hotel Spa: Resort/hotel spa is located within a resort or hotel providing professionally administered spa services, fitness and wellness components.

Resort: Resort is a hotel located in a leisure tourism destination offering extensive guest facilities, recreation and full service.

Responsible Tourism: Responsible tourism is an approach to manage tourism in destinations, with an aim to maximize economic, social and environmental benefits while minimizing costs to destinations.

Rural Tourism: Rural tourism is essentially a holiday which takes place in the countryside and may indicate many types of leisure holidays such as soft adventure, farm visits, home stays, fishing, boating, literary festivals, local festivals and events, and activities like bird watching and village visits.

Sales: Sales is a process by which a product is sold for a consideration and it not only includes the price of a product, but also other details of interest to the customer such as warranties, support, delivery timelines and training.

Services: Services are products that are intangible, invisible and person dependent.

Skimming: Skimming is a product pricing strategy by which a firm charges the highest initial price that customers will pay, and as the demand of the first customers is satisfied, the firm lowers the price to attract another, more price-sensitive segment.

Spas: Spas can be defined as destinations people visit for renewal of body, mind and spirit.

Special Interest Tourism: Special interest tourism is the provision of customized tourism activities that caters to the specific interests of groups and individuals.

Specialist Tour Operator: A Specialist tour operator is one who offers specialized tourism products to a 'niche' clientele or market.

Staged Authenticity: Staged authenticity is the recreation of events and rituals for the benefit of the visitor.

Statistics of Characteristics: Data related to personal information, consumer preferences and visitor satisfaction constitute statistics of characteristics.

Statistics of Expenditure: Statistics of expenditure shows all data related to tourist spending in the destination.

Statistics of Volume: Statistics of volume shows the number of arrivals made by tourists in a destination as well as their average length of stay.

Sustainable Development: Sustainable development is development that meets the needs of the present without compromising the ability of future generations to meet their own needs.

Sustainable Tourism: Sustainable tourism is tourism that seeks to minimize ecological and socio-cultural impacts while providing economic benefits to local communities and host countries.

Tele Marketing: Tele marketing is a method of direct marketing in which a salesperson solicits prospective customers to buy products or services, either over the phone or through a subsequent face to face or Web conferencing appointment scheduled during the call.

The Global Sustainable Tourism Council Criteria: The criteria acts as the global baseline standards to have a common understanding for sustainability in travel and tourism.

Time Charter: Time charter is one where a single tour operator contracts an aircraft for the season.

Time Share: Time share is a scheme in which the customer purchases a period—typically a week or its multiples—in a property, retaining the right to use the unit annually, for a number of years.

Tourism Demand: Tourism demand can be defined as 'the total number of persons who travel, or wish to travel, to use tourist facilities and services away from their places of work and residence'.

Tourism Products: Tourism products are a combination of goods and services that are demanded by a tourist during travel to and stay in the destination.

Tourism Stakeholders: Tourism Stakeholders refers to players like local community members, the business owners and employees, the local government who have a stake in the development of a destination.

Tourism: Tourism comprises the activities of persons travelling to and staying in places outside their usual environment for not more than one consecutive year for leisure, business and other purposes not related to the exercise of an activity remunerated from within the place visited.

Tourist: Tourist is a visitor if his/her trip includes an overnight stay.

Transit Destinations: Transit destinations are those which offer brief stays as part of a larger holiday elsewhere, adding a facet to the holiday experience.

Travel Frequency: It measures the average number of trips taken for tourism purpose by the population over a specific period of time.

Travel Propensity: It specifies the effective or actual demand for tourism in a given population while measuring the demand for tourism.

Traveller: Someone who moves between different geographical locations, for any purpose, and for any duration.

Trekking: Trekking or hiking refers to multiday trips through rural, often hilly or mountainous territory.

Turnaround Time: Turnaround time is the time needed for the aircraft to arrive at the gate for passengers to disembark, unloading of baggage, onboard of new passengers and their baggage as well as cleaning and freshening up of aircraft before making a new trip.

Variable Costs: Variable costs are those which change according to the level of output.

Vertical Integration: When enterprises operating at different points of distribution channel come together, it is called vertical integration.

Villa: A villa is a luxurious country residence, but nowadays used to refer to a detached suburban house.

Visa: A visa is an entry in a passport or other travel document made by an official or government, indicating that the bearer has been granted authority to enter the country concerned.

Visitor: A traveller making a trip outside his/her usual environment, for less than a year, for any purpose other than for employment, is termed a visitor.

Weather: Weather is the state of the atmosphere at a moment in time, as determined by the simultaneous occurrence of several meteorological variables like temperature, wind, cloud cover, precipitation at a specific geographical location.

Wildlife Sanctuary: A wildlife sanctuary (WLS) is declared for the purpose of protecting, propagating or developing wildlife on its environment.

Wine Tourism: Wine tourism includes visits to wineries, vineyards and restaurants known to offer unique vintages, tasting wines, as well as organized wine tours which involve taking part in the harvest, wine festivals or other special events.

Index